Skills
for Living

Frances Baynor Parnell
Educational Consultant and Author
Wilmington, North Carolina

Contributor for Sewing Chapters
Joyce Honeycutt Wooten
Burgaw, North Carolina

Publisher
The Goodheart-Willcox Company, Inc.
Tinley Park, Illinois
www.g-w.com

Library of Congress Cataloging-in-Publication Data
Parnell, Frances Baynor.
  Skills for living / by Frances Baynor Parnell; contributor for sewing chapters, Joyce Honeycutt Wooten.
     p. cm.
  Includes index.
  ISBN 1-59070-668-4
  1. Home economics. 2. Life skills. I. Title: Skills for living.
II. Wooten, Joyce Honeycutt. III. Title.
TX167 .P38 2008
640--dc22   2005040240

Introduction

Skills for Living is a comprehensive text designed to help you meet the challenges of daily life with confidence. It will help you develop a range of skills related to interpersonal and family relationships, healthy living, getting and keeping a job, foods and nutrition, management, clothing, and housing.

Each chapter in the text is divided into several topics. Topics begin with a set of objectives and a list of vocabulary terms to help prepare you for reading. At the end of each topic, a few questions are given to help you review important concepts. Further review of important information is provided at the end of each chapter.

Each chapter includes two types of features: "The More You Know" and "Setting the Scene." "The More You Know" provides additional information related to the Topic. "Setting the Scene" features will help prepare you to make important decisions in your life.

Another feature, which appears at the end of each part of the book, is called "**career.**guide." These features describe career opportunities in the various fields of family and consumer sciences. Descriptions of the rewards and demands of the career field, personal qualities needed for success, and preparation requirements are just a few of the types of information you will read about in "**career.**guide."

About the Author

Frances Baynor Parnell was a secondary family and consumer sciences teacher for 32 years and served as department chair. She is president of Natural and Family Resources, Inc., which provides opportunities to be involved in cultures around the world. She has conducted research and completed a project on work and family skills to supplement family and consumer sciences education programs in North Carolina. In addition to writing this text and its supplements, Frances coauthored the book *Guarding Your Own Mental Health in a Fast-Paced World*. She has written numerous articles for professional publications. She has conducted many workshops and given frequent presentations. She has also contributed her expertise and leadership to a number of professional and civic organizations, which have earned state and national recognition in areas of environmental concerns.

During her years of teaching, Frances has received such awards as the North Carolina Home Economics Teacher of the Year, the Outstanding Educator Award (from East Carolina University, where she received her B.S. and M.S. degrees), and the Frances Hutchinson Teacher of the Year Award.

Contents in Brief

Contents

Part Four
Nutrition and Food
Preparation

The More You Know:

Setting the Scene:

career.guide

Part One

A Better You

Chapter 1
Understanding Yourself

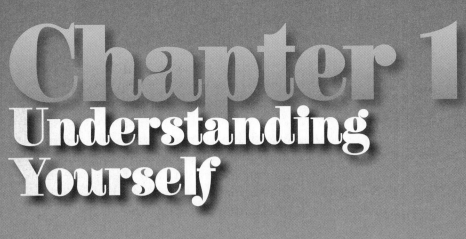

Careers

These careers relate to the topics in this chapter:
- ▼ summer camp counselor
- ▼ teacher's aide
- ▼ caseworker assistant
- ▼ family and consumer sciences teacher

As you study the chapter, see if you can think of others.

Topics

Topic 1-1
All About You

Objectives

After studying this topic, you will be able to
▼ identify the factors that help make you a unique person.
▼ describe how personality develops.
▼ list ways to improve self-concept.
▼ relate self-esteem to a positive self-concept.

Topic Terms

heredity
environment
cultural heritage
ethnic group
personality
character
empathy
self-concept
self-esteem

You are a unique person. From the moment you were conceived, you have been unique. No other person is exactly like you—you look, think, and act differently from anyone else. This makes you special. Like you, all other people are unique. They, too, are special in that they look, think, and act differently from everyone else.

Part of learning about yourself is understanding the different factors that make you a unique person. These include your heredity, environment, cultural heritage, personality, character, and self-concept.

Your Heredity

All people are influenced by their heredity. **Heredity** is the sum of all traits passed on through genes from parents

to children. Heredity causes people to be alike in many ways. Almost everyone is born with two arms, two legs, two eyes, two ears, a nose, and a mouth. Heredity also causes people to be different. Some are tall; others are short. Some have black hair; others have blond hair. Some have great intellectual potential; others have limited intellectual potential. See 1-1.

Your Environment

Your inherited traits are influenced by your environment. Your **environment** is made up of everything that surrounds you. As an infant, you had little control over your environment. As you are growing older, you are gaining more control. In the future, you will probably be able to choose the environment in which you will live.

1-1
Heredity causes both similarities and differences in people. How does your heredity influence you?

Two different types of environments influence your personal development: psychological and physical. Both affect the way you look, think, and act.

Your *psychological environment* is composed of attitudes expressed by people around you. It includes the feelings and beliefs of your family members, teachers, classmates, and friends. These people influence the attitudes you have.

Your *physical environment* is composed of objects around you. One main factor in your physical environment is the place where you live. You had little control of your physical environment as a young child, but as you grow older, you have more options.

Your Cultural Heritage

Your **cultural heritage** is made up of learned behaviors, beliefs, and languages that are passed from generation to generation. Your family helps you learn about the culture of your society. Their guidelines and beliefs become part of your heritage. The foods you eat, the holidays you celebrate, and the traditions you observe are part of your culture. Through all these cultural experiences, you learn appropriate behavior for your culture.

Most people are strongly influenced by their cultural heritage. It helps to make everyone unique. Part of learning about yourself is understanding how your own cultural heritage shapes your development. Understanding cultural differences between you and others is equally important.

An **ethnic group** is a group of people who share common racial and/or cultural characteristics such as national origin, language, religion, and traditions. Ethnic groups are important as they help to maintain a culturally healthy society. This is because a blending of all these groups' cultures makes American culture truly unique. Understanding this may help you appreciate your own cultural heritage. It also may help you appreciate others as they model their cultural heritages, 1-2.

Your Personality

Your personality results from a special blending of your heredity, environment, and cultural heritage, 1-3. **Personality** is the total of all the behavioral qualities and traits that make up an individual. It includes the way you feel, think, speak, dress, and relate to others.

Your personality is a combination of all the traits that make you unique. These traits develop over a period of time. Some are considered more desirable than others. Are you cheerful, cooperative, or easy-going? These are examples of desirable personality traits. On the other hand, laziness, moodiness, or grumpiness are less desirable traits. How would you describe yourself?

Your Character

Some parts of your personality are described as *character traits*. **Character** refers to inner traits, such as conscience,

1-2
Cultural diversity among people helps to maintain a healthy society.

1-3
The way you interact with your friends is a part of your personality that makes you unique.

moral strength, and social attitudes. It is the inner you—the force that guides your conduct and behavior toward acceptable standards of right and wrong.

Character development, like other personality traits, begins in childhood. Children are taught that certain behaviors are acceptable while others are not acceptable, 1-4. For example, young children may be told not to hit others. As they begin to internalize the message, they conform because an internal control tells them what is appropriate. As character continues to grow, children develop acceptable standards of behavior that they use voluntarily. They can then face new situations and know right from wrong. This happens even when no one is there to guide their behavior.

Character Traits

Common character traits include caring, fairness, respect, trustworthiness, responsibility, and citizenship. *Caring*

1-4
As children interact with parents and other adults, they develop acceptable standards of behavior.

Respect means to hold someone or something in high regard. Every individual deserves the respect of others and should be treated with courtesy. You may not agree with someone on a particular issue, but you can respect his or her right to see the issue differently. You still remain friends. You admire others for standing up for what they believe, and you respect them for it. Respect for personal property means caring for it. If it is borrowed, it is returned in the condition it was received. Respect for authority means obeying the rules and laws established for the well-being of all. Acting with consideration and even admiration toward people, laws, and property describes a respectful person.

Trustworthiness means you can be relied upon. For instance, if a friend tells you a secret, you do not tell anyone else, 1-5. Your friend trusts you. Trustworthy people can be relied upon to keep their promises. Trustworthiness is important in building strong relationships. Employees are expected to be trustworthy. They can be trusted to do their jobs to the best of their abilities.

is a trait that describes people who are kind to others. Caring people are friendly to everyone, not just their close friends. They are helpful and respond quickly to the needs of others. Caring people have empathy. **Empathy** means they understand how others feel even when their own personal feelings may differ. They also show sympathy. They know to give a caring hug when others are hurting.

Fairness is the ability to be honest and impartial—to act in an objective, unbiased way. Those who are fair show no prejudice toward others' opinions, ideas, or ways of doing things. All people are treated impartially.

1-5
Most people expect their good friends to be trustworthy.

Responsibility means being accountable for your actions and obligations. Whether you like your responsibilities or not, you are accountable for them. That means you can be counted upon to complete your assigned tasks. There are many duties or obligations that you are responsible for at home, school, and work. These may include taking care of your belongings and performing work assigned to you. Responsibility for your actions means you accept the consequences for what you do, good or bad. Responsibility and trustworthiness are traits that work together. If you take care of your responsibilities, you are a trustworthy person. However, it is also important not to accept more responsibilities than you can handle.

Citizenship (as a character trait) refers to the quality of a person's response to membership in a community. Citizenship is usually conferred on you at birth. You become a citizen of the country and state in which you are born. You are also a citizen of the community in which you live. Loyalty to country and community is expected of its citizens. When you complain yet fail to do your part, you show disloyalty. If services or facilities are not as you would like, you have a duty to make them better. You can work to make needed changes. This is the mark of good citizenship at any level of government.

Your Self-Concept

At an early age, you began developing your own self-concept. Your **self-concept** is your view of yourself. This view was largely influenced by people around you and the way you interpreted their behaviors toward you.

Positive and Negative Self-Concept

When people show approval of you and the things you do, you receive a positive message such as, "You're all right. People like what you do." Positive feelings like these help you develop a *positive self-concept*, 1-6.

If you have a positive self-concept, you will see yourself as a lovable and worthwhile person. You will expect most people to accept you. Chances are they will receive you and want you for a friend.

When people show disapproval, you receive a negative warning. You may feel a sense of personal rejection. You may think, "They don't like me, because they don't

1-6
Friends who accept you for who you are help you develop a positive self-concept.

seem to like what I do." Many messages such as these would tend to promote a *negative self-concept*. Every person receives some positive and some negative messages. However, it lies within the individual to measure his or her own self-worth.

If you have a negative self-concept, you will feel uncertain. You may not see yourself as lovable or worthwhile. You will hesitate to reach out to others in fear of possible rejection. You may feel a little uncomfortable about yourself. You may even make others feel uncomfortable when they are with you.

Improving Your Self-Concept

Because your self-concept continues to be formed throughout your life, having a positive self-concept is important. Liking yourself and feeling good about yourself allows your personality to grow and develop even more. See 1-7.

If you would like to feel better about yourself, you can learn to improve your self-concept. Doing so can help you deal with negative feelings and make desired changes. As you learn more about yourself and learn to accept yourself, you will gain more self-confidence. You will have the confidence to try new activities and accept any challenges you face. As a result, your self-concept will become more positive. There are several steps you can take to start improving your image of yourself.

Be Realistic About Your Expectations of Yourself

This is one way to improve your self-concept. Remember that no one is perfect. Know that you will do some things well. Know, also, that you may not do some things as well as other people. In other words, look for balance in your life. Know that some times in your life will be great, while other times will be fair. Feel

1-7
As you mature, you will begin to explore ways to improve your self-concept.

good about yourself whenever you do something, whether or not you are the best at doing it.

Don't be afraid of failure. Failure can be beneficial if it forces you to take a fresh look at yourself. Think about what went wrong. Find a way to make a comeback. With that comeback, you can experience a sense of freedom that allows you to take new risks. You may find untapped inner resources as you redirect your plans for your life.

Develop Your Talents and Abilities

Another way to improve your self-concept is to work to develop your talents and abilities, 1-8. If you are a member of Family, Career, and Community Leaders of America, take on a special project that will give you an opportunity to develop a new skill. Who knows—you might be the top salesperson in the fund-raiser. Maybe you will help others fight hunger by collecting double the number of canned products for the local food bank.

1-8
You can improve your self-esteem by getting involved in an activity you do well. If you know you are a good musician, take lessons and become even better.

Look for Positive Relationships with Others

All people need positive reinforcement to develop a healthy self-concept. While people determine their own self-worth, they weigh the attitudes expressed toward them by others. Living in a negative psychological environment and maintaining a positive outlook is difficult. Therefore, surrounding yourself with some positive people who support you is important.

Spend Time Doing Activities You Enjoy

All people need to spend time alone to think about their lives, hopes, and dreams. Learn to enjoy being alone and doing activities by yourself. Maybe you like reading poetry or playing the piano. These activities will help you relax and give you pleasure. You may enjoy running. Many people find exercise a way to help them relieve tension and see things more clearly.

Develop a Sense of Humor

Most importantly, develop a sense of humor. Learn to laugh at yourself. Don't become embarrassed. A sense of humor adds a soft touch to otherwise hurtful situations. It can take the sting out of cutting remarks and sarcasm. It can help you be comfortable in touchy situations. Finally, it can help others feel comfortable with you.

Your Self-Esteem

Self-esteem is the sense of worth you attach to yourself—it's a word used to describe a positive self-concept. Taking pride in yourself and your accomplishments shows self-esteem.

Your self-esteem is an important part of you. It is a personal statement you make to yourself that describes your self-worth. You are a worthy person. If you feel that you are worthwhile, it will show in your relationships with others. If you accept yourself, you are more likely to accept others. Those who lack self-esteem think little of themselves. Therefore, they don't think others will like them. Sometimes in an attempt to make friends, they give in to negative peer pressure. They may get involved in behaviors that are not in their best interest.

An important fringe benefit of self-esteem is that you are likely to demonstrate more responsible behavior. You have the strength to make your own decisions. Knowing that you are not dependent on others for your sense of worth, you can use

Setting the Scene: Humor Can Help

Imagine you are a member of a dance-planning committee. You enjoy serving on the committee. It makes you feel included and allows you time to socialize with some of the older students you admire. However, at today's meeting you are distracted by thoughts of your upcoming term paper. You don't even realize the other committee members are trying to get your attention until they burst into laughter. You are wildly embarrassed to be singled out in this negative way, especially in front of people you want to impress.

Analyze It: How can you use humor in this situation? What effect might this have on the other committee members? What might your reaction suggest about your self-concept?

1-9
People with strong self-esteem often choose careers where they can help others.

Check It Out!

1. Explain how heredity causes people to be alike and to be different.
2. How does your cultural heritage help make you unique?
3. What three factors blend together to form a person's personality?
4. Describe a person with a positive self-concept.
5. Explain the relationship between self-esteem and self-concept.

your best judgment. You are less likely to be influenced by negative peer pressure. Your demonstration of responsible behavior makes you a better person, and it also makes you a positive example for others, 1-9.

Having self-esteem does not mean that everything you do will be successful. However, it does help you to maintain a realistic view of your successes and failures. You will be more likely to try harder to reach your goals and fulfill your responsibilities if you have self-esteem.

Topic 1-2
Your Growth and Development

Objectives
After studying this topic, you will be able to
▼ identify different types of growth.
▼ describe how human needs influence behavior.
▼ relate how wants differ from needs.
▼ explain how values and standards are interrelated.

Topic Terms
maturation
chronological growth
physical growth
puberty
adolescence
hormones
emotional growth
intellectual growth
social growth
peers
needs
wants
values
standards

If growth and development can be summarized in one word during the teen years, that word would be *change*. The change that occurs between childhood and adulthood is frequently described as **maturation**. Changes that occur will be chronological, physical, emotional, intellectual, and social. As you mature, your physical, personal, and behavioral characteristics will become more adult.

Growing Chronologically

Chronological growth refers to a person's age. This is the only type of growth that takes place at the same rate for all people. Each birthday automatically adds another year to your age. Chronological maturity is often used for legal purposes. People have to prove their age to obtain a driver's license, vote in government elections, or enlist for military service.

Growing Physically

Physical growth refers to the changes in your body stature. See 1-10. Your physical growth is influenced by heredity and health habits. The way you choose to eat, exercise, and care for your body will influence your physical development.

An important stage of physical growth is called **puberty**. In this stage of development, an individual becomes capable of sexual reproduction. This stage lasts two to three years and is characterized by rapid growth—the fastest rate of growth since infancy. Puberty ends when sexual reproduction becomes possible, but growth continues. Puberty generally begins between the ages of nine and eleven for girls. It begins between the ages of eleven and thirteen for boys.

Adolescence is a term used to describe that period from puberty until growth ceases and adulthood is reached. This period usually lasts until young women are 15 to 17 years of age. Adolescence usually lasts until young men are 17 to 20 years of age.

1-10

Everyone develops at different rates. Your physical growth is probably different from that of your friends.

Physical Changes

Physical changes that take place during adolescence are caused, in part, by hormones. **Hormones** are chemical substances in the body that trigger certain types of physical growth. The most noticeable changes are a sudden growth spurt and the development of adult characteristics. Visible signs of sexual development appear. Members of both sexes experience an increase in their muscle tissue that results in a weight gain. Skeletal development causes increased height and wider shoulders among males.

Other physical changes among males include the enlargement of the genitals, the appearance of pubic hair, and a deepening of the voice. Facial and underarm hair appear later.

Females increase in height. They also have an increase in fat, or *adipose tissue*.

Breasts enlarge, and pubic and underarm hair appears. The menstrual cycle begins shortly after these physical changes occur.

Growing Emotionally

Emotional growth refers to development in the range of feelings and the ability to express these feelings. The hormones that stimulate changes in physical development during puberty and adolescence stimulate changes in the emotional state as well.

Emotional Changes

It is common during adolescence to have significant emotional swings. Perhaps you will feel moody—up one minute, but down the next. You may find yourself desperately wanting independence from your family. A little later, however, you long for the security that your family offers. There are times you will want to express your own identity. You may want trendy clothes or a new haircut. At other times you will want to be just like everyone else, 1-11. You may feel you are on an emotional roller coaster.

Sensitive is a key word to describe teens' emotions. Adolescents crave acceptance and are sensitive to criticism. They are sensitive about their personal appearance and want to know they are attractive to others. Sometimes they are critical of themselves. Their self-concept may be weak at times, like the young man who was feeling down when he said, "I'm a real

loser." A caring friend pointed out some of the young man's strengths. After reflecting on this, the young man replied, "I do some things really well, but some I don't do well at all. I guess I'm really pretty balanced."

Growing Intellectually

Intellectual growth means developing the ability to reason and form complex thought patterns. It is influenced by your heredity, environment, and desire to learn. When your environment offers learning experiences, you are stimulated to think and look for new solutions to problems. When you were younger, you needed to see concrete examples for any problem to be solved. Now you can understand more abstract concepts.

If you have a desire to learn, intellectual growth will occur throughout your life. Many older adults are still enthusiastic about learning new things. If your environment lacks stimulation, or if you lack the desire to learn, your intellectual growth will be impaired.

Growing Socially

Social growth means developing the ability to get along with other people. You begin this process in early childhood as you learn to take turns and share. Through years of playing and working together, people learn to get along with others. They also learn that different people like different activities, 1-12.

Social Changes

Growing socially is sometimes complex in the teen years. As you mature in other ways, your relationships with adults change. You no longer wish to be treated

1-11
The desire to be like your peers but still have your own identity is a natural part of growing up.

1-12
How well do you get along with others? A socially mature person has good times with others and enjoys life.

as a child by parents, teachers, and other adults. You want more control over your social situations; you want to spend more time with your peers. **Peers** are other people who are your age.

With added control comes added responsibilities. You must learn to interact with adults on a more mature level while showing respect for their wisdom and authority. You must learn to interact with your peers in ways that foster your positive development and theirs.

Influences on Behavior

All humans share certain needs. These needs cause people to behave as they do. Most behaviors are attempts to satisfy a need or to remove something that is not needed. In an effort to satisfy needs, you will establish values and standards for your life.

Human Needs

Needs are basic items that are required for living. All people have the same basic needs. These needs must be met for proper growth and development.

Abraham Maslow, a famous psychologist, identified five levels of human needs. He then ranked these needs in order of priority. As you read chart 1-13, notice that more needs are related to the psychological environment than to the physical environment. Observe, however, that physical needs are more urgent. They must be fulfilled before the psychological needs can be considered.

Comparing Needs and Wants

Do you know the difference between *needs* and *wants*? Sometimes the meaning of these words is confusing. However, each one has a distinct meaning. Understanding the relationship between both terms is important as both affect your behavior.

Everyone has the same basic needs. However, people have different wants. **Wants** are those things people desire, but don't need. They are not necessary for survival. They may bring satisfaction, but

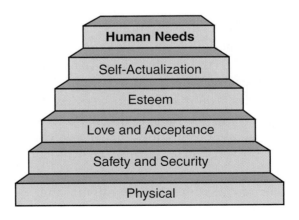

1-13
In Maslow's ranking of human needs, physical needs have first priority.

life will go on without them. Sometimes people want something they don't really need. The latest computer game or an expensive piece of jewelry might be an example.

The Relationship of Needs and Wants

There is a relationship between wants and needs that affects your behavior. For example, you need food in the morning before you begin your schoolwork. You may want to eat at home, or you may want to eat in the cafeteria after you arrive at school. Either way your need has been satisfied, but you chose the way you wanted to satisfy it.

Wants for some people may even be needs for others. For example, in most families an adult needs to work to provide a family income. Such an income is used to provide for the family's needs and perhaps some of the items the family wants. A teen in that same family may want to work too, but for different reasons. The teen's basic needs, however, would be met whether or not he or she earned an income. The adult who works to supply family needs may want to work outdoors—perhaps in a construction trade. Another adult who works to meet certain needs may want to work indoors drafting house plans.

As you define your needs and wants, you may recognize the necessity to meet the basic needs of dependent family members. You may have to sacrifice some wants to be able to do this. Good management techniques will enable you to balance needs and wants. This allows the family to satisfy its needs and have some resources left to help satisfy some wants, 1-14.

1-14
Would you be satisfying a want or a need by buying a CD?

Values

People satisfy their needs in different ways. If this were not so, everyone would eat the same kind of food and live in the same kind of house. Instead, life is full of variety. Each person is unique with his or her style of living. Each person's decisions and behaviors are different from those of anyone else. Factors that contribute to the differences between people include their values and standards.

Values are the beliefs, feelings, and experiences you consider to be important and desirable. Honesty, friendship, freedom, happiness, popularity, health, or education may be values you consider important. The combination of values you have and the importance you give each one makes you unique. Your values become a part of your personality.

Your values affect your behavior. Consciously or unconsciously, they guide the decisions you make every day. If education is important to you, you might choose to spend an evening studying rather than watching TV. If adventure is something you value, you probably would choose an exciting hobby, 1-15.

Your values were not given to you at birth; they have developed over time. All the experiences you have had throughout your life have contributed to your set of values. Your future experiences will also affect your values. Some values will become more important to you. Others will become less important. Your set of values will never be final. They will change just as you change.

Factors Affecting Your Values

Many factors influence the development of your values. One important factor is your relationships with other people. Your first basic values were learned from the people who took care of you as a young child—your parents, other family members, babysitters, and preschool teachers. You may not have always understood the words they were saying. However, you could recognize the love, warmth, honesty, and other personal traits they demonstrated. Children imitate people they admire.

As you grew older, you probably began to adopt the values of other children who were your friends. As you made new friends, they may have encouraged you to change some of your values. (This is why parents are often concerned about their children's friends.) A similar pattern probably will occur throughout your life. The people you meet, especially your peers and friends, will continue to influence what you consider to be important.

Your experiences, along with your education and knowledge, also affect your values. Something can't be important to you if you don't know anything about it. Once you have experienced or studied something, you can then decide if it will become a part of your values.

Needs are another factor that influence values. If you had not eaten for three days, you would put a high priority on food. You likely would trade two tickets to the best rock concert of the summer for a good dinner. Someone who has just moved from a rural area to a city may have the need to feel secure. That person may place a high priority on home security measures.

Your values are also influenced by your religious beliefs and morals. The presence or absence of religious teachings and experiences can affect your choice of values. These, in turn, affect your concepts of right and wrong and of good and bad.

Values are affected by the family life cycle. When a couple first marries, material possessions may be important to them.

1-15
Wakeboarding is a sport for people who value adventure and excitement.

They may want a house, furnishings, a car, and other possessions. If they have children, their values are likely to change, 1-16. Being financially secure and having nearby playgrounds, friends, and schools for their children may take on new importance. When their children have grown and left home, their values will change again. Convenience, nearness to family members and friends, and leisure activities may become more important.

Value Conflicts

People are constantly faced with conflicts in their values. These conflicts can create many frustrations. See 1-17. For instance, someone whose values include both honesty and friendship may be torn when choosing between telling the truth and saving a friendship.

Values can have an impact on your interests. For instance, if you think education is more important than sports, you may choose to join the math club instead of the volleyball team.

Value conflicts often arise in families. For example, a family's values might include job success, prestige, and close

1-17
If you value good physical health, you may feel frustrated when you have to pass on high-fat foods that you enjoy.

friendships. A job promotion may create a conflict among these. The promotion would be a mark of success and would add to the family's prestige. However, it would mean moving to another state and leaving good friends. The family must decide which values are more important to them. This will determine whether or not the job promotion is accepted.

Value Judgments

When you make a value judgment, you assign a level of importance to a certain item or action. You may think a flower is pretty, a song is good, a cake tastes terrible, or a person is mean. When you make value judgments, you should remember that you are a unique person with a unique set of values. Your particular values cause you to behave in a certain way. They influence the choices you make. They affect your reactions to ideas and objects.

Before you criticize other people for making judgments that differ from yours, stop and think. How well do you know those people? Do you know what

1-16
A family with children may prefer to live in a neighborhood with many children and nearby parks.

is important to them? Do you know what prompts them to make their decisions?

Values vary from person to person. Try to keep an open mind about the personal values of each individual. If you do, you will be able to understand and get along with other people better.

Standards

Standards are accepted levels of achievement. There are many different kinds of standards. People have standards for their appearance and how well they do certain skills. They have standards for the quality of their possessions, too. Different people have different standards. For instance, one student might have a standard to answer every test question correctly. Another student might have a standard to simply get a passing grade. See 1-18.

Standards and Values

People's standards are related to their values. Their standards will be high for the items they value. For instance, a person considers cleanliness a value. That person will probably have high standards related to the upkeep of the house.

Like values, people acquire their standards through personal contacts and their experiences. Therefore, people from the same culture, and especially the same family, often have similar standards.

Knowing your own standards and what you expect from life can help you understand yourself more fully. In a similar way, you can have a better understanding of other people if you notice what standards they apply to their own lives.

1-18
This student has set high standards for academic performance. Maintaining this standard takes careful preparation.

Check It Out!

1. Name the type of growth that refers to changes in body stature.
2. Explain the difference between emotional growth and intellectual growth.
3. _____ growth is how you relate to other people.
4. List five factors that influence the development of a person's values.
5. Describe how standards are related to values.

Chapter Review

Summary

Learning all about you means looking at yourself and your present stage of development. You are growing toward adulthood, so you are in a state of change. Your heredity, environment, cultural heritage, personality, character, and self-concept are factors that help make you a unique—and special—person. All teens grow and develop at different rates physically, emotionally, intellectually, and socially.

As a unique person, you have needs, values, and standards. Each one affects your behavior. The way you meet your needs, the values you adopt, and the standards you set for yourself will have a great effect on your life.

Think About It!

1. Summarize some ways you are influenced by each of the following: (A) heredity, (B) environment, (C) cultural heritage, (D) personality, (E) character, (F) self-concept
2. What advice would you give to a friend who makes this statement: "I really feel down! I'm the shortest one in gym class, my grades aren't that great, and I don't feel like I fit in!" Base your response on the five areas of growth and development.
3. How do your character traits influence your personality?
4. How can a sense of humor improve your self-concept?
5. What is the difference between adolescence and puberty?
6. What are some of the ways you think you have grown socially?

7. Why is it important to understand how needs, values, and standards are interrelated?

Try It Out!

1. Select a character from a movie, book, or TV program. Explain how this character has been influenced by his or her environment.
2. Use magazine pictures to make a class bulletin board depicting cultural heritage. Choose an appropriate caption for the bulletin board.
3. Trace around your hand on a sheet of paper. Within the lines, write at least 10 words or phrases that describe you. Ask a friend to review the words you wrote to determine whether they tend to reflect a positive or negative self-concept. Determine how you can convert the negatives to positives.
4. Describe what you would consider the ideal person—someone who is at the peak in all five types of growth. Compare your ideas with those of your classmates. How do your ideas differ from their ideas?
5. List all the activities you did yesterday. Then list the needs you were trying to fulfill—either consciously or subconsciously—by completing these activities.
6. Describe how people might show they have the following values: beauty, love, religion, security, adventure.
7. Work in small groups to list some common value conflicts teens have to resolve. Perform skits to show possible solutions to the conflicts.

Chapter 2
Your Health and Fitness

Careers

These careers relate to the topics in this chapter:
▼ health spa attendant
▼ recreation aide
▼ health records technician
▼ public health professional

As you study the chapter, see if you can think of others.

Topics

2-1 Your Physical Fitness
2-2 Your Mental Health
2-3 Health Risks
2-4 Strategies for Healthful Personal Development

Topic 2-1

Your Physical Fitness

Objectives

After studying this topic, you will be able to
▼ explain why good health is important.
▼ describe two areas on which physical activity should focus.
▼ use suggestions for getting adequate sleep.
▼ determine good grooming practices.

Topic Terms

physical wellness
physical fitness
aerobic capacity
insomnia
grooming

While some people are not born with good health, everyone wants to be healthy. Most people know good health means more than merely being free from disease. A concept known as *wellness* describes a desired state of health. **Physical wellness** means the body is able to fight illness and infection and repair damage. This state of health makes you feel and look better. It gives you energy to do your daily tasks and helps you enjoy life more fully. Only a small percentage of people currently enjoy this level of good health. However, attaining physical wellness is a worthy goal that all people should try to achieve.

Two key factors can help you achieve physical wellness. First, you need professional medical care. This includes preventive health care with regular checkups and any needed emergency treatment. Second, you need self-care. This

means meeting your body's needs through good nutrition and weight management. It also means getting enough physical activity and rest as well as learning to manage stress. See 2-1. Finally, self-care includes grooming and personal hygiene.

Physical fitness refers to the condition of your body. When you are physically fit, your muscles are toned, your heart is strong, and your lungs are clear. You are able to perform a variety of tasks.

Fitness and wellness go hand in hand. You cannot be healthy if your body is not strong. Likewise, you cannot keep your body strong if you are not healthy.

Many factors play a role in determining your state of physical wellness and physical fitness. However, the care you give yourself has the greatest impact on both areas of your well-being. You need to assume responsibility for your health and fitness.

2-1
Getting enough physical activity is part of the self-care needed to achieve physical wellness.

The Importance of Good Health

Your health can affect you in a number of ways. Your ability to succeed at school depends on your health. When you are physically fit, you are better able to stay alert and learn. Poor health can prevent you from attending classes regularly. Your grades may suffer if you are not able to attend lectures and participate in labs. This can affect any plans you may have to go to college or technical school.

Good health is important to career achievement. Some careers require excellent health and physical fitness, 2-2. You need to be in your workplace daily. If poor health causes you to miss work, you may have trouble keeping your job. If you stay healthy, you will be more likely to advance in your career.

Your personal and family life will also be more satisfying if you have good health. You will be able to more fully enjoy interacting with people and taking part in activities. You will feel better as you do your daily tasks. Good health will help you get more enjoyment from daily living.

Being Physically Active

Getting daily physical activity is a key part of building and maintaining physical fitness. Regular physical activity can

2-2
People whose jobs involve physical labor need to stay in excellent health to do their jobs well.

Setting the Scene: Getting Back in the Game

After a summer where you had a job working on computers all day, you decide to try out for an athletic team. The coach welcomes you but restricts you to short, simple workouts and limited practice. You know you will not make the beginning lineup at this level. You mention this to the coach, state that you are disappointed, and hint that you might drop out if things don't change.

Analyze It: Why would the coach limit the activity of a player who has been fairly inactive all summer? How can you use the situation to still become the best player you can be? How can you use this outcome to help with future goals?

enhance your posture. It can improve your blood circulation and increase your lung capacity. Building more movement into your day can help relieve stress, boredom, and depression. Physical activity can help you build strength and flexibility. It can also help you manage your weight. Besides all that, physical activity can be fun, especially if you do it with friends.

Physical activity does not have to be a strenuous exercise program. Many of the tasks that are part of your daily routine are forms of moderate physical activity. For instance, walking, bicycling, raking leaves, and cleaning the house will all help you develop fitness. See 2-3. If you enjoy activities that are more vigorous, you might try dancing, swimming, or playing tennis.

2-3
The chores you do every day are types of physical activity.

You need to include at least 60 minutes of activity in your daily schedule. (Urge adults in your family to include at least 30 minutes of activity in their schedules.) You do not have to spend 60 minutes all at once. You can accumulate a number of 10 to 20-minute segments of activity throughout the day.

Aerobic Capacity

Physical activity is most worthwhile when it focuses on two areas. One of these areas is aerobic capacity. **Aerobic capacity** is a measure of the condition of your heart and lungs. One way to test your aerobic capacity is to measure your pulse rate. Your pulse rate reveals the number of times your heart beats per minute. People who enjoy a high aerobic capacity have a lower pulse rate than those who are out of shape. The time it takes for an increased pulse rate to return to normal is another sign of aerobic capacity. The faster your pulse rate returns to normal, the higher your capacity. Activities that improve aerobic capacity include walking, running, jogging, bicycling, swimming, and aerobic dancing.

Muscle Strength and Flexibility

The second focus of physical activity should be on muscle strength and flexibility. Muscular strength relates to your muscles' ability to do work. It is often measured by how much weight you can lift, 2-4. You do not have to lift weights to build strength. You can also lift common objects such as bags full of groceries or backpacks full of books.

Flexibility refers to your range of motion. A broad range of motion can help you avoid muscle injuries. Dancing and doing stretches can help you increase flexibility.

2-4
Lifting weights helps build muscle strength, which is one of the goals of physical activity.

The Importance of Leisure Activities

Leisure is freedom from chores, homework, jobs, and other responsibilities. It is the time you have to do something just because you want to do it. Leisure is not only fun—it is also good for you. The greatest benefit derived from leisure is the reduction of stress. Leisure activities help keep the body, mind, and spirit ready to fight any challenging forces you might face.

Many busy people fail to plan for leisure. Some think it is selfish to claim time for themselves when they could be doing something more important. This is a mistake. The ability to be productive requires you to first care for yourself.

Leisure can be used to do anything you like as long as it is not a responsibility. Some teens may choose to watch a favorite TV show or read. Others might use their leisure time for skateboarding or bicycling. You may spend your leisure time alone or with others. Many families use their leisure time to enjoy recreational activities together. See 2-5.

The Importance of Sleep

Teenagers and adults often fall into the trap of not getting enough sleep. You need to find time to sleep, even if it means

2-5
Strengthening family relationships can be one effect of enjoying leisure time together.

The More You Know: Leisure Activities Affect You Physically

Enjoyable activities cause the brain to release chemicals such as serotonin and endorphins, which create a sense of well-being. When you feel stressed, try to find ways to make the stressors enjoyable. For one person, an outing with the family might be leisure. Another person might find it stressful. Look for the best in situations at hand. When the differences between enjoyment and stress is your attitude, try to develop a positive outlook. Do what you must do and do it as cheerfully as possible. Relieving stress may be as simple as changing your attitude.

cutting down on your activities. People who lack sleep may become irritable or show a decline in muscle coordination. The quality of their work usually suffers, too.

The amount of sleep a person needs is an individual matter. Some people get by with six hours a night. Others need nine or ten hours. Most people feel best when they sleep seven to eight hours a night.

Insomnia is the inability to get the amount of sleep you need when you need it. Taking sleeping pills is a poor solution to the problem. Most sleeping pills become ineffective after a few weeks of use, and they can be addictive. If you have trouble sleeping, try the following suggestions listed.

▼ Make physical activity a part of your daily routine. It can help you sleep deeper and longer.

▼ Establish regular times for going to bed and waking up. You can program yourself into a sleeping schedule.

▼ Form a habit of doing a relaxing activity just before bedtime. Read, listen to soft music, or take a hot bath.

▼ Use your bed strictly for sleep. This will help program your body to know that getting into bed means "it is now time to sleep." If you want to read or watch TV, do so before getting into bed. See 2-6.

▼ Stay away from coffee, tea, or cola in the evening. The caffeine in these beverages may keep you awake.

2-6
If you have trouble sleeping, avoid using your bed for studying or any other activity besides sleep.

▼ Sleep on a mattress that is neither too soft nor too firm.
▼ Keep the temperature in the bedroom at a moderate setting—not too cold and not too warm.

The Importance of Personal Hygiene

Other people's impressions of you are influenced by the way you look. Your appearance can also have a great impact on your self-image. However, you do not need beautiful features to be attractive. Your appearance is largely determined by the way you care for yourself.

Grooming means cleaning and caring for the body. To be well groomed, you must take action. You must pay attention to all aspects of personal care, from head to toe.

Basic Hygiene

Basic *hygiene*, or cleansing practices that promote good health, includes your whole body. You need to take a bath or shower every day. Soap and warm water will remove dirt, oils, and dead skin cells. This will help you feel and smell fresh. Deodorants and antiperspirants will help control body odor throughout the day.

Caring for Your Skin

Your face is likely to be the first feature people notice about you. There are four skin types—normal, oily, dry, and combination. To care for your skin properly, you will first need to determine your skin type. Cleanse skin using products formulated for your skin type. Follow cleansing with a moisturizer. See 2-7.

2-7
The oily areas of combination skin may require extra cleansing.

Your Skin and the Sun

Another important aspect of skin care is avoiding prolonged exposure to the sun. The sun is damaging to the skin and is a leading cause of skin cancer. People of all ages and skin colors should take precautions to avoid too much sun exposure. Wear long sleeves, pants, and hats to help cover the skin. Also, apply a good sunscreen to exposed skin.

Caring for Your Teeth

Regular dental checkups and daily brushing and flossing should be a part of your health routine. Brush teeth at least twice daily and floss once a day.

Caring for Your Hair

Hair care is basic to a healthy, attractive appearance. Hair care involves a number of steps. Proper shampooing, conditioning, and styling all play an important role in your appearance, 2-8.

2-8
Taking good care of your hair can enhance your appearance.

2-9
Teens who take part in sports need to choose easy-care hairstyles that suit their active lifestyles.

Your lifestyle will affect your choice of a hairstyle. You should be able to care for your hair within a reasonable amount of time. Your hairstyle should be suited to your activities. It should not be a safety hazard as you work. It should not be an inconvenience to you if you participate in sports. See 2-9.

Check It Out!

1. True or false. A person's health can affect his or her ability to get and keep a job.
2. Name five benefits of daily physical activity.
3. How many hours of sleep do most people need each night in order to feel their best?
4. Why is it important for you to know your skin type?

Topic 2-2
Your Mental Health

Objectives

After studying this topic, you will be able to
▼ describe a healthy mental state.
▼ demonstrate ways to cope with stress and depression.
▼ identify warning signs of depression that indicate a need for help.

Topic Terms

defense mechanism
stress
depression

2-10
People who are mentally healthy have a positive outlook on life.

Your health involves more than being fit physically. You need to be fit mentally and be able to recognize good mental health. You must realize that factors such as stress can affect your mental health. Also be aware that serious mental conditions, such as depression, require psychiatric help.

Maintaining a Healthy Mental State

People who are mentally healthy look for, and find, the best in their surroundings. They understand themselves and what makes them think and act as they do. They can accept their weaknesses and recognize their strengths. People with healthy mental states are self-confident. They are more likely to follow their principles than to respond to peer pressure. They also have a sense of humor and seem to enjoy life. See 2-10.

Mentally healthy people are able to deal with change. When they have difficulties, they are able to analyze the causes of the problems. They find solutions and put them into action. Once they solve problems, they can look back on the problems as learning experiences. This approach allows them to avoid similar problems in the future.

Maintaining a healthy mental state is an important aspect of self-care. Mentally healthy people know how to relieve frustration. They try not to think self-defeating thoughts. They are able to peaceably resolve conflicts with others to avoid negative feelings.

Using Defense Mechanisms

Sometimes situations occur that can challenge your healthy mental outlook. Wanting to guard yourself against pain, stress, and frustration in these situations is only natural. Using defense mechanisms is one way you care for your mental health. **Defense mechanisms** are behavior patterns people use to protect their self-esteem. See 2-11.

Defense mechanisms can be positive or negative solutions to problems. It depends entirely on how they are used. When people are aware they are using defense mechanisms, they are in control of their actions. They are using the defense

Defense Mechanisms

compensation. Using a substitute method to achieve a desired goal.
Example: You are too short to excel in basketball. However, if you work out and lift weights, maybe you will make the football team.

conversion. Transferring an emotion into a physical symptom or complaint.
Example: You fear you do not know the material to be covered on the test and you get a headache.

daydreaming. Accomplishing through the imagination something you have not accomplished in reality. Daydreaming can provide both positive and negative solutions. When daydreams are used to find creative solutions to problems, this is positive. When they are used frequently to escape reality through fantasy, they are negative.
Positive example: Sue was daydreaming about having the "latest look" for her party outfit. She suddenly thought of how she could combine some of her old clothes to get just the look she wanted.
Negative example: Maggie turned down Sam's invitation to the school party. Sam went with another girl and daydreamed he was with Maggie.

direct attack. Overcoming obstacles or problems through realistic efforts to find solutions.
Example: You are overweight because you snack on high-calorie foods all the time. You decide to cut out snacking and eat only nutritious food at regular mealtimes.

displacement. Transferring an emotion connected with one person or thing to another person or thing.
Example: You get upset with a friend and take it out on your sister.

giving up. Allowing discouragement to get you down.
Example: You try to lose weight. After two weeks, you have not lost an ounce. You just give up the idea of losing weight and go back to your old eating habits.

idealization. Placing a value on something or someone that is beyond its worth.
Example: You lose a favorite piece of jewelry and lie in bed and cry for two days.

projection. Placing the blame for your failures on other people or things.
Example: You blame the teacher when you fail a test because he did not tell you what would be covered on the test.

rationalization. Explaining your weaknesses or failures by giving socially acceptable excuses.
Example: You tell your parents you went to a movie they had forbidden you to see because all your friends were going.

regression. Reverting back to a less mature stage of development.
Example: You get angry with someone and slam the door as you leave.

2-11

These defense mechanisms are sometimes used to hide or counterbalance feelings or behaviors.

mechanisms in an attempt to maintain a healthy mental state. However, some people fail to realize they are relying on defense mechanisms. In these cases, defense mechanisms can cause people to lose touch with reality.

Stress and Your Health

Stress is your body's reaction to the events of your life. When something bad happens, such as forgetting your homework or losing your job, you feel stress. You also feel stress when good things happen, like winning a race or meeting someone special. See 2-12. In either case, your body responds. Your heart beats faster. Your face flushes. You perspire more. Perhaps your stomach tightens.

Change is frequently a cause of stress. Graduating from high school, taking a new job, getting married, and moving into a new apartment are all major changes. Doing all these at the same time would be likely to cause you stress.

You need stress in your life to add excitement, but too much can affect your physical and mental well-being. Excessive amounts that are not managed can result in physical and emotional problems. Someone under stress may experience headaches, stomachaches, high blood pressure, or changes in sleep patterns. Emotional signs of stress include tension, anger, and an inability to concentrate.

Coping with Stress

Learning to manage the stress in your life can help you become more mentally fit. When physical or emotional problems result from stress, look at your lifestyle. Ask yourself the following questions:

▼ Am I following good health practices? Am I able to eat regular meals and to get plenty of physical activity? Do I get an adequate amount of sleep?

▼ Am I realistic about the goals I have set for myself?

▼ Am I managing my time and energy efficiently in order to meet my commitments?

▼ Are there many changes occurring in my life at one time?

Answering these questions will help you identify the events in your life that cause stress. Once you have recognized these situations, you can work to resolve them. This will help you reduce any symptoms that have resulted from too much stress in your life. See 2-13 for some suggestions that may help you handle stress.

2-12
Even happy events can be stressful.

Techniques to Reduce Stress

- Be physically active each day to help relieve the pressures of stress. Go for a brisk walk or play a game of basketball or tennis.
- Be your own person. Do not let others put too much pressure on you. Learn to say no.
- Talk to someone about your concerns. When you have trouble solving a problem, other people may be able to offer suggestions you had not considered. A family member, friend, teacher, or counselor might be able to help. You might also want to seek professional advice.
- Take time off to escape from your everyday worries. Your mind will feel refreshed and ready to tackle anew what lies ahead. You might try listening to soft music, reading a fantasy story, or taking a warm bath.
- Manage your time. Set realistic goals for the tasks you need to accomplish. Prioritize the tasks. Then work toward your goals—do not procrastinate!
- Take care of your health. Eat right and get plenty of sleep and physical activity. Stress is easier to handle when you are rested and in good health.

2-13
A variety of techniques can be used to help people manage daily stress.

Depression

Depression is an emotional state that ranges from mild, short-lived feelings of sadness to a deep, despairing sense of dejection. Becoming depressed after a failure or loss is normal. However, a lingering depression whose onset does not seem to be triggered by a particular event is not normal.

Clinical depression has a number of symptoms, 2-14. Patients generally feel tired. They may not feel like doing anything. They may express no interest in favorite activities. They often experience feelings of isolation and desire to withdraw from others.

Clinical depression may have several causes. Some people experience seasonal depression. Treatment for these people may begin by adjusting their living environments. Sometimes depression is due to a chemical imbalance in the body. Such imbalances may be treated with therapy and drugs.

The impact of having clinical depression is different for each person. One person may react with intense emotion, viewing this situation as a crisis. Another person may see a diagnosis of clinical depression as only a slight setback.

Symptoms of Depression

- continual sadness, anxiety, or empty moods
- feelings of hopelessness and helplessness
- lack of interest in pleasurable activities
- sleeplessness or oversleeping
- decreased appetite or overeating
- difficulty concentrating, remembering, or making decisions
- headaches, digestive disturbances, nausea, or chronic pain
- feelings of isolation from family members and friends
- excessive crying

2-14
Prolonged symptoms of depression indicate a need for professional help.

Overcoming Depression

In both mild and clinical depression, a person must take much of the responsibility for his or her feelings. In this way, a person has an active role in his or her eventual recovery. Many of the techniques described for relieving stress can help a person beat a simple case of the blues. However, clinical depression requires professional treatment. A psychiatrist can determine appropriate therapies based on the needs of the patient. The psychiatrist may prescribe antidepressant drugs. He or she may also advise the patient to check into a psychiatric ward or hospital.

It may take months or even years for a patient to recover from clinical depression. During the recovery period, he or she will need patience and support from friends and family members. A depression patient might need encouragement to keep busy. Family members can urge the patient to follow a normal routine of grooming, eating, and sleeping. They can suggest leisure activities that will help keep the patient from thinking about his or her depression. A patient who is unable to work due to his or her illness can still be involved in household tasks. If tasks seem overwhelming, family members can suggest ways to break them into smaller, more manageable parts.

A depression patient might be encouraged to do something for other people, such as volunteer work. Doing something for others will force the patient to make human contacts. It will also help the patient see that he or she is needed—that life really does matter. See 2-15.

2-15
Becoming involved with volunteer work can be therapeutic for someone suffering from depression.

Suicide

Sometimes depression goes beyond a person's capacity to cope. The person may think everything will go wrong and nothing will help. The individual feels hopeless and powerless. Thus, he or she becomes reconciled to total failure and stops trying. This response is illogical, but intense emotions impair the ability to reason. When a person is in this type of mental state, he or she may have thoughts of suicide.

Suicide attempts are often cries for help. Victims are asking someone to understand and care. People who attempt suicide rarely wish to die. They just wish to end life as they know it. They fail to realize suicide is permanent and will allow them no opportunity to live a more satisfying life.

Teen Suicides

Some teen suicides correspond to a breakdown of the family support system. When the family structure is not intact, teens have fewer chances to communicate with parents. When problems arise, teens may feel no one is available to help them deal with their overwhelming feelings.

Competition is also regarded as a factor that affects suicide rates. Teens have to compete for leadership roles, sports teams, part-time jobs, college admissions, and scholarships. Competitive losses become very depressing for some teens. Relationships with others are another factor. Teens are sensitive about their peer relationships. They can also be easily hurt in relationships with members of the opposite sex. Feelings of rejection can lead some teens into a deep depression.

Some teens express feelings of anger, depression, and anxiety through harmful behavior. They may become delinquent or sexually promiscuous. They may run away from home or abuse alcohol and other drugs. Such actions prevent teens from forming bonds with others. Intense feelings of rejection, isolation, and despair may develop. A sense of failure at life can breed thoughts of suicide.

Suicide Prevention

Talk of suicide should not be taken lightly. If you suspect someone is suicidal, immediately seek the help of an adult. School counselors, members of the clergy, and medical professionals can point you in the direction of help. Suicide prevention hot lines are also available to help people deal with thoughts of suicide.

When People Need Help

People may need to seek help when they are not in top mental health. First, they should try talking with family members or trusted friends. If this does not resolve the feelings, a visit to a family physician may

be in order. The physician can rule out the possibility of a physical illness that could cause depression. He or she will be helpful in locating a mental health counselor if one is needed.

Maintaining mental health may not always be easy. However, people should not feel they have to do it by themselves. Many mental health specialists are available for counsel. Most regions have psychiatrists, mental health associations, and mental health centers. Most school systems also have psychologists and psychiatrists available for students who need specialized care, 2-16.

2-16
A school psychologist can help teens who have trouble handling problems such as stress and depression.

Check It Out!

1. Describe what is meant by a healthy mental state.
2. True or false. Stress is your body's reaction to both good and bad events in your life.
3. List five symptoms of depression that should not be ignored.

Topic 2-3
Health Risks

Objectives

After studying this topic, you will be able to
▼ list health risks associated with tobacco, alcohol and other drugs, and sexually transmitted diseases.
▼ explain how routine decisions can affect your health.

Topic Terms

passive smoking
smokeless tobacco
sexually transmitted disease (STD)
acquired immune deficiency syndrome (AIDS)
human immunodeficiency virus (HIV)

Practicing health habits to promote wellness involves avoiding certain health risks. These risks include tobacco as well as alcohol and other drugs. They also include sexually transmitted diseases.

Tobacco

Cigarette smoking is the largest preventable cause of illness and premature death in the United States. Many thousands of deaths each year are linked to cigarette smoking. People who smoke are more likely to suffer from heart disease, respiratory infections, and lung cancer.

Smoking during pregnancy can be harmful to the unborn child. Pregnant women who smoke have a higher risk of miscarriage and premature delivery. Babies born to women who smoke often weigh less, and their future growth and development may be impaired.

Passive smoking is also a health concern. **Passive smoking** is the inhaling of smoke in a smoke-filled environment. For people with lung and heart problems, breathing smoke-filled air can be very irritating, 2-17. Small children are also highly affected by passive smoking. Studies show that children of smokers are more likely to suffer from respiratory ailments than children of nonsmokers.

The use of **smokeless tobacco** products involves health risks as well. These are products such as chewing tobacco and snuff, which are chewed or placed against the gums. Their use has been linked to gum cancer and irritations of the gums and lips.

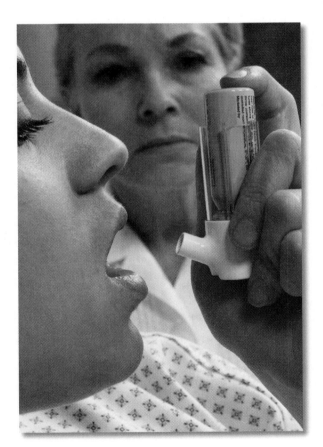

2-17
Asthma patients are likely to suffer more breathing problems if they live or work in smoke-filled environments.

For people who have never used tobacco products, continuing to avoid these products is the most health-conscious choice. For people who have used tobacco products, quitting is one of the best steps they can take for their health. People who quit smoking enjoy almost immediate health benefits. Within 24 hours, the risk of heart attack decreases. After three days, breathing becomes easier and lung capacity increases. Within weeks, the body's energy level increases.

Alcohol

Alcohol is a depressant drug that is a serious health risk. Health care for alcohol related illnesses and accidents costs millions of dollars every year. Alcohol can damage the brain, liver, stomach, and other organs. It also interferes with judgment, vision, muscle coordination, and reaction time. This is why it poses such great danger to people who drive under its influence. See 2-18.

Another health problem related to alcohol is alcoholism. Alcoholism is an addiction to alcohol. It is a disease that affects teenagers as well as adults. Alcoholics lose control of their drinking. They become dependent on alcohol. Alcoholism interferes with health, personal relationships, and ability to function.

Once alcohol has entered the body, coffee and cold showers will not help lessen its effects. Alcohol will continue to circulate in the body until the liver burns it up. This occurs at the rate of about one drink every two hours for a 150-pound person.

Alcohol has legal risks as well as health risks. It is illegal for teens to buy alcohol. It is illegal for *anyone* to drive under the influence of alcohol.

2-18
Safe drivers avoid the use of alcohol.

You can protect your health and your legal status by avoiding alcohol. You can also protect yourself by refusing to ride in a car with a driver who has been drinking.

Other Drugs

Alcohol is not the only drug that poses a health risk to teens. A variety of other drugs—both legal and illegal—can be hazardous to health.

Drug abuse is the use of a drug for a purpose other than it was intended. Even legal drugs purchased over the counter or with a prescription can be abused. These drugs should be used only according to package directions or as directed by a doctor. Also, never use someone else's prescription drugs.

Some legal products not sold as drugs are, nonetheless, used as drugs. Some people consume coffee, tea, and soft drinks for the stimulating effect of the caffeine they contain. Some people inhale paint, glue, and nail polish remover for their intoxicating effects.

Drug abuse can damage your health, interfere with your ability to function, and affect your mind. Some drugs cause *addiction*, which is a dependence of the body on a continuing supply of the drug. After an addiction has developed, taking the drug away will cause agonizing withdrawal symptoms.

Even experimenting with drugs can be dangerous. Experimenting often leads to more frequent drug use. If an addiction develops, serious health and legal problems may result. Some of the long-term health risks of drug abuse are listed in Chart 2-19.

Sexually Transmitted Diseases

As a health risk, **sexually transmitted diseases (STDs)** are a major concern in the United States. This concern is especially great for young adults. STDs are spread mainly through sexual contact. They can also be passed from pregnant women to their infants. They are not spread through casual contact, such as hugging or shaking hands.

The main STDs that are of concern are AIDS, gonorrhea, syphilis, chlamydia, and herpes. The symptoms and side effects of these diseases range from an outbreak of blisters to blindness to death.

You have a responsibility to prevent the spread of STDs. You can do this by becoming educated about STDs. If you know of someone who has an STD, encourage him or her to get prompt, effective treatment. Also encourage this person to behave responsibly and avoid spreading the STD to others. The only sure way to prevent STDs is to abstain from

Long-Term Health Risks of Drugs

- **Caffeine:** headaches, nervousness, stomach disorders
- **Depressants such as PCP, tranquilizers, quaaludes, and barbiturates:** fatigue, confusion, paranoia, addiction
- **Hallucinogens such as LSD:** hallucinations
- **Inhalants:** damage to the nervous system, kidneys, and blood
- **Marijuana:** learning difficulties, lung damage, possible damage to reproductive organs, psychological addiction, possible link to use of other illegal drugs
- **Narcotics such as heroin and other opiates:** addiction, malnutrition, risk of overdose and hepatitis, severe withdrawal symptoms
- **Steroids:** acne, stunted growth, sterility
- **Stimulants such as cocaine and amphetamines (speed):** nervousness, severe depression, nose damage, hallucinations, damage to the heart and brain

2-19
Abuse of both legal and illegal drugs can have negative, long-term effects.

sex. The risk of contracting STDs becomes higher as a person has more sexual partners. You owe it to yourself to stay healthy and avoid contracting STDs.

AIDS

The most deadly STD is **acquired immune deficiency syndrome (AIDS)**. This disease is caused by the **human immunodeficiency virus (HIV)**, which breaks down the body's immune system. This leaves the body vulnerable to diseases a healthy body could resist. Most people with AIDS eventually die from one or more of these diseases.

HIV is transmitted through such body fluids as blood and semen. HIV can be contracted through sharing contaminated intravenous needles as well as through sexual contact. Infants can contract HIV during the birth process or through breast-feeding.

In the past, some people contracted HIV from blood transfusions. However, this risk is now very small since all blood is screened for HIV. There is no risk of contracting HIV from donating blood because fresh needles are used for each donation.

Decisions That Affect Your Health

You make many routine decisions every day. You decide what to eat, where to go, and what to wear. Take a minute when making these decisions to think about how they might affect your health. For instance, keep in mind that limiting high-fat foods can reduce your risk of heart disease. Remember that using crosswalks and traffic lights can help you avoid being hit by a car. Do not forget that dressing warmly in winter will help you prevent hypothermia. Keeping your health in mind will help you make decisions that will promote wellness.

Not all health-related decisions are routine. You might have to decide if you want to go skydiving or bungee jumping. Some people have no desire to participate in such high-risk activities. Others are thrilled by the potential danger.

If you are intrigued by a certain degree of risk, take precautions. You do not have to avoid all potentially dangerous activities to protect your health. However, you have a responsibility to be fully aware of the risks you are taking. Then you need to do whatever is necessary to make the activity as safe as possible. Take lessons from trained professionals to learn how to do activities properly. Wear protective clothing. Plan what you will do if problems arise.

Avoid risks when you can. When you must take risks, address them sensibly. This will help you protect your health and make your life more fulfilling. See 2-20.

2-20
Knowing traffic laws and wearing protective clothing will help take the risk out of riding a motorcycle.

Check It Out!

1. Inhaling smoke in a smoke-filled environment is called _____.
2. True or false. Drinking coffee will help sober up someone who is experiencing the effects of alcohol.
3. List three long-term health risk of each of the following: marijuana, stimulants, inhalants, steroids, and caffeine.
4. What is HIV and how is it transmitted?
5. Give an example of a routine decision and explain how it can affect your health.

Strategies for Healthful Personal Development

Objectives

After studying this topic, you will be able to
▼ summarize factors that contribute to a quality life.
▼ identify roadblocks to personal development.
▼ explain the consequences of risk-taking behavior.
▼ relate the importance of supportive relationships.

Topic Term

quality of life

Quality of life is a phrase used to describe many factors that work together to foster personal well-being. How would you describe a good life? What do you want out of life? What is most important to you and your family? These are questions you might ask yourself in forming your view of a quality life.

What Contributes to Quality of Life?

The following are some of the factors people mention when describing a quality of life:

▼ *Good health.* Your health and the health of the other members of your family is very important. Remember the last time you were ill. Did you tell yourself "if I can just get better, everything will be okay"? People often don't realize how important their health is until they lose it.

▼ *Environmental factors.* Clean air and water, a safe neighborhood, and access to recreational facilities are just some of the environmental factors that can impact the quality of your life.

▼ *Emotional closeness.* To feel you are loved and to feel love for others is important to most people. Without this emotional tie to at least one other person, life may not be as satisfying as it could be. People who feel loved are usually happier, more enthusiastic, healthier, less prone to illness, and generally live longer.

▼ *Social ties.* Having friends and feeling like a member of a community is part of a fulfilling life. Those who feel isolated and alone are usually less likely to be satisfied with their lives.

▼ *Educational opportunities.* Everyone has the right to a good education in a safe school environment. Qualified teachers and up-to-date classroom materials allow you to reach any educational goals you set for yourself. A variety of educational opportunities are available after high school. If you choose to pursue these, they can greatly impact the quality of your life in the years to come.

▼ *Satisfying work.* Wages bring buying power and essential needs, such as nutritious food and health care. A work environment that is free of hazards to your physical and emotional health is also important. Being a productive member of a work group can give you personal satisfaction, 2-21.

You cannot always change the circumstances under which you live. However, you can look for ways you can

2-21
Having a job you enjoy and that brings satisfaction is often an important part of a quality life.

change your life to bring it closer to the quality you desire. A positive attitude helps. Those who think of their glass as half full will enjoy a better quality of life than those who feel their glass is half empty.

What Roadblocks Might Lie Ahead?

As you strive to achieve the quality of life you desire, there will be roadblocks along the way. These may interfere with the quality of your life. There may be temporary setbacks that can be overcome with hard work. Some people will be challenged to do so, whereas others may give up altogether.

Some roadblocks may be permanent obstacles. If such a roadblock occurs, you must find a way to cope with the situation. No matter what the obstacle, you can find a way to bring quality and meaning to your life.

The roadblocks typically encountered are usually the opposite of those factors that make for a quality life. For example, poor health can present special challenges. If you or someone close to you is injured or develops a major health problem, it will significantly impact your life. You may be challenged in new ways to live a normal life.

The abuse of alcohol or other drugs can be a roadblock. Such abuse can interfere with personal relationships, educational goals, and employability. Drug addictions, which lead to physical dependence on a drug, can seriously interfere with people's lives. Other types of addictions can also occur, such as addictions to gambling. These can be as difficult to overcome and as destructive of people's lives as physical addictions.

Emotional closeness may be difficult to attain if you lack self-esteem. If you have not learned to love yourself, it may be difficult for you to love someone else. Your challenge will be to find ways to improve your self-esteem in order to overcome this roadblock. Emotional dependencies can also leave people feeling unable to control their destinies. These feelings of inadequacy can lead to severe depression.

Stress in the workplace can be a debilitating factor for some people, 2-22. Such stress can be caused by work that is too demanding, keeping people away from family and friends. Working extremely long hours and spending days and even weeks away from home can make it difficult to have a normal family life. A threatening psychological environment or sexual harassment can also create an intolerable work situation. Another work situation that can create roadblocks is

2-22

A stressful period at work may interfere with the quality of your life.

a low-paying job that makes it difficult to meet living expenses. The stress of living from paycheck to paycheck can impact many aspects of a person's life. The prospect of unemployment is also a possibility.

Violence or the threat of violence is another potential roadblock. Anyone who lives in fear for his or her health and safety cannot live a satisfying life. Violence can occur on the street or within the home. It can be gang violence or violence within the family, such as spouse or child abuse. Just the threat of violence can create an intolerable situation. Those who live with such threats cannot move forward with their lives until the threats to their safety are removed.

These are just some of the potential roadblocks that you may be facing now, or may face in the years ahead. Others may also lie in your path as you move toward adulthood.

What Tactics Can Aid Personal Development?

Learning some tactics that can aid in your personal development may be helpful to you in overcoming these roadblocks, should any occur. Avoiding risks along the way is one of the keys to avoiding roadblocks. Building relationships with people is another skill that will help you in your personal development.

Avoid High-Risk Behavior

Risks involve uncertainty, and they often have an element of danger. There may even be the possibility of harm or loss. Risk-taking behaviors are common among teens. It is a normal part of their desire for independence. Some teens get a natural high from taking risks. They feel alert, excited, and alive. Others like to take risks to prove they can stretch the limits and succeed. See 2-23.

Not all risks are bad. There is a positive side to risk-taking. The kicker on the football team took a risk when the coach asked him to attempt a difficult field goal. Imagine how proud he was when he made it! Shawn risked being turned down when he invited someone new to the fall dance. The acceptance was enthusiastic.

Many risks, however, are quite serious due to their consequences. They can result in physical or mental harm to a person, cause injury or death, and even affect the lives of innocent people. These

2-23
A roller coaster provides the excitement of taking a risk but very little danger.

consequences are severe. Young people should carefully analyze the risks they take and consider the possible outcomes. Some risks, such as having sex, using illegal drugs, drinking alcohol, smoking cigarettes, and driving while intoxicated, can have lifetime consequences. Some risks can endanger the health and well-being of others. No one has the right to take risks that might cause harm to others.

Some teens think they are immune to danger, but no one really is. Consider any risk seriously. Then, if you choose to proceed, plan ahead to reduce the gravest consequences. For instance, if you want to raft a dangerous river, train for it and go with a team of rafters who are also well trained. Before you take off, secure your helmet and life vest, know how to avoid falling off, and know how to get back on if you do.

Choose your risks wisely and think through all possible outcomes. Riding in a car is a routine risk, but doing so without fastening your seat belt raises the risk factor. Riding with someone who has been drinking raises the risk level even higher. Going to a party can be great fun. Using drugs while you are there increases the risk factor. The use of illegal drugs can lead to serious health consequences and even death. There is also the risk of possible arrest for possession of drugs. When people are under the influence of drugs or alcohol, they are also less able to make good decisions involving their behavior. None of these consequences can lead to positive outcomes concerning the quality of your life.

Build Supportive Relationships

You will come in contact with many people throughout your life. Some of these people will be very close to you. They are the people who will love you, encourage you, support you, and make you feel worthwhile. These are likely to be your parents, your close friends, a dating partner, and may eventually include a marriage partner. Even in the workplace, you may find a mentor who will help you along in your career.

The relationships you share with these people have a great effect on the quality of your life. You are healthier, both physically and mentally, when you have these supportive relationships in your life. Your happiness and success in life are closely related to your ability to form meaningful relationships with others.

The caring people in your life will support you in times of stress, 2-24. They will help you solve problems and find direction. Supportive relationships go both ways. That means both people in the relationship meet needs and contribute to the personal development of the other. Relationships involve sharing feelings, experiences, problems, interests, and activities. People share and work toward common goals. They respect each other. They also trust each other, knowing that each is honest and reliable. Openness is also important to any relationship. Sharing thoughts, opinions, and feelings is key to a successful relationship.

Unfortunately, some people lack this supportive network of people. They are unable to form meaningful and positive relationships with others. What happens when people lack these relationships? Self-esteem suffers. They feel unworthy of anyone's love. They may attempt to fill

2-24
Having a parent who will support you when problems arise is important to your overall well-being.

this void in various ways. For instance, a young woman may feel if she gets pregnant and has a baby, she will have someone to love her. She thinks her baby will always be there for her. This is the wrong reason for having a baby. She is choosing to have a baby for selfish reasons and is not considering the welfare of her child. Some young people join gangs to fill their need to be a part of a group. Once they are in the gang, they get trapped into participating in unhealthy or illegal activities that may include violence. Many times it is difficult to get out of a gang safely.

As you can see, it is important to surround yourself with people who will support you in a positive manner. Some young people feel they are lacking such a support group. If you feel this way, try to connect with some caring adults. Remember that adults other than parents can help you. An older sibling, a grandparent, a favorite teacher, a religious leader, a neighbor, or your employer are all possible candidates. Close friends should also be an important part of your support group, 2-25.

To enlarge your circle of supportive relationships, be the first to smile and say hello to new acquaintances. You may get a few negative responses, but most people are waiting for someone to make the first move. It only takes a few words to initiate a relationship, but it can also be accomplished through deeds. When you perform an act of kindness—expecting nothing in return—it may lead to a long-lasting friendship.

Check It Out!

1. List three factors that can contribute to a quality life and give an example of each.
2. Identify three roadblocks to personal development.
3. Give an example of a positive risk and an example of a risk that can have negative consequences. Explain your answers.
4. Give three characteristics of a supportive relationship.

2-25
For many young people, close friends can provide support in both good times and bad.

Chapter Review

Summary

You need to take an active role in keeping yourself physically fit. Maintaining good health can have a positive effect on your school, work, and family life. Getting daily physical activity that improves aerobic capacity and builds muscle strength and flexibility will help you stay in shape. Enjoying leisure activities and getting adequate sleep will also help you perform at your highest level. Your daily grooming routine will affect your appearance as well as your health.

Your mental health as well as your physical health can affect your overall well-being. Occasionally using defense mechanisms and learning to cope with stress can help you protect your mental health. Clinical depression is one type of mental illness. Severe depression can lead some people to thoughts of suicide. Counseling and other sources of help are available to people who are having trouble maintaining a healthy mental state.

Some people knowingly take health risks. Using tobacco products can cause heart disease and various types of cancer. Drinking alcohol can impair muscle coordination and cause organ damage. Abusing other legal and illegal drugs can lead to a range of long-term health risks. Behavior that causes the spread of sexually transmitted diseases is also an extreme health risk. When faced with decisions regarding risky substances or behaviors, carefully consider how your health might be affected.

Your health and fitness include deciding what makes a quality of life for you. You need to be aware of possible roadblocks that may lie ahead. Developing tactics that can aid your personal development will help you along the way. You need to be aware of certain high-risk behaviors that can have negative consequences. It is best to avoid these risks. Finally, building supportive relationships can have a positive effect on the quality of your life.

Think About It!

1. Why is good health important to you?
2. What types of activities do you enjoy that improve aerobic capacity? What types of activities do you enjoy that build muscle strength and flexibility?
3. How do you like to spend your leisure time?
4. What techniques do you find most effective for helping you get to sleep?
5. What is your skin type? How do you care for it?
6. Give an example of a time when you used a defense mechanism to protect your self-esteem.
7. Which of the coping strategies for stress do you think are more useful for teens? Which are more useful for adults?
8. The health risks associated with tobacco, alcohol and other drugs, and sexually transmitted diseases are widely known. However, people still take these risks. How do you think people could be encouraged to show more consideration for their health regarding these risks?
9. How can a person's state of health affect his or her employment opportunities? List ten careers related to the topics in this chapter.

10. List some "quality of life" factors that are important to you. Be prepared to explain why you selected each factor.

11. Why is it important to have supportive relationships?

Try It Out!

1. Set up two columns on a sheet of paper. Title one column *Aerobic Capacity* and the other *Muscle Strength and Flexibility*. Then list all the moderate or vigorous physical activities you have done today under the appropriate column. Are you getting enough of both types of activity? What improvements do you need to make?

2. Research grooming habits in another culture. Write a brief paper describing any differences you find and the reasons for those differences.

3. Create a poster that illustrates a healthy mental state. Use the characteristics listed in this chapter as a guide.

4. Interview people in five occupations, such as a teacher, homemaker, businessperson, construction worker, and waiter. Ask about the factors that cause stress in their jobs and how they manage that stress. Share your findings with the class.

5. Survey nonsmokers in your school to determine how they feel when they are forced to inhale cigarette smoke produced by smokers. Report your findings in an article for the school newspaper.

6. Set up a classroom exhibit on sources of help for people who want to stop using tobacco, alcohol, and other drugs.

7. Choose a song, story, book, or movie that illustrates a supportive relationship. Write a paper describing the relationship and the role the relationship played in each person's development.

Chapter 3
Developing Your Interpersonal Skills

Careers

These careers relate to the topics in this chapter:
- ▼ reading tutor
- ▼ youth services worker
- ▼ consumer services representative
- ▼ editor

As you study the chapter, see if you can think of others.

Topics

3-1 The Communication Process
3-2 Communication in Relationships
3-3 Conflict Resolution

Topic 3-1

The Communication Process

Objectives

After studying this topic, you will be able to

▼ improve your listening and speaking skills.

▼ begin and develop conversations more easily.

▼ use several forms of nonverbal communication to communicate more effectively.

▼ describe the use of several types of electronic communication.

Topic Terms

communication
verbal communication
nonverbal communication
active listener
feedback
passive listener
reflection
manners
body language
personal space
technology
Internet
online

To develop good relationships with other people, you have to be able to communicate. **Communication** is the process of conveying information in such a way that the message is received and understood. Through communication, you can share ideas, opinions, and facts with others. In close relationships, you can also discuss and share your problems and feelings. See 3-1.

Good communication is a skill you will use throughout your life. It is based on a mutual effort between people to understand one another. Speakers must try to make their messages relevant to the listeners. At the same time, listeners must open their minds to the messages being sent.

All forms of communication—speaking, listening, reading, writing, and body language—can be grouped into two different categories. The first is **verbal communication**, which involves the use of words. **Nonverbal communication** is the second category; this involves sending messages without words. In this topic, you will learn more about these two forms of communication.

Verbal Communication

Communication skills are just like word processing skills or baseball skills. You can learn them, practice them, and improve them. The first steps in improving your verbal communication skills are learning to listen and to speak well.

Listening

Listening plays an important role in communication. A spoken message is worthless unless someone hears it and listens to it. *Hearing* and *listening*, however, have two different meanings. You hear many sounds all day long. Radios, kitchen appliances, cars, and airplanes are just a few examples. If you really listened to all these sounds, you would not have time to think about anything else. Instead,

3-1
How much time do you spend every day communicating with family, friends, classmates, and teachers?

you have developed the habit of ignoring unimportant sounds. This is usually a good and helpful habit. If you aren't careful, however, you may find yourself slipping into this habit more often than you should. You may be ignoring spoken messages that people are trying to send to you.

Barriers to Good Listening
Recognizing what gets in the way of good listening can help you learn to overcome these barriers. The habit of ignoring sounds is just one barrier to good listening. Forgetting all or part of the message is a common communication barrier. Even if you listen to what is being said, there is a chance for a communication failure. Studies show that people remember as little as 25 percent of the information they receive through listening. People remember more when they see, read, or verbally repeat the message they hear.

Listening by itself does not always ensure good communication.

Another barrier to good listening is not understanding the message being sent. The message a person sends to you may not be the same message you receive. The speaker may pronounce words differently if he or she is from a different part of the country. The speaker may use slang expressions or words that are unfamiliar to you. You may think the speaker is joking when he or she is serious. Even the tone of voice can change the meaning of what is said. These are just a few of the factors that can interfere with good listening.

Become an Active Listener
Listening is important to good communication because you listen more often than you speak. With practice, you can develop good listening skills.

A good listener is an **active listener**. This means the listener gives the speaker some form of feedback. **Feedback** lets the speaker know the message is getting through to the listener and how it is being received. The feedback can be a nod, a smile, or even a comment that lets the speaker know the message is received.

A **passive listener** may hear the spoken words, but not the meaning of the words. A passive listener does not respond to the speaker in any way. The speaker doesn't know if the message is being received or not. Have you ever spoken to someone who didn't seem to really be listening to you?

By using active listening, you improve the entire communication process. The following are some tips to help you:

▼ *Ask questions to clarify the message.* This shows you are not only hearing what the speaker is saying, but also processing it. You are trying to understand the speaker and preparing to act on the message. Speakers should try to present information clearly. Listeners have the responsibility of seeking clarification if the information is confusing. Receiving the right message is a two-way process. As you listen, ask for added details. Ask the speaker to go over any points you have not clearly understood.

▼ *Pay attention.* Focus your attention on the speaker. Use eye contact. Do not let your mind race ahead of what is being said. Avoid daydreaming or letting your mind wander to other topics. See 3-2.

▼ *Be interested.* You will listen better if you have a sincere desire to know what the other person is saying and feeling. With genuine interest in the speaker, it becomes easier to focus attention on him or her.

▼ *Be patient.* Give the speaker time to present his or her message. Do

3-2
A good listener shows sincere interest in what the speaker is saying.

not interrupt and take over the speaking role.

▼ *Keep the speaker in mind.* Expect the information to come from the speaker's background of experiences or point of view. To listen, you have to put aside your previous thoughts and biases for the moment. Concentrate on the person who is speaking to you.

▼ *Stay focused.* Some people are too busy thinking about what they will say in response to a speaker. As a result, they fail to listen to what is said. When someone is speaking, listen. When the person stops, you can collect your thoughts and then respond. The speaker will respect you for listening, thinking about what was said, and making a thoughtful response.

▼ *Use reflection*. When you use **reflection**, you repeat in your own words what you think was said. The speaker sees in a "mirror" the message that was sent, but in words reflected back by the listener. The receiver might say, "If I understand you correctly, you are saying…" With reflection, the speaker can easily see if a message was misinterpreted.

▼ *Listen to the speaker's tone of voice*. Sometimes the way something is said is just as important as what is said. For instance, a comment such as "You look sad" might be judged as sarcastic, critical, or sympathetic, depending on how it was stated.

3-3
Good communication skills are important in both personal and business relationships.

Speaking

Speaking is the most widely used form of verbal communication. Speaking and listening are equally important in the two-way communication process.

You spend much of your day speaking with others. The way you speak affects your life in many ways. It affects your relationships with your family members and your friends. It affects your daily interactions with teachers, classmates, coworkers, and employers, 3-3. Speaking clearly will help you express your thoughts, feelings, and ideas to others.

Have you noticed that some people have better speaking skills than others? You could listen to them for hours and not lose interest. With practice, you too can develop your speaking skills.

Developing Speaking Skills

How good are your speaking skills? Do you send clear messages when you speak to others? Do others interpret your messages correctly? The way you speak affects the impressions people form of you.

If your skills need improvement, try using some of these techniques:

▼ *Keep the listener in mind*. Use words the listener will understand. This is especially important if the listener has a different cultural or educational background from you or if the listener is a child. To communicate clearly, you need to be aware of the meanings others may attach to the words you use.

▼ *Keep messages short and simple*. Use simple language and proper grammar. Explain your message clearly. Leave no room for confusion and you are more likely to be understood.

▼ *Be considerate of others' feelings*. Think before you speak. Avoid making comments that may hurt someone. If criticism is needed, try to make it constructive. Try to suggest ways to improve or change a behavior that is bothering you. Sometimes praise works better than criticism. Praise what you do like, and that action will probably be repeated. Ignore what you do not like, and that action will probably be stopped.

▼ *Be open and honest*. This is especially true when you are talking to your close friends, 3-4. Don't expect them to read your mind. They can't. If you want them to know what you want or how you feel, you will have to tell them.

▼ *Respect the listener*. Good rapport between a speaker and a listener aids good communication. Good rapport is built on respect and sincerity. Talking down to a person or showing disrespect will cut off communication lines.

▼ *Be positive*. People enjoy listening to someone who has a positive outlook on life. On the other hand, people become bored listening to someone who complains all the time. Using a

pleasant tone of voice and maintaining eye contact are ways of conveying a positive attitude. This encourages others to listen and respond positively to the speaker.

▼ *Check to see whether your message is being received accurately*. Questions such as "What do you think?" or "How do you feel about this?" will draw your listener into a speaking role. He or she will then reflect on what you have said and give you some feedback. This will tell you if your message has been understood. You will know if you should go back and explain something again or go ahead with new information. Concentrate on one communication skill at a time. Listening and speaking skills improve with practice.

How to Start a Conversation

Another way to develop your speaking skills is to practice starting a conversation. Good conversation skills are useful in many situations. For instance, you notice an interesting-looking person standing alone at a party. You would like to talk to the person, but you don't know what to say. Does this situation sound familiar? To be prepared, have a few conversation openers in mind, such as the following:

▼ *Ask questions*. Questions work in almost any situation, 3-5. When you use questions to start conversations, ask questions that require more than a yes or no answer. Examples are, "What do you think about…?" "How do you feel about…?" "What do you think would happen if…?" Ask the person a key question about himself or herself. Ask about his or her work, hobbies, or family. Almost everyone has a good personal story to tell. Most people enjoy talking about themselves.

3-4
Open and honest communication is especially important among friends.

3-5
Asking a question that requires an explanation is a good conversation starter.

▼ *Make a sincere compliment.*
Another good conversation starter is to compliment the person about something—appearance, clothing, possessions, or accomplishments. Compliments make people feel good about themselves. When they feel good, they are likely to relax and begin talking.

▼ *Mention something you have in common with the other person.* If you know the person, mention a subject you know the person thinks is interesting. Discussions of current events, movies, books, and sports events can keep a conversation going.

If you and the person to whom you are talking both know some of the same people, you can talk about them. However, this type of conversation can be risky. Be sure to say only positive things. Don't begin by criticizing someone who may be this person's neighbor, cousin, or best friend!

▼ *Discuss one topic.* A personal conversation is more likely to be successful if you explore just one key point of common interest. Look for an interesting depth in that topic rather than trying to cover many topics. A constant change of subjects may drive the other person away.

Practice will help you feel more comfortable talking with people. Try not to be shy. Chances are the person you want to meet would like to meet you, too. Try not to be afraid of saying the wrong words. Just relax and be yourself. Concentrate on enjoying the conversation and the other person's company.

Nonverbal Communication

People communicate in many ways other than the spoken or written word. Communication that does not involve

Setting the Scene: Communicate Without a Word

You hear footsteps coming closer. You turn and see your best friend walk into the room. His shoulders and slumped and his arms are folded. One of his hands is clenched in a fist. He is frowning, and he avoids making eye contact with you.

Analyze It: What nonverbal messages are being sent? What would be your response to these messages?

words is called nonverbal communication. The way a person looks, dresses, acts, and reacts are forms of nonverbal expression.

Your Appearance

Does your appearance send the message you want it to send? When people meet you, what is their first impression? People form their impressions of you based on the way you look. Often these judgments are made quickly. Before you say anything, your appearance is sending a message to them. Are you communicating a positive message about yourself? See 3-6.

Good grooming is one way to send a positive message. It shows you care about yourself and the way you look. The clothes you wear communicate a message about you, too. They are clues to your lifestyle and personality. Neat, clean clothes that fit well help create a positive image. Studies show people generally respond more favorably to those who are well groomed and well dressed.

Your Actions

The actions you take can send messages to others. For instance, **manners** are rules to follow for proper conduct. Using good manners sends the message that you want others to feel comfortable. In most cases, having good manners is as simple as being kind to others and using common sense.

Other actions will send the message that you care about people's feelings. Using the words *please*, *thank you*, and *excuse me* shows courtesy and respect to others. Sending a note of thanks or a card to cheer someone up reflects thoughtfulness, 3-7. Giving a gift on a special occasion tells people you are considerate. Using a pleasant tone of voice lets others know you want them to feel at ease.

3-6
Being well-groomed and neatly dressed sends a positive nonverbal message.

3-7
A card can help you communicate your feelings of concern for another.

Body Language

When you nod your head, shake your fist, or point your finger, you are communicating without words. With **body language**, you are using body movements, such as facial expressions, gestures, and posture, to send messages to others.

Although you are not using words, your messages can be crystal clear. The expression on your face can convey your mood before you even begin to talk. Direct eye contact with someone can convey honesty and straightforwardness. When you walk into the kitchen and find that someone has prepared your favorite dinner, a kiss and a hug can help you say thank you. With a smile and a shake of your head, you can let someone know that you agree. With a wink, you can say "I like you." Some people use hand gestures to make their spoken messages clearer.

People from different cultures have developed certain body language that is unique to their culture. Because we live in a multicultural society, it is important to be aware of possible differences in body language. In some cultures, the way a message is delivered is more important than the actual content of the message.

Personal Space

Your **personal space** is the area around you. When others enter this space, your reaction is a form of nonverbal communication. The way you allow people to use your personal space depends on the way you feel about these people. You may enjoy the closeness of a hug from a special person, or a whisper in your ear from another. A quick handshake may be as close as you wish to be with others. When a person enters your personal space you feel either comfortable or uncomfortable. Your behaviors reveal the way you feel. See 3-8.

The More You Know: Body Language Around the World

Some communications are influenced by cultural diversity, so being aware of cultural differences is important. For example, in some cultures people are taught to never make eye contact with someone in authority. A friendly hug may also be off-limits. In large U.S. cities, people avoid making eye contact with anyone on the streets. While some specific body language does vary, a person from any culture is likely to understand gestures meaning *yes*, *no*, *come*, *stop*, *up*, *down*, and *thank you*.

Have you ever hugged family members or friends you hadn't seen for a while? You knew they didn't feel you were invading their space. Conversely, have you ever touched a person who quickly withdrew from you? This reaction said you were getting too close for their comfort.

The place or situation you are in also affects the use of your personal space. For example, when your date puts an arm around you, you may respond by snuggling a little closer. You may like the warmth of the touch. If he or she tries the same hug at school, you may respond by withdrawing. Perhaps you feel this behavior is inappropriate in public. You may also respond positively to a friendly hug, but negatively to a forceful hug.

Most Americans like to stay about an arm's length from each other when they

3-8

You would probably be comfortable letting a close friend or dating partner enter your personal space.

speak. This is not the case in other cultures. People from some cultures like to stand closer when they speak. This closeness makes some Americans feel uncomfortable. An awareness of this cultural difference can help you avoid any misinterpretation of another's actions.

Technology and Communication

Technology, the use of scientific knowledge for practical purposes, has led to many new ways for people to communicate with each other. No longer do you have to wait a week or more to receive a written response for a letter you sent. You can send a message around the world in an instant. It is possible to receive a reply equally fast.

These communication devices are popular because they are time-savers for those who use them properly. On the other hand, their prevalence in people's lives can make them time-wasters as well. Their impact has been significant both in the home and in the workplace. Though most people see many benefits to these methods of communication, others see some drawbacks. The following are some popular electronic devices used for communication.

Cellular Phones

Cellular telephones provide two-way voice communication without the direct wire connections required of standard telephones, 3-9. Voice transmissions are sent by radio waves to towers and switching centers that relay the messages to their destinations. Cell phones and monthly rate plans can be purchased from a provider. If you use more minutes than are included in your rate plan, the costs can be high.

Pay-as-you-go phones are another option. You purchase the phone and a certain number of minutes. The minutes can be used at any time until you have used all you purchased. Then, you can buy more minutes. This option can be more cost-effective than monthly rate plans for people who do not use their cell phones often.

3-9

Many people enjoy the convenience of cell phones.

The portability and small size of cell phones have made them very popular. They can be carried easily in a pocket, briefcase, or backpack and used practically anywhere. This allows instant communication from wherever you are, which is particularly beneficial in emergency situations. Cell phones are also being paired with global positioning devices to provide emergency assistance and information to travelers.

The use of cell phones can be disturbing to other people if used in public places. Though popular with students, many schools ban their use. If you use a cell phone, have consideration for the people around you when at school or in a public place. Phones should be turned off when ringing will disturb others. Conversations on cell phones should not take place where other people can hear them. It is inconsiderate to talk on your cell phone in movie theaters or restaurants. Other people are trying to watch the movie or are having their own conversations. They should not have to listen to yours.

Voice Mail

Voice mail is an electronic version of a telephone answering machine. If no one answers the phone, the caller leaves a recorded message for the recipient to listen to later. The message can be played back or accessed from another telephone.

Voice mail has several advantages. Family members can eat meals together undisturbed and allow their voice mail to record messages. Family members who need to communicate with other family members can also leave messages. For example, if parents are at work, children can leave messages about where they will be and when.

When leaving a voice mail message, there are certain courtesies you should follow.

▼ Speak clearly and distinctly.
▼ Give your name and telephone number.
▼ Keep your message brief (30 seconds is ideal), but explain the reason for your call.
▼ Minimize the need for a call back if possible. For instance, if a meeting date has changed, give the date for the postponed meeting.
▼ Give the date and time.
▼ Let the person know the best time to reach you.

Computers

The **Internet** is an international network of computers that are linked to share information. It is available to anyone who has a computer, an Internet service provider, and a means of connection. Types of connection include dialup service using a phone and modem; DSL (digital subscriber line); and high-speed cable. When you access the Internet, you are **online**.

The Internet allows instant communication to anywhere in the world through e-mail. E-mail is an important method of communication in the workplace. It often replaces in-house office memos or written correspondence to customers or clients. See 3-10 for some points to keep in mind when using e-mail at work.

Extended family members who live distances apart have found e-mail to be an excellent way to stay in touch. Grandparents can e-mail their grandchildren in their homes or college dorm rooms. Parents can e-mail important messages to their school-age children at home or spouses in other workplaces.

E-Mail Etiquette

- Grammar, spelling, and punctuation must be accurate, as in any written form of communication.
- Use a single-subject line so the receiver can easily decide the importance of the message.
- Begin with a friendly and appropriate greeting. Use a first name only if you know the person.
- Do not yell (using all uppercase letters is considered YELLING). It is not appropriate in business reports or letters.
- Avoid using emoticons in business communications. *Emoticons* are keyboard characters that are typed in configurations to indicate body language, such as :-) for a smile. Use them in personal e-mail messages only.
- Do not use e-mail to deliver extremely sensitive information. A face-to-face message or telephone conversation is better to prevent misunderstandings.
- Be aware that e-mail is not secure. If using e-mail at work, your employer can read your mail.

3-10

If you use e-mail to communicate at work, follow these guidelines.

The Internet is a popular source of knowledge and entertainment. *Web sites* can be used to find all kinds of information. These sites are maintained by educational institutions, companies, organizations, government agencies, and individuals. You can locate information needed for research assignments without leaving your home. Online resources also allow you to access current news, weather, or your own bank account. Online shopping is another possibility for the Internet user. From your computer, you can purchase almost anything from grocery items to airline tickets.

Though access to the Internet can lead you to vast amounts of information, there are some precautions. The Internet is not owned or controlled by any one organization. Anyone can place any type of information on the Internet, whether accurate or not. Therefore, if you are using it for research, you should focus on using reliable sources. Check the accuracy of information provided by unfamiliar sources. The government currently does not regulate the Internet, and little information is censored. Children can accidentally wander into sites that are meant for adults only.

Check It Out!

1. Name two barriers to good listening skills.
2. True or false. People are more likely to remember a message they hear if they do not repeat it verbally.
3. Briefly describe five techniques for improving speaking skills.
4. List four suggestions for starting a conversation.
5. Explain how nonverbal communication is related to your appearance.
6. List three electronic means of communication. Give an example of how each can be used to benefit communication.

Topic 3-2
Communication in Relationships

Objectives

After studying this topic, you will be able to
- ▼ state the importance of open communication in relationships.
- ▼ list ways to communicate positive feelings.
- ▼ describe barriers to communication.
- ▼ suggest methods for handling negative feelings.
- ▼ give tips for communicating in the workplace.

Topic Terms

open communication
stereotypes
prejudices
coded messages
role expectations
diverse

People often speak of **open communication**. This means a free flow of ideas, opinions, and facts among the people involved. They may not agree on everything, but they respect one another's point of view. They can have intelligent discussions about views that differ from their own. All ideas are treated with interest, curiosity, and respect.

Clearly communicating your thoughts and feelings is part of open communication. In this topic, you will learn more about skills you can use to develop open communication in your relationships. These include communicating positive feelings, overcoming barriers, and handling negative feelings.

The Importance of Communication in Relationships

Open communication has many benefits, especially in personal relationships. It allows people to learn more about themselves and other people. It helps people express their feelings to their friends and family. Using it helps strengthen relationships. Overall, it can lead to richer, more satisfying relationships. See 3-11.

Communicating Positive Feelings

Each person is responsible for his or her own happiness. Do you want to be happy? If so, you must work toward that goal. Thinking positively about most situations in life will help you be happy. Your positive attitude encourages open communication.

Good feelings are contagious. If you are a positive person and communicate this to others, they will feel happier, too. See 3-12.

3-11
Open communication allows people to express their ideas and feelings freely.

3-12
People who communicate their positive feelings enrich the lives of others.

The following list suggests ways to communicate positive feelings. Decide which suggestions would be most helpful to you.

▼ Whenever you meet someone, be the first one to say hello.
▼ Offer praise and compliments when they are deserved.
▼ Defend people who are the object of harmful gossip.
▼ Smile and look happy. Show your positive personality traits.
▼ Look others in the eye when you talk to them and speak clearly.
▼ Show concern for others by asking them about matters that are important to them.

Barriers to Open Communication

Communicating with others is not always easy. Many barriers stand in the way of open communication. A few of the barriers are physical in nature, such as speech and hearing disabilities. However, most barriers to open communication are social or psychological. Understanding these differences can help you avoid them. Some of the most common ones are described on the following pages.

Stereotypes

One barrier to open communication is stereotyping. A person who **stereotypes** others has a set belief that all members of a group will behave in the same ways. Stereotypes put labels on groups of people. These labels may be based on a group's age, sex, race, or religion. For instance, some people may believe that all young men should participate in sports or all older people are forgetful.

Because every person is different, neither of the above statements can be true for all people within these groups. If you pay attention to stereotypes like these instead of accepting individual differences, you may misinterpret messages. To be a good listener, you must have an open mind. You must ignore stereotypes and give people the chance to communicate as individuals.

Prejudices

Another barrier to open communication results from prejudices. **Prejudices** are opinions that people form without complete knowledge. They are usually based on a lack of facts and a lack of understanding. People with prejudices do not accept that others' beliefs can be different from theirs. Prejudices might include negative attitudes toward religions, races, cultures, nationalities, socio-economic groups, cities, geographic regions, or foods.

Many prejudices lead to negative behaviors such as name-calling. Prejudiced people may choose to avoid certain groups or individuals. They usually do not seek understanding or new meanings. They have already made up their minds. It's as if they are saying "I already know about that" or "I already know about your kind." These actions set up barriers and prevent good communication from taking place.

Here is an example of a man who had a prejudice toward certain foods. When the man took his date out to dinner, she ordered roast lamb. She soon realized he was embarrassed to be seen with a date who ate lamb. He did not eat meat and thought of it as unwholesome. He also felt prejudice toward her because she ate a food that he didn't consider acceptable. Because of his prejudice, the couple never dated again. Such a prejudice toward people and objects—in this case food—hampers good communication.

Some prejudices come in the form of love. For example, parents are naturally proud of their children. They may think their son or daughter is the best looking, most talented, and most personable individual. This may be true, but such an attitude is usually padded with a little pride and prejudice. Loving people is important. However, maintaining an ability to be rational about all people and objects is important, too.

Coded Messages

When people try to communicate without saying what they really mean, they are using **coded messages**. Listeners are forced to make assumptions as they decode the speakers' messages. Although coded messages hinder good communication, some people continue to use them. See 3-13.

One tricky statement to decode is "Give me your honest opinion." Some people may really want your opinion. Others say this when they really mean "Tell me I am right. Support me in what I have done." You must decode the message according to the situation. Your clues may be the person's tone of voice and facial expression.

Another example of coding is when a young man asks a young woman "What are you doing Saturday?" His message is a coded one. He doesn't really want to know what she is planning to do. This is his way of saying "Will you be free on Saturday? I would like to see you then." He hopes the girl will recognize the coded message and interpret it correctly. However, she may respond with another coded message. Then he must decode her message. Does she have time to see him on Saturday? Is she too busy to see him or doesn't she want to see him? As you can see, communicating with coded messages is risky.

Teasing is a type of coded message. The way a person teases is the key to decoding the real meaning of the message. Teasing is a means of getting someone's attention.

3-13
Good friends know their friendship depends on open communication. They avoid using coded messages to express their thoughts and feelings.

It's usually a way of saying "I like you." Teasing can almost always be decoded as a type of compliment. However, some forms of teasing and joking can cause problems in personal relationships. Some people say harsh things in a joking manner when they really mean what they are saying. They don't have the nerve to say it otherwise. This type of joke is cruel and can easily hurt someone's feelings.

Gender Differences

Sometimes, differences between males and females create some barriers to communication. These barriers may be related to role expectations. **Role expectations** are patterns of socially expected behavior. In other words, people learn to behave the way they think society expects them to behave. They also expect certain role behaviors from others.

Certain roles are associated with being male or female. For males, some of these roles include brother, son, boyfriend, husband, and father. Female roles include sister, daughter, girlfriend, wife, and mother. Both men and women also have expectations as to how the opposite sex should fulfill their roles. For instance, some husbands may expect their wives to cook and do household chores. A girlfriend may expect her boyfriend to pay for every date.

Role expectations can create confusion. This is because people don't always agree on the behavior for certain roles. See 3-14.

Handling Negative Feelings

There are many ways you can resolve negative feelings. You must first wish to communicate effectively and be willing to take the first steps to resolving these feelings. As you read the following suggestions, think about yourself. Which of these guidelines would be most helpful for you?

▼ Discuss your negative feelings with the person whose behavior is bothering you. Don't complain to others until you have spoken with that person. People who are not involved in a problem usually can't do anything about it.

▼ Keep a simple issue simple. Don't add other issues to it, building it up until it becomes a major problem.

▼ Do not reopen old issues that have already been settled.

▼ Discuss the problem without making nasty comments and accusations that would hurt the other person. Recognize your own faults and accept them. Don't blame them on others. Try to be pleasant rather than grouchy. Help people see that you like them, even though you don't like their behavior.

▼ Say what must be said and stop. Don't continue talking about one issue and repeating yourself.

▼ Try to end on a positive note. Make a positive comment about the person or the situation.

3-14
In the past, men may have considered cleaning and child care a female role. Today, however, those views are quite different.

Today, some of the barriers created by gender differences are diminishing. As society's view of male and female roles continues to change, people's views of role expectations will change, too.

When Negative Feelings Occur

Every person has negative feelings at times. When you hold back negative feelings, they may become stronger and more frustrating. You need to know how to vent your emotions. Even negative feelings can be communicated in a useful, constructive way.

Communication in the Workplace

The communication skills you have learned to use in your personal life can help you communicate at work. The circumstances differ, however. You have known your family and close friends for a long time, and you have learned how to communicate with them. When you begin a job, you will meet many new people. In today's world, the workforce is likely to be very **diverse** (differing from one another). Workers differ by age, ethnicity, and gender. Increasing numbers of workers have disabilities. Due to the diverse nature of the workforce, communication can be more challenging. See 3-15.

The goals of communication at work are to pass along information and to build effective work relationships. Different styles of communicating and different interpretations of communications can interfere with attaining both of these goals. People from different backgrounds may define problems differently. They bring their personal goals, priorities, and standards to their jobs. When diverse people form team-based work groups, disagreements may occur. It is important to remember that every person is different. That does not mean they are difficult. By thinking of someone as just different, you become less judgmental. You can be more open to their opinions and ideas.

Many of the effective communication techniques that you use in other settings can also be used on the job. In addition, the following points can be helpful:

▼ Keep conversations unrelated to work to a minimum. These prevent you and other employees from doing your work. Your personal life should be kept private. Workplace gossip should be avoided. Professionalism is expected of employees.

▼ Show courtesy to customers and clients, 3-16. Do not keep them waiting while you finish a conversation with a fellow employee.

▼ Use good listening skills. Listen carefully when directions are given. Ask questions to prevent any misunderstandings.

▼ Use standard English at work, not slang. For example, say *yes* rather than *yeah*.

3-15
Clear communication in the workforce can be challenging, but it is necessary for a team to function well.

3-16
When communicating with customers, their needs always come first.

▼ Avoid telling jokes at work. Because of the diverse nature of the workforce, some people may be offended by an innocent joke.

▼ If misunderstandings occur, discuss them with the person involved. It is possible to respectfully disagree.

Check It Out!

1. True or false. In open communication, people know each other so well that they agree about everything.
2. Give five examples of ways to communicate positive feelings.
3. A communication barrier based on opinions that people form without complete knowledge is known as _____.
4. Identify five ways to communicate negative feelings.
5. What makes communication in today's workplace challenging?

Topic 3-3
Conflict Resolution

Objectives

After studying this topic, you will be able to

▼ identify some types and causes of conflict.
▼ explain possible negative and positive reactions to conflict.
▼ describe constructive and destructive methods of conflict resolution.
▼ list the steps in the conflict resolution process.
▼ explain the use of mediation.

Topic Terms

conflict
scapegoating
negotiation
compromise
conflict resolution process
mediation
peer mediators

Each person has a unique way of viewing and reacting to every situation. When people live and work closely, as they do in families, in friendships, and on the job, conflicts are bound to arise. A **conflict** is a struggle between two people or groups who have opposing views. The ability to resolve a conflict is an important skill in good communication.

Types of Conflicts

There are all types of conflicts. Some are small, such as a disagreement between two people over a trivial matter, 3-17. You

3-17

Even good friends can have conflicts because they are together so much of the time. What's important is to choose a method of resolving the conflict that is fair to all.

and a friend may disagree over where to go after school. Disagreements can grow into larger conflicts if the two people are not willing to reach an agreement peacefully.

Conflicts can also occur within families—between husbands and wives, parents and children, or among siblings. Again, the conflicts can be small and easily resolved. They can also be over important issues. Maybe you and your parents disagree about how late you should be able to stay out on weekend nights. Bringing up an issue that is causing a conflict is a good way to begin to deal with the problem. Listening to each other's views and talking about them can usually lead to good solutions.

Conflicts are not confined to interpersonal relationships. They can occur between larger groups—even entire nations. Throughout the world, there are nations that are at war with other nations. These, too, are conflicts, but on a much larger scale. Many times the conflicts between nations are based on some of the same differences that cause conflicts between individuals. Differences

in religious beliefs and practices are often at the core of many national conflicts. Disagreements over government policies can also lead to major disputes.

Causes of Conflict

Causes of conflict can be trivial or significant. It is important to take an objective look at the conflict and try to determine the cause. Knowing why the conflict occurred will likely help in resolving it. Many conflicts occur because of poor communication. Have you ever made arrangements to meet some friends, and they never showed up? You may have been really angry until you found out they never received your message, or they misunderstood where you were to meet. Many times a failure to communicate can be more serious. Has anyone ever said to you "If you had told me, all this could have been avoided"? If a parent or your boss said this to you, you may have been in real trouble!

Some conflicts result from specific situations. For instance, perhaps you and your friend both like the same boy. He starts paying more attention to you than to your friend. She starts acting weird, complaining about everything. She never used to be like that. Suddenly you're arguing all the time, and then you have a really big fight. The situation has led to a conflict between the two of you.

If people have very different personalities, they could be on a collision course. For instance, consider this couple. She is neat and organized, likes to be on time, and always seems to be in control. He is completely disorganized, can never find anything, and is always running late. These two people could be very happy together, each benefiting from the other's strengths. On the other hand, they could be miserable together. Their very different personalities could lead to some major conflicts.

Conflicts often occur between parents and their children during the teenage years. The role of parents is to guide their children as they grow toward adulthood. Parents are responsible for their well-being until they are adults. The role of teens is to develop independence. They are anxious to be able to make decisions for themselves. Finding a happy medium between these opposing roles is often difficult. Parents and children often pull in opposite directions. Conflicts frequently occur during these tumultuous years. See 3-18.

Differences in values can lead to conflicts, as you learned in Chapter 1. Your values are important to you. If someone else does not have the same values as you, conflicts can arise. The degree of conflict depends on the importance of the value to you. For instance, your parents may think good grades are most important, while you think your performance on the volleyball team is most important. You want to spend

time practicing when they want you to study more. This difference in values can lead to disagreements. A friend may value having a good time, while you may value getting into a good college. This could lead to disagreements about how you spend your free time together.

Some conflicts can be traced to cultural differences. For example, the American culture encourages quick decision making. This is not characteristic of all cultures. The American culture is one where people are always busy and active. People from many other cultures do not believe in this active lifestyle. They prefer a more relaxed pace. The concept of time also varies among cultures. Americans follow daily schedules timed to the minute. They expect punctuality, 3-19. Other cultures place more emphasis on relationships than on schedules. Being late is not a problem for them. These are just a few examples of cultural differences that can lead to conflict if people are unaware of them.

Reactions to Conflict

Conflict is normal. There will always be disagreements between people. It is how people react or respond to these disagreements that determines whether they ignite into major conflicts or just go away. Negative reactions can escalate conflicts and lead to hostility and personal attacks. Some even end in violence. Positive reactions can lead to solutions that both parties can accept. Many actually lead to personal growth.

Negative Reactions

Avoidance is a common reaction to conflict. Some people just walk away. This might be a good response if a person is concerned that an argument could escalate

3-18
When teens are learning to drive, it is an especially stressful time for them and their parents.

3-19
Many Americans become frustrated if they cannot keep to their planned schedules.

into violence. A cooling-down period might be good for everyone involved. In most cases, however, avoidance simply puts off resolution. It does not solve the problem. Instead, resentment builds up as the person tries to suppress hurt feelings. If this continues over a period of time, it can lead to an explosion of emotions when the person finally reaches a breaking point.

Some people attempt to resolve conflicts by blaming others. This is called **scapegoating**. The person blamed for the problem is the scapegoat. Everyone else is freed of the responsibility for the problem because they can blame this other person. This is not a resolution because no one tries to solve the conflict. The conflict goes on with both parties feeling it is "not my problem."

Some responses to conflict include arguing, becoming angry, and name-calling. When one person becomes angry and begins yelling, the other person is likely to become angry as well. Verbal attacks fly back and forth. People say hurtful things they often regret later. They feel belittled when their self-esteem is under attack. It is sometimes hard to forgive people when such outbreaks occur. An atmosphere of hostility prevails.

The most destructive reaction to conflict is violence. If tempers flare out of control, shoving, hitting, or pushing can result. Some people first experience hitting as children. They think this is an acceptable form of reaction because their parents hit them. They also see more violence portrayed in the media—on television and in movies. As they become older, they may use this same form of behavior. A violent reaction to conflict is never the answer. It can lead to child abuse, spouse abuse, or elder abuse. It can also lead to violence outside the home.

Positive Reactions

There are ways people can react to conflict that will help the situation. First, you can learn to control your emotions. Lashing out in anger usually solves nothing. You can also ask the other person to remain calm. Both people need to stop, take a deep breath, and quiet their emotions. See 3-20.

It is also important to listen. Instead of shouting, stop and listen to what each person is saying. Focus on the real problem as you exchange views. Don't bring up other issues. Focus on the current conflict.

Try to remain neutral. Do not jump to a judgment before everyone has his or her say. Then you are ready to find a real solution to the conflict.

Learning to react positively when a conflict occurs is an important life skill that can lead to personal growth. It is a sign of maturity when you can control your emotions, listen to other viewpoints, and avoid jumping to conclusions. These skills will help you in your personal relationships as well as in work situations. Teamwork is stressed in today's workplace. You might someday be working closely with other employees in a work setting. Because conflicts will arise, reacting positively can lead to constructive resolution of these conflicts. An employer will recognize and appreciate your ability to handle conflict in a mature manner.

Constructive Methods for Handling Conflict

To resolve a conflict, each person has to assume responsibility for his or her feelings. The emotions you feel may be caused by others, but they belong to you. If you wish to lessen stress that occurs in conflict, you must be willing to resolve the conflict. Try these techniques for starters.

Use "I" Messages

Use "I" messages instead of "you" messages. This means you take ownership for your feelings. You state what you feel or think instead of criticizing the other person. Say "I think you are ignoring me" rather than "You are ignoring me". You might further say, "When I think you are ignoring me, I feel hurt. I don't like being ignored." As you express your feelings, you are taking credit for them.

3-20

Being calm and using humor are ways to soothe the heated emotions of a conflict.

"You" messages, on the other hand, come across as accusations. "You are ignoring me" places blame on the other person and may aggravate the situation. When taking ownership and saying "I think" or "I feel" you avoid accusing the other person of negative behaviors.

Learn to send "I" messages. For example, "When you tell so-called funny stories about me to my professional friends, I am embarrassed." Can you see in this example that you are assuming responsibility for your feelings of embarrassment? A "you" message sounds like an accusation. "You embarrass me when you tell your so-called funny stories about me to my professional friends." The "you" message places the blame on the other person.

Decide Who Owns the Problem

Whose problem is it? When a problem exists between two people, both own the problem. Even when one person creates the problem, he or she makes it a problem for the other. State your point of view in a way that will not create an argument. Seek feedback to determine how the other person is receiving your message. To avoid misunderstandings, use clarifying messages periodically, 3-21. Try comments such as: "If I am hearing you correctly, you are saying that..." or "I think I heard you say..."

Learn to Negotiate and Compromise

An important method for resolving conflicts is negotiation. **Negotiation** means communicating with others in order to reach a mutually satisfying agreement.

3-21
When resolving a conflict with another person, state your point of view calmly and clearly. Then ask for feedback.

Such an agreement usually involves a compromise. In a **compromise**, both parties agree to give up something. Each person gives up something of importance to obtain something else that also has importance.

Negotiation and compromise must be considered carefully. Some issues may be so important to you that you will be unwilling to negotiate and compromise. For example, you may not wish to compromise your moral views or spiritual views. For this reason, you will not enter into a negotiation that would require you to make a compromise. What is important is that you negotiate and compromise when it is appropriate.

The purpose of negotiation and compromise is to remove conflict. Four methods are commonly used.

▼ *You win/I lose*. The person who wins is happy with this compromise. The person achieved what he or she wanted. However, you may feel the person took advantage of you. You may feel like a loser. You are likely to be unhappy about your loss. The conflict is likely to resurface at a future time. A power struggle is likely to persist.

▼ *I win/you lose*. This is the opposite of the above situation. You feel happy because you achieved what you wanted. However, the person who loses may not be happy about being the loser. This conflict is likely to resurface. One person had to compromise too much.

▼ *I lose/you lose*. Negotiations apparently became very difficult this time. Both you and the other person are losers. So many compromises were made that neither person's wishes were met. No one is happy.

▼ *I win/you win*. This is the ideal way to resolve conflicts. Both parties were able to talk through the situation. You were able to negotiate in such a way that each achieved what he or she wanted. Neither person forced his or her ideas on the other. Both parties probably made compromises. Neither was forced to compromise anything that was cherished. Those items that were lost were not highly valued, so there were no losers. Both are now happy winners.

You must recognize that some conflicts cannot be resolved. There are people who create conflicts and refuse to resolve them. Some people make unfair demands on others. If this happens, you may have to give up your responsibility toward resolution. You may have to recognize that the problem is not yours and leave it with the person who owns it.

In these situations, relations between the people involved will suffer. Perhaps the relationship is already weak. Remember that relationships are between at least two people. Sometimes every person has to be willing to stand alone. When efforts toward negotiation and compromise don't work, you can still feel you tried your best. In spite of the outcome, you have gained some experience from having tried to resolve the issue.

Use the Conflict Resolution Process

In some instances, a more formal process may be needed to resolve the conflict. The **conflict resolution process** is a step-by-step form of communication that allows conflicts to be worked out in a positive manner. The process should be used as soon as possible after a conflict occurs. This prevents anger and tension from building. It should also take place in private with only the individuals or parties involved present. Everyone needs to remain calm and be willing to listen to each other. These are the steps to follow.

1. *State the problem*. All participants must have the opportunity to tell their view of what is causing the problem. Each person must listen carefully and stay focused on the main issue. All must agree on exactly what the problem is.

2. *List possible solutions*. The next step is to suggest all potential solutions. Think of as many solutions as possible even if some seem unworkable. An idea can sometimes spark a better solution. Everyone should be able to speak freely and without criticism.

3. *Evaluate each possible solution*. Take a closer look at the best possible solutions. Which ones do both parties

like? Which ones seem to solve the problem? Use negotiation skills until a compromise solution can be reached.

4. *Pick the best solution.* Finally, both parties must agree to the best solution. It won't be a solution unless everyone is in agreement.

5. *Carry out the solution.* A plan should be made to carry out the solution. State what each party will do and when they will do it. Keep it simple. Also, decide what actions the parties will take if a conflict occurs again.

6. *Evaluate the results.* The process does not end until the solution has been put into action and the results are evaluated. If a conflict is still occurring, the process needs to begin again. Following these steps, where everyone involved is allowed to speak freely, should lead to satisfactory solutions. More serious and escalating conflicts can be avoided.

Mediation

Some efforts to resolve conflicts between parties just do not work without outside help. Mediation may be needed. In **mediation**, a third person is called on to help reconcile differences between the conflicting parties. This person is called a mediator. Through mediation, an attempt is made to settle the dispute and find a peaceful solution to the conflict, 3-22. The opposing parties talk to each other with the help of the mediator. Mediators can assist in school, work, and even international disputes. They are often included in the conflict resolution process.

A mediator is sometimes needed to settle family disputes. Family members live under the same roof, share meals and living space, work together, and play together. Conflicts are bound to occur. The conflict resolution process can be used by family members to resolve their conflicts. The two family members can talk about the problem and find a solution acceptable to both. Sometimes mediation may be needed. Who becomes the mediator? Anyone who is not emotionally tied to the issue can become the neutral third party. When a mom and daughter have a strong difference of opinion, the dad or son might be the mediator who helps bring about a win/win solution.

Peer Mediation

Many schools use **peer mediators**. These are students who are trained in the conflict resolution process. They listen and act in an unbiased manner to help fellow students settle their differences. Peer mediators are selected for their leadership skills, emotional maturity, and interest in helping others. They are often preferred as mediators because students feel more comfortable with a peer. They may feel another student can understand their problems better than an adult. Hopefully, solutions can be found. When conflicts cannot be resolved, the parties involved may have to agree to disagree, but in a peaceful manner. This necessitates respect for all concerned.

Violence: A Destructive Method of Handling Conflict

You have learned of constructive ways to deal with conflict. Is there such a thing as a destructive method of dealing with conflict? If a conflict is settled, how can it be destructive? The answer is if an act of violence is used. If physical force is used against another person or group that harms them to the point where they are completely subdued and afraid to speak up, then a

3-22
Sometimes a teacher acts as a mediator to resolve conflicts between students.

destructive method of handling conflict has been used. The conflict is ended only because one person or party has been injured or even killed by another person or group.

Gangs often use this form of conflict resolution. It also happens within some families. It may take the form of spouse abuse, child abuse, or elder abuse. If conflicts arise, one family member may attempt to completely dominate another family member. Physical force is often used, but emotional abuse can be equally devastating. Suicide also falls into this category. A person may feel there is no way out and attempt suicide.

Remember that violence does not solve a conflict. Violence is costly to society in terms of tax dollars spent on criminals in prisons. It is also costly to people in terms of lowered self-worth and lost dignity in addition to physical pain and suffering.

Always strive for positive resolutions of conflicts where differences are settled peacefully and friendships and families are kept intact. Conflict resolution skills will benefit you throughout your life as they foster relationships, increase job productivity, and prevent violence.

Check It Out!

1. State three possible causes of conflict.
2. Give an example of a negative reaction to conflict and an example of a positive reaction to conflict.
3. Why are "I" messages more successful than "you" messages in resolving conflicts?
4. Name the most ideal negotiation and compromise method.
5. List the steps in the conflict resolution process.
6. Why is mediation sometimes needed to resolve conflicts?

Chapter Review

Summary

Developing your ability to communicate well will help you throughout your life. To do this, you will want to improve your verbal communication skills. This involves speaking and listening. As a speaker, you need to send clear messages. As a listener, you want to receive and understand messages.

Nonverbal communication is an important part of the communication process as well. As you talk with people, you will become aware of the many messages you receive through nonverbal communication. Your appearance, manners, and body language are just a few of the ways you convey messages without words.

Technology has led to new forms of communication. These include cellular phones, voice mail, and e-mail. Remember to use these mediums of communication cautiously and courteously.

Open communication is important in personal relationships. Sharing positive feelings with others encourages open communication. Recognizing common communication barriers such as stereotypes, prejudices, coded messages, and gender differences helps people overcome them.

Negative feelings can occur in relationships. Learning to handle these feelings in a positive way is another important communication skill. Because of the diversity of today's workplace, communication in the workplace is especially important.

No matter how well people communicate, conflicts are still going to occur. There are many types and causes of conflicts, just as there are negative and positive reactions to them. Conflicts can best be resolved through negotiation and compromise. The conflict resolution process can also be used to resolve conflict. Mediation by a neutral third party is sometimes necessary. Violence is a destructive method of conflict resolution.

Think About It!

1. Why do you think good communication is easiest when people know one another and have similar backgrounds?
2. How would you rate your verbal communication skills at school and at home? Based on your rating, what steps would you take to improve your listening and speaking skills?
3. Choose conversation openers that you think would help you begin and develop a conversation with each of the following:
   A. A soccer player.
   B. A child in a pet store.
   C. A teacher whose class you enjoy.
   D. Parents of your dating partner.
4. In your opinion, is it fair to judge people on the basis of nonverbal communication? Explain your answer.
5. Apply the concept of open communication to an employee/employer relationship. When will open communication help this relationship? When will it hinder the relationship?

6. Summarize the benefits of communicating positive feelings. How do you communicate positive feelings to others?

7. Select and rank any five barriers to communication listed in this chapter. Use the number one as the most frequently observed barrier. Use the number five as the least frequently observed barrier.

8. Imagine that someone is very angry with you. Suggest ways that you would want that person to handle his or her negative feelings.

9. What in your opinion is the least desirable way to resolve a conflict?

10. In what careers would good communication skills be especially helpful? Explain your answer.

Try It Out!

1. Try to improve your listening and speaking skills by having a conversation with another person about any topic. When one partner speaks, the other listens. Neither person may respond to any statement without first summarizing what the partner has said. Incorrect summaries must be clarified before the conversation continues.

2. The same words can be used to convey different meanings by changing the tone of voice. Ask classmates to say one statement three different ways to convey three different meanings. Examples are: "I like the new youth director." "That's a nice looking outfit you're wearing."

3. Ask classmates to demonstrate desirable skills in communicating the following messages. Discuss each message after it is delivered. Tell why you think the speaker chose a certain phrase, speaking style, or tone of voice.
   A. Describe your favorite meal to your best friend.
   B. Describe your favorite meal to your grandparent.
   C. Ask a restaurant waiter to recook a hamburger that is too rare.
   D. Ask a salesclerk to recheck a sales slip that you think is wrong.
   E. Communicate with a four-year-old who wants to eat cookies just before dinner.
   F. Role-play a situation in which a talkative young man is dating a quiet young woman.

4. Work in a small group to develop a list of communication barriers. Exchange lists with another group. As a team, discuss some ways to overcome barriers.

5. Brainstorm as a class and suggest as many stereotypes as you can. Discuss how such stereotypes could limit your ability to communicate with others.

6. Select a possible conflict between two students who are working together on a class project. Demonstrate the four methods used to negotiate and compromise.

7. Role-play the use of the conflict resolution process. Describe a hypothetical situation that might occur in your school where the conflict resolution process could be used. Have classmates take roles as the two groups in conflict. If your school has peer mediators, ask one of them to participate in the role-play.

▼career.guide

Employment Opportunities | Entrepreneurial Opportunities | Rewards and Demands | Preparation Requirements

Food Science, Dietetics, and Nutrition Careers

Career Ladder for Food Science, Dietetics, and Nutrition

▶ **Advanced Degree**

Nutrition researcher
Health inspector
Clinical dietitian
Food production chemist
Quality control director

▶ **Bachelor's Degree**

Registered dietitian
Food technologist
Food inspector
Test kitchen supervisor
Quality control technician

▶ **Associate's Degree**

Laboratory technician
Dietary aide
Foodservice assistant

▶ **High School Diploma**

Food processing worker

▶ **Pre-High School Diploma**

Volunteer in a community kitchen or a meal delivery service for shut-ins
Participate in local science clubs and 4-H programs related to science

---

Food scientists apply the principles of science to maintaining a food supply that promotes health and satisfies consumers. Dietitians help people improve their health and well-being through more nutritious diets.

Employment Opportunities

Many food scientists help manufacturers produce, process, preserve, and package food products. They research new food sources and develop products that meet consumer demands for taste and convenience. Food scientists also inspect handling operations to make sure safety standards are met. In government agencies, they conduct basic research to improve food sources. Scientists also monitor compliance with nutrition labeling laws and health standards to enforce government regulations.

Dietitians can serve many roles depending on their work setting. In hospitals, nursing homes, and other care facilities, they plan diets to address patients' needs. Community dietitians counsel individuals and groups as part of local public health programs. Management dietitians direct the foodservice operation for hospitals, schools, restaurant chains, and other institutions. They handle all hiring, training, budgeting, planning, and purchasing to prepare nutritious, appealing meals.

Entrepreneurial Opportunities

With a background in food science, a self-employed person can offer research services to food companies on a project basis. This type of arrangement allows them to work the hours they prefer. Self-employed dietitians offer consulting services to food companies, airlines, hotels, weight-loss centers, and private clients. Those with writing skills sometimes become the authors of cookbooks, textbooks, or newspaper columns.

Rewards and Demands

Many workers in this field make significant health contributions to the food supply and the diets of individuals. These workers are rewarded by knowing they are helping people live longer, healthier lives.

Demands of this career area involve standing for many hours and making sure all work is done accurately. There is no room for error. Some jobs may require working evenings or on weekends.

Preparation Requirements

Few jobs are available in this professional field without a college degree or special training. In high school, students can prepare for college entry by taking as many science classes as possible. If offered, food science is a good choice. Math classes are very important, too.

Entry-Level Jobs

A high school education may qualify workers for jobs in food processing plants.

Midlevel Jobs

There are several job possibilities for graduates of community college programs. Dietary aides help dietitians assemble meals in hospitals and nursing homes. Large schools that employ foodservice directors use trained lunchroom assistants to help prepare and serve the menus. Research technicians help scientists set up laboratory experiments.

Professional-Level Jobs

Beyond a four-year degree, food scientists and dietitians who wish to work in a research lab, clinic, or public health office usually need a master's degree or a doctorate. Requirements vary by state, but most dietitians need a license to practice. This requires completion of a college program approved by the American Dietetic Association (ADA), an internship, and a certification exam. The license allows the dietitian to become a registered dietitian (RD).

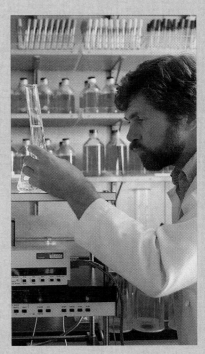

Some scientists conduct research aimed at improving the nutrient quality of the food supply.

Personal Qualities Needed for Success

Food science and dietetics careers require above-average ability in science and in communicating scientific principles to the general public. Laboratory scientists prefer solitary work, but dietitians and other food scientists must enjoy working with people. Curiosity, imagination, patience, and persistence are important traits for workers in this field.

Future Trends

The rapid growth of scientific knowledge touches all fields, especially food and health. Scientists are finding new ways to add more-nourishing ingredients to food products. As facts increase about preserving health and preventing disease, dietitians play important roles in helping people make informed food choices. With adults living longer and the population growing, demand by seniors for nutrition counseling will increase. As health and fitness become more important aspects of everyday life, foodservice providers, restaurant chains, and catering companies will need more nutrition consulting from dietitians.

Career Interests, Abilities, and You

A good way to pursue a career in this field is to take food-related and science courses in high school. You might also ask to shadow someone working in one of the occupations. Seek part-time employment or do volunteer work in a food-related program.

Part Two
Family and Community Relationships

Chapter 4
Understanding Families

Careers

These careers relate to the topics in this chapter:
- ▼ home companions
- ▼ family programs coordinator
- ▼ family life educator
- ▼ marriage counselor

As you study the chapter, see if you can think of others.

Topics

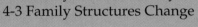

Topic 4-1

What Is a Family?

Objectives

After studying this topic, you will be able to
▼ describe roles of family members.
▼ name functions the family unit performs for individuals and society.
▼ analyze how people with a single lifestyle meet their needs for the functions provided by families.

Topic Terms

family
procreation
socialization

The family unit forms the foundation of society. Most people are raised in family settings. In these settings, they learn skills and share experiences that will shape the rest of their lives. See 4-1.

The term **family** can be defined in a number of ways. One common definition is: two or more people related by blood, marriage, or adoption. This definition emphasizes the structure of the family unit. Other definitions emphasize the roles, responsibilities, rights, and relationships of family members. For example, a family can be described as two or more persons committed to one another over time who share resources, responsibility for decisions, values, and goals.

What makes the family such an important unit? To answer this question, you must take a closer look at the roles family members fulfill. You must also consider the functions families provide for individuals and society.

4-1
Skills children learn in a family setting are often used throughout their adult lives.

Roles of Family Members

Each member of a family has special roles to play. Such roles include parent, child, spouse, sibling, and income provider. The behaviors expected of people in these roles vary from family to family. Many of your family roles were inherited when you were born. At birth, your sex determined your role as son or daughter, brother or sister, and niece or nephew. See 4-2.

Some of your family roles are assigned to you. You are expected to fulfill certain responsibilities as a result of assigned roles. For instance, if you are an older sibling, you may have to fill the role of caregiver to younger siblings. You might have the responsibility of watching them from time to time.

Some roles are chosen. If you have talent in the kitchen, you might choose the role of family cook. If you enjoy being outdoors, you may take on the responsibility of caring for the lawn.

4-2
In this family, the girls fulfill roles as daughters and as sisters.

Functions of the Family

Through their various roles and responsibilities, family members form an interactive unit. This unit provides for the physical, mental, emotional, social, and spiritual well-being of its members. It also provides a number of functions for society. Culture, society, and technology are strong influences on the family. Besides these, demographic factors, economic forces, and world events can also affect the family.

Procreation

One of the basic functions of the family is **procreation**, or the bearing of children. Most people are born into a family environment. Parents have children to express their love for each other. They desire the experience of raising children and watching them grow into unique adults. They want their children to carry on the heritage and traditions of their family line. See 4-3.

The function of procreation assures the continuation of society. As children are born into families, the population is maintained. As the children become adults, they join the workforce to produce goods and services. They spend dollars to stimulate the economy. They have children of their own who will follow the same cycle.

Physical Care

When parents supply their children with food, clothing, and shelter, they are providing the function of physical care. This function also includes providing medical care and creating a safe and healthy environment.

4-3
Parents choose to have children to fulfill their desire to share their love and help shape the life of another human being.

Society helps families with the function of physical care. If parents cannot afford food, shelter, or medical care, public assistance and charitable programs try to meet those needs. If families face unsafe situations, police and fire departments can assist them.

Society is not set up to provide complete physical care for all people. Therefore, families serve a vital function by satisfying some of these needs themselves.

Socialization

Another important function of families is the **socialization** of children. This means teaching children to conform to social standards. As parents socialize their children, they act as authority figures in the home. In this role, they establish reasonable rules of conduct. Parents set limits that protect their children and teach them appropriate behavior.

Teaching children about their heritage is part of socialization. Children need to learn about their cultural background. Parents can share family traditions with children and help the children develop pride in their ancestral roots.

Education is also part of the socialization process. Parents provide infants and young children with general guidance and moral education. They act as role models to provide career and vocational training. Parents are also responsible for enrolling their children in formal education programs. As children get older, therefore, schools and other agencies assume part of the responsibility for socialization.

Emotional Support

Perhaps the most critical function of families in today's society is the emotional support of family members. No other social unit can replace the family for providing children with love and nurturing. Parents form a bond with their infant children. As children grow, parents are there to comfort children when they are sad. They can reassure children when they have doubts. They can forgive children when they make mistakes. See 4-4.

Children are not the only family members who require support. Parents rely on their children to let them know they are loved and appreciated. Parents also count on support from each other. Parents need to make their marriage a priority. Partner-centered marriages provide stability in the home and create a secure atmosphere for all. Children as well as parents benefit from a family that is led by a strong partnership.

4-4
Helping children feel secure is one way parents provide emotional support.

Single Living

Not all people live in families. Many adults are single. They may live alone or with roommates. These adults must find other resources to meet their needs for functions provided by the family.

Choosing the Lifestyle

People choose a single lifestyle for different reasons. Some single people want time to explore their own interests. Some people want the flexibility to travel. Some people want a single lifestyle while they finish their education or establish careers.

Some see a single lifestyle as a temporary one. Others want to remain single permanently. They may choose this lifestyle because they value their privacy and enjoy being alone. These people may like to relax in peace and quiet. They prefer the personal freedom offered by a single lifestyle, 4-5. They would rather be alone with their thoughts than feel obligated to interact constantly with another person.

People who are committed to their careers or to civic, social, or religious activities may also choose a single lifestyle. Such people devote all of their attention, time, and energy to their special interests. They do not have enough time for the types of relationships involved in marriage or parenting.

Accepting the Lifestyle

A single lifestyle is not always chosen. Widowed people are forced to accept a single lifestyle when their mates die. Likewise, people must make a transition to a single lifestyle when a divorce occurs. Some people who would like to be married must accept a single lifestyle. Some of these people never find the right person to be a marriage partner. Some had a painful

4-5
Many single people value their independence as well as quiet personal space.

relationship in the past and are afraid to develop a new relationship. Some become involved in caring for aging parents and do not have time to meet potential partners. Others travel so much with their careers that they are never in one place long enough to develop a relationship, 4-6.

Meeting Needs for Family Functions

Regardless of the reasons for their lifestyle, single people need the functions provided by families. They must find other means of meeting these needs.

Adult single people must work to earn a living and provide for their own physical care. They pay for their own housing. They buy their own food and clothing. They rely on physicians when they get sick. They turn to public agencies, such as police and fire departments, for help with their needs for safety.

4-6
Some people who are highly involved with their careers do not have time to establish relationships with potential marriage partners.

Many single people have a strong network of friends. These friends serve as a source of emotional support. They provide love and encouragement when family members are not available. Some single people live with roommates. Roommates help share the expenses of food, housing, and other physical needs. They provide one another with a sense of security. They also help meet emotional needs by providing companionship. Although people in a single lifestyle do not live with family members, they often maintain close relationships with them. Visits, letters, e-mail, and phone calls provide the family contact many single people require.

Check It Out!

1. What are the three ways family members get their various roles?
2. What are the four main functions of the family?
3. List four reasons people choose a single lifestyle.

Topic 4-2
Family Structures Vary

Objectives
After studying this topic, you will be able to
▼ describe characteristics of various family structures.
▼ name six factors that can influence family responsibilities.

Topic Terms
family structure
nuclear family
single-parent family
stepfamily
extended family
childless family
media
demographics

How would you describe a typical American family? Your answer to this question is likely to differ from the answers given by your classmates. This is because there is no "typical" American family. Some families have two parents and some families have one parent. Some families have stepparents and stepchildren. Some families have grandparents, aunts, uncles, and cousins. Some families have children and some families do not.

Family Structures

Family structure refers to the makeup of a family group. It is based on the relationships of the members in the family. Each of the five basic structures is able to provide the main family functions for its members.

Nuclear Families

A **nuclear family** is a family group that consists of a man and woman and their children, 4-7. This structure gives children the comfort and security of family ties with both parents. It gives them a solid base for the development of human relationships. The nuclear family also gives children a view of adult roles modeled by their parents.

In nuclear families, husbands and wives usually seek their chief companionship and emotional support from each other. Children receive attention, love, encouragement, and guidance from their parents. Close family interaction in this structure can promote a feeling of togetherness. It can help family members build strong, healthy relationships.

Single-Parent Families

In the **single-parent family** structure, one adult lives with one or more children. The adult may be widowed, separated, divorced, or never married. The single parent must provide the functions of a family without the aid of a spouse.

The lack of adult role models is a concern in many single-parent families. Children learn gender-appropriate behavior from adults. A little boy living with his single mother misses opportunities to learn male role behavior from his father. Likewise, a little girl living with her single father misses opportunities to learn female role behavior from her mother.

Organizations designed to help fill the vacant adult roles in single-parent families exist in many communities. Big Brothers and Big Sisters are organizations with this purpose. The Big Brothers organization matches adult men with young boys who

4-7
The nuclear family structure can provide an excellent environment for rearing children.

lack male influence in their homes. The Big Sisters organization operates in the same way to match adult women with young girls. The adults help to provide friendship and guidance to young people.

The parents in single-parent families often miss the companionship of other adults. They can find support and understanding in organizations like Parents Without Partners (PWP). Local chapters of this international organization sponsor many social and educational activities. These events help group members adjust to their roles as single parents. Some activities include children to allow them to interact with adults of the sex opposite that of their own parents.

Cooperation is the key to success in single-parent families. Each member should be aware of the needs and concerns of other members. When one family member has a problem, another member may be able to understand and offer help. See 4-8.

4-8

A single-parent family structure can encourage a high degree of sharing and a strong commitment between family members.

Stepfamilies

When a single parent marries, a **stepfamily** is formed. The husband, the wife, or both spouses have children from other marriages. Thus, the stepfamily structure includes the roles of stepparents and stepchildren.

The members of a stepfamily must be flexible enough to adjust to a new lifestyle. In most cases, at least some of the family members were previously part of a nuclear family. They may have faced the crisis of death or divorce. They have adjusted to a single-parent family structure. Making the adjustment to a stepfamily may be stressful for them. To cushion this adjustment, each family member must try to be understanding and cooperative.

A stepfamily is usually a new experience for everyone involved. Each person brings his or her hopes and doubts into the family. New relationships form. Besides adjusting to each other, husbands and wives must adjust to each other's children. The children must adjust to a new parent as well as new brothers and sisters.

Without cooperation, the adjustment to a stepfamily could be difficult. Even with cooperation, there may be some problems at first. If everyone in the family keeps trying, however, the result could be a strong, healthy family unit. The new combination of interests, skills, and other resources could make the stepfamily lively and exciting. See 4-9.

Extended Families

In an **extended family** structure, other relatives live with parents and their children. Grandparents, aunts, uncles, and/or cousins might be part of an extended family. This family structure is less common today than in the past.

4-9
Adjustment to a stepfamily can be easier if everyone makes a sincere effort.

An extended family takes care of its own members. Aging parents receive care from their children rather than from nursing homes. Grandparents and other adults care for the children. Children gain general knowledge and learn specific skills from the adults.

In most extended families, members offer one another economic support. The family can take advantage of each member's knowledge, skills, time, and energy. One person may be interested in gardening and cooking. Someone else may enjoy sewing clothes for the family. Other members might be talented in home or car maintenance or in handling financial affairs. By combining the resources of all the family members, the household can be run economically.

Childless Families

A fifth family structure is the childless family. A **childless family** is a couple without children. Some childless couples are not able to have children and prefer not to adopt. Other couples choose not to have children. In the past, relatives and society might have criticized this decision. Today, this has become an acceptable option. See 4-10.

People who do not have children of their own may choose to interact with children in other settings. They might spend time with nieces or nephews. They might also do volunteer work with children in their community.

4-10
Childless couples may prefer to concentrate on goals other than raising children.

Factors Influencing Families

Families are affected by outside forces, both good and bad. Parents try to take advantage of the positive influences to enhance the family's well-being. They also try, to the extent possible, to shield family members from negative influences.

Cultural Influences

Perhaps the strongest influence in shaping family structure is the cultural heritage of the individuals involved. Culture shapes a person's expectations for the different roles of various family members. The U.S. population includes people from cultures throughout the world. Therefore, newlyweds may have different expectations for their new life together if they come from different cultural backgrounds.

Respect for the extended family is a strong influence among people of many cultures. The benefits of the extended family include help with housekeeping and child care tasks. While the son or daughter raised in an extended family may feel comfortable with this living arrangement, his or her spouse may not.

The cultures that value extended families are also likely to emphasize family interests over the individual's. This may be expressed by the family deciding what career their son or daughter eventually pursues. The parents may regard these decisions as theirs to make since they will rely on the children's earning power in their old age. A family-arranged marriage is another sign of a family that emphasizes family interests over the individual's. See 4-11.

Societal Influences

Through the socialization process, parents teach children the do's and don'ts of society. The family interprets the standards of society to help children understand what behaviors are expected of them. By learning these important lessons through teaching and training, children understand how the standards apply to their lives. With parental love and support, children then grow into productive members of society.

In a democratic society, free expression is allowed and encouraged. Sometimes the ideas and values expressed are not consistent with what children learn from their families. Peers, for example, can strongly influence individuals to join group activities, for good or bad.

4-11
Couples contemplating marriage would benefit from meeting each other's families to experience their customs and values firsthand.

Advertising and other forms of media can also influence individuals to behave contrary to their training. **Media** are channels of mass communication, such as magazines, television, radio, and the Internet. These influences can convey beliefs, priorities, and standards of conduct contrary to a family's view of what is right and proper.

When negative influences from society begin to make an impact, parents are challenged to work harder in the role of socializing their children.

Technological Influences

Many of the time- and energy-saving tools and appliances used in homes are the result of technology. These devices help families manage their lives and provide physical care to their children.

Telecommuting, discussed further in Chapter 9, is also possible as a result of technology. Telecommuting allows parents to earn income while staying home. When parents work from their homes, they can tailor their schedules to include both roles of parent and income producer. As a result, they mesh the responsibilities of being a parent with those of being an employee, 4-12.

One of the most important benefits of new technology is the ability to communicate easily with others. Using the Internet, family members living apart can stay in touch through e-mail. They can share family photos and custom-made sound clips, such as thank-you messages or birthday greetings. The latest technology in

4-12
Mothers of young children especially value telecommuting careers.

home computers can even send live-action pictures and sound anywhere. Broadcasts of holiday celebrations and family events help family members throughout the world share common experiences. Communication technology increases the ability of families to provide emotional support to distant members.

Demographic Factors

Many demographic factors indicate that families are changing. **Demographics** are statistical qualities of the human population. By checking demographics, many trends can be observed.

A major trend affecting the family is the high percentage of women working away from home. Historically, the man was the "breadwinner" while the woman tended to the home and family. Today the majority of mothers hold jobs outside the home. If fathers are also away at work, some outside help is needed to care for young children. Extended families are very helpful in this situation. With one or more other adults living with the family, someone may always be present to care for the children. Without this help, parents often share— with a babysitter, child care worker, or teacher—their responsibilities for providing physical care and socialization to children.

Another trend that impacts families is the growing population of older adults due to increasing lifespan. When older adults are healthy, they can lead independent lives. When their health begins to fail, their lifestyles must change, too. Older adults with physical or mental disabilities must be watched closely so they do not fall prey to accidents or safety hazards. As older adults move in with their middle age "children" to watch over them, extended families are created, 4-13. Many middle-age adults have the double responsibility of raising children and providing care to aging parents.

4-13
When an aging parent decides to live with his or her child's family, an extended family is formed.

Another important demographic trend is the high mobility of the U.S. population. Compared to past generations, when moving once or twice was common, today's families move five or more times. Often they move so parents have better job opportunities. The move may benefit the family financially, but it can negatively impact members emotionally. Left behind are cousins, aunts, uncles, and grandparents that provided emotional support. Often they provided physical support, too, especially in helping with child care. In these situations, parents must fill the void created by moving away from beloved family members.

Economic Forces

Economic forces have much to do with a family's well-being. The absence of good jobs causes some families to leave familiar surroundings, seeking opportunities else-where. Left behind is the family support system that helped in times of need.

If one salary does not satisfy family needs, one parent must work multiple jobs or both parents must earn incomes. In these cases, parents are often faced with finding alternatives for handling part of their child care responsibilities. When older children are present, more household and child care responsibilities are usually assigned to them.

World Events

Family development is influenced not only by events within the country, but also by world situations. People of the world are no longer isolated from one another. New communication systems make worldwide information readily available. Therefore, events that occur in one country become common knowledge around the world within minutes.

Social and political unrest in one area of the world can influence countries on the other side of the globe. Family members can be separated when there is a need to send military troops abroad. Natural disasters such as floods or earthquakes can devastate whole cities. After such events, families from distant countries may donate money, clothing, and food to assist the victims.

The family is no longer an independent economic unit, 4-14. Families depend on global markets to satisfy needs for many products. For example, consider what happens when a war interferes with shipments of petroleum from oil-producing countries. Less fuel is available to drive cars and heat homes, causing prices to skyrocket. Families have little choice but to pay the higher prices. Often they must alter their lifestyles and postpone unnecessary purchases, too. Higher fuel

4-14
A high price on in-season produce usually indicates bad weather in the areas where the produce was grown.

costs eventually increase the prices of all goods and services, affecting everyone's pocketbook. This, in turn, influences the general economy. When the public has less spending power, companies respond by producing less and, thus, cutting jobs. Events in other parts of the world can have long-term effects on families in your area.

Check It Out!

1. A married couple with children describes the _____ family structure.
2. Name three organizations that can help fill the gaps in single-parent families.
3. List six factors that can affect the responsibilities of family members.

Topic 4-3

Family Structures Change

Objectives

After studying this topic, you will be able to
▼ list the six stages of the family life cycle.
▼ determine the consequences of divorce.
▼ explain why second marriages are more likely to be successful for people whose first marriages ended in divorce.

Topic Term

family life cycle

Family structures do not always remain the same. They may change as new members are added to a family or as present members leave. For instance, a nuclear family may become an extended family or a single-parent family. Some of these changes occur as a result of the natural passage of time.

Family Life Cycle

While family structures vary, each structure includes basic stages of growth and development called the **family life cycle**. See 4-15. Studying this cycle can help people prepare for the challenges that may exist in their own families.

Stages in the Cycle

The family life cycle contains six main stages and a number of substages. The first main stage is known as the *beginning stage*. Families in this stage consist of a husband and wife. While in this stage, couples

Setting the Scene: Readjusting

Your family believes your older sister has been successfully launched. She has chosen a career, achieved the required education, completed training, and accepted a job within driving distance of her apartment. To your parents' surprise, she announces that she will be moving back home with them…and you.

Analyze It: How will this affect you? What rules and expectations might apply to your sister that don't apply to you? Which rules and expectations might apply to you that don't apply to your sister?

make adjustments to marriage and form foundations for their future families. There may be many money pressures as couples try to establish a new home. There may be time pressures, too, as spouses try to build careers, finish a higher education, or perhaps do both.

During the years when a family is growing, it is in the *childbearing stage*. This stage includes the birth of the first child through the birth of the last child. This is a very busy period since attention to the child is full-time. If a parent cannot stay home with the child, arrangements must be made so the child receives quality care. Whether a career couple hires outside help or one spouse stays home full-time, there is considerable money pressure.

The family continues to grow in the *parenting stage*. Parents provide for the children, while the children pursue their

Family Life Cycle

Beginning Stage	Child-bearing Stage	Parenting Stage	Launching Stage	Mid-Years Stage	Aging Stage
• Married couple without children	• Couple from birth of first child through birth of last child	• Couple with child(ren)	• Couple with child(ren) leaving home	• Couple with independent child(ren) living away from home	• Couple during retirement until death of both spouses

4-15
Family life follows a series of stages as couples age and children come and go.

individual interests and school activities. This tends to be the most expensive stage of the family life cycle. Food and clothing costs increase as children grow. Having enough space for everyone to live comfortably may require remodeling the family home or moving to a larger one. School activities and sports often involve extra fees. Saving money for the children's college educations occurs during this period. Also, tension between the spouses can develop if there is no plan for handling the many housekeeping and child care duties.

The *launching stage* is when children begin to leave home and become independent of their parents. They may leave for college and continue after graduation in their chosen careers. Some may find jobs and move to their own housing; others marry and start their own families. However, today it is not unusual for adult children to return home at some point.

The launching stage is followed by the *mid-years stage* when all children have left and the couple is again independent. During this period, couples enter their peak earning years. They can spend more of their income on themselves instead of the children. They may do so by upgrading their homes or taking more frequent vacations. They may also become grandparents in this stage.

The final stage of the family life cycle is the *aging stage*. This stage begins at the time of retirement and continues until both spouses die. During this stage, one spouse may live alone after the death of the other. When the spouses are financially secure and enjoying good health, it is a very rewarding period. Time can be devoted to lifelong interests at whatever pace is comfortable. When problems begin to surface over finances and/or health, life can become unpleasant. Tensions may develop with other family members who try to offer assistance.

Variations in the Cycle

Families are unique and do not always fit a given mold. Many families have overlaps in the stages and substages of the life cycle. For example, a family may include a baby, school-age children, and teenagers all at one time. A family may launch an older child while a preschooler is still at home.

Sometimes many years separate the stages of a family's life cycle. For example, a couple may have a teenager before their second child is born. This family experiences the qualities of both the childbearing and parenting stages.

As individuals progress through the stages of the family life cycle, they are faced with different roles and responsibilities. Roles change as family members grow older. For example, in the beginning stage, a man has the role of husband and provider. In the childbearing family stage, he takes on the additional role of father, 4-16. In the aging stage, he no longer has the role of provider and may have to accept the role of widower.

4-16
A man takes on a new family role with new responsibilities when he becomes a father.

Divorce

Changes in family structure are not always the result of time passage. A change from a nuclear family to a single-parent family is often the result of divorce. Divorce is common in today's society. Many couples decide they have problems and differences that cannot be resolved. They believe they would be happier living apart, so they get a divorce. Divorce rates are high among people of all ages, economic levels, and religions.

The More You Know: Who Gets Divorced?

Certain groups of people are more likely to divorce than others. Teen marriages have a high divorce rate, especially when the bride is pregnant. Many of these couples are not ready to handle the responsibilities of marriage and parenthood. Marriages in which spouses have a low level of education also have a high divorce rate. A lack of education often prevents people from getting good jobs that pay higher wages to cover their cost of living. This adds stress to a couple's marriage relationship. Spouses who have mixed or no religious ties are also more likely to get divorced. On the other hand, spouses who share strong religious beliefs are more likely to have stable marriages.

Adjusting to Divorce

Divorce creates many changes for many people. The two former spouses have to break their emotional ties to each other. They have to go through the legal process of ending their marriage. They have to set up two separate households. This means changing their budgets and usually leading simpler, less costly lifestyles.

Divorced persons have to learn to think of themselves as individuals again. They have to adjust to independence. They have to learn to make decisions by themselves and lead their own lives. See 4-17.

Divorce affects not only the couple, but also the people they know. Friends, neighbors, and colleagues of the couple may choose sides and become either "his" or "her" friends. Some people who have a negative view of divorce may not want to remain friendly with either member of the divorce. Other people may remain supportive and help the divorced persons make new social contacts.

Children of a divorced couple face many changes, too. They have to adjust to living with one parent and visiting the other parent. They may have to move to a new home. They may have to go to a new school and meet new friends. In addition, they have to adjust to the changes in their parents' social lives.

Remarriage

Remarriage is another event that causes family structures to change. Many single-parent families become stepfamilies when divorced people remarry.

Second marriages are usually more successful than first marriages. One reason is that spouses are older and usually more

4-17
Divorced persons must adjust to establishing a home without the former spouse.

mature. They are more willing to invest the time and energy needed to make their marriages work. They have learned from their mistakes. They have a better idea of the kind of person they want for a marriage partner. They also have more realistic views of what they can and cannot expect of a spouse and of a marriage.

Second marriages have just as many challenges as first marriages have. When children from previous marriages are involved, second marriages may have even more challenges. Cooperation and communication can help spouses successfully handle these challenges. Spouses in second marriages may be more willing to cooperate with each other. They may try harder to keep communication lines open. This helps them keep in touch with each other's thoughts and feelings. Communication also prevents minor problems from growing and becoming major problems. With good cooperation and communication, any marriage can be successful. See 4-18.

4-18
Communicating and spending time together can help a couple build a successful marriage.

Check It Out!

1. What are the six stages of the family life cycle?
2. True or false. When a couple divorces, their friends, neighbors, and colleagues are affected.
3. What are two reasons that second marriages are more likely to be successful for people whose first marriages ended in divorce?

Chapter Review

Summary

The family is the most important social unit in cultures throughout the world. Each person fulfills various inherited and assigned roles as a family member. The family provides the functions of procreation, physical care, socialization, and emotional support for its members.

Families take the form of different family structures. A nuclear family includes a husband, wife, and their children. A single-parent family has one parent and one or more children. A stepfamily contains stepparents and stepchildren. An extended family includes one or more relatives outside the nuclear family, such as an aunt or a grandmother. A childless family consists of a couple without children. Single people do not live in any of these family structures. They must meet their needs for the functions provided by a family in other ways.

Various outside forces may affect the roles and responsibilities of family members. Culture, society, and technology are strong influences. Some demographic factors that affect families include more women working outside the home, the longer lives of older family members, and more families moving more often. Economic forces and world events can also affect families.

Throughout their lives, the structures of families change. Some of these changes occur as a family goes through the stages of the family life cycle. Other changes in family structure are the result of divorce or remarriage.

Think About It!

1. What are three ways family members might demonstrate commitment to one another?
2. Describe your family roles and the roles of two of your family members.
3. Which of the functions provided by families do you think is most important? Explain your answer.
4. How do people with a single lifestyle meet their needs for each of the functions provided by families?
5. Which of the family structures discussed in this chapter do you feel is best equipped to provide the functions of the family? Explain your answer.
6. Which of the factors that influence families most affects yours? Explain.
7. If you were going to choose a family-related career, which one would you choose? Why?
8. Which stage in the family life cycle do you think would be the most exciting stage for parents? Explain your answer.
9. List two consequences a divorce would have for each of the following: a husband, a wife, and children.
10. If your first marriage ended in divorce, what would you do to help avoid divorce in your second marriage?

Try It Out!

1. Using your library resources, prepare a bibliography of books and magazine articles that classmates can use for further research about families.
2. Write a story about a family in the year 2030. Describe how roles of family members and functions provided by the family might change in the future.
3. As a class, prepare a series of posters, each portraying a different family structure.
4. Role-play a scene or two depicting the advantages and disadvantages of single living.
5. Prepare a bulletin board using magazine pictures or family photos contributed by class members. Write clever captions to identify the various stages of the family life cycle represented.
6. Research the current statistics on divorce and remarriage. Share your findings in an oral report.
7. Look in the yellow pages of the telephone directory to find family and marriage counseling services available in your area.

Chapter 5
Strengthening Families

Careers

These careers relate to the topics in this chapter:
- ▼ community service worker
- ▼ companion for the homebound
- ▼ child welfare research assistant
- ▼ family crisis counselor

As you study the chapter, see if you can think of others.

Topics

5-1 Building Functional Families
5-2 Balancing Family and Work
5-3 Handling Family Crises

Topic 5-1

Building Functional Families

Objectives

After studying this topic, you will be able to
▼ describe characteristics of functional families.
▼ list techniques family members can use to build a functional family.
▼ explain how functional families fulfill their family rights and responsibilities.

Topic Terms

functional family
dysfunctional family
codependency

In today's complex world, people face the challenge of keeping the family unit strong. This challenge is not always easy to meet. However, many families face the challenge by making family life a top priority. Family members know and accept the responsibility they have for one another. They are committed to working together and making special sacrifices to help one another.

Making and Keeping Families Strong

A strong, healthy family is also called a **functional family**. A functional family provides a positive environment. Each family member is encouraged to grow and to reach his or her fullest potential, 5-1. A functional family tries to stay balanced.

The family works together to meet the needs of each member. In turn, each family member carries out his or her roles and responsibilities. Together, the family works to keep their unit strong, healthy, and happy.

Functional families have certain qualities in common. They communicate effectively. When problems arise, they try to solve them. Spending time together is important to them. Family members appreciate and support one another. Each member tries to understand the roles of other family members. Above all, they value family life.

Functional families also realize they are not perfect. Their lives don't always run smoothly. However, they have a sense of purpose. They work hard to overcome obstacles and stay strong. They feel the rewards are worth the effort they put into the relationship.

Have you thought about what you can do to strengthen your family and help keep it that way? Some helpful techniques you and your family can use to achieve this goal are described below.

Communicate Effectively

You can find ways to communicate more effectively with your family, 5-2. Make a point to talk with other family members. Listen carefully to make sure you understand the other person's viewpoint. Plan to have mealtimes together to talk about daily events, or set up a regular family meeting. When schedules are hard to coordinate, try using notes, e-mail messages, and telephone calls as a pleasant surprise. This method may also help your family stay in touch with members who are away from home. Communicate positive feelings by planning special events the family can enjoy together. Communicate your understanding of

5-1
Functional families provide for the physical, social, emotional, and spiritual needs of their members. They put the family first.

The More You Know: How Can Families Communicate?

Functional families communicate effectively. This means they talk about problems, express their needs and feelings, and listen to one another. Members respect each other's opinions, even if those opinions differ from their own. They use open communication to solve the problems when they disagree. They also communicate in ways that help them develop a sense of trust in one another.

others' feelings. Sincere words like "I love you" accompanied by a hug or a kiss can lift spirits or mend hurt feelings. Good communication promotes growth for all family members.

Solve Problems

Functional families try to resolve problems and conflicts in positive ways. When all family members tackle problems together, they develop a feeling of joint ownership. Jointly owned problems are usually easier to solve. There are more people to identify possible solutions.

Get Help When Needed

Functional families admit they have as many problems as less-healthy, or dysfunctional families. A **dysfunctional family** provides a negative environment that discourages the growth and

5-2
Effective communication is one factor in building strong family relationships.

development of family members. The difference between a functional family and dysfunctional family is the way they look at problems and solve them. For example, some dysfunctional families try too hard to help their members. They may assume responsibility for family members who have serious problems by covering for them. This is called **codependency**. A pattern of unhealthy behaviors is used by family members to cover up the problem. This adversely affects the emotional health of everyone in the family and does not help the family member who has the problem.

Functional families look for positive outcomes in all types of situations—even problem situations. They deal with the problems instead of being destroyed by them. When they cannot solve a problem themselves, they seek outside help.

When your family faces what you consider a real problem, try using the problem-solving process. Openly discuss the problem; don't let it build up inside. State your feelings using I-messages. Avoid name-calling or blaming someone else for your problem. Try for an I win/you win situation by compromising or negotiating for a satisfactory solution. If a serious problem arises that cannot be resolved within the family, suggest seeking help outside the family.

Spend Time Together

Functional families spend time together whenever possible. They bring a sense of play and humor into their leisure time. Family interactions are balanced, so all members feel involved. Some families go to the movies, work on hobbies together, or have a family game night. What is most important is they do something together as a family. See 5-3.

You can find ways to spend time with your family, too. Look for special activities you and your family can share, like biking or preparing evening meals. Help plan a family vacation or outing. Share family celebrations like birthdays and anniversaries. Celebrate religious and patriotic holidays together. Start a new family tradition that will help create happy memories, such as visiting a museum or planting trees. Plan ahead with your family so everyone can get involved.

Show Appreciation

Functional families find ways to show appreciation. This form of emotional support encourages a secure and loving environment. Showing appreciation through words or actions contributes to each member's well-being and self-esteem, 5-4.

You can show family members appreciation in your everyday actions. Offer to help out without being asked. Thank others when they help you. Give sincere compliments about a job well done or when someone looks nice. Create your own special event for a family member. Let others know they are special in your life by the things you say and do.

5-3
Many families enjoy spending time together by taking an annual vacation trip.

5-4
Helping with raking the leaves is one way to show appreciation.

Show Respect

No two members of a family are exactly alike. To keep families strong, members need to show respect for one another. This can be done in a number of ways. They can respect one another's ideas and opinions, recognizing that not everyone will agree on every matter. Listening to what everyone has to say, no matter how old they are, is important. Each individual will have likes and dislikes. These, too, should be respected.

Family members can respect one another's privacy, as well as their personal belongings. Asking if you can borrow an item that belongs to a brother or sister rather than taking the item without a word shows respect. Showing respect for older members of the family is important in most cultures. When you show respect for family members, they feel valued and loved. Respect is an important part of emotional support and leads to feelings of trust.

Understand One Another

Functional families try to understand the changing roles of each family member. They recognize that family tensions may increase during the period of adolescence. The adolescent is learning independence, while parents are beginning to give up some controls. It is a period of uncertainty and adjustment for both adolescents and parents. Both parties must try harder to understand and accept the changes that occur during this period. All must make an extra effort to show respect for one another and trust one another.

Understanding your changing role may help you understand your parents' point of view. Your parents are watching you grow from a child to an adult. During this time, you and your parents won't always agree. Being patient and understanding may be helpful. Try speaking and acting in ways that help make this transition smoother for both sides. You may find some of the tips listed in 5-5 helpful.

Strengthening Parent-Teen Relationships

- Conduct family meetings so everyone will have opportunities to bring up issues for discussion.
- Recognize potential problems and be willing to talk about them.
- Encourage open discussion by listening and trying to understand the other's point-of-view.
- Communicate honestly and truthfully.
- Respect one another.
- Negotiate fairly.
- Communicate without manipulating one another. For example, avoid trying to get your own point across by making others feel guilty.
- Use a normal tone of voice.
- Maintain self-control. When tempers flare, communications close.
- Try to read and respond to nonverbal communication.
- Seek clarification when you do not understand.
- Learn to laugh and cry together.
- Always remember—in good times and bad—that you are a family.

5-5
It's not always easy for parents and teens to relate well to each other. For those who can, however, the rewards are worth the efforts. Here are some tips that can help parents and teens strengthen their relationships.

Fulfilling Family Rights and Responsibilities

In most families, family rights and responsibilities are closely linked. For each right a family member has, a responsibility comes with it. Functional families are committed to fulfilling these rights and responsibilities. They do so by sharing values and goals, responsibility for decisions, resources, and a commitment to one another.

Sharing Values and Goals

Family members have a right to expect support and guidance as they establish values and goals. Family members also have a responsibility to provide this support and guidance for one another.

Functional families share what is important to them both directly and indirectly. Parents directly teach their children *morals*—a sense of what is right or wrong. Children also learn what is important to their parents indirectly by watching what goes on around them. When family members live with certain values, these become important to all members. As a result, family members share many values even if they are not actually discussed. See 5-6.

Functional families help members develop values by being supportive. When a family member says "I think…" or "I believe…" others listen with respect and understanding. As a family, they are able to discuss issues openly. Open discussions

5-6
Families who share values and goals create a positive environment that keeps the family strong.

also help family members develop good communication skills, self-respect, self-confidence, and self-esteem.

When family members share what they feel is important, they are likely to share goals, too. Families set goals that reflect their values. These goals give direction to their lives. When they share certain goals, it's easier for family members to work together with enthusiasm. Each person may try a little harder if the family is planning a vacation or saving for a new house.

Functional families encourage people to share goals. Family members can offer one another companionship as they work toward their goals. They can also celebrate together when their goals are reached.

Sharing Responsibility for Decisions

Family members have a right to learn and practice decision-making skills within the warm and supportive setting of the family unit. They also have a responsibility to provide input for family decisions that need to be made. Together, members of functional families can discuss ideas and explore alternatives. They can make wise decisions that are best for the entire family.

Sharing Resources

Functional families work together for the well-being of all members. Each member has a responsibility to contribute the special resources he or she has to offer. Each member also has a right to share in the resources contributed by others. Family members enjoy a sense of fulfillment in giving and receiving. See 5-7.

The time, energy, interest, knowledge, and skills contributed by family members have economic value. When family members exchange these resources, they

5-7
Children who learn about sharing family resources are more likely to contribute to the family group when they get older.

also help one another grow emotionally, intellectually, and socially. They all become better people. They help ensure economic security for their members.

Functional families use their resources for home management. They establish realistic expectations and set priorities.

Preparing work schedules and assigning responsibilities to all family members helps establish a balanced workload. Working together to manage the home gives members a sense of belonging. It also teaches job skills that will be useful when family members become wage earners.

Sharing a Lasting Commitment

Sharing commitment to one another is a right and a responsibility of family members. In functional families, a lasting commitment is the tie that binds family members. Commitment is an expression of love. It provides individualized attention to the needs of each person. This lasting commitment adds to a person's sense of security. At the end of a hard day, a worker needs to know that emotional support can be found at home. After surgery, a patient needs to know that family members will help make the recovery easier. People need to know they are not alone—their family will always be there for them.

The commitment among family members provides opportunities for giving as well as receiving. Cooking a special meal or mowing the lawn without being asked are thoughtful gestures that make everyone feel good. Just being there to listen is also important.

Check It Out!

1. Identify five qualities functional families have in common.
2. Explain the difference between a functional family and a dysfunctional family.
3. Explain how functional families fulfill their family rights and responsibilities.

Topic 5-2
Balancing Family and Work

Objectives

After studying this topic, you will be able to
▼ explain the relationship between family and work.
▼ recognize ways working families can manage multiple roles.
▼ identify ways employers can help dual-career families manage work and family roles.

Topic Terms

dual-career families
multiple roles
priorities
job sharing
flextime
flexible workweeks
tailored paychecks

Families face challenges every day. One of the biggest challenges they face today is balancing the roles and responsibilities of family life and work. Not only do working parents provide economic support for family members, they must also fulfill their parental roles. Work should be an enjoyable part of a well-rounded life. Work rewards and responsibilities should be balanced with those of personal and family life.

As employers face changing trends in the economy, they are trying to support harmony between work and family life. Family-oriented employers are adapting new programs and benefits to meet the needs of working parents. By allowing more choices, employers are helping working parents balance their family and work responsibilities.

The Relationship of Work and Family Life

The relationship between family life and work is complex. Each affects the other in both positive and negative ways. Work affects the quality of family life; in turn, the quality of family life affects work performance.

The Effects of Work on Family Life

Work has both positive and negative effects on family life. Many workers find satisfaction in developing their professional roles as well as contributing to the family's income. Job satisfaction is one positive effect that carries over to family life. People who find jobs for which they are well-suited receive more satisfaction from working. This helps them focus more positively on family responsibilities when they are at home. Work satisfaction gives them more confidence in managing everyday tasks and problems.

Parents who enjoy their work can convey this attitude to their children. They can encourage children to perform work tasks at home and praise them for well-done jobs. This helps children develop positive attitudes about work. Positive attitudes and skills that family members learn at home can be carried over into the workplace.

Work can have a positive effect on family relationships. Managing work and family time effectively becomes a shared effort among family members. Family relationships are often strengthened if members strive to be more supportive of one another in meeting responsibilities. Children often become more self-reliant and independent when both parents work. Sharing household tasks may improve relationships among family members, especially fathers and children, 5-8.

Work can have negative effects on a worker's personal and family life, too. Time management and role overload are two common challenges faced by families with working members. Workers' job demands may leave them little time for themselves, family members, socializing, recreation, and household chores. Job demands may leave them too busy or too tired to devote enough time to family responsibilities.

Trying to fulfill too many roles can lead to role overload. Role overload can cause physical and emotional strain, which can lead to fatigue and irritability. Households with two working parents, single parents, and mothers with young children often experience the most difficulty with role

5-8
This father and daughter are working together to complete family chores.

overload, 5-9. These households have fewer family members with time available to handle child care, household, and job tasks.

When both spouses work outside the home, meeting family needs becomes even more challenging. Families in which both spouses are employed are called **dual-career families**. Spouses in these families must try to balance their work and marriage roles. If they have children, they also must manage their parenting roles. Dual-career families often need to make special efforts to keep communication open. Since family members may be away from home often, they must make the most of their time together.

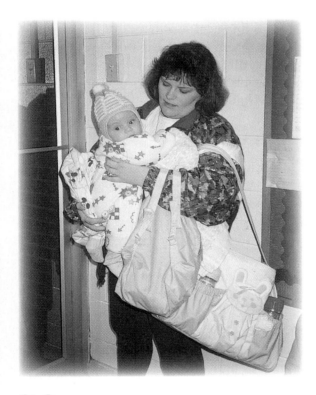

5-9
Because a working mother with young children has many responsibilities to fulfill, she is more likely to experience role overload.

The Effects of Family Life on Work

Just as work affects family life, family life affects work in positive and negative ways. Strong family relationships have a positive effect on work performance. A supportive family gives workers added energy to meet job demands.

Some aspects of family life can have negative effects on work performance. Having overly demanding family responsibilities is one example. Responsibilities such as caring for small children, older family members, or family members with disabilities place added role strain on workers. Work performance may suffer as the worker may be more tired, absent more often, and more focused on family matters.

Managing Multiple Roles

People who combine family roles with their career roles have **multiple roles**. Balancing multiple roles is not easy since work roles often conflict with family roles. Fulfilling each of these roles places demands on all family members. Careful planning is needed for these families to meet their responsibilities. Managing family resources, such as time and energy, also becomes important. See 5-10.

Working parents face many decisions about how to manage their responsibilities at home and at work. Good managerial skills and relationship skills are the keys to balancing their busy lives. Setting priorities and making choices about household tasks, child care, and family schedules can help them make wiser decisions.

5-10
Working parents plan their time carefully in order to avoid role conflict.

5-11
Many families value their time together and make this time a priority.

Set Priorities

To manage multiple roles, families have to learn to manage their time. This means the family must set priorities and then make choices accordingly. **Priorities** are important tasks ranked in order of importance. To set priorities, they must decide which tasks are most important to the family and then rank them in order of importance. Successful families need priorities to help them keep their focus and complete tasks. They must ask "What is of greatest importance to this family?" The answers will vary for different families. Decisions will be based on many factors, including family responsibilities. Some families may decide spending more time together is important. Others may choose to focus on meeting other basic needs. See 5-11.

In making career-related decisions, parents must consider their children's needs, their own personal needs, and their career needs. Will their jobs provide enough financial resources? Will a job change interfere with the time they can spend with their children? Can they take on new job responsibilities and still devote quality time to family members?

Make Choices

Setting priorities is bound to create some priority conflicts that will need to be resolved. For instance, working late at the office might help a parent get a promotion and earn more money. However, this would mean spending less time with the children. This creates a conflict between the priorities of money and family interaction. Family members will have to pull together to make a choice.

Basic relationship skills help families work through situations when choices need to be made. Support, open communication, negotiation, and compromise help families make choices and keep responsibilities in balance. Family members can support one another to avoid feelings of guilt or resentment about work responsibilities. Single parents may look to close friends and relatives for extra support. All family members may have to accept responsibility for household tasks such as laundry, cleaning, and cooking. Parents may sometimes need to adjust work responsibilities so they can spend more time with the family. They might have to make choices about working less overtime, changing to a part-time job, or working from home.

Working families must realize they can't have it all. That is, in balancing family and work, they must have realistic expectations. They must be prepared to face potential problems. There are trade-offs between family life and work. Combining both is not always easy. Family time will have to be carefully planned. Housekeeping standards may have to be lowered. Some family activities may have to be missed. Job and career advancement may be slower.

Find Child Care

Working parents may need to make child care arrangements for their children. They must choose child care arrangements that best fit their needs and their children's needs. Some of the options available are discussed later in Topic 11-2.

The Role of the Employer

In today's economy, employers are finding it more beneficial to help employees balance work and family roles. One way they do this is by offering flexible work arrangements that help employees handle family responsibilities. Offering family-related employee benefits is another option many are taking.

Such programs and benefits help both businesses and employees. Businesses are looking for new ways to increase

productivity and cut costs. Hiring and training new, less-skilled workers can be costly for them. Not only do employers want to keep skilled employees, they want to increase employee morale. If employees are satisfied with their jobs, they are often more productive and committed to their employer.

Flexible Work Arrangements

Employers are more willing to accommodate working parents by offering flexible work options. Such options provide more opportunities for working parents to be available to their children and other family members as needed.

Telecommuting is one option. In this type of arrangement, an employee works from an office set up at home, 5-12. The employee is connected to the office with the office using a phone and the Internet. Companies are finding telecommuting makes good business sense. Work-at-home employees tend to work more hours, have better morale, and take fewer sick days.

5-12
For employees seeking a flexible work schedule, telecommuting is a popular choice.

Job sharing is another option growing in popularity. In **job sharing**, two people divide the work responsibilities of one job. Each person works on a part-time basis rather than full time. This enables working mothers to remain in the workforce and still spend time with their children.

Flextime plans mean employees can set their own work schedule within certain terms. Some may choose to start later in the day to avoid heavy morning and evening traffic. Parents with school-age children can benefit from this plan, too. One parent can start work earlier and arrive home by the end of the school day. The other parent can start work later and be home to see the children off to school in the morning.

Core hours are observed by companies that allow flextime. The total workday may run from 7:00 A.M. through 7:00 P.M. All employees must be on hand during core hours. Core hours may be from 10:00 to 11:30 A.M. and from 1:30 to 3:30 P.M. Employees are free to schedule the remaining hours to their convenience. This plan allows flexibility for parents to arrange their work schedules around their children. Medical appointments, school visits, and even parent volunteer hours at school can be easily arranged around core hours.

Flexible workweeks are in use at some companies. Some employees are now moving to four-day, 40-hour workweeks. They work a 10-hour workday rather than a traditional eight-hour workday.

Employee Benefits That Help Families

Employee benefits provided by the employer are known as *fringe benefits*. Fringe benefits are regarded as hidden pay. Life and health insurance, profit-sharing plans, and paid vacations are traditional fringe benefits offered by employers. On-site child care and parent education seminars are popular, family-oriented fringe benefits. See 5-13. Some companies provide college scholarships for children of their employees. Fringe benefits may even include family discounts for club memberships or amusement park tickets.

Tailored paychecks allow employees to plan benefits that meet their own wants and needs. A married employee or parent might need and want different benefits from those wanted by a single employee. The stage in the family life cycle also affects the type of benefits chosen. For example, the McRaes are a young, career-oriented couple with young children. They need

5-13
Some employers offer child care assistance or on-site child care facilities as a benefit for their employees.

cash to meet living expenses. They also need income protection for a spouse and children in the event of disability or death. A tailored paycheck plan would allow the McRaes to receive more cash and more income protection. These benefits are needed by their young and dependent family.

The Moengas have different needs as they approach retirement. At age 55, they are eager to build their retirement income. Their children are living independently. A tailored paycheck would allow the parents to receive less cash and to contribute a larger sum to a retirement program.

Check It Out!

1. Describe one effect of work on family life.
2. When both parents are employed outside the home, the family is called a _____-_____ family.
3. List four flexible work options offered by some employers that help employees balance work and family.

Topic 5-3
Handling Family Crises

Objectives

After studying this topic, you will be able to
▼ describe the types of events that can lead to a crisis.
▼ describe skills and resources for handling family crises.
▼ summarize the effects of various types of crises on families.

Topic Terms

crisis
support system
physical neglect
emotional neglect
physical abuse
emotional abuse
sexual abuse
substance abuse
addiction
drug abuse
alcoholism
alcoholic
enabler
support group

As you have read, a family's life is filled with challenges. Some of these challenges are fairly routine and easily managed. Others are much more serious, affecting the whole family system.

Facing difficult challenges is not easy. However, difficult challenges can occur at any time in your life. That's why learning about these challenges and the changes that can result is important. This can help you prepare for and manage these events in your own life. Knowing what resources are available to help you deal with challenges is also worthwhile.

What Is a Crisis?

At some point in their lives, most people face some type of crisis. A **crisis** is an event or experience that greatly influences people's lives. These events cause people to make difficult changes in their lifestyles. The greatest challenge of a crisis is knowing how to handle these changes.

A crisis affects families in different ways. That is, a crisis to one family may not be a crisis to another. How the family views the situation and adjusts to it determines the impact it will have. For example, an unexpected baby may be a crisis in one family, but a welcome addition for another. Moving to a new home may be an adventure for one family, but an extremely stressful adjustment for another. Loss of a job may mean a temporary loss of income for one family, but the stepping stone to a better job for another.

Characteristics of Crises

What types of events can lead to a family crisis? Crisis-producing events have certain traits that make it difficult for families to adjust to change. Four of these traits are described below.

- *A devastating event that causes a great loss for the entire family.* Property loss from a fire, a tornado, or an earthquake is an example. An automobile accident resulting in the disability or death of a family member or friend would be another example, 5-14.
- *A stressful event that affects the entire family.* For example, moving and adjusting to a new home would be

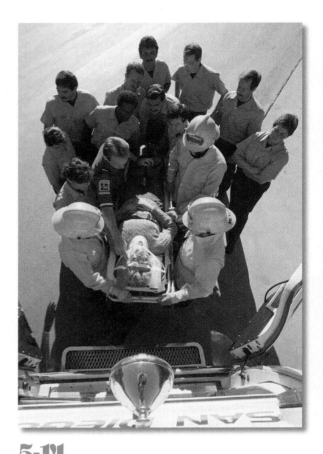

5-14
A serious accident can be the devastating event that causes a family crisis.

stressful for the entire family. A long period of unemployment would have serious effects on all family members.
- *An event that requires major adjustments by family members.* A major change in the family structure, such as separation, divorce, or remarriage would affect the way a family functions.
- *An event that occurs suddenly or unexpectedly.* A sudden loss of income, sudden illness, or the death of a loved one can be difficult for family members to face.

Sometimes a crisis is not triggered by a single event. It may be caused by a series of stressful events that build up over a period of time. The family may not realize a crisis is building until it actually happens. For instance, the combination of ending a relationship, moving to a new home, and starting a new job could lead to a crisis. How does a crisis event affect the family? The entire family system is affected. This is because the whole family's ability to function normally is changed. Family members are unable to carry out their roles and responsibilities. They need to use coping skills to adjust to the changes that have taken place. These skills help return balance to their lives as quickly as possible.

Skills for Coping with Crises

Why do some families seem to cope well during a crisis, while others let it destroy their lives? Functional families face a variety of crisis situations; they cope well because they communicate and cooperate. They have the confidence to meet any challenge. They deal with a crisis in three ways. First, they join together as a family to face the crisis head-on. Second, they focus on a positive aspect of a problem situation. They react positively and try to make the best of the situation. Third, they make use of their support system.

A **support system** is a network of people and organizations that family members can turn to during a crisis. The primary support comes from relatives, friends, neighbors, teachers, coworkers, and members of religions groups. These are individuals a family can contact in an emergency. For instance, a neighbor might look after a child on a moment's notice if the parents are suddenly called away. A support system also includes public and private agencies that help families. These agencies may provide health care, child

care, financial aid, or legal assistance. Professionals at these organizations are trained to provide assistance to families during a crisis.

Dysfunctional families are unable to deal with crises in healthy ways. Many are poor problem solvers. They become locked into one way of responding to family problems. Anger, violence, and alcohol abuse are common responses. Some of these responses create new crisis situations. Dysfunctional families often depend on other people to rescue them from crises.

A crisis event cannot be ignored—it requires some type of response. A family who uses coping skills learns to handle these challenges. Learning how to handle change and unexpected events when they occur is the key to surviving any crisis. Families can use various resources to help them pull through difficult situations. One resource is developing effective coping skills. A number of techniques may be helpful.

▼ *Plan how to handle a crisis before it happens.* To be prepared for change, families need to anticipate how to handle crises. As a family, they can plan how they would handle certain crisis situations. This helps the family in two ways. First, they can plan strategies that might help when the unexpected happens. Second, it prompts them to do as much as possible to prevent the problems from occurring.

▼ *Have clearly defined family goals.* This technique helps the family remain focused when emergencies arise. For example, the Browns have four family goals. They are to communicate openly, respect and support one another, deal fairly with problems, and get the best education possible. A major job transfer will not impact this family heavily; they can meet these goals in many different settings. However, having a child flunk out of college might be a major upset for them. How would they handle this crisis? They would discuss it, respect and support the child, and perhaps encourage the child to find other educational opportunities. The Browns' family goals helped them solve their problem in a sensible way.

▼ *Maintain family unity.* In a crisis situation, family members need to band together, get involved, and help out. Family members that are supportive of one another have stronger emotional ties. They are better able to survive difficult times. Once they begin working together to solve a problem, they are likely to stay unified.

▼ *Build on previous successes.* Families should use whatever techniques worked best for them in the past to help them through a crisis. For instance, if relatives or friends offered emotional support in the past, families should seek their help again. See 5-15.

▼ *Maintain feelings of affection.* Feelings of affection among family members are especially important during difficult times. Although each family has its own way of expressing affection, an extra effort by each member can be helpful.

▼ *Place family needs before personal needs.* During a crisis, some family members may want to put their personal plans on hold. This is especially important if those plans would place additional stress on the family. For instance, a family member might delay moving out or buying a car until the crisis has passed.

▼ *Find ways to get help with family responsibilities.* Working together to share decision making and other family

5-15
Emotional support from friends can help teens work through a crisis.

responsibilities is important. However, if extra help is needed, let others who have offered to help do so. Call on people in your support system.

▼ *Seek help for problems.* Some problems cannot be resolved within the family or seem too large to handle. In these cases, a family should not be afraid to seek outside help. Families should also know that many resources are available to help them. Knowing what help is available, where to find it, and how to ask for it are important coping skills.

Where can a family seek help? Friends, relatives, and neighbors can provide emotional support or emergency assistance. Many families seek guidance through their religious faith. Professional help can be found through local community services and government agencies. It is important to develop a support system of groups and individuals to whom you can turn for help.

Types of Crises

All families face different types of crises. Some of these—family violence, substance abuse, and death—are more difficult to face and manage than others. Learning more about each type can help families cope if one occurs.

Unemployment

A family's financial situation can change suddenly if a main provider becomes unemployed. This can happen for a number of reasons, many of which the individual has little control over. For example, a company may have to downsize and eliminate jobs if the economy declines. Sometimes, a serious health problem can force an individual into unemployment. Whatever the reason, unemployment drastically changes the income level of the family, and that can lead to a crisis. If a new job cannot be found right away, bills may not be paid. The family may find it harder to buy essentials such as food.

While a new job is sought, communication and cooperation among family members can help. With communication, the family can decide which wants and needs they can forego. The unemployed person could provide services that the family might otherwise hire others to do, such as child care, laundry, or lawn care. Teens might find part-time jobs. Families who band together and support one another can usually find ways to work through the crisis.

Family Violence

In some dysfunctional families, poor family relationships can lead to violence within the family. A family member may resort to violence as a way of expressing anger or resolving conflicts. Unfortunately, this behavior often becomes a pattern that is repeated over and over.

Types of Family Violence

Family violence may take several different forms. One form of family violence is *neglect*. Neglect is a less violent but still serious form of abuse. It threatens the physical and mental well-being of family members. Neglect occurs when the needs of family members are not met. Not providing proper food, clothing, shelter, medical care, and parental supervision are forms of **physical neglect**.

Another form of neglect is emotional neglect. **Emotional neglect** is the failure to provide loving care and attention. A neglected family member who receives no signs of affection may grow to feel unloved and unlovable.

Abuse is the most damaging form of family violence. There are different forms of abuse. **Physical abuse** happens when one family member physically injures another family member. Abusive behavior includes hitting, kicking, biting, or throwing objects. This form of abuse often causes serious injury or sometimes death.

Emotional abuse happens when one family member purposely damages another member's self-concept. It destroys the abused person's self-esteem and makes the person feel worthless. This happens when the abuser constantly yells, teases, or insults the abused. It can also occur in parent-child relationships when parents have unrealistic expectations of a child. They expect the child to perform tasks that the child cannot do. Then they blame and punish the child for failing.

Sexual abuse in families occurs when one family member forces another family member to engage in sexual activities. One type of sexual abuse is *incest*. This is sexual activity between people who are closely related, such as between a father and a daughter.

Acts of physical violence within a family can occur among all family members. Children and wives are the most frequent victims. Children may be physically or emotionally abused by one or both parents. Husbands may batter wives, causing serious physical injuries. Sometimes children are the abusers rather than the victims. Adolescent children may assault their parents when something they want is withheld from them. Siblings may attack each other to settle an issue.

Why Family Violence Occurs

Why does family violence happen? The reasons vary. Abusive family members often have low self-esteem. They may feel unloved by other family members. Some adults may have been abused as children,

so they have not learned to express their emotions properly. The abuser cannot deal with his or her emotions through acceptable behavior, so he or she becomes aggressive.

In families where physical violence is common behavior, the children may adopt the same type of behavior. Unemployment, financial problems, marital problems, job pressures, substance abuse, or illness are also contributing factors.

Where to Get Help

With help, neglect and abuse can be prevented. Various programs, facilities, and support groups are available to help families break out of the cycle of family violence.

Many types of programs are available in local communities. Community service organizations are listed in the Yellow Pages of local phone books. Look under the heading *Social Service Organizations*. Information about individual and group counseling services is also available from local mental health associations. Government programs and services are listed under the local county name in the phone book. Emergency shelters are located across the country for providing temporary housing to abused women and their children.

Parents Anonymous is a self-help group that helps abusive parents and abused children. Most cities have chapters of this national organization.

If you know parents who are experiencing a great deal of stress, you can help. First, offer your friendship. Individuals who abuse or neglect their children often feel unloved themselves. Another way to help is to offer to babysit for them. Urge them to get out of the house—to go places and do things.

There may be times when you must protect abused children. This may mean reporting the abuse and neglect of parents to a social service agency. Most agencies have special counselors to help parents and their children when cases are reported. Reporting is the key to such service. Counselors cannot help a family unless the situation is brought to their attention by a report.

Substance Abuse

One of the most serious crises affecting families involves substance abuse. **Substance abuse** is the use of illegal drugs or the misuse of legal drugs such as alcohol. The misuse of a substance, such as alcohol, can lead to physical and psychological addiction. An **addiction** is a dependence of the body on a continuing supply of the drug. After an addiction has developed, taking the drug away will cause agonizing withdrawal symptoms. When one family member becomes addicted, the entire family is affected.

Drug abuse is the use of a legal or illegal drug for a purpose other than its intended use. Illegal drugs include heroin, cocaine, and marijuana. Legal drugs, such as over-the-counter medications and prescriptions, can be abused as well.

An addiction to alcohol is called **alcoholism**. Like diabetes or cancer, alcoholism is a type of disease. A person who suffers from this disease is an **alcoholic**.

People become addicted to alcohol and other drugs for many different reasons. In response to the drug or alcohol, some may feel more relaxed. Some use it to deal with or overcome problems, such as job-related stress or family problems. However, addiction can trigger other stressful problems, such as losing a job. This added stress can cause the addict to drink or abuse drugs even more, which may lead to another more serious crisis.

Substance abuse seriously affects all family members. The spouse and children of an addict may have a hard time accepting the problem. They may blame themselves for the problem. As a result, they may avoid seeking help because they are too ashamed or embarrassed. A spouse may deny that his or her mate is an alcoholic or drug user. Younger children may not understand an alcoholic parent's behavior. Teens may try to hide the problem from others or avoid spending time at home. Because of their problems at home, children's schoolwork may suffer, 5-16.

Codependency often occurs in families of addicts as family members try to find ways to survive the crisis. A

5-16
Because of problems they are experiencing at home, some teens may find it hard to concentrate on schoolwork.

family member may become an **enabler**—someone who unknowingly acts in ways that contribute to an addict's drug use. The enabler wants to help the alcoholic or drug addict with his or her problem. In so doing, they make the problem worse by denying that a problem exists. Enablers cover up for the behavior of the addict, allowing the addict's behavior to manipulate their own. They may lie for the addict or give excuses for the addict's actions. They unknowingly perpetuate the addiction.

To help an alcoholic or drug addict, family members should seek assistance from outside sources. Learning about the disease, talking about it, and learning coping skills can help family members handle the crisis. They may need professional help to identify any codependency behaviors.

Overcoming alcoholism or drug addiction is not easy, but it can be done. However, the user must make the decision to stop. They must first admit they have a problem and need help before anyone can help them. During the recovery period, an alcoholic or drug addict needs strong family support combined with professional help to overcome the illness.

Where to Get Help

Professional help is available from many local sources. Treatment and prevention services are available through community hospitals and health centers, family service agencies, and the National Council on Alcoholism (NCA). For more information, look in the Yellow Pages of the phone book under "Alcoholism Information and Treatment" or "Drug Abuse Information and Treatment."

A **support group** is a group of people who share a similar problem or concern. *Alcoholics Anonymous (AA)* is a nationwide support group for alcoholics. *Narcotics Anonymous (NA)* is a support group for

Setting the Scene: Helping or Hurting?

You know a friend has been taking drugs, and you fear that addiction may result. You have promised not to tell anyone about the drug use. You try to cover for your friend, thinking this will benefit everyone involved. You know the truth will cause some full-blown crises for the family and a lot of trouble for your friend.

Analyze It: Whom are you helping? Whom are you hurting? Who is being manipulated? What should you do at this point?

drug addicts who want to recover from their addiction. The goal of AA and NA is to help alcoholics and drug addicts help themselves to recovery. Help for family and friends of alcoholics is available through *Al-Anon*. Teen children of alcoholic parents can seek support by joining *Alateen*. *Nar-Anon* is for family members and friends of drug addicts.

By seeking out a support group, people find other individuals who are experiencing a similar crisis. Members of the support group come together to discuss common concerns, problems, and issues. People benefit from support groups by learning they are not the only ones with certain problems. They are able to talk with others who truly understand their situations. They share helpful information and resources while they listen and learn from one another.

Serious Illness or Accidents

A serious illness or accident can be a crisis for a family. The emotional drain of watching a loved one suffer or the anxiety felt when awaiting the outcome of an operation can be stressful for family members. Even the physical care of the patient at home can take a huge toll on the care provider—both physically and emotionally. The high costs of medical care can be a significant drain on a family especially if the income provider is the one who is sick or injured.

Support groups may be a source of strength for the family during this type of crisis. Learning more about a certain illness from other people who have had family members with this illness can be very beneficial. Spiritual ties help some families. The support of friends and relatives becomes even more important.

Death

Death is another crisis that all families face. Although death is as much a part of the family life cycle as birth, dealing with the loss can be difficult. However, families must learn to accept death as a reality of life, 5-17.

When a loved one dies, family members often experience a variety of emotions. Feelings of sadness, anger, and guilt are common. Such feelings are normal responses to a loss and are part of the grieving process. Family members may feel sadness because they miss the person. Some may feel angry that the person died and left them behind. Others may feel guilty about unfinished business, such as owing an apology or saying "I love you." Caregivers might feel an emptiness because they are no longer needed.

Accepting the reality of the loss can be hard. However, acceptance is an important

5-17
Everyone must eventually face the crisis of death in his or her family.

part of adjusting to the loss. Then family members can take action to handle those feelings and get on with their lives. Although time will help ease the pain, family members can take other steps to work through their grief. They can

▼ accept the support of friends, relatives, and other people around them.
▼ talk about their feelings of sadness. They should not be ashamed to cry if they feel sad.
▼ recall the happy memories they shared with the deceased person with other family members and friends.

Check It Out!

1. List four traits of crisis events.
2. List eight coping skills that can help families survive a crisis.
3. Explain how alcoholism affects all family members.
4. List three steps family members can take to work through grief.

Chapter Review

Summary

Making and keeping the family strong and healthy is a challenge faced by all families. Functional families don't just happen—family members must work together to achieve this goal. They are committed to communicating with one another, solving problems, showing appreciation, understanding one another, and sharing with one another. Families face many different types of challenges. Balancing family and work roles and responsibilities is a continuing challenge, especially for dual-career families and single parents. For these families, good management and relationship skills are the keys to balancing their busy lives. To accommodate working parents' needs, more employers are offering flexible work schedules and employee benefits.

Of all the challenges families face, crises are the most difficult. The key to surviving a crisis is learning coping skills. Coping skills help families handle the changes a crisis causes. However, some types of crises, such as family violence, substance abuse, and death, are much more difficult to handle. Knowing how to cope and where to get help can help families work through these situations.

Think About It!

1. Do you think it's important for families to build strong, healthy relationships? Explain why or why not.
2. Evaluate how your parents balance their work and family roles. What types of problems do they encounter in trying to balance these roles? Why do you think it's important for them to balance these roles? What steps can you take to help them manage family responsibilities?
3. Functional families tend to cope better with crisis situations. Why do you think these families cope better with crises than others? What steps can a family take to prepare for a crisis?
4. Think of a crisis situation you have experienced in your family. How did you cope with the situation? How did other family members handle the situation? If the same crisis happened again, how would you handle it?
5. Suppose a friend confides in you that he or she suspects the children he or she babysits are being abused. What advice would you give to your friend about this situation?

Try It Out!

1. Review the qualities of functional families in Topic 5-1. For each quality, suggest one activity teens could do at home to help strengthen their families. Then develop a poster based on your suggestions titled *Ways to Strengthen Your Family*.
2. Contact the personnel departments of several businesses in your local area. Determine what policies or programs these employers are offering to help workers balance work and family responsibilities. Which employee benefits are most popular? As a class, evaluate whether employers are meeting the needs of families in your area. What other types of family benefits do you think would be helpful for them to offer employees?

3. Survey several dual-career families to determine how they manage their work and family responsibilities. Summarize your results in a report to the class.

4. Research a family crisis that you have heard or read about recently. Write a report about your findings. Include information about possible causes, the effect on family members, coping skills, and where to get help.

5. As a class, develop a list of resources that are available in your community to help families with crises. Use your local phone book to compile the list of social service agencies, organizations, and services available. Develop a master list that can be made available to students in your school.

6. Invite a panel of professionals from various social service agencies to discuss their careers. What type of education and training is needed in this career area? What do they consider most satisfying about their careers? What do they consider least satisfying about their careers?

7. Interview a social services counselor to determine how that agency provides help for families in crisis.

8. Research resources available on the Internet that can help families during a crisis. Prepare a report to share with the class.

Chapter 6
Personal Relationships

Careers

These careers relate to the topics in this chapter:

▼ peer counselor
▼ social caseworker's aide
▼ youth director
▼ school counselor

As you study the chapter, see if you can think of others.

Topics

Topic 6-1
Developing Positive Relationships

Objectives

After studying this topic, you will be able to
▼ discuss types of relationships.
▼ list benefits of positive relationships.
▼ describe how to develop key elements that form the basis of positive relationships.

Topic Terms

sibling
networking
mutual respect

6-1
Spending time with friends helps people become more aware of the needs of others during the teen years.

Think about your current relationships. Now imagine all the relationships you have yet to develop in the future. That adds up to *many* different relationships you will be involved in throughout your life! Most of them will be positive relationships. This means they are healthy and satisfying for you and the people with whom you relate.

Positive relationships do not happen automatically. You have to work to develop them. In order to build positive relationships, you must feel true concern for other people. This sense of concern increases during adolescence. During the teen years, people become less self-centered and more aware of the needs of others. See 6-1.

Types of Relationships

Learning to get along with others begins at an early age. Most people learn to develop positive relationships at home with their parents and siblings. Later, they expand their relationships to include peers, romantic partners, coworkers, and others. Learning about these different types of relationships can help you form successful bonds with others.

Parents

Infants form their first relationships with their parents. Infants are totally dependent on their parents and other caregivers to fulfill all their needs. These include the physical needs of food and clothing, as well as emotional and social needs, 6-2. Children need to feel secure and loved. Because of this, they tend to behave

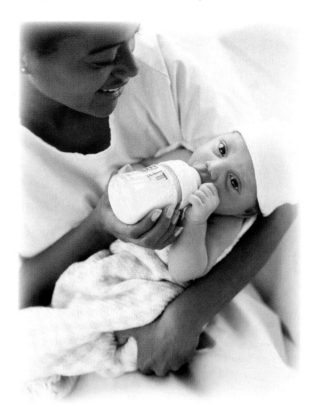

6-2
Infants begin their first relationships—with their parents—almost immediately after birth.

in ways that will assure their parents' love. As they grow older, they become more and more capable of supplying some of these needs themselves.

In early adolescence, children begin to demonstrate a measure of independence. Parents are still responsible for their children. However, the weight of responsibility begins to shift away from parent toward the child.

This change in the parent-child relationship often causes conflict between parents and children. Parents may relinquish too much or too little control. Children may want too much or too little responsibility. Communication is needed to maintain a positive relationship between parents and their children during this period.

Relationship patterns established between parents and teens are often followed by teens in their later relationships. Studies show that young people who get along well with their parents tend to relate well to their own children. Girls who form good relationships with their fathers have good relationships with their future husbands. Boys who get along well with their mothers interact well with their future wives. Families who build positive relationships tend to produce future families who also build positive relationships.

Siblings

Young children also begin building relationships with their siblings at an early age. **Siblings** are brothers and sisters. Siblings relate to one another on more equal terms. This type of interaction often leads to competition. Sometimes jealousies emerge as siblings compete with one another.

Building positive relationships with siblings prepares children to build positive relationships with their peers. Learning to handle jealousy and competition with siblings helps children know how to handle these situations with friends. See 6-3.

Peers

Relationships with peers become very important during the teen years. Positive peer relationships form a support system for teens. Having friends reassures teens that other people are facing the same changes and decisions they are.

You cannot choose your family members, but you can choose your friends. You are likely to choose friends with whom you can build positive relationships. Most people tend to choose friends who have characteristics similar to their own. Perhaps

6-3

Sibling relationships prepare children to interact with peers.

you look for friends who are dependable, honest, sincere, thoughtful, and willing to help others.

You must have realistic expectations of others if you want to build positive relationships with them. Do not expect your peers to be perfect or to fit your exact mold. You must learn to accept your friends as they are. You may not always like what your friends do. You may not always agree with their opinions. However, they have rights just as you do. You grow by being exposed to their different attitudes and beliefs.

Not all of your peers will be your friends. You will not have enough in

common with some of your peers to build friendships. However, even acquaintances can become an important part of your relationship network.

Romantic Relationships

During the later teen and adult years, romantic relationships become important to many people. Romantic relationships are positive because caring for someone and knowing he or she cares for you adds meaning to life. Sharing the joys and sorrows of daily experiences helps couples grow closer. Partners encourage each other to develop to their full potential as human beings.

Some romantic relationships lead to marriage. Marriage relationships grow and change as the people in them grow and change. To keep marriage relationships positive, couples need to work on keeping lines of communication open. Each partner must make his or her needs known. Each partner must also strive to meet the needs of his or her spouse.

Work Relationships

People form less intimate relationships with their coworkers. Coworkers can enjoy working together even if they do not have much in common outside of work. They can enjoy job-related successes together. See 6-4.

Positive work relationships are based on respect for the feelings of others. A good attitude will help you relate to those with whom you work. Accept your fair share of responsibilities. Do not expect others to do your work for you. On the other hand, do not assume that you can get along without your coworkers. Most jobs are a team effort. If you show consideration to coworkers, they will be likely to cooperate with you.

6-4

Relationships with coworkers center around shared job experiences.

Benefits of Positive Relationships

Positive relationships produce many benefits. Research has shown that relationships can affect a person's physical and emotional well-being. People who maintain positive relationships have fewer physical illnesses. They are also less prone to diseases and tend to live longer. Their emotional well-being is enhanced because they know people care about them. They can share their problems and thereby reduce the stress of daily living.

Positive relationships also provide social benefits. You are more likely to go places and get involved in activities when someone can join you. Your present relationships can serve as bridges to future relationships. Your social circle will expand as you meet new people, 6-5.

6-5

You might be more likely to join a team if a friend joins with you. You then make new relationships with your other team members.

The More You Know: What Makes a True Friend?

If you're looking for positive relationships, consider people

- with whom you feel you can talk about anything
- who make you feel peaceful just by being with them
- with whom you can have fun—even when you are not doing anything special
- to whom you can tell a secret and know it won't get spread around
- who understand and support you whether you're feeling up or down
- who tell you what you need to hear, not what you want to hear

Economic well-being can be a benefit of positive work relationships. People who relate well on the job are likely to enjoy their work. This will encourage them to stay on the job. They will increase their chances of being promoted and getting more pay raises.

Networking is another benefit of positive relationships. **Networking** means forming an interconnected group whose members work together to help one another. Some networks are social. The people involved help one another make social contacts. This type of network might help a new student feel welcome in school.

Other networks are business related. Participants try to help each other succeed in the world of work. Members of the network may help one another find jobs, learn new skills, or get promotions. These relationships can impact career success.

Qualities Needed for Positive Relationships

As you read earlier, positive relationships do not happen automatically. Both people involved must work to develop key qualities that form the basis for positive relationships. These qualities include a positive self-concept, mutual respect, trust, openness, and reliability.

Positive Self-Concept

As you have read, a positive self-concept means that you see yourself as worthwhile. Confident people who care for others may anticipate that others will care for them in return. In addition, when others see that you think highly of yourself, they are likely to think highly of you as well. They may realize that they would enjoy forming a friendship with you.

A positive self-concept usually results from positive feedback. Therefore, an important part of friendship is providing positive feedback to your friend. This will continue to help build your friend's self-concept. At the same time, a true friend will do the same for you.

Mutual Respect

Mutual respect means each person regards the other with honor and esteem. People in positive relationships do not expect each other to agree on everything. Neither person tries to force an opinion or idea on the other. They respect each other's right to differ. They respect each other for who they are.

Building mutual respect between teens and adults is sometimes a challenge. Some teens feel threatened by the experience and maturity of adults. They think adults judge them unfairly. On the other hand, adults fear that teens believe adults are not in touch with current youth culture.

Teens and adults both need to feel they are valued by one another. Teens can benefit by seeking wisdom from adults. Likewise, adults can be inspired by the enthusiasm of youth. Such worthwhile exchanges can help teens and adults build mutual respect and develop positive relationships, 6-6.

Trust

Trusting people means having confidence in them. In a positive relationship, you must trust the other person. However, you must also prove that you are trustworthy. You must be careful not to betray the confidence that is vested in you. You must be able to keep secrets. You must not laugh at friends who share serious concerns with you. You must not encourage others to participate in activities that are not in their best interests.

Trust in a relationship can be fragile. If you give advice that backfires, you may not be trusted in the future. When advice is sought, it may be better to help friends view situations from several different perspectives. Allow them to analyze the possible alternatives and choose their own plan of action.

Openness

Openness in a relationship refers to an atmosphere in which people feel free to share their thoughts and feelings. You must create this atmosphere for people with whom you relate. You must make them feel comfortable about opening up to you.

You must also be willing to open up to others. No one can second-guess what you think or feel. People cannot meet your needs unless you tell them what your needs are. See 6-7.

6-6
Teens and adults both benefit from spending time together.

6-7
Being able to communicate openly helps people build positive relationships.

Reliability

People in positive relationships must be reliable. If you say you will do something, people must be able to count on you to do it. If you say you will be somewhere, people must be able to depend on you to be there.

Reliability goes beyond keeping your word. It also refers to routine patterns of behavior. For instance, perhaps people can rely on you to take a leadership role in a group. Maybe they can count on you to remain calm, even in frantic situations. Reliability helps people know what to expect from others in relationships.

Check It Out!

1. True or false. Relationships between parents and teens can affect teens' future relationships.
2. Forming an interconnected group whose members work together to help one another is known as _____.
3. What are the key qualities that form the basis for positive relationships?

Topic 6-2
Developing Friendships

Objectives

After studying this topic, you will be able to
▼ name three types of friends.
▼ describe factors that lead people to form friendships.
▼ explain three types of dating.
▼ explain the difference between love and infatuation.
▼ analyze factors involved in a responsible relationship.

Topic Terms

multicultural society
group dating
random dating
steady dating
infatuation
abstinence

Friends make successes more exciting and failures less painful. They are an important influence in your life.

Friendships

Friends are people who know, like, and trust each other. They are people who spend time together, sharing thoughts and feelings. Friends complement one another's positive traits. They also care enough to tactfully point out habits and attitudes that may need to be changed.

Friendship is the bond that forms between friends. This bond is built through a process of give and take as two people learn to appreciate each other. The best friendships develop between people who share experiences, interests, and values.

Types of Friends

The type of friendship two people share is determined by the strength of the bond between them. An *acquaintance* is someone you know, but who is not a close friend. You know your acquaintances by name, but you probably do not spend much social time with them.

You may think of many of your friends as *good friends*. These are people with whom you share common interests. You talk, have fun, and enjoy social activities together, 6-8. Acquaintances may become good friends if you spend time with them.

One or two of your good friends might become your *best friends*. These are the friends with whom you share your deepest thoughts and feelings. They are the ones you ask for advice when you have a problem. Best friends often share a common background and lifestyle.

Meeting New People

The first step in making friends is meeting people. You might admire a certain person in your school. However, you can't be friends unless you can first meet the person. Do not overlook opportunities to meet people of different ages, cultures, and ethnic backgrounds.

You are most likely to meet people in your classes, at club meetings, and at

6-8
People enjoy sharing time with their good friends.

parties. See 6-9. These groups will be close to you in age. However, you will have the opportunity to meet people of different ages, too. Don't exclude older or younger people from your friendships. You may find that you share interests and values with people who are not your age. These are the qualities on which friendships are built. On the other hand, sometimes people of other ages can also provide other viewpoints that you had not considered.

Most of the people you meet are likely to live close to you. For instance, if you live in Utah, you will meet more people from Utah than from Texas, Maine, or France. Likewise, you will meet more people from

6-9
You may become good friends with the people you see every day.

your neighborhood than from the other side of town. If you do meet people from other neighborhoods, states, or countries, take advantage of the opportunity.

We live in a **multicultural society**. That means there are people from many different cultures living in the same communities. Be open to forming friendships with people from different backgrounds. Through these friendships, you can learn about other cultures, including different religions, beliefs, and customs. You can learn about likenesses and differences. As you do so, you will probably discover there are more likenesses than differences. Differences are more likely to be limited to dress, food habits, and social traditions. You may not agree with all you learn, but be open to this wider view of the world. You will probably see that most cultural groups have much in common.

Forming Friendships

You don't form friendships with everyone you meet. Friendships are more likely to form between people who have similar personalities, common interests, and like values.

You are likely to form a friendship with someone who has a personality similar to yours. If you are quiet, you will probably prefer being with someone else who is quiet. If you are outgoing, you will probably enjoy being with someone who is outgoing. When people think and act alike, they usually enjoy being together.

Friendships are also likely to develop between people who have common interests. Friends generally share the same interests. You can meet new people with similar interests while doing those things you enjoy, 6-10. For example, you might take your pet for a walk and meet another pet owner. If you volunteer with a group

6-10
These two students met through their common interest in video production.

that is working on a project that interests you, you will meet others with similar interests.

You will probably form friendships with those who share your outlook on life. They will think about issues in the same way as you. Your values are likely to be similar, as are your goals.

You want to develop friendships with those who have values similar to yours because your friends influence your behavior. You want to do things together, so you need to be with a friend who has behavior standards similar to yours. If you go to a party, will your friend act in the same manner as you? Peer influence is at its greatest during the teen years. Be alert to the influence your friends have on you. Do these influences help you grow to your fullest potential? Friends should not drag each other down. Friendships should be mutually beneficial.

How to Make Friends

Have you ever gone to an event where you did not know anyone? You were probably nervous and even a bit scared. However, this is the best way to meet new people. If you are afraid to go up to someone you do not know and start a conversation, you need to make yourself approachable. People are more likely to approach you when you are alone than when you are in a group. Those who hesitate to break in on a group conversation have no barriers when you are by yourself.

No one wants to be rejected or made to feel silly if they do make an effort to talk to you. They need to feel that they will be received warmly. Strangers are more likely to strike up a conversation with you if you

▼ show you are interested in them
▼ focus on what they are saying
▼ ask questions
▼ provide feedback to keep the conversation moving
▼ are open-minded

Remember, you don't have to wait for someone to speak to you. You can make that important first move. What do you have to lose?

Dating

The factors that attract people to friends also attract them to dating partners. Spending time with dating partners can teach people lessons that help them prepare for marriage.

While people are dating and having fun, they are also learning about themselves. Through dating, people learn how to give and take in personal relationships. They become aware of why these relationships are important to them. They learn to recognize the impact their words and actions can have on the lives of other people.

Dating helps people learn about members of the opposite sex. Dating shows a man that all women are not like his mother and his sisters. It shows a woman that all men are not like her father and her brothers.

Group Dating

First dating experiences for young people often take the form of **group dating**. This is when a number of people of both sexes go out together. Each member of the group has fun without feeling especially close to any one person. Each person is free to get to know all the members of the group. Teens today may refer to group dating as "hanging out."

Group dating is an easy way to begin dating. Young people can interact with members of the opposite sex without pressure. For instance, with a whole group to carry on conversations, no one feels on the spot to keep talking. After learning to feel comfortable in a group, most people become ready to date as couples.

Random Dating

Random dating, also called *casual dating*, allows people to date more than one person at a time. See 6-11. For instance, suppose Terry takes Sara to a dance on Friday night. Sara not only socializes with Terry, she also meets and interacts with his friends. Terry may go with Maria to a picnic on Saturday. Here he meets and interacts with Maria's friends. If Terry continues random dating, he will have the chance to socialize with many different people. If Sara and Maria continue random dating, they too will meet more new

6-11
Random dating partners can have fun without becoming seriously involved.

people. This in no way reduces the fun or the value of the social experiences they share with Terry.

In casual dating, everyone grows socially, and no one feels disloyal or jealous. The dating objectives are fun and entertainment. Everyone is learning about getting along with other people, but no one is falling in love.

Steady Dating

Through random dating, two people may meet and find that they like each other very much. They may agree to date only each other. This is called **steady dating**, but may be referred to as "going out." If someone is said to be going out with another person, they are probably in a steady dating relationship.

Steady dating provides several types of security. For instance, you know that someone likes you and cares about you. You know that someone understands you and enjoys being with you. You can relax and be yourself without fear of rejection.

Another type of security is not having to worry about spending the evening with someone you do not know. When you date someone for the first time, you take some risks. The person's idea of fun may be different from yours. You may spend the evening watching a baseball game when you really wanted to go to a movie. The person may cause trouble between you and your parents by keeping you out too late. When you date someone steadily, there are fewer chances for problems. You have a good idea of what to expect from your date.

Some teens may feel that steady dating gives them the security of having a date when they "need" one. They won't have to go to dances or parties alone. However, this is not a good reason to date. First, you may lead your dating partner to believe you

care for him or her more than you really do. Second, going places by yourself can build your self-esteem. You may even meet new people who recognize and admire your confidence!

Although steady dating provides some security, it does not guarantee perfect peace and unity. Conflict occurs in any relationship. When a conflict occurs in random dating, the couple may just stop seeing each other. The commitment involved in steady dating encourages the couple to resolve their conflicts. By learning to handle conflicts in a positive manner, the couple's relationship can continue.

Sometimes even steady dating partners cannot resolve their conflicts. This is normal. When this happens, partners may decide to end their relationship—perhaps willingly, perhaps not so willingly. Either way, former partners must adjust to the change. They also need to seek new interests. See 6-12.

What Is Love?

Suppose you have met and been attracted to someone. You have dated each other for a long time. You like each other very much. Now you are wondering if you are in love with each other. How can you be sure?

Unfortunately, a person's affection cannot be measured by any objective standards. It has no height, weight, or volume. A person's affection cannot be compared against a standard definition of love, either.

The word *love* has many different meanings. It can mean the way you feel when your brother mows the lawn for you. It can mean the way you feel when your friend lets you borrow a new sweater. It can mean the way you feel when you are going steady with someone.

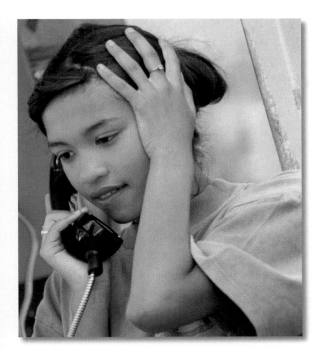

6-12
Calling friends and focusing on other interests can help a person adjust to the change after the end of a steady relationship.

Love involves caring more about your mate than yourself. You want your mate to be happy. You look for ways to express your affection. You may send flowers. You may cook a special dinner. You may just give your mate an unexpected hug and say "I love you."

Is It Love or Infatuation?

Infatuation is often confused with love. **Infatuation** is an intense feeling of admiration. Although both of these emotions are directed toward another person, they differ in many ways.

You can be infatuated with someone you have never met, such as a political leader or a famous singer. You can also be infatuated with a fantasized image of someone you know. For instance, you may know the star of your school's wrestling team. You could build a fantasized image around him. You could view him as an ideal blend of good looks, strength, and courage.

Infatuation in a relationship is often short-lived. It may begin quickly and focus on just one trait, such as a person's appearance or special skill. It may end just as quickly if one person becomes impatient, bored, or dissatisfied with the relationship.

People may fall into infatuation, but they rarely fall into love. People are more likely to grow into love slowly as they learn more about each other. The focus of love is on the other person as a whole. When you love someone, you know the person well. You have a realistic view of the person's strengths and weaknesses. Since time and care are needed to build a love relationship, people are likely to try to make it last longer.

Perhaps the surest sign of infatuation is that it is self-centered. A person is concerned about his or her own feelings and desires. Love, on the other hand, is unselfish. A person in love thinks about the other person first. The other person's wants, needs, and feelings are most important, 6-13.

Responsible Relationships

Steady dating usually means that two people spend a great deal of time together, often alone. As they do so, they may develop feelings of love for each other. When this happens, it is only natural that the two will want to express their affection in some way. Certain hormones become active during the teen years, and the body changes as well. Sexual urges may become strong, especially between two people

6-13
A couple who is in love focuses on meeting each other's needs.

who are attracted to each other. In some relationships, there may be pressure for sexual relations.

It is normal to experience sexual desires, but it is important to think through how you feel about having a sexual relationship. You need to think about this in case you find yourself in a situation where you are being pressured to have sex. If you know where you stand, you will be able to make a decision quickly, if necessary. You should also have a plan of action that will help you out of any difficult situation.

Some teens are pressured into a sexual relationship they are not ready for. They may feel pressure from their date or even pressure from their friends. They may feel they are being left out if they do not give in

to sexual pressures. Messages from movies, television, and music seem to imply that "everyone is doing it," even though this is not the case.

If young people give in to these pressures, they may experience many emotions. They may feel shame and experience feelings of guilt. They may feel used rather than loved. Their self-esteem may suffer if they have compromised their values, standards, and morals.

In addition to emotional consequences, there are physical consequences. Sexually transmitted diseases (STDs) can sometimes occur as a result of sexual activity. Some STDs are life threatening. Another possible consequence is pregnancy. A pregnancy can alter the future of both partners. Anyone involved in a sexual relationship must be aware of these possible consequences.

Facing Sexual Decisions

Every day you make decisions. Some are important decisions; others are not. If you decide to skip lunch, the decision will impact you for about six hours (if you don't skip lunch regularly). Deciding to have a sexual relationship can affect the rest of your life. The lives and health of both partners may be jeopardized when they make a careless choice.

Self-esteem impacts almost all the decisions you make. If you feel good about yourself, you trust yourself to make good decisions. Having self-esteem can help you make important decisions that are right for you. If you always need the approval of others, you may tend to let others make decisions for you. If you lack self-esteem, you may let them pressure you into doing what they want you to do. If you think you lack self-esteem, plan now to make changes in your life. You need to be able to make decisions for yourself and stick to them.

Sexual **abstinence** is a choice to refrain from sexual intercourse until marriage. There are many reasons young people are choosing abstinence. Many choose abstinence for moral reasons, believing that sexual relations belong only in marriage. Abstinence fits with their values and standards and frees them from guilt. Others choose abstinence for reasons of health and safety. They recognize that sexually transmitted diseases and infertility can result. They do not want to risk their health nor their chances of having children later on. Many teens see abstinence as a matter of personal integrity and an expression of self-esteem. They have control of their lives. They have goals they want to reach. They don't want to risk a pregnancy until they are ready for this responsibility.

Because teens are aware of the negative impact that sexual activity can have on their lives, there is a growing movement for sexual abstinence. Contracts are even available. Teens sign declarations stating they will abstain from sexual activity until marriage. This movement, plus other educational programs, are making a difference. The rate of teenage pregnancies is starting to decline.

Dealing with Sexual Pressures

When you make the decision not to have sex, you need to be prepared to follow through with your decision. Others must respect your decision. Make sure your date knows what your limits are. Talk about how you both feel. Knowing your limits can help you both stop before you go too far.

Practice saying no. You can just say "No." It's your right. You do not need to give any explanations or reasons, but you need to be firm. Other suggestions for what to say are given in 6-14. If you know what you will say and do, it will be easier for you.

Avoid situations that may be difficult to handle. Do not spend time alone together in either of your homes when no one else is there. Go out with other couples or groups. Also stay away from parties where alcohol and drugs are available. Their use can cloud judgment.

Showing Affection in Other Ways

How do you let your partner know that you really care for him or her without having sex? There are as many ways as there are people. Talk about your lives, hopes, and dreams. Be there to listen when he or she is going through a difficult time. Go dancing. Put a note in his or her locker. Make special greeting cards. Be creative! There are many ways to say "You are truly special to me." See 6-15.

Ways to Say No to Sexual Activity

"I'm not ready for sex."
"If you love me, you won't pressure me."
"You mean a lot to me, and I want to keep it that way."
"I don't want to lose respect for you."
"I respect myself too much."
"I believe in waiting for marriage."
"I'm more comfortable in a group of our friends. We're spending too much time alone."

6-14

If someone is pressuring you to have sex, use one of these ways to say no.

6-15
Just spending time having fun together can let people know you care about them.

Check It Out!

1. Name and describe three types of friends.
2. List two ways dating helps people prepare for marriage.
3. True or false. Infatuation is based on reality, not fantasy.
4. State three reasons why young people are choosing sexual abstinence.

Topic 6-3
Negative Relationships

Objectives

After studying this topic, you will be able to
▼ describe a negative relationship.
▼ explain how to end and recover from a negative relationship.
▼ explain how a code of behavior can help you manage negative peer pressure.
▼ give examples of sexual harassment.
▼ explain what rape is and how to avoid being a rape victim.

Topic Terms

peer pressure
sexual harassment
rape
acquaintance rape
date rape

So far in this chapter, you have read about positive relationships, including friendships and dating relationships. Unfortunately, not all relationships are positive. Learning how to identify and end negative relationships can help you protect your social, emotional, and sometimes physical health.

What Is a Negative Relationship?

A *negative relationship* is one that is neither healthy, satisfying, nor successful for one or both of the people involved. A negative relationship goes beyond simply being annoyed with another person or being tired of the relationship. A negative relationship threatens a person's physical and/or emotional well-being.

Negative relationships often involve some level of abuse. This abuse can range from name-calling and put-downs to physical violence. Verbally humiliating someone can cause emotional scars. The person may begin to feel unworthy, or even deserving of the abuse. He or she may lose self-esteem. Physical violence can result in cuts and bruises, broken bones, or even death. To avoid these destructive forces, negative relationships must be ended.

Ending a Negative Relationship

You may think that anyone who is in a negative relationship would want to end the relationship immediately. A person can detach himself or herself from a peer or coworker who is causing a negative relationship. However, ending a relationship with a parent, sibling, or dating partner can be much more difficult.

Some people find it hard to end even the most harmful relationships. A child may feel trapped by financial dependence on his or her parents. A wife may fear further abuse from her husband. Dating partners may be ashamed to turn to family or friends for help.

The first step in ending a physically abusive relationship is to get away from the abuser. Children and youth may need help with this step. Teachers, doctors, police officers, and religious leaders can guide young people to sources of assistance.

A plan should be formed to get away from an abuser in advance to avoid panic in a moment of crisis. Some clothes and a few personal items might be left with a

Setting the Scene: Can a Friendship Be Bad?

Nicole and Shauna have been friends since they met in seventh grade and spend as much time together as they can. They love being the center of attention and are the loudest in every group. They think poor grades are hilarious. Lately, they have begun trying to outdo each other's outrageous behavior. They started having shoplifting competitions. At school, their last prank ended with the injury of a classmate. Nicole's parents have announced that they will be starting counseling sessions with her.

Analyze It: In what ways can you identify Nicole and Shauna's behavior as negative peer influence? What actions should their parents take? How might the girls actually develop a mutually beneficial friendship?

friend. Money, keys, and important papers should be safely stored. These items can then be retrieved quickly if an emergency escape becomes necessary. Following an abusive incident, a police report should be filed as soon as possible. Any needed medical care should be obtained. Victims can then move into a shelter. There they will be able to get counseling and legal advice.

Emotionally abusive relationships are not life threatening. However, they must still be ended to preserve the well-being of the people involved. Again, getting away from the abuser is the first step. This gives the abused person a chance to regain some of his or her self-esteem. It gives the abuser a chance to face his or her use of negative relationship patterns.

Not all negative relationships must end unhappily. Relationship patterns that lead to negative relationships can be stopped. Counseling can help people change negative patterns of interaction.

Recovering from a Negative Relationship

Recovering from a negative relationship takes time. Spending some of this time alone can help begin the recovery process. People can use time alone to think about what may have led to the negative relationship patterns. They can consider how these patterns might be avoided in future relationships. See 6-16.

6-16
Spending some time alone can give a person the chance to reflect on the causes of a negative relationship.

Taking time to look back on the relationship may be helpful. However, this time should not drag on too long. People recovering from negative relationships need to get on with their lives. Pushing themselves to get involved in group activities will help them avoid spending too much time alone.

Not all of a person's relationships will be negative. His or her positive relationships may become more important during the recovery period. The support of family and friends can provide comfort during this time of healing.

Some negative relationships leave lasting scars. Some people find it hard to build new relationships. Their self-esteem has been damaged. Counseling may be needed to help these people regain a sense of self-worth. Only after learning to love themselves will these people be able to love and trust others again.

Negative Peer Pressure

Negative relationships are sometimes the result of negative peer pressure. **Peer pressure** is the influence a person's peers have on him or her. Peer pressure is positive when it is used to encourage someone to adopt acceptable behavior. For instance, someone might use positive peer pressure to prompt a friend to study for a test. See 6-17. Peer pressure is negative when it is used to urge someone to adopt unethical behavior. For instance, someone might use negative peer pressure to persuade a friend to shoplift.

6-17
Positive peer pressure might be used to encourage students to show support for their school teams.

Managing Negative Peer Pressure

Managing negative peer pressure is a skill all people need to develop. The first step to managing negative peer pressure is to identify when it is being used. Some teens have trouble with this step. This is because they have not decided what types of behavior they think are unethical. In other words, they don't know what activities they consider to be right and wrong.

Developing a code for your behavior will give you a defense against negative peer pressure. You won't have to make quick decisions about whether or not something is right for you. You will simply follow your code.

Your code will be based on your values. It will define what unethical behavior means for you. For instance, you may decide it is okay to tease people about things they say. However, you might decide it is wrong to tease people about their appearance or their skills. Therefore, if your friends start booing a basketball player for missing a shot, you won't feel pressured to join them. Booing goes against your code of not teasing people about their skills.

Parents and other trusted adults can help you form a code of behavior that is right for you. Talking to these adults can also help reassure you when your code is tested, 6-18.

You will probably adapt your behavior code and beliefs from time to time. However, it is best not to do so when you are under pressure. Try to choose friends who will not urge you to act irresponsibly. Also, learn to avoid situations that might pressure you to break your code of behavior. When you run into unexpected

6-18

Talking to an adult can help reassure a teen about his or her code of behavior.

pressure, try using your sense of humor. You can jokingly resist peer pressure without sounding afraid or unsure.

Sexual Harassment

A very difficult negative relationship is one that involves sexual harassment. **Sexual harassment** is defined as unwanted or unwelcome sexual advances, requests for sexual favors, or other verbal or physical sexual conduct. Sexual harassment can be a leering stare. Comments with sexual overtones are considered sexual harassment. Body contact, such as brushing too close to another person or deliberately touching someone in a sexual manner, are other examples of harassment. Sometimes demands are made for sexual favors with the promise of certain benefits if the person complies. This, too, is sexual harassment. All types of sexual harassment are illegal.

You probably hear more about sexual harassment in the workplace, but it can happen anywhere, between people of all ages. It can happen at school, home, and social functions.

Being a victim of sexual harassment can be very frightening. Some victims feel ashamed and think they somehow are responsible. They may also try to ignore it, hoping it will stop on its own. Sometimes people are unsure whether or not sexual harassment is actually happening. To help you recognize behaviors that are often considered sexual harassment, review the list in 6-19.

If you think you are a victim of sexual harassment, speak up. Tell the harasser that you resent the behavior, and you will take action if it continues. The person may not realize that you feel sexually harassed. If you do not say anything, the person may think you welcome the behavior. If you say something, it might stop.

If the harassment does not stop, talk to a person in charge. At home, you can tell a parent; at school, you should speak to a counselor. If sexual harassment occurs at work, speak to your supervisor. If your supervisor is the harasser, talk to

Identifying Sexual Harassment

Behaviors that are often considered sexual harassment include unwanted and unwelcome

- sexual language
- sexual name-calling
- pressure to engage in sexual activity
- personal questions about someone's sexual behaviors
- sexist or sexual remarks about a person's clothing, body, or sexual activities
- demands for sexual favors
- staring at, touching, or grabbing a person in a sexual manner

6-19

Any of these behaviors can be considered sexual harassment if they are unwanted and unwelcome.

the person designated by your employer to handle sexual harassment complaints. The important thing is to speak up. Do not allow the harassment to continue. You have the right to expect others to respect you as a person.

Rape

Rape is one of the most serious types of personal attacks. **Rape** is the crime of forcing another person to submit to sexual relations. During recent years, rape has increased rapidly. Young people under the age of 18, especially women, are often the victims. The majority of rapes occur at night. Many occur in the victim's home, at or near a friend's home, or on the street. Persons who rape strangers are more interested in gaining power over their victims than in satisfying themselves sexually. The victim may be in danger of being killed by the attacker.

Date and Acquaintance Rape

Rape committed by someone the victim knows is far more common than rape by a stranger. In over half of all reported cases involving teens, the rapist was someone the victim knew. **Acquaintance rape** occurs between people who know each other. This may be a friend, someone at school, a coworker, or someone the victim just met. **Date rape** is the rape of a dating partner. In most cases of date or acquaintance rape, victims thought they could trust their attackers because they knew them.

When a person says no, yet is forced to have sex, it is rape. What the victim chooses to do to get through the rape encounter does not change the charge. Even if the victim used poor judgment, it is still rape. Rape is illegal; poor judgment is not.

How can you prevent acquaintance or date rape from happening? Take extra precautions to avoid situations where you could be attacked. Learn to recognize situations that could get out of control. If someone tries to take advantage of you, or if the person's actions make you uncomfortable, be prepared to leave. Learn to say no. Let the other person know you mean what you say.

Rape can be an extremely traumatic experience for the victim, with serious long-term effects. Many victims are afraid to report rape by strangers and are even less likely to report date rapes. They may be afraid of getting into trouble with their parents, or may blame themselves for the incident.

Reporting incidents, however, is important for preventing other rapes. Medical care and counseling are needed to help victims recover from the experience. *Rape crisis centers* are community agencies that provide for victims' needs. They can arrange for medical help as well as counseling. Counseling provides emotional support that helps victims regain their self-esteem and trust in others.

Check It Out!

1. True or false. Being angry with a dating partner is an example of a negative relationship.
2. Give three reasons why some people find it difficult to end negative relationships.
3. What is the first step to managing negative peer pressure?
4. Give three examples of sexual harassment.
5. True or false. Rape is usually committed by a stranger.

Chapter Review

Summary

Building positive relationships with parents, siblings, peers, romantic partners, and coworkers will help you throughout your life. These relationships will build your self-concept and bring you physical, emotional, social, and economic benefits. Mutual respect, trust, openness, and reliability will help you build relationships that are positive.

Many of your positive relationships will be with acquaintances, good friends, best friends, and dating partners. You will be attracted to these people partly because you meet each other's complementary needs. Through group dating and random dating, you will find partners with whom you want to have steady relationships. As you learn the difference between love and infatuation and learn how to have a responsible relationship, you will build more mature, lasting relationships.

Unfortunately, many people experience negative relationships. If you recognize that a relationship is damaging for you or the other person involved, it should be ended. Some negative relationships are the result of negative peer pressure. Forming a code for your behavior will help you manage this peer pressure. You should know how to recognize sexual harassment and how to avoid being a victim of either sexual harassment or rape.

Think About It!

1. Evaluate the relationships between you and your parents, siblings, peers, romantic partners, or coworkers. Give five suggestions for improving relationships with the group you choose.
2. Which of the benefits of positive relationships do you consider to be most important? Explain your answer.
3. Explain how you can develop each of the key elements that form the basis for positive relationships.
4. Evaluate the importance of acquaintances, good friends, and best friends in your social life. Describe how you would be affected if your best friends moved away.
5. Identify three complementary needs that you and a friend or dating partner meet for each other.
6. Which type of dating do you think most helps people to mature socially? Explain your answer.
7. Describe a situation in which you were infatuated with someone. How were you able to identify your feelings as infatuation rather than love?
8. What are some possible consequences of continuing a negative relationship?
9. What would you say to a best friend who was hesitant to end a negative relationship?
10. Give two examples of negative peer pressure faced by students in your school.
11. Name a career that is of interest to you. Tell how the skills taught in this chapter could help you become successful in that field of employment.

Try It Out!

1. Write a short essay describing your most significant positive relationship. Explain how you have benefited from this relationship and what elements helped you build it and keep it strong.

2. Select two couples from movies, TV shows, or books that have complementary needs. Discuss how their complementary needs affect their relationship.

3. Create a bulletin board display of pictures and cartoons related to random and steady dating.

4. Research the characteristics of infatuation and love. Design a poster to illustrate your findings.

5. Write a fictitious letter to an advice columnist. Ask for advice on how to end a negative relationship, recover from a negative relationship, or manage negative peer pressure. Exchange letters with a classmate. Write a response to the letter you receive using information you learned in this chapter.

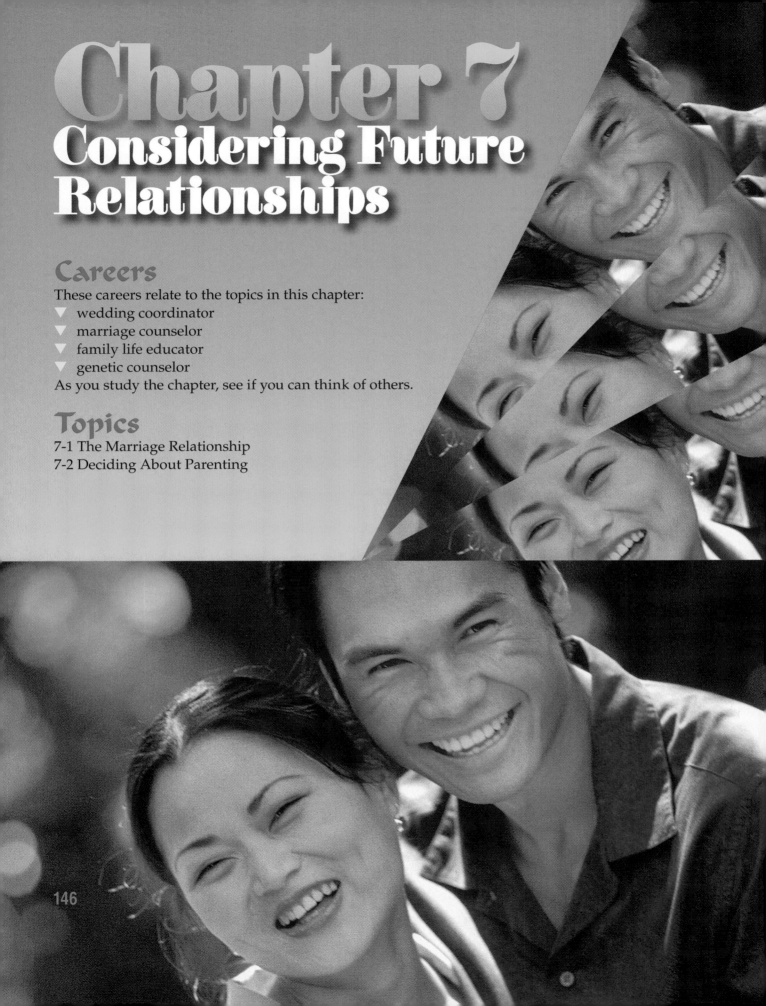

Chapter 7
Considering Future Relationships

Careers

These careers relate to the topics in this chapter:
- ▼ wedding coordinator
- ▼ marriage counselor
- ▼ family life educator
- ▼ genetic counselor

As you study the chapter, see if you can think of others.

Topics

146

Topic 7-1
The Marriage Relationship

Objectives

After studying this topic, you will be able to
▼ identify the role of love in a marriage relationship.
▼ describe factors that influence mate selection and marital success.
▼ explain the importance of the engagement period and the process of adjusting to married life.

Topic Term

intermittency of love

Marriage can be the closest and most satisfying relationship between two people. Loving someone and being loved in return can make life more meaningful and enjoyable.

In marriage, you can share the experiences of daily life with someone you love. You can laugh together and cry together. You can share your thoughts and feelings. You are encouraged to do your best and to be your best—to develop your full potential as a human being. You, in turn, encourage your mate to develop to his or her full potential.

Getting married does not magically end all problems. Marriage does not guarantee you love, happiness, and security forever. It is a growing, changing relationship. It has to grow and change because people grow and change. The challenge of marriage is to grow closer together rather than farther apart. If a couple meets this challenge, the marriage will be strong and healthy. If the couple does not meet this challenge, the marriage may end in unhappiness or even divorce.

Marriage is a part of most people's lives. They prepare for marriage by dating. They learn to love, and they choose a mate. They announce their engagement and plan their wedding. Then they work together to build a successful marriage.

Learning to Love

In American culture, dating serves many important functions. It helps people learn more about interpersonal relationships. Besides encouraging positive peer relationships, it helps people evaluate the personality traits they like or dislike in others. People learn to recognize the give-and-take involved in getting along with members of the opposite sex. The entire dating experience helps people prepare for marriage and be more successful marriage partners.

After dating for a while, two people may decide they are in love. They may wonder if they really love each other enough to spend the rest of their lives together. The surest sign of love is that it's unselfish. If you are in love, you think about the other person first, not about your own feelings and desires. The other person's wants and needs are most important. You enjoy making the other person happy and find special ways to express your affection.

Sharing is an important part of the kind of love that leads to marriage. When you are in love, you and your mate enjoy spending time together, 7-1. You find that activities are more fun and chores are less boring when you share them.

Communicating is one way of sharing. By communicating, you and your mate can

7-1
Activities are more fun and chores are more bearable when you share them with someone you love.

Factors That Influence Marital Success

Many factors will help determine whether your future marriage succeeds. Having several positive factors is not a guarantee that your marriage will be happy. Having several negative factors does not necessarily mean that you will have a bad marriage. However, a couple who have several positive factors working for them have a better chance to make their marriage last. The following factors are known to influence marital success.

share each other's thoughts and feelings. When one is happy, the other can share in that happiness. When one is upset, sad, or confused, the other can help by listening with empathy.

Good communication helps you and your mate know each other better. By staying in touch with each other's thoughts, you and your mate can grow closer and closer together. Without good communication, each of you may become involved in your own thoughts and plans. You and your mate may drift apart. Eventually, you may find that you have little in common.

The More You Know: What Do You Expect from Marriage?

People tend to find what they seek in relationships. Successful relationships happen between people who believe the relationship will work. A couple who seek a long-lasting relationship tend to focus on the positive attributes of their relationship. They seek ways to make their marriage last. Parents who understand both the demands and rewards of parenting are more likely to look for the positive aspects of parent-child relationships. They can view both the joys and challenges realistically.

Family Background

Similar family backgrounds can strengthen a marriage relationship. At first, you may think that your family is not that important. After all, your mate should be interested in you, not your family. However, your family background has left lasting marks on you. See 7-2.

Family Lifestyle

Where you have grown up affects you in many ways. People from different regions of the United States have slightly different lifestyles. They dress differently, talk differently, and eat different foods. They have different occupations. People from large cities, suburbs, small towns, and farms have slightly different lifestyles, too. They may have different views on subjects such as privacy, recreation, and politics.

Family Relationships

Another aspect of your family background is the relationships within your family, 7-3. How do you get along with your siblings? Have you learned to compromise? If you are female, have you learned something about men from your

7-3

Relationships among members of your present family may influence the relationships that will form within your future family.

brothers? If you are male, have you learned something about women from your sisters? The lessons you learn from your siblings will help you adjust to living with your mate.

The relationship you have with your parents may form the pattern for your future relationship with your own children. Do you have a good relationship with your parents? Can you talk with them? Can you settle conflicts in positive ways? Have you proven to them that you are responsible? Do they trust and respect you?

The relationship between your parents may affect your relationship with your mate. Do your parents communicate well? Do they show affection to each other often? How do they settle conflicts? Do they compromise, or does one parent always win? People learn from their parents and often imitate them. If your parents have a good relationship, you have the advantage of seeing how a good relationship works.

7-2

Your family background is likely to influence your choice of spouse and your marriage relationship.

If your parents do not have a good relationship, you aren't doomed. You can learn from their mistakes and make your marriage a good one.

Family Customs

Family customs are another part of your family background. How do you celebrate birthdays and holidays? What kinds of vacations do you take? Who handles the money matters in your family? Who does the cooking and cleaning? Who is in charge of disciplining the children? You may take your family customs for granted now. However, they will affect the customs you follow when you establish your own family.

Values and Standards

To live in peace and harmony, marriage partners need to have similar values and standards. You have to know a person well before you begin to learn about his or her standards and values. This is why the time you spend dating someone is so important.

Values

A person's values affect many day-to-day matters. Someone who considers career success important may put extra time and energy into college classes and part-time jobs. Someone who feels that close family ties are important may be involved in many family activities. Someone who values physical fitness may spend time and money playing golf, tennis, and basketball. The list could go on and on. People invest effort, time, money, and other resources in the activities that are important to them, 7-4.

Standards

Couples should share similar standards. Standards can affect daily routines. For instance, some people have

7-4
A couple who share values, goals, and standards for family unity have a better chance for a successful marriage.

high standards for cleanliness. They may expect everyone to help keep the home clean and neat. Following rules is another kind of standard. Some people never break a rule or law. Other people don't mind bending rules as long as they don't hurt anyone and they don't get caught.

As time passes, values and standards become more and more important in a relationship. Unless they are shared, resentment may grow. A marriage has a better chance for success when the partners have similar values and standards.

Emotional Maturity

Another factor relating to marital success is emotional maturity. The more emotionally mature couples are, the better their chances are for successful marriages, 7-5.

7-5
As individuals mature, they are usually better prepared to build a successful marriage.

Emotionally mature persons are in control of their own lives. They make their own decisions and accept responsibility for the consequences. They recognize their own needs, values, and goals. They have self-discipline.

Emotionally mature people have their share of frustrations, failures, and disappointments. They accept these problems as part of life. They bounce back quickly from their problems and move on.

Because emotionally mature people have their own lives under control, they can be more understanding of others. They recognize other people's needs and values in addition to their own. They can offer emotional support to their mate so the mate can fulfill needs and meet goals, too.

Emotionally mature individuals deal with reality rather than fantasy. They do not expect people to be perfect. They know that everyone has both strengths and weaknesses. They are willing to share, cooperate, and compromise to get along with others. They do not ignore or run away from problems. When a conflict arises in marriage, an emotionally mature couple deals with it. They talk about it and resolve it in a way that satisfies both of them.

Age for Marriage

Age is an important factor in marital success. It is often a sign of emotional maturity. The younger couples are when they marry, the less likely they are to have successful marriages. Because marriage requires maturity, older couples usually have greater chances of success in their marriages.

Teenage Marriages

A couple without emotional maturity will have trouble building and maintaining a strong, healthy relationship. Many teen

Setting the Scene: Working It Out

Nikiah resents all the time her husband, William, spends at work. She does not like staying home alone on weekends and thinks having a baby would help.

William is getting quite tired of his long hours at work. However, he thinks they need the income to pay their bills.

Analyze It: What threats to marital success do you see in this relationship? What misconceptions do William and Nikiah seem to have? What are some possible options for them?

couples lack this emotional maturity. As a result, few teens are able to handle the pressures and responsibilities of marriage.

Financial demands are another reason for the failure of teenage marriages. Money can be an especially important issue to teenage couples. Neither spouse may have received enough education or training to get a good job. If both spouses remain unskilled, their financial pressures will grow. If one works while the other goes to school, their financial situation will gradually improve. However, the mate without the education may resent working so hard for the education of the other. At the same time, the mate with the education may begin to feel superior to the uneducated mate. The emotional pressures may destroy their marriage.

Emotional maturity grows with age. This is why emotionally mature people are usually better prepared for married life. They have had more time to handle responsibilities and become independent. They have had more chances to interact with people and are more likely to choose compatible mates. They have had time to receive education or training. They may have even had time to establish careers.

Common Interests

Having fun is an important part of married life. You don't have to do everything together, but you should have some common interests. You might enjoy going to concerts, playing cards, riding bikes, or watching sports. See 7-6.

A healthy social life includes activities with other people, too. Both you and your mate will bring some friends into the

7-6
Sharing the activities they both enjoy can help marriage partners strengthen their relationship.

marriage. These friendships are important and should be continued. After you are married, your friends and your mate's friends may socialize with both of you. In addition, you will make some new friends together. Developing these mutual friendships is one of the adjustments you will need to make early in marriage.

Parental Approval

Parental approval is a positive factor in a marriage. Studies show that most successful marriages have the consent of all parents.

Why is parental approval important? It shows that the parents realize their child is mature enough to be married. It shows they are willing to entrust their child's well-being to the care of the future mate. It also shows they are supportive of the relationship.

Why do parents sometimes disapprove? Parents want their children to live happy lives. They may recognize some weak traits in the person their child wants to marry. They feel that in time, the child will recognize the weak traits, too. Disapproval is often their way of saying you should wait a while and learn a little more about this person before you commit yourself to marriage.

In any marriage, the spouses will have many adjustments to make. They will have many conflicts to settle and many compromises to make. If the parents do not approve of the marriage, the spouses have less incentive to settle their differences. They may give up easily. They may think, *Our parents said this marriage would be a mistake, and it is. We might as well give up.*

On the other hand, spouses seem to compromise more readily if their parents approve of their marriage. They may think, *Our parents thought this marriage would work. We don't want to disappoint them by giving*

up so easily. What's wrong with our marriage? What can we do to make it better? This positive viewpoint can save a marriage that might otherwise fail.

Attitude Toward Marriage

The attitude spouses have about marriage plays a major role in their marital success. Too often people think that marriage means living happily ever after. However, all marriages have conflicts and challenges. Marriage means bringing two different people together. The process of give-and-take is a part of daily life.

The Engagement Period

The engagement period helps couples prepare for marriage. It marks the end of dating and the start of a couple's plan for married life.

In American society, the engagement period has several functions. It is a time for a couple to discuss important issues such as the ones listed in 7-7. It is a time for them to establish good relationships with their future in-laws. They will also make plans for their wedding and future home.

While an engagement is considered preparation for marriage, not all engagements end in marriage. Many couples who approach engagement seriously find that they are not ready to commit themselves to marriage. They may find their differences are too great to resolve. For a couple in this situation, a broken engagement is better than a broken marriage.

Making Marriage Work

People continually grow and change. It makes sense that a marriage relationship would continually grow and change, too. The most obvious changes occur early in marriage. Throughout a marriage

Issues to Discuss During Engagement

Your attitudes toward marriage

Your readiness, as a couple, for married life

Your expectations
   of your husband or wife
   of your first year of marriage
   of your fifth, tenth, twentieth, and fortieth
   years of marriage

Educational goals

Career goals

Family goals
   having or not having children
   establishing family customs
   relationships with in-laws

Friendships
   old and new
   individual and shared

Social activities

Differences in
   age
   where you were raised and where you live
      now
   nationality
   race
   religion
   social class

Marriage roles
   sharing responsibility
   resolving conflicts
   sharing household chores
   caring for and disciplining children

Financial matters
   present financial status
   financial goals
   your monthly budget
   how financial decisions will be made
   who will handle the money

Where you will live

What transportation you will need

7-7

Open communication about important issues helps a couple prepare for marriage.

relationship, the greatest challenge for most couples is to grow closer together, not farther apart.

Early Marital Adjustments

Whenever two people start a new life together, adjustments have to be made. Since no two people are alike, this is to be expected. Most newlyweds will be faced with several adjustments as they adapt to their new lifestyle. Their success in making these adjustments will affect the quality of their relationship.

Adjusting to a new home is one change for newlyweds. If they had been living with their parents, their new dwelling may seem small. Their furnishings may seem simple and sparse. The couple will have to adjust to housing they can afford. With a good attitude, the couple can enjoy the challenge of gradually improving their home.

Newlyweds have to adjust to some new daily living habits and routines, 7-8. Morning and evening schedules will have to be adjusted to fit the couple's needs. Meal patterns will have to be adjusted according to food preferences, cooking skills, and time schedules. Plans will have to be made so household chores such as doing laundry, dusting, and mowing the lawn are done. Good communication and cooperation will help the couple make these adjustments easily.

Social activities tend to change and become less expensive. Married people tend to set many long-range goals. These goals may include further education, home ownership, and parenthood. Such goals require financial commitments. To meet their long-range goals, a couple may spend less money for recreation.

Relationships with family members and friends may change, too. A spouse usually receives top priority in marriage. Wise

7-8
Sharing household duties helps this couple build a closer relationship.

parents, other family members, and friends realize this is an important adjustment for newlyweds. This does not mean that others are forgotten. Since newlyweds tend to spend more time together, they have less time for family and friends.

Nurturing a Marriage

Subtle changes occur continuously in marriage. As people grow older, they face new challenges and accept new responsibilities. Some of their interests and attitudes change. Good communication helps marriage partners keep in touch with each other's changing personality.

Then they can change together. Their relationship can become closer and stronger. See 7-9.

Two people can grow closer together in marriage, but they cannot achieve perfection. No person is perfect. No marriage is perfect. A couple should not expect to feel total love for each other all the time. They should not be disappointed if love seems to fade and then reappear. This is called **intermittency of love** and is normal in a relationship.

Sometimes a couple's love will have periods of growth; other times it will level out. If they have a strong relationship and keep communication lines open, their love will return.

Just as love has its ups and downs, so does happiness. Trying to maintain constant happiness can drain a marriage relationship. Married people should stay in tune with each other's feelings, supporting each other through these ups and downs.

7-9
People change over time. Adjustments in the marriage relationship are therefore also necessary.

They may find happiness together in special occasions, such as anniversaries and holidays. They may also find happiness in simple acts of kindness and thoughtfulness. Sometimes one spouse may feel unhappy or upset. This is a normal part of most relationships. By offering love and understanding during these times, a couple can work through these feelings.

Any marriage will have good times and bad times. A successful marriage is one in which both partners want success and are willing to work for it. They focus on their love for each other and the good times they share. They make an effort to communicate their thoughts and feelings to each other. When problems or differences arise, they work together to resolve them.

Check It Out!

1. Name three factors that influence a person's choice of a marriage partner.
2. True or false. The relationships among members of a person's family may influence the relationships that will form within his or her future family.
3. Name two reasons for the high rate of failure in teenage marriages.
4. True or false. In successful marriage relationships, couples continually grow and change.

Topic 7-2
Deciding About Parenting

Objectives

After studying this topic, you will be able to
▼ state the goal of parenthood.
▼ describe the challenges of parenthood.
▼ recognize the challenges faced in youth parenting.
▼ analyze the factors that influence parenthood decisions.

Topic Term
parenting

Parenting is the name given to the process of raising a child. It includes all of the love, care, and guidance given by parents in this process. Parenting begins with the birth or adoption of a child and lasts a lifetime. Even if the marriage breaks apart, parents are still the parents of their child.

Before committing themselves to parenting, people should have a full understanding of the demands and rewards of this important role. Any goal started without knowledge and planning has little chance for success. Likewise, people who begin parenting without knowledge and planning may fall short of their parenting goals.

The Goal of Parenting

The primary goal of parenting is to help children grow and become mature, independent individuals who can make their own decisions and accept responsibility for their actions. In simpler words, it might be stated in this way: The goal of parenting is to help children grow up responsibly.

There is no step-by-step recipe you can follow to reach this goal of parenting. Each child is unique, and each situation is unique. The best way to prepare yourself for parenthood is to learn as much as possible about children. The more knowledge you have, the better able you will be to handle any situation that occurs.

Helping Children Grow Up Responsibly

Helping children grow up responsibly is not always easy. One of the most important—and most difficult—tasks for parents is to teach their children values and standards. Another difficult task is to allow children to learn through new experiences. Parents also need to help their children learn to interact with other people.

Teaching Values and Standards

To teach children how to evaluate the importance of something, parents first must have firmly established values and standards of their own. They must be living a lifestyle that reflects their beliefs. Then their children will be able to follow their examples and adopt similar values and standards. See 7-10.

Letting Children Learn Through New Experiences

Parents have a strong urge to cushion the path for their children. They should realize, however, that their help may actually hinder their children's development. Whenever possible, a child who demands "Let me do it myself" should be allowed to try. The child may not do the job perfectly, but perfection is not always necessary. Having the child learn to do it may be more important than having it done perfectly.

7-10
These children are learning the importance of family mealtimes shared together.

Recognizing the Importance of Other People in Children's Lives

This is an important factor in helping children grow up responsibly. Babies are happy to be completely dependent on their parents. As children mature, however, they want and need to meet many different people. Parents with a healthy attitude about their children recognize this as a positive mark of growth. Parents with a less healthy attitude may feel jealous about the loss of their children's attention.

The Challenges of Parenting

Being a parent involves commitments of love, time, energy, patience, and money. Most people gladly accept these commitments in order to have the rewards of parenthood, 7-11. They look forward to rocking a baby to sleep and to watching their children play. They want to take pride in the accomplishments of their children. When the children reach adulthood, their parents look forward to the companionship they will all share.

Parenting Is an Expression of Love

For many couples, having a child is a way of fulfilling the deep love they have for one another. After the child is born, creating an atmosphere of love and acceptance is important to the child's emotional development. Parents need to show their love and affection to one another and to their child. A climate of love in the home lays the foundation for self-esteem and trust. See 7-12.

7-11
Both father and mother play important roles in the development of their children.

Parenting Requires Patience

One frustration of parenthood is the hundreds of questions that children ask. One young couple decided to take their child to a playground. They expected to relax and talk while their child played. Instead of going off to play, the child sat at their feet and began asking questions. Some of the questions seemed silly to the parents. In cases like this, however, parents must remind themselves that this type of behavior is normal for young children. They must try to avoid becoming impatient.

Parenting Involves a Major Financial Commitment

The costs of having and rearing a child are increasing. The costs for clothing, furniture, and toys the child will need add up quickly. As children grow, their financial needs increase. Housing, food, transportation, medical care, and recreation become major expenses, 7-13. Education costs can be great if private schools are chosen, or if the child wishes to pursue a college degree.

An additional financial consideration is the loss of one spouse's income. This can happen if one of the parents gives up a job to stay home and care for the child. If both parents continue to work, child care will be an expense. It is important for couples to consider how they will meet these financial commitments.

Youth Parenting

Parenting in the teen years presents many challenges for young couples. Few teenage parents are aware of the time, energy, and money required to rear a child. Many are not prepared to face the physical,

7-12
Babies who experience love in the family unit will learn to trust.

Parenting Involves Commitments of Time and Energy

Babies have to be fed, bathed, and clothed. Their cries have to be answered, even in the middle of the night. Sometimes the tasks involved in caring for a child seem endless, and parents become discouraged. One young parent said, "All my life, I looked forward to having a baby. I didn't have a realistic view of parenthood, though. I only thought about the good points. Now I sometimes feel guilty. I get so tired that I don't enjoy caring for my baby as I always thought I would."

7-13
For parents, expenses for instruments and lessons for their children must be considered.

emotional, social, and financial challenges of parenthood.

Teenage mothers face several physical health risks during pregnancy. A lack of medical care or poor nutrition during pregnancy puts both mother and child at risk. Pregnancy-related illnesses, such as toxemia, and other complications are also more common for teen mothers. *Toxemia* is high blood pressure caused by the pregnancy. Because their own bodies may still be developing, teens have higher risks of having premature, low-birthweight babies. The infant death rate is also higher for teen mothers than for mothers in their twenties. As research shows, a mother's age does make a difference in pregnancy. The best childbearing years for women are from ages 20 through 32.

Emotional Challenges

Teen parenthood will affect the young parents emotionally. Many teenage marriages occur because the young woman becomes pregnant. Because of emotional and financial pressures, these marriages have a fairly high divorce rate. The addition of a child adds even more pressures. Young couples, who are still growing up themselves, are often unable to deal with all the pressures they face. See 7-14.

Teen parents must cope with sudden changes in their roles from adolescents to parents. This often causes more emotional stress. They are faced with the challenge of growing up overnight to assume adult roles as parents. Their own parent-child roles are often conflicting. They are parents to their babies while they remain children of their own parents.

7-14
Many of the emotional pressures involved with parenting are overwhelming to teens.

One frustrated teen mother said it this way. "The baby is mine when she needs care. No one babysits so I can go out on weekends; I just have to stay home. When decisions that affect the welfare of the baby have to be made, my mother makes them. I need her help very much, but I'm resentful when she acts like my baby is really her baby."

Social Challenges

The arrival of a baby greatly hinders teen parents' social life. Working and child-care responsibilities mean they are less likely to experience a normal social life with friends their age. Their opportunities to socialize with their friends are limited. They see that their friends have more freedom and fewer responsibilities. This sometimes creates feelings of frustration and even anger.

Financial Challenges

Teen parents face many financial difficulties as they enter the adult world. Many lack stable financial resources, such as secure jobs. In trying to meet expenses, they are more likely to drop out of school and have low-paying jobs. Many also lack the skills and training needed to advance in their jobs.

Although some teenage parents choose to marry, a large percent do not. This usually means the father is separated from his child and may not offer any financial support. If the mother chooses to raise the baby, she assumes most of the responsibility for the baby's daily care. Many young mothers drop out of school to care for their babies. With little formal education, most do not find jobs to support themselves and their children. They cannot afford child-care services either. Many need to resort to federal aid programs such as Social Services for financial support.

Many states have laws requiring fathers to support their children. In these states, teenage fathers are responsible for paying child support. Many are likely to drop out of school in an effort to earn the money for payments. With little formal education, their chances of finding employment to support themselves and pay child support are not good. These conditions can lead to living in poverty.

Education and Career

While some teen parents who have strong support at home are able to finish their high school education, many drop out of school. Without a high school diploma, they find it difficult to obtain good-paying jobs. They will also be unable to further their education beyond high school. Without at least a high school education, the young parents will find it hard to achieve their career goals. This may severely limit their lifetime earning potential. Not only do teen parents suffer the economic consequences, but their children suffer also.

The Children of Youth Parents

Teens are still developing physically, intellectually, emotionally, and socially. They are usually not yet financially independent either. Because of such factors, their children are subject to more risks than children born to older parents.

▼ *Health risks.* A young mother may not be aware of certain prenatal behaviors that could put her unborn child at risk. For example, taking certain medications not prescribed by your doctor may harm a fetus. A poor diet can result in an underdeveloped or low-birthweight baby. Smoking cigarettes can lead to a premature birth. Excessive alcohol consumption can cause *fetal alcohol syndrome*, a condition that includes physical and mental disabilities.

▼ *Academic risks.* The first two years of life are critical because the child is building the mental foundation that will dictate behavior through adulthood. Young parents may lack the time to adequately guide the development of their child, especially if they must work, attend school, and also care for their child's other needs.

▼ *Emotional risks.* Recent research has shown that emotional development is the foundation of intelligence. Even newborns have emotional needs. They are best met through activities such as rocking, touching, soothing, talking, and singing. Young parents may again be unable to spend this quality time with their babies.

▼ *Social risks.* Studies show that children born to teen parents are more likely to become parents themselves when they are teenagers.

▼ *Economics.* Because teen parents may lack education and job skills, their children have a greater chance of living in poverty.

▼ *Child care.* The children of teen parents are likely to have caregivers other than their parents while parents are in school or working. Finding quality care for children may be difficult and expensive. If the children are cared for by their grandparents, they may start to bond more with the grandparents than their parents.

▼ *Neglect and abuse.* It is difficult to meet the needs of another when your own needs may be unmet. A lack of experience in child care may result in a teen parent neglecting his or her child. In addition, a teen parent may find the pressures of parenthood too much to handle. He or she may take out frustrations on the child in abusive ways.

Deciding Whether to Have Children

One of the most important decisions a couple will make together is whether to have children. Although this decision is a personal one, parenthood should also be a joint decision made by husband and wife together. Many personal factors need to be considered, including reasons for having or not having children. To make a wise decision, each partner needs a clear understanding of each other's feelings and goals as they relate to parenthood.

Reasons for Having Children

Why do so many people choose to have children? For many parents, bringing a child into the world is an expression of love. Sharing the joys and responsibilities of rearing a child brings many couples closer together. The desire to have a family lifestyle is another reason for having children. Many people want to enrich their lives and share their experiences with children. They don't want to miss the special experiences of life that children make possible, 7-15. Fulfilling role expectations is also a reason for having children. People who have grown up in a stable family setting know that someday they will be parents, too.

Reasons for Not Having Children

Most couples choose to have children. However, after careful evaluation of their feelings, others choose not to become parents. Some couples may prefer the freedom of a childless lifestyle. The demands of a career may make others unwilling to take time to rear a child. Others may have physical traits or

Besides determining if they want to have children, couples also need to decide if they are ready to have children. They should not feel obligated to have children just to satisfy their friends and relatives. They also should not feel selfish if they decide to remain childless. Couples who decide they are ready to have children begin the process of family planning. See 7-16.

7-15
Sharing experiences with his child fulfills the life of this parent.

hereditary diseases they do not wish a child to inherit. The expense of rearing a child may deter some. An unhappy childhood or fear of rearing a child may influence other couples' decisions.

Other Factors Affecting Parenthood Decisions

Couples making a decision about parenthood will consider many personal factors. Each factor can affect their final decision. One factor they should discuss is the short- and long-term goals they have set for their life together. How will children fit into these goals? Another factor a couple needs to evaluate is their own relationship. Is it strong and growing? Are they secure in their roles as husband and wife? Would a child enrich their relationship? Are they both ready to accept the roles of father and mother?

7-16
Couples who want children and are prepared to handle the responsibilities should be encouraged to have children.

Check It Out!

1. State the primary goal of parenthood.
2. Name two typical challenges faced by teen parents.
3. List three reasons why many people choose to have children.
4. Identify two personal factors affecting a couple's decision about parenthood.

Chapter Review

Summary

Marriage can be the closest and most satisfying relationship between a couple. However, it takes prior preparation and continual effort to maintain this relationship.

Several factors influence marital success, including having similar family backgrounds, values, and standards. Sharing common interests, having emotional maturity, and having parental approval also help marriages succeed. The engagement period is a time to examine relationships, establish positive in-law relations, and plan for the wedding.

Examining attitudes toward parenthood is important. Like marriage, parenting involves many goals and challenges. Parenthood challenges are likely to be magnified among youth parents. Many personal factors affect a couple's decision about whether or not to have children.

Think About It!

1. What factors do you think have the most influence on a person's choice of marriage partner?
2. List ten issues you think are especially important for a couple to discuss during engagement. Explain your responses.
3. What steps can newlyweds take to make their marriage adjustments easier?
4. Describe the responsibilities of parents to their children.
5. Discuss the pros and cons of youth parenting.
6. Why do you think deciding about parenthood may be more difficult than deciding about other major lifestyle factors, such as careers?

Try It Out!

1. Assign two sets of values and two standards to an imaginary engaged couple. Write a short story describing how the values and standards of these two people would affect their relationship.
2. Describe a typical day for an imaginary couple in the first week of their marriage (after the honeymoon). Then describe a typical day after six months, after three years, and after ten years of marriage. Show how the couple has grown and changed.
3. List several factors people should consider before they become parents. Compare your list with those of your classmates.
4. Write a character sketch of an imaginary couple who should *not* have children. Share your ideas with your classmates.
5. Create a booklet for prospective parents entitled *The Challenges of Parenthood*. Find pictures to illustrate the booklet and write descriptive captions under each picture.
6. Interview parents and childless couples. Based on your findings, discuss
   ▼ the advantages and disadvantages of having children
   ▼ the reasons for not wanting children
   ▼ the best age for becoming parents
   ▼ the consequences of unwanted pregnancies

Chapter 8
Community Living Skills

Careers

These careers relate to the topics in this chapter:
- ▼ restaurant crew leader
- ▼ community affairs director
- ▼ personnel manager
- ▼ city supervisor

As you study the chapter, see if you can think of others.

Topics

Topic 8-1

Leaders and Followers

Objectives

After studying this topic, you will be able to
▼ explain the roles of leaders and followers.
▼ demonstrate the qualities of effective team members.
▼ identify three types of leadership.
▼ describe five functions performed by group leaders.

Topic Terms

team
leader
follower
diversity
autocratic leadership
democratic leadership
laissez-faire
motivation
brainstorming
tact

8-1
Group involvement is an important part of life for many people.

Throughout life, you will be a member of several groups. Your family is a group. Your classes are groups. You may also be involved with clubs, bands, sports teams, and choral groups. See 8-1.

Each member of a group can affect the success of group activities. Learning how to work with others will allow you to contribute to a group's effectiveness. In the process, you will develop positive relationships with your peers. Participating in group activities will also promote your social and emotional development.

Being a Team Member

A **team** is a group of people organized around a common goal. Every good team has leaders and followers. No team can exist with just one or the other. When team leaders and followers work toward the group's goal, they are practicing good teamwork.

A **leader** is a person who influences the behavior of others. Leaders take charge and help group members set and achieve group goals. Good leaders inspire the trust of their followers and respond to their teammates as friends. They involve all group members in planning, conducting, and evaluating group activities.

No person is a leader in all situations. A leader in the drama club may be a follower in the band. An athletic leader may be a follower on the yearbook staff. A business leader may be a follower in a social setting. You will be needed to lead in some cases and follow in others.

A **follower** is a person who supports a group by helping put goals into action. The best plans of any group will not yield results without the support of dedicated followers. Followers are needed to supply time, talents, energy, and other resources to achieve team goals. Followers take direction, but also help leaders determine the best course of action. Most people develop team skills by first assuming a follower role. They grow into leadership positions gradually as they develop self-esteem.

For a team to function effectively, leaders and followers must show a spirit of give and take. Followers must be willing to take a leadership role when their expertise is needed to achieve the team's goal. Likewise, leaders must recognize that sometimes a follower is better suited to temporarily take charge. When team members work well together, they do what needs to be done, no matter what titles they have. See 8-2.

Both leaders and followers are needed to build strong teams at school, in the community, and in the workplace. Teams are especially important in the workplace. Consequently, employers try to hire individuals who have good teamwork skills.

Qualities of Effective Team Members

Team members put the interests of the team first and always emphasize "we" instead of "me." They keep open minds and come to meetings willing to discuss all ideas. They expect others to have different ideas and opinions. They do not become offended when their ideas are criticized. They use humor whenever appropriate, but never in a way that offends someone. They do their share of work, complete assignments on time, and keep a positive attitude. Effective team members try to do what is best for the team.

Members of teams that operate effectively pay close attention when others speak. Sometimes ideas expressed by teammates of different cultural backgrounds do not immediately make sense. People of every culture have unique beliefs, values, customs, traditions, and religious practices that are often reflected in their views. Sometimes a language barrier exists, making it difficult for people to express ideas clearly. When communicating with individuals of other cultures, extra patience and understanding is needed by everyone.

You will encounter people from other cultural backgrounds throughout life. This influence is the result of a multicultural society. Sometimes the term **diversity** is used to refer to the condition of a team whose members represent many different cultures. Diversity presents opportunities to share cultural traditions and customs.

8-2
Someone who is usually a follower may emerge as a leader for certain projects.

When everyone's culture is respected, individuals feel free to express opinions and views. The team benefits from the open, honest discussions. Often more and better ideas result.

On the other hand, diversity can create team conflict unless there is an effort to understand other cultures and a strong commitment to cooperation. Some additional ways to demonstrate team commitment are listed in 8-3.

Opportunities for Leadership

Leaders are people who step up and take charge of a situation. They are needed at all levels of human organization. Countries, states, cities, businesses, schools, and clubs all need leaders. Your skills as a leader may be used in a number of ways, both now and in the future.

Qualities of Committed Team Members

- Smile and use a pleasant tone of voice.
- Remain quiet until you have the floor.
- Think highly of every team member including yourself.
- Make an effort to bring out members who may be shy.
- Seek clarification when something is not clear.
- Be willing to compromise on issues that can be handled effectively in several different ways.
- Celebrate your team's successes and the ability of members to work well together.

8-3

These personal qualities are signs that members are committed to their group.

Right now, you may be needed to lead class discussions, club meetings, or athletic rallies. You may know a student who has personal problems and needs your encouragement to seek counseling. You may serve on a team headed by a weak leader and have some ideas for motivating the group.

If you become a parent later in life, you will be a leader to your children. You may serve a leadership role in your community and possibly run for an elective office. No doubt you will join community and social groups devoted to your interests and possibly hold leadership positions.

In the workplace, you will have many opportunities to lead. Unlike the past, when supervisors told workers what to do, today's workplace uses a teamwork approach. Employees are expected to work well as teammates and share the leadership role as assignments dictate. Group members must possess the teamwork skills of creative thinking, decision making, and conflict resolution. A leader must know how to organize and manage the team's resources. Participation in school clubs and organizations, discussed in Topic 8-2, will help prepare you for leadership.

Types of Leadership

There are three basic types of leadership. The first type, **autocratic leadership**, demands the cooperation of others. The autocratic leader has full control of the group and makes all the decisions for the group. Autocratic leadership stresses meeting goals. It demands that team members perform as directed to reach goals. Autocratic leaders may seem harsh at times. However, their followers receive the satisfaction of knowing they have done more than they thought they could do. Some people would never try unless, in a kind but firm manner, a good leader says "Do it."

Democratic leadership stresses the needs and wishes of individuals. The group discusses matters of policy. Members are encouraged to participate in decision making by voting. See 8-4.

In a democratic group, members have the power to select a leader to act in their best interest. They trust the leader to make good decisions for the group. If the leader fails to consider the group's wishes, however, the members have the power to choose a new leader.

The third type of leadership is called **laissez-faire**. Laissez-faire leaders play down their roles in groups. They are on hand only to serve as resources. Laissez-faire leadership allows true freedom. Members may do whatever they want to do. The group is not pressured to move forward on a schedule. An active group may fail to reach goals due to a lack of organization. In the end, members may feel that little has been accomplished in spite of their individual efforts.

All three types of leadership have good points. Autocratic leadership may be needed to help some people become productive and meet fixed deadlines. Democratic leadership takes advantage of members' ideas and provides the organizational structure to accomplish goals. Laissez-faire leadership fosters individual creativity, even though it may result in a low degree of productivity. See 8-5.

The secret to involving all members is to know how and when to use all three types of leadership. You must vary your leadership style to fit the people in the group as well as the situation. Take care not to become a bossy autocrat. Do not get carried away with the laissez-faire style or your group may not accomplish anything. Democratic leadership usually works best, but you cannot expect it to work in every situation.

8-4
In the democratic style of leadership, decisions are discussed by all group members.

8-5
Laissez-faire leadership works well in situations where group members need to use their creativity.

The More You Know: Leadership in Action

All three types can be used to achieve a single goal. See if you can recognize the types of leadership in the following example.

The members of a club vote to replace the worn draperies in the student lounge. The club leader asks a small task force to research the group's options for raising funds. Once the membership hears and discusses the alternatives, the group votes.

The leader suggests group members get prices for ready-made and custom-made draperies. They can compare these prices with the cost of the materials needed to make the draperies themselves. Group members meet several times to discuss the possibilities. However, the decision is theirs to make.

Effective Leadership

Leaders perform a number of functions in a group. They must set a good example, motivate followers, and guide group planning. Leaders also need to use tact and give recognition to those who deserve it.

Set an Example

When you are the leader of a group, you need to set an example for the other members. Although you have extra responsibilities as leader, you also have the responsibility of doing your share of the work. If you fail to participate, you set a poor example for your followers. They may see no reason to help with projects if you are not helping. They may also lose respect for you and begin to resent you. See 8-6.

On the other hand, you should not try to do all the work by yourself. If you are a good leader, you will get other people involved. Try to place all members on one or more active committees. Give others the chance to participate and have the satisfaction of being useful and needed. Involving more people will allow more work to be done and more goals to be achieved.

Another way you can set an example is by cooperating with everyone. Some large groups tend to divide into little groups of friends. You, too, may feel more comfortable working with your friends. However, you must remember that you are leading the entire group. You must go outside your usual circle of friends to include everyone. Your example will encourage others to work together for the good of the group.

Motivate Followers

As a leader, you may need to motivate followers to get involved in group projects. **Motivation** is a force that gives people a reason to take action.

Some people have *intrinsic motivation*. Their motivation comes from within themselves. They set many goals for themselves and willingly work to achieve those goals. Group members who are intrinsically motivated show enthusiasm. They never need to be prodded. Instead, they always look for ways to help.

Other people need *extrinsic motivation*. This motivation comes from a person's environment. Leaders can provide followers with extrinsic motivation by

8-6
Leaders as well as followers must participate in group efforts.

helping them notice their environment. A choir director may say the choral group sounds better when members are smiling. A scoutmaster may comment that the flowers in the city park need weeding. Such suggestions from leaders can motivate followers to take action. See 8-7.

Some followers are very willing to help but have no idea what needs to be done. Watch for these individuals and recommend tasks to them so they can enjoy being productive team members. Without positive direction, these people often get lost in confusion.

What about those who refuse to get involved? If you know their reasons, you may be able to motivate them. For instance, some people may not think they are capable of doing a job. You could help these people find tasks that better match their skills. This will allow them to develop more self-confidence.

Some people may refuse to get involved because they are too busy. They may have numerous other commitments. You might

8-7
This choir director uses extrinsic motivation to encourage his group to prepare well for a concert.

motivate these people to take on small tasks. This will allow them to participate without devoting a large amount of time. These people can take on larger tasks when their schedules are less hectic.

Guide Planning

Being involved in the planning motivates group members to participate. With careful planning, a group can successfully handle several projects and activities. Your role as leader is to guide the planning. Be sure the group thinks through a plan and is able to carry it out. Summarize thoughts frequently to ensure that all members understand the same meaning.

During a planning session, a leader can encourage a group to express ideas by brainstorming. **Brainstorming** is a group problem-solving method in which individuals offer all ideas that come to mind. It is a technique that requires rapid thinking and a constant expression of ideas. Some of the ideas will be really wild, but that does not matter. The goal is to develop many ideas, not a few well-planned thoughts. No one is allowed to criticize any ideas, so members offer them without fear of embarrassment. Later, the group decides which ideas to pursue, sometimes combining two or more brainstorming thoughts. The ideas that motivate the most members will be put into action.

Brainstorming has two benefits. First, the group is likely to find answers to its problems or challenges. Secondly, the opportunity to offer suggestions promotes member participation and motivation.

Use Tact

Successful leaders need to have tact. **Tact** is knowing what to do or say to avoid offending others. If being tactful is not one of your strong qualities, work on developing it. Tact will help you work with others without hurting them or making them angry.

Getting group members to do their share of tasks often requires tact. Most people like being *asked* to do something rather than being *told* what to do. Some leaders are afraid that if they ask followers to do something, the followers will refuse. Therefore, they just tell the followers what to do, even though this approach often causes friction. Eventually group members may not cooperate willingly.

Tact is necessary whenever you deal with people. Being kind and considerate is always appreciated. A smile with a pleasant tone of voice is important in all situations. This is true whether you are a leader or a follower.

Give Recognition

Leaders also need to give followers the recognition they deserve. Your encouragement can help bring out the best in others. When their efforts enable the group to reach a goal, give them the credit. See 8-8.

One way leaders can give recognition is with a sincere "thank you." People need to know their personal efforts are important and truly appreciated. The leader should

8-8
Giving awards is one way a leader can recognize the efforts of individual group members.

take the time to congratulate the person in front of the group so everyone knows that individual efforts are noticed and valued.

Promote Cultural Diversity

One of the responsibilities of a group's leader is to promote cultural diversity. The acceptance of other cultures begins with an understanding of them. Therefore, a leader might encourage group discussion about cultural differences. The leader might also plan cultural activities, asking group members of differing backgrounds to plan the events. This will help bring down barriers in the group, enabling group members to work better together.

Check It Out!

1. True or false. A strong leader always performs as a leader, never as a follower.
2. Suggest five qualities of effective team members.
3. List and describe the three basic types of leadership.
4. A force that gives people a reason to take action is _____.

Topic 8-2
Organizations That Work!

Objectives

After studying this topic, you will be able to
▼ name three youth organizations and three professional organizations and tell the purpose of each.
▼ explain how a group's constitution and bylaws act as guidelines for electing officers and holding meetings.
▼ demonstrate how a group can use the planning process to establish a goal around which programs and activities can be organized.

Topic Terms

constitution
bylaws
parliamentary procedure

What makes an organization successful? Its purpose is a key factor. A group's purpose is its reason for existing. A group sets goals to help achieve its purpose.

Youth and Professional Organizations

One purpose of most youth organizations is to help prepare young people for their adult roles in society. Perhaps you are a member of such a group. Most schools offer a range of organizations that encourage student participation. Chart 8-9 describes several popular youth organizations.

Youth Organizations

Business Professionals of America (BPA)	Promotes skills and aptitudes needed by a world-class business workforce.
DECA—An Association of Marketing Students	Helps students learn about marketing, merchandising, management, and related subjects.
Future Business Leaders of America (FBLA)	Assists students in choosing business occupations and helps them become competent, successful business leaders.
Family, Career and Community Leaders of America (FCCLA)	Encourages personal growth, leadership development, family and community involvement, and preparation for the multiple adult roles of family member, wage earner, and community leader. It is the only student organization with the family as its central focus.
Health Occupations Students of America (HOSA)	Helps members build their physical, mental, and social well-being while developing into competent leaders and health care workers.
National FFA Organization	Teaches leadership, character development, sportsmanship, cooperation, service, improved agriculture, and citizenship to students studying agriculture.
Technology Student Association (TSA)	Develops the leadership and personal abilities of students as they prepare for their roles in a technological society.
SkillsUSA	Helps students develop leadership and teamwork skills and prepares them to enter trade, industrial, technical, and health careers.

8-9

These career and technical student organizations help prepare teen members for future work roles.

As an adult, you may become involved in an organization that enhances your profession. The purpose of these organizations is to promote the career areas in which their members work. Professional organizations may achieve this purpose by funding research, offering scholarships, and sponsoring meetings to keep members updated. Chart 8-10 lists a number of professional organizations related to the field of family and consumer sciences. Many of these have chapters that students can join to get an inside view of the profession.

Getting Organized

Organization is another factor that contributes to a group's success. Members know what to expect when a group follows set guidelines for electing officers and holding meetings. These guidelines are stated by the group's constitution and bylaws.

Many groups are local chapters of national organizations. All the chapters share the same purpose as the national organization. They also follow the same basic constitution and bylaws.

Family and Consumer Sciences Professional Organizations

American Dietetics Association (ADA)	Serves dietitians who work in hospitals, schools, colleges, universities, business institutions, and industry.
American Association of Family and Consumer Sciences (AAFCS)	Serves individuals working in all areas of family and consumer sciences to help individuals and families develop living skills and adjust to limited resources and a changing environment.
American Society of Interior Designers (ASID)	Serves interior designers interested in establishing a professional code of ethics and an educational standard for all designers.
Association for Career and Technical Education (ACTE), Family and Consumer Sciences Division	Serves career-focused family and consumer sciences educators.
Consumer Science Business Professionals (CSBP)	Serves business professionals who integrate consumer trends and perspectives into business solutions.
Family and Consumer Sciences Education Association (FCSEA)	Serves supervisors and teachers of family and consumer sciences.
International Association of Clothing Designers (IACD)	Serves designers of apparel for a variety of markets.
National Association for the Education of Young Children (NAEYC)	Serves administrators and teachers in schools for very young children.
National Extension Association of Family and Consumer Sciences (NEAFCS)	Serves employees of the Cooperative Extension Service interested in opportunities to improve their skills as family and consumer sciences educators.
National Restaurant Association (NRA)	Serves those involved in one of the many aspects of the foodservice industry.
Society of Consumer Affairs Professionals (SOCAP)	Serves those in industry responsible for creating and maintaining maximum customer satisfaction and loyalty.

8-10

These professional organizations promote the careers of members working in various areas related to family and consumer sciences.

The **constitution** is a set of laws that govern an organization. In its simplest form, a constitution usually includes the following:

▼ name and purpose of the group
▼ membership requirements
▼ the group's officers, their duties, and the method of election

▼ basic meeting requirements, such as the number of people that must be present before a meeting can be held
▼ procedures for changing the constitution

Many groups also have bylaws that accompany the constitution. The **bylaws** are a set of specific rules that expand the constitution by giving more information. For instance, bylaws list the names and functions of committees. They state the order of business and any other information that is needed to make the constitution clear. The rules stated in the bylaws are more likely to need changing from time to time.

Electing Officers

Your group's constitution and bylaws will state the officers to elect and their duties. Knowing the duties expected of various offices will help you nominate people qualified to handle the jobs if elected. See 8-11.

Different groups nominate candidates for offices in different ways. Some groups simply accept nominations from the

8-11
A group's constitution will describe the duties of the group's president and other officers.

members during a business meeting. Other groups have interested persons submit requests to run for offices. Many groups have a nominating committee that prepares a list of candidates to present to the full membership. In every case, members vote to determine the winners.

In addition to officers, most groups need to elect or appoint chairpersons for the *standing*, or permanent, committees. Membership, publicity, and fund-raising committees are examples of standing committees. Your group's method for selecting chairpersons will be described in your bylaws. Some groups elect all committee chairpersons. In other groups, the president or a committee appoints chairpersons.

Chairpersons are also needed for ad hoc committees. An *ad hoc committee* is one that is appointed to perform a specific task. When that task is completed, the committee dissolves. A committee to plan this year's homecoming float is an example of an ad hoc committee.

Holding a Meeting

Most groups follow guidelines to help them conduct meetings in an orderly fashion. The guidelines most often used by groups are called **parliamentary procedure**. Using parliamentary procedure, a meeting usually begins with a call to order. Then the minutes of the last meeting are read. The *minutes* are an official record of what took place at the meeting. The minutes are followed by reports from standing and ad hoc committees. Any unfinished business from the previous meeting is discussed next. Finally, the group discusses any new items of business.

Before a group can take action, members must vote. Before the vote, a motion must be made. A *motion* is a suggestion to take action. One group member makes a motion and another member seconds it. To *second* a motion means to show support for it. After a motion has been made and seconded, group members have an opportunity to discuss the motion. Under parliamentary procedure, the discussion must focus on the topic of the motion. Only one person can speak at a time. All members must be given an equal opportunity to state their opinions. During the discussion, a member may move to *amend*, or change, the motion. When the discussion is over, a vote is taken. The group must follow the decision of the *majority*, 8-12. Usually a majority equals half the total number of members present plus one.

8-12
Group decisions are reached by a majority vote.

Choosing Effective Programs and Activities

Some people join organizations because they need outlets for their energy and ideas. Unfortunately, it seems there are never enough of these people. According to research, about 10 percent of the members in a typical group do most of the work. About 80 percent tag along and enjoy belonging to the group. The other 10 percent criticize and complain about what is being done.

As a leader, your job is to be sure to keep the interest of the active members and involve the others more. If you succeed, your group will be doing better than most. As you work toward this goal, try not to let the criticism of a few members squelch your enthusiasm.

The key to keeping members involved is planning good activities. The activities of a group should be planned around one main goal for the year. The goal should relate to the personal needs and priorities of group members. It should make a difference in the lives of the members. Having one main goal provides a standard for measuring the group's progress throughout the year. It also creates a focus that builds interest.

A good way to involve members in establishing a group goal is through the planning process. See 8-13. It was developed by Family, Career and Community Leaders of America and is widely used by their chapters. However, the planning process will work equally well with any group. It is not a foolproof formula for a successful project. Rather, it is a process designed to get your group started. You may need to rearrange, revise, or repeat the steps to make the process work for you.

Group Planning Process

Identify Concerns

Discuss concerns related to a problem that bothers your group, such as:
- If youth in your community are littering, why?
- What does littering have to do with your group?
- How are littered areas currently being cleaned?
- What is currently being done to reduce the littering problem?
- What effects does littering have on the community as a whole?

Set Your Goal

Narrow down your concerns. Decide what you can realistically do and set a goal, such as:
- Design materials to help other youth make intelligent decisions about littering.
- Develop a campaign to promote the understanding of the need for a clean environment.
- Volunteer in civic cleanup programs.

Form a Plan

Decide the *who, what, when, where,* and *how* of your project:
- Consider how to finance your project, who to reach, how to reach them, what resources to develop, and how to publicize your project.

Act

Put your plan into action:
- Make a workable timetable to keep track of your progress. Revise it if and when necessary.

Follow Up

Evaluate:
- Evaluate your efforts as you work on your project. Learn from your mistakes as well as from your successes. Make changes when necessary.

8-13

The steps of this planning process can help any group plan a project. An example is shown for studying the problem of littering.

A group's goal can be represented in every program and activity. For instance, your group's goal might be to improve communications. Programs could be built around ways to communicate with people. Emphasis could be placed not only on verbal communication, but also on body language, music, and poetry. A fund-raising project might be selling note cards or stationery. A related activity could be becoming pen pals with people of other cultures. You might sponsor a fashion show that features clothes that communicate. You could communicate food customs by preparing international dishes. Going on a picnic with preschoolers might help you improve your communication with children. Although the activities are varied, they all relate to communication. Questions that guide the selection of programs and activities appear in 8-14.

Selecting Programs and Activities

Is this program or activity consistent with the overall purposes of the group?

Will it help us attain our goals?

In what ways will members benefit?

In what ways will others benefit?

Will the program or activity be enjoyable?

Can it be completed within a reasonable length of time?

Will it provide opportunities for members to grow as individuals?

Will all people who wish to work on this program or activity be permitted to do so?

Will it be so difficult that members will become discouraged?

Will this program or activity provide a break from the usual routine?

8-14

Asking these questions can help group members select worthwhile programs and activities for their organization.

Stay Within the Limits

All groups have to operate within limits. You have limited amounts of time and money to spend on activities. You have a limited number of members who can participate. In order to have a successful group, you must avoid planning projects that are beyond your resources.

Certain school rules often limit what a group can and cannot do. When planning programs and activities, it is important for your group to follow these rules. You should not do anything that jeopardizes your group's relationship with others. You want to keep on good terms with other groups in your school. You need to preserve the respect of school officials. You also need to maintain the support of the community.

If you have concerns about whether or not your group is operating within the rules, investigate before proceeding. Sometimes the limits can be stretched a bit to accommodate special situations. However, it is best to get approval in advance. Your group is likely to suffer negative consequences if it tries stretching the limits without permission.

There may be times when your group cannot do something you want it to do. Accept the facts. Part of learning about group participation is learning to cope with disappointments.

Publicize

You need to let people know about your group's exciting programs and activities. Your group should have a publicity committee to help get the word out. Publicizing your group's plans can also attract new members to the group. Publicity can help build support for your group in the community, too.

You may want to announce upcoming events in your school and local newspapers. If you plan something very newsworthy, you might want to contact local radio and TV stations. The yearbook is another important place to publicize school groups. If your group is part of a national organization, you might submit stories for their state and national publications. Once you start, you will find many interesting ways to publicize your group. See 8-15.

At the beginning of the year, get the names of contact people at newspaper offices and media stations. Ask these people to describe the types of information they want to receive. This will help you know how to prepare material and where to send it when events are happening.

Be sure your announcements include all the information needed to enable people to participate. Tell who sponsors the

8-15

A display is an effective way to publicize past projects and attract interest in the group.

event. Describe the plans and state when and where the event takes place. Pictures make news articles more interesting. When possible, include a large black-and-white glossy photo with your story. Be sure to identify the people in the photo. This type of publicity does more than attract the attention of people outside the group. It also increases the pride group members feel for their organization.

Evaluate Your Accomplishments

Make a point of evaluating your group's programs and activities. Check to see how much your group has accomplished toward achieving your goal. Groups that do not take time to do this miss one of the real satisfactions of work. You may be surprised at all you have done.

Evaluating your accomplishments can help you improve in the future. As you think back, try to remember some activities

that sounded great but did not work. Discuss why those activities failed. Discuss how your group can prevent similar failures in the future.

Did you have some projects that were not as great as they could have been? Was more careful planning needed? Did you have too few resources? Were some committees too busy? Were some committees bored? Asking these questions will help you determine how the group can have more success with future projects. See 8-16.

8-16

One way to evaluate the success of a charity fundraiser is to count the number of participants and amount of contributions raised.

Check It Out!

1. What is the purpose of most youth organizations?
2. List five types of information an effective constitution should include.
3. What is the key to keeping members involved in a group?

Topic 8-3

Your Rights and Responsibilities as a Citizen

Objectives

After studying this topic, you will be able to

▼ explain the importance of being an informed citizen and exercising your right to vote.

▼ summarize the role of the court system in interpreting public and civil laws.

▼ describe several types of taxes.

▼ list conservation measures you can take to help protect the environment.

▼ consider why community involvement is important to individuals, especially teens.

Topic Terms

public law
misdemeanor
felonies
civil law
progressive tax
direct tax
indirect tax
volunteers

School groups are not the only place where you have the opportunity to be a leader. You can also be a leader in your community in your role as a citizen.

You are a citizen of your city or town, your state, and your country. As a citizen, you have certain rights and responsibilities. You have a right to enjoy the freedoms that are protected by laws. You have the responsibilities of becoming informed, voting, obeying laws, paying taxes, and protecting the environment. Fulfilling your responsibilities will help you protect your rights and the rights of others.

To Be Informed

You have a right to information about the world around you. You have a responsibility to use that information to be an informed citizen.

Laws and government policy affect how you live. You need to be aware of how new and revised laws and policies might affect your rights and the rights of others. For instance, a change in the education policy could affect the schools you attend. Factors in the economy can limit your ability to find a job and purchase goods and services. New environmental standards will affect the air you breathe and the water you drink. International events can alter your sense of security.

As an informed citizen, you can work to resist negative conditions and make positive changes. When you are knowledgeable, you can speak to other citizens about issues that concern you. You can write to your political leaders to express your views. By being informed, you can take steps to defend your rights. See 8-17.

To Vote

Voting is both a right and a responsibility. It is a privilege to be able to help choose your government leaders. People in many nations do not have that freedom. It is your duty to cast your ballot on election days. If you do not vote, you will be letting other people choose your leaders for you.

Many people do not exercise their right to vote. A lack of information keeps them from knowing the candidates and

8-17
Citizens can stay informed of their rights and responsibilities by researching laws and government policy in a library or on the Internet.

their views. You can avoid this problem by reading newspapers and watching the news on TV. Find out what the issues are. Make a point of learning how candidates stand on the issues. You will then be able to determine which candidate's views are most like yours. This will help you know how to cast your vote.

Registering to Vote

If you are 18 years old and a United States citizen, you may register to vote. Registering puts your name on a list showing that you are allowed to vote in a certain place.

You are responsible for registering to vote. Even if you are eligible to vote, you will not be able to do so unless you register. In most states, you must register about

30 days before an election in order to vote. Once you have registered, however, you will not need to register again unless you move. You can find out where to register in your area by contacting your local government offices.

To Obey the Law

Although people sometimes complain about laws, life would be chaos without them. You have a right to the benefits that laws provide. You have a responsibility to obey laws that govern your behavior. For instance, you have a legal right to a public education. However, you also have a legal responsibility to attend school until you reach a certain age.

Public Laws

Two main categories of laws govern people in the United States. These are public laws and civil laws. **Public laws** govern the relationship between people and their government.

Criminal Laws

Criminal laws are a type of public law. They protect citizens from acts that are considered wrong or unfair. Traffic violations and kidnapping are examples of such crimes. In criminal law, the government is always the *prosecution*, or accuser. The person being charged with the crime is called the *defendant*.

Criminal cases involve two kinds of crimes—misdemeanors and felonies. **Misdemeanors** are minor criminal offenses. Speeding, disorderly conduct, and petty theft are misdemeanors, 8-18. The punishment for such crimes may be a fine or short jail sentence.

Serious crimes are called **felonies**. Rape, robbery, murder, and arson are felonies. The punishment for most

8-18
In some states, driving a car without wearing a safety belt is a misdemeanor.

felonies is a long prison sentence. In some states, the most serious felonies may be punishable by death.

Civil Laws

The other main category of laws is **civil law**. This area of law deals with disputes between private citizens. Divorce suits and contract disagreements are examples of cases involving civil laws. In civil law, the person making the complaint is the *plaintiff*. The other party is known as the *defendant*.

Every person has the right to protection by both civil and criminal law. Every person has the responsibility to obey the law. When people obey the law, they protect one another without the need for court action. Because people do not always act responsibly and follow the law, the court system stands ready to hear cases and make rulings that uphold the law.

The Court System

The U.S. Constitution and the constitutions of the various states established the court system. This system gives courts the power to review and settle disagreements about civil laws. It also gives them the power to try and punish people for disobeying criminal laws.

There are two separate court systems in the United States. *Federal courts* primarily hear cases dealing with federal law. *State courts* hear most criminal and civil cases involving people within a state. There are several different types of courts in both the state and federal court systems. The nature of a case determines the type of court that hears it. See 8-19. Cases are first heard in *trial courts*. A judge or a jury may decide trial cases. People who disagree with verdicts reached in trial courts can take their cases to an *appellate court*. A panel of judges who reach a decision by majority vote hears appeals. The judges look for legal errors that might have occurred during the previous trial. If they find such errors, they have the power to reverse the previous verdict.

Small Claims Court

Minor disputes over small amounts of money may be settled in small claims court. These courts are rather informal. Plaintiffs and defendants present their cases directly to a judge. Lawyers are not necessary and court fees are low. This makes small claims court an affordable option for most people.

To Pay Taxes

Like laws, people often complain about taxes. Also like laws, taxes are needed to create the type of society to which U.S. citizens have grown accustomed. Federal,

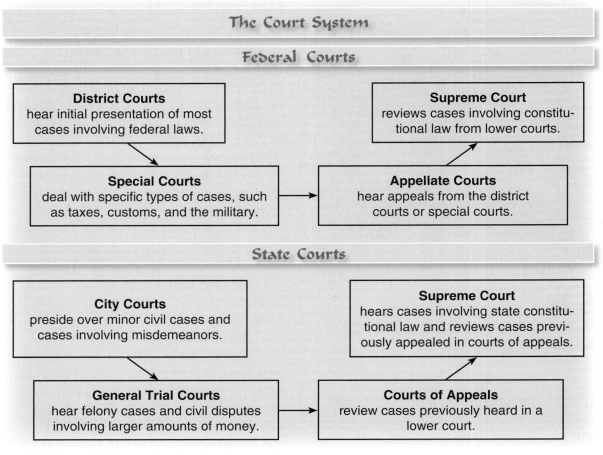

The Court System

Federal Courts

District Courts
hear initial presentation of most cases involving federal laws.

Special Courts
deal with specific types of cases, such as taxes, customs, and the military.

Supreme Court
reviews cases involving constitutional law from lower courts.

Appellate Courts
hear appeals from the district courts or special courts.

State Courts

City Courts
preside over minor civil cases and cases involving misdemeanors.

General Trial Courts
hear felony cases and civil disputes involving larger amounts of money.

Supreme Court
hears cases involving state constitutional law and reviews cases previously appealed in courts of appeals.

Courts of Appeals
review cases previously heard in a lower court.

8-19
Each level of the state and federal court systems handles different kinds of cases.

state, and local governments collect taxes. Tax dollars are used to pay for national defense, postal services, health inspection services, and police and fire protection. Roads, parks, and schools are all funded by taxes, 8-20.

As a citizen, you have a right to the services provided by tax dollars. You also have a responsibility to pay taxes. Monitoring the fairness of tax laws is both a right and a responsibility.

Types of Taxes

A number of different taxes are collected to generate money for government services, 8-21. These taxes can be classified in different ways. Some taxes are **progressive taxes**. In other words, as the item being taxed increases, the rate of tax increases. For instance, income tax is a progressive tax. The more you earn, the higher is the percentage of tax you pay.

8-20
Parks are just one of many public facilities that are funded by tax dollars.

Direct taxes are those charged directly to the people who are to pay them. Sales tax is an example of a direct tax. **Indirect taxes** are included in the price of taxed items. Excise tax is an example of an indirect tax. To get an idea of how these taxes affect citizens, consider the following example. Suppose gasoline and antifreeze both cost $2.50 a gallon. Excise tax of 20 cents a gallon is *included* in the price of the gasoline. However, a sales tax of 6 percent is *added* onto the price of the antifreeze. Therefore, you will have to pay $2.50 for a gallon of gasoline. A gallon of the antifreeze, on the other hand, will cost you $2.65.

To Protect the Environment

You are not just a citizen of a city, state, and nation. You are also a citizen of the world. As such, you have a right to live in a clean, healthy environment. You also have a responsibility to help keep your environment clean and healthy.

Protecting the environment means doing your part to help keep the air and water supply clean. It also means conserving the land and its resources. See 8-22.

Measures you can take to protect the environment include using environmentally safe products. Choose nontoxic cleaning agents and biodegradable detergents. Use rechargeable batteries.

Waste from product packaging takes up a lot of space in landfills. You can lessen the environmental impact of packaging by following the slogan *reduce, reuse, recycle*. Reduce the amount of packaging material you bring home by choosing products with minimal packaging. For instance, select unpackaged fruits and vegetables instead of produce sold on foam trays wrapped in plastic. Reuse empty product containers whenever possible. Recycle as many product containers as possible. Glass, metal, paperboard, and many plastics can be recycled into other materials.

Types of Taxes

Income tax	Provides the greatest source of government income. The tax is deducted from a worker's paycheck. Income tax is also collected on sources of income, such as investment dividends and interest.
Social Security tax	Is paid jointly by employers and employees. The employee's portion is deducted from each paycheck. This tax provides income to those no longer working because they reach retirement age or become disabled. It also provides survivor's benefits to a worker's dependents.
Sales tax	Is collected by some state and local governments. It is added to the cost of many goods and services when purchases are made.
Excise tax	Is included in the price of specific items and services. Gasoline and cigarettes are among the items on which excise taxes are paid.
Property tax	Is levied by state and local governments on real estate and personal property, such as cars, boats, and jewelry. It is paid by property owners, but is included as part of the rent charged on leased properties.

8-21
Different types of taxes pay for a wide range of government services.

Conservation measures at home can help save electricity, gas, and water. You can preserve limited natural resources by turning off lights, television, and other power-operated items not being used.

8-22
FCCLA members pick up trash around their school and in other areas of their community.

When no one is home, adjust your heat and air conditioner settings accordingly. Take short showers to save water. Be aware of how much water is running needlessly when brushing teeth and shaving. Make sure the dishwasher is full before running it. Always adjust the clothes washer's water level to each load. Walk, ride a bicycle, use public transportation, or carpool to reduce the use of gasoline. Always try to take the most direct route when driving.

To Be Involved in Your Community

Taxes provide most of the public services needed, but never stretch far enough to cover everything. This is why volunteers are welcomed in many government and nonprofit agencies. **Volunteers** are people who provide valuable services by offering their time, talents, and energy free of charge.

People who become involved in their communities take pride in them. They enjoy knowing they make a positive contribution. Such contributions can make the community more beautiful, such as freshly painted park benches, litter-free sidewalks, and holiday decorations. Volunteering also makes a noticeable difference in people's lives. Examples include making food baskets for the needy and helping people learn to read.

Most communities have a roster of volunteer opportunities available. However, you might see a specific need and simply inform the people in charge that you want to fill it. Think about your interests and abilities in deciding where you want to devote your efforts. That will lead you to find a volunteer opportunity that matches your enthusiasm.

Volunteering can benefit you in more ways than you imagine. You learn more about your community and your neighbors. You meet new friends and receive the personal satisfaction of seeing that your help really matters. You also perfect your skills and can also gain new skills.

Volunteering can help you determine your career interests. By gaining firsthand experience in related areas, you can better decide which direction in life appeals most to you. For example, if your interests include working with children and oil painting, you could seek a job that includes both. Some possible jobs that merge these interests are likely found in community recreation programs and local child care centers. If your interests change, you can always shift to other types of volunteer work to explore new areas.

Your volunteer experience will be a valuable asset when you try to obtain your first job. See 8-23. First-time job seekers who have no previous job experience to report can always list their volunteer work. Such work is just as important to employers as job experience gained in a paid position. Also, some of the people you help by volunteering may keep you informed of job openings in your field of interest. They can vouch for your ability to do a good job to a potential employer you may want to impress. They may even offer you a full-time job when you leave school.

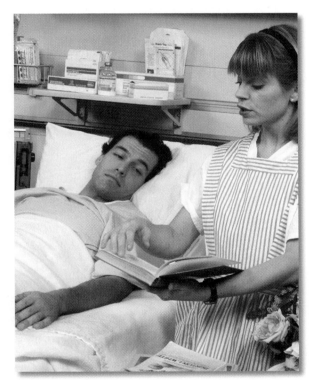

8-23

In addition to the job skills learned while volunteering, you also develop important interpersonal skills by working with the general public and cooperating with coworkers.

Later, when you meet the age requirement, you may wish to serve on a local committee or run for an elective office. Most of the big issues affecting a community are resolved in the political arena. The many different roles of public service are important, and dedicated people are always needed to fill them.

Setting the Scene: Volunteering for the Future

You do not have an after-school job, but you know the importance of having work experience to list on college and job applications. You are considering doing some volunteer work in your community instead. This could be a fun and meaningful opportunity to help others while building an attractive resume.

Analyze It: What factors should you consider in choosing the best volunteer options for yourself? How will you benefit from the experience now? How might volunteer work help you get a job later? How might it help you identify your future career goals?

Check It Out!

1. What requirements must a person meet to register to vote in the United States?
2. Minor criminal offenses are called _____. Serious crimes are called _____.
3. List five services provided by tax dollars.
4. What steps can citizens take to lessen the environmental impact of waste from product packaging?
5. State three results of volunteering that can help teens get a full-time job in the future.

Chapter Review

Summary

Both leaders and followers are needed to create teams. An effective team is the result of committed members who put team goals first. Diversity among team members is viewed as a positive factor instead of a negative influence that divides the team. Through teamwork, members can develop leadership skills.

Leaders are likely to use a combination of autocratic, democratic, and laissez-faire leadership styles. Leaders are expected to set an example to motivate group members. They need to use tact and give recognition as they guide group planning as well.

As a teen, you may belong to one or more youth organizations. You may join a professional organization when you enter the workplace. These and all organizations need to follow some guidelines in order to be effective. Groups need to elect officers who will hold meetings and plan worthwhile programs and activities. Group events need to be publicized to generate interest and evaluated to improve future planning.

Leadership skills used in youth and professional groups are also used by citizens in the community. As a citizen, you have a responsibility to be informed, vote, and obey laws. You also have a responsibility to pay taxes and protect the environment. Performing these tasks will help you protect your personal and legal rights. Volunteering allows you to give back to your community. It can also help you gain experience and friendships that will be beneficial in getting a job in the future.

Think About It!

1. Describe an instance when you filled the role of a follower. How did you act in that role? Then describe an instance when you filled the role of a leader. How did you act in that role?
2. What type of leadership would you recommend in each of the following situations? Explain your choices.
   A. Organizing the planting of a vegetable garden with a group of young 4-H members who have no prior gardening experience.
   B. Planning a fund-raiser for a church youth group.
   C. Serving as a campaign manager for a friend who is running for a seat on the student council.
   D. Teaching a new play to a football team.
3. Imagine you are the captain of the volleyball team that is selling candy to raise money. As an effective leader, explain how you might set an example, motivate followers, guide planning, use tact, and give recognition for this project.
4. Imagine that your Family, Career and Community Leaders of America chapter has a concern about traffic along Main Street where young children walk to school. Use the planning process described in Figure 8-13 to form a plan that addresses this concern.
5. What rights do you value most as a citizen? What responsibilities can you fulfill to help protect those rights?
6. Write a brief reaction to this statement: taxes should be abolished.

7. Why should protecting the environment be a global effort rather than a local effort?
8. In what ways can leadership skills be helpful to homemakers? In what other careers do you see leadership skills being particularly helpful?

Try It Out!

1. Read a biography or an autobiography of a famous leader. Share the story with your classmates. Work together to identify the leadership style he or she used most often. Also list the leadership skills the leader used to involve his or her followers.
2. Present a brief skit to the class to illustrate a good leadership skill.
3. Make a list of extrinsic motivators you think would be most effective for people in your age group.
4. Work in a small group to investigate the rules of parliamentary procedure. Role-play the proper use of parliamentary procedure for discussing an issue and taking a vote at a meeting.
5. Contact the office of a local newspaper or radio station. Find out what format an announcement for a school club event should follow. Prepare an announcement in the proper format, making sure you include all necessary information. Exchange your announcement with a classmate for critiquing.
6. Design a poster encouraging citizens to fulfill one of their responsibilities.
7. Complete each of the following sentences:
   A. I will know and exercise my rights and responsibilities as a citizen because…
   B. I will be an informed citizen because…
   C. I will be a voting citizen because…
   D. I will be a law-abiding citizen because…
   E. I will be a tax-paying citizen because…
   F. I will protect the environment because…
   G. I will become a volunteer because…
   H. I will run for elective office some day because…

Chapter 9
Job Readiness Skills

Careers

These careers relate to the topics in this chapter:

▼ human resources assistant
▼ personnel assistant
▼ career counselor
▼ training director

As you study the chapter, see if you can think of others.

Topics

9-1 Career Planning
9-2 Finding a Job
9-3 Succeeding on the Job

191

Topic 9-1
Career Planning

Objectives

After studying this topic, you will be able to
▼ explain how your interests, aptitudes, and abilities relate to your career choices.
▼ identify resources used for career planning.
▼ determine factors to consider in making career decisions.

Topic Terms

job
career
interests
aptitude
abilities
job shadowing
cooperative education
apprenticeship
Tech prep
internship
mentor
career plan

Are you ready for the world of work? Have you thought about what type of career you want to pursue after you graduate? Do you know what types of jobs can help you reach your career goal? Now is the time to begin thinking more seriously about your career options.

How will you match yourself with the career that is right for you? In this topic, you will take a closer look at all the factors affecting your career choice so you can make a wiser decision. Your career choice will require careful thought and planning. After all, it will have long-term effects on your future lifestyle.

How do you get started in planning a career? You begin by evaluating yourself. What interests you? What do you do well? Then you gather career information through different sources and explore the options that interest you.

Understanding Career Planning

As you begin your career planning, you will hear the terms *job* and *career*. Do you know the difference between them? The meanings are easily confused. Understanding the difference is important.

If you work now, your **job** is whatever you do to earn a living. Your job consists of many tasks—all the duties you perform while you work. Perhaps you wait on customers, take inventory, and operate a cash register. Other people who have the same type of job would do similar tasks. See 9-1.

9-1
Anyone who rings up merchandise must be able to work the cash register.

A career is a much broader concept than a job. Your **career** will be a series of jobs you hold over a period of years, often in the same or a related field. Through career planning, each job you have will help you prepare for your career goal. During your career, you may change jobs several times. As your career progresses, you may be promoted to higher-level positions and your responsibilities may increase. Career-focused planning in high school will help you gain insights into the skills and education needed for the career of your choice. You will then know what courses will best correlate with your career plans.

9-2
People who prefer working with children would probably not be happy working with computers.

Know Your Interests, Aptitudes, and Abilities

Start your career planning by getting to know yourself better. Evaluate your interests, aptitudes, and abilities. This will help you make a more satisfying career choice.

Your Interests

The first step in career planning is to identify your interests. Your **interests** are all the activities you like to do. What do you most enjoy doing? How do you spend your free time? What hobbies do you like? What subjects most interest you in school? Your answers to these questions are important. These preferences, which are based in part on your personal priorities, will affect your career choice. See 9-2. Once you recognize what brings you satisfaction, you can look at jobs that would provide the same type of satisfaction.

You can learn more about your interests by taking an *activities preference inventory*.

Most school guidance departments can give this type of test to students. The test is designed to help you determine if you prefer working with people, objects, or ideas. Most jobs fit into one of these areas.

The inventory is like a multiple-choice test. You are given several choices and must select the one choice that most appeals to you. After completing the test, you are given a key to score yourself. The results will give you some ideas about your main interests relating to people, objects, or ideas. If the inventory shows you enjoy working with people, you might like a career in sales, social work, teaching, or nursing. If you enjoy working with objects and tools, you might enjoy constructing buildings, sewing, or operating office or laboratory equipment. If you enjoy planning or evaluating projects more than actually doing them, you enjoy working with ideas. A career in research, marketing, or publishing might be best for you. Although you should look for a career that deals with your main interests, many jobs involve all three areas. For instance, sales associates work mostly with people, but they must have objects to sell and ideas about how to sell them.

Your Aptitudes

You need to have more than an interest in a career to be successful in it. You also need an aptitude for it. **Aptitude** is your natural talent and your potential for learning. When you have an aptitude for a certain skill, you can learn the skill easily and perform it well.

Aptitudes are often related to job success, 9-3. If you have a natural talent for writing, you would have a good chance for success in a journalism career. If you have an aptitude for working with numbers, perhaps you could become a successful accountant. On the other hand, if you do not have an aptitude for music, a singing career might not be your best choice.

Aptitudes are often tested in schools. The guidance counselor can discuss your test scores if you want to know more about your aptitudes. Keep in mind, however, the results will not give you definite answers to your career questions. They will not

tell you that you will be a success in one field and a failure in another. Rather, the results will indicate your strong areas. That information will give you an idea of the kinds of careers in which you have the best chances for success.

Your Abilities

Although you have certain natural aptitudes, you must develop your abilities. **Abilities** are your powers to perform. They are your skills in doing tasks. You develop your abilities through training and practicing. See 9-4. Abilities may be mental or physical. For example, you may have the ability to easily solve complex math problems or to be a gymnast.

Developing an ability to perform a task is easier if you have an interest and an aptitude. However, a strong interest and hard work can help to overcome low aptitudes.

9-3
A person with a musical aptitude may quickly learn to play an instrument.

9-4
With advanced training and education, you could develop the abilities needed for a health-related career.

Interests, aptitudes, and abilities are interrelated. When considered together, they help indicate several possible career choices that would suit you well. Ideally, you will select a career that addresses your interests and uses your aptitudes and abilities.

Learn About Careers

When you have a better understanding of yourself, you can begin considering careers that interest you. If you wonder how to find the career that is best for you, the answer may be found through research.

Taking advantage of the many resources available will help you make the choice that is right for you.

Career Information Resources

Many school and community resources are available to help you learn more about careers. Talking with people and gathering information at the library are two ways to get started.

Talk with People

People are valuable sources of career information. Begin with yourself. Have you had a job? If so, did you like it? What did you most like about the job? What did you dislike? Would you like a career that is somehow related to that job?

Your friends, relatives, neighbors, and other people in the working world are good resources. Ask them about their jobs. This will help you learn about different jobs. Ask how they chose their careers. What are the good and the bad points of their jobs? As you talk with others, consider which types of jobs you might enjoy.

Talking with a school guidance counselor about your interests, aptitudes, abilities, and career goals may be helpful, 9-5. The counselor can answer your questions about career opportunities. He or she can tell you about the education and experience needed for various careers. The counselor can suggest several schools that offer programs in your area of interest. Most counselors have files of career information from various schools. They may even set up meetings for you with recruiters from various schools.

Use Library Resources

Most libraries are rich sources of career information. Look in both school and public libraries. A good place to begin your research is the computer subject index or

9-5

School guidance counselors often assist students in making career decisions.

the card catalog. Look under *careers, jobs,* or *vocations* for general information. If you are interested in a certain field, such as nursing or electronics, look under that topic.

Another library resource is the *Readers' Guide to Periodical Literature,* which indexes magazine articles. It lists the articles that appear in major magazines by subject, such as employment or careers. Each reference gives the title of the article, the name and date of the magazine, and the page number. The advantage of magazine articles is that they have current information.

Check the reference section for career information guides. These guides help people explore career options and identify occupations of interest. One commonly used guide is the *Occupational Outlook Handbook,* published by the U.S. Department of Labor (DOL). It gives information about occupations, training requirements, expected earnings, work conditions, and future job prospects.

The DOL provides the latest information on today's occupations through an online database called the O*Net. This valuable information can be accessed at online.onetcenter.org. The O*Net describes the occupations and the training and education requirements for each.

Exploring Careers in Family and Consumer Sciences

Exploring different career options now will help you make a future career choice. Have you thought about using the skills you have gained in this course in your career? If so, you may want to take a closer look at family and consumer sciences.

The field of family and consumer sciences is devoted to improving the quality of individual and family life. Careers in this field are often divided into six smaller groups according to subject matter. They are

▼ child development and family relations
▼ foods, nutrition, and hospitality
▼ money management and consumerism
▼ textiles and clothing
▼ housing and interior design
▼ education and communication

The chart in 9-6 shows careers in family and consumer sciences at three different levels. The course you are taking now will help prepare you for an entry-level position, such as a caseworker's aide. One to two more years of training and education would prepare you for an intermediate-level position. A food service assistant or home health aide are examples. A four-year college degree is required for many professional positions, such as a teacher.

As the chart shows, you can choose careers within one career area, or *cluster* (group of related jobs). Suppose careers in textiles and clothing interest you. There are many choices. You could operate a sewing machine to tailor garments or make new clothes in your home. You could be a salesperson in a clothing store or a fashion buyer for a chain of stores. You could be a clothing and textiles teacher, fashion editor, apparel designer, or textile scientist.

Using Your Family and Consumer Sciences Skills

You will be able to use your skills in family and consumer sciences in whatever career you choose. If, however, you choose a career in this field, many of the same skills overlap into the six subject areas. For example, an extension specialist who teaches nutrition would have career skills in education as well as foods and nutrition. Even if you choose a career outside family and consumer sciences, you can use the skills you learn in this course both in your career and at home. For example, business careers related to marketing food products require knowledge of foods, business practices, and consumer trends. You may not want a career in food service or family services, but you will still need the abilities to cook for yourself and care for your own family.

Your Education Choices

As you learn more about various careers, you should consider the type and amount of education and training needed. How much education will you need to achieve your career goal? Is specialized training required? Finding the answers to these questions is the next step in the career planning process.

Today's workplace is a complex and competitive environment. It is wise to develop knowledge and skills that can be applied to several jobs since the job market keeps changing. New technologies are creating new jobs while making some traditional jobs *obsolete* (out-of-date). A good education offers a person many more job advantages, such as more interesting work with higher wages. Most jobs require extra training and education after high school.

Sources of Education

In Chapter 8, you learned that volunteering in your community could prepare you for the workplace. Holding a part-time job provides work experience, too. In addition to these job-learning opportunities, there are several other ways to learn about jobs firsthand.

Career Preparation During High School

Often students begin exploring career options through **job shadowing** programs. These give students knowledge of a particular career area through a one-day visit to a job. The student accompanies an experienced person to work and observes that person's activities. Teens are sometimes given opportunities to shadow parents for a day to develop a deeper understanding of their work responsibilities. Job shadowing can help teens improve their employability skills.

Some high school programs provide students with actual job experience in their respective fields of interest. These are called *work-based learning programs*. The programs combine classroom instruction with on-the-job experience.

There are several different types of work-based learning programs, but they share many qualities. For example, the student spends several hours per week both in the classroom and at a specified work site. Students receive school credits

Careers in Family and Consumer Sciences

	Child Development	Family Relations	Foods, Nutrition, and Hospitality
Entry-Level Positions	Babysitter Parent's helper Nursery school aide Child care center aide Playground assistant Camp counselor's aide	Homemaker's aide Caseworker's aide Senior citizens' center aide Camp counselor	Busperson Dishwasher Cook's helper Short-order cook Stock clerk Restaurant server Host Caterer's helper
Positions That Require More Training	Playground director Teacher's aide School food service worker Scout leader Recreational leader	Help-line counselor Counseling paraprofessional Senior citizens' center staff worker Youth services worker Homemaker services director	Dietitian's helper Food service manager Restaurant manager Food purchaser Sanitation supervisor Quality control supervisor Pastry and dessert chef Chef or chief cook Baker Restaurant owner Demonstrator
Positions That Require a College Degree	Nursery school teacher Designer of children's clothing, furniture, or toys Writer of children's books, stories, or games Child care center or nursery school administrator Child welfare worker	Social worker Crisis center counselor Family budget counselor Family/marriage therapist School counselor Family health counselor	Dietitian Executive chef Sales manager Marketing executive Advertising manager Caterer Editor or writer Food technologist Nutritionist Product developer Food stylist

(Continued)

9-6

You can obtain the skills needed for an entry-level position in a family and consumer sciences careers while still in high school. With additional training and education, you can advance to higher-level positions.

Careers in Family and Consumer Sciences

Money Management and Consumerism	Fashion and Apparel	Housing and Interior Design	Education and Communications
Consumer affairs aide Consumer survey assistant Office worker Consumer product tester assistant	Stock clerk Salesclerk Cashier Alterationist's assistant Laundry attendant Display assistant Clothing repair specialist Fabric salesperson	Upholsterer's helper Designer's aide Home lighting aide Home furnishings salesperson	Babysitter Nursery school assistant Youth counselor
Consumer service representative Consumer product specialist assistant Credit bureau research clerk Loan officer assistant Bank teller Collection agent	Sewing machine operator Presser/finisher Buyer Fashion photographer Fashion writer Store manager Dry cleaner Alterationist Tailor/reweaver	Drapery/slipcover maker Designer's assistant Upholstery and carpet cleaner Appliance/furnishings salesperson Home lighting designer Real estate agent	Teacher's aide 4-H leader
Retail credit manager Money investment adviser Consumer survey specialist Consumer affairs director Loan officer Consumer product specialist Consumer money management director Financial planner	Fashion designer Textile designer Marketing specialist Market researcher Display artist Researcher or tester Clothing consultant Merchandise manager	Textile designer Kitchen designer Home furnishings adviser Home furnishings editor Home furnishings buyer Interior designer Merchandising specialist Home service director Public housing consultant Home planning specialist	High school family and consumer sciences teacher Family and consumer sciences professor Curriculum specialist County extension agent Adult educator

for their work experience. Usually they receive pay, too, but not always. The student's on-the-job training is carefully supervised. The program coordinator, usually one of your teachers, makes sure all key parties support the student's training agreement. Key parties include the school, employer, student, and the student's parents or guardians. Work-based learning programs include the following:

▼ **Cooperative education**, frequently called a co-op program, prepares students for an occupation immediately after high school through a paid job experience.

▼ **Apprenticeship** programs provide training for a skilled trade. Apprenticeships usually require a legal agreement that you will work for the employer for a designated length of time in exchange for the instruction.

▼ **Tech prep**, or the technical preparation education program, often combines two years of high school courses with two years of postsecondary education. This program of study prepares students for a wide range of technical careers.

▼ An **internship** offers paid or unpaid work experience to learn about a job or industry. An internship is usually a more advanced program of study.

At the job site, a supervisor is responsible for the student's performance, 9-7. The supervisor may appoint an

9-7
On the job, students will learn from a supervisor or mentor.

employee to train the student or may choose to do the training alone. A person who knows how to do the job and teaches the student to do it well is called a **mentor**. This person often answers the student's day-to-day questions.

Career Preparation After High School

Sometimes high school graduates obtain job experience by joining the military. Others may gain job experience by volunteering for the Peace Corps or a similar organization. Usually, though, graduates go on to schools of higher education to prepare for their careers.

▼ *Professional schools* offer training in a specialized field, such as becoming a chef, fashion designer, or computer technician. Schooling consists of classroom training and hands-on experience. You receive a certificate or diploma at the end of the course. You may be required to pass a test to receive a license to work in the profession.

▼ *Community colleges* offer skills training or comprehensive programs. At the end of the two-year programs, students usually receive a certificate or associate degree. Community colleges offer many areas of study, which often reflect the job needs of the area. Graduates include medical and legal secretaries, child care workers, hairdressers, practical nurses, and hotel managers. See 9-8. Some students transfer to a university for additional education.

▼ Most *college* or *university programs* are designed for four years of study. They give students a broad background of general knowledge and extensive instruction in a specific subject. Bachelor's degrees are given in many categories. Examples are interior design, textiles and clothing, food and nutrition, counseling, journalism, computer technology, advertising, and education.

9-8
Students in community college programs can learn skills related to specific career areas, such as data processing and office administration.

Some companies offer on-the-job training to employees. Sometimes this training helps new employees learn the unique work methods and philosophy of their employer. At other times, on-the-job training prepares employees to handle more challenging jobs. However, when individuals are hired by a company, they already possess the skills they need for an entry-level job in their field.

Your education will be a major factor in determining your job choices. You need to choose the right type of education for the career you want.

Other Factors Affecting Your Career Choice

When making any career decision, you will consider many factors. First, you consider your interests, aptitudes, and abilities. Then, you consider the educational requirements and training needed. Finally, you will consider other important factors, such as your lifestyle, potential income, and working conditions.

Your Lifestyle

How will your career affect the way you live? In matching yourself to the right career, think about your desired lifestyle, 9-9. What personal priorities and goals are important to you? In addition to liking your job, consider the impact it will make on your future life. Where do you want to live? Some jobs may be easier to get in a large city or certain parts of the country. Do you plan to marry and have a family? If so, consider the working hours that will be required for some careers. If you value time with your family, would nighttime or long working hours interfere with your family life? Your friendships and how you spend your leisure time will also be affected.

9-9
If you are considering a career in retail sales, you may have to work longer hours. How will this affect your lifestyle?

Potential Income

Income is another factor to consider in your career choice. How much income do you want to earn? What income can you expect to earn in your chosen career? This will affect how much money you will have available to spend. Will it provide for personal and family needs? What is the income potential of this career?

Be cautious about making high income your top goal. Many people who achieve top-paying jobs do not find the satisfaction they expected. Their ties to their family, friends, and community often bring greater personal rewards. Obtaining a good income is a very worthwhile goal, but not if it replaces important goals in other areas of your life.

Working Conditions

Besides working hours, it is important to consider working conditions in your career choice. Are there certain environmental conditions to which you would object? For instance, would it bother you to work in noisy, dusty conditions? Would you prefer to work in a quiet office setting? Do you want the same type of responsibilities every day or a variety of tasks? Do you like a great deal of independence or constant team interaction? Every job has certain desirable and undesirable conditions. Your choice should be the most satisfying for you. See 9-10.

Consider the effect your career could have on your physical and mental health. Some careers are very stressful while others

9-10
What would you like most about working in this environment? What would you like least?

are not. Some people work well under intense pressure while other individuals do not. If stress reduces the quality of your productivity at work, it will probably affect your lifestyle as well.

Making a Career Decision

Choosing a career can be one of the hardest decisions to make. However, making a decision now will give you a head start on career planning. As a result, you will have a better idea of where you want to direct your life. You can start setting your career goals now and working toward them.

Throughout your working life, you will consider different jobs and even different careers. This is very common today. It is rare for a person to stay in the same job for a lifetime. Consider new opportunities as they arise and the career direction that is best for you at that time.

Making a Career Plan

As you explore your interests, aptitudes, and abilities, look for career options that seem to fit you. Once you decide what type of career you want to pursue, begin identifying what it will take to achieve that goal. A list of steps to follow to achieve a career goal is called a **career plan**. You would take a step every few years of your life, identifying the following for each step:

▼ job experience
▼ education and training
▼ extracurricular and volunteer activities

The chart in 9-11 shows a career plan for a person wanting to become a kindergarten teacher. It represents one of

The More You Know: Shaping a Career

It is easier to look back on a person's life and observe a common theme rather than identify what lies ahead. However, by making plans now, you can direct your life along the path you want. When new opportunities or interests arise, you can then adjust your plans.

Look at Beth's career changes. During high school, she worked as a salesclerk in a clothing store. She liked fashion and decided to study fashion design in an area college. She used her knowledge to create fashion displays for the store's merchandise. Her abilities in displaying fashions became useful when a local drama group needed help developing costumes for their play. As a hobby, Beth helped design the costumes for that play and several others. Soon she realized she wanted to know more about historical costume design. She went back to school for an advanced degree in clothing and textiles, with a specialization in historical clothing. After graduation, she took a job at her state's capitol building. She is now responsible for displaying and preserving her state's historical clothing collection. Beth's love of clothing fashion was the motivating force behind her career decisions. If her primary interest were salesmanship instead of fashion, her career would have taken a different course.

Career Plan for Kindergarten Teacher			
	Job Experience	Education and Training	Extracurricular and Volunteer Activities
During Junior High School	Babysitter	Choose topics related to early childhood education for extra credit or when subjects are optional.	Play with and help guide younger children in the family as well as the neighborhood.
During High School	Playground assistant	Take a college preparatory exam.	Teach neighborhood children to read better and enjoy team sports.
During College	Part-time nursery school aide	Obtain a bachelor's degree in elementary education with an emphasis in early childhood education. Also obtain a teacher's certificate.	Help direct activities at a summer camp.
After College	Kindergarten teacher	Consider obtaining an advanced degree (to become a teacher of kindergarten teachers).	Help develop preschool and after-school programs for young children.

9-11

A career plan is a guide to the career-related goals you want to accomplish in the foreseeable future.

many different career plans that could be developed to reach that same goal.

Every student can begin preparing for his or her career now by making a career plan. This is also the time to take the first step. Mapping a career plan on paper helps a person develop a course of action and stick to it.

A well-developed career plan can eliminate some of the frustration of planning a career because you always know where you want to go and what you need to do next. As with any other goal setting, you make a plan, implement it, and evaluate your progress along the way. You may want to adjust your plan as your interests or goals change.

Creating a Career Ladder

You can see how one job in a career field often leads to another. A career ladder illustrates this concept. The career ladder shown in 9-12 is for careers in child development. A student considering a career as a kindergarten teacher could also use it.

The bottom rung of the ladder shows jobs requiring little or no experience. Traveling up the ladder leads to related jobs of increasingly greater responsibility. You will notice that these jobs require more education and experience. The top of the ladder shows jobs that require education beyond a bachelor's degree—either a master's degree or a doctorate.

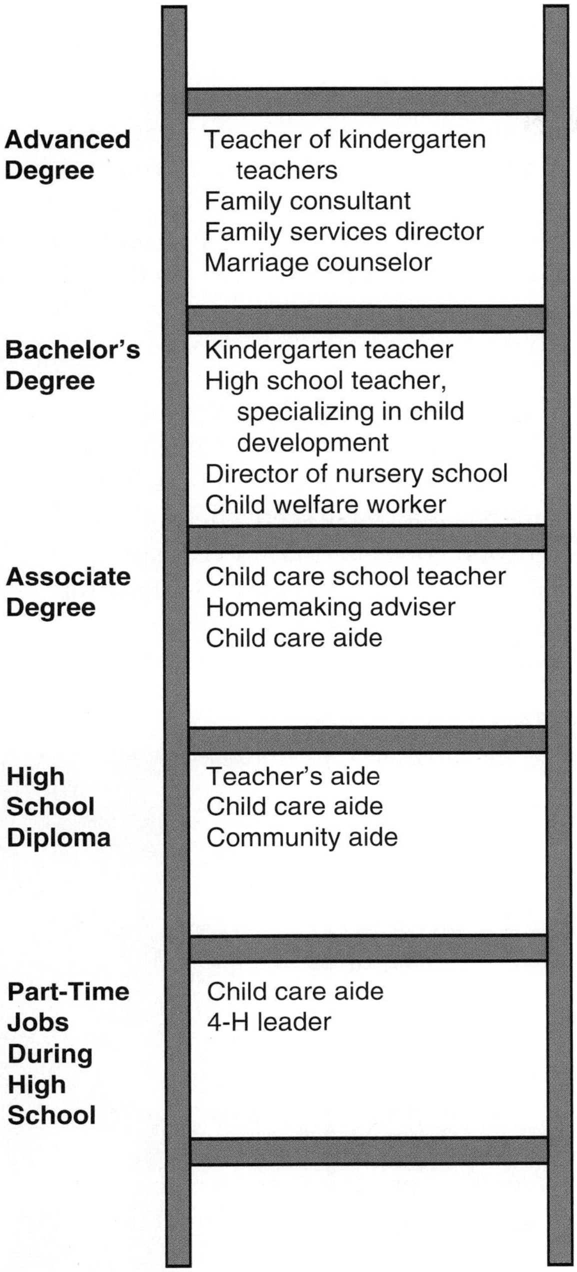

Advanced Degree	Teacher of kindergarten teachers Family consultant Family services director Marriage counselor
Bachelor's Degree	Kindergarten teacher High school teacher, specializing in child development Director of nursery school Child welfare worker
Associate Degree	Child care school teacher Homemaking adviser Child care aide
High School Diploma	Teacher's aide Child care aide Community aide
Part-Time Jobs During High School	Child care aide 4-H leader

9-12

This career ladder in child development shows how a person can advance from job to job.

As you make your career decisions, try to consider the overall picture. Try to make choices that will give you the greatest satisfaction. In doing so, you create the quality of life you desire.

Check It Out!

1. Explain how a person's interests, aptitudes, and abilities affect his or her job satisfaction.
2. List five sources of career information.
3. Name the six subject matter areas in the field of family and consumer sciences.
4. True or false. Most students receive a bachelor's degree after two years of study at a community college.
5. Besides interests, aptitudes, and abilities, name three other factors to consider in making a career decision.

Topic 9-2
Finding a Job

Objectives

After studying this topic, you will be able to
▼ describe sources used to find job openings.
▼ complete a job application form neatly and accurately.
▼ prepare for a successful job interview.
▼ list the advantages and disadvantages of being an entrepreneur.

Topic Terms

personal fact sheet
references
resume
entrepreneur

Once you have a career plan in mind, your next step is to find a job that fits it. Perhaps you would like to hold a part-time job while in high school. This can help you gain valuable skills and experience while you explore your career choice. Having a job provides some income and helps you learn job responsibilities and communication skills.

Finding a job takes work. You must make the effort to find job openings that fit your qualifications—do not wait for an employer to come to you! Next, you need to apply for positions that interest you. Finally, you must interview with an employer. If you receive a job offer, you must then decide whether to accept it.

Finding Job Openings

The first step in getting a job is finding job openings. How do you find an employer who is looking for a worker with your qualifications? Job openings can be found through a variety of sources. Some of the most common sources are listed here.

People

If you want a job, let people know. Tell everyone you know—your friends, parents, relatives, and neighbors. See 9-13. Someone may have seen a help-wanted sign. Someone else may have heard about a new business that is looking for employees. Another person may know about a job opening where he or she

9-13
Family and neighbors can be great resources when you start your job hunt.

works. Many personnel directors say the best information about a company's plans comes from current employees.

School

Your school can be another source of job leads. Some schools have job placement programs. If your school does not have one, contact a person who could help you. This could be a counselor, teacher, or the person in charge of community relations. These are the people that employers would probably call about job openings. If the key people in your school know you want a job, they can tell employers about you.

Want Ads

To get an idea of the job market in your area, look at the want ads in local newspapers. These ads are located in the classified section of the newspaper. They give brief descriptions of all kinds of jobs,

9-14. If you see an ad that interests you, respond right away. Job openings listed in want ads are often filled shortly after the ads appear.

The Internet

The Internet is one of the easiest places to find job openings all over the country. Companies may post jobs on their own Web sites. Newspapers usually have a Web site that includes the same want ads they print. In addition, many Web sites are devoted exclusively to job openings. These sites may even offer tips on preparing your resume and interviewing.

Employment Agencies

Going to an employment agency is a more formal approach to job hunting. State and federal agencies provide free employment services to job seekers. Private agencies may charge a fee for their services.

9-14
Reading the want ads in your local newspaper is one way of finding job leads.

State and Federal Employment Services

Check the telephone book for the location of your nearest state employment service office. Counselors there can review your education and experience. They can talk with you about job requirements and help you set realistic career goals. Placements are made for all kinds of jobs.

The Civil Service Commission is a federal agency. It hires the people who work for the United States government. Civil service jobs are available throughout the country. They are available in almost any line of work. To get a civil service job, you may be required to pass an exam. You must meet certain education and experience requirements. The requirements vary for different types of jobs. The placement services of the Civil Service Commission are free.

Military recruitment offices can be considered a type of employment agency. They offer jobs and careers. They also offer educational benefits and options for education that could lead to other careers.

Private Employment Agencies

Another option to consider is a private employment agency. These charge the employer or the job seeker a fee for their services. Most agencies are specialized. Some may handle just one type of job, such as office jobs. If an agency offers you a position, use caution. Read any contract that is offered to you carefully. Do not sign it until you understand all the terms of the agreement.

Direct Contact

If you want to work for a certain company, try a direct approach. Contact the head of the company or the personnel director. Write a letter, make a phone call, or visit the company in person. Sometimes a combination of methods works best. For instance, you may write a letter and follow it with a personal visit. The company and the situation will determine how you apply for work.

Applying for a Job

Before you apply for any job, you need to gather and organize some personal information about yourself. Write down this information neatly on a sheet of paper. Then you can take it with you whenever you fill out a job application. Your **personal fact sheet** should include your Social Security number, education, work experiences, skills, honors and activities, hobbies, and interests. Also list at least three **references**. These are people who know you well and can vouch for your good work. Good choices include a teacher, club adviser, former employer, or family friend. Ask in advance for permission to use their names.

When you find a job opening that interests you, apply for it. Depending on the type of position, this may be done by sending a letter of application and resume, using the telephone, or applying in person.

Sending a Letter of Application and Resume

For many jobs, you will need to write a letter of application to the person in charge of hiring. In it, be as brief and concise as possible. Begin by expressing your interest in the job. Then briefly describe your qualifications for the job opening. Finally, request an appointment to discuss your qualifications in person. Most good letters of application contain no more than three paragraphs.

Be sure to send a resume with your letter of application, 9-15. A **resume** is a

Terry C. Pinkham
204 Quail Run Road
Oak Park, TN 30241
(321) 555-4567

tpinkham@provider.com

Employment Objective	Day camp counselor
Education 2006-present	Oak Park High School, Oak Park, TN
Work Experience 2006-2007	Babysitter for two school-age children
Summer 2006	Volunteered in church nursery with school-age children
Honors and Activities	Member of Family, Career and Community Leaders of America for two years
	Member of Spirit Club for three years
	Member of Student Council during junior year
	Member of choir for three years
	Member of National Honor Society for one year
	Student of the Week, Oak Park Center for Youth

References available upon request.

9-15
A resume is a brief overview of your qualifications for employment.

brief account of your education, work experience, and other qualifications for employment. The information from your personal fact sheet can help you prepare your resume. Your resume should be neatly typed, well organized, and easy to read. A good resume sparks the employer's interest in you. It should get the employer interested in asking you for an interview. As a teen you may have no job experience to report. If so, focus on your volunteer activities as well as your interests and abilities.

Your list of references should be typed on a page separate from your resume. At the bottom of your resume, state: "References are available upon request." When you are successful in obtaining an interview, be prepared to list your references at that time.

Wait at least 7-10 business days after you send your letter of application to see if you receive a call from the company. If you do not, you may want to call them for further information. This will remind them of your interest.

Applying by Telephone

When calling an employer, state your name and the position that interests you. Have ready your list of questions to ask about the position. Take notes during your conversation. Being polite and courteous will help you make a good impression. If you are interested in the job, ask for an interview. Be sure to set up the date, time, and location for the interview with the employer.

Filling Out a Job Application

When you apply in person for a job, you will be asked to fill out an application form. Completing an application form neatly and accurately is important, 9-16. If

9-16
It is a good idea to practice completing job applications before you apply for the job you want.

you do not fill it out correctly, you may not be considered for the job.

In some cases, you may be interested in working for a company that has no current job openings. Some companies accept applications even if they do not have openings. When an opening does occur, they look through the applications and pick out the best.

When you are asked by an employer to complete an application form, keep the following tips in mind:

▼ Read through the entire application before you write anything on it. Be sure you know the correct information to write for each of the questions. You do not want to give the same responses for two or three different questions.

▼ Look for specific directions on how to fill out the form such as *write, print,* or *use black ink*. Follow the directions carefully. Be as neat as possible.

▼ Refer to your personal fact sheet or resume as you complete an application form. It should include most of the information you need.

▼ Never leave a question unanswered. The reader may think you were careless and overlooked it. If a question does not apply to you, write "does not apply" or draw a line through the space.

▼ Give complete and accurate information. If you have no full-time work experience, mention part-time jobs like babysitting and volunteer work you have done. If you are asked for information you do not know, get the answer from your personal fact sheet.

▼ Carry a pocket-size dictionary with you so you can check your spelling.

▼ Be prepared to give the name, title, address, and phone numbers of people for whom you have worked, either for pay or for volunteer work. Provide the same information about your references.

The Job Interview

When you visit a company to complete an application form, it is a good idea to be prepared for an interview. The employer might want to interview you right away. If you get this chance, you will want to take advantage of it. In other cases, the employer may look over your application first and contact you later. He or she may call you at home to set up an appointment for another day.

Be Prepared

How can you prepare for an interview? Do some research related to the company, 9-17. Learn about the products it sells or the services it offers. Talk to people who work there or know others who work there.

9-17
Prepare yourself for a job interview by researching the company's background.

Find out all you can about the job opening. Review your own qualifications for the job.

Be ready to answer questions the employer may ask: "What do you know about our company?" "What kind of work are you seeking?" "Why do you want to work for us?" "Why do you think you are right for the job?" When an interviewer sees that you have researched the company, he or she learns two important facts about you. One is you really want the job. The other is you are willing to practice and put extra effort into something that is important to you.

Look Your Best

First impressions are important when you meet someone. This is just as true for employers as for new friends or dates. You will want to look your best for an interview. Good looks begin with good grooming. Your hair should be clean and neatly styled. If you wear makeup, keep it to a minimum. Jewelry, too, should be kept to a minimum. Your hands should be clean, and your fingernails should be trimmed neatly. Clothes are a major part of your appearance. Again, cleanliness and neatness are key. Clothes should also be appropriate for the occasion. If you are applying for a job in a bookstore, dress the same way you would dress to work in the store, but slightly better. If you are applying for a job as an auto mechanic, you can wear casual clothes, but they should be clean and neat. Looking your best shows self-respect. You may have one idea of how to look your best and the interviewer may have another. Avoid dressing in a way that may invite criticism. Body piercings, tattoos, extreme hairstyles, and very tight or skimpy clothing may prevent you from getting the job you want.

Show Confidence

How you act is an important factor in any interview. You can show your self-confidence right away by coming to the interview alone. If family or friends come with you, it may appear that you cannot handle responsibilities on your own.

Arrive at least five minutes early for your appointment. Tell the receptionist or person in charge your name and the name of the person you are meeting. Then wait patiently to be welcomed into the interviewer's office.

Greet the interviewer with a firm handshake. When you are offered a seat, sit up straight on the edge of the chair with feet flat on the floor. Use good posture and look alert. Never chew gum or smoke. Speak clearly to be heard and understood.

An interview is your chance to "sell" yourself. Speak positively about yourself and your experiences. Be prepared to discuss your work experiences, abilities, interests, and career goals. If you believe you can do the job and you want the chance to try, say so. See 9-18.

Have a Positive Attitude

Your attitude tells the interviewer as much about you as your words do. Try to express a positive, "can do" attitude. Act interested in what the interviewer is saying. Be enthusiastic about the job. You do not have to overdo these emotions. If you really want the job, you will be able to express your feelings naturally. Trying too hard will make you look insincere, pushy, or desperate.

You can answer some interview questions with a *yes* or *no* answer. Other questions will require more complete answers. Speak slowly and clearly, using good grammar. Be completely honest. It is never to your advantage to lie.

9-18
Showing confidence during a job interview makes a good impression on the interviewer. Be prepared to tell the interviewer how your skills relate to the job.

As the interview continues, you will have a chance to ask questions. You may want to ask about specific job duties, the hours you will work, and possibilities for advancement. If the job is offered and you are interested, you may then ask about pay, vacation time, and other benefits.

The interviewer should bring up the topic of pay. If the job is available at a specific pay rate, your decision should be easy to make. Either you will accept or reject the rate. By rejecting a fixed rate, you reject the job. However, if the pay level is flexible and the job appeals to you, you should say "salary is negotiable." This means you are willing to discuss pay after all the benefits and other features of the job are discussed. See 9-19.

Do not feel obliged during the interview to declare the specific pay you expect. You will want to consider all that you learned about company benefits and weigh them accordingly. If the interviewer presses you to declare a salary level, state a range that is not excessive. For example, you may say, "Somewhere between (state two amounts), but I am flexible." You will not want to make the mistake of quoting a pay so high that the interviewer eliminates you from consideration.

At the end of an interview, you should thank the interviewer for considering you for the job. Do not be disappointed if you are not offered the job right away. In most cases, other people will be interviewed, too. You may even be asked to come in for a second interview. If this is the case, expect your desired salary to be discussed. A final choice may not be made for several days or even longer.

Before you leave, be sure to ask the interviewer when a final decision will be made. The interviewer may promise to contact you on a certain date to let you know if you will be hired. You can also ask the interviewer if you may call him or her in a few days. In either case, sending a follow-up letter after the interview is a good idea.

Sending a Follow-Up Letter

Sending a follow-up letter after every interview is a matter of courtesy. It is a way to thank the interviewer as well as remind him or her of your interest in the job.

A *follow-up letter* is a brief letter written in business form. See 9-20. It thanks the interviewer for taking the time to talk with you about the job opening. More importantly, it reminds the interviewer of your interest in the job. If you remember an important point you wish you had mentioned during the interview, you may add that to the letter.

If the interviewer does not contact you as promised, follow up with a telephone call. When you make the call, be brief. Just say something like, "Good afternoon, Mr. Smith. This is Roberta Jones calling. I filled out an application and had an interview with you on (state the date). I am still interested in the position and wonder if you have made your decision." Whatever

9-19

Be honest yet flexible when discussing compensation during an interview.

204 Quail Run Road
Oak Park, Tennessee 30241
June 3, 2006

Mr. C.L. Stone, Personnel Manager
Camp McGhee
106 S. Main Street
Oak Park, Tennessee 30241

Dear Mr. Stone:

Thank you so much for taking time to interview me yesterday.

I am excited about the possibility of working as a camp counselor during the summer. My interview made me more certain that this would be a good place for me.

I eagerly await your decision and look forward to hearing from you.

Sincerely,

Terry C. Pinkham

Terry C. Pinkham

9-20

Sending a follow-up letter after a job interview is a courtesy the interviewer will appreciate.

the interviewer's response, be as pleasant and positive in your manner as you were during the interview.

Do not be discouraged if you do not receive a job offer right away. Looking for a job takes time and patience. Learn from the experience. You may interview with several employers before you find the best job for you. In the meantime, keep looking for jobs and going to interviews. Follow up on each one. Eventually, you will get a job.

Creating Your Own Job

Another option to finding a job is creating your own job. Many people fulfill their career goals by creating their own jobs rather than working for other people. They are called entrepreneurs. **Entrepreneurs** start and manage their own businesses. They also assume all risks and responsibilities. For many people, entrepreneurship is a rewarding and satisfying experience.

Entrepreneurship: Pros and Cons

Being an entrepreneur has both advantages and disadvantages. One main advantage is that you are your own boss. You make your own decisions, rules, and business policies. You can be as creative as you want to be in trying out new ideas. You create your own work schedule. If you manage your business well, you have the potential to make as much money as you want.

Being an entrepreneur has some disadvantages as well. Managing a business is a big responsibility that takes hard work and dedication. Until the

Setting the Scene: Starting a Business

You need to earn money to attend the national meeting of the Family, Career and Community Leaders of America. You know how to bake, decorate cakes, and plan parties. You decide to start a temporary business.

Analyze It: How can you publicize your business? What personal qualities might help you succeed? How can this experience help you pursue a career?

business develops a good reputation, entrepreneurs must work during many evenings and weekends without taking vacations. Entrepreneurs have no health benefits; they must buy their own insurance. Entrepreneurs are also responsible for paying the benefits of other employees. Often no profit is made in the first year. Most entrepreneurs live off their savings until their businesses start to make money. If you make a wrong decision, you cannot blame anyone else. Financial problems and poor management decisions are two common reasons why small businesses fail.

Getting Started

If you think you have what it takes to succeed as an entrepreneur, you can start right now. Make a list of all your interests and skills. Your business should be something you enjoy doing. Next, survey your market. Make a list of all the people you know who might pay for the products you make or the services you deliver.

Consider the start-up costs and how much work you can handle. Then check to make sure you have the equipment and space needed to get started. Decide how much you will charge for your product or service. Estimate the profits you expect after paying business expenses. Finally, find ways to promote your business. See 9-21.

While in college earning a forestry degree, Rashon started an outdoor service business to support himself. He enjoyed being able to study and work at the same time. He also liked being financially independent. When he was too busy, he hired other college students to help him.

There are a number of ways to use interests and skills to start a business. By the time he graduated, Rashon knew what career he wanted. His college education had given him a solid business background. He liked being his own boss and he was willing to work hard for long hours. His wide variety of outdoor services included surveying land, building speed bumps in parking lots, and painting lines to mark parking spaces. He enjoyed the

9-21
These enterprising teens decided to use their skills to become entrepreneurs. They find entrepreneurship a challenging and rewarding experience.

challenge of learning new tasks. Also, he was willing to approach people and offer his services. He decided to become a full-time entrepreneur.

Few people combine their interests, aptitudes, and abilities into a truly customized job. However, people who acquire the needed skills and work hard can achieve their goals.

Are you interested in creating your own job? Sometimes the hardest part is deciding what to do. You must study your interests, aptitudes, and abilities to make a good decision. The suggestions in 9-22 may spark your imagination. The examples listed in the chart show only a few of the many ways you can earn money on your own. Once you decide what you want to do, you must also make sure there is a demand for your business. For instance, a children's party service would not be profitable in a neighborhood where there are no children. Another part of starting a business is setting appropriate fees. They should be high enough to cover expenses and deliver a profit. At the same time, they should be low enough to attract clients. In creating your own job, you must use the same good judgment needed in setting any other goal.

Be an Entrepreneur

Gift Shopping Service
Do not have time to shop for those special gifts? Local teen will do your shopping for you! Gift wrapping and mail service also available. Hourly fee charged. 555-1212

Vacation Service
Going out of town? Let me take care of those routine household tasks. I can collect mail, care for pets, water plants, and do yard work—all for one low fee. Call for more details. 655-9881

Letter Addressing Service
Talented teen with neat handwriting. Will address wedding invitations, party invitations, and holiday greeting cards. Call for a free sample of my work. 656-6200

Baking Service
If you do not have time to prepare homemade baked goods you like to eat, call me. I will bake and deliver your favorite breads and desserts. 555-3754

Fruit Basket Service
A thoughtful way to welcome houseguests or show a friend you care! Personalizes fresh fruit baskets arranged and delivered for you. Local delivery to hospitals, hotels, or your home. Call for more details. 555-1492

Lawn and Garden Care
One time or all-the-time yard care. Grass mowing, weeding, edging, planting, raking, or clean-up. Free estimates. 565-0321

Birthday Party Catering Service
Celebrate your child's birthday with no hassles! For one set fee, I arrange a party for up to 15 children. The fee covers your expenses, including the cost of the cake, punch, cups, napkins, favors, and entertainment. A variety of party themes available. 565-2387

9-22
Have you ever thought about becoming an entrepreneur? If so, one of these ideas might appeal to you.

Check It Out!

1. List five sources a job seeker might use for finding job openings.
2. Name three ways to apply for a job.
3. True or false. If a question on an application form does not apply to the applicant, the applicant should leave it blank.
4. List five points job applicants should keep in mind about their behavior during an interview.
5. Explain the purpose of writing a follow-up letter after an interview. What points should the letter include?
6. List two advantages and two disadvantages of becoming an entrepreneur.

Topic 9-3

Succeeding on the Job

Objectives

After studying this topic, you will be able to

▼ identify the qualities and skills needed for job success.

▼ determine the effects of technology on the workplace.

Topic Terms

work ethic
telecommuting

What qualities are needed for job success? The same personal qualities that help you get a job can also help you keep it. Most employers look for certain qualities when they hire employees. They want employees who have skills to get the job done and work well with others. Most successful employees share many of these same qualities. As you read this topic, think about the personal qualities you have now. Developing these qualities will increase your chances of being a successful employee, too.

Qualities of Successful Employees

Several qualities are key factors in job success. Having a positive attitude, being dependable, being honest, and getting along well with others will contribute to your becoming a successful employee.

Positive Attitude

Your attitude plays a big role in your success on the job, 9-23. It shows how you think and feel about other people and situations. A positive attitude will help you learn your job duties, work with others, and get ahead in your career.

If you have a positive attitude, you always try to do the best job possible. You accept your fair share of the responsibility without complaining. You accept criticism as a means of improving your job performance. You are willing to try new tasks. If you enjoy your work, you are more likely to do a better job. This makes you a more valuable employee.

A positive attitude helps you get along with others, too. People enjoy working with someone who is friendly and cheerful most of the time. Being courteous and showing respect for others are positive qualities to have.

Dependability

If you are dependable, your employer can count on you to be reliable and responsible. You get your work done and do not expect others to do it for you. You have a good attendance record and start work on time every day.

Honesty

Another personal quality of a good employee is being honest. Employers want employees they can trust. That means telling the truth, keeping any promises you make, and dealing with people fairly. Being honest also means putting forth your best effort on the job. You do the job you are assigned and do not waste time. Employers expect you to give an honest day's work for an honest day's pay.

9-23
People who have positive attitudes are willing to tackle any job task.

Ethics

A **work ethic** is a standard of conduct for successful job performance. Your concepts of fairness, right and wrong, and good and bad affect your work ethic. A strong work ethic will help you achieve personal satisfaction, 9-24. Successful employees work not only for the company but also for personal satisfaction. Chances are that your boss will not compliment you daily for your work. Consequently, you need to develop personal feelings of satisfaction from the work you do. You need to set high standards for your work and take pride in meeting them. In turn, personal satisfaction will make your work seem more important and more enjoyable.

Cooperation

An ability to work well with all people is important for job success. This means you can work with people of all

9-24
Successful employees develop feelings of personal satisfaction from doing their work well.

ages, of both genders, and of different backgrounds. You show respect and courtesy to your boss, coworkers, and customers. See 9-25.

Part of getting along with others is working as a team member. To show others you want to be cooperative, you accept your share of the work. You make an effort to contribute to the group's goal. Each group member should feel free to make worthwhile contributions. Combining the special traits and skills of each person allows the group to achieve the best results.

Good working relationships are based on respect for others' feelings. Follow directions carefully. Ask questions when you do not understand how to do a task. Do not expect your coworkers to do your work for you. On the other hand, never assume that you can get along without your coworkers. If you willingly cooperate with them, they will cooperate with you. Being friendly, respectful, and enthusiastic will help you become part of a team.

Job Readiness Skills

What skills are required of people who enter the workforce? What do they need to know to perform well on the job?

9-25
Because you will encounter so many different people on the job, cooperation is a necessary quality.

These questions were examined by the U. S. Department of Labor. The group that handled the study was the Secretary's Commission on Achieving Necessary Skills (SCANS), also called the SCANS commission. It identified five skills needed to become an effective employee in today's workplace. These skills, called SCANS competencies, include competence with

▼ resources
▼ interpersonal skills
▼ information
▼ technology
▼ systems

The SCANS commission also identified three foundation elements workers need before they can use the competencies well. These include basic skills, thinking skills, and important personal qualities. Considered together, they are known as *workplace know-how*. They are also called *job readiness skills*. See 9-26.

The skills people need for success in the workplace cannot be developed separately. Each builds on and supports another. You can develop job readiness skills at school and through part-time jobs, but there are other ways. Extracurricular activities, community involvement, volunteer activities, and projects at home can help prepare a student's job readiness.

Good Appearance

Whether fair or not, others judge you by your appearance, either consciously or subconsciously. What you wear to work reflects how you feel about your work. Try to look your best every day because neatness shows respect for yourself and others.

Most employers enforce dress codes that list clothing styles and items inappropriate for the workplace. They know the importance of clothing to maintaining a businesslike atmosphere.

Workplace Know-How

For effective, on-the-job performance, workers need the five competencies and three part foundation of skills and personal qualities listed below.

SCANS Competencies

Workers with job readiness skills know how to use

- **resources**—They know how to allocate time, money, materials, space, and workers.
- **interpersonal skills**—They work well on teams, teach others, serve customers, lead, negotiate, and interact well with people from culturally diverse backgrounds.
- **information**—They know how to acquire and evaluate data, organize and maintain files, interpret and communicate, and use computers to process information.
- **systems**—They understand social, organizational, and technological systems. They can monitor and correct performance. They can design or improve systems.
- **technology**—They can select appropriate equipment and tools, apply technology to specific tasks, maintain equipment, and troubleshoot equipment problems.

The Foundation

Developing scans competencies requires

- **basic skills**—reading, writing, arithmetic, mathematics, speaking, and listening.
- **thinking skills**—the ability to learn, reason, think creatively, make decisions, and solve problems.
- **personal qualities**—individual responsibility, self-esteem, sociability, self management, and integrity.

9-26

Employees are expected to have these skills and abilities.

Customers, too, expect business people to dress appropriately. They do not want to be served by workers who appear sloppy or dressed for some other occasion. Customers often take their business elsewhere if a company does not maintain businesslike surroundings.

Becoming a Professional

When you display all the positive qualities discussed, you are on the road to becoming a professional. A professional is an employee who keeps a courteous, conscientious, and businesslike manner. When companies hire new employees, they look for people who fit this description. They want to maintain a good public image and seek employees who share their concern.

Becoming a professional is not a goal reserved for certain careers. Any employee can, no matter what his or her job is. A professional is easy to spot, 9-27. It is the person who demonstrates the following qualities:

▼ smiles and greets everyone pleasantly
▼ remembers and uses correct names and titles
▼ treats everyone with respect
▼ keeps a calm disposition
▼ avoids talking negatively about coworkers and customers
▼ wears conservative clothing from head to toe
▼ chooses a becoming and conservative hairstyle
▼ avoids excessive use of perfume and cologne
▼ limits jewelry and makeup
▼ practices good hygiene
▼ uses proper etiquette

Professionals uphold the standards of the company and set positive goals for themselves. They avoid doing anything

All jobs are affected by innovative technology. In factories, computerized robots perform the most dangerous and monotonous jobs efficiently. Sales teams receive records of purchases as soon as they are made anywhere in the company and can readily determine future inventory needs. Exciting new technologies such as *nanotechnology*, which includes devices built at the molecular and atomic level, are on the horizon. In the workplace, people can use e-mail, facsimile (FAX) machines, wireless phones, GPS (global positioning systems) and video conferencing to stay in touch with coworkers and clients. See 9-28. People can also use these devices to work out of their homes. This is called **telecommuting**.

With every technological device comes a need for specialists who can operate and service it. In some businesses, new job positions are created to fulfill these needs. In other cases, job roles are expanded to include new duties. Job expansion also creates a need for more education. People must have the knowledge and training necessary to operate new equipment.

9-27

A well-groomed appearance and a pleasant smile are two clues that this person is a professional.

that disrupts the work environment. They focus on doing their jobs well and helping the company succeed.

Technology in the Workplace

Advances in technology have changed many aspects of life. Computer technology is used in every industry and in most classrooms and homes to make time-consuming and demanding tasks easier. As technology continues to change our world, people must adjust to new roles and responsibilities.

9-28

A webcam, microphone, and Internet connection allows people to work together even though separated by long distances.

There is great demand for people who excel in the use of today's technologies. Competition among employers for these skills increases the salary employees can command. The salary for a position will also increase as the education and duty requirements for the position increase.

Instead of being apprehensive about learning how to use new tools in their jobs, employees are advised to expect and welcome change. The latest innovations in technology soon become obsolete. Future changes may occur even more rapidly. Technological progress is occurring at an accelerating rate. Any new technology will probably lead to other new technologies. Workers must stay flexible enough to adopt new procedures and work methods.

As devices are developed to perform tasks more accurately, some jobs are eliminated. Thus, people can no longer prepare for one career or know what new technologies will affect their jobs in the future. Lifetime learning is essential for those who plan to hold wage-earning jobs during all of their productive years.

Occasionally technological changes bring some negative results. Physical ailments such as carpal tunnel syndrome increase with the growth of technology. Repetitive body motions can cause this work hazard over extended periods. Also, telecommuters who have limited opportunities for personal interaction sometimes feel isolation and loneliness.

Technology impacts every aspect of the workplace. It promotes greater speed, efficiency, and accuracy. However, competence with technology is just one of five skills that effective workers are expected to have. Employees with workplace know-how also need competence with resources, interpersonal skills, information, and systems.

Check It Out!

1. List three qualities needed for job success. State some examples of each quality.
2. Why is a work ethic important to job success?
3. Using technological devices to work from home is known as _____.

Chapter Review

Summary

Learning more about yourself, your interests, aptitudes, and abilities is the first step in matching yourself to the right career. Many resources are available for gathering career information. As you get closer to making a career decision, you may want to explore careers in family and consumer sciences. In setting your career goals, consider the training you will need. Making a career decision now will help you get started in reaching your goals.

Use resources such as people, agencies, and want ads to find job openings. Applying for job openings may involve sending a resume, calling the employer, or applying in person. A job interview is your chance to make a favorable impression on the interviewer. After the interview, sending a follow-up letter is important. Another option in job hunting is to create your own job by becoming an entrepreneur.

Once you have a job, you will want to be successful at it. A positive attitude, dependability, honesty, and an ability to work with others will help ensure your success.

Think About It!

1. Why is evaluating your current interests, aptitudes, and abilities an important part of career planning?
2. How could family and consumer sciences skills be used in your career?
3. Briefly summarize the factors you think will affect your career choices.
4. What preparation(s) for finding a job do you think will be most important for you? Why?
5. What recommendations would you make to a friend who is thinking of starting a business?
6. If you were an employer, what three qualities would you most want in an employee? Explain your answer.
7. What type of technological skills do you think will be most important in the workplace in 10 years? 20 years?

Try It Out!

1. Choose a career that interests you and write a career profile. Include the following information in your profile: nature of the work, places of employment, training and qualifications needed, advancement opportunities, typical salaries, and social and psychological factors related to this career choice.
2. Make a list of five careers that interest you. Then show how you would use a career ladder to reach these career goals.
3. Collect several different job application forms. Complete one of them.
4. Role-play several different job interviews. As a class, evaluate each interview situation.
5. Write a follow-up letter to the interviewer in one of the role-play interviews described in the previous activity.
6. Brainstorm a list of possible jobs you could have as a teen entrepreneur.
7. Interview a successful employee about his or her attitude, dependability, honesty, ethics, cooperation, and appearance on the job. Ask how these factors have impacted the employee's performance.

Family and Community Services Careers

Career Ladder for Family and Community Services

▶ **Advanced Degree**

Alcohol and drug abuse
counselor
Family therapist
Social welfare administrator
Marriage therapist

▶ **Bachelor's Degree**

Cooperative extension
agent
Rehabilitation counselor
Social worker
Child advocate

▶ **Associate's Degree**

Recreational therapist
Camp counselor
Family services aide
Volunteer services
coordinator
Caseworker's aide

▶ **High School Diploma**

Adult care assistant
Companion to seniors living
alone
Playground assistant

▶ **Pre-High School Diploma**

Babysitter
Tutor
Lifeguard
Volunteer in family- and
community-related
agencies

People in family and community services help improve the well-being of the community. They work to create a better quality of life for individuals and families.

Employment Opportunities

Workers in this field are employed by social service groups, schools, businesses, and government agencies. They usually focus on one area, such as youth services. Some employees, however, develop a broad knowledge of family and community services.

Entrepreneurial Opportunities

Those desiring self-employment can serve as counselors in private practice. Often they narrow their practice to certain age groups, such as teens or older adults. Other entrepreneurs focus on counseling couples or families. Lobbying for family and community issues is another option for those wanting to become self-employed.

Rewards and Demands

People who work in family and community services find it rewarding to touch people's lives in positive ways. These workers enjoy seeing members of families become healthy and work toward common goals. Some feel especially fulfilled after helping troubled people find ways to deal with their problems.

Some jobs in family and community services can be emotionally draining. For instance, many workers find it stressful to work with clients who are in constant physical or emotional pain. Workers may need to put in long days and work evenings to meet the needs of their clients. This type of schedule can place a strain on a worker's personal life.

Preparation Requirements

People can start preparing for family and community services careers when they are in high school. The training needed depends on the kind of work a person wants to do. Preparation also depends on the needs of the people a worker will serve. Taking classes to prepare for college is a good start.

Some workers in the family and community services field specialize in assisting older adults. Courses in business and psychology may also prove helpful. Taking part in the school's chapter of Family, Career and Community Leaders of America (FCCLA) can help build leadership skills.

Entry-Level Jobs

Most entry-level jobs in family and community services require little formal training. For instance, a child care aide or a camp assistant is likely to receive on-the-job training. Workers in entry-level jobs generally receive training through workshops sponsored by the employer.

Midlevel Jobs

People working in mid-level careers need some training beyond high school. Someone working as a home companion may have training from a vocational school. A caseworker's aide might be expected to have a two-year degree. An associate's degree in human services technology would prepare a worker for a job at this level.

Professional-Level Jobs

Family and community services jobs at the professional level require at least a four-year degree. A family and consumer sciences teacher has at least an undergraduate degree. Cooperative extension agents and social services directors also need four-year degrees. A counselor, such as a substance abuse counselor, needs an advanced degree. College programs such as social work, youth services, and family studies provide the required degrees.

Personal Qualities Needed for Success

An ability to understand human nature will help employees succeed in this career area. Workers need a true concern for individuals and their problems. Counselors and social workers must communicate well with clients. The ideal employee has excellent listening skills and doesn't get discouraged when there seems to be no or slow progress. All workers must respect the need to keep client records confidential. Those in leadership roles need skill in guiding people and managing resources. All workers in this field will benefit from a desire to be life-long learners. Having good judgment and being objective and flexible also help workers succeed in this field.

Future Trends

The number of jobs in the field of family and community services is expected to increase. Some jobs will be in the area of research. The impact of technology on the family and the effect of violence on children are current topics of study. Services for older adults will be in greater demand as the population ages. A larger number of immigrants will increase the need for workers who can speak more than one language. Employment counselors will be needed to help people look for jobs. In many of these careers, the pay will remain low for the level of responsibility.

Career Interests, Abilities, and You

Assess your skills, interests, and abilities to learn if a career in family and community services is for you. Taking a family and consumer sciences course in family relations might help you decide. Shadowing a cooperative extension agent or a social worker will give you an idea of what the job involves. Volunteer work can also help you assess your interest in helping others. Offer your services to the Salvation Army or the Red Cross to experience a common setting for this career field.

Social workers may be employed by senior living centers.

Part Three
Understanding Children

Chapter 10
Meeting Children's Developmental Needs

Careers

These careers relate to the topics in this chapter:
- ▼ children's apparel retail associate
- ▼ pediatric aide
- ▼ nursery school director
- ▼ pediatric nurse

As you study the chapter, see if you can think of others.

Topics

227

Topic 10-1
The First Year

Objectives

After studying this topic, you will be able to
▼ describe the characteristics and basic needs of newborns.
▼ summarize the physical, emotional, social, and intellectual development of infants.

Topic Terms

pediatrician
newborn
sudden infant death syndrome (SIDS)
infant

The first year of life is an exciting time for babies and their parents. Babies have changing needs as they grow and develop. Parents can create a nurturing environment to help meet those needs.

Parents will have many questions as they observe the development of their babies. A **pediatrician** is a doctor specializing in the care and development of children. He or she can be a vital source of information for parents when problems arise.

Newborn Babies

For the first month of life, a baby is called a **newborn**. Having a newborn in their home will be a big adjustment for parents and other family members. Parents must be prepared to care for this new little person.

Characteristics of Newborns

Newborns look different from older babies. The average newborn weighs about 7½ pounds and is about 20 to 21 inches long. The newborn's skin may appear red and wrinkled. The head may be misshapen. The chin recedes, the nose is flattened, and the ears are pressed against the head. (Some of these characteristics are less apparent on babies delivered by cesarean section.) The eyebrows and eyelashes may be barely visible. Some newborns are nearly bald.

Newborns have large heads compared to their bodies. They often have bowed legs and bulging abdomens. Newborns also have very short necks, sloping shoulders, and narrow chests.

Care of Newborns

Newborns have relatively simple needs. They need to eat and sleep. They need to be kept clean, warm, and dry. Above all, they need to be loved, 10-1.

Feeding

Babies are not able to digest solid foods until they are four to six months old. Therefore, parents must choose breast milk or formula to provide all the nutrients their newborn needs. Newborns need to be fed six to eight times a day. They generally wake up once or twice during the night to be fed.

Sleep

Newborns sleep about 18 to 20 hours a day. They tend to sleep about four to five hours at a time. Then they awaken for an hour or so to be changed and fed before going back to sleep.

Babies need a firm, flat mattress for support and posture development. The mattress should fit inside the crib very

10-1
Newborns' needs are very basic, but their main need is for love and affection from all family members.

snugly. There should be no way for children to get their heads caught between the crib and the edge of the mattress.

Sudden infant death syndrome (SIDS) is a concern of parents. SIDS is the sudden death of an apparently healthy baby during sleep. Although the cause is still unknown, several factors may be involved. As a precautionary measure, caregivers should place babies on their backs rather than their stomachs when placing them in the crib to sleep. This practice has reduced the rate of SIDS significantly. Also keep stuffed toys, pillows, and soft bedding out of the crib to prevent suffocation in bedding.

Bathing

For the first few weeks after birth, babies should be given sponge baths several times a week. Once a baby's navel has healed, he or she may be given tub baths. The baby's eyes, ears, nose, and face

are cleaned first. Then the baby is carefully lowered into a small tub containing a few inches of warm water. The baby's body should be gently washed with a mild soap. Caregivers should be sure to clean the diaper area and the folds of the baby's skin. After a thorough rinsing, the baby is lifted out of the tub and gently patted dry with a soft towel, 10-2. Baby oil or lotion may be applied to moisten a baby's tender skin.

Clothes

Clothing for newborns should be made of soft, flame-retardant fabrics. Garments should be loose fitting and easy to put on and take off. Clothing should be appropriate for the existing temperature. Infants can quickly become too hot or too cold. Use sweaters and blankets as needed.

10-2
Wrapping an infant in a soft towel will give him or her a feeling of security after a bath.

Diapers

Diapers are a basic clothing need of babies for two or more years. Parents may choose cloth or disposable diapers. Newborns need to be changed about 10 times a day. Changing diapers promptly and thoroughly cleansing the diaper area will help prevent diaper rash.

Infants

Babies up to 12 months old are called **infants**. During these months, babies change in many ways. When watching for signs of development, parents need to remember that each child is an individual, 10-3. The signs of growth mentioned here are averages. Each child will develop at his or her own rate.

Early Brain Development

Scientists have recently discovered that experiences soon after birth affect much of the brain's development. The first two years of life are critical in determining how the circuits of the brain are wired. How the brain grows is dependent on emotional interaction, which involves the parents and other caregivers. Babies whose parents and caregivers talk and read to them and play simple games with them have enhanced intellectual, physical, and emotional development.

The first few years of a baby's life are the most important ones for brain development. Some abilities are acquired more easily during certain time-sensitive periods. These are sometimes referred to as "windows of opportunity." Time taken to interact with the baby then will have lifelong positive effects. Time lost can be difficult to make up later.

If physical and emotional needs are met in a predictable, responsive way in the first years of life, the foundation is set for healthy emotional development. Emotional health is necessary for the development of intelligence.

10-3
Infants grow very quickly, but at their own developmental rates.

Setting the Scene: Early Start

You are planning a baby shower for your sister Melanie and her husband Manchester. The shower theme is "Books for the Baby." Melanie and Manchester have already started *in utero* reading to their unborn child. You are trying to decide what types of books are most appropriate for small children.

Analyze It: Which types of books seem appropriate for *in utero* reading? Why? What type of book do you think Melanie and Manchester would most enjoy reading to their child? Who should be the primary reader, Melanie or Manchester?

Physical Growth of Infants

In their first year of life, infants will triple in weight. They will grow to 1½ times their length at birth. Their large and small muscle skills develop at an amazing rate. Parents can notice changes almost daily.

Infants progress from reflex actions to controlled muscle movement. Newborns are not able to hold up their heads. For this reason, their heads must be carefully supported when they are being held. By six months, infants can roll over. At seven months, many babies are beginning to crawl. (Once infants reach this stage, increased supervision will be needed to protect them from hazards.) Eight-month-old babies can sit alone for a period of time, 10-4. By 10 months, infants may be able to stand up by themselves. Many children are able to start walking by their first birthdays.

Emotional and Social Growth of Infants

Emotionally and socially, infants, like all people, need love and attention from others. From birth, infants respond to human contact and a warm, loving environment. Infants begin to show emotions at a very young age. Two-month-olds can show when they are distressed, excited, or happy. By five months, the range of emotions has expanded to include fear, disgust, and anger. Eight-month-old infants often demonstrate fear of strangers and may seek the comfort of parents in a stranger's presence. By the time infants are 10 months old, they begin to cry less frequently. At one year, babies begin to develop their own identities. They are also able to recognize emotions expressed by others.

Socially, newborns can recognize a parent's voice. As they grow older, infants respond to familiar faces. They also begin to show sensitivity around strangers. By five or six months, infants start to enjoy playing games like peek-a-boo. At nine months, they begin to show interest in play activities of others. At 12 months, infants socialize by practicing communication skills with adults.

Intellectual Growth of Infants

Newborns receive information and show intellectual development through their senses. They follow moving objects with their eyes and listen attentively to sounds with their ears, 10-5. By two months, infants are able to discriminate between different voices. They also show preference for people over objects. At

10-4
As the large muscles develop, babies will be able to do more on their own.

10-5
Babies' visual world begins with black and white. The sharp contrast is easier to perceive and provides needed visual stimulation.

three months of age, infants begin to show signs of memory. As infants grow older, they remain alert for increasingly longer spans of time. By six months, infants show improved eye-hand coordination. At eight months, infants understand simple concepts, such as *in* and *out*. Ten-month-old infants will search for hidden objects. By their first birthdays, many children can put nesting toys together correctly. They may also show a preference for one hand over the other.

Toys provide infants with intellectual stimulation. Babies like toys that appeal to the senses. Bright colors, varied textures, and interesting sounds attract their attention. Since infants tend to put objects in their mouths, toys need to be kept clean. Children should not be allowed to play with small objects that could be swallowed.

Language development is a sign of intellectual growth. Newborns cry to express their needs. By three months, infants make vowel sounds, like *ooh* and *ah*. Consonant sounds begin to appear in the fourth month. Five-month-olds understand their own names. Infants begin to recognize some words at eight months. At nine months, infants may say *mama* and *dada*. They can also follow simple directions. By the end of the first year, most infants have a vocabulary of several words. They begin to use language to express themselves.

Speaking to infants will have a great impact on their language development. Newborns do not understand words, so the content of your message is unimportant. However, speaking to them allows them to enjoy human contact and helps them become familiar with specific voices, 10-6. Newborns can perceive a parent's mood. Therefore, parents should speak in pleasant tones that reflect an interest in and love for the child.

The content of messages becomes increasingly important as infants grow older. Infants begin to understand the

10-6
Speaking to and interacting with infants is important to their intellectual growth.

words being spoken to them at about eight months. They begin to repeat the words they hear by 11 or 12 months. Parents have a responsibility to use messages that provide guidance with love. They must also teach children to use appropriate terms.

Check It Out!

1. Describe three characteristics of newborns.
2. About how many hours will an average newborn sleep each day?
3. Explain briefly what has been learned about early brain development.
4. How much will a baby's weight and length increase in the first year of life?
5. Give three examples of intellectual growth of infants.

Topic 10-2
Children from One to Five

Objectives

After studying this topic, you will be able to
▼ explain patterns of growth and development.
▼ give examples of physical, emotional, social, and intellectual characteristics of toddlers and preschoolers.
▼ describe types of special needs children might have and how to meet those needs.

Topic Terms

sequential steps
individual rates of growth
interrelated development rates
toddler
solitary play
parallel play
object permanence
preschooler
cooperative play
children with special needs
physical disability
mental disability
learning disability
emotional disorder
gifted or talented
inclusion

Caregivers need an understanding of what they might expect from children within a given age range, 10-7. Knowing about patterns of growth and behavior is helpful. Caregivers should also remember that all individuals are unique. Sometimes a toddler will behave as a five-year-old. At other times, the same toddler may behave

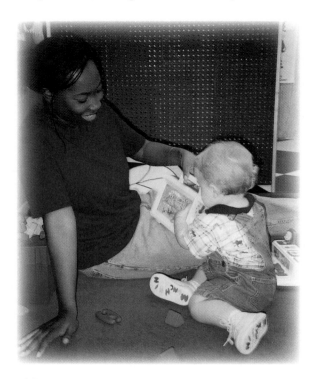

10-7
Caregivers should expect different behaviors from children of different ages.

as an infant. Caregivers must always maintain a flexible attitude as they work with individual children.

Children have much to learn about themselves, other people, and the world. Children do not need to be pushed to learn. They absorb much of what they need to know from their environments. Thus, a rich environment offers rich learning experiences. (See Appendix.)

Patterns of Growth and Development

Growth and development occur in a series of patterns called **sequential steps**. Each new response is based on existing capabilities and skills learned in prior

steps. For example, to learn to shake a rattle, a baby must already know how to grasp it.

Growth and development rates vary from child to child. One baby may grasp and shake a rattle at an earlier rate than another baby of the same age. This is called **individual rates of growth** because each child is unique. Factors such as heredity, environment, and motivation influence individual rates of growth.

Growth is also influenced by **interrelated development rates**. Physical, emotional, social, and intellectual growth are all happening all the time. For example, imagine you are babysitting an infant who is crying. You try to console the baby by giving him a rattle. The rattle is recognized intellectually and his hand grasps it physically. Emotionally, the baby is appeased by the distraction of the rattle. As you can see, there are strong and complex interactions between physical, emotional, social, and intellectual aspects of growth.

Toddlers

One- and two-year-old children are called **toddlers**. This term comes from the unsteady way children move, or toddle, when they begin to walk. As children gain mobility, they have more opportunities to develop mentally and socially.

Physical Growth of Toddlers

During the toddler years, parents will see steady improvements in their child's large muscle skills. As leg muscles develop, toddlers become able to run, jump, kick, and climb as well as walk. Strengthening arm muscles enable 18-month-old toddlers to throw a ball and 36-month-old toddlers to catch one.

Small muscle skills also improve as children grow. They become able to fill and empty containers, turn knobs, and build block towers. They like to scribble, paint, play with modeling clay, and string beads. By the time a toddler is 30 months old, he or she can turn the pages of a book. See 10-8.

Toilet Learning

One important physical skill most children master toward the end of the toddler years is toilet learning. As children learn to control their muscles, toilet learning will come naturally. Children should not be pushed to learn how to use the toilet. At some point, children will begin showing signs of awareness of their

10-8
Books with large, easy-to-turn pages help toddlers develop small muscle skills.

bowel movements. At this time, caregivers can begin offering the "potty" about every two hours. This helps a child stay dry. The child may have frequent bathroom accidents, but caregivers should not show disappointment. It's best to praise desired behaviors and to let undesired ones pass with minimum attention. Success in toilet learning, like other successes, will come in time.

Emotional and Social Growth of Toddlers

A toddler's emotions are difficult to predict. Many toddlers have strong reactions and react differently at different times. Their expanding range of emotions includes pride, affection, stubbornness, jealousy, and sympathy. Toddlers are quite self-centered and are often demanding, possessive, aggressive, and insecure. They seek approval and are easily hurt by criticism.

You may have heard older toddlers called the "terrible twos." Behaviors displayed at this age may be caused by insecurity. Perhaps their growing knowledge of the world makes two-year-olds suddenly feel small. To cope with this new feeling, they try to act big. They become very independent and do everything loudly. They frequently respond by saying no, even when they plan to do what is asked. Wise adults learn to phrase conversations so children are not given a chance to say no as a response.

Young toddlers like playing alone. This is called **solitary play**, 10-9. Toddlers also like to play beside other children rather than with them, which is called **parallel play**. Two children may be playing the same thing, but there is little to no interaction between them. This pattern of play may continue to preschool.

10-9
Young toddlers enjoy playing by themselves.

Toddlers prefer the company of family members to the company of others. Two-year-olds can be expected to be socially aggressive. They do not like to share and have not learned to say please. Instead, they snatch the toys they want.

Intellectual Growth of Toddlers

Intellectually, toddlers have an increasing attention span. They begin to show signs of memory. They are able to recognize **object permanence**. This means children learn that objects and people still exist even when they cannot see them. For example, imagine you are hiding a toy under a blanket, then bringing it back out and showing it to the child. A toddler understands that the toy is simply under the blanket; it hasn't disappeared forever.

This is also a time when children learn to identify shapes and familiar objects. Toddlers enjoy imitating others, and by 20 months of age, they begin to enjoy imaginative play. Concepts learned during the toddler years include the differences between *one* and *many* and between *before* and *after*. Toddlers display active curiosity. They use thought processes to solve simple problems, and they enjoy putting puzzles together.

Toddlers show rapid increases in their language skills. They understand more words than they can say. Between the ages of one and three, however, toddlers' vocabularies will grow from three or four words to over 500 words. Two-year-olds use language to show their understanding of simple concepts. They begin to speak in two- and three-word sentences.

Preschoolers

Three-, four-, and five-year-old children are called **preschoolers**. During the preschool years, children become increasingly independent as they acquire new skills.

Physical Growth of Preschoolers

Physically, preschoolers do not gain weight and height as fast as younger children. However, large muscle skills continue to become more refined as children grow. Preschoolers have better balance and coordination. Large muscle skills expand to include hopping, skipping, dancing, and jumping rope. Preschoolers have improved accuracy in throwing and catching, 10-10. They are able to use tricycles and other pedal toys. They enjoy playing on playground equipment, such as swings, slides, and jungle gyms. They can also dress themselves with greater ease.

Improved small muscle skills allow preschoolers to unbutton buttons and pull up large zippers. By age four or five, they

10-10
Games that involve throwing and catching become more fun for preschool-age children.

can also lace their shoes and may be able to tie knots. They can brush their teeth and feed themselves with spoons and forks. Preschoolers can draw shapes and cut on lines with scissors. They can put puzzle pieces together and turn pages in a book.

Emotional and Social Growth of Preschoolers

Three-year-olds are generally cooperative and like to perform simple chores. Being a helper seems special at age three. Four-year-olds tend to be emotionally unpredictable. Four-year-olds are friendly one minute and quarrelsome the next. They like being independent and resist pressures placed on them by demonstrating stubbornness and temper.

Five-year-olds generally try to please, so this is a pleasant age. They tend to be more patient and generous and less combative. They express their feelings through language rather than emotional outbursts.

Preschoolers are proud of their parents. They seek comfort, approval, and emotional support from parents. However, friends are important to preschoolers, too, 10-11. Preschoolers make friends easily and begin to seek status among their peers. They play with their friends, which is called **cooperative play**. Two or more children play complementary roles and share play activities. They make rules, assign roles, and create new games and activities. Competitive games become popular.

To encourage social growth, pre-schoolers should be given opportunities to practice sharing. They need to learn to assume responsibilities and develop dependability.

Intellectual Growth of Preschoolers

Throughout the preschool years, attention span and concentration skills continue to improve. By age five, many

10-11
Preschoolers enjoy playing with other children their age.

children are eager to go to school. Intellectual growth at this age is shown by a child's ability to plan in advance. A five-year-old can tell you what he or she is going to draw before drawing it.

Preschoolers ask many questions in order to learn about their environments. Caregivers must show an interest in children and give honest but simple answers.

Caregivers can show an interest in preschoolers' intellectual growth by asking questions as well as answering them. Which is larger? Which is smaller? Which is taller? Which is shorter? Which is near? Which is far? What color is this? Which one is blue? Questions such as these are often called *reading readiness exercises*. They help prepare children for reading lessons that will come later.

Preschoolers learn how to count and begin to understand number concepts. Their vocabularies expand to over 2,000 words. They enjoy listening to rhymes and stories. They also enjoy games and puzzles that allow them to use their word and number skills.

With their larger vocabularies, preschoolers begin to speak in complete sentences. Their grammar reflects that used by people around them. Therefore, caregivers have a responsibility to use correct grammar since they are serving as role models for children.

Children with Special Needs

All children have needs. Some have greater needs than others. Children with disabilities and gifted and talented children are often called **children with special needs**. These children may need more or different care than average children, including extra support, instruction, or guidance.

Some special needs are described below:

▼ A **physical disability** limits a person's body or its functions. Limitations include either leg or arm movements or both. Physical disabilities also include vision, hearing, or speech impairments.

▼ A **mental disability** limits the way a person's brain functions. The child's intellectual abilities, when compared with the average, are a year or more delayed. These children have a limited learning capacity. Learning takes place slowly. Mental disabilities range from mild to severe.

▼ A **learning disability** is a limitation in the way a person's brain sorts and uses certain types of information. It does not affect overall brain function. Dyslexia, for example, impairs the ability to read. The dyslexic person sees certain letters and numbers either backwards or inverted. Learning disabilities may also affect math skills. Many learning disabilities can be treated. Others can be overcome with training in ways that compensate for the disability.

▼ An **emotional disorder** limits the way a person functions emotionally and socially. An emotional disorder may cause a child to be too insecure or fearful to play with other children. On the other hand, the child may be too aggressive. Emotional disorders are often marked by extremes of behavior and can limit a child's ability to concentrate. Unfortunately, these disorders do not go away on their own. They require a diagnosis by a health care professional.

▼ A **gifted or talented** child shows outstanding ability in either a general sense or in a specific ability. A gifted child may have above-average intelligence overall or excel in a specific academic area. A talented child may possess extraordinary skill in an area such as art, music, or athletics.

Children with special needs require the same basic care as other children. They need love and support. They need encouragement to develop their skills and overcome their weaknesses. They may also need some extra attention in certain areas. For instance, a child with a mental disability may need directions to be given one step at a time. This child may also need to have directions repeated more often. However, caregivers should resist the urge to do a child's tasks for him or her. The child needs to do as much as possible on his or her own, 10-12. This will help the child develop independence and a strong self-concept.

Inclusion

There was a time when educators thought it was best to teach special needs children with others who had similar needs. There were separate classes for the gifted and for those with specific disabilities. Today, many children with special needs are placed in classes with nondisabled children for at least a part of each day. This practice is called **inclusion**—the placing of students of varying abilities in the same class. It is believed that all children benefit from being together.

Including all children in the same classrooms helps them all experience and value diversity. Nondisabled children learn valuable lessons in understanding, caring, and compassion. Children with disabilities benefit from the acceptance and assistance of their nondisabled peers. Special needs children learn valuable social skills that prepare them for society at large. Children with special needs create unique challenges for their caregivers. They even create hardships at times. Caregivers must treat each child according to his or her needs. Professionals can assist caregivers in meeting the unique needs of a special child. Every child deserves an opportunity to be the best person he or she is capable of being.

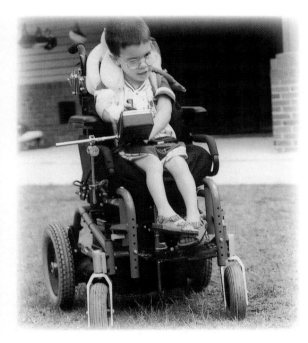

10-12
Providing ways for children with physical disabilities to do things on their own helps their self-esteem.

Check It Out!

1. List four small muscle skills that develop during the toddler years.
2. By age three, how many words does the average toddler have in his or her vocabulary?
3. True or false. Five-year-olds tend to express their feelings through emotional outbursts.
4. Explain the difference between a mental disability and a learning disability.
5. What is inclusion?

Topic 10-3

Meeting Children's Physical Needs

Objectives

After studying this topic, you will be able to

▼ describe how a child's likes can be used to encourage good eating habits.

▼ explain factors to consider when selecting clothes for children.

▼ identify benefits children gain from physical activity.

▼ list guidelines to help parents maintain a healthy and safe environment.

Topic Terms

self-help features
active-physical play
manipulative-constructive play
immunizations
communicable diseases
first aid

A child's basic physical needs must be met before other needs can be satisfied. Parents have a responsibility to provide for their children's physical needs. They must supply adequate food, clothing, shelter, and medical care. Parents must also teach children how to eat, dress, and care for their bodies. This will help children develop independence and assume responsibility for their own physical care.

Serving Food

Food is one of a child's primary physical needs. Parents need to provide nutritious meals for their children. However, children have small stomach capacities. Therefore, they may not be able to eat all the foods they need at meals. Thus, snacks become an important part of a child's food plan each day, 10-13.

Mealtime Psychology

Children sometimes need to be persuaded to eat foods that are good for them. Parents can use a bit of mealtime psychology to accomplish this goal.

Parents should try to avoid making an issue over food habits. When a fuss is made over behavior—even bad behavior—children enjoy the attention. Children will repeat the behavior to get more attention. Children eat best when parents praise their good habits and ignore undesirable ones.

Some children do not like to drink milk. However, their developing bodies need the calcium and phosphorus found in milk. Parents can serve milk-rich foods to make up for a lack of milk in the diet. Ice cream,

10-13
Healthy snacks help meet a child's nutrient needs.

custard, cream soups, and cheese are alternatives to milk that are popular with children.

Children like small servings of food. Many children are discouraged from eating by the sight of a large plate of food. Providing children with small portions allows them to ask for second helpings when they enjoy a food.

Children like bright colors. Foods like bright yellow peaches or bright green broccoli often appeal to them. Children are also likely to enjoy eating from a table set with brightly colored plates and glasses. They may even prefer one special plate and always want to be served from it.

Children like foods prepared especially for them. Parents may try making a smaller biscuit or a mini pizza for a child. They can draw a funny face on a hamburger with mustard and ketchup. Syrup can be used to write a child's name on a pancake. Children will find such foods more fun to eat.

Involving Children in Meal Preparation

Children like to choose their own food. Adults can encourage small children to eat by allowing them to help with the menu plan. They can provide children with a variety of healthy food options. For instance, parents might ask children whether they would rather have carrot sticks or celery sticks. They could offer bananas or apples. Then the children can choose which foods they want to eat.

Children are more likely to eat foods they help to prepare, 10-14. Children can spread peanut butter on crackers. They can prepare vegetables for a raw salad or beat

10-14
Involve children in the preparation of easy foods, such as peanut butter sandwiches.

eggs that are to be scrambled. These tasks teach children food preparation skills as well as encouraging them to eat.

Snacks

Snacks supplement the foods children eat at meals. To avoid interfering with meals, snacks should not be given near mealtimes. They should be served at least an hour before meals are to be served. Snacks should be nutritious and help meet the body's requirements for a balanced diet. See 10-15.

Children like snacks that can be eaten with their fingers. Many ready-to-eat breakfast cereals make good finger foods. Raisins, orange sections, and crackers are also good choices to offer.

Choosing Clothes

Clothes are another basic physical need for children. However, clothes provide more than just physical protection. Clothes

Healthy Snacks

Fruit juices
Fresh fruits
Raisins
Toast
Strips of turkey or lowfat ham
Frozen yogurt
Pudding
Pretzels
Popcorn
Cheese cubes
Carrot and celery sticks
Crackers with peanut butter
Peanuts
Sunflower seeds
Unsweetened dry breakfast cereal

10-15

A variety of foods that appeal to children can be served as nutritious snacks.

can help children develop decision-making skills. As with foods, children like to choose the clothes they wear. Parents can offer two options and allow children to select the outfit they wish to wear.

Clothes can also help stimulate intellectual development. Children can be asked to identify the colors of their clothes. They can name items pictured in fabric prints.

Parents need to provide children with clothes that are warm and comfortable. They must consider the fit, fabric, and construction of the garments they select for their children. They also need to look for features that will make it easy for children to dress themselves. Following a few guidelines can help parents select clothes that their children will enjoy wearing.

Fit

Parents need to think about how a garment fits a child. Children grow very rapidly. Keeping up with their changing sizes can be expensive. However, parents should resist the temptation to buy large clothes in the hopes that children will be able to wear them longer. Instead, parents should try to buy clothes that fit, but also allow a little extra room for growth. See 10-16.

A child's clothes must fit properly to allow for comfort and safety. Children need clothes that allow freedom of movement as they play. Clothes that are too tight can bind and restrict them. Clothes that are too loose may cause children to trip and fall.

Children's clothes are often sized according to the age of the child most likely to wear them. Since children grow at different rates, however, this is not always a valid guide. The best way to check for correct fit is to allow children to try on garments. When this is not possible, clothing can be chosen by a child's

Parents also need to look at the construction of children's clothing. Garments need to be sturdy enough to withstand hard use and frequent laundering. Double-stitched seams, well-made buttonholes, and securely attached fasteners are signs of durable construction.

Self-Help Features

Children can be encouraged to gain independence by being allowed to dress themselves. In fact, most children insist on dressing themselves by the age of three.

When selecting clothes for children, parents can look for self-help features. **Self-help features** are clothing design details that make clothes easier for children to put on and take off. They include elasticized waistbands and large neck and arm openings, 10-17. Large buttons or snaps that are easier for little fingers to manipulate are self-help features, too.

10-16
Shoulder straps can be adjusted to extend the wear of garments as children grow.

measurements. A child's height, weight, chest, and waist should be considered when evaluating fit.

Fabric and Construction

Parents should consider the fabrics used to make garments when choosing clothes for their children. Children prefer soft fabrics that feel good against their skin. Knits are quite popular because they give with the child's movement. Play clothes made of absorbent fibers help absorb perspiration. Firm weaves and close knits help clothes resist the wear and tear children put on them.

10-17
An elasticized waistband and stretchable neck and arm openings are self-help features that make this outfit easy for a child to put on.

Size of Wardrobe

Parents may wonder how many clothes a child should have. This depends on many factors. The climate, the availability of laundry facilities, and the family's values affect the size of a child's wardrobe.

Because children grow rapidly, new clothes must be purchased often. If children have large wardrobes, they may not get much use out of each garment. Many parents prefer to buy a few sturdy garments that can be washed and worn repeatedly. Children can get full use out of such garments before outgrowing them.

The Role of Play in Physical Development

Meeting children's physical needs includes providing them with opportunities to play. Both active-physical play and manipulative-constructive play are important to physical development.

Active-physical play helps children develop their large-muscle skills. They use their large muscles for movements like walking, running, hopping, jumping, and skipping. Movement helps them gain an understanding of space and the position of the body in space. They learn to understand concepts such as *front, back, side, up, down, high, low, through*, and *between*. Children learn to react quickly. They also gain more control over their body movements. As children get older, this control allows them to master more refined physical skills, such as skiing, skating, and dancing.

Manipulative-constructive play helps children develop small-muscle skills. The small muscles are those that control the wrists, hands, thumbs, fingers, and ankles. As smaller, finer muscles develop, you will see children picking up blocks with their fingers. As their skills develop, they begin to stack the blocks. By manipulating objects, children learn about the world around them.

Small-muscle development encourages eye-hand coordination. For instance, children learn to pick up shaped objects and drop them into containers with matching shapes for openings. Other small-muscle tasks include writing, drawing, stacking, stringing beads, and fitting puzzles and building pieces together. Caregivers need to provide children with play materials that will help them develop these small-muscle skills.

Physical skills improve as a child grows and develops. For example, an infant will crawl after a rolling ball. A preschooler might run after a ball. An older, more surefooted child might kick a ball. Each child has demonstrated a higher level of physical development.

Games and play activities can be chosen to help build physical skills. Children enjoy walking, running, jumping, balancing, and swinging their arms. They like to throw, catch, roll, and bounce balls. Riding tricycles and playing with outdoor equipment are also fun physical activities, 10-18. The appendix suggests other appropriate play activities to introduce at various stages of a child's skill development.

Social, emotional, intellectual, and physical development are all interrelated. Therefore, activities that stimulate physical growth will stimulate growth in other areas as well.

10-18
Physical activity, such as using a walkabout, helps children develop large muscle skills.

should be taught not to fear doctors, dentists, and other health professionals who might provide this care. See 10-19.

Children can be taught to be responsible for their own health. Parents can teach children proper eating and sleeping habits and dressing skills. Parents can also set a positive example by practicing good health care themselves. The following guidelines will help parents establish a healthy routine for their children:

▼ Maintain a clean environment.
▼ Teach children the importance of body cleanliness.
▼ Take children for regular medical checkups.
▼ Keep children's immunizations up to date. **Immunizations** are injections or drops given to a person to provide immunity from a certain disease.
▼ Keep children away from people who have **communicable diseases**. These are illnesses that can be passed on to other people, such as colds and sore

Creating a Healthy and Safe Environment

Physical needs include the need for proper health care and a safe environment. Failure to meet these needs can result in illnesses, accidents, or even death.

Health Care

Parents have a responsibility to protect their children's health. Providing nutritious food, adequate clothing, and a warm home will help keep children healthy. However, children are still likely to become ill from time to time. When this happens, parents have a duty to see that their children receive proper medical care. Children

10-19
Children can handle an unexpected hospital stay better if they have been taught not to fear doctors.

throats. Also, discourage habits that might spread communicable diseases, such as sharing drinking cups.

▼ Have a knowledge of common childhood illnesses and diseases. Be familiar with their symptoms and how to treat them.

▼ Treat wounds, bites, and stings promptly.

▼ Avoid foodborne illnesses by carefully selecting, preparing, and storing foods.

Safety

Caregivers have two responsibilities regarding children's safety. They must make the environment as safe as possible for children. Also, they must teach children to recognize and avoid safety hazards.

Parents need to look for safety hazards from a child's low vantage point. They should look for possible hazards to a child who is learning to sit, creep, stand, or walk. Parents must remove all items that could be dangerous to young children. They must teach older children to avoid dangerous items and to stay out of harmful areas.

The following guidelines will help parents maintain a safe environment for their children:

▼ Supervise children at all times. Their mobility, desire for independence, and curiosity prompts them to explore items that could be hazardous.

▼ Teach safe use of toys and play equipment.

▼ Avoid giving children toys that are sharp or fragile or that have small pieces that can be swallowed.

▼ Place gates at the top and bottom of stairs to prevent falls.

▼ Keep sharp and breakable objects out of the reach of children.

▼ Keep hot water, hot food, and other hot objects out of children's reach to prevent burns.

▼ Keep medicines and cleaning agents in a locked cabinet. Do not remove product labels.

▼ Place fencing around swimming pools, garden ponds, and other bodies of water to prevent accidental drownings. Supervise children constantly when they play near water.

▼ Provide safe, sturdy places for children to climb. Watch children closely when climbing is allowed.

▼ Keep plastic bags and large sheets of plastic away from children to prevent suffocation.

▼ Protect children from electrical hazards. Unused outlets should be capped with a safety device or covered with electrical tape. Keep appliance cords out of a child's path to prevent tripping. Do not allow cords to hang where children could grab them. If an appliance has a retractable cord, leave only the length that is needed outstretched. Use electrical appliances near the back of the counter where children will find it hard to reach them.

▼ Check fire extinguishers regularly and know how to use them.

▼ Plan and practice evacuation procedures for the home in case of fire.

▼ Secure children in a car seat for even short distances. The middle of the back seat is the safest spot for the car seat. Older children should always use safety belts. See 10-20.

Protecting Children from Strangers and Abductions

Unfortunately, there is a fine line between teaching children to love and accept all people while also teaching them to act with caution. While children are young, caregivers are charged with protecting them from strangers who might

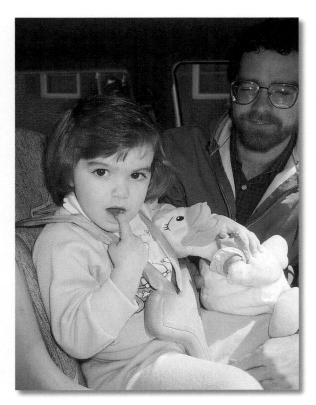

10-20
Car seats help protect children while traveling.

abuse or abduct them. Caregivers must keep an eye on children at all times.

As children grow and are allowed to accept some independence, there are times when an adult is not there to protect them. Teach children not to open the door to strangers. Explain why they should not get into a car or go anywhere with people without first getting approval from a caregiver. Teach children how to politely hang up the phone without saying their parents are not home. They also need to know how to speak to strangers without getting into a conversation that reveals personal information. Children should not accept gifts of food unless one of their caregivers is present. Teach them that it is appropriate to respond to such offers by smiling and politely saying "No thank you."

First Aid in Emergencies

No matter what you do as a caregiver to prevent injuries to children, accidents are bound to happen. When they do, you need to know how to react. **First aid** is emergency care or treatment given to people right after an accident. It relieves pain and prevents further injury. Caregivers need to know basic first aid procedures so they can treat minor injuries promptly. The following are some basic first aid techniques:

▼ *Small cuts and abrasions:* Wash area with soap and water. Apply mild antiseptic and bandage.

▼ *Deep cuts or puncture wounds:* Place a clean cloth or bandage over the wound. Press the wound with the palm of your hand to stop the bleeding. Then get medical help.

▼ *Minor burns:* Place the burned area in cool water for a few minutes until the pain subsides. Do not apply ointment.

▼ *Severe burns:* Have the child lie down. Do not put anything on the burn or try to remove any material stuck to the skin. Get medical help right away.

▼ *Broken bones:* If you think the child has a broken bone, get medical help. Do not move the child.

▼ *Splinters:* Wash the area with soap and water. Using a pair of tweezers, remove the splinter at the same angle it entered the skin. Cover with a bandage.

▼ *Insect stings:* If the child is stung by a wasp, bee, hornet, or yellow jacket, watch for an allergic reaction. A rash or swelling is a mild reaction. If the child is weak and collapses and has abdominal cramping, get prompt medical help.

▼ *Electric shock:* Do not touch the child with your bare hands until the electrical connection is broken or you, too, will be shocked. Either turn off the electricity or use a wooden stick, a cloth, or a rope to pull the child away from the source. If the child is not breathing, give *cardiopulmonary resuscitation (CPR)* if you are certified to do this. This technique includes rescue breathing and forcing the victim's heart to pump blood. Get medical help immediately.

▼ *Choking:* If a child cannot speak or breathe, he or she may be choking on something. Another sign is bluish lips and fingernails. You should immediately perform an abdominal thrust (Heimlich maneuver). The steps in this procedure are outlined in 10-21.

Have the phone number for the poison control center posted near the phone. If a child swallows a substance that could be poisonous, you will need to call this number immediately. Be prepared to tell the staff member what the child swallowed. Then follow his or her directions.

If serious illness or injury occurs, seek professional help immediately. You may need to call for an ambulance. For some emergencies, you may want to take the child to a hospital emergency room or clinic for treatment. The severity of the injury will determine which action you should take.

Check It Out!

1. True or false. Parents should repeatedly scold children who refuse to eat foods that are good for them.
2. List four factors to consider when selecting clothes for children.
3. Explain the difference between active-physical play and manipulative-constructive play.
4. List five health and five safety guidelines parents should follow to protect their children.

Performing the Abdominal Thrust (Heimlich Maneuver)

Infants and Toddlers

1. Place the child over your arm or thigh so the child's head is down. The child's abdomen should be against your arm or thigh. Support the head and neck with one hand.
2. Strike the child sharply with the heel of your hand three or four times between the shoulder blades until the object is dislodged.

Older Children

1. Pick the child up from the rear around the waist, or kneel over the child.
2. Place fist of one hand above navel, but well below rib cage. Cover fist with other hand. For a very small child, use two fingers from each hand.
3. Pull upward with both hands quickly but gently three to four times. Use less force for smaller children.
4. Repeat if necessary to dislodge the object from the windpipe.
5. Watch breathing and check pulse. Be prepared to give mouth-to-mouth breathing.

10-21

Knowing when and how to perform an abdominal thrust is important when a child is in your care.

Topic 10-4

Meeting Children's Social and Emotional Needs

Objectives

After studying this topic, you will be able to

▼ explain how to help children develop independence and responsibility.

▼ summarize techniques for communicating with children.

▼ give suggestions for guiding children's behavior.

▼ describe the role of play in social-emotional development.

▼ describe ways to help children overcome their fears.

Topic Terms

self-image
guidance
developmentally appropriate practices
modeling
setting limits
consistency
positive reinforcement
redirection
prompting
consequences
time out

The social and emotional development of children is an important part of their overall development. *Social development* is the process of learning to relate to other people. Very early in life, children begin to interact with their parents and siblings. As they get older, they interact more with people outside their family, including caregivers, teachers, playmates, and school friends. As they interact with others, they learn to cooperate, share, and follow directions. They develop their communication skills. Children become friendly and confident as they spend time with other people.

Emotional development refers to feelings and emotions and the way children express their emotions. Children show such emotions as love, fear, happiness, and frustration from a very early age. As they get older, they learn to control some of their emotions. Learning to express anger and frustration in acceptable ways shows emotional growth. For example, preschoolers might cry if they are unable to have the toys they want. Older children understand and accept explanations of why they can't have the things they want. Though disappointed, they control their emotions and are much less likely to cry. See 10-22.

As children interact with parents, siblings, and others, they experience and express many emotions. They feel love from their parents, and they respond in a similar manner. They develop a sense of trust. Children need to know that their caregivers will act in their best interests and be there for them at all times. They learn this through observing caregivers' actions as well as hearing caregivers' words. When children learn that caregivers are dependable, they trust them. The need to sense trust in another and to feel trustworthy is important to developing strong relationships.

All children need to feel loved for emotional growth to occur. Without this feeling of love, other aspects of development will be adversely affected. Recent studies have shown that emotional development lays the foundation for intelligence. At each stage of development, emotions lead the way, and learning facts and skills follow.

Helping Children Develop Independence and Responsibility

A child's social needs include learning skills that will help him or her become an independent person. Children also need to learn to accept responsibility for their actions as they begin to interact with others. Caregivers can use a number of techniques to help children develop independence and responsibility.

Young children want to become independent. This is evidenced by two-year-olds who insist "I can do it myself." Caregivers can help children build independence by giving help only when children need it. Caregivers often perform chores for children even though the children could do the chores themselves. In many cases, a better approach would be to wait for the children while they do the chores. Then the caregiver can praise the children for their efforts. Children want the praise and approval of their caregivers.

Decision-making skills are needed for independent living. Caregivers can help children learn these skills by allowing them to make as many choices as possible. The choices don't have to be major ones. For instance, children can help choose the foods they eat, the clothes they wear, and the activities they do. See 10-23. By being involved in the decision-making process, they gain self-confidence.

Children can help make many decisions every day. However, you should offer a choice only when you plan to abide by the decision. It is unfair to ask children to make decisions and then disagree with their choices. This harms children's

10-22
Older children show greater control over emotions such as anger, disappointment, and frustration.

The development of esteem begins early. Children form opinions of themselves by picking up on feelings and attitudes from their caregivers and others. By the way they are treated, children sense they are loved and valued by others. Children translate the messages they receive into a **self-image**—the way they see themselves. As children grow, they reassess their self-image from time to time. They get a more fully developed picture of themselves.

10-23
Children learn decision-making skills when they are allowed to choose their own toys.

self-concepts. It leads them to believe that you don't care what they think. It makes them feel their decisions are invalid.

One way to avoid this situation is to offer a child two equally acceptable alternatives. For instance, don't ask a child what he or she wants to eat for dinner. The child might say "Candy," which you are unlikely to consider a worthwhile entree. Instead, ask if the child would rather have turkey or ham. This allows the child to choose between two nutritious options.

Another way caregivers can help children build independence is by allowing them to solve their own problems when possible. When given a chance, many children are able to find satisfactory solutions.

A father told of his children who quarreled about who would sit in the front seat of the car. He decided to let them try to work it out. After much fussing, they came to a decision. One child would always sit in the front seat when they were leaving home. The other child would always

sit in the front seat for return trips. The children's own solution worked out very well.

A goal of child care is helping children prepare to become responsible adults. An important part of being responsible is accepting the consequences of decisions. Children need to learn that they will have to live with the results of their decisions— good or bad.

Suppose a child was given a choice of an apple or a banana for snack time, and the child chose the apple. After taking a few bites, the child said, "I don't want this apple. May I have a banana instead?" One good way for a caregiver to handle the situation would be to say, "You don't have to finish the apple now. I will put it away, and you can eat it later. However, you cannot have a banana. You chose an apple for this snack time. When it is snack time again, you may have a banana." This shows the child that he or she must accept the consequences of the decision that was made.

Another way children develop responsibility is by being encouraged to care for their own belongings. This can be done by providing storage within their reach. Low closet rods and dresser drawers help children to keep their clothes in place. Easy-to-reach shelves allow children to store their own toys, 10-24.

Providing Guidance

Meeting children's social and emotional needs includes helping them learn behavior that others will find acceptable. Children need guidance to help them handle life's experiences. **Guidance** includes everything caregivers do and say to promote socially acceptable behavior.

Factors in a child's environment that guide his or her behavior are called *extrinsic guidance*. This is the type of guidance

10-24
Accessible storage helps children develop responsibility as they learn to care for their own belongings.

caregivers provide. A caregiver's goal is to encourage children to begin guiding their own behavior. When children adopt a socially acceptable behavior pattern, they are practicing *intrinsic guidance*. Intrinsic guidance is also known as self-control or *self-discipline*.

Communicating with Children

Caregivers communicate with children in order to guide them. Children can be guided by both verbal and nonverbal messages. The following techniques can help make communication with children more effective:

▼ *Maintain eye contact during conversations.* Eye contact makes listening easier for a child. It also helps you, the speaker. By looking into a child's eyes, you can usually tell when the child understands. You may need to kneel down to a child's level in order to do this.

▼ *Keep messages simple and brief.* When talking with a young child, use small words and short sentences.

Give children only one or two simple instructions at a time. Children become confused when too many difficult words are used or too many directions are given at one time.

▼ *Speak in a relaxed voice.* Use a calm, quiet, relaxed tone of voice with children. They are more likely to listen to this type of voice. Then when you must raise your voice in an emergency, they will be more likely to pay attention to you.

▼ *Reinforce words with actions when necessary.* Remember that actions speak loudly. For instance, suppose Tommy is busy playing when you call him to dinner. He ignores your call. You may need to go to him, take him by the hand and say, "Let's eat now." By walking the child to the table, your message is made clear.

▼ *Use positive statements.* Emphasize what children should do rather than what they should not do, 10-25. For instance, suppose two children were throwing sand in the sandbox. You could say, "Don't throw the sand." Since throwing was fun, however, the children are likely to begin throwing something else. A more effective approach might be to say, "Instead of throwing the sand, try using it to build a sand castle." Another positive approach might be, "I see you want to throw something. Here is a ball. See if you can throw it instead." Children are easy to distract—especially if the tone of your voice makes your idea sound like fun.

▼ *Answer children's questions briefly and truthfully.* No matter what children ask, a simple answer is likely to satisfy their curiosity. Answer any question in a manner appropriate for the child's level of understanding.

Using Positive Statements	
Negative	**Positive**
"Don't spill your milk."	"Hold your glass steady."
"Don't talk with your mouth full."	"Wait until you have swallowed your food before you begin talking."
"Don't put your feet on the chair."	"Keep your feet on the floor."
"Don't yell."	"Please talk softly."
"Don't push and shove."	"Keep your hands by your side."
"Don't interrupt when others are talking."	"Wait for your turn to talk."
"Don't throw blocks."	"Keep the blocks on the table, please."
"Don't pull the kitten's tail."	"Pet the kitten gently."
"Don't leave the toys on the floor."	"Put the toys on the shelf."
"Don't get paint on your clothes."	"Put on a smock."

10-25
Positive statements clearly tell children what they should do.

Developmentally Appropriate Guidance

Caregivers need to use different guidance techniques for children of different ages. A technique that is effective with four-year-olds may not work with toddlers. **Developmentally appropriate practices** are those that are suited to the developmental characteristics and needs of the individual child.

By the time children reach the toddler stage, they are old enough to understand simple words. Caregivers can use brief statements, such as "Pet the bunny gently." Toddlers should be able to follow such simple directions.

Caregivers need patience when they are with toddlers. Children of this age have a very short attention span. Caregivers may need to repeat a suggestion many times before a toddler adopts the desired behavior.

By the age of four, children are beginning to be able to reason. Briefly explaining why a certain behavior is or is not appropriate will help children use acceptable behaviors.

Guidance Techniques

Caregivers can use a number of techniques to guide children's behavior. Caregivers must first act as positive role models. Children learn by imitating others. Whenever you speak, you are **modeling** behavior. At an early age, children are aware of the actions of the adults around them, 10-26. They copy the behavior of the adults they see every day. If you want their behavior to be positive, you must model that behavior yourself and set a good example. Also remember that children are probably listening and watching you when you don't realize it. For example, if the rule is to chew with your mouth closed, all caregivers should also be sure to chew with closed mouths.

10-26
Children are eager to receive attention from caregivers and are likely to model their behavior.

Children need to know what they may and may not do. This is called **setting limits**. These may be also be called *rules*. They are made to keep children safe. For example, a young child may be allowed to play only in the fenced backyard away from the street. This is a limit set to protect the child. Limits should be reasonable and appropriate for the child's age. An older child may be allowed to play anywhere within the caregiver's view. With permission, an older child may even play at another child's home.

If rules are made, they must be enforced with **consistency**. This means the same behavior is expected at all times. Children feel secure when limits are enforced consistently. If they are not, the child becomes confused. Using the above example, a young child may play in the front yard one day instead of the backyard. If the rule is not enforced, the child will play in the front yard on other days. The child broke the rule and nothing happened. When limits are consistent, children are more likely to respect them. When they are not consistent, children will ignore them.

Children's behavior can often be molded by rewarding positive behavior. This is called **positive reinforcement**. Caregivers should try to reward good behavior with attention and praise. Undesirable behavior should be ignored if possible. Gestures as well as words can be used to guide behavior. A smile, a nod, or a gentle hug will reinforce positive actions.

Even babies realize that if an action brings a desired response, repeating the action will bring a repeated response. For instance, a baby sitting in a high chair may throw a spoon on the floor. If you give the spoon back to the baby, he or she may throw it on the floor again. If you give the spoon back a second time, the baby is likely to think you are playing a game. The baby is too young to understand if you say "Keep your spoon on the tray." The best way to handle this situation is to simply stop giving the spoon back to the baby.

Another guidance technique is **redirection**, or focusing the child's attention on something else. For instance, suppose a child wants a toy another child has. Offering the child a different toy is a way of turning his or her attention in a different direction. The key to redirection is providing an appealing substitute.

Caregivers can use a technique called **prompting**. Questions can prompt children to exhibit desired behavior. A caregiver might ask "Where does the ball belong?" A child may respond by putting the ball on the proper shelf. Asking "What are you supposed to do when you are finished painting?" may encourage children to wash their hands.

Caregivers need to give children time to make a transition from one activity to another. Play is important to children, and they do not like to be suddenly interrupted. If possible, a warning should be given five or ten minutes before a change of activities. This gives children time to finish what they are doing.

Children tire of activities quickly due to their short attention spans. A caregiver may need to provide new activities for children to encourage positive behavior, 10-27. Positive reinforcement should be used as much as possible to guide children's behavior. When misbehavior occurs, however, consequences may become part of the guidance process.

10-27
Providing children with interesting activities reduces behavior problems.

Using Consequences

Consequences are results that follow an action or behavior. When using consequences, the negative results of the child's own actions influence future behaviors. If a child's health or safety is at risk, a caregiver must step in at once. However, if a child's well-being is not at risk, consequences can act as a deterrent to inappropriate behavior. For instance, playing with food is inappropriate behavior at the dinner table. Suppose a child plays with his or her food until it becomes cold. He or she then asks to have the food reheated in the microwave oven. The request is not honored. The child learns that the consequence for not eating promptly is to eat cold food.

Caregivers can set up consequences that relate to misbehaviors. These are called *logical consequences*. For instance, a child who throws blocks may not be allowed to play with the blocks for a period of time. Once consequences are imposed, they must be enforced. Otherwise, children will not learn from the consequences of their behavior.

Another logical consequence might be a time out. A **time out** involves moving a child away from others for a short period of time, 10-28. It should be used only when a child's disruptive behavior cannot be ignored. The child needs time to calm down and gain self-control. A time out is not appropriate for children younger than the age of four. Younger children are not able to understand their behavior can have negative consequences. The time out should be limited to three minutes.

A caregiver should be careful never to threaten to withdraw love. A child needs to feel loved regardless of his or her behavior. Love should not be used as a reward that has to be earned by a child. It should be given freely.

10-28
A time out is a guidance technique that teaches young children about negative consequences.

Parenting Styles

Parents tend to develop a parenting style they use to guide their children's behavior. Parenting styles can be grouped into three categories:

▼ *Authoritarian parents* tend to rule single-handedly. They maintain control and expect conformity. The children are not encouraged to negotiate or present different views.

▼ *Permissive parents* allow children to set their own rules. Children are allowed to make most of their decisions. Without boundaries, these children may feel insecure. They sometimes fear the natural consequences of decisions they are not prepared to make.

▼ *Democratic parents* allow freedom within structure. Rules are established and explained. Children are allowed to ask questions and present their views. Children feel secure because they know what to do and why they are doing it.

The Role of Play in Social-Emotional Development

Though extrinsic guidance is important in helping children develop socially and emotionally, children also learn through their play. As children play, they interact with the world of people and objects. As they do so, they develop socially and emotionally. For instance, a game that babies enjoy playing is peek-a-boo. They will play this game with their caregivers. It helps them develop a sense of trust. The face of the caregiver reappears after it disappears. This is an important learning for infants.

Caregivers can promote social-emotional development by initiating play activities appropriate for the age of the child. Peek-a-boo games with infants can be followed with games such as pat-a-cake. Still later, the game might be rhyming words. The actual game is not as important as the social interactions and the trust that forms between caregiver and child.

As children get older, they play more with other children, 10-29. This group play promotes skills such as cooperation, sharing, and property rights. Playing with others helps children learn to give and receive. Self-esteem develops when there is a balance between giving and receiving. The goal is to help children learn to make and maintain relationships where they also develop healthy self-concepts.

Helping Children Overcome Fears

Children between the ages of two and six are quite likely to develop a number of fears. Meeting children's emotional needs involves helping them handle their fears. A caregiver needs to respect a child's fears.

A caregiver can try to find out the reason for a child's feelings. This may suggest ideas for helping the child overcome his or her fright. For instance, a boy had a fear of swimming. His parents asked why he was afraid. The boy said he wouldn't be able to breathe if his head went under the water. The parents used this information to gradually introduce the boy to shallow water. Soon the boy felt safe enough to get his head wet.

A caregiver can encourage a child to overcome a fear. However, the caregiver should avoid forcing the child into a situation that he or she finds frightening. Children will try new experiences when they feel ready. Forcing them only prolongs their apprehension.

The majority of children's fears are fears of unfamiliar objects and situations. As children gain experience with something, they typically lose their fear of it. Caregivers need to clearly explain

10-29
A group of neighborhood children may work together to set up a lemonade stand.

new circumstances before children have a chance to become fearful. For example, children are often afraid of doctors. A caregiver can use a toy medical kit to show a child tools similar to those used by doctors. This will help the child feel more relaxed when he or she sees these tools in a doctor's office.

A caregiver may be able to distract a child's attention away from his or her fears. A two-year-old cried when riding over a bridge on the route to her home. Her caregiver asked her why she was afraid of the bridge. The child said, "It goes hmmm." The caregiver said, "Since the bridge hums to us, maybe we can hum to it next time." They rehearsed their humming sound several times. On the next trip, the child looked forward to humming so much that she did not cry. Through distraction, the child's attention was diverted from her fear of the bridge to humming.

Check It Out!

1. Describe three ways caregivers can help children develop independence.
2. Everything caregivers do and say to promote socially acceptable behavior is called _____.
3. Describe three guidance techniques you can use to guide children's behavior.
4. True or false. Most fears among children are caused by bad experiences they have had.

Topic 10-5
Meeting Children's Intellectual Needs

Objectives
After studying this topic, you will be able to
▼ explain the role of play in intellectual development.
▼ describe various enrichment activities that stimulate children intellectually.
▼ list guidelines for selecting toys for children.

Topic Terms
imitative-imaginative play
dramatic play
socio-dramatic play
multicultural book

As children grow, they develop intellectually. They gain the ability to reason and use complex thought processes. They also learn how to use their imaginations and think creatively.

Caregivers need to provide children with stimulating activities. However, they should be careful not to challenge children to do too many difficult tasks. Children need to value themselves and feel good about what they do. This helps them develop self-esteem.

The latest research shows that it is more important for children to be confident, curious, motivated, and persistent as they enter school than to be able to recite numbers, letters, and colors. Intellectual development will occur when there is a positive social-emotional foundation.

The Role of Play in Intellectual Development

Children learn through their play activities. They experiment to see how things work. They use their imaginations and try new ideas. Play allows children to experience different sights, sounds, textures, smells, and tastes. Children are introduced to their environment and objects in their environment. They learn to use these resources. Through play they learn number concepts such as *more* and *less* and *large* and *small*. Puzzles and nesting toys help them see size and shape relationships. Many activities encourage creative thinking. Some activities can also be chosen to help children build reasoning skills. All these activities lead to learning, but without any pressure to succeed.

Children play in many ways. In active physical play, children use their large muscles as they run, hop, jump, and skip. They use their small muscles as they play with toys, such as puzzles, beads, and blocks.

In **imitative-imaginative play**, children use their imaginations as they pretend to be other people or objects. This form of play begins at about two years of age. At this age, children are capable of having an object stand for something else. For instance, a cardboard box might represent a car or a plane. By three or four years of age, children begin **dramatic play**. This form of play involves role playing. A child imitates another person or acts out a situation, but does so alone. See 10-30. **Socio-dramatic play** involves several children imitating others and acting out situations together. They mimic such adult roles as mommy, daddy, doctor, or astronaut. They make decisions and learn problem-solving skills.

10-30
This child is playing the role of a television announcer.

Language concepts also develop as they generate plots and story lines. Creativity and imagination are fostered.

Enrichment Activities for Children

Not all activities provide the same types of intellectual stimulation. Books, stories, music activities, art activities, and toys all give children different learning experiences. Offering children a variety of activities gives them the opportunity to use a range of skills.

Books

Children develop an interest in books at an early age. The content of books should be chosen with a child's age in mind, 10-31. Very young children enjoy books about objects that are familiar to them. Animal stories are favorites. Children like to identify the animals pictured and make animal noises.

10-31
Children enjoy books from a very early age.

Books can expose children to a wide range of ideas. Look for books that show both men and women in various careers. This will allow children to explore nontraditional work roles. Also select **multicultural books**. These are stories that involve characters from a variety of racial and ethnic groups. Such books can help children develop positive attitudes about sex roles and other cultures.

Children should be permitted to handle their own books. Books for small children should be sturdy. Heavy cardboard and fabric pages are easy to turn and will not tear easily. When reading books with paper pages, teach children to turn pages carefully. Repair torn pages with clear tape so children will not be tempted to tear them more.

Stories

Stories can provide intellectual stimulation by encouraging children to use their imaginations. Children might be motivated to memorize stories and repeat

The More You Know: How Does Reading Affect Other Skills?

Reading to children is one of the best ways to help them learn language skills. Children build their vocabularies as they associate pictures with words in a book. They practice communication skills by talking about stories. They develop reasoning skills when they answer questions about a story. In addition, reading time offers opportunities for the reader and listener to strengthen their bonds.

them. They can use dramatic skills by acting out a story as it is told. Children may also develop creativity by illustrating a story with art.

Caregivers can show regard for children by preparing stories that meet the children's interests. Good storytellers put a lot of action into stories. They change the tone of their voices to fit the moods of the story. They use their hands to create sounds as needed. Stories can be chosen to create a desired setting. Exciting stories are best before playtime. Happy, peaceful stories are best before bedtime.

Some stories are old favorites that have been told to children for generations. Others are created on the spot. Young children like stories about themselves. A recap of their day's activities can become a story.

Art Activities

Art activities teach children about colors, lines, and shapes. They also provide children with an opportunity to develop creativity.

Children are not always able to verbalize their thoughts and feelings. Art materials can help children express emotions when they do not have words to say what they mean.

Children should use a variety of art materials. Modeling clay is a favorite medium for artistic expression. Crayons and paints are also popular, 10-32. Caregivers can give children some basic guidelines about how art materials should be used. For instance, they might require children to wear smocks when working with these materials. They may show children how to avoid dripping paint or

10-32
Painting gives children a chance to express their creativity.

how to make different shapes with clay. However, adults should not control art activities too carefully. They should not tell children what to make or how to make it. Children should be given freedom to be creative.

Caregivers should not criticize children's artwork. They should also avoid trying to guess what children have made. A child's confidence can be shaken when a caregiver incorrectly identifies something the child has made. A wise alternative would be to say, "This is interesting. Tell me about it." The child may explain what a sculpture or drawing represents. The child might also tell what he or she was thinking as the object was being created.

Music Activities

Music introduces children to a number of concepts. Children develop an awareness of rhythm as they play with instruments. They gain an understanding of pitch and can identify high and low notes. They learn about rhymes as they sing the words of songs.

Music has appeal to children of all ages. Even babies seem to find soft music relaxing and soothing. They like musical toys. They wave their arms and kick their legs in response to the sound of music.

Children like songs they understand. Sometimes they will enjoy singing with a caregiver. At other times, they will want to perform alone. Children especially like action songs so they can use their bodies. Caregivers shouldn't worry if they cannot sing well. Children will still enjoy the rhythm of music.

Musical instruments also provide fun learning experiences for children. Children love to participate in rhythm bands. They can take turns beating drums, shaking tambourines, or ringing triangles. Children also enjoy making rhythm sounds with sandpaper blocks, rhythm sticks, finger cymbals, shakers, and bells.

Music, like stories and books, can help create a desired mood. Exciting music can help awaken a sleepy child in the morning. Soft, quiet music can help an excited child relax at bedtime.

Watching TV and Videos

Some people think watching TV and videos is a negative activity for children. However, these mediums have several positive traits. They give children a chance to slow down after an active day of play. Many TV shows and videos are educational, too. They teach children such basic concepts as numbers and letters. They present examples of accepted social behavior, like sharing and telling the truth. They also inform children about current issues, such as the environment.

Caregivers should resist the temptation to use the television as a babysitter. Whenever possible, caregivers should watch programs with children. They can ask children questions about programs to stimulate the children's thinking.

Caregivers should be actively involved in helping children select appropriate programs. Children need to be able to understand the programs and videos they watch. Those that will confuse or upset them are not recommended.

Programs must be selected according to the maturity of children. Shows that are frightening or contain adult subject matter should be avoided. Children cannot always separate fiction from reality. Watching scary videos and TV shows may cause children to have nightmares. They may fear the frightening events they have seen will happen to them. The easiest way to prevent such fears is to control which shows children watch.

Selecting Toys

Toys are tools to help children grow physically, emotionally, socially, and intellectually. They should be chosen to stimulate—but not overstimulate—a child's total development.

Age Appropriateness

Caregivers should select toys that are appropriate for a child's age. Age is a clue to a child's skill level. For instance, one-year-old children do not have the strength or coordination needed to ride a tricycle. However, most one-year-olds are able to walk. Therefore, a pull toy is a good choice for a one-year-old. The child can play with the toy while walking. The tricycle would be a better choice for an older child who has developed more muscle skill, 10-33.

10-33
This boy is proud that he is able to ride this car and make it "go."

Toy manufacturers often state on the label the age of the child for whom the toy was designed. Look for these age suggestions on labels as you consider the purchase of toys. The need for a lot of adult assistance is a sign that a toy is too complicated. Wait and purchase such a toy when the child is able to handle it with less supervision.

The interests of a child should also be considered when selecting toys. Some children prefer quiet activities, such as puzzles. Many children enjoy role-playing. For this group, housekeeping toys and occupational toys, such as tool chests, might be good choices. Active children like climbing toys and wheel toys. As children get older, many begin to enjoy scientific toys.

Safety

Safety is another key consideration when choosing toys for children. Avoid the following:

▼ toys with small parts that can be swallowed
▼ sharp points that can poke
▼ rough or sharp edges that can cut
▼ long cords or strings (for infants and young children)
▼ flammable materials
▼ nonwashable dolls and stuffed toys
▼ toxic paints
▼ poorly made toys that can easily fall apart

Children are disappointed when toys break. Broken toys are also hazardous. Therefore, look for durable, well-made toys. See 10-34.

Caregivers should check the instructions that accompany toys. They can demonstrate the safe use of toys to children.

10-34
The softness of these foam blocks makes them safe toys for young children.

All toys are hazardous when they are left on floors, stairways, and driveways. Children should be taught responsibility for their own belongings. Caregivers can insist that children keep all toys stored when not in use. Providing adequate and safe storage space will help children with this task.

Check It Out!

1. Explain the difference between dramatic play and socio-dramatic play.
2. What are three concepts children can learn through music activities?
3. List three guidelines to follow when selecting toys for children.

Chapter Review

Summary

Parents must quickly learn how to care for their newborns during the first year of life. Then as infants grow physically, emotionally, socially, and intellectually, parents will enjoy watching for signs of development.

Although growth is fastest in the first year, children from ages one to five continue to develop with amazing speed. Parents must provide an atmosphere that will foster growth in all areas. Parents will also have to address any special needs that their children might have.

Parents must make sure that children's physical needs are met. They need to offer children a variety of nutritious and appealing foods for meals and snacks. They must consider the fit, features, fabric, and construction of the clothes they select for their children. Parents need to encourage their children to be physically active. They also need to create a healthy and safe environment for their children.

Parents must meet children's social and emotional needs as well as their physical needs. They need to communicate with their children and teach them independence and responsibility. They need to provide guidance to direct their children's behavior. Parents also need to help their children learn to overcome fears.

Parents must not overlook their children's intellectual needs. They can stimulate children's intellectual development by reading to them and telling them stories. Art and music activities can be intellectually stimulating. When choosing toys that promote intellectual growth, parents must consider age appropriateness and safety.

Think About It!

1. What do you think would be the greatest challenge of caring for a newborn?
2. What would you expect if you were babysitting a toddler? What would you expect if you were babysitting a preschooler?
3. How would you encourage children who are fussy eaters to eat foods that are good for them?
4. What types of games and play activities would you use to help children develop physically?
5. What are some ways you could help a child develop a positive self-image?
6. Describe some problems you have had when working with small children. How might good guidance techniques have simplified the situations?
7. What techniques do you think would be most effective for guiding a child's behavior? Explain your answer.
8. What types of activities would you prefer to use to stimulate a child intellectually? Explain your answer.

Try It Out!

1. Investigate how to feed, bathe, clothe, or diaper a newborn. Use a doll to give a demonstration to the class.
2. Investigate programs in your school district that are available to assist children with special needs. Find out if any of these programs are designed for preschool children. Report your findings in class.
3. Develop a checklist of factors that would help you select clothes for children.

4. Plan some activities designed to teach children independence and responsibility. Invite some children to class or volunteer to work in a preschool program and conduct the activities. Write a report about the results.

5. Write a story about a child. In the story, describe factors in the child's environment that provide extrinsic guidance. Also describe a situation in which the child practices intrinsic guidance.

6. In a small group, discuss fears that you had as a young child. Talk about what you think motivated the fears. Describe the role older individuals played as you overcame them.

7. Observe a children's story hour at your local library. Give a brief oral report describing how the librarians stimulate interest as they read.

8. Visit a toy department and compile a list of five toys that would be appropriate for preschoolers. Briefly describe how each toy will foster the development of a child.

Chapter 11
Caring for Children

Careers

These careers relate to the topics in this chapter:
▼ infant care assistant or babysitter
▼ nanny
▼ Head Start teacher
▼ social worker

As you study the chapter, see if you can think of others.

Topics

11-1 Being a Responsible Caregiver
11-2 Child Care Options

Topic 11-1

Being a Responsible Caregiver

Objectives

After studying this topic, you will be able to
▼ name possible caregivers for children.
▼ list characteristics of a responsible caregiver.
▼ describe the responsibilities of caregivers.
▼ identify helpful resources for caregivers.

Topic Terms

caregiver
hot line
foster care

11-1
Many different people will provide for a child's care through the growing years.

A **caregiver** is a person who provides care for someone else. A caregiver may be responsible for an older person, a person with disabilities, or a young child. In this chapter, you will learn about caregivers who provide care for young children.

A child may have many different caregivers, including parents, grandparents, babysitters, and teachers, 11-1. You, too, may be a child's caregiver. You may have younger brothers and sisters. You may babysit for children in your neighborhood. You may even choose a career that involves working with children.

Who Are the Caregivers?

Many people may fill the role of caregiver for a child. The primary caregivers are the parents. They have the main responsibility for providing for their child's needs. There are times, however, when they cannot be with their child. Then other caregivers fulfill this important role.

Many of a child's caregivers are related to the child, such as siblings, grandparents, aunts, uncles, and other relatives. Older brothers and sisters may occasionally be left in charge of their younger siblings. After-school care is often provided by older siblings. Grandparents, if they live near their grandchildren, may have an important role in their grandchildren's lives, 11-2. They may care for the child for a short time on an as-needed basis, or for a longer, more regular period of time. In the case of a single parent, the grandchild and his or her parent may even live with

11-2
This grandfather is happy to fix his granddaughter's bike.

the grandparents. They may provide much of the child's care if the parent must finish school or work.

Other caregivers may be employed by the family to care for the child in their absence. These include babysitters, child care providers, and preschool teachers. Babysitters generally provide care in the child's own home for a few hours at a time. Sometimes children are dropped off at a sitter's home. Many more children today are spending a portion of each day in a child-care center or preschool. Here professional child-care workers become the caregivers.

Guardians and foster parents may be responsible for a child's care. These individuals are legally required to care for a child if the parents are unable to do so. Sometimes the role of caregiver is more informal. For example, a caring neighbor

may invite a child to go on an outing to give the parents some much-needed free time together. The neighbor becomes a caregiver for the time they are out.

Characteristics of Responsible Caregivers

Every person is not equally qualified to be a caregiver. Some people are uniquely talented in the care of children, while others may have some skills to learn. Where do you fit in the picture? The characteristics of responsible caregivers fall into four categories: personal qualities, personal skills, knowledge and experience, and health.

Personal Qualities

A person who is responsible for the care of children should have certain personal qualities. Responsible caregivers

▼ *enjoy children.* They find each child to be unique and fascinating. They feel energized in the presence of children. Good caregivers have a sense of humor and have fun with children. People who enjoy children find them easy to love.

▼ *are patient.* They do not count the times a child asks "Why?" They can read the same books aloud, tell favorite stories, and play the same game again and again. They know that children learn at different rates. They can patiently wait for children to learn to do things for themselves, like tie their shoelaces. See 11-3.

▼ *are flexible.* Children can be unpredictable. Caregivers must be prepared for anything and be willing to adapt to changing circumstances.

11-3
Caregivers must be patient and allow children to learn skills for themselves.

▼ *are alert to children's needs.* Children must be supervised at all times. Caregivers are always watchful to foresee and prevent problems that may occur. In the event that a child's safety is endangered, they are there to immediately offer aid and comfort. Emotional and social needs are also met promptly.

▼ *exercise self-control.* Caregivers should exhibit a calm and gentle demeanor. Caring for children can be stressful and tiring at times. Good caregivers know when to take a personal time out and calm themselves down. Sometimes caregivers need to "count to ten" to keep their emotions under control.

▼ *are consistent.* A responsible caregiver establishes routines and rules that are followed regularly. This prevents children from becoming confused. Bedtime, mealtimes, and other daily activities become rituals. This means they are conducted in the same manner each time. Children learn to depend on these routines. For instance, if children follow a certain bedtime routine night after night, they are more likely to go to bed without a problem. Rules also must be enforced consistently. This gives children a sense of security. If not, children learn that rules are meaningless and can be ignored.

▼ *set good examples.* Children like to imitate the behavior of adults because it makes them feel grown up. They especially imitate those whom they admire. They learn what to do—right or wrong—from watching others. Good caregivers know this and are careful to set good examples.

Personal Skills

Certain personal skills are needed to give care to young children. The skills needed by responsible caregivers include communication skills, judgment skills, and management skills.

Caregivers must be able to communicate with both children and adults. When communicating with children, they need to speak clearly and use words the children can understand. Using simple language is important. Young children have limited vocabularies. Also using positive statements will help children know what is expected of them. In other words, they tell children what to do rather than what not to do. For example, instead of saying "Do not run," they say "Please walk." See 11-4.

Caregivers may also need to communicate with other adults. Babysitters and child-care professionals need to be able to communicate with the child's parents or guardians about the care and needs of the child. They also may need to communicate with other caregivers if they are in a group child-care facility.

11-4
Children respond best to caregivers who communicate clearly.

Judgment skills are important for caregivers to have. Every day child caregivers are required to make decisions on how to handle situations involving the children in their care. For example, they must help children deal with conflicts. All children have differences from time to time. The caregiver must know how and when to get involved. Sometimes children can be allowed to work through conflicts on their own. At other times, a decision must be made quickly to avoid a dangerous situation.

Conflicts between adults and children are bound to occur as children enter their toddler years. Again, judgment skills are needed. Caregivers are expected to use mature judgment in handling these disagreements. They need to know effective guidance techniques and how to use them. To foresee and prevent is the best way to avoid problems. Making sure children have a healthful, safe environment is another preventive measure. If children have ample age-appropriate toys and materials to explore, it is less likely that problems will arise.

Certain management skills can benefit caregivers. It helps to plan ahead. There may be moments when everything seems to happen at once. A responsible caregiver should try to foresee possible needs and prepare for them. For instance, having a good supply of diapers on hand shows good planning. Having activities planned to keep children actively involved shows planning, 11-5. Knowing where the first aid supplies are kept and making sure all supplies are available is another example. Then, when unexpected events happen, the caregiver is ready.

A responsible caregiver also knows how to manage time well. Caregivers can organize their time, set priorities, and distinguish between important and urgent matters. There is always more that could be done. If caregivers are to be ready for their responsibilities, they will need to make choices that make good use of their time. They will need to use basic time management skills. You will learn more about time management in Chapter 17.

Knowledge and Experience

Some knowledge about child growth and development is important for caregivers no matter what their role. All child caregivers need to know what children are like. Knowledge is basic to knowing what to expect of children at different ages—their needs, abilities, and interests. This understanding helps

11-5
Quality caregivers plan a variety of activities to keep children actively involved.

caregivers plan appropriate activities to meet their developmental needs. It helps them understand children's behavior and how to respond. For instance, if caregivers know children start becoming afraid of leaving their parents at about eight months, they can plan ways to help children through this stage.

The more experience caregivers have in being with children, the more they will learn about caring for them. New parents who have not been around babies are always very nervous when they become parents for the first time. They are afraid at first to even hold their babies for fear they might harm them. Newborns seem so fragile. Soon parents become quite comfortable with their babies. After the second or third child, they are experienced caregivers and feel much more comfortable in their role as parents.

This is true for all caregivers. Experience is often the best teacher. The more caregivers are around children, the more they learn about how to care for them. They become more comfortable in their presence. When you babysit a child for the first time, you probably feel nervous. After a while, you feel much more at ease as you get to know the child. You know more of what to expect from the child and how best to guide him or her.

New caregivers can learn about children by reading books on child development. Many child care classes are also available. Your school probably offers a child development or parenting class that you could take. Classes are also available for adults.

Professional child care workers must meet state licensing requirements in order to work with young children. A few positions require little training or experience. Most child care jobs, however, require a person to have additional education beyond high school. A two-year associate's degree in child development or a related area is often a minimum requirement. In order for a child care facility to be licensed by the state, the child care workers must meet these educational requirements. Licensing requirements vary from state to state.

Good Health

Health is an important factor for caregivers. Much energy is expended physically, mentally, and emotionally during a day spent with children. The physical movement involved is almost continuous. Staying mentally alert to a child's ongoing needs gives little time to relax. The responsibility of helping each child develop to his or her fullest potential can be challenging. A lot of energy is expended. Good health is vital in order for caregivers to function to the best of their ability.

Responsibilities of Caregivers

Parents and other caregivers have tremendous responsibilities in their roles as caregivers. It is not an easy task. Anyone taking on this role must be ready to fulfill some very important jobs. They are responsible for meeting children's many needs, including the following:

▼ *Physical needs.* A child's physical needs must be met. These include providing the child's food, clothing, shelter, and medical care. Caregivers are responsible for the health and safety of the children in their care.

▼ *Social needs.* A child must learn to interact with other children and adults. Children need to learn valuable lessons in sharing, communicating, and compromising, 11-6. Children also need to develop character. They have to learn to behave in ways that are acceptable to society. Children are not born knowing right from wrong. Caregivers have the responsibility to guide children in ways that will promote their moral development.

▼ *Emotional needs.* Children need to feel loved no matter what they do. They also need to learn how to express their emotions in acceptable ways. This sometimes requires caregivers to set limits. Through love and guidance, parents and other caregivers help children grow toward independence.

▼ *Intellectual needs.* Caregivers must provide children with opportunities that will help them grow and learn. They can help children develop their language and thinking skills by providing them with suitable learning opportunities.

11-6
Caregivers are responsible for helping children develop the social skills of sharing and communicating.

Resources for Caregivers

How can you learn to be a responsible caregiver? Don't assume knowing how to care for a child is intuitive. Be prepared to learn as much as you can using the many resources available to you. As stated earlier, there are many classes you can take to learn about children, but there are other resources as well. Some can be used to gain general information about child care. Others may be called on in special situations.

You might begin by checking your local library for books and magazines you think will be helpful, 11-7. In addition, you can go online and check out various Web sites for information. You must be very cautious, however, in selecting Web sites. Some you can count on for reliable information; others you cannot.

Get acquainted with the various public and private agencies available in your community. There are services for child care and parent education, and even recreation. Most will also have educational literature to distribute. Many of these agencies provide services for families in times of need. Some agencies can diagnose and treat health problems. Others offer financial advice and assistance. Look in the Yellow Pages or Blue Pages of your local phone directory to find the names and locations of the various agencies in your community. City, county, and state government agencies will be listed. These agencies can also refer you to volunteer organizations and support groups that provide various types of assistance.

In emergency situations, you might want to call a hot line. A **hot line** is a number people can call for information or other assistance with a specific problem. Many hot lines operate 24 hours a day.

11-7
Books about child care can be valuable resources for caregivers.

Persons familiar with the particular crisis will answer the phone, offer guidance, and refer callers to local services. If an emergency occurs with a child in your care, you may need to call 911 for medical assistance, 11-8.

A support group might also be a resource for a caregiver. As you have read, a *support group* is a group of people who share a similar problem or concern. Members join together regularly to discuss the concern they have in common. The group might be led by a professional counselor who has special knowledge of the problem.

There are many kinds of support groups. Many are organized to provide support for people who have a family member who has a certain illness. Others are organized for parents dealing with certain problems. For example, *Share* is a support group for parents who have lost a newborn through miscarriage, stillbirth, or infant death. *Child Find* is for parents trying to find missing children. Support groups meeting in your local community are often listed in the phone book. Medical professionals can also refer you to support groups.

The Role of Society in Protecting Children's Rights

Children are a precious resource. They are our hope for the future. Parents and other adults care for them while they are young. Children are easily hurt because they are physically weaker than adults and cannot reason as adults. It is society's responsibility to protect them.

In the United States, parents have the rights of guardianship and determine their children's upbringing. They are responsible for their physical care and their financial support. They provide moral teachings, provide for their education, and make health care choices. If the parents do not provide for these needs of their children, the state can act on the child's behalf and provide protection. This might mean the state would require foster care in extreme situations. **Foster care** is care provided for a child who needs a home temporarily. Children may be placed in foster homes because they have been abandoned, abused, or neglected by their parents. In other situations, children's parents may be temporarily unable to care for them and ask the state for help.

Laws are also passed to protect children's rights. School attendance, for example, is required by law up to a certain age. There are child labor laws that protect children from unsafe working conditions or jobs that interfere with their education. States also provide child welfare services. These services offer food and assistance to families who are unable to make provisions on their own.

All caregivers are responsible for the well-being of the children in their care. It is society's responsibility to make sure all children receive that care. If the parents cannot provide it, other adults will. Legislative policies are made to protect children as they grow to adulthood.

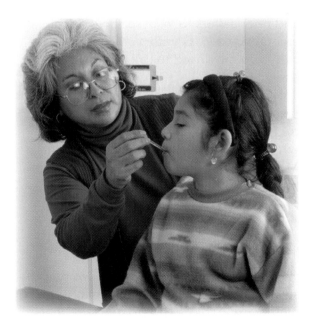

11-8
A child in your care may need to be taken to a health clinic if there are signs of serious illness.

Check It Out!

1. Name four types of caregivers for children.
2. List five characteristics of a responsible caregiver.
3. Describe the four main responsibilities of caregivers.
4. State four helpful resources for caregivers.

Topic 11-2
Child Care Options

Objectives

After studying this topic, you will be able to
▼ identify child care options.
▼ list factors parents should consider when choosing a child care facility.

Topic Terms

nanny
child care cooperatives

Many child care experts feel the ideal environment for child rearing is in the home with at least one parent present. However, this arrangement is not always possible, especially in dual-career or single-parent families. The numbers of women entering the workforce are increasing every year. With this increase comes a rapidly growing demand by parents for quality child care. There are several options available to parents for child care. To choose the option that best meets their needs, parents must consider each one carefully.

Types of Child Care

Many types of child care options are available to parents. Once parents identify the options available, they should evaluate the pros and cons of each one. This will help them make the best choice for their child's needs.

Child Care in the Parent's Home

This is the most desirable and convenient type of child care. In this option, the caregiver comes to the parent's home. Often the caregiver is a relative, grandparent, or close friend. Whomever the parents select, the caregiver should be a warm, loving person who interacts well with children, 11-9. This person should have similar viewpoints as the parents about child rearing.

Many parents prefer this option, especially for their infants and toddlers. Children feel more secure in a familiar setting where they receive individualized attention. They receive more consistent care. Their physical, social, emotional, and intellectual needs can be met more easily.

Some families obtain the services of a nanny. A **nanny** is a trained caregiver who provides quality care for children in the parent's home. Live-in nannies receive room and board, plus a salary for their services. Although this type of care is expensive, it is consistent. Some nannies also do household chores, which lightens

11-9
Parents want a caregiver who will interact with their child as they would.

the parents' workload when they are home. This allows the parents more time to spend with their child when they are home.

Child Care in the Caregiver's Home

This has been the most common type of child care in the United States. Most parents like having their young children in a family-type setting. This encourages children to develop a close relationship with the caregiver. Other benefits include less structure that allows time for play and relaxation. The hours are usually more flexible and the care costs less. Children are less likely to be over-stimulated by the activities of a large group of children. Most states require these homes to be licensed, but this is difficult to enforce.

Child Care Cooperatives

Child care cooperatives are formed by groups of parents who share in the care of the children. These programs allow parents more control over the child care program. They formulate policy, establish the budget, determine the instructional program, and provide care for the children. Parents also hire teachers or other personnel who may be needed. Cooperatives are often formed so parents can take turns caring for children. They pay for the care of their children by working in the center. Instead of paying a fee for child care, many volunteer for a certain number of hours.

School- or University-Sponsored Child Care Programs

Some parents enroll their children in a school- or university-sponsored program where student teachers are being trained in child care. These programs offer high quality in both staff and curriculum, 11-10. Availability is limited to university towns or school systems that provide the caregiver training.

11-10
College child care programs offer quality care for children and excellent training for future child care workers.

Church or Social Group Programs

Child care programs sponsored by church or social groups usually cost less because the sponsor helps fund the costs. For example, church-sponsored child care would likely be based in one of the church buildings. Eliminating the cost of providing a facility cuts the operating expense greatly. The staff for these programs are not only responsible to the parents, but also to the sponsor. These are usually high-quality programs.

Government-Sponsored Child Care Programs

Programs such as Head Start are sponsored by the government. These programs are offered to lower-income working families who may need low-cost child care. Again, the sponsor underwrites the expense of operating the facility. However, the program must meet strict guidelines to be licensed. Fees charged for participation are very low or nonexistent.

Employer-Sponsored Child Care Services

Businesses are becoming more involved in helping working parents meet child care needs. These programs are increasing as records show that employees are more dependable when child care is provided for their children. Companies who provide child care have less turnover and less absenteeism among workers.

Employers sponsor different types of child care facilities. On-site child care facilities are located on the company grounds, so parents are close at hand if their children need them. Some facilities are off-site, near the workplace. Others are existing child care facilities contracted by the company for their employees. In each of these options, employers may pay all or part of the child care costs.

Privately Owned or Franchised Child Care Centers

These child care facilities are profit motivated. Privately owned child care centers are operated as any other business except they provide child care. Most franchised child care centers started as privately owned centers. Entrepreneurs saw an opportunity to meet a need, so they created a larger group of centers. These chains try to offer uniform facilities,

Setting the Scene: Assessing Child Care Options

Your sister needs child care for her two-year-old son. You visit a facility with her. When you arrive, the door is open wide so you can walk in. A child with a runny nose comes over to greet you. The teachers are talking and laughing among themselves. They speak to you warmly after they finish their conversation

After showing you the facility, the director assures you they offer the lowest rates for child care in town.

Analyze It: What evidences of quality child care have you observed? Are there problem areas? How important is the cost of child care? Is this the center for your nephew?

equipment, and programs. Similar services are often provided in all centers under the franchise. If parents like the franchise in New York, for instance, they can expect the same services in Oklahoma.

Selecting Quality Child Care

Putting time and effort into choosing quality child care is important for parents. They need to consider their own needs as well as their children's needs. They realize that their children's development will be affected by the child care environment and the caregivers. The health and safety of their children is a concern as well. Knowing what to look for in a quality program and knowing the right questions to ask are the keys to successful child care experiences, 11-11.

When deciding among the child care options, parents need to consider many factors. The four major factors include the setting, programs, adult-child ratios, and caregivers.

Comfortable, Homelike Setting

The physical setting of the room should be comfortable and appeal to children. Furnishings should be child-sized and the decor cheerful and bright in color. A homelike and flexible setting is needed to provide for active play, quiet play, group play, and independent activities.

Age-Appropriate Programs

Although programs differ in content and approach, children should be in programs appropriate for their stage of development. Infants and toddlers have some unique needs. Programs for these children should not be scaled-down versions of programs designed for preschoolers. Activities for younger children should help them to trust the adults who care for them. Programs for older children should offer a variety of learning experiences.

Adequate Adult Supervision

Because children need personalized care, the adult-child ratio should be considered. Many states outline requirements regarding the adult-child ratio for licensed facilities. In most cases, one adult is considered appropriate for three infants, four toddlers, or eight preschoolers.

The More You Know: The Role of Caregivers

Some caregivers see their role in child care as a physical one. They expect to provide food, clothes, shelter, and toys. They know they are responsible for children's cleanliness, safety, and health. All of these are indeed important. However, caregivers also serve as role models. Children learn to behave by the examples set for them by their caregivers. Children are dependent on their caregivers to help them grow socially, emotionally, and intellectually as well as physically.

Selecting Quality Child Care

The Facility

- Does the care facility meet state, county, and city licensing requirements? Is it checked regularly by authorities to see that certain standards are maintained?
- Does the care facility have a good reputation?
- Is the care facility in a convenient location?
- What is the cost for each child?
- Are alternative schedules available to meet various needs for hours per day and days per week?

The Setting

- Does the setting have a warm, homelike atmosphere?
- Are the rooms and play areas designed and decorated with children in mind?
- Is the care facility equipped with a variety of safe play equipment and arranged with safety in mind?
- What precautions are taken to prevent children from wandering away and to prevent strangers from entering the premises?
- Are the restrooms clean, easy for children to use, and in good repair?
- Do the children have a comfortable and quiet place for naps?
- Is there an isolated place for an ill child?
- Is good emergency care available for the children if the need arises?
- Is the food nutritious, well prepared, and suited to the age of the children?

The Programs

- Are the children grouped according to age? Are suitable activities planned for each age group?
- Are children allowed to choose some of their own activities? Are they allowed time for quiet individual play as well as active group play?
- Is each child respected as an individual?
- Are the needs of the parents recognized by the caregivers?

The Adult-Child Ratio

- What is the adult-child ratio?
- Are all areas of the care facility supervised at all times?
- If a child needs individual attention at times, would this be available?

The Caregivers

- Are the caregivers well trained and experienced?
- Are interactions between caregivers and children pleasant?
- Do the caregivers encourage the physical, intellectual, emotional, and social development of the children?
- Do the caregivers attend promptly to children's needs?
- Are the caregivers calm, gentle, and fair to the children? Do they have a good sense of humor?
- Do the caregivers use guidance techniques without the use of harsh punishment?
- Do the children seem happy?

11-11

Parents should carefully evaluate each of these factors before selecting a child care program.

Consistent, Quality Care Provided by Caregivers

The quality of care given by child care workers is important. They should be well trained and experienced for their work with children. They should enjoy interacting with young children and be friendly and affectionate toward them. Each child should feel appreciated and be given encouragement and praise. See 11-12.

11-12
Child care workers should demonstrate a positive attitude toward their work. They should enjoy interacting with children, as well as encourage each child's development.

Caregivers should understand that building trust and self-confidence is important in the early years. They should provide opportunities for children to experiment and to be creative. Children should be urged to ask questions, investigate, make decisions, and assume responsibilities. Guidance should be firm, fair, and consistent with the child's needs.

The quality of care can be observed by visiting a child care facility. High-quality facilities should be busy, happy places. Children should be seen learning and playing under the supervision of friendly, alert adults.

Other Factors

The location of the care facility and the fees charged for care are other factors parents may also consider. These two items are important. However, they must not be weighed too heavily against the goals of parenting. Parents want to be sure that their children will grow and learn. They want to provide their children with a safe, healthy setting. When parents are working, they also want their children to receive warm, loving care.

Check It Out!

1. True or false. Many people think the ideal environment for child rearing is in the home with at least one parent present.
2. List eight child care options.
3. List four factors parents should consider when choosing a child care facility.

Chapter Review

Summary

Many people may fill the role of caregiver for a child. The primary caregivers are the parents. Responsible caregivers have certain personal qualities, skills, knowledge, and experience. The responsibilities of caregivers include meeting children's physical, social, emotional, and intellectual needs.

Many types of child care options are available for families. In selecting quality child care, parents must consider several factors. Selecting the option that best meets their needs and their child's needs is important.

Think About It!

1. Imagine you are an adult who just had your first child. Other than yourself, who would you most want to be your child's caregivers?
2. Rank the characteristics of responsible caregivers from the most important to the least important in your view. What did you choose as the most important characteristic and the least important characteristic?
3. Would you ever consider becoming a foster parent? Why or why not? What factors would help you make this decision?
4. If you were a working parent, how would you select child care for your children? What factors would you consider in making your selection?
5. Think about the pros and cons of hiring a live-in nanny. Do you think this would be an option you would consider in the future? Why or why not?

Try It Out!

1. Many parents and caregivers today use the Internet as a source for child care information. Visit several Web sites for parents and caregivers. Set up a check sheet for evaluating the Web site. Which would you rate the highest for accuracy, objectivity, currency, and coverage?
2. Use the Yellow Pages to create a list of community resources for caregivers. Include government agencies, volunteer organizations, support groups, and hot line numbers.
3. Research the requirements for becoming a foster parent in your state.
4. Pretend you are a working parent who needs to select child care. Visit both an in-home service and a child care facility in your local area. Develop a checklist to evaluate the caregivers, programs, and services each provides. Then list the pros and cons of each facility. Based on your comparison, which type of child care would you choose for your child? Explain your answer.

Early Childhood Education and Services Careers

Career Ladder for Early Childhood Education and Services

▶ **Advanced Degree**

Children's librarian
Child life specialist
Teacher trainer

▶ **Bachelor's Degree**

Child care administrator
Preschool teacher
Toy designer

▶ **Associate's Degree**

Math or language tutor
Head start teacher
Recreational director
Library assistant

▶ **High School Diploma**

Bus driver
Recreation aide
Teacher's assistant
Craft demonstrator

▶ **Pre-High School Diploma**

Babysitter
Day camp assistant
Library volunteer

Workers in this field work with children up to six years of age. Some provide physical care and emotional comfort, while others address these needs and actively promote normal growth and development. This field also includes workers who develop toys, books, and other materials for children.

Employment Opportunities

Preschool teachers and their assistants work in public or private centers. Teachers help children learn basic physical, mental, emotional, and social skills. Assistants help teachers with record keeping, preparing instructional materials, and setting up learning centers to give teachers more time for teaching. Some child care workers feed, diaper, comfort, and play with babies. Managers supervise the staff, perform administrative functions, and make sure the center meets state regulations.

Family child care providers care for children in their homes and may do all the tasks described above. Nannies may also perform a variety of tasks for children while living in their homes.

Entrepreneurial Opportunities

Workers in this field may provide family child care in their homes or in the child's home. Running a cleaning, catering, or transportation service for a child care center are other options for an entrepreneur.

Rewards and Demands

Children have unique ways of rewarding those they love with smiles, hugs, and words of affection. People who work with children are also rewarded by knowing they make a big difference in these young lives.

Caring for children can take its toll on patience and physical stamina since each child is unique and makes different demands. Attending to each child's interests and problems requires a great deal of standing, walking, bending, stooping, and lifting. Providing fair but firm discipline and staying alert to potential problems can also be demanding. Child care workers often face stressful conditions, low pay, and few benefits. Employee turnover in this occupation is high, and those who stay are frequently asked to help train new employees.

Preparation Requirements

A few entry-level jobs require only a high school diploma, but most jobs require further child care training and education. Some states require training in health and first aid, fire safety, and child abuse detection and prevention. Future workers in this field need to check the job requirements in their states.

High school students wishing to work with young children would be wise to take at least one child-related course. Those who want to become preschool teachers should take college preparatory courses.

Entry-Level Jobs

All entry-level jobs are positions that are heavily supervised or have no responsibilities in dealing directly with children.

Midlevel Jobs

People in mid-level careers often learn needed skills through a two-year program or specialized training. A nanny and most child care positions require at least this level of training.

Professional-Level Jobs

As a rule, a person working at the professional level has at least a four-year degree. This includes preschool teachers and managers of child care centers. A university professor who trains child care teachers usually has a doctorate.

From assistants to administrators, positions in a child care center fall at all levels of the career ladder.

Personal Qualities Needed for Success

People who work with children should genuinely like children and enjoy being with them. They should understand and promote childhood growth and development. This requires creativity, resourcefulness, flexibility, and organization.

Good health, physical stamina, and emotional stability are essential. Patience is also a needed as well as positive attitude to expect the unexpected. Since child care workers are role models, they must set a good example. They should also be interested in art, music, dancing, singing, and crafts.

Future Trends

The large percentage of mothers in the workforce has created a great demand for child care services. The current shortage of child care workers is expected to continue as long as wages in this field remain low.

Career Interests, Abilities, and You

To find out if working with young children interests you, take a child development course in high school or consider doing volunteer or part-time work that involves children. Ask others who have chosen a child-related career about their duties and experiences. This will help you see if you have the necessary skills, interests, and traits.

Part Four
Nutrition and Food Preparation

Chapter 12
Healthful Eating

Careers

These careers relate to the topics in this chapter:
- ▼ volunteer for meal delivery service for shut-ins, such as Meals on Wheels
- ▼ dietary aide
- ▼ nutrition assistant
- ▼ food chemist

As you study the chapter, see if you can think of others.

Topics

12-1 Nutrients at Work for You
12-2 Making Daily Food Choices
12-3 Nutritional Needs Change
12-4 Balancing Calories and Energy Needs

Topic 12-1
Nutrients at Work for You

Objectives

After studying this topic, you will be able to
▼ explain the importance of choosing nutritious foods.
▼ identify good food sources of various nutrients and describe how your body uses them.

Topic Terms

nutrient
nutrition
carbohydrate
protein
amino acid
fat
saturated fat
unsaturated fat
cholesterol
mineral
legume
vitamin
fortified
enriched
Dietary Reference Intakes (DRIs)

Pizza, milk, apples, and popcorn— these foods, and all the other foods you eat, provide nutrients for your body. **Nutrients** are chemical substances from food, which the body uses to function properly. After your body digests food, your bloodstream absorbs nutrients from the digestive tract and carries them to body cells. In the cells, nutrients help maintain and regulate body processes and promote growth.

Nutrition is the science of how nutrients support the body. The nutrients that keep your body working properly are divided into six major classes:

▼ carbohydrates
▼ proteins
▼ fats
▼ minerals
▼ vitamins
▼ water

Each of the nutrients performs special functions in the body. You get different nutrients from different foods. Therefore, you need to eat a variety of foods to get all the nutrients you need. By knowing the functions and sources of the nutrients, you will be able to make nutritious food choices.

Carbohydrates

Carbohydrates are the major sources of energy in your diet. Most carbohydrates come from plants. There are three kinds of carbohydrates: sugars, starches, and fiber. Your body can change both sugars and starches into energy.

Sugars are *simple carbohydrates* found in foods such as milk, fruits, candy, and cookies, 12-1. Your body can use some sugars right away for energy. Other sugars must first be broken down into simpler sugars.

Starches are often called *complex carbohydrates*. Cereals, bread, rice, pasta, and starchy vegetables are good sources of starch. Before your body can use starches for energy, it must convert the starches into simple sugars during digestion. Nutrition experts recommend most people get more than half of all their daily calories from complex carbohydrates. (People who are diabetic must monitor their carbohydrate intake and follow a prescribed diet.)

12-1
Milk and brownies are both sources of simple carbohydrates.

Like starch, *fiber* is a complex carbohydrate. Although your body cannot digest fiber, you need fiber in your diet. This is because fiber provides roughage that stimulates the normal activity of your intestines. Fiber moves food through your body and helps your body get rid of solid wastes.

When you eat more carbohydrates than your body can use, some of them are changed to *glycogen*. Glycogen is stored in your body for times when you need quick energy, such as when you run to catch a bus. Your body maintains only a small amount of glycogen. Excess carbohydrates that are not stored as glycogen are changed to fat for storage in the body.

You need to eat carbohydrates, especially complex carbohydrates, every day. A diet low in carbohydrates will not provide the best energy source to fuel your body. Your body will use protein for energy instead. This will deplete protein

supplies needed for growth and repair of body tissues. A diet low in fiber will not promote proper activity of the intestines and may result in constipation.

Proteins

Proteins are a nutrient found in every cell in your body. They are needed for growth, maintenance, and repair of body tissues. Proteins are made up of **amino acids**, which are building blocks for your cells. Your body uses proteins to produce enzymes and hormones. These help the body maintain its chemical balance and build antibodies to fight infections. The amount of protein you need depends on several factors.

You need extra protein when you are recovering from an injury or illness to help replace and repair cells. Periods of growth also require additional protein to build new cells. Without adequate protein, growth is stunted. As your rate of growth slows, you require less protein. However, you never outgrow the need for protein in your diet.

Not all protein sources are the same. There are two classes of proteins—complete proteins and incomplete proteins. *Complete proteins* supply all the amino acids your body needs. Foods that come from animals, such as meat, poultry, fish, milk, cheese, and eggs, are sources of complete proteins. *Incomplete protein* sources contain some, but not all, of the amino acids your body needs. Plant sources of protein, such as dried beans, peas, and nuts, provide incomplete proteins.

When incomplete proteins are combined with complete proteins in a meal, all the needed amino acids are provided. As an example, pasta (an incomplete protein) combined with cheese (a complete protein) can supply all the amino acids you need. See 12-2.

12-2

This creamy soup combines the incomplete protein of peanuts with the complete protein of milk to supply all the needed amino acids.

Sometimes incomplete proteins can work together to supply needed amino acids. A peanut butter sandwich is a good example. Peanut butter and enriched bread are both sources of incomplete proteins. When they are combined, however, they provide all the amino acids your body needs.

Protein foods should be eaten each day. People whose diets are low in protein experience poor muscle tone, lack of energy, and reduced resistance to disease. Severe protein shortages may result in a disease called *kwashiorkor*. Protein consumed beyond the body's needs is stored in the body as fat.

Fats

Fats are concentrated sources of food energy. They provide slightly more than twice as much energy per unit of weight as carbohydrates and proteins.

Fats do more than provide food energy. Fat is stored beneath the surface of the skin to insulate the body from shock and temperature changes. It protects and cushions the organs in your body from injury. Fats are needed in the diet to help the body distribute and use some vitamins. They also supply *essential fatty acids*, which are needed for normal growth.

Fats are divided into two classes. **Saturated fats** are solid at room temperature. **Unsaturated fats** are most often liquid at room temperature. As a rule, foods from animal sources, like meat and butter, tend to be higher in saturated fats. Foods from plant sources, like corn oil and soybean oil, tend to be higher in unsaturated fats.

Sometimes manufacturers process unsaturated fats to make them solid. This process is called *hydrogenation*. Solid vegetable shortenings and margarines are products that have been hydrogenated.

Cholesterol is a fatty substance found in every body cell. The body uses cholesterol to make a number of important materials, including sex hormones and vitamin D. Your body manufactures all the cholesterol you need. However, you also get cholesterol from your diet when you consume foods from animal sources, such as eggs and shellfish.

Saturated fats and dietary cholesterol both tend to raise blood cholesterol levels. Excessive cholesterol in the blood can form deposits on the inside of blood vessels. This causes the flow of blood to be restricted or blocked completely. A heart attack can result. Therefore, health experts advise people to limit their intake of saturated fats and cholesterol.

When the diet is deficient in fat during infancy and childhood, growth can be stunted. A diet too low in fat can cause skin problems and the poor utilization of some vitamins. Of the fats needed in the diet, fish, nuts, and seeds are good sources. However, excessive amounts of any fat can cause weight problems. People who eat such amounts tend to eat less of other needed foods. This should be avoided because a well-balanced diet is important for good health. See 12-3.

12-3
Pairing high-fat foods, like sausages, with lowfat foods, like vegetables and whole grains, helps keep a diet in balance.

Minerals

Minerals are inorganic substances needed for building tissues and regulating body functions. They are an essential part of bones, teeth, and red blood cells. Minerals also aid in the proper functioning of muscles and nerves and in the clotting of blood. Like proteins, minerals are needed for growth and repair of body tissues. Unlike the nutrients previously discussed, minerals do not provide the body with energy. They do not have to be broken down by digestion for the body's use, either. Your body can absorb minerals directly from the foods you have eaten.

Calcium and Phosphorus

Calcium and *phosphorus* are the most abundant minerals in the body. Reserves are stored in the bones. Calcium and phosphorus are also found in teeth, soft tissues, and body fluids.

Calcium is used to regulate the use of other minerals in the body. Without calcium, the blood would not clot. Calcium also helps the nervous system function. All muscles are dependent on calcium for their activity.

If a person's diet is low in calcium, his or her bones will serve as a reserve to fill immediate calcium needs. However, a low calcium intake over a long period could lead to *osteoporosis*. This is a disease characterized by weak, brittle bones, which are more likely to fracture. As osteoporosis progresses, bones become too weak to support the body's weight. They are unable to withstand force from routine chores like lifting and bending. See 12-4.

Milk is an excellent source of calcium. Other good sources are yogurt, cheese, pudding, and dark green leafy vegetables.

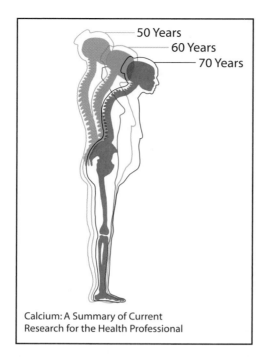

50 Years
60 Years
70 Years

Calcium: A Summary of Current
Research for the Health Professional

12-4
Osteoporosis weakens bones and can cause an increased risk of fractures and curving of the spine.

These foods, and foods that are high in protein, are also good sources of phosphorus.

Fluorine

Fluorine is needed for the proper development of bones and teeth. When added to the diets of children, it helps reduce tooth decay. Fluorine is not readily available in foods. Therefore, many cities add fluorine to the supply of drinking water.

Iodine

Iodine is present in very small amounts in the body, but it is essential for good health. Iodine is used to make *thyroxine*. Thyroxine is a hormone produced by the thyroid gland, which is located at the base of the neck. Thyroxine controls the rate at which the body uses nutrients. When the diet is low in iodine, the thyroid gland enlarges. This condition is called a *goiter*. Seafood and iodized salt are good sources of iodine.

Iron

Iron is another essential mineral. Iron combines with protein to make hemoglobin. *Hemoglobin* is a substance in the blood that carries oxygen from the lungs to cells throughout the body.

A diet that is constantly low in iron results in a condition known as *iron-deficiency anemia*. Symptoms of this condition include extreme fatigue, pale skin, and poor appetite.

Foods rich in iron include organ meats, lean meats, dried beans and peas, dark green leafy vegetables, and eggs. Women generally require more iron than men. To meet their needs, some women may need to take iron supplements prescribed by a doctor.

Sodium

Sodium works with other minerals to help maintain the balance of fluids in the body. It also plays a role in transmitting nerve impulses to the brain. Few people get too little sodium in their diets. In fact, many people get too much. Diets high in sodium are linked with high blood pressure. The main sources of dietary sodium are table salt and processed foods, which often contain a lot of salt. See 12-5.

Zinc

Zinc has a number of functions in the body. It is important for normal growth and development. It helps the immune system work properly. Zinc also helps wounds heal. Too little zinc in children's diets can stunt their growth. An excess of

12-5
French fries and other salty foods contribute sodium to the diet.

zinc can be toxic. Meat, fish, poultry, whole grains, and some legumes are good sources of zinc. **Legumes** are seeds that grow in the pods of some vegetable plants.

Other Minerals

The body needs a number of other minerals to maintain good health. These include copper, potassium, chlorine, magnesium, and selenium. Each of these minerals performs specific functions. Eating a variety of foods is the best way to make sure you get all the minerals you need.

Vitamins

Vitamins are organic substances needed in small amounts for normal growth and the maintenance of good health. Vitamins are regulators of body processes. Like minerals, they do not directly supply energy. Vitamins are necessary to enable the other nutrients to do their work. Most vitamin needs can be met by eating a variety of foods.

Fat-Soluble Vitamins

Vitamins can be divided into two groups. The first group is *fat-soluble vitamins*. These are vitamins that can be stored in your body in fatty tissues and in the liver. The fat-soluble vitamins are A, D, E, and K.

Vitamin A

Vitamin A is needed for good vision, normal growth, and healthy skin. A deficiency of vitamin A can cause night blindness and drying of the eyes and skin. *Night blindness* occurs when the eyes cannot adjust from bright to dim light. This can be very hazardous to a person who drives at night.

Excesses of vitamin A from food are not common. However, an excessive intake of vitamin pills containing vitamin A can be dangerous. People who get too much vitamin A over a long period may experience fatigue, headaches, and vomiting.

Good sources of vitamin A are liver, whole and fortified milk products, and fish oils. Foods that are rich in carotene are also good sources of vitamin A. *Carotene* is an orange pigment the body can convert to vitamin A. Carotene is present in orange fruits and vegetables, like apricots, carrots, and sweet potatoes. It is also present in dark green vegetables, like spinach and broccoli. See 12-6.

Vitamin D

Vitamin D helps your body absorb calcium and phosphorus and deposit them into cells. Vitamin D works with calcium and phosphorus to form and maintain bones and teeth.

12-6
Carrots, which are rich in carotene, are a good source of vitamin A.

A prolonged shortage of vitamin D in the diets of growing children can cause weakened bones. Extreme shortages can result in a condition called *rickets*.

Extra vitamin D is stored in the body. Excessive amounts of vitamin D may cause diarrhea, nausea, and headaches.

Vitamin D is often called the "sunshine vitamin." This is because your body can manufacture vitamin D when your skin is exposed to sunlight. However, foods such as eggs, butter, fish liver oils, and fortified milk are more reliable sources. (**Fortified** means nutrients have been added to a food to improve its nutritional value.)

Vitamin E

The main function of vitamin E in the human body is to act as an *antioxidant*. This is a substance that protects compounds from the damaging effects of oxygen. Vitamin E protects blood cells and cells in the lungs from oxygen damage. It also protects vitamin A and fats in the body.

Vitamin E is found in vegetable oils, whole grain cereals, liver, and green leafy vegetables. It is so widely distributed in foods that humans rarely have deficiencies. Because excess vitamin E is stored in the body, large doses from supplements may be harmful.

Vitamin K

Vitamin K is needed for proper blood clotting. Vitamin K deficiencies are not common because vitamin K is widely available in most diets. A severe deficiency could cause bleeding, but deficiencies are rare. Although vitamin K excesses are also rare, they can be toxic. Bacteria in the human digestive tract make about half of the body's needed vitamin K. The rest of vitamin K needs must be met by food sources such as spinach, cabbage, eggs, and liver.

Water-Soluble Vitamins

The second group of vitamins is the *water-soluble vitamins*. These vitamins are not stored in the body to a great extent. Excess amounts of water-soluble vitamins are excreted in the urine. Therefore, you need to eat good sources of these vitamins every day.

The B vitamins and vitamin C are water-soluble vitamins. These vitamins can be lost during cooking. This is why it is a good idea to cook most foods quickly, using as little water as possible. After cooking, do not throw away cooking liquid. Instead, save it for use in a sauce or soup.

B Vitamins

The B vitamins are a group of vitamins that are similar. However, each vitamin in this group plays its own role in helping your body function properly. Thiamin, riboflavin, and niacin may be the most well known B vitamins. Folate and vitamin B₁₂ are also members of this vitamin group. See 12-7.

Thiamin helps you obtain energy from the foods you eat. It is important in promoting a normal appetite and good digestion. It also helps the nervous system function properly. A deficiency of thiamin can result in nausea, depression, loss of appetite, and fatigue. A severe deficiency can lead to a disease called *beriberi*. This disease causes numbness in the ankles and legs and leads to paralysis and heart failure. Good sources of thiamin include pork, legumes, and whole grain and enriched grain products. (**Enriched** means nutrients that were lost during processing have been added back to a product.)

Riboflavin is also needed by your body to obtain energy from foods. It is needed for healthy skin and normal vision. A deficiency of riboflavin can cause cracked lips, a skin rash, and extremely sensitive eyes. The best sources of riboflavin are dairy products, meats, and leafy green vegetables.

Niacin, like thiamin and riboflavin, is needed to help you obtain energy from foods. It is also needed for healthy skin, good digestion, and proper functioning of the nervous system. A deficiency of niacin can cause *pellagra*, which affects the skin and digestive system. Good sources of niacin include meat, poultry, fish, nuts, dried beans, and whole grain and enriched grain products.

The body uses *folate* to make all new cells. This function has a special significance for pregnant women. The spine and brain of a baby growing in its mother's womb may not develop properly if the mother's diet lacks folate. Damage to the spine and brain can occur in the first few weeks of pregnancy. This is before most women even know they are pregnant. Therefore, all women of childbearing age are urged to be sure they are meeting their folate needs. Fresh fruits and vegetables, especially leafy green vegetables, are good sources of folate. A form of folate is also added to enriched grain products.

Vitamin B₁₂ helps the body make red blood cells. This vitamin also protects nerves. A vitamin B₁₂ deficiency can result in anemia and nerve damage. Vitamin B₁₂ naturally occurs only in foods of animal origin, such as meat, fish, poultry, eggs, and dairy products. See 12-8. People who do not eat these foods may obtain the vitamin from supplements or fortified soy milk.

12-7
Breads made with enriched or whole grain flour are good sources of the B-vitamins thiamin, riboflavin, niacin, and folate.

12-8
Poultry and other foods from animal sources provide vitamin B$_{12}$.

Vitamin C

Vitamin C helps hold body cells together and keeps the walls of the blood vessels strong. Vitamin C is important in the healing of wounds. It also helps your body fight infection. A lack of vitamin C over time may result in bleeding gums, loose teeth, bruising, and sore joints. A severe deficiency of vitamin C can lead to a disease called *scurvy*. To prevent a deficiency, be sure to eat at least one serving of a food high in vitamin C each day. Citrus fruits, strawberries, cantaloupe, peppers, broccoli, and tomatoes are all good sources of vitamin C.

Water

Perhaps you do not think of water as a nutrient, but it is one of the most important nutrients. Over half the body's weight is water. As a basic part of blood and tissue fluid, water helps carry nutrients to the cells and waste products from the cells. Water also aids in digestion and regulates body temperature.

You should try to drink six to eight glasses of water each day. You get additional water from the foods you eat.

Foods such as soup, watermelon, tomatoes, and even breads and meats contain water. Water is also a product of chemical reactions that take place in your body.

You can get the water your body needs from drinking other beverages in addition to water. However, limit your intake of soft drinks and fruit punches. These beverages are high in added sugars. Sugars promote tooth decay and may be a source of excess calories in the diet.

You should also avoid drinking large amounts of caffeinated beverages, such as coffee, tea, and cola. Excessive intake of caffeine has been linked to such symptoms as anxiety, restlessness, and headaches. Read labels and choose caffeine-free beverages, which are now widely available.

Chart 12-9 provides a summary of the basic functions and important sources of nutrients discussed in this text. Review this chart to help make sure your diet includes the variety of foods you need for good health.

Dietary Reference Intakes

To help you determine your daily nutrient needs, the *Recommended Dietary Allowances (RDA)* were established in 1941. The Food and Nutrition Board of the National Academy of Sciences developed the RDA through much scientific study. From time to time, the RDA are revised to reflect the latest nutrition studies.

A revision in the late 1990s made RDAs one of four types of reference values jointly called **Dietary Reference Intakes (DRIs)**. The other three types of values in the DRIs are the *estimated average requirements (EAR)*, *adequate intakes (AI)*, and *tolerable upper intake levels (UL)*. These four types of values can be used for planning and assessing diets.

Nutrient	Function	Sources
Carbohydrates	Supply energy. Help the body digest fats efficiently. Spare proteins so they can be used for growth and maintenance. Provide bulk in the form of cellulose (needed for digestion).	Sugar: Honey, jam, jelly, sugar, molasses Starch: Breads, cereals, corn, peas, beans, potatoes, pasta Fiber: Fresh fruits and vegetables, whole grain breads and cereals
Proteins	Promote tissue growth and repair. Help make antibodies, enzymes, hormones, and some vitamins. Regulate many body processes. Regulate fluid balance in cells. Supply energy when needed.	Complete proteins: Meat, poultry, fish, eggs, milk and other dairy products Incomplete proteins: Cereals, grains, nuts, dried beans and peas
Fats	Supply energy (most concentrated energy in food). Carry fat-soluble vitamins. Insulate the body from shock and temperature changes. Protect vital organs. Add flavor to foods. Serve as a source of essential fatty acids.	Butter, margarine, cream, whole milk, cheese, marbling in meat, bacon, egg yolks, nuts, chocolate, olives, salad oils and dressings
Minerals Calcium	Helps build bones and teeth. Helps blood clot. Helps muscles and nerves to work. Helps regulate the use of other minerals in the body.	Milk, cheese, other dairy products, leafy green vegetables, fish eaten with the bones
Fluorine	Helps in proper development of bones and teeth. Helps reduce tooth decay.	Fluoridated drinking water
Iodine	Enables normal functioning of the thyroid gland.	Iodized table salt, saltwater fish and shellfish
Iron	Combines with protein to make hemoglobin. Helps cells use oxygen.	Liver, lean meats, egg yolk, dried beans and peas, leafy green vegetables, dried fruits, enriched and whole grain breads and cereals
Phosphorus	Helps build strong bones and teeth. Helps regulate many internal bodily activities.	Protein and calcium food sources
Sodium	Helps maintain the balance of body fluids. Helps transmit nerve impulses.	Table salt, processed foods
Zinc	Promotes normal growth and development. Helps the immune system work properly. Helps wounds heal.	Meat, fish, poultry, whole grains, some legumes *(continued)*

12-9

All the nutrients work together to build, maintain, and repair the body and provide it with strength and energy.

Nutrient	Function	Sources
Vitamins **Vitamin A**	Helps keep skin clear and smooth and mucous membranes healthy. Helps prevent night blindness. Helps promote growth.	Liver, egg yolk, dark green and yellow fruits and vegetables, butter, whole milk, cream, fortified margarine, ice cream, Cheddar-type cheese
Vitamin D	Helps build strong bones and teeth in children. Helps maintain bones in adults.	Fortified milk and margarine, butter, fish liver oils, liver, sardines, tuna, egg yolk, the sun
Vitamin E	Acts as an antioxidant.	Liver and other variety meats, eggs, leafy green vegetables, whole grain cereals, salad oils, shortenings and other fats and oils
Vitamin K	Helps blood clot.	Organ meats, leafy green vegetables, other vegetables, egg yolk
Thiamin	Helps promote normal appetite and digestion. Forms parts of the coenzymes needed for the breakdown of carbohydrates. Helps keep nervous system healthy and prevents irritability. Helps body release energy from food.	Pork, other meats, poultry, fish, eggs, enriched or whole grain breads and cereals, dried beans, brewer's yeast
Riboflavin	Helps cells use oxygen. Helps keep skin, tongue, and lips normal. Helps prevent scaly, greasy areas around the mouth and nose. Forms part of the coenzymes needed for the breakdown of carbohydrates.	Milk, all kinds of cheese, ice cream, liver, other meats, fish, poultry, eggs, dark green leafy vegetables
Niacin	Helps keep nervous system healthy. Helps keep skin, mouth, tongue, and digestive tract healthy. Helps cells use other nutrients.	Meat, fish, poultry, milk, enriched or whole grain breads and cereals, peanuts, peanut butter, dried beans and peas
Folate	Helps the body make all new cells. Protects unborn babies from damage to the brain and spinal cord.	Fresh fruits and vegetables, enriched and whole grain breads and cereals
Vitamin B$_{12}$	Helps the body make red blood cells. Protects nerves.	Meat, fish, poultry, eggs, dairy products, fortified soy milk
Vitamin C	Is needed for healthy gums and tissues. Helps heal wounds and broken bones. Helps body fight infection. Helps hold body cells together.	Citrus fruits, strawberries, cantaloupe, broccoli, green peppers, raw cabbage, tomatoes, green leafy vegetables, potatoes, sweet potatoes
Water	Is a basic part of blood and tissue fluid. Helps carry nutrients to cells. Helps carry waste products from cells. Helps control body temperature.	Water, beverages, soups, most foods

12-9
(Continued)

The DRIs outline nutrient requirements for each sex and for several age groups. Allowances include needs for energy, protein, and many vitamins and minerals. Another goal of the DRIs is to help reduce the risk of some diseases. Allowances given in the DRIs are designed to meet the needs of healthy people. The DRIs are not useful guides for people who have special dietary needs. See 12-10.

12-10

Choosing a variety of nutritious foods for meals throughout the day will help you meet the DRIs for needed nutrients.

The More You Know: What Do the DRIs Tell You?

The estimated average requirement (EAR) is a level of a nutrient estimated to meet the requirements of half the healthy people in a group. RDAs are based on EARs. Adequate intake (AI) levels are set for the nutrients for which no RDA has yet been determined. The tolerable upper intake level (UL) is the highest amount of a nutrient a person can consume daily without health risks. All of these values are based on consumption by a healthy person.

Check It Out!

1. Chemical substances from food, which the body uses to function properly, are called _____.
2. What are the three kinds of carbohydrates?
3. What is the difference between a complete protein and an incomplete protein?
4. Which nutrient serves as a concentrated source of food energy?
5. What are three good sources of calcium?
6. Which type of vitamins cannot be stored in the body to a great extent and need to be consumed daily?
7. What are two main functions of water in the body?
8. The Recommended Dietary Allowances (RDA) are one of four types of reference values included in the _____.

Topic 12-2
Making Daily Food Choices

Objectives

After studying this topic, you will be able to
▼ describe how food choices are influenced by physical, emotional, social, and cultural factors.
▼ plan a well-balanced diet based on the MyPyramid food guidance system.
▼ list the Dietary Guidelines for Americans.

Topic Terms

MyPyramid
Dietary Guidelines for Americans

Eating right requires more than knowing the names of the nutrients. You also need to know how to choose a variety of foods that will supply those nutrients.

Influences on Food Choices

You have probably noticed that all people do not eat the same foods. Food choices vary because of the different influences that affect individual food preferences. Some of these influences include physical, emotional, social, and cultural factors.

Physical factors include a person's age, level of activity, and state of health. An active young athlete would choose foods not included in his or her grandmother's diet. Someone with diabetes must choose foods more carefully than someone who does not have diabetes. A person whose metabolic rate is high can eat many foods without gaining weight. Conversely, a person with a low metabolic rate may gain weight more easily. Wise people choose foods that they know are best for their physical health.

Emotional needs may influence foods you choose to eat. For instance, some people may eat more when they are happy or sad. Others may have no appetite when they are upset.

Social influences impact food choices because people tend to eat the foods others around them are eating. You may avoid high-fat foods at lunch if your friends are weight-conscious. On the other hand, you may overeat at a party where everyone is eating appetizers and snacks all night.

Cultural factors will also affect the foods you eat. For example, a Jewish family might eat traditional potato latkes, but avoid eating shrimp because of dietary law. A family living close to the coast might eat lobster regularly because it is affordable. A family in the Midwest might order lobster only on special occasions because of the expense.

Every person makes personal food choices. Think of the influences that help direct your choices. There are many acceptable food patterns. Be sure you choose foods that will keep you healthy.

MyPyramid

An easy way to plan a nutritious diet is to choose foods using the MyPyramid food guidance system developed by the U. S. Department of Agriculture. **MyPyramid** symbolizes a personalized approach to healthy eating and physical activity, 12-11. It groups foods based on their similarity in nutrient content.

12-11
The MyPyramid symbol illustrates the relationships among five main food groups that should make up the bulk of your diet.

The groups are
▼ grains
▼ vegetables
▼ fruits
▼ milk
▼ meat and beans

The MyPyramid symbol represents the recommended proportion of foods from each of the five food groups. Wider bands suggest a larger proportion of the diet. Oils are also included in the symbol as they provide essential nutrients.

The plan also aims to help people balance food intake and physical activity to promote healthy weight. Your level of physical activity influences the amount of food you should consume. To manage body weight, engage in up to 60 minutes of moderate to vigorous physical activity most days.

The Web site at MyPyramid.gov helps you create a personalized eating plan based on your age, sex, and activity level. After you enter this data, a daily food intake plan is created. It indicates what and how much you need to eat.

Grains

The grains group, which includes bread, cereal, rice, and pasta, provides carbohydrates for energy. Whole grain products are important sources of thiamin, niacin, folate, and iron. Whole grain foods are also high in fiber.

According to MyPyramid, differing amounts of grains are recommended for your age group and activity level. Check www.MyPyramid.gov to see specific recommendations.

Vegetables

The vegetable group includes all forms of vegetables: raw, cooked, canned, frozen, dried, and juices. Different vegetables provide different nutrients. However, cooking causes the loss of some nutrients. Fresh raw vegetables tend to provide good amounts of nutrients and fiber.

Many vegetables are good sources of vitamins A and C. Excellent sources of vitamin A include dark green and deep yellow vegetables, such as spinach, broccoli, carrots, and squash. Cabbage, peppers, and tomatoes are good sources of vitamin C.

According to MyPyramid recommendations, most teens need 3 to 4 cups of vegetables daily. Try to eat a wide variety of vegetables each week. Choose from all five subgroups: legumes and dark green, orange, starchy, and other vegetables.

Fruits

The fruit group includes all forms of fruits. Like vegetables, fruits are excellent sources of fiber. The richest sources of vitamin C are citrus fruits, such as oranges and grapefruit. Cantaloupe, strawberries, and kiwifruit are also good sources of vitamin C. Bananas are a good source of potassium.

Two to two-and-a-half cups of fruits are recommended each day for teens. Again, these recommendations may vary with personal activity levels. Also remember to go easy on fruit juices, which often contain added sugars. See 12-12.

Milk

Along with milk, yogurt, and cheese, the milk group includes milk-rich desserts such as puddings and custards. These foods provide calcium, riboflavin, phosphorus, protein, and many other nutrients. Fortified milk is the major source of vitamin D in the diet.

Children under 8 years of age need two cups from this group each day. It is recommended that all other age groups get 3 cups every day of lowfat or fat-free choices.

12-12
When you choose a fruit juice, make sure it is 100% juice and not juice drink. Also check for added sweeteners.

Meat and Beans

The meat and beans group includes meat, poultry, fish, and eggs. Other protein sources, such as nuts, dried beans, and dried peas, can be used as meat alternates. Protein, iron, and B vitamins are found in this group. Teen boys need the equivalent of 6 to 7 ounces of lean protein each day. Teen girls need 5 to 7 ounces.

When choosing the recommended number of daily servings from each food group, you need to know portion sizes. Chart 12-13 identifies ounce and cup equivalents for the food groups.

Oils

Many foods in the meat and milk groups also contain high amounts of fats that should be avoided. These are the saturated fats. However, your body needs certain oils that come from vegetables and some fish, but only in small quantities. Common sources of the healthy oils are nuts, olives, avocado, cooking oils, margarine, and certain salad dressings. You need to be aware of all sources of fats in your diet when planning your food choices.

Understanding Ounces and Cups	
Food Group	**Ounce or Cup Equivalents**
Grains	• 1 slice of bread • 1 cup ready-to-eat cereal • ½ cup cooked cereal, rice, or pasta • 5 whole wheat crackers • 3 cups popcorn
Vegetables	• 2 cups raw leafy vegetables • 1 cup other raw or cooked vegetables • 1 cup vegetable juice
Fruits	• 1 medium apple, banana, orange, or pear • 1 cup chopped, cooked, or canned fruit • ½ cup dried fruit • 1 cup fruit juice
Milk	• 1 cup milk, yogurt, or calcium-fortified soy milk • 1½ ounces natural cheese • 2 ounces processed cheese
Meat and beans	• 1 ounce cooked lean meat, poultry, or fish Count the following as 1 ounce of lean meat: • ¼ cup cooked dry beans • 1 egg • 1 tablespoon peanut butter • ½ ounce nuts

12-13

Becoming familiar with what counts as ounce or cup equivalents for each food group will help you make sure you are meeting your daily nutrient needs.

Setting the Scene: How Can MyPyramid Help You Manage Your Weight?

It seems that everywhere you look, a different weight management plan appears. You wonder how to evaluate each one in terms of healthy living. You refer to the MyPyramid Web site and study the groups and suggestions.

Analyze It: In what ways do government research and recommendations help you make wise food choices? How does knowledge of the MyPyramid recommendations affect your perception of other weight management plans? According to MyPyramid, how can you make food intake and physical activity work together to achieve a healthy lifestyle?

The Dietary Guidelines for Americans

To help people choose healthful diets, the U.S. Departments of Agriculture and Health and Human Services have suggested **Dietary Guidelines for Americans**. See 12-14. The Dietary Guidelines are described in the following paragraphs.

Adequate nutrients within calorie needs. Consume a variety of nutrient-dense foods and beverages within and among the basic food groups. Choose foods that limit the intake of saturated and *trans* fats, cholesterol, added sugars, salt, and alcohol.

Weight Management. To maintain body weight in a healthy range, balance calories from foods and beverages with calories expended. If you are overweight or underweight, you are more likely to develop health problems. Overweight is linked with high blood pressure, heart disease, stroke, certain cancers, and other illnesses. Underweight people have little to lose in the event of a wasting illness. You will read about how to manage your weight in Topic 12-4.

Physical activity. Regular physical activity helps promote health, psychological well-being, and a healthy body weight. It also builds and maintains strong bones and muscles. Throughout your teen years, you need to spend at least 60 minutes a day of moderate to vigorous-intensity physical activity. As you grow older, you need to keep including at least 30 minutes of moderate activity in your daily schedule.

Food groups to encourage. No single food can supply all the nutrients in the amounts you need. For example, milk supplies calcium but little iron. Meat supplies protein but little calcium. To have a nutritious diet, you must eat a variety of foods. This is the best way to get the range of nutrients you need.

In general, at least half the grains you eat daily should come from whole grains. These foods are rich in complex carbohydrates—your body's best source of energy. Whole-grain foods, such as oatmeal and whole-wheat bread, supply fiber to help your digestive system work properly. Consume three cups per day of fat-free or lowfat milk or equivalent milk products.

Choose a variety of fruits and vegetables daily. Eat different types of fruits and vegetables to get the full range

Dietary Guidelines for Americans

Adequate Nutrients Within Calorie Needs

- Consume a variety of nutrient-dense foods and beverages within and among the basic food groups. Choose foods that limit the intake of saturated and *trans* fats, cholesterol, added sugars, salt, and alcohol.
- Meet recommended intakes within energy needs by adopting a balanced eating pattern, such as MyPyramid.

Weight Management

- To maintain body weight in a healthy range, balance calories from foods and beverages with calories expended.
- To prevent gradual weight gain over time, make small decreases in food and beverage calories and increase physical activity.

Physical Activity

- Engage in regular physical activity and reduce sedentary activities to promote health, psychological well-being, and a healthy body weight.
- Achieve physical fitness by including cardiovascular conditioning, stretching exercises for flexibility, and resistance exercises or calisthenics for muscle strength and endurance.

Food Groups to Encourage

- Consume a sufficient amount of fruits and vegetables while staying within energy needs. Two cups of fruit and 2½ cups of vegetables per day are recommended for a reference 2,000-calorie intake, with higher or lower amounts depending on the calorie level.
- Choose a variety of fruits and vegetables each day. In particular, select from all five vegetable subgroups (dark green, orange, legumes, starchy vegetables, and other vegetables) several times a week.
- Consume 3 or more ounce-equivalents of whole-grain products per day, with the rest of the recommended grains coming from enriched or whole-grain products. In general, at least half the grains should come from whole grains.
- Consume 3 cups per day of fat-free or lowfat milk or equivalent milk products.

Fats

- Consume less than 10 percent of calories from saturated fatty acids and less than 300 mg/day of cholesterol. Keep *trans* fatty acid consumption as low as possible.
- Keep total fat intake between 20 to 35 percent of calories, with most fats coming from sources of polyunsaturated and monounsaturated fatty acids, such as fish, nuts, and vegetable oils.
- When selecting and preparing meat, poultry, dry beans, and milk or milk products, make choices that are lean, lowfat, or fat free.
- Limit intake of fats and oils high in saturated and/or *trans* fatty acids, and choose products low in such fats and oils.

(continued)

12-14

Following the Dietary Guidelines for Americans can help people form eating and activity habits that contribute to good health.

Carbohydrates

- Choose fiber-rich fruits, vegetables, and whole grains often.
- Choose and prepare foods and beverages with little added sugars or caloric sweeteners.
- Reduce the incidence of dental caries by practicing good oral hygiene and consuming sugar- and starch-containing foods and beverages less frequently.

Sodium and Potassium

- Consume less than 2300 mg (approximately 1 teaspoon of salt) of sodium per day.
- Choose and prepare foods with little salt. At the same time, consume potassium-rich foods, such as fruits and vegetables.

Alcoholic Beverages

- Alcoholic beverages should not be consumed by some individuals, including those who cannot restrict their alcohol intake, women of childbearing age who may become pregnant, pregnant and lactating women, children and adolescents, individuals taking medications that can interact with alcohol, and those with specific medical conditions.
- Alcoholic beverages should be avoided by individuals engaging in activities that require attention, skill, or coordination, such as driving or operating machinery.

Food Safety

To avoid microbial foodborne illness:
- Clean hands, food contact surfaces, and fruits and vegetables. Meat and poultry should not be washed or rinsed.
- Separate raw, cooked, and ready-to-eat foods while shopping, preparing, or storing foods.
- Cook foods to a safe temperature to kill microorganisms.
- Chill (refrigerate) perishable food promptly and defrost foods properly.
- Avoid raw (unpasteurized) milk or any products made from unpasteurized milk, raw or partially cooked eggs or foods containing raw eggs, raw or uncooked meat and poultry, unpasteurized juices, and raw sprouts.

12-14
(Continued)

of nutrients these healthful foods provide. Include dark green vegetables, orange fruits and vegetables, and dried beans and peas in your diet regularly. A varied diet based on these foods supplies vitamins, minerals, fiber, and complex carbohydrates. Such a diet is also generally low in fat.

Fats. Choose a diet that is low in saturated fat and cholesterol and moderate in total fat. Diets high in saturated fat, cholesterol, and *trans* fatty acids increase the risk for heart disease. High-fat diets are also linked to obesity and certain types of cancer. The total fat in your diet should not provide more than 20 to 35 percent of the calories you consume. No more than 10 percent of your total calories should be from saturated fat. You should also limit your intake of foods high in cholesterol, such as butter, liver, and egg yolks.

Carbohydrates. Choose fiber-rich fruits, vegetables, and whole grains often. Choose foods and beverages with little added sugars or caloric sweeteners. Many beverages and foods that are high in sugar supply calories but are limited in nutrients. Such foods include soft drinks, cookies, ice cream, and candy. Limiting your use of these foods may help you avoid unwanted pounds and cut down on tooth decay. Watch for ingredient labels that list brown sugar, honey, corn syrup, molasses, sucrose, dextrose, glucose, and fructose. These are all forms of sugar.

Sodium and potassium. Choose and prepare foods with little salt. Salt contains sodium, which contributes to high blood pressure in some people. At the same time, consume potassium-rich foods, such as fruits and vegetables. Sodium is naturally present in many foods. It has been added to others during processing. You should use salt sparingly in cooking and at the table, 12-15. You can read labels to avoid selecting foods that are high in sodium. Convenience foods, such as packaged mixes, frozen entrees, and canned soups and vegetables, tend to be high in sodium. Many snack foods, such as chips, crackers, pretzels, and nuts, are also highly salted.

12-15
Make foods flavorful by seasoning them with herbs instead of salt.

Alcoholic beverages. Alcoholic beverages supply little more than calories. Many health problems are linked to alcohol consumption, including addiction, liver disease, and some cancers. Many accidents also result from the use of alcohol.

Food safety. Eating food that has not been handled properly can sometimes make people sick. To keep foods safe to eat, you need to follow four safety measures—clean, separate, cook, and chill. Use hot soapy water to keep hands, utensils, and surfaces clean throughout food preparation. Keep raw foods separated from cooked and ready-to-eat foods while shopping, preparing, and storing. Use a food thermometer to make sure foods are cooked to a safe internal temperature. Chill perishable foods by storing them in the refrigerator or freezer within two hours of purchase or preparation. You will read more about how to keep foods safe to eat in Topic 14-2.

The Dietary Guidelines are based on research about how diet may relate to health problems such as heart disease, hypertension, and cancer. Their aim is to help people in the United States form healthful eating and activity patterns. Following the Dietary Guidelines cannot guarantee people they will never get sick. However, eating and activity habits do have an effect on health. Forming good habits can keep healthy people feeling well.

Check It Out!

1. List the five main food groups in MyPyramid. Give the recommended number of daily portions for each group for teen girls.
2. On what are the Dietary Guidelines for Americans based?

Topic 12-3
Nutritional Needs Change

Objectives

After studying this topic, you will be able to
▼ identify dietary needs of people in different stages of life.
▼ describe special nutrient needs of athletes.
▼ explain how some diseases can be related to diet.

Topic Terms

vegetarian diet
dehydration
food allergies
food intolerance
lactose intolerance

All people need the same nutrients. However, the amounts needed vary from person to person. For instance, women need more iron than men. Someone who has a large body build needs more food than someone who has a small build. People who perform hard physical work need more nutrients than those who lead less-active lives, 12-16. A person who has a disease or is recovering from illness needs more nutrients than one who is in good health.

Nutritional needs vary with age as well as with gender, body size, activity level, and health. Needs change throughout the life cycle. Meal managers need to know how to meet the needs of people at different ages.

12-16
People who do work that is physically demanding need more calories to fuel their high level of activity.

Needs of Pregnant Women and Infants

Nutritional needs begin before birth. Pregnant women must eat foods that will supply nutrients for their babies as well as for themselves. Once babies are born, they have tremendous nutrient needs to support their rapid growth.

Nutrition Before Birth

An unborn child has no way to get nutrients except through the mother's diet. Thus, the mother's body needs to be well nourished prior to and during pregnancy. Pregnant teenagers have more difficulty meeting the needs of their developing babies than pregnant adults. This is because teenagers must fulfill their own nutrient needs for growth as well as the needs of the growing baby.

Women who have good eating habits will not need to make drastic dietary changes before or during pregnancy. Consuming two to three daily servings from the milk group will provide the calcium needed during pregnancy. Two added servings from the grains group will help meet increased calorie needs. An extra serving from both the fruit and vegetable groups will provide needed vitamins, minerals, and fiber. Doctors may also prescribe nutrient supplements to help meet increased needs during pregnancy.

Nutrition in Infancy

Every part of a child's body grows and develops most rapidly during the first year of life. Good nutrition is most important during this year to build a strong foundation for a healthy lifetime.

Breast milk or formula is a baby's first food. Breast milk is perfectly designed to meet most of a baby's nutrient needs. Formula also provides needed nutrients, but health professionals agree that breast milk is the best choice for infant nutrition. To protect her health while breast-feeding, a mother needs to maintain a good diet. See 12-17.

Babies need vitamin C early in life. Breast milk contains vitamin C. However, fortified apple juice may be given when babies reach about six to eight months of age. Doctors may also recommend vitamin supplements for babies.

Doctors have differing opinions as to when solid foods should first be offered to infants. However, most doctors agree that babies should not be given solid foods before four months of age. Cereals are generally introduced first. Other foods are then introduced gradually. Babies can soon begin eating a variety of foods from all the food groups.

12-17
By eating well, a nursing mother gets the extra nutrients her body needs to make milk for her baby.

As children grow teeth and learn to control chewing and swallowing, table foods can replace strained baby foods. Foods should be cut into small pieces and offered in small servings. As energy needs increase, larger servings can be offered.

Needs of Children and Teens

As children grow, their nutritional needs continue to change. Their food preferences also change. Caregivers must help children select a variety of well-liked foods from each of the food groups.

Nutrition During the Preschool Years

Adults and children need the same nutrients. However, preschool children need larger proportions of nutrients to support their rapid growth. Caregivers need to make a special effort to include vitamins A and C in the diets of preschoolers. Raw fruits and vegetables, which are good sources of these vitamins, can be offered as snacks.

Most preschoolers cannot eat enough at mealtimes to meet all their nutrient needs. Thus, snacks are needed to supplement nutrients provided by meals. In addition to fruits and vegetables, cheese cubes, cereals, and crackers spread with peanut butter make nutritious snacks.

Adults play a key role in teaching preschoolers good eating habits. Children are great imitators. If an adult refuses a certain food, a preschool child is likely to refuse it, too. Adults can encourage good nutrition by offering children a variety of nutritious food choices. Adults also need to set an example by eating nutritious foods themselves.

Nutrition During the Early School Years

Starting school changes a child's daily routine and eating schedule. A nutritious, energy-packed breakfast is needed to help children stay alert in class.

While at school, children are exposed to the eating habits of others. They may refuse a food simply because their peers do not eat it. Children may sometimes need to be encouraged to eat well-balanced lunches in the school cafeteria. They need the energy and nutrients provided by milk, breads, meats, fruits, and vegetables. See 12-18.

12-18
Balanced meals provided by the school lunch program are designed to meet the nutrient and energy needs of young children.

Nutrition During the Teen Years

Like infancy, adolescence is a period of rapid growth. Teens are growing taller and gaining weight. Their bones are increasing in density. Their muscles are developing in size and strength.

All this growth creates great nutritional needs for teens. However, busy schedules often cause teens to skip meals. Many teens also select snack foods that are high in fats and sugars and low in other nutrients. Therefore, nutrient needs do not always get met.

Meals and snacks for teens need to be carefully planned. They must provide all the nutrients needed for growth and maintenance of strong, healthy bodies. Foods must also supply enough energy to meet a teen's high level of activity.

Special Needs of Vegetarians

During the teen years, many young people try new eating patterns. One of these patterns for a number of teens is a **vegetarian diet**. This is a pattern of eating that is made up largely or entirely of foods from plant sources. People choose to follow vegetarian diets for various reasons. These reasons include health, economy, religion, animal rights, and availability.

People who follow vegetarian diets may be called *vegetarians*. Several types of vegetarians exist. They are described by the types of animal foods they consume.

▼ *Vegans* consume no foods of animal origin.
▼ *Lacto vegetarians* exclude meat, poultry, fish, and eggs but include dairy products.
▼ *Ovo vegetarians* omit meat, poultry, fish, and dairy products but include eggs.
▼ *Lacto-ovo vegetarians* do not eat meat, poultry, or fish. However, they include eggs and dairy products in their diets.

The key to good eating is a variety of foods from many sources. Thus, total exclusion of animal food sources may lead to some deficiencies. Vegetarian diets can be healthful, but they require planning.

As you have read, animal foods serve as main sources of complete protein as well as other nutrients. By combining incomplete proteins, vegetarians can get all the amino acids they need. Vegetarians who consume eggs and/or dairy products can usually meet their needs for other nutrients, too. Those who omit dairy products from their diets may have difficulty getting enough

calcium and vitamin D. Vegans may also have trouble meeting their needs for iron, zinc, and vitamin B_{12}. Some vegetarians may need fortified foods or supplements to meet all their nutrient needs. Refer again to Chart 12-9. It will help you review some rich sources of protein, calcium, iron, zinc, vitamin B_{12}, and vitamin D.

Sports Nutrition

Many people take part in athletic activities. These athletes often ask how added physical activity affects nutritional needs. In most cases, athletes do not need dietary supplements. Eating a nutritious diet each day is the best way to meet nutrient needs. Athletes need to follow the same Dietary Guidelines suggested for all healthy people, with four minor changes, 12-19.

12-19
Making a few small adjustments to a healthful diet can help teen athletes meet their nutrient needs.

Increase Daily Calorie Intake

Athletes need extra calories to fuel high levels of activity. For best performance, 65 to 70 percent of calories should come from complex carbohydrates, such as breads, cereals, and pasta. Protein should supply 5 to 10 percent of calories. Fat should provide the remaining 20 to 25 percent.

Eating a small meal three to four hours before a workout or competition will provide needed energy. This meal should be high in carbohydrates, which are stored in the body as glycogen. Excess fats and proteins from the meal will be stored as body fat. During activity, the body can more easily release energy from glycogen than from body fat.

Drink Plenty of Fluids

Drinking fluids during activity helps prevent **dehydration**, or an abnormal loss of body fluids. Athletes lose a lot of water through sweating. They need to be sure they drink enough to replace those losses. Thirst does not always indicate fluid needs. Fluid intake should begin two hours before exercise and continue at fifteen-minute intervals throughout exercise. Liquids should also be consumed after exercising.

Water is a good fluid choice for athletes. It is easily absorbed and rarely causes cramping. Beverages containing caffeine should be avoided because they can cause dehydration.

Eat Plenty of Iron-Rich Foods

Iron helps the blood carry needed oxygen to muscles during physical activity. Good sources are lean meats, leafy green vegetables, and enriched and whole grain breads.

Meet Daily Calcium Needs

Meeting the daily requirement for calcium is especially important for female athletes. Calcium helps build strong bones that are more resistant to stress fractures. Dairy products and leafy green vegetables are good calcium sources.

Supplements

Athletes should avoid depending on supplements to replace a well-balanced diet. Supplements such as vitamins, high-energy bars, and sports drinks are not dangerous. However, they should not be consumed instead of healthful foods and water.

Anabolic steroids are powerful but dangerous drugs that some people take to boost athletic performance. Such drugs mimic the natural male hormone testosterone. This helps build muscle tissue and body mass. However, steroids do not improve agility or skill. They may also cause many serious health problems, such as high blood pressure, heart disease, and liver damage. Steroid use may cause adolescents to stop growing. Males may begin producing less of their own testosterone, and females may show the effects of increased male hormone. For these reasons, steroids should not be used to attempt to boost athletic ability.

Needs of Adults

By the time people reach their early twenties, their bodies are generally considered to be physically mature. Gradually, metabolism begins to slow, causing adults to need fewer calories. If adults do not decrease their food intake, they are likely to put on weight.

The need for nutrients during adulthood does not diminish along with the need for calories. The body tissues that have been developed must now be maintained. The diet needs to supply adequate amounts of protein, minerals, and vitamins. These nutrients will help keep the body healthy.

Meals and snacks for adults need to include foods that will supply nutrients along with calories. For instance, fruit juices are better choices than cola beverages, which provide little more than calories. For desserts, fresh fruits are a nutritious alternative to pies, cakes, or cookies.

Nutrition for Older Adults

Many older adults are less active than younger adults. This causes them to need fewer calories. However, older adults still need about the same amounts of most other nutrients as they did when they were younger. The need for calcium actually increases for adults over age 50. See 12-20.

Physical changes caused by the aging process can affect the eating habits of older adults. Such obstacles need to be kept in mind when planning meals. For instance, people who have trouble chewing may find it easier to eat softer foods, such as pudding and applesauce. People who have sensitive stomachs may prefer milder versions of spicy foods like chili.

While some changes may be necessary in the diets of older adults, it is important that foods remain appealing. Older adults must be willing to eat the foods they are served for their nutrient needs to be met.

Nutrition Needs of People Who Are Ill

People who are sick usually have additional nutrient needs. Fevers, vomiting, or diarrhea create the need for more water

12-20
Because older adults are often less active than younger adults, they need fewer calories from foods.

than usual to replace lost fluids. People recovering from some illnesses, as well as surgery, need additional protein. The need for some vitamins and minerals, such as vitamin C and zinc, also increases.

Those with diseases such as diabetes mellitus, cancer, and HIV/AIDS require a medical diet. These diets are prescribed by doctors and registered dieticians.

Food Allergies

Food allergies are abnormal reactions of a body's immune system to a particular food. Symptoms usually come on quickly, often in only a few minutes. They can range from nausea to rashes, shortness of breath, or even sudden death. Allergies usually develop in stages. When you first encounter a food that you are allergic to, there will likely be no symptoms or very mild symptoms. With later exposures, symptoms are likely to appear and will then occur every time you eat the food. Symptoms are usually the same every time, but in some cases the severity of symptoms may increase. Some of the most common foods causing allergic reactions are milk, eggs, wheat, and corn.

Food Intolerances

Food intolerance is an adverse reaction to the consumption of certain foods. Usually symptoms appear more slowly than in the case of food allergies. Symptoms are also usually milder, including upset stomach, minor headaches, and loss of sleep. High-protein foods are often involved. People on low-carbohydrate or low-protein diets may be more likely to experience these problems.

Lactose intolerance is a form of food intolerance in which the body is unable to digest dairy products that contain lactose. *Lactose* is a sugar that is broken down into glucose by the enzyme *lactase*. Some people's bodies produce insufficient amounts of lactase. Instead of being broken down, lactose ferments in the intestines. This causes symptoms ranging from bloating and nausea to diarrhea. Lactose intolerance is controlled by limiting lactose intake or omitting it from the diet.

High Blood Pressure

Blood pressure is the force of blood pushing against the walls of the arteries. High blood pressure usually has no symptoms until it leads to problems with the heart, brain, or kidneys. High blood pressure can cause arteries to harden, leading to a heart attack or stroke. Once high blood pressure develops, it usually lasts a lifetime. However, it can often be controlled.

Many times, the cause of high blood pressure is not known. Weight loss, physical activity, and a healthful diet are usually recommended to help prevent and control high blood pressure. A healthful diet includes foods low in sodium, fat, and cholesterol.

Diabetes

In a healthy body, the hormone insulin helps move the glucose used for energy throughout the body. In the body of a person with diabetes, the production of insulin is limited, or the body cells do not respond properly to insulin. Glucose stays in the blood where it can cause serious damage to body organs. Complications include the destruction of small blood vessels in the eyes, the slow deterioration of the kidneys, cardiovascular complications, and nerve damage.

There is no cure for diabetes. People with diabetes must monitor their blood glucose level. They must learn to carefully control their sugar intakes while still eating a diet high in complex carbohydrates. Weight control and regular exercise are also important factors. Some people with diabetes must receive insulin to replace the natural supply.

Osteoporosis

Osteoporosis is a disease that weakens bones, often causing severe fractures. It occurs primarily in people over 50 years of age. Osteoporosis is caused from a depletion of calcium in the body. This results in porous and brittle bones that break easily. Osteoporosis is more common in women than in men.

Almost all cells of the body require calcium. The body absorbs calcium directly from the food consumed. However, if there is insufficient calcium in food, the body will withdraw calcium from the bones. When supplies are insufficient, the body will also slow the loss of calcium through the urine. Gradual loss of calcium in bones is a normal part of aging. A diet rich in calcium and vitamin D promotes healthy bones, 12-21. This can slow bone loss and lessen the risk of fracture.

Cancer

Cancer refers to a disease in which abnormal cells divide uncontrollably and invade other body tissues. The abnormal cells may also spread to other parts of the body. The development of abnormal cell masses are called *tumors*. In some cases, no tumors develop. Instead, uncontrolled cell growth occurs in the blood and blood system.

12-21
Milk and other dairy products provide calcium needed to fight osteoporosis.

In most cases it is not known what causes cancer, but there are risk factors that are often associated with an increased prevalence. One such risk is a diet high in fat. The American Cancer Society recommends that you eat an abundance of fruits and vegetables each day, as well as whole grains and beans. Limit fat intake, especially animal fat. Use alcohol in moderation or not at all. It is also recommended that you stay active and maintain a healthy weight.

Check It Out!

1. Why do pregnant teenagers have more difficulty meeting the needs of their developing babies than pregnant adults?
2. What are four modifications athletes need to make in their diets?
3. True or false. Adults need more calories than teenagers.
4. What diet-related recommendations will help prevent or control high blood pressure?

Topic 12-4

Balancing Calories and Energy Needs

Objectives

After studying this topic, you will be able to

▼ identify factors that affect energy needs for metabolic and physical activity.

▼ outline guidelines for healthy weight loss and healthy weight gain.

▼ describe two common eating disorders.

Topic Terms

calorie
basal metabolism
body mass index (BMI)
overweight
obese
underweight
anorexia nervosa
bulimia nervosa

Energy is needed to support every activity of your body. From sleeping to running a marathon race, your body constantly requires energy. You obtain needed energy from carbohydrates, fats, and proteins in the foods you eat. This food energy is measured in units called **calories**. Learning to balance your calorie intake against your calorie needs will help you maintain a healthy weight.

When choosing foods, you need to be aware that some foods produce more energy per serving than others. Foods high in fats, such as fried foods and ice cream, are higher in calories than other foods. Foods with high water content, such as watermelon, tomatoes, and lettuce, are lower in calories per serving. See 12-22.

12-22
Tomatoes, lettuce, and the other ingredients in this salad are high in water content and thus low in calories.

Meeting Energy Needs

People differ in their calorie needs. Needs are based on a person's age, sex, body size, and level of physical activity. The body needs energy to support both metabolic and physical activity.

Metabolic Energy Needs

Even when you sleep, your body is working. Your heart keeps pumping blood. Your lungs keep drawing oxygen. Your tissues are being built and repaired. These life-sustaining activities are collectively called **basal metabolism**. Basal metabolism accounts for the energy required when your body is at physical, emotional, and digestive rest.

The *basal metabolic rate (BMR)* varies greatly from person to person. The BMR is higher while a person is growing. Thus, the BMR of children and teenagers is greater than that of adults. This is why people need to decrease the amount of food they eat when they get older. Older people do not need as many calories to sustain their body processes as younger people.

Other factors, such as glandular secretions and body temperature, can affect your metabolic energy needs. For instance, when there is an undersecretion by the thyroid gland, basal metabolism is lower. When there is an oversecretion, basal metabolism is higher. The higher your body temperature is, the greater your metabolic needs are. Therefore, when you have a fever, your basal metabolism will be higher.

Energy for Physical Activities

Physical activity raises energy needs above basal requirements. Whenever you use your muscles, you use energy. The amount of energy you need is related to the amount of work you do. For instance, you need more energy to walk than to sit and rest. You need more energy to run than to walk. If your level of physical activity is light, you will need fewer calories to fulfill your energy needs. If you are very active, you will need more calories to meet your energy needs.

Controlling Your Weight

Weight management involves both eating and physical activity. The foods you eat give your body energy, which is measured in calories. When you are active, you burn these calories. To control your weight, you need to compare the calories you eat to the calories you burn.

How Much Should You Weigh?

To set goals for weight management, you need to know what weight range is considered healthy for you. Health professionals determine this by using a calculation called **body mass index (BMI)**. The BMI is very useful for measuring body fat.

For adults age 21 and older, the BMI is a number that simply relates weight to

height. As shown in Chart 12-23, an adult BMI of 18.5 to 25 refers to a healthy weight. A BMI of 25 to 30 is viewed as **overweight**. A BMI over 30 is considered **obese**.

For people age 2 to 20, healthy weight is determined differently. The reason is children and teens have different body-fatness levels as they grow and mature. Their BMI, called "BMI for Age" or "BMI for Children and Teens," is plotted on age- and gender-specific growth charts. These charts are far more complex than the simple chart used for adults. Four weight classes exist for 2-to-20-year-olds: *underweight, normal, at risk of overweight,* and *overweight*. The term *obese* is only used with adults.

Overweight adults are encouraged to lose weight, but overweight children and adolescents are not. This is because young people can "grow into" leaner bodies by slowing their weight gain as they grow and develop. Weight loss could negatively affect normal growth. Overweight adults, however, are advised to lose weight and stabilize their weight at a healthy level.

In addition to fat, the body's bone and muscle also contribute to its weight. These two body components actually weigh more than fat tissue. An athlete's BMI, therefore, may fall in the overweight range due to a large muscle mass. For nonathletes, however, a high BMI usually indicates excess body fat.

Overweight and obesity are common at all age levels, but not everyone needs to lose weight. People at a healthy or normal weight should try to maintain it. Those who are underweight should focus on gaining weight.

Healthy Weight Loss

Many people have a goal to lose unwanted pounds. Sometimes these pounds are the result of glandular activity

Body Mass Index (BMI)

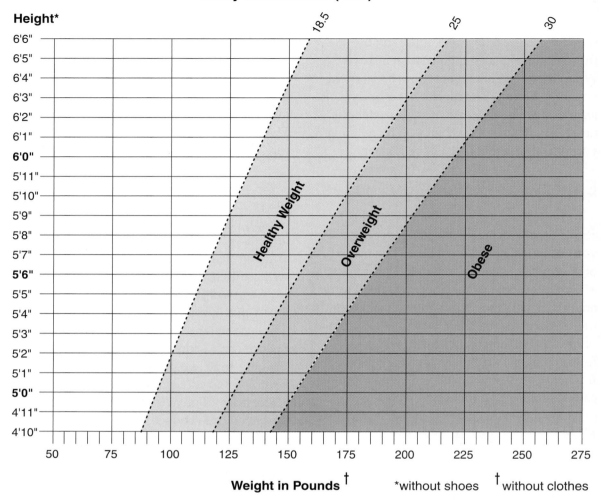

12-23

Balancing calories and energy needs allows people to stay within a healthy weight range for their height.

that affects metabolism. However, most people gain weight because they consume more calories than they burn. The excess calories are stored as fat. As fat stores accumulate, weight gain occurs.

Obesity is one of today's major health problems. Obese individuals are more likely to develop high blood pressure, diabetes, and heart disease. Obesity may also have a negative impact on a person's self-concept.

For many overweight people, reaching a healthy weight is easier said than done. Promises of quick weight loss in the form of fad diets are often tempting for these people. They may be attracted by diet aids and diet plans that promise fast results. Overweight people should beware of such promises. Dietitians agree there is no fast and easy way to lose weight. Weight loss should be a gradual process. It is best achieved by increasing physical activity and choosing sensible portions of healthful foods.

The following guidelines may help people who are trying to lose weight:

▼ Try to maintain a balance between food intake and physical activity. Avoid eating more calories than you burn.

▼ Try to spend at least 60 minutes each day in moderate physical activity. Plan to walk briskly, bike, swim, or jog. The more active you are, the more calories you burn. Schedule your physical activity about an hour before dinner. Vigorous activity helps suppress the appetite. See 12-24.

▼ Base your diet on grains, vegetables, and fruits. Then select moderate portions of lowfat dairy products and lean meats, poultry, and fish. Limit foods that are high in fat and/or sugar. Read labels to determine the fat and sugar content of foods you eat.

▼ Avoid omitting any group of foods from your diet. You can reduce portion sizes, but continue eating a variety of nutritious foods.

▼ Avoid making drastic changes in your food intake without the advice of your doctor. A high percentage of people who lose weight by radically changing their diet habits regain the weight.

12-24
Although exercise is important for everyone, it can have extra benefits for people who are trying to lose weight.

▼ Beware of fad diets that focus on one or two foods. A variety of foods are needed for overall health and well-being.

During the teen years, your body is growing rapidly. You need calories to support this growth and to fuel your daily activity. Therefore, health experts generally recommend that teens avoid restricting calories or trying to lose weight. Instead, experts encourage most overweight teens to follow the tips above to avoid gaining more excess weight. The goal is to increase physical activity and make healthful food choices. These steps will help overweight teens grow into their present weight.

Healthy Weight Gain

Being underweight can have adverse effects on health just as being overweight can. Adults who have a BMI below 18.5 are considered **underweight**. People who are underweight may suffer from more infections. They also tend to have low energy levels and may chill easily.

People who are underweight should consult a physician before adjusting their eating habits to gain weight. This will help them determine if a physical or emotional problem is preventing them from gaining weight. To gain weight, choose nutritious foods that provide more calories per serving. Increasing portion sizes and adding nutritious snacks will add calories to the diet. Eating five or six small meals rather than three large meals each day will also foster weight gain.

Eating Disorders

Many people have poor eating habits. They may not eat a wide variety of foods, or they may eat too many high-fat foods. However, an *eating disorder* is an abnormal eating pattern that actually threatens a person's health.

Eating disorders are not limited to a certain group of people. However, those most likely to develop eating disorders are young women and teenage girls.

Two common eating disorders are anorexia nervosa and bulimia nervosa. These disorders are mental as well as physical illnesses. They often involve skewed views of food and body shape and unnatural fears of weight gain.

Anorexia nervosa is an eating disorder in which a person avoids eating, sometimes to the point of starvation. This complex problem is based on a strong need to feel thin. Anorexics often have psychological problems that cause them to have distorted self-images. No matter how much weight they lose, they still see themselves as fat.

The effects of anorexia nervosa on health can be devastating. Body temperature drops, and females may stop menstruating. Skin becomes dry and hair becomes dull. Failure to meet nutrient needs can cause heart damage and loss of bone and muscle tissue. Severe cases can result in death. Even those who recover may have sustained permanent physical damage.

Bulimia nervosa is also known as the *binge-purge syndrome*. People who have this disorder go on eating binges and consume excessive amounts of calories. They then take steps to avoid weight gain. Some bulimics purge themselves of the food by vomiting or taking laxatives or diuretics. Other people with this disorder fast or exercise intensely to avoid weight gain. This binge-purge pattern is repeated at least twice a week. See 12-25.

Bulimia nervosa can take quite a toll on health. Frequent vomiting can erode the teeth and irritate the esophagus. Imbalances of body fluids can damage the heart and kidneys.

The earlier eating disorders are detected, the better the chances victims have of recovering with no serious medical problems. Treatment of an eating disorder may involve a team of health professionals. If needed, treatment begins with a hospital stay to combat malnutrition. Physicians attend to health problems that have resulted from the disorder. A dietitian can advise the patient on how to choose a healthful diet. A psychologist can offer counseling to address the underlying causes of the disorder. This helps victims understand their problems and learn to cope with them in healthy ways.

12-25
Rather than enjoying a single serving, someone who has bulimia nervosa might eat an entire dessert and then purge to avoid weight gain.

Check It Out!

1. A _____ is the unit used to measure food energy.
2. List five guidelines for people who are trying to lose weight.
3. True or false. Anorexia nervosa and bulimia nervosa require both physical and mental treatment.

Chapter Review

Summary

To eat a healthful diet, you need to be aware of the various nutrients that are in foods. The six basic nutrients are carbohydrates, proteins, fats, minerals, vitamins, and water. Each of these nutrients serves different functions in the body. Each can be obtained from a number of food sources. Knowing your nutrient needs will help you meet them through the foods you eat each day.

MyPyramid symbolizes a personalized approach to healthy eating and physical activity. MyPyramid divides foods that have similar nutrient content into groups. These groups are grains; vegetables; fruits; milk; meat and beans; and fats. Eating the recommended number of ounces or cups from each group every day will help you meet your nutrient needs. The Dietary Guidelines for Americans are a set of pointers that can help you form healthful eating and activity patterns.

Dietary needs vary at different stages of life. During childhood and the teen years, people have increased needs for some nutrients to support rapid growth. As people reach adulthood, their needs for many nutrients remain high, but their calorie needs decrease. As dietary needs change, be prepared to adjust your eating habits.

Your body needs energy for both metabolic and physical activities. Balancing these needs with the calories you get from foods will allow you to control your weight. Being either overweight or underweight can cause health problems.

People who need to lose or gain weight need to take steps to do so in a healthful manner. Dramatic, unhealthy weight loss or gain can be the result of an eating disorder.

Think About It!

1. Why do you think some people do not eat the proper nutrients? What could be done to change this?
2. Which nutrient would be the most likely to be lacking in your diet? Why?
3. How could the MyPyramid system be used by teens to plan meals when parents work outside the home?
4. Which of the Dietary Guidelines for Americans do you think is hardest to follow? Explain your answer.
5. What dietary advice would you give to a friend who is an athlete?
6. How will you change your eating habits as you become an adult?
7. How would following a daily program of physical activity affect your calorie needs and your weight?
8. The "Iced Tea Diet" promises you will lose 15 pounds in three weeks. You simply have to replace two meals a day with a glass of iced tea. If you needed to lose weight, would you follow this diet? Explain why or why not.
9. Explain how the MyPyramid system could be used to meet dietary needs in another culture.
10. How could a person's career choice affect his or her eating habits?

Try It Out!

1. Prepare a booklet about the six classes of nutrients. Use pictures to illustrate foods containing the nutrients and tell why each nutrient is important to the body.

2. List five of your favorite snacks. Identify what major nutrients you receive from each snack.

3. List all the foods you ate yesterday. Tally the number of servings you ate from each group in MyPyramid. Write a paragraph describing how you might alter your meals to include any missing servings.

4. Log on to the www.MyPyramid.gov Web site. Select MyPyramid Plan and enter your personal data. Print the PDF version of your results. Using this data, plan a nutritious diet for one day, including breakfast, lunch, dinner, and three snacks.

5. Work in a small group to discuss the nutritional needs of people at a specific stage of life. Compare and contrast your group's findings with the nutritional needs of people at different stages identified by other groups.

6. Read an article about food's effect on an athlete's performance. Report your findings to the class.

7. Make a poster illustrating helpful guidelines people could follow to lose or gain weight.

Chapter 13
Meal Management

Careers

These careers relate to the topics in this chapter:
- ▼ cook's helper
- ▼ foodservice worker
- ▼ restaurant manager
- ▼ test kitchen director

As you study the chapter, see if you can think of others.

Topics

Topic 13-1
Planning Meals

Objectives

After studying this topic, you will be able to

▼ use a meal pattern based on MyPyramid to plan meals throughout the day.

▼ write a menu illustrating variety in color, flavor, texture, shape, size, and temperature.

▼ evaluate your cooking skills, food budget, and preparation time as they apply to meal management.

Topic Terms

meal management
convenience food

Imagine this situation: You arrive home at six o'clock to prepare dinner. Then you must rush to meet a seven o'clock appointment. Unfortunately, today's hurried lifestyles often result in this type of schedule. A nutritious, attractive, and economical meal may be a small concern when you are in a hurry.

To guard against the pitfalls of busy days, meal management is a must. **Meal management** involves using resources of skills, money, and time to put together nutritious meals. A meal manager must plan well-balanced menus; shop for healthful, economical foods; and prepare meals in the time available.

How do you begin to plan great meals? Cookbooks, magazines, and the food sections of newspapers often give many good menu suggestions, 13-1. You might also keep a collection of your family's favorite recipes and add to it as

13-1
Great meals begin with advance planning. Cookbooks, magazines, and newspapers often contain good menu ideas.

you discover new favorites. However, finding tasty menus and recipes is just the beginning of meal planning.

You need to consider five factors when you plan meals. You want meals to be both nutritious and appealing. You also want meals that suit your cooking skills, food budget, and available preparation time. Thorough planning is the key to preparing and serving good meals.

Planning for Nutrition

You know the foods you eat provide your body with carbohydrates, proteins, fats, minerals, vitamins, and water. However, no one food contains all the nutrients you need. You must plan carefully to have meals and snacks that will supply all the essential nutrients.

Using a Meal Pattern

You can make your meal planning easier by using a meal pattern. A *meal pattern* is a guide that outlines the basic foods normally served at a meal. Many nutrition experts currently recommend a meal pattern based on MyPyramid. This pattern includes

▼ two to three servings from the grains group
▼ one to two servings from the vegetable group
▼ one to two servings from the fruit group
▼ one serving from the milk group
▼ one serving (the equivalent of 1 to 3 ounces of cooked, lean meat) from the meat and beans group

You can use the MyPyramid meal pattern whether you are planning a menu for breakfast, lunch, or dinner. Remember to select a variety of foods from each group to get the suggested number of servings each day. Breakfast should provide about one-fourth of your daily nutrients and calories to get you going in the morning. Lunch and dinner should each provide about one-third of your daily nutrient needs. Include snacks in your meal planning to satisfy between-meal hunger and supply your remaining nutrient needs. See 13-2.

Grains Group

Grain products should be the foundation of each day's meal plan. When including foods from this group in your meals, choose whole grain products often. They provide more fiber and other protective substances than refined grain products.

Ready-to-eat and cooked cereals, bagels, and muffins are great choices for breakfast. You can use all types of breads to make sandwiches for lunch. For a change of pace, wrap sandwich fillings in pita bread or a tortilla. Rice and pasta are versatile, economical, and nutritious options for dinner. These grains can be used alone and

in a variety of main dishes. Crackers and popcorn are popular snacks from the grains group.

Vegetable Group

Vegetables are easy to include in meals and snacks. Fresh vegetables can be added to tasty egg dishes for breakfast. At lunch, you might enjoy raw vegetables or vegetable salads. Cooked vegetables can play a leading role on your dinner plate or be served in main dish soups and casseroles. Vegetable juice makes a nutritious snack.

Different vegetables provide different nutrients, so include a variety in each day's meal plan. Include good sources of vitamin C, such as broccoli and peppers. Choose good sources of vitamin A, such as leafy green vegetables and carrots. Dried beans and peas, which are high in protein, and starchy vegetables, which provide complex carbohydrates, are also good choices.

Fruit Group

Include a variety of fruits in each day's meal plan. Fruit juice is a common choice for breakfast. Fresh whole fruit or fruit salad is a refreshing addition to a lunch menu. Warm fruit compote or a baked fruit dessert would add color and nutrients to dinner. Raisins, dried apricots, and other dried fruits make sweet, chewy snacks. Choose good sources of vitamin C each day, such as citrus fruits, strawberries, and melons. See 13-3.

Milk Group

Include foods from the milk group in meals throughout the day by serving milk as a beverage. You can also serve milk with cereal at breakfast and use it in creamy soups for lunch. Pudding made with milk makes a favorite dessert with dinner. An alternative to milk is lowfat cheese. Cheese makes a great addition to a

MyPyramid Meal Pattern					
Meal	Grain Group (2-3 servings per meal)	Vegetable Group (1-2 servings per meal)	Fruit Group (1-2 servings per meal)	Milk Group (1 serving per meal)	Meat and Beans Group (1-3 ounces per meal)
Breakfast	1 English muffin	1 cup sautéed onions, peppers, and potatoes* ½ cup vegetable juice	½ cup cantaloupe	1½ ounces lowfat cheese	1 scrambled egg
Snack	1 bran muffin		½ cup orange juice		
Lunch	2 slices whole-wheat bread	1 cup spinach salad 2 tomato slices	1 banana	1 cup lowfat yogurt	2 ounces sliced turkey
Snack	5 whole-grain crackers	½ cup carrot and celery slices			1 tablespoon peanut butter
Dinner	1½ cups brown rice	1 cup stir-fried broccoli, carrots, and mushrooms	2 pineapple rings	1 cup fat-free milk	3 ounces shrimp*
Snack	3 cups unbuttered popcorn				
Total Daily Amounts	10 ounces	4 cups	2½ cups	3 cups	7 ounces

13-2

Use a meal pattern based on MyPyramid. This will help you make sure you get your total recommended number of servings each day.

breakfast omelet, luncheon sandwich, or dinner casserole. You can use lowfat yogurt to meet your daily servings from the milk group, too. Yogurt is a great snack, whether you eat it alone or layered with fresh fruit.

Meat and Beans Group

Many meal managers begin their menu plans by choosing a main dish from the meat and beans group. Then they select foods from the other groups as accompaniments. If you take this approach, be sure to keep current health guidelines in

13-3
Servings from the vegetable and fruit groups can fit into any meal.

mind. Nutrition experts recommend that foods from animal sources take up no more than one-third of the space on your plate. Grains, vegetables, and fruits should fill two-thirds or more of your plate. Following these proportions can help you create filling, nutritious meals that are high in fiber and low in fat.

Ham and eggs may be the first breakfast foods that come to mind from the meat and beans group. However, do not limit yourself to only familiar dishes when planning meals. Be adventurous by trying new recipes that include more plant-based foods from this group in your diet. You might try a breakfast bean burrito or a smoothie made with tofu. Chickpeas and kidney beans would be delicious ingredients in a salad for lunch. For dinner, you might prepare lentil chili or black bean burgers. Of course, peanut butter is a time-honored snack food from the meat and beans group.

When planning meals, consider any special nutritional needs of family members or guests. For instance, older children, teens, and adults require three cups daily from the milk group. Children aged two to eight need only two servings per day. If you are planning meals for a person trying to lose weight, you might select foods that are lower in calories. People with food allergies, diabetes, or heart disease may require special diets. People who are ill or recovering from surgery may also have particular food needs.

Variety in Meals

Color, flavor, texture, shape, size, and temperature are important points to consider in planning meals with variety. Keeping these factors in mind will help you plan meals that are attractive as well as delicious. Choosing foods that appeal to the senses (sight, smell, and taste) will make meals enjoyable. Foods that complement each other also add interest to mealtime, 13-4.

13-4
The colors, flavors, textures, shapes, and temperatures of the foods in this attractive meal complement one another.

Color

Color adds eye appeal to meals, so plan meals with a variety of colors. For instance, if your meal includes rice, serve carrots or green beans instead of cauliflower for color contrast. Garnishes can add color and variety to a meal. A sprig of parsley or a sprinkle of shredded cheese can add interest to a casserole. A lemon wedge or carrot curls can make a main dish platter look attractive. Fresh fruit makes a colorful dessert topping.

Flavor

The flavors of foods should complement each other. A sweet flavor blends well with a sour flavor. A mild flavor offsets a strong flavor. For instance, the mild flavor of baked fish combines well with the strong flavor of tangy salsa. Use well-liked combinations of foods that taste good together, such as pasta with a zesty tomato sauce. Vary the flavors of food items to avoid repeating one flavor. In other words, if you are serving steamed carrots as a vegetable, avoid serving shredded carrots in your salad.

Texture

Textures of foods should offer variety. *Crisp*, *tender*, *soft*, *creamy*, *smooth*, *crunchy*, and *chewy* describe common food textures. Try to serve at least three textures in each meal. For instance, crispy stir-fried vegetables with tender chicken over granular brown rice makes a good combination. On the other hand, creamed chicken and vegetables over soft white rice would offer little variety in texture.

Shape and Size

Use your creative flair to combine a variety of shapes and sizes in your meals. Avoid serving several foods at the same meal that are the same shape and size. For instance, meatballs, small whole potatoes, and Brussels sprouts would be too similar in shape and size. Serving sliced potatoes and green beans with the meatballs would be more appealing.

Temperature

Plan to include foods that differ in temperature as part of the meal plan. Cold foods, such as crisp vegetable salads, contrast well with hot foods, such as sliced ham and a baked potato. Serve hot foods hot and cold foods cold for the greatest appetite appeal.

Cultural and Societal Influences

Variety in colors, flavors, textures, and shapes plays a role in foods of all cultures. However, the specific foods and seasonings that make up this variety differ from one culture and society to another.

Culture and society have been influencing people's food choices since prehistoric times. Early people did not have access to foods from all over the world. They had to eat whatever was available. Those who lived in coastal areas ate seafood. Those who lived in woodlands might have eaten deer, caribou, and other wild game. As time passed, people moved to different regions where new foods were available. However, the regional foods people first became used to eating remained their cultural preferences.

You can still see regional and cultural influences on food choices today. Foods are shipped all over the United States. However, you are still more likely to see lobster tanks in a grocery store in Maine than in a store in Wyoming, 13-5. Cheese soup is more common on restaurant menus in Wisconsin than in Georgia. You will find

13-5
Grilled lobster is a more typical entrée in New England than in the Southwest.

few Asian markets in an area with a large Latin population. Markets in a Latin district are more likely to feature tortillas, beans, peppers, and other ingredients used in Latin dishes.

If you are like most people, you tend most often to choose foods that reflect your culture. You also select foods that are typical of the society in which you live. As a meal manager, you can add variety to your family's meals by choosing to serve foods from other cultures.

When You Are the Meal Manager

As a meal manager, you need to consider more than the nutrition and appearance of the food. You also need to consider your skills, your budget, and the amount of time you have available.

Your Cooking Skills

The meals you plan are often determined by the preparation skills you have developed. People who have little cooking experience tend to plan meals that require little preparation. As experience increases, they become more confident and try more detailed recipes.

If you are a beginner, trying to prepare three new recipes for one meal could be frustrating and confusing. One new recipe at a time is enough for adventure. After you master a new main dish recipe, you may wish to try a new salad recipe to accompany it. Later, you may want to try a new dessert recipe to accompany the main dish and salad.

Have patience with yourself as you learn to cook. If you can manage to cook only one dish, then plan to serve it with other foods that require no cooking. With practice, your cooking skills will develop. In time, you will be able to cook anything you wish.

Your Food Budget

Preparing a juicy sirloin steak may be as easy as preparing a hamburger, but the cost varies greatly. The amount of money budgeted for food is an important factor in planning meals. Most people have a limited food budget. You must use care to select foods that are economical as well as nutritious. Planning well-balanced meals on a budget is a challenge, but it can be done. Here are some helpful tips to get you started.

Before planning menus, check newspaper, television, and radio advertisements for weekly specials. Look and listen for sale prices on foods your family enjoys. Then plan your menus around these advertised specials. Check newspapers and magazines to find coupons for items you need and use regularly, 13-6.

13-6
Clipping coupons for food products you buy regularly can help you stretch your dollars at the grocery store.

Plan menus including seasonal foods. Fresh produce (vegetables and fruits) is plentiful, tasty, and less expensive when it is in season. For instance, strawberries may be a real bargain in late spring; potatoes are a bargain at harvest time. During off-seasons, canned or frozen produce may be cheaper.

Stretch your food budget by planning menus that include less-expensive cuts of meat. Meat alternates, such as eggs and legumes (beans and peas), can be used in many types of meatless main dishes. Stretch the number of meat servings in main dishes by using bread crumbs, cereals, rice, or pasta as meat extenders. For instance, combine bread crumbs with ground meat to make a meat loaf. Add meat to a sauce and serve it over spaghetti.

Energy Costs

When planning meals, do not forget about energy costs. Energy not only costs money, it uses limited natural resources. The longer foods cook, the more energy is used. Therefore, consider required cooking times of foods when choosing a menu.

The method used to prepare foods can affect the cooking time. For instance, you can steam rice on top of the range in 15 minutes. If you bake rice in the oven, it will take about an hour. However, if you were already baking a cake, it would be more economical to bake the rice at the same time.

Foods that can be cooked together can save energy. Try preparing one-dish meals, such as vegetable and meat dishes, stews, or casseroles.

Your Preparation Time

With careful planning, you can control the use of time to prepare meals. Here are some ways to save preparation and cooking time by planning ahead.

Consider using some convenience foods to save time. **Convenience foods** are food products that have some preparation steps done to them. The manufacturer has done most of the measuring and combining. With only a few steps, you can prepare the food successfully. For instance, a frozen dinner requires only reheating. Canned and frozen vegetables have already been cleaned, pared, and chopped. They are usually ready to heat and serve, which greatly reduces preparation time. Mixes for muffins, cakes, cookies, breads, soups, and puddings are other examples. These foods still require some preparation, but they require less time than made-from-scratch foods. Although convenience foods save time and energy, they are often more costly than foods prepared from scratch.

Plan foods that require no cooking. A cottage cheese and fruit salad served with wheat crackers and a beverage makes a complete, timesaving meal. A nutritious breakfast featuring ready-to-eat cereal is also quick and easy to prepare. See 13-7.

When you have extra time, prepare large portions of food so they can be used

13-7
Making a quick salad is a nutritious meal idea when you are short on time.

for more than one meal. For instance, leftover ham, turkey, or beef can be used later in sandwiches, casseroles, and soups.

Plan meals that suit the time you have available for preparation. If you have only enough time to heat a plate of leftovers, do not try to prepare an entire meal.

A Variety of Eating Schedules

Everyone in your family may not be able to eat meals at the same time. In many families, all adults may be employed outside the home, and their work schedules may vary. Some adults may work nights or evenings. Children may be involved in activities that take them away from home during normal mealtimes. In these busy households, traditional eating patterns may be difficult to follow. Meals will have to be planned to meet these various schedules. Keep in mind that young children and older family members often prefer to eat on a regular schedule. Teenagers and most adults can usually be more flexible.

When planning meals for a variety of eating schedules, select foods that taste good when reheated. Family members who are unavailable to eat when meals are served can reheat foods in the microwave oven later. For instance, many one-dish meals can be refrigerated and reheated. Some one-dish meals, such as chili or beef stew, can also cook all day in a slow cooker. Family members can serve themselves as their schedules allow. Prepare menu items on weekends and freeze them for use during the week. Make recipes in large quantities and freeze individual portions for later use.

Plan to have food items on hand for family members to make their own meals. You can keep sandwich and salad items in the refrigerator. Fresh fruits, cheeses, and canned or dry soups can also form the basis of quick meals.

Check It Out!

1. List the food groups that make up a meal pattern based on MyPyramid.
2. Name five points to consider in planning meals with variety.
3. List three ways to plan well-balanced meals on a budget.

Topic 13-2
Shopping for Food

Objectives

After studying this topic, you will be able to

▼ plan and organize a shopping list.
▼ describe different types of food stores.
▼ list factors to consider when deciding how much food to buy.
▼ explain how to recognize quality in foods.

Topic Terms

national brand
house brand
generic product

13-8
Use store ads to write a shopping list that will save you money by taking advantage of advertised specials.

Shopping for food is an important part of meal planning. Whether you shop in a supermarket or neighborhood store, grocery shopping involves many decisions. You must decide what to buy, where to shop, and how much will meet your needs. As a smart shopper, you must also be able to evaluate the quality of food products.

Preparing a Shopping List

A *shopping list* is a detailed list of the kinds and amounts of food you want to buy. You can save three valuable resources—time, energy, and money—by planning your shopping list carefully. You will not have to decide what you need to buy. You will not be tempted to buy items you do not need, either.

You should write your shopping list before you go grocery shopping, 13-8. As you make out your list, review all the recipes you are planning to prepare. List all the items you need for your weekly menus and snacks. Add any staple items you have used during the week, such as bread, milk, and eggs.

As you prepare your list, use weekly food ads to compare food items and prices. You may want to stock up on items that are on sale. However, read carefully to find out if you are really saving money on an item. Some foods featured in ads are not on sale. Also, note special promotions and clip coupons you want to use. A coupon can save you money, providing you need the item and plan to buy it.

Save time and energy by organizing your shopping list according to the grocery store's layout. List the items you will need in each aisle or department of the store. For instance, keep all fresh produce and all frozen foods grouped together on your list. This step will help you avoid going back and forth to find items. It will also help you avoid overlooking needed items on your list.

Deciding Where to Shop

Once you have prepared your shopping list, you must decide the best place to shop. Different types of stores offer different product selections, prices, and customer services.

Types of Food Stores

Five of the most common types of food stores are supermarkets, discount supermarkets, specialty stores, warehouse clubs, and convenience stores. Comparing them will help you decide which type will best meet your shopping needs.

Large *supermarkets* sell a wide range of food and household products, 13-9. They often charge lower prices because

13-9
Because supermarkets offer a full range of fresh food products, finding the exact item you need is easier.

they do a high volume of business. Many supermarkets offer customer convenience services, such as check cashing or home delivery.

Discount supermarkets are sometimes known as warehouse supermarkets. These stores sell foods and household items at discounted prices. To keep prices low, many offer less variety and fewer customer services. For instance, shoppers may have to bag their own groceries.

Specialty stores specialize in carrying one type of food item. A seafood store or bakery is an example of a specialty store. Prices are often higher, but shoppers may prefer the quality and personalized service.

Warehouse clubs sell a variety of products in fixed quantities. The products are often sold in bulk at lower prices. Customers usually must purchase a membership to the warehouse club that allows them to shop there. Services are minimal.

Convenience stores offer convenient locations, longer hours, and fast service. However, product selection is limited, and prices are higher than supermarkets. Shoppers must decide if the added conveniences are worth the cost.

Evaluating Store Features

When choosing a place to shop, ask yourself a few questions. Does the store offer courteous service and helpful employees? Is the store clean and well maintained? Are meats, produce, and dairy products always fresh? Does the store stock a variety of foods in various package sizes to meet your needs? Is the checkout fast and efficient?

After evaluating the types of stores available, you may narrow your choices to one or two stores. You will become familiar with the products and services available at these stores. You will know just where to locate the items on your shopping list.

You will not waste time and gas driving to a store on the other side of town just for a bargain.

Deciding How Much Food to Buy

One of the most challenging aspects of shopping is deciding how much food to buy. Your decision should be based on your food budget. Three other factors you will want to consider are serving sizes, storage space, and shelf life.

Refer to your recipes to determine how many servings each one makes. If you need to make a larger or smaller number of portions, adjust your recipe before you go shopping. This will enable you to buy the correct amounts of ingredients. Read product labels for items you are not using in recipes. Labels state how many servings are in each food container to help you decide how much you need.

The amount of storage space you have available will help determine the quantity of foods you can buy. Some shoppers stock up when their favorite items are on sale. This saves money, but such foods must be stored until needed. If you do not have enough space for storage, large sale purchases are not practical.

A product's shelf life is also a factor to consider when buying food. For instance, buying a large box of cereal may be more economical than buying a smaller box. However, if the cereal gets stale before you can use it, the cost savings are wasted. The cost per serving of the eaten cereal rises sharply.

Recognizing Quality in Foods

To be a good shopper, you must be able to recognize quality. Many foods, such as meat, eggs, and dairy products, are graded. A grade is an indication of the quality of a food. The grade of a food does not affect its wholesomeness or nutritive value. For instance, a tough cut of beef may be just as wholesome and nutritious as a tender cut. However, its grade will not be as high.

Many foods are not graded. In these cases, you must evaluate quality based on your knowledge of food. For instance, fresh apples may not be graded. However, if you know high-quality apples have a firm texture and bright color, you can look for those features.

Wise buying includes knowing which quality is best suited to your needs, 13-10. For example, you may prefer top quality, tender beef for broiling. On the other hand, beef to be used in a stew could be less tender and of a lower quality.

13-10
One way to select the best value in meats is to compare quality. Look for the quality best suited to your needs.

Stores stock various brands of products. These include national brands, house brands, and generic products. **National brands** are often advertised nationwide. These products are generally of high quality, but they often cost more than other brands. **House brands** are brands that are sold by a store or chain of stores. Their quality is similar to national brands, but they usually cost less. **Generic products** have plain labels containing only the names of the products and other required label information. See 13-11. These products are nutritionally equivalent to national and house brands, but they may not be of the same quality. Generic products often cost less than branded products.

Damaged packaging can affect the quality of any food product. If a box is crushed, the food inside may be crushed, too. If a can is dented, the seal may be broken and the food may be contaminated. If frozen food packages are perforated, the contents may have lost quality due to freezer burn. For best quality, avoid buying damaged packages.

Check It Out!

1. True or false. A carefully planned shopping list saves time, energy, and money for the shopper.
2. List the five types of grocery stores you may consider in deciding where to shop.
3. What factors should you consider in deciding how much food to buy?
4. True or false. Food is graded to indicate its wholesomeness.

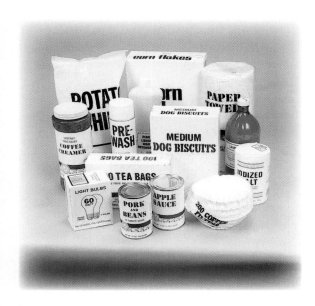

13-11
Generic products are characterized by their plain labels.

Topic 13-3

Buying Information

Objectives

After studying this topic, you will be able to
▼ use unit pricing to compare the cost of food products.
▼ describe four types of open dating used to indicate the freshness of food products.
▼ identify the types of information found on food product labels and tell how it can be used to make wise purchase decisions.
▼ list three sources of consumer information about food products.

Topic Terms

unit pricing
open dating
pack date
pull date
freshness date
expiration date
food additive
universal product code (UPC)

As you have read, many factors influence the food choices you make. Many resources are available to help you get the most for your food dollars. These resources include unit pricing, open dating, and package labeling.

Unit Pricing

Comparison shopping is made easier with unit pricing. **Unit pricing** shows the cost per standard unit of weight or measure. You can use unit pricing to compare prices among brands, package sizes, and product forms (fresh, frozen, canned). Unit pricing labels are usually posted on the shelves beneath food items. See 13-12.

Open Dating

You can judge the freshness of perishable foods through **open dating**. This dating process gives you information about the freshness of foods. It appears in four forms.
▼ Canned foods are often stamped with a **pack date**. This tells you when the food was processed.
▼ A **pull date** is often used on dairy products and cold cuts. This is the last day a store should sell the product. The pull date allows for some storage time at home, 13-13.

13-12

Unit pricing allows you to compare prices of various products.

13-13
Open dating helps you determine the freshness of the foods you buy.

13-14
Is fruit juice more nutritious than fruit drink? Food labels will give you the answer to this question, along with other useful information.

▼ Bread and baked goods usually have a **freshness date**. It indicates the end of the product's quality peak, but the product can be used beyond this date.

▼ **Expiration dates** appear on products such as yeast and baby formula. An expiration date is the last day a product should be used or eaten. When shopping, avoid buying outdated foods.

Food Labeling

You cannot examine the contents of a box or can of food before you buy it. However, you can learn a great deal about the foods you buy by reading labels, 13-14.

Food Label Information

According to government regulations, certain information must appear on food labels, 13-15. Every food label must include

▼ the common name of the product and its form, such as whole, sliced, or diced

▼ the net contents or net weight

▼ the name and address of the manufacturer, packer, or distributor

▼ a list of ingredients

Ingredients must be listed on the label in descending order by weight. For example, *peas, carrots, water,* and *salt* may be printed on a can label. This means the can contains more peas than carrots, more carrots than water, and more water than salt.

Descriptive terms used on food labels have often created confusion for consumers. As a result, the Food and Drug Administration (FDA) has set uniform definitions for descriptive terms such as *light, reduced,* and *free*. This assures consumers that terms appearing on food products are accurate.

Some foods are labeled *organically grown*. This means they were grown without the use of manufactured fertilizers or pesticides. Natural versions were used instead of chemicals. Organic foods are more expensive than non-organic foods. However, they taste the same and have similar nutritional value.

Parts of a Food Label

Description: The FDA has set specific definitions for descriptive terms, assuring shoppers that they can believe what they read on the package:
- free
- light
- more
- good source
- high
- low
- reduced
- less

For fish, meat, and poultry:
- lean
- extra lean

Health Claims: Food labels are allowed to carry information about the link between certain nutrients and specific diseases. For such a "health claim" to be made on a package, the FDA must first determine that the diet-disease link is supported by scientific evidence.

Ingredients, listed in descending order by weight, are required on almost all foods.

Health claim message referred to on the front panel is shown here.

"While many factors affect heart disease, diets low in fat and cholesterol may reduce the risk of this disease."

13-15

This example of a food label shows the information required by government regulations.

Understanding Food Additives

Food additives may be among the items found in a food product ingredient list. **Food additives** are substances that are added to food for a specific purpose. For instance, some food additives help keep foods from spoiling. Other food additives are used to enhance flavor, color, or texture; add nutrients; or aid processing.

Food additives may be added during any phase of producing, processing, storing, or packaging. Many familiar substances, such as salt, sugar, and vinegar, are common food additives.

Food additives are a subject of concern to some people. However, laws require substances to be carefully tested before they can be used as food additives. Additives must be proved safe for their intended uses. Certain additives must be identified on ingredient lists, as some people may be allergic to them.

Nutrition Facts Panel

By law, almost all packaged food products are required to include nutrition labeling. The Nutrition Facts panel found on food labels offers much useful information. It is designed to help consumers choose healthful diets. Consumers can use this panel to learn about the nutritional qualities of the food products they buy. See 13-16.

The panel includes the following nutrition facts:

▼ serving size
▼ servings per container
▼ calories per serving and calories from fat
▼ nutrients per serving, including total fat, saturated fat, *trans* fat, cholesterol, sodium, total carbohydrate, dietary fiber, sugars, and protein
▼ percent Daily Values of nutrients based on a 2,000-calorie diet

The More You Know: What Do Terms on Food Products Mean?

Descriptive terms used on food labels often create confusion for consumers. As a result, the Food and Drug Administration (FDA) provides definitions for descriptive terms such as *free*, *light*, *reduced*, and *high*. This assures consumers that terms appearing on food products are accurate and easy to compare.

A label describing a product as *sugar free* or *fat free* means the food has less than 0.5 gram of the component per serving. Either the component is missing or it is present only as a trace amount. The terms *zero*, *no*, or *without* may be used in place of *free*.

The label term *light* means the product has one-third fewer calories or half the fat of the regular product.

A product labeled *reduced calories* has 25% fewer calories than the same amount of the regular product. Another term to describe this reduction is *fewer*.

Use of the term *high* means the food has at least 20% more of the Daily Value for a given nutrient per serving. For example, grape juice labeled *high in vitamin C* has 20% more vitamin C than one would normally find.

To get a quick idea of how a food product rates for certain nutrients, look at the percent Daily Values. A food that contains 5 percent or less of a nutrient is considered low in that nutrient. A food that provides 20 percent or more of a nutrient is considered a good source of that nutrient. Use this information on food labels to help you limit total fat, saturated fat, cholesterol, and sodium. Also, use it to make sure you are getting enough fiber, vitamins A and C, calcium, and iron in your diet.

By using nutrition labeling, you can compare the nutritive values of various foods. This will enable you to get the most nutrition for your food dollar.

Universal Product Code

Another item found on most product labels is the **universal product code (UPC)**. This is a group of bars and numbers that contains price and product information, 13-17. In stores using a computerized checkout system, the grocery checker passes each UPC over a scanner. The computer reads the bar code and automatically records the information. The customer's receipt lists the items purchased and their prices, along with the total. This type of checkout is faster and more accurate. The labor savings may be passed on to customers through lower prices.

Other Sources of Information

Sometimes the information on shelf tags and product labels may not be enough to answer all your questions. Where can you find the information you need? The Food and Drug Administration (FDA) and the United States Department of Agriculture (USDA) offer a wealth of information. Your local cooperative extension agent or

Nutrition Panel Information

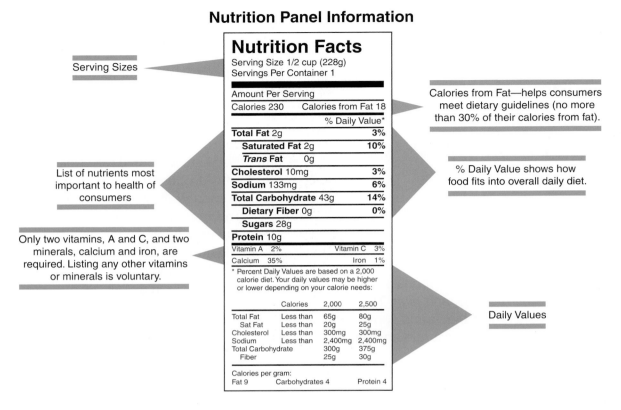

Serving Sizes

Calories from Fat—helps consumers meet dietary guidelines (no more than 30% of their calories from fat).

List of nutrients most important to health of consumers

% Daily Value shows how food fits into overall daily diet.

Only two vitamins, A and C, and two minerals, calcium and iron, are required. Listing any other vitamins or minerals is voluntary.

Daily Values

Nutrition Facts
Serving Size 1/2 cup (228g)
Servings Per Container 1

Amount Per Serving

Calories 230   Calories from Fat 18

% Daily Value*

Total Fat 2g	**3%**
Saturated Fat 2g	**10%**
Trans Fat 0g	
Cholesterol 10mg	**3%**
Sodium 133mg	**6%**
Total Carbohydrate 43g	**14%**
Dietary Fiber 0g	**0%**
Sugars 28g	
Protein 10g	

Vitamin A 2%		Vitamin C 3%
Calcium 35%		Iron 1%

* Percent Daily Values are based on a 2,000 calorie diet. Your daily values may be higher or lower depending on your calorie needs:

		Calories	2,000	2,500
Total Fat	Less than		65g	80g
Sat Fat	Less than		20g	25g
Cholesterol	Less than		300mg	300mg
Sodium	Less than		2,400mg	2,400mg
Total Carbohydrate			300g	375g
Fiber			25g	30g

Calories per gram:
Fat 9   Carbohydrates 4   Protein 4

13-16

A Nutrition Facts panel is found on most food labels. Using the information on it can help you compare the nutritional values of various products.

DEL MONTE PROOF OF PURCHASE
16 OZ. FRENCH GREEN BEANS

0   24000 01394

13-17

The universal product code (UPC) appears on various products as a group of lines, bars, and numbers.

family and consumer sciences teacher can answer many of your questions. Many food firms will also provide information about their products. You can use the Internet to quickly find Web sites for all these sources.

Check It Out!

1. A consumer aid that shows the cost per standard unit of weight or measure for a food product is known as _____.
2. List the four forms of open dating.
3. List the information required to appear on a food label.
4. Name three sources of consumer information about food products.

Topic 13-4
Storing Foods

Objectives

After studying this topic, you will be able to
▼ describe general guidelines for storing foods.
▼ identify two examples of technology in food packaging.

Topic Terms

food rotation
aseptic packaging
retort packaging

13-18
Food should be properly stored as soon as you bring it home from the grocery store.

Storing food properly is just as important as selecting it. In general, the foods you buy should be stored at home as they were stored at the grocery store. Proper storage at home will help maintain the quality of food, 13-18.

Properly Storing Foods

The types of foods you buy will determine the proper storage method. Foods can be stored in the refrigerator, in the freezer, or on a shelf. (More information on how to store specific types of food will be given in Chapter 15.)

In the Refrigerator

Foods such as meats, dairy products, and some fruits and vegetables spoil easily. Store these *perishable foods* in the refrigerator. Keep refrigerator temperatures at 35°F to 40°F. Most foods kept in the refrigerator should be packaged in airtight wraps or containers.

In the Freezer

Most types of food can be stored in the freezer. Tightly wrap foods in heavy-duty freezer wrap or aluminum foil or place them in airtight freezer containers. Label and date all frozen foods so you can easily identify them and avoid storing them too long, 13-19. To maintain food quality, keep freezer temperatures at 0°F or below. Keep frozen foods frozen until you are ready to prepare or serve them.

On a Shelf

Some foods require no refrigeration or freezing. You can store them on shelves in a cool, dry place. Place foods such as flour, cereals, pasta, dried beans, and peas in tightly sealed containers. Keep onions and potatoes in net bags or other containers that allow air to circulate. You can store bread and rolls on shelves for a few days. For longer storage, however, you should

13-19
Labeling and dating frozen foods will help you use them before they lose their peak quality.

freeze them to prevent mold growth. You can also store fruits and vegetables in cans and jars on shelves. However, you need to refrigerate these products after opening them.

When properly stored using any of the above methods, many foods will keep for months without spoiling. See 13-20. A loss of flavor may occur, however, if food is stored over a long period. For this reason, make **food rotation** a part of your storage routine. Store the freshest food at the back of the shelf. Use the oldest foods stored at the front of the shelf first.

Storing Leftovers

Leftover food that you want to save for a later meal can be stored at home as it was in the store. For example, uneaten popcorn and most breads can be stored on a shelf in a tight container. Meats will need to be refrigerated or frozen, depending on how soon you plan to eat them.

Store leftovers within two hours after the time they were served. Bacterial growth may contaminate hot foods that have cooled off or cold foods that have warmed up to room temperature.

Setting the Scene: Meal Management in Action

You are planning a drop-in buffet between 5:00 and 8:00 p.m. in honor of your parents' anniversary. You want to keep food preparation and service simple so you can greet and mingle with family friends. Your menu includes the following family favorites:

Roast beef slices with French rolls, mayonnaise, mustard, pickles, and tomato
Raw vegetable tray with salsa dip
Trays of red, white, and black grapes
Dry-roasted almonds
Fruit punch
Cupcakes with a wedding motif

Analyze It: Which food groups are included in the menu? Is there variety in color, flavor, texture, temperature, shape, and size? Which foods will be easy to prepare? Which foods can be left on the buffet all evening without fear of spoilage? Which foods should be left in the refrigerator and replenished as needed? Will you have time to mingle among the guests?

Food Storage Times	
Refrigerator	**Storage Time**
Beef, pork, lamb	2 to 4 days
Poultry, fish	1 to 2 days
Bacon, ham	5 to 7 days
Milk	1 week
Butter	2 weeks
Natural, process cheeses	4 to 8 weeks
Fruits and vegetables	Varies according to type
Freezer	
Beef	6 to 12 months
Pork	3 to 6 months
Lamb	6 to 9 months
Ground beef, pork, lamb	3 months
Ham, hot dogs	2 months
Poultry	6 to 8 months
Fish	3 to 4 months
Fruits and vegetables	9 to 12 months
Bread	2 to 3 months
Ice cream	2 months
Shelf	
Dried foods (cereal, flour, sugar)	1 year
Food in jars (catsup, jelly, pickles)	1 year
Onions and potatoes	4 weeks
Unopened cans	1 year
Aseptically packaged products (milk products, juices, soups)	6 months

13-20

Foods can be stored for various lengths of time.

Technology in Food Packaging

Food technologists and packaging specialists have come up with a number of new packaging techniques in recent years. These packaging methods allow some perishable foods to be stored on pantry shelves. These methods also allow for improved flavor and nutrition at a reduced cost.

One type of modern packaging technology is **aseptic packaging**. In this type of packaging, foods and containers are sterilized separately. Then the food is packed in the container in a sterile chamber. The foil-lined boxes commonly used for juices and milk are examples of aseptic containers. Many other products, such as soups and tofu, are also packaged aseptically.

A second type of packaging technology is **retort packaging**. In this technique, foods are sealed in foil pouches and then sterilized. This type of packaging is used for some shelf-stable entrees, 13-21. Food items sold in these types of packages can be stored on shelves for up to six months.

Check It Out!

1. Foods that should be stored in the refrigerator because they may spoil are known as _____ foods.
2. True or false. Foods stored in the freezer should be labeled and dated.
3. Explain the meaning of the term *food rotation*.

13-21
Foil retort pouches allow food products containing perishable ingredients to be stored on a shelf.

Chapter Review

Summary

Basic meal management skills are an important part of meal planning. Following a meal pattern based on MyPyramid can help you plan meals to meet your family's nutrient needs. Meal management skills can also help you plan varied meals that suit your food budget and available preparation time.

Following a carefully planned shopping list will save you time and energy when you shop. Listing what you need and avoiding impulse buying will save you money. Save both time and money by shopping at a store that offers reasonably priced foods, customer services, and a convenient location. Learning to recognize the quality of food can help you compare products to determine the best buy. When quality is not important, choosing lower-quality foods can save on the food budget.

Buying information helps you compare products and make wiser food choices when you shop. Unit pricing, open dating, food labeling, and UPCs are sources of information. Understanding this information will also help you save money as you shop.

Proper storage of food at home is the key to preserving its quality. An easy guide is to store food at home as it is stored in the supermarket. Modern packaging technology has made some perishable foods easier to store.

Think About It!

1. Why do you think meal management skills are an important part of meal planning?

2. Describe a meal that includes variety. Why is variety desirable in planning meals?

3. Suggest some ways to cut the costs of preparing meals at home.

4. How can the order of a shopping list save time, money, and energy?

5. What factors do you consider most important when choosing a place to buy food products?

6. Which information do you find most helpful to you as a food shopper? Why?

7. What do you think is the most important reason to know how to store foods properly?

8. In what careers do you think meal management skills would be required? In what other careers do you think these skills might be helpful?

Try It Out!

1. Choose three of your family's favorite recipes. Plan and organize a shopping list as if you were going to buy the ingredients for these recipes.

2. In class, discuss factors that usually affect the price of food. Suggest ways to get the best buys for your food dollars.

3. Plan a nutritious, economical meal that offers variety and is easy to prepare. Compare your ideas to those of your classmates.

4. Ask the butcher in a meat department to point out signs of quality used to establish the grade of various meats on display.

5. Ask the manager of your school cafeteria to share how meal management practices are part of his or her job.

Chapter 14
Before You Cook

Careers

These careers relate to the topics in this chapter:
▼ cooking school aide
▼ housewares demonstrator
▼ housewares department manager
▼ appliance sales trainer
As you study the chapter, see if you can think of others.

Topics

Topic 14-1

Know Your Equipment

Objectives

After studying this topic, you will be able to

▼ explain how to select, use, and care for major kitchen appliances.

▼ use portable appliances in the foods lab.

▼ identify various types of kitchen utensils and explain their uses.

Topic Terms

convection cooking
portable appliance
kitchen utensil
cookware
bakeware

Meal preparation can be made easier by using the right tools for food preparation tasks. With the help of various kitchen appliances and utensils you can save time. Knowing how to select, use, and care for your kitchen tools can make meal preparation run smoothly.

Major Appliances

Major appliances are the most costly kitchen tools. They are used for storing and cooking foods and for kitchen cleanup tasks. Refrigerators, ranges, and microwave ovens are found in most kitchens, 14-1. Dishwashers, food waste disposers, and trash compactors are also widely used major appliances.

14-1

A range is a major kitchen appliance found in every kitchen.

The Refrigerator

The refrigerator is the main food storage appliance. Its primary job is to keep food cold and retard food spoilage. It does this by using a system of circulating cold air. The temperature inside the refrigerator should be maintained at 35°F to 40°F.

Selection

Many sizes and styles of refrigerators are available. Look for easy-to clean surfaces both inside and outside. Compare energy costs with similar models. Decide whether you need special features, such as an automatic icemaker.

To choose the right size refrigerator, keep your family size in mind. Also think about how often you shop for groceries and how much freezer space you may need. Make sure the refrigerator you choose will fit the space available in your kitchen.

Decide which refrigerator style you need. Refrigerators are available in single-door, refrigerator-freezer (two-door), and compact-portable styles. See 14-2.

Use and Care

To keep foods safe, keep the refrigerator clean. Wash and dry inside and outside surfaces often. If the refrigerator has coils, vacuum them at least twice a year. (Coils are usually located on the back of the refrigerator.) Follow the manufacturer's use and care instructions for properly defrosting the refrigerator.

14-2
This two-door refrigerator-freezer has the freezer on the bottom. This keeps refrigerated foods at eye level.

You can take two key steps to maintain the proper temperature inside the refrigerator. First, do not open the door unnecessarily. This wastes energy by causing the refrigerator to work too hard. Second, try not to overcrowd the refrigerator. This may interfere with air circulation.

The Range

The range is a basic meal preparation appliance. Most ranges have four surface units, an oven, and a broiler. The range may use either electricity or gas for fuel. Your cooking and baking needs and available fuel hookup will determine which fuel and features you need.

Selection

In an electric range, electricity flows through coils of wire called heating elements. Some cooktops feature *quartz halogen* elements, which heat faster than standard electric coils.

In a gas range, gas and oxygen are mixed and burned in burners. Gas ranges have an energy-saving *pilotless ignition*, which requires electricity to work. Some gas ranges feature high-efficiency burners sealed into the cooktop for easier cleanup.

A *freestanding range* has an oven below the cooktop. There may also be a second oven above the cooktop. Freestanding ranges can either stand alone or be placed between two counters.

Drop-in ranges sit on a cabinet base. *Slide-in ranges* sit on the floor. Both styles have ovens below cooktops. These range styles have unfinished sides. The appliances fit snugly between two cabinets, giving the appearance of being built into the counter.

Cooking appliances are also available as separate built-in cooktops and ovens. Cooktops are built into a countertop. Ovens are built into a wall. See 14-3.

14-3

A built-in cooktop that is separate from the oven gives a kitchen greater flexibility by creating multiple work centers.

Some ranges may include special features or optional accessories. A rotisserie, a griddle, or thermostatically controlled surface units are some examples. Some ovens have a convenient self-cleaning feature. All these features add to a range's cost, so carefully determine which ones you really need.

Another oven option is the *convection oven*. This type of oven is available in gas and electric models. **Convection cooking** involves circulating hot air over all food surfaces. This allows the convection oven to cook more quickly and evenly than a conventional oven. The convection oven uses lower temperatures to cook food than a conventional oven. When using a convection oven, be sure to adjust cooking times and temperatures.

Technological advances have brought several high-speed ovens to the consumer market. Some use powerful *halogen lamps*, which cook with super-hot light waves. Some high-speed ovens combine halogen cooking with convection or microwave technology. The result is ovens that cut conventional cooking times by 30 to 80 percent. The light of the halogen lamp aids browning while allowing foods to stay moist. This makes many foods more appealing than they would be if prepared in a microwave oven. However, most high-speed ovens are at the high end of the consumer price range.

Use and Care

Follow the manufacturer's instruction manual for proper use and care of your range. Wipe up spills on cooktop surfaces immediately with a damp sponge. Clean the oven surfaces as recommended or set the self-cleaning cycle.

Practice energy-saving habits when cooking or baking. Match the cooking utensil size to the surface unit size. When baking, keep the oven door closed. Opening the door to peek inside lets heat escape, and this wastes energy.

Practicing safety habits when using a range is important. If you must light a match to light a gas range, always light it before turning on the gas. If the controls are turned off and you smell gas, ventilate the room and call a repairperson.

The Microwave Oven

A microwave oven cooks food using microwaves. *Microwaves* are high-frequency energy waves that cause food molecules to vibrate rapidly. The friction produced by these molecules creates heat that cooks the food.

Cooking with a microwave oven saves time and energy. See 14-4. You can defrost, reheat, and cook food in much less time than in a conventional oven. Because heat is created inside the food, the oven stays cool.

Selection

Many sizes, styles, and features are available in microwave ovens. Your choice will depend on your cooking needs.

Two main styles of microwave ovens are available. *Countertop* ovens are the most popular style with the best feature choices. Some models can be mounted under a cabinet to save counter space. *Over-the-range* microwave ovens hang over the range or are the upper oven on a two-oven range.

Use and Care

Follow the manufacturer's cooking guidelines. Because microwave ovens cook foods quickly, you must time foods carefully to guard against overcooking.

Do not turn on a microwave oven when it is empty. This could damage the oven. Also avoid using metal utensils in the microwave oven. Metal reflects microwaves and could damage the oven. Use paper, glass, and plastic cooking utensils. These materials allow the microwaves to reach the food being cooked.

Because food spills do not cook onto the oven interior, cleanup is easy. Wipe up spills with a damp cloth. Keeping the oven interior clean is important for another reason. Food spills may damage the door seal.

The Cleanup Appliances

The cleanup appliances include dishwashers, food waste disposers, and trash compactors. These appliances aid in making cleanup quick and easy. Follow the manufacturer's use and care instructions when using these appliances.

14-4
A microwave can cook most foods faster than a conventional oven and it uses less energy.

Dishwashers

Dishwashers offer many benefits. They save time and energy. Hot water and strong detergent help sanitize dishes. Dishwashers are available as either *portable* or *built-in* models. Both types operate in cycles and can be used to wash most kitchen utensils, 14-5.

For best cleaning results, load the dishwasher properly and use automatic dishwasher detergent. Avoid overcrowding dishes so water and detergent can circulate freely.

To save energy, operate the dishwasher only when you have a full load. To save more energy, turn off the dry cycle. The heat created in the dishwasher by the hot water will dry the dishes.

Food Waste Disposers

Food waste disposers are used to dispose of soft food waste. Two types of food waste disposers are available. A switch turns on a *continuous feed disposer*. Then food is pushed into the disposer in a continuous manner. When operating a *batch feed disposer*, food is added in small amounts. The disposer is then turned on when the lid is placed over the opening.

Operate food waste disposers carefully. Before using a disposer, check to be sure there are no foreign items in it. When operating a disposer, use cold running water. Use a rubber spatula to push foods into the disposer. Never use your fingers or metal objects to place food in the disposer.

Trash Compactors

Trash compactors are used to compress disposable wastes into a neat bundle. Compacted trash takes up about one-fourth the space of waste that has not been compacted. Food scraps and nonrecyclable containers can go in a trash compactor. However, do not place aerosol cans or flammable materials in this appliance.

Portable Appliances

A number of portable appliances are found in most kitchens. **Portable appliances** can be easily moved from one place to another. These appliances are designed to help people save time and energy when preparing foods.

Some portable appliances, such as popcorn poppers, are designed to do special jobs. Others, such as mixers and food processors, can perform a variety of tasks. See 14-6. Other common portable appliances include electric skillets, toasters, toaster ovens, blenders, food processors, coffeemakers, and electric mixers.

When selecting portable appliances, asking yourself a few questions can help you choose wisely. Will the appliance perform desired tasks quickly and safely? How often will I use it? How much

14-5
A built-in dishwasher is permanently installed under a counter.

 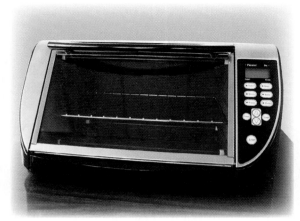

14-6
Small appliances can perform many tasks or one specific task. The food processor can shred, slice, mix, chop, or puree foods. The toaster-oven can warm, toast, bake, and broil.

storage space will it need? Is it easy to assemble, disassemble, and clean? Look for appliances that will give you the most satisfaction for your money.

Kitchen Utensils

A **kitchen utensil** is a handheld kitchen tool used for measuring, cutting, mixing, cooking, or baking tasks. Specialized utensils are available to perform almost any food preparation task.

The storage space in your kitchen is likely to be limited. Therefore, you need to choose wisely which utensils you will own. When selecting utensils, decide which ones best fit your needs. Think about your quality requirements and your budget. To get the most satisfaction from your cooking utensils, read and follow the manufacturers' use and care instructions.

To make utensils convenient to use, store them near where you will be using them. For instance, store a soup ladle near the range. Store measuring cups near your electric mixer. Be sure to store utensils

safely, too. Keep knife blades covered and sharp edges pointing down.

Measuring Utensils

Measuring utensils will help you correctly measure recipe ingredients. Each type of utensil has a specific measuring function. See 14-7.

Dry measuring cups are used for measuring dry ingredients, such as flour and sugar. They are also used for measuring shortenings and chopped foods.

Liquid measuring cups are used to measure liquid ingredients, such as water, milk, oil, and syrup. They are clearly marked with levels to allow accurate measurement of various amounts of ingredients. Liquid measuring cups should have a lip and a handle to make pouring easy.

Measuring spoons are used to measure small amounts of liquid, dry, and solid ingredients. These spoons are made of metal or plastic.

Although spatulas are not measuring utensils, they can assist you with measuring tasks. Use a *straight-edged spatula*

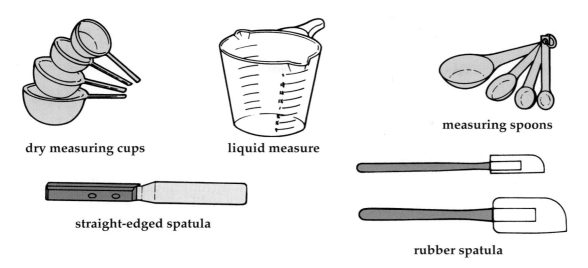

dry measuring cups

liquid measure

measuring spoons

straight-edged spatula

rubber spatula

14-7

Use of standard measuring utensils helps assure the success of a recipe. The most common ones are shown here. Spatulas are used to level off or scrape out measured ingredients.

for leveling dry and solid ingredients in measuring cups or spoons. A *rubber spatula,* or rubber scraper, can help you scrape wet or solid ingredients from measuring utensils.

Cutting Utensils

In meal preparation, cutting utensils are used to peel, pare, chop, slice, shred, carve, and debone foods. One type of cutting utensil that can do all these tasks is the knife. However, there are many types of knives, and each one is designed to handle particular cutting tasks. Some knives are long; others are short. Some have straight blades; others have *serrated,* or toothed, blades. The style of each knife depends on the preparation tasks for which it is used. See 14-8. The most popular types of knives are described below.

You can use a *paring knife* to pare (cut the skin off) vegetables and fruits, such as cucumbers and apples. It will also help you with small slicing and trimming jobs.

1. paring knife
2. French knife
3. utility knife
4. carving knife
5. serrated knife

14-8

A variety of cutting tools are used for food preparation tasks.

A *French* or *chef's knife* can chop, dice, and mince such foods as fruits, vegetables, nuts, and garlic. It is one of the most versatile knives you can own.

A *utility knife* is also versatile. It is a good choice for slicing foods, such as tender vegetables and cheeses.

A *carving knife* is used mostly for meats and poultry. Choose this type of knife when slicing ham, turkey, roasts, and other large food items for serving.

You need at least one *serrated knife* in your kitchen. Use this type of knife for slicing bread, sponge-type cakes, and soft vegetables like tomatoes.

Keeping the cutting edges of knives sharp is important. Sharp knives produce smoother, cleaner cuts with an easy hand motion. Exerting pressure to cut with a dull knife may cause an accident.

A *cutting board* should be used when cutting food with a knife. It protects your hand, the countertop, and the cutting edge of the knife. Cutting boards are made of wood, acrylic, and glass-ceramic. The only wooden boards to consider are hardwoods such as oak or maple. Softwoods such as pine are too porous. Bacteria can collect in porous wooden boards as well as deeply worn or grooved hardwood or acrylic boards. A glass-ceramic board resists the buildup of bacteria, but it dulls knives. All cutting boards should be washed and sanitized after each use.

Another type of cutting tool is *kitchen shears*. Use them for cutting dried fruits. They are also useful for snipping herbs, cutting meat or pizza, and opening food packages.

A *peeler* with a floating blade is used to remove the skin of fruits and vegetables. Because it removes a very thin layer, the nutrients near the surface are preserved. Peelers are also used to make garnishes such as carrot curls.

A *shredder-grater* is a four-sided utensil used for shredding, grating, and slicing tasks. Use it to grate lemon rind, shred cheese or cabbage, and slice potatoes.

Mixing Utensils

Mixing utensils are used for tasks such as mixing, combining, stirring, beating, blending, and whipping. Basic mixing utensils include bowls, spoons, scrapers, and beaters.

Use a *mixing bowl* to hold the recipe ingredients you want to mix. These bowls come in various sizes. A large *mixing spoon* makes it easy to mix, stir, or blend ingredients. *Rubber scrapers* are versatile tools. They are useful for folding ingredients and cleaning the sides of your mixing bowl. *Rotary beaters* have a crank, which you turn to make the beaters rotate. Use a beater to blend, beat, and whip ingredients in a mixing bowl. Another utensil that can do these mixing tasks is a *whisk*.

Cookware and Bakeware

Special equipment is needed for cooking food. **Cookware**, which includes saucepans and skillets, is used for cooking on top of the range. **Bakeware** is used for baking foods in the oven. Chart 14-9 gives some general tips for selecting cookware and bakeware.

Cookware

Saucepans and pots with tight-fitting lids serve many uses. Both are used for cooking foods over direct surface heat. Saucepans usually have one handle while pots have two handles. Several sizes are commonly used in most kitchens.

A *double boiler* is a small pan that fits inside a larger pan—usually a saucepan. Food is placed in the top pan. Water is placed in the bottom pan. The steam

Selecting Cookware and Bakeware

When you select cookware, look for these features:

- durable materials that distribute heat evenly
- sturdy designs with flat bottoms and smooth edges
- heat-resistant handles that are securely attached
- tight-fitting lids with easy-to-grip knobs
- durable pieces that are light enough to handle comfortably
- easy-to-clean design that will maintain appearance with proper use and care

When you select bakeware, look for these features:

- appropriate materials (glass, metal, glass-ceramic) that suit your specific baking needs
- the correct size for the intended use
- lightweight yet durable utensils that are easy to handle comfortably
- easy-to-clean designs that will maintain appearance with proper use and care

14-9

Follow these helpful tips when selecting cookware and bakeware.

produced when the water is heated cooks the food in the top pan. This gentle heat is less likely to burn delicate foods, such as milk and cream-based dishes.

Skillets, or frying pans, are used for shallow fat frying, panbroiling, searing, and braising foods. Heavy materials that distribute heat evenly, such as cast iron or cast aluminum, are desirable for skillets.

Griddles are skillets without sides. They are used for grilling sandwiches and cooking pancakes and French toast.

Large kettles are used when cooking foods in quantity, such as soups and pastas. Some of these pots come with a basket that is useful for steaming foods.

Bakeware

Several baking utensils are customized for specific tasks. Bakeware includes loaf, muffin, tube, pie, springform, pizza, and round and square cake pans.

When selecting bakeware, consider the surface of the utensil. If the surface is light and shiny, part of the heat will be reflected away from the food. Foods baked in shiny pans will have light, soft crusts. Dull, dark surfaces absorb heat and cook faster. Foods baked in dark pans will have crisper crusts. Glass also absorbs heat and cooks faster. Most recipe baking times are based on using light and shiny cooking surfaces.

Cookie sheets have a low rim on one or more sides of the baking sheet for strength. They are used for baking cookies, rolls, and biscuits and for heating frozen foods such as pizza.

Most *roasting pans* have high domed lids to cover meats. They also have removable racks to hold meat out of the drippings that form during cooking. Roasting pans may be oval or rectangular in shape and can be purchased in various sizes.

Casseroles are baking dishes with high sides. You can use them for both baking and serving foods. Some casseroles are designed for freezer-to-oven use. They may be made of glass, glass-ceramic, or earthenware. Sizes range from single servings to several quarts.

A *cooling rack* is an important accessory for baking. A cooling rack allows air to circulate around food so it can cool evenly.

Cookware and Bakeware Materials

Learning about the materials used to make cookware and bakeware can help you make wiser choices. Well-constructed, high-quality materials will likely last many years, 14-10. Read and follow the use and care instructions that come with the products.

All materials are not suited for every use. For instance, plastic bakeware is often used for microwave cooking. It is easy to clean, sturdy, and dishwasher safe. However, most plastic bakeware cannot be used in a conventional oven at high temperatures. When choosing cookware and bakeware, look for materials that are versatile.

14-10
High-quality cookware is a good investment. With proper use and care, it will provide years of service.

Check It Out!

1. List four major appliances commonly found in a kitchen.
2. How does a portable appliance differ from a major appliance?
3. List and state the specific use of four cutting tools.
4. Explain the difference between cookware and bakeware.

Topic 14-2

Safety and Sanitation

Objectives

After studying this topic, you will be able to

▼ follow safety practices in the kitchen when preparing foods.

▼ list specific guidelines that fall under the steps *clean*, *separate*, *cook*, and *chill* for keeping foods safe to eat.

Topic Terms

sanitation
foodborne illnesses
cross-contamination

A safe kitchen is one that is as free as possible from risks of injury. Taking precautions can help you keep your kitchen work area safe and free from accidents. Handling food properly and keeping food safe to eat are important sanitation practices. **Sanitation** is the process of maintaining a clean and healthy environment. Following sanitary food preparation measures assures that food is safe to eat.

Make It Safe

Following safety practices will help you prevent accidents in the kitchen. The most common types of accidents in the kitchen are electrical shocks, fires, burns, falls, cuts, and poisonings. Remember to practice safety habits when using appliances and utensils.

Using Appliances and Utensils Safely

Many accidents in the kitchen are caused by the misuse of equipment. Accident prevention depends on your knowing how to safely use each appliance. You must follow all manufacturers' use and care instructions carefully. You also need to know how to use all utensils, cookware, and bakeware correctly. Knowing how to use and care for equipment is only the first step. Follow up by practicing safety procedures. Some important kitchen safety guidelines are listed in Chart 14-11.

Keep It Sanitary

Many cases of foodborne illness occur each year. **Foodborne illnesses** are sicknesses caused by eating contaminated food. The contaminants that cause illness are often bacteria. If you suspect any food is spoiled, do not taste it. Throw it out immediately.

Signs of foodborne illness often include vomiting, diarrhea, stomach cramps, and headaches. These symptoms can occur within 30 minutes of eating contaminated food. However, sometimes symptoms take a few weeks to appear. Most foodborne illnesses usually last no more than a couple days, but some can have lasting effects. Pregnant women, young children, older adults, and people with weakened immune systems are at greater risk of foodborne illness. These groups of people need to take extra precautions to handle food safely.

Food safety involves four basic steps—clean, separate, cook, and chill. If you remember these steps and observe the following tips, you can help prevent foodborne illness.

Kitchen Safety

Preventing Cuts and Minor Injuries

- Hold the tip of a knife down when carrying it.
- If you drop a knife, step back and let it fall.
- Keep knife blades sharp.
- Store knives in a rack or drawer with the cutting edges down.
- Chop, dice, and slice foods on a cutting board.
- Use knives for cutting only. If a can opener or screwdriver is needed, find the appropriate tool.
- Cut down and away from yourself when using a knife.
- Wash sharp knives separately.
- Wrap broken glass in heavy paper before putting it into the trash.
- Do not leave drawers and cupboard doors standing open.
- Turn off appliances such as electric mixers, blenders, and food processors before cleaning the sides of the container with a rubber scraper.

Preventing Fires

- Avoid wearing loose clothing and roll up long sleeves when cooking.
- Tie back long hair.
- Dip a burned match in water before putting it into a trash can.
- When manually lighting a gas burner, strike the match before turning on the gas. Never leave food cooking on the range unattended.
- Keep aerosol cans away from heat.
- Clean grease from the exhaust fan to prevent grease fires.

Preventing Falls

- Wipe up spills immediately.
- Keep a sturdy step stool handy for reaching high places.

Preventing Burns

- Use a pot holder, not a dishcloth or towel, to handle hot utensils.
- Keep a fire extinguisher near the kitchen entrance.
- Lift pot lids away from your body to avoid steam burns.
- Dry foods before putting them into hot fat to avoid spatters.
- Do not put water on a grease fire. Cover it with the lid of a pan or smother it with salt or baking soda.
- Do not carry a container of hot food across the room without first giving a loud warning to others.
- When draining hot food from a pan, use the lid as a shield from the steam.
- Open the oven door flat and pull out the oven rack when removing foods from a hot oven.
- Keep pan handles turned away from the front of the range when cooking.

Preventing Electrical Shocks

- Read and follow manufacturer's directions before using any electrical appliance. Plug electrical cords into appliances before plugging them into wall outlets. Disconnect appliances by pulling on the plug rather than the cord.
- Avoid overloading electrical outlets. Unplug an electrical appliance before cleaning it.
- Handle electrical appliances only when your hands are dry.

Preventing Poisonings

- Keep all chemicals, such as medicines, household cleaners, and pesticides, away from food storage areas.
- Keep food out of range when spraying chemicals. Wipe counters thoroughly when spraying.

14-11

Following safety guidelines while preparing and serving foods can help protect you and others from injury.

Clean Hands, Utensils, and Surfaces

Cleanliness is essential. Keep utensils and work areas clean. Pay attention to personal cleanliness. Wash your hands with warm water and soap for 20 seconds before handling food. Make sure your fingernails are clean, too. Some other important principles of sanitation are listed below.

▼ Tie back hair or wear a chef's hat or hairnet to keep hair from falling into food.

▼ Wear a clean apron to avoid transferring bacteria from your clothes to the food. Use clean equipment.

▼ Do not use a hand towel to dry dishes.

▼ Do not touch food with your hands if you could use tongs, a fork, or a knife. Rewash hands after handling raw meats, poultry, fish, or eggs.

▼ Wear plastic gloves when working with food if you have an open sore on your hand.

▼ Do not lick fingers or cooking utensils. Use one spoon for stirring and another spoon for tasting.

▼ Cover coughs and sneezes with a tissue and wash your hands afterward. Also wash hands after using the bathroom, changing diapers, or playing with pets.

▼ Replace cutting boards when they become worn and hard to clean.

▼ Wash dishes thoroughly with hot soapy water and sanitize eating utensils with scalding water or sanitizer. See 14-12.

▼ Keep kitchen counters clean.

▼ Wash tops of cans before opening them to keep dust and bacteria out of food.

▼ Wash fresh fruits and vegetables under running water to flush away dirt and pesticides before preparation.

Pest Control

Pests can transfer disease-causing bacteria to food during storage. Therefore, you need to take steps to keep mice, rats,

14-12
The hot water and strong detergent used in a dishwasher sanitizes dishes.

ants, flies, and cockroaches out of your home. You must prevent these pests from contaminating surfaces, utensils, or food supplies.

Methods for pest control vary. You can use a variety of traps or sprays. However, you must exercise great caution because chemicals can also contaminate surfaces, utensils, and food. If pest problems persist, contact your local health department for their suggestions. You may need to call a professional exterminator to keep pests away.

Separate Raw and Cooked Foods

You must handle all foods properly to prevent contamination. However, you must handle perishable protein foods (meat, poultry, fish, and eggs) with extra care as they are easily contaminated. When these foods are raw, you must also keep them separate from other foods. If these foods happen to be contaminated, keeping them separate will help you prevent cross-contamination. **Cross-contamination** is the spread of bacteria from a contaminated food to other food, equipment, or surfaces.

▼ Place fresh meats, poultry, and fish in individual plastic bags at the grocery store. This will keep juices from getting on other foods in your shopping cart. Place these foods in sealed plastic containers and store them on a lower shelf in the refrigerator. This will prevent them from dripping on other foods.

▼ Wash cutting boards and other equipment immediately after using them to prepare raw meats, poultry, fish, or eggs. This will help you avoid transferring bacteria from uncooked foods to other foods.

▼ Never serve cooked meat, poultry, or fish on the same plate that held these foods before cooking.

Cook Foods Thoroughly

Raw and undercooked meat, poultry, fish, and eggs may contain disease-causing bacteria. Thoroughly cook these foods and all dishes that contain them. Also, be sure food you order in restaurants is completely cooked. The temperatures used for cooking can kill many harmful bacteria.

▼ Use a food thermometer to be sure meat, poultry, fish, and egg products are cooked to the recommended internal temperatures. Color is not an accurate indicator of doneness. See 14-13.

▼ Do not partially cook meats, poultry, or fish. Cook them thoroughly and serve immediately.

▼ Stuff meats, poultry, and fish just before baking. Remove stuffing promptly after baking; refrigerate leftovers separately.

▼ Never set the oven lower than 325°F when cooking meats.

▼ Keep hot foods hot—above 140°F. Bacteria grow fast in warm foods at lower temperatures.

▼ If you are heating leftovers, be sure to heat them to at least 165°F before serving. Heat sauces, soups, marinades, and gravies to this temperature as well.

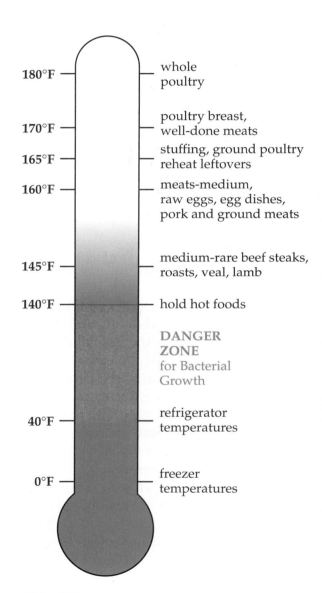

180°F — whole poultry

170°F — poultry breast, well-done meats

165°F — stuffing, ground poultry reheat leftovers

160°F — meats-medium, raw eggs, egg dishes, pork and ground meats

145°F — medium-rare beef steaks, roasts, veal, lamb

140°F — hold hot foods

DANGER ZONE for Bacterial Growth

40°F — refrigerator temperatures

0°F — freezer temperatures

14-13
Thoroughly cooking food to the proper temperature kills harmful bacteria.

Chill Foods Promptly

Refrigerator temperatures slow the growth of harmful bacteria. This is why it is important to keep perishable foods chilled until you are ready to prepare or eat them. It is also important to chill leftover foods as soon as you are done eating.

▼ Put frozen and refrigerated foods in your shopping cart last.
▼ Get foods home as quickly as possible. In warm weather, carry a cooler in your car to keep foods cool until you get home.
▼ Promptly store foods that should be chilled and frozen.
▼ Wrap foods properly for freezer and refrigerator storage.

▼ Use thermometers to monitor storage temperatures. Be sure your freezer is kept at 0°F or lower and your refrigerator is kept at 40°F or lower.
▼ Thaw perishable foods overnight in the refrigerator or in the microwave oven just before cooking. Never thaw on the counter or in the sink.
▼ Marinate meat, fish, and poultry in the refrigerator.
▼ Never leave perishable foods out over two hours. This includes takeout foods and foods on a buffet table.
▼ Place leftovers in shallow containers to promote rapid cooling. Then refrigerate or freeze leftovers promptly. See 14-14.
▼ Keep cold foods cold—below 40°F. Bacteria grow fast in cool foods at higher temperatures.

14-14

Storing foods in shallow containers helps them quickly reach safe, cool temperatures.

Setting the Scene: Cultural Differences in Food Handling

You have watched movies and news reports featuring other cultures and countries. You have noticed that some people use food preservation, cooking, and storage techniques that differ from the concepts most familiar to you. For example, refrigerators are not available in many cultures.

Analyze It: What ways can you think of to preserve other food without refrigeration? How might this apply to you if your home lost electricity due to a natural disaster? What other cultural differences related to food can you name?

Check It Out!

1. List three safety practices that help prevent kitchen accidents.
2. Explain how foodborne illnesses occur.
3. List the four basic steps to food safety and give two specific guidelines for each step.

Topic 14-3
Using a Recipe

Objectives

After studying this topic, you will be able to
▼ identify the information found in a recipe and follow it successfully.
▼ demonstrate proper measuring techniques for different types of ingredients.
▼ define cooking terms used in recipes.
▼ describe two categories of cooking methods.

Topic Terms

recipe
measurement equivalents

Cooking, like other skills, is learned through practice. Before you begin to cook, you need to know certain information about the food product you want to make. What ingredients do you need, and in what amounts? What utensils do you need to use? What steps should you follow? All this information is included in a recipe. A **recipe** is a list of ingredients with a complete set of instructions for preparing a food product.

Learning to use a recipe correctly is the key to good meals. If you can read and follow recipe instructions, you can prepare almost any food product. With experience, you can even develop your own recipes. See 14-15.

14-15

Smart cooks use simple recipes as they first learn to cook. As they develop their cooking skills, they will be able to try more involved recipes.

Understanding How to Use Recipes

All recipes include certain information, 14-16. The *ingredient list* tells you what food items you need. It also lists the exact amount of each ingredient you need to make the product. Preparation directions for combining the ingredients are next. Utensil sizes for cookware or bakeware are given, as are oven temperatures and cooking times. The recipe *yield* tells you how many servings the recipe makes.

Steps for Using Recipes

Many factors—measurements, preparation methods, cooking utensils, temperatures, and cooking times—can affect the outcome of a recipe. That is why it is important to follow all instructions.

Taco Frittata
(2 servings)

1   tablespoon butter
4   eggs
2   tablespoons chopped green chilies
2   tablespoons water
½   teaspoon Worcestershire sauce
¼   teaspoon salt
¼   teaspoon ground cumin
      dash pepper
⅓   cup chunky taco sauce

Melt butter over medium heat in a 6- to 8-inch omelet pan or skillet with ovenproof handle.* Beat together remaining ingredients, except taco sauce, until blended. Pour into pan. Cover and cook over low to medium heat until eggs are almost set, about 6 to 8 minutes. Pour taco sauce over top. Remove pan from heat. Cover and let stand 5 minutes or broil about 6 inches from heat until eggs are completely set, about 2 to 4 minutes.

*To make handle ovenproof, wrap completely with aluminum foil.

14-16

A recipe includes all the information you need to successfully prepare a food product.

Following the guidelines below can help you get great results from the recipes you prepare. Here are some steps to help you get started.

▼ Read the entire recipe carefully *before* you start to cook. Make sure you have all the ingredients and utensils listed on hand. Check the preparation and cooking times in the recipe to make sure you have enough time to prepare it.

▼ Note any abbreviations used in the ingredient list. Be sure you understand what each one means. Abbreviations often used in recipes are given in 14-17.

▼ Before you start measuring and mixing, gather all the ingredients and cooking utensils you will need.

▼ If your recipe tells you to *preheat* the oven, turn the oven on before you begin to cook. Set the temperature given in the recipe. The oven will then be hot when you are ready to put the food in it.

▼ For successful results, follow recipe directions exactly. Measure the exact amounts of each ingredient. Mix ingredients in the order listed, using the method given. Use the correct utensil sizes.

Abbreviations Used in Recipes

tsp. or t.	teaspoon
tbsp. or T.	tablespoon
c. or C.	cup
pt.	pint
qt.	quart
gal.	gallon
oz.	ounce
lb. or #	pound

14-17

Recognizing the abbreviations used in recipes will assist you in measuring ingredients accurately. The most common abbreviations are listed here.

▼ For best flavor and appearance, accurate timing is important. Follow cooking or baking times as stated in the recipe. If your range has a timer, use it to remind you when cooking times end.

In the early stages of learning to cook, using simple recipes is smart. Simple recipes have few ingredients and easy preparation steps. As you develop your cooking skills, you can try more difficult recipes and experiment with some of your own ideas.

Using Ingredient Substitutions

As you assemble your recipe ingredients, you may find you do not have a certain item on hand. In some recipes, you may be able to substitute one ingredient for another. In some cases, a substitution may affect the results of the finished product. If you are in a pinch, however, the substitution may be necessary.

Measuring Techniques

Learning to measure ingredients accurately is important for successful results, especially in baked products. Dry, liquid, and solid ingredients each require special measuring techniques. Chart 14-18 lists the right technique to use for each type of ingredient.

For measuring dry ingredients, such as flour and sugar, use dry measuring cups. Use measuring spoons for measuring leavening agents, spices, and small amounts of dry ingredients. The general technique for measuring dry ingredients is to overfill the cup or spoon. Then level it off with a straight-edged spatula or knife.

Measure liquid ingredients in glass or clear plastic liquid measuring cups. Place the measure on a flat surface and then carefully fill it to the correct measurement

The More You Know: What Can You Substitute?

Have you ever started to prepare a recipe and discovered you were missing an ingredient? Many times a substitution can be made that will save you a trip to the supermarket. For example, 1 whole egg can be used instead of 2 egg yolks. Make 1 cup of buttermilk by adding 1 tablespoon of vinegar to milk to make 1 cup. Two tablespoons of flour can be used in place of a tablespoon of cornstarch. If you need one cup of cake flour, use ⅞ cup of all-purpose flour. A cup of heavy cream can be replaced by ¾ cup of milk plus ½ cup of butter.

line. Check the accuracy of your measurement at eye level. Use a measuring spoon for measuring small amounts of liquids.

Shortenings and other solid foods, such as peanut butter, are measured with dry measuring cups. Measuring spoons work well for small amounts. Press the ingredient into the cup or spoon so no air space remains. Level it off with a straight-edged spatula or knife. For sticks of butter or margarine, cut through the wrapper at the correct measurement line.

Understanding Recipe Terms

As a beginning cook, you may come across recipe terms or directions you do not understand. Understanding these terms will help you use the right method

Measuring Techniques

Brown sugar	Pack firmly into a dry measure and level off top with straight edge of spatula or knife.
Granulated sugar	Spoon sugar into a dry measure until it is overfilled. Level off the top of the measure with a metal spatula or knife.
Flour, powdered sugar, fine meal, or crumbs	Stir lightly with a fork or spoon. Spoon lightly into dry measure until it is overflowing. Do not shake or tap measure. Level off top with straight edge of spatula or knife.
Baking powder, cornstarch, spices	Dip small measure into container and bring it up heaping full. Level off top with straight edge of metal spatula or knife.
Solid fats	Pack fat firmly into a dry measure and level off top with straight edge of metal spatula or knife. Remove fat with a rubber spatula. Butter and margarine usually come in sticks with measurements marked on the wrapper.
Liquids	Place liquid measure on a flat surface. Pour liquid into the measure until it reaches the desired level. View at eye level.

14-18

Proper measuring of ingredients will help ensure good results when cooking.

for preparing the recipe correctly. Some common terms used in recipe directions are defined in 14-19.

Changing the Yield

What do you do if you need more or fewer servings than your recipe makes? You can double or halve the ingredient amounts to change the recipe yield if you understand measurement equivalents. **Measurement equivalents** are amounts that are equal to other amounts, 14-20. For instance, one-fourth cup equals four tablespoons. To halve one-fourth cup, you would use two tablespoons.

When doubling or halving a recipe, write down the amounts of ingredients

you will be using. This will help you avoid confusion while you are preparing the food.

Learning Cooking Methods

When preparing food, you want it to be both appetizing and nutritious. Some foods can be served raw. Others require cooking. Cooking is a science as well as an art. When heat is applied to food, certain changes take place. When different foods are combined, physical or chemical changes may also take place. Knowing various cooking methods will help you create tasty, nutritious meals.

Recipe Terms to Know

baste. To keep food moist during cooking by spooning or pouring melted fat, meat drippings, fruit juice, or sauce over it.

beat. To make a mixture smooth by adding air using a brisk stirring or whipping motion with a spoon or an electric mixer.

blend. To combine two or more ingredients until smooth and of uniform consistency.

bread. To dip food into a mixture, such as beaten eggs and milk, and then roll it in crumbs.

brown. To cook food quickly at a high temperature so the surface becomes brown.

chop. To cut into pieces with a knife, scissors, or food chopper.

cream. To stir or beat solid fat, such as shortening or butter, with sugar until the mixture is soft, smooth, and creamy.

cut in. To mix dry ingredients into shortening by using a pastry blender, two knives, or a fork.

dice. To cut into small even pieces, smaller than ½ inch.

dredge. To dip into or sprinkle with flour.

fold. To combine ingredients into a light, airy mixture using a down, across, up, and over motion with a rubber spatula.

knead. To use a fold-push-turn motion when working with doughs.

marinate. To let a food, such as meat, stand in a liquid to increase the flavor and/or tenderness of the food.

mash. To crush food until it has a smooth texture.

mince. To cut with a sharp knife or scissors into very small pieces.

mix. To combine ingredients until evenly distributed or blended.

reconstitute. To restore foods to their normal state by adding water.

scald. To heat milk just below the boiling point.

sear. To brown the surface of meat quickly with intense heat.

sift. To pass dry ingredients through a mesh or screen to add air or to combine dry ingredients.

slice. To cut or divide into flat pieces.

stir. To mix foods with a circular motion.

whip. To beat rapidly to incorporate air and to increase volume.

14-19

As you learn to cook, it is helpful to know the meaning of these terms.

Basic Cooking Methods

Foods can be prepared in a variety of ways. The method you use depends on the food you are preparing.

The basic methods of cooking food can be grouped in two general categories. The first category is *moist heat cooking methods*. In these methods, food is cooked in a humid environment. Moisture may be due to water or a water-based liquid being added to the food. Moisture may also result when steam released from the food is trapped in the cooking utensil or appliance. Boiling or stewing, braising, simmering, and steaming are all moist heat cooking methods. Basic microwave cooking is also considered a moist heat cooking method. This is because steam is enclosed in the sealed microwave oven cavity during cooking.

The second category of cooking methods is *dry heat cooking methods*. In these methods, food is cooked in hot air or

Common Measurement Equivalents

1 tablespoon	= 3 teaspoons
⅛ cup	= 2 tablespoons
¼ cup	= 4 tablespoons
⅓ cup	= 5⅓ tablespoons
½ cup	= 8 tablespoons
⅔ cup	= 10⅔ tablespoons
¾ cup	= 12 tablespoons
1 cup, ½ pint	= 16 tablespoons
1 pint	= 2 cups
quart	= 2 pints, 4 cups

14-20

Knowing equivalent measures can help you change recipe yields.

on a hot surface without added moisture. Baking or roasting, broiling, deep-frying, grilling, panbroiling, panfrying, and stir-frying are all dry heat cooking methods. These methods allow food products to become brown and develop crisp crusts, which cannot form in a moist atmosphere.

Moist and dry heat cooking methods are described in Chart 14-21. More information on cooking methods for specific types of foods is presented in Chapter 17.

General Cooking Guidelines

A general rule to follow when cooking food is to avoid overcooking it. Overcooking makes protein foods, such as meat and eggs, tough and causes milk to curdle. Baked products become dry. Fruits and vegetables become mushy and discolored when overcooked. Overcooking also causes foods to lose water-soluble vitamins.

Try to conserve nutrients when preparing food. If foods are simmered, use as little water as possible. When foods are boiled, plan a way to use the liquid in which they were cooked. Valuable vitamins and minerals are often discarded when cooking liquids are poured down the drain. Use these liquids in soups, sauces, and gravies.

Microwave Cooking

Most foods cook much faster in a microwave oven than they do in a conventional oven. Therefore, you need to use some special cooking techniques when preparing foods in a microwave oven to achieve best results.

The defrost cycle is a popular feature on most microwave ovens because you can defrost foods at the last minute. *Defrosting time* is determined by the size and density of the food you wish to defrost. You will need more time to defrost a four-pound roast than four pounds of individually wrapped steaks. This is because the roast is larger and denser than the steaks.

Many microwave ovens have an automatic defrost cycle. A sensor measures the steam generated as a food product defrosts. This sensor automatically stops the defrost cycle at the right time. Most microwave ovens have a chart in the use and care manual to help you determine correct defrost times. Many food packages also give directions on how to defrost the products in a microwave oven.

Foods such as eggs, apples, potatoes, and many prepackaged foods are covered with a tight skin or wrapper. Moisture in foods turns into steam during the cooking process. If this steam is trapped inside the skin or wrapper covering a food, the encased food can explode. Exploding food items can be dangerous as well as messy and unattractive. *Piercing* the skin or wrapper of such foods before microwaving allows the steam to escape slowly as the food cooks.

You read earlier that you should not use metal utensils in a microwave

Cooking Methods

Moist Heat

Method	Procedure	Foods
Boil/Stew	To cook in water or liquid in which rolling bubbles have formed	Vegetables, meats, pasta
Braise	To cook in a small amount of liquid in a tightly covered pan over low heat	Meats, vegetables
Microwave	To cook in a microwave oven	Vegetables, meats, fruits, casseroles
Simmer	To cook in liquid just below the boiling point	Eggs, meats, soups
Steam	To cook in steam, with or without pressure	Vegetables, meats, fish

Dry Heat

Method	Procedure	Foods
Bake/Roast	To cook in an oven in a covered or uncovered container	Cakes, cookies, breads, eggs, some vegetables, meats
Broil	To cook uncovered by direct heat	Meats, seafood, fruits, and vegetables
Deep-fry	To cook in a large amount of hot fat	Meats, seafood, vegetables, doughnuts, fritters
Grill	To roast slowly over coals or another intense heat source	Meats, vegetables
Panbroil	To cook uncovered in a fry pan, pouring fat off as it accumulates	Bacon, sausage, and similar meats containing a large amount of fat
Panfry	To cook in a small amount of fat	Meats, seafood, vegetables, eggs
Stir-fry	To cook foods quickly in a small amount of fat at a high temperature	Thinly cut meats, fish, vegetables, rice

14-21

Choose the cooking method best suited to the food you are preparing.

oven. However, you can use foil in small amounts if you do not allow it to touch the walls of the oven. For example, you might cover chicken wing tips or the small ends of drumsticks with foil. This technique is known as *shielding*. The parts of a food that you shield with aluminum foil are prevented from overcooking. Other foods you might shield include the bone area in a large meat cut. You can also shield the corners of a square baking dish to keep the food in the corners from becoming dry.

Covering foods in a microwave oven prevents them from drying out due to loss of moisture. There are several popular coverings. You might simply cover foods in a microwavable dish with the lid to the dish. Plastic wraps work well for covering many foods. However, they can form tight seals, so you will need to leave a loose corner to allow steam to escape. This is called *venting*. Paper towels are used for covering foods that produce fats, such as bacon, or breads that produce moisture. The paper towel absorbs the fat or moisture so the food does not become soggy. Wax paper can be placed atop a casserole in a microwave oven for efficient cooking.

Microwaves cook the outer edges of foods first. Microwave ovens also tend to cook faster in the center of the oven. You can compensate for these deviations and promote even cooking by stirring, rearranging, or rotating the food. *Stirring* will bring food from the center of a dish to the outer edges for faster cooking. You cannot stir some foods, such as chicken pieces. *Rearranging* these foods halfway through the cooking cycle will help them cook more evenly. What about a pineapple upside down cake, which cannot be stirred or rearranged? *Rotating* such foods a quarter or half turn several times during the cooking cycle will help distribute microwaves more evenly. Many microwave ovens come with a turntable to rotate foods for you.

Hot foods continue to cook as long as they are hot. Therefore, many microwave recipes recommend *standing time* to allow the food to finish cooking. Standing time should begin just before a food has finished cooking. Failing to allow for standing time can result in overcooked foods.

Many of today's microwave ovens cook even faster than models sold a few years ago, 14-22. You may need to alter the cooking times of your favorite microwave recipes if you get a new microwave oven. You should always read the recipe you are using and the directions that come with a new oven.

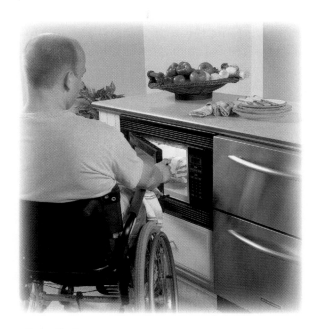

14-22
Today's powerful microwave ovens cook foods faster than ever.

Check It Out!

1. What is the first step to follow in using a recipe?
2. Describe the technique used for measuring flour.
3. Briefly explain each of the following recipe terms: blend, mix, and stir.
4. What are the two general categories into which cooking methods can be grouped?
5. Using small amounts of foil to cover areas of a food product and prevent them from overcooking is called ____.

Topic 14-4
Cooking Smart

Objectives

After studying this topic, you will be able to
▼ plan a meal management time plan at home.
▼ demonstrate how to work as an effective team member in the foods lab.

Topic Term
work plan

14-23
Working together in the school foods lab requires cooperation from each group member.

Cooking smart means getting foods prepared with a minimum of time and a maximum of efficiency. Some tricks that will help you master these skills can be used both at home and at school.

There is one major difference between meal preparations at home and at school. At home, you may prepare foods your way. At school, you are a part of a team. Besides learning cooking skills, you learn the importance of teamwork. See 14-23.

At Home

The key to successful meal preparation at home lies in planning. Timing is one of the most difficult skills in meal preparation. This means having all the food ready and at the right temperature at serving time. You can achieve this goal, but it takes careful scheduling.

Using a Time Plan

As a beginning cook, you will want to write out a time plan. A time plan helps you coordinate your cooking schedule. You will know exactly when you must complete certain preparation tasks to serve the meal on time. You will also avoid the confusion and frustration of having several tasks to complete at the same time.

Try to pace your cooking activities according to the clock. You can do this by establishing the time the meal is to be served. Then count back in time to decide when you should start each part of the meal.

Suppose you want to prepare this meal: baked chicken, hot rolls, a salad, and chocolate pudding. Here is how your time plan would work. Because the chicken will take the longest to cook, prepare it first and place it in the oven. Then prepare the pudding. You can prepare the salad next. Chill both the salad and the pudding in the refrigerator until serving time. About 15 minutes before you plan to eat, heat the rolls in the oven. During this time, you can set the table and prepare the beverage. At mealtime, the chicken and rolls should be hot, the salad crisp, and the pudding chilled. When serving many foods that are to be cooked in the oven, choose foods that have compatible oven temperatures. For instance, stuffed pork chops, green bean casserole, and a quick bread can all be baked at 350°F.

As you gain experience, you will find it easier to prepare simple meals without a time plan. Do not allow relying on a time plan to make you feel uncomfortable, however. Good cooks with years of experience still use them when they prepare food for special occasions.

Making Meal Preparations

Making meal preparations means doing meal-related tasks ahead of time. It could mean baking a large ham, roast, or turkey on the weekend to eat during the week. It could mean preparing a salad or casserole the night before you plan to serve it. It might also mean setting the table in the morning before you go to work or school. Use any time available to prepare for meals. You will be glad you did when it is mealtime.

Many foods lend themselves to being prepared and stored ahead of time. By preparing large amounts of foods such as soups and casseroles, you can freeze leftovers for other days, 14-24. This is a real time-saver. Most cooking time is spent assembling ingredients and utensils and then cleaning up afterwards. By preparing several dishes at once, you save much time and effort. On a busy day, all you have to do is allow time to heat the dish in the oven or microwave.

Using Computer Technologies

Time planning is crucial for people with busy lifestyles. As a result, many people are using the convenience of computer technology to save time in the kitchen. Both

14-24
The effort required to make one large pot of stew can provide several meals for a family.

large and small appliances and personal computers are used to perform daily kitchen tasks.

Many modern appliances use microprocessors to make meal preparation easier. A *microprocessor* is a tiny computer control. Both large and small appliances use these computer controls to simplify many cooking tasks. For instance, you can program a range or microwave oven to operate at certain times and temperatures. You can set a coffeemaker to turn on in the morning or evening.

Personal computers (PCs) offer many timesaving uses in the kitchen, too. Instead of using cookbooks, you might use a special software program to store recipes and menu plans in your computer's memory. When you are ready to cook, you can call up the recipe file. The program can calculate the amount of each ingredient needed and even prepare a shopping list. You can also look up recipes and meal preparation tips on the Internet. See 14-25.

At School

When you prepare food at school, you learn two important skills: cooking and teamwork. Thorough planning and good cooperation are needed for a successful foods lab experience.

Working with Others

Learning to work well with others in your foods lab is an important skill. Because your class time is limited, lab time must be carefully scheduled. In the foods lab, you are likely to be working with a larger group than you work with at home. You may not be familiar with your classmates' work habits, so planning lab time eliminates confusion. You need to know what is expected of you as part of

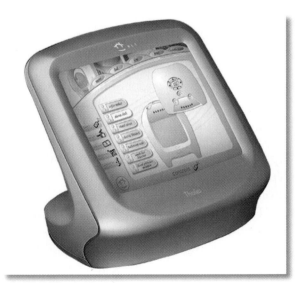

14-25

This computerized console can communicate with other kitchen appliances as well as sending and downloading information through the Internet.

the team. You also need to know when to complete your tasks.

Make the most of this opportunity to be part of a team. Such an opportunity improves your ability to get along with others, now and in the future. Be cooperative and keep a positive attitude. If you have a concern about an assigned task, talk with your group.

Planning the Lab

To have a successful lab experience, you need a work plan. A **work plan** is a detailed list of all the duties that must be completed during the lab. The list also includes who will perform each task as well as the ingredients and utensils needed. Your teacher will probably ask you to complete the plan at least a day before you will be cooking.

Making Out the Shopping List

The first task in your work plan is determining what foods you will prepare. Most likely your teacher will plan this portion of the lab. Locate the necessary recipes and make an accurate list of all the ingredients needed. Your teacher may inform you that some staple ingredients are already on hand. You may be asked not to write those ingredients on your list.

Making a Time Schedule

Next, make a time schedule that includes all the tasks to be done. Prioritize the tasks in order of importance. List first those tasks that require the greatest amount of time. Allow enough time for preparation, serving, and cleanup. As a group, decide who will perform each task. For each lab planned, rotate job tasks. This way each member has the experience of performing each task. Once your schedule is complete, your lab group will be ready to prepare your planned food. See 14-26.

14-26
A successful foods lab depends on good planning and teamwork.

Evaluating the Lab Experience

Evaluation is an important individual and group process. It gives you an opportunity to identify your strengths and weaknesses. This process also reinforces the positive aspects of the lab experience.

Evaluate yourself first; ask yourself what you did well. Did you use utensils, appliances, and food preparation techniques correctly? Identify areas in which you can improve. Second, evaluate the performance of your group as a whole. Be sure to discuss how, as a group, you can improve on the weak areas. Do not hesitate to admit your strengths and weaknesses. This is how members of your group can learn from one another.

Check It Out!

1. True or false. A time plan helps people determine what preparation tasks must be completed so their meals are prepared on time.
2. Name two ways in which computer technologies can assist with meal management.
3. List three steps to follow for planning a successful foods lab.

Chapter Review

Summary

Before you begin cooking, you need to know how to choose the cooking equipment that will best meet your needs. Kitchen appliances include major and portable appliances. Utensils are used for measuring, cutting, and mixing tasks. Cookware and bakeware are used for cooking and baking foods. With proper use and care, all these kitchen tools will provide many years of service. The more you know about cooking equipment, the greater your chances are for a successful cooking experience.

Good safety and sanitation habits must also be a high priority when you cook. Following the steps of clean, separate, cook, and chill when handling food will help you avoid foodborne illnesses. Your health and the health of others depend on the way you practice these habits.

Knowing how to read and use recipe information is another basic cooking skill. Learning to measure accurately is essential for preparing a recipe properly. Understanding cooking terms, making substitutions, and adjusting yields are other important techniques for cooking success.

Techniques for cooking smart can be used at home or at school. At home, it means using a time plan and making preparations. At school, it means practicing teamwork and preparing a work plan.

Think About It!

1. If you could only have one oven in your kitchen, which type would you choose: a conventional oven, microwave oven, or convection oven? Explain your choice.
2. Name three portable appliances you consider versatile. Then suggest different ways you can use each one to take advantage of the versatility.
3. What is the advantage of buying high-quality kitchen utensils?
4. Chart 14-11 lists seven guidelines for preventing fires. List the three guides you think are most frequently ignored. What happens as a result of ignoring fire prevention principles?
5. What types of foods are most likely to become contaminated if they are not handled properly?
6. Why should you gather all the ingredients and cooking utensils you will need before you start preparing a recipe?
7. How does a time plan make work in the kitchen more efficient?
8. Give several examples of early preparations that will be helpful as you attempt to serve family meals.
9. In what careers do you see the information in this chapter being helpful? Share these insights with your classmates.

Try It Out!

1. Select one major appliance, portable appliance, or kitchen utensil. Study the use and care instructions that came with it. Demonstrate the correct use and care of that piece of kitchen equipment.

2. Conduct a safety and sanitation check of your foods laboratory at school and your kitchen at home. What can you do to improve the safety and sanitation standards at school and at home?

3. Create a kitchen safety poster for the foods lab that shows safety rules for using, washing, and storing knives.

4. Find a recipe you would like to prepare. Read it thoroughly and
   A. translate the abbreviations
   B. explain the correct procedure for measuring each ingredient
   C. identify the key preparation terms

5. Choose any recipe and adapt it by
   A. doubling the ingredients
   B. cutting the ingredients in half

6. Write a menu for a family meal to be served at 6:30 p.m. Prepare a time plan. (You will need to refer to the recipes for the required cooking times.) As you prepare the time plan, ask yourself these questions: When will you complete certain tasks? Which tasks can be done ahead of time?

Chapter 15
Buying, Storing, and Preparing Foods

Careers

These careers relate to the topics in this chapter:
- ▼ family food shopper
- ▼ food product demonstrator
- ▼ food technician
- ▼ food editor

As you study the chapter, see if you can think of others.

Topics

15-1 Meat, Poultry, Fish, and Alternates
15-2 Fruits and Vegetables
15-3 Grain Products
15-4 Milk and Milk Products

Topic 15-1
Meat, Poultry, Fish, and Alternates

Objectives

After studying this topic, you will be able to

▼ list factors to consider when buying meat, poultry, fish, and alternates.

▼ use proper storage methods for meat, poultry, fish, and alternates.

▼ describe cooking methods used to prepare meat, poultry, fish, and alternates.

Topic Terms

meat
poultry
finfish
shellfish
meat analog

Meat, poultry, fish, eggs, dry beans, and nuts are major sources of protein in your diet. In addition, protein foods are often the main dish of a meal. See 15-1.

Some protein foods can be the most costly part of your food budget. Wise selection, storage, and preparation will help you get the most for your money.

Buying Meat, Poultry, Fish, and Alternates

Meat, poultry, and fish are the most costly protein foods, so you should select them carefully for the best value. Less costly but equally nutritious protein alternatives are also available. Eggs,

15-1
Protein foods, such as steak, are often served as the main course of a meal.

dry beans, and nuts are good sources of protein, vitamins, and minerals. To stretch your food dollar, plan some menus around these alternates.

Meat

Meat is the edible portion of animals, including muscles and organs. Beef, veal, pork, and lamb are the most common forms of meat. Mature cattle provide beef, while young cattle provide veal. Pork comes from swine. Lamb comes from young sheep.

You should consider two major factors when buying meat. One is the quality of the meat; the other is the cut of the meat.

Meat Inspection and Grading

In the United States, all meat shipped across state lines must be inspected. This is done by the United States Department of Agriculture (USDA) to certify that the meat is wholesome. An inspection also indicates the plant and processing conditions were sanitary.

In addition to an inspection stamp, beef, veal, and lamb may be stamped with a grade shield, 15-2. (Pork is considered

15-2

The USDA stamp on the top certifies that meat is wholesome. The grade shield below is an indication of quality.

tender, so it is not graded for retail sale.) This shield indicates the meat was voluntarily graded for quality. Grades help consumers determine the tenderness and juiciness of the meat. Meat from a young animal is usually tender; meat from an older animal is usually tougher.

The three top grades for beef established by the USDA are prime, choice, and select.

▼ *Prime* beef has the best quality and flavor. It is the most tender because it has the most *marbling* (fat that is mingled throughout the lean). This grade is mainly sold to restaurants.
▼ *Choice* beef has excellent quality, but has less fat and flavor than prime. It is the highest quality found in grocery stores and meat markets.
▼ *Select* beef has less flavor and marbling than prime and choice. However, it has less fat and a lower cost, so it is a good buy from health and budget angles.

Meat Selection

In selecting meat, you can be sure the quality is good if the lean has good color and is marbled with fat. Meats are generally pink to red in color. Quality meat also has firm fat that is creamy white in color. Meat with yellow fat is of poorer quality.

Regardless of the grade, some cuts of meat are more tender than others. The location of the meat in the animal determines tenderness. Cuts from the less-used muscles along the back are more tender. These include rib and loin cuts. Cuts from the muscles that are frequently used are less tender. These include leg and shoulder cuts.

You can also determine whether a meat cut comes from the tender part of an animal by looking at bone shape. T-shaped bones, flat bones, and wedge bones indicate tender cuts. Round bones (from the arm and leg area) and blade bones (from the shoulder area) indicate less-tender cuts of meat.

Buy the cut of meat best suited to your needs by reading meat labels. See 15-3. Meat labels make meat identification easy.

MEAT DEPARTMENT		
WEIGHT Lb. Net	PAY	PRICE Per Lb.
2.45	$5.12	2.09
BEEF CHUCK BLADE ROAST		

15-3

A meat package label shows the names of the wholesale and retail cuts, the weight, and the price.

By reading the meat identification label, you can find out the

▼ type of meat
▼ wholesale cut (location of the meat in the animal)
▼ retail name of the cut

The tenderest cuts of meat make up a very small portion of the animal. They are also more highly sought by the consumer. This is why these cuts are most expensive. When buying meat, consider the cost per serving rather than the cost per pound. If two cuts of meat cost the same, the cut with less fat and less bone will yield more servings.

Poultry

Poultry describes any domesticated bird raised for meat and/or eggs. Chicken, turkey, duck, and goose are the most popular types of poultry in the United States. Like meats, poultry must be federally inspected for wholesomeness. It may also be voluntarily graded for quality. Only U.S. Grade A poultry is sold at the retail level. However, "ungraded" poultry is usually equal in quality to Grade A poultry.

Ready-to-cook poultry is sold fresh-chilled or frozen. Poultry should look moist and plump and have clean, blemish-free skin. Choose birds with meaty breasts and legs. See 15-4. Avoid buying frozen birds that show signs of thawing or freezer burn (brownish spots). When buying chicken or turkey, whole birds are usually a better buy than pieces, such as breasts and legs.

Fish

Finfish and shellfish are two forms of fish that are eaten as food. **Finfish** have fins and backbones. **Shellfish** have shells instead of backbones. Both are available in many forms, depending on where you live.

15-4
High-quality poultry should have meaty breasts and legs and clean, blemish-free skin.

Be alert to the visible signs of freshness and quality when selecting fish and shellfish. Inspection and grade seals can help you determine quality. You should also consider appearance and form when making a purchase decision.

Finfish

The most popular finfish are cod, flounder, halibut, salmon, sole, snapper, and trout. When buying fish, however, look for regional specialties. They will usually cost less than varieties that must be shipped in from other areas. When buying fresh finfish, you will want to watch for the following signs of quality:

▼ Eyes should be bright and clear.
▼ Gills should be reddish in color.
▼ Scales should be tight to the body and shiny.
▼ Flesh should be firm enough to spring back when gently pressed.
▼ Odor should be fresh. See 15-5.

15-5
Look for signs of quality when buying fresh fish.

Fish are marketed in a variety of forms. The most popular choices are drawn, dressed, fillets, and steaks. *Drawn fish* have the entrails (guts) removed. *Dressed fish* have been cleaned. In addition to the entrails, they have had the head, tail, fins, and scales removed. *Fillets* are sides of the fish, which are cut away from the bone lengthwise from head to tail. Fillets are popular because they are usually boneless and ready to cook. *Steaks* are cross-sectional slices of larger fish with one large, central bone. Steaks are also ready to cook.

Fish is available frozen, canned, or dried as well as fresh. Fish sticks are a common form of frozen fish. Canned tuna, salmon, sardines, and mackerel are economical buys. In some areas, dried, salted, and smoked fish are popular menu items.

Shellfish

Clams, crabs, lobsters, mussels, oysters, shrimp, and scallops are all varieties of shellfish. If oysters, clams, scallops, and mussels are purchased fresh, the shells should be tightly closed. Fresh shellfish

such as crabs, lobsters, and shrimp should retain their natural color. You can also buy shellfish in canned or frozen form.

Eggs

When buying eggs, size and condition are important factors to consider. Choose the size that best meets your needs. Open the carton to be sure eggs have clean, uncracked shells.

Size and Color

Eggs are classified by size according to weight per dozen. Medium, large, and extra large are the sizes most commonly sold in grocery stores. Recipes are usually based on using large eggs.

Eggshells may be either white or brown. The color of the shell has nothing to do with the quality or nutritive value of the egg. (The breed of chicken determines the egg color.) See 15-6.

Grades

The USDA has set up standards of quality for grading eggs. The grade of an egg is based on interior quality and the

15-6
White eggs and brown eggs have the same quality, nutritive value, and taste.

condition and appearance of the shell. Most eggs sold in grocery stores are Grade AA or A and are suitable for all uses.

Plant-Based Meat Alternates

Some plant-based foods provide low cost, high-protein alternatives to meat, poultry, fish, and eggs. Legumes and meat analogs are becoming more popular choices in the market today. They help consumers make the most of their protein food buys.

Legumes

High in essential amino acids, legumes are seeds that grow in the pods of some vegetable plants, 15-7. Legumes include

15-7
Legumes, which play a major role in the global diet, are economical sources of protein.

beans, lentils, peas, and peanuts. Served alone, they are nutritious; however, they provide incomplete protein. Team them up with a grain or animal food and you have a complete source of protein.

Legumes are often purchased dried. When buying dried legumes, look for high quality. Uniform color and size ensure freshness and even cooking. High-quality legumes are free from debris (stones, sticks, and dirt) and visible defects (cracks, insect holes).

Meat Analogs

Meat analogs are plant-based protein products made to resemble various kinds of meat. These products are made from soybeans, wheat, yeast, and other vegetable sources of protein. Bacon bits and soyburgers are common meat analogs.

When you buy these products, read the nutrition labels carefully. The food values vary depending on the products from which the meat analogs were made.

Storing Meat, Poultry, Fish, and Alternates

Because protein foods are highly perishable and expensive, proper storage is important. Improper storage can lead to flavor and nutrient loss, spoilage, and foodborne illness. Knowing how to store these foods properly will prevent costly waste.

Prepackaged meats and poultry can be stored in the original wrapping. Store them in the coldest part of the refrigerator. Meat should be used within three to four days. Use poultry within one to two days. Never store stuffed poultry (cooked or uncooked) in the refrigerator. Stuffing should be removed from the bird and refrigerated separately.

Fresh fish is more perishable than meat or poultry. When stored in the refrigerator, fish must be tightly wrapped in foil or plastic wrap. Otherwise, the odor of the fish will penetrate other foods stored in the refrigerator. Fresh fish should be eaten within one or two days.

For longer storage, meat, poultry, and fish can be frozen. Wrap each food item tightly before freezing it.

Properly stored fresh eggs will keep up to four weeks in the refrigerator. The best way to store eggs in the refrigerator is in the original carton. Store them with the large end up to keep the yolk centered. Keep the carton away from foods with strong odors, which eggs can absorb. Eggs should not be washed.

Store unopened packages of dried legumes in a cool, dry place. After opening packages, transfer the legumes to an airtight container. This will keep the unused portion fresh and free from insects. See 15-8.

Because of their high oil content, nuts may become *rancid* (develop a bad flavor). Storing nuts in the refrigerator is best if you plan to keep them for a few months. For longer storage, freeze them.

15-8
Airtight storage keeps legumes fresh and pest-free.

Preparing Meat, Poultry, Fish, and Alternates

Choosing the right cooking method for the type of protein food is the key to successful preparation. Meat, poultry, fish, and eggs are high in protein. Therefore, these foods require low to moderate cooking temperatures. Such temperatures will prevent protein foods from becoming tough and dry.

The two main cooking methods for preparing protein foods are dry heat and moist heat. *Dry heat methods* include roasting or baking, grilling, broiling, pan-broiling, and frying. *Moist heat methods* include braising, steaming, and poaching.

Meat

When you prepare meat, you want it to be tender, juicy, and flavorful. Meat that is cooked at high temperatures becomes dry and tough. High cooking temperatures also cause meat to shrink and lose some B vitamins. When you cook meat at low temperatures, there is less shrinkage.

Choosing a Cooking Method

The type of cut will determine the cooking method you will use to prepare meat, 15-9. Tender cuts of meat are often prepared using a dry heat cooking method. Less tender cuts are usually cooked using a moist heat cooking method. The addition of water or other liquid in these methods helps reduce toughness in less tender meats.

Cooking by Cut

Tender Cuts—Cook with Dry Heat

Beef	Lamb	Pork
Chuck top blade steak	Center-cut leg steaks	Chops
Ground beef patties	Ground lamb patties	Cutlets
Porterhouse steak	Kabobs	Ground pork patties
Rib roast	Loin chops	Ham
Rib steak	Rib chops	Ham slices
Sirloin steak	Shoulder chops	Kabobs
T-bone steak	Sirloin chops	Leg roasts
Tenderloin roast	Sirloin steaks	Loin roasts
Tenderloin steak		Shoulder roasts
Top loin roast		Tenderloin medallions

Less-Tender Cuts—Cook with Moist Heat

Beef	Lamb	Pork
Beef for stew	Breasts	Loin chops
Chuck pot roast	Neck slices	Shoulder cubes
Chuck short ribs	Riblets	
Corned beef brisket	Shanks	
Cubed steak	Shoulder Cuts	
Flank steak		
Round steak		
Round tip roast		
Shank cross cuts		
Skirt steak		

15-9

The method you use to prepare meat often depends on the cut of the meat.

Less tender cuts of meat are tough due to *connective tissue*. They can be tenderized by marinating them, which also adds extra flavor.

Judging Doneness

Using a *meat thermometer* is the best way to judge when meat has reached the desired degree of doneness. Color is not an accurate indicator of doneness. When using a meat thermometer, insert it into the thickest part of the meat. The bulb of the thermometer should not rest in fat or touch the bone. Meats are done when they have reached the recommended internal temperatures. See 15-10.

Poultry

Properly prepared poultry is tender and juicy. Virtually all poultry sold in grocery stores is young and tender. Dry heat cooking methods, such as frying and roasting, are popular ways to prepare poultry. However, moist heat cooking methods, such as stewing and braising,

Meat Doneness Temperatures

Meat	Temperature (°F)
Beef and lamb	
ground	160
medium rare	145
medium	160
well done	170
Pork	
fresh, medium	160
fresh, well done	170
ground	160
ham, fresh	160
ham, precooked	140

15-10
Using a meat thermometer correctly can help you determine when meat has reached the proper degree of doneness.

are desirable for many poultry dishes. Regardless of the method you choose, do not overcook poultry as it will become dry and flavorless.

If you plan to roast poultry with stuffing, stuff the poultry just before roasting. (If you buy frozen commercially stuffed poultry, do not thaw it before cooking.)

Judging Doneness

A food thermometer is the only reliable guide for judging doneness of poultry. The thermometer should be centered in the thickest part of the breast or thigh. Whole poultry is done when it reaches an internal temperature of 180°F. When poultry is properly cooked, the meat should be fork tender and the juices should run clear.

Fish

Properly prepared fish is moist, tender, and flavorful. Both moist heat and dry heat methods can be used when preparing fish.

Avoid overcooking fish to keep it from becoming dry and tough. Finfish is done when the flesh is firm and flakes easily when pressed with a fork. Shellfish should be cooked for a short time at moderate temperatures.

Eggs

The secret to cooking eggs properly is to use low to moderate heat for just the right amount of time. Undercooked eggs may contain bacteria that can cause foodborne illness. Therefore, it is important to cook eggs and egg dishes thoroughly. When properly cooked, egg whites are set and egg yolks are thickened. Egg dishes should reach an internal temperature of 160°F as measured on a food thermometer. If cooked too long or if the cooking temperature is too high, eggs become tough and rubbery.

Eggs are a versatile food. They can be scrambled, fried, poached, baked, hard cooked, or soft-cooked. They can be used alone or as ingredients in other foods. See 15-11. Omelets, custards, and souffles are examples of foods made with eggs. Eggs are also used as a

▼ *thickening agent* to help thicken mixtures such as custards, sauces, and puddings

▼ *leavening agent* to make products such as cakes, souffles, and quick breads rise

▼ *glaze* on breads or pastries

▼ *coating* on foods for frying (Foods can be dipped into a beaten egg mixture and then dredged in flour, cornmeal, or bread crumbs. The egg holds the coating in place and makes a crispy crust for fried foods.)

▼ *binder* to hold ingredients together, such as in a meat loaf

▼ *garnish* to make other foods more attractive and nutritious

Legumes

Properly prepared legumes are tender, but not mushy. Wash dried legumes and remove any foreign matter, such as sticks and stones. Dried beans need to be soaked before cooking. Read package directions to determine how much water to use. You do not need to soak dried peas and lentils.

To soak dried beans, quickly boil them for two minutes. Then remove them from the heat and let them stand for one hour.

15-11
Eggs are a key ingredient in this quiche.

You can also soak dried beans overnight. After cooking, you may simply season and eat them. You may also combine cooked beans with other ingredients to make dishes such as baked beans, 15-12.

15-12
Cooked dried beans can be combined with other foods in a variety of dishes.

Check It Out!

1. Describe the appearance of high-quality poultry.
2. How can legumes be served as a complete source of protein?
3. True or false. The best way to store eggs is in the carton with the small end up.
4. Why does the cooking temperature matter when preparing meat, poultry, fish, and eggs?
5. What factor should be used to determine the cooking method for preparing meat?
6. How do you judge the doneness of cooked finfish?

Topic 15-2

Fruits and Vegetables

Objectives

After studying this topic, you will be able to
▼ list factors to consider when buying fruits and vegetables.
▼ use proper storage methods for fruits and vegetables.
▼ describe preparation and cooking methods for fruits and vegetables.

Topic Term

produce

15-13
To get the most from your money when buying fruits and vegetables, take time to select items carefully.

Fruits and vegetables are nutritious and tasty mealtime favorites. Besides providing vitamins and minerals, most have no fat, few calories, and a lot of fiber. By carefully choosing, storing, and preparing fruits and vegetables, you will get the most for your money.

Buying Fruits and Vegetables

Fruits and vegetables are available in fresh, frozen, canned, and dried forms. With so many choices, how do you decide what to buy? Learning how each form differs and following some basic selection tips can help you make smarter choices. See 15-13.

Fresh Fruits and Vegetables

Fresh fruits and vegetables, which are called **produce**, are available year-round. Buy produce *in season*, or during the time

of the year when it is harvested. In-season produce is fresher, higher in quality, and lower in price.

When shopping for produce, always look for the highest quality. Learn to judge produce by its appearance. All fresh produce should feel firm and have bright colors. Mature, ripe produce has the best flavor. Bruised, wilted, or decayed produce is a sign of poor quality. See 15-14.

When selecting produce, handle it carefully to avoid bruising it. Buy only amounts of produce that you can store and eat before it spoils.

Frozen Fruits and Vegetables

Frozen fruits and vegetables retain much of the same appearance, flavor, and quality as fresh produce. However, the texture of thawed or cooked fruits and vegetables may be less crisp. Frozen fruits and vegetables are available in plastic bags or paper cartons.

You should select frozen fruits and vegetables with care. Buy packages that are undamaged and frozen solid. A soft

Buying Fruits and Vegetables

Type of Produce	Look For:	Avoid:
Fruits		
Apples	Bright color, firm texture	Bruised spots, shriveled skin
Bananas	Bright color, firm texture	Bruised skin
Berries	Bright color, plump fruit	Soft, moldy, or leaky fruit
Cantaloupe	Yellowish rind, pleasant aroma	Soft spots
Citrus fruits	Bright color, heavy for size	Dull or shriveled skin, soft spots, lightweight for size
Grapes	Bright color, plump fruit	Soft, shriveled, or leaky fruit
Peaches	Slightly firm flesh	Bruised spots; hard, immature fruit; greenish skin
Pears	Firm flesh, good color	Bruised spots; hard, immature fruit
Watermelon	Smooth outer surface, firm texture, juicy fruit	Pale color, dry flesh
Vegetables		
Asparagus	Closed, compact tips; rich green color; tender stalk	Open tips, moldy spots
Beans (snap)	Bright color	Limp, dry pods; blemishes; thick, tough pods
Broccoli	Tight flower clusters, uniform green color	Yellow or brownish color, wilted stalks
Cabbage	Firm head, heavy for size, bright color	Wilted, decayed, or blemished leaves
Carrots	Bright orange color, smooth skin, firm texture	Limp texture, discolored skin
Cauliflower	Tight flower clusters, white color	Discolored appearance
Celery	Crisp stalks, bright color	Discolored or limp stalks
Corn	Plump kernels	Wilted husks, small kernels
Cucumbers	Bright green color, firm texture	Yellow color, limp texture
Lettuce	Bright color, heavy for size, crisp leaves	Blemished or wilted poor color
Onions	Smooth skin, firm texture	Soft spots
Potatoes	Smooth skin, firm texture, appropriate shape	Bruised spots, shriveled skin, signs of sprouting
Tomatoes	Bright red color, firm texture, smooth skin	Soft spots, cracked surfaces, bruised skin

15-14

Use this selection guide for choosing these popular fruits and vegetables.

package is an indication of thawing. Thawing affects quality, taste, and storage time.

Canned Fruits and Vegetables

Canned fruits and vegetables come in many convenient forms, such as whole, sliced, and pieces. Fruits may be packed in heavy syrup, light syrup, or fruit juices. Fruits packed in juice are lower in calories and higher in nutrients than those packed in syrup. Vegetables are usually packed in water. Look for those packed without added salt to help avoid excess sodium in your diet.

How do you get the best buys in canned fruits and vegetables? Several factors affect cost, including brand, can size, and packing liquid. House brands and generic products are often priced lower than national brands. Large cans often cost less per serving than small cans. Plain canned fruits and vegetables are usually a better buy than those packed in flavored sauces.

Dried Fruits and Vegetables

Dried fruits and vegetables are light in weight because the water has been removed. The flavors and textures are slightly different from fresh, frozen, and canned forms. However, they can be *rehydrated* (have the water content restored) for a softer texture. Both dried fruits and vegetables are packaged in sealed bags or boxes. Look for well-sealed packages that are free of moisture. Dried fruits should feel soft and pliable in the package. Dried vegetables are brittle and hard.

Storing Fruits and Vegetables

As a smart shopper, you must choose high-quality fruits and vegetables. To maintain this quality, however, you need to store fruits and vegetables properly.

Proper storage protects the nutrients, flavors, and freshness of perishable produce. The quality of most fruits and vegetables is maintained by storing them in the crisper section of the refrigerator. Do not wash fruits and vegetables before storing them as this may hasten spoilage. See 15-15.

Some vegetables with high water content, such as lettuce and celery, need to be kept moist. Wrap lettuce with damp paper towels. Sprinkle celery with water. Store both of these vegetables in perforated plastic bags to retain moisture without trapping it.

Some fruits and vegetables are stored at room temperature. You can store bananas on a countertop. They will continue to

15-15
Use care when handling and storing fresh fruits and vegetables to maintain their quality.

ripen during storage. Banana skins turn dark quickly when refrigerated. This makes them less attractive, but the flavor remains good for a few days. Store vegetables that do not require refrigeration in a cool, dry place. Onions, potatoes, sweet potatoes, tomatoes, and hard-rind squash are examples of vegetables that do not need to be refrigerated.

Frozen fruits and vegetables should be stored in the coldest part of the freezer. Store canned products on a shelf in a cool, dry place.

After opening canned goods, store any leftovers in an airtight container in the refrigerator. Store dried products in a cool, dry place. After opening packages, reseal them tightly. Then check package directions for proper storage.

Fresh Fruits and Vegetables

Fruits and vegetables are versatile. They are easy to prepare, and you can serve them in a variety of ways. You can eat them raw or cooked. You can also use fruits and vegetables for salads and snacks or mix them with other foods.

The cooking process changes the flavor, color, and texture of fresh fruits and vegetables. Choose the method that best suits your planned use.

Vegetables

Before eating or cooking fresh fruits and vegetables, wash them thoroughly, 15-16. Use cool running water to remove dirt, pesticides, and bacteria. You should even wash produce with inedible rinds and skins, such as citrus fruits. Avoid soaking vegetables while cleaning or storing them as this causes nutrient loss.

The More You Know: Plan for Snack Attacks

One way to practice self-control when snacking is to pack your snacks first! Buy, prepare, and store foods in measured snack portions. Buy foods that are high in nutritional value specifically for snacking. Look for foods that are already bite-size pieces, such as almonds, grapes, blueberries, strawberries, broccoli florets, and baby carrots. Add some low-fat cheese and crackers. Choose snacks that fit with foods you would eat at mealtime. Plan so that your snacks are not "extras" but an integral part of your daily meal plan.

15-16
Thoroughly wash fresh produce in cool running water to remove dirt and pesticide residues.

Some fruits, such as apples and bananas, may become discolored when exposed to air. Dipping them in an acid, such as orange, lemon, or pineapple juice, can prevent this.

Crisp, crunchy raw fruits and vegetables taste best when they are served cold. Prepare them and then store them in the refrigerator until serving time.

Serve fruits and vegetables soon after you cut, peel, or cook them. Vitamins are lost when these foods are allowed to stand.

Cooking Methods

Although most fruits and vegetables are tasty and more nutritious when eaten raw, some require cooking. Cooked fruits may be served as desserts or side dishes at any meal. Cooked vegetables are often served as side dishes, in soups, or in casseroles.

Both moist heat and dry heat cooking methods can be used to cook fruits and vegetables. They can be simmered, steamed, microwaved, baked, or broiled. Two common cooking methods—simmering and microwaving—are described here.

When *simmering* fruits and vegetables, use a small amount of water or liquid and a short cooking time. Heat the liquid to boiling before adding fruits or vegetables. (Adding a small amount of sugar adds flavor and helps fruit hold its shape.) You can reduce cooking time and nutrient loss by covering the pan. However, you should leave the lid off strongly flavored vegetables, such as turnips and onions. You should also cover these vegetables with water. These steps will help some of the strong flavors to escape. Cook fruits and vegetables until they are tender, but slightly crisp.

The liquid in which fruits and vegetables are cooked contains nutrients. Save it and use it later in gravies, sauces, soups, and stews.

Microwaving fruits and vegetables is a popular cooking method. This method helps retain the colors, flavors, and nutrients because produce cooks quickly using little or no water. Pierce whole fruits or vegetables before cooking to allow steam to escape. When cutting up fruits or vegetables, cut them into same-sized pieces for more even cooking. Cover and cook until crisp-tender, stirring once or twice during the cooking time. Whether whole or cut up, let fruits and vegetables stand a few minutes before serving to complete the cooking process. See 15-17.

Preparing Other Forms of Fruits and Vegetables

Canned fruits are ready to serve right from the can. You can drain them or serve them in the fruit juice or syrup in which

15-17
Fresh vegetables cooked in a microwave oven retain their nutrients and bright colors.

they were packed. If you are heating canned fruits, heat them in their juice or syrup. Drain canned fruits before using them in baked products.

Canned vegetables are precooked, so you can simply heat them through before serving. Avoid overcooking as this makes canned vegetables mushy.

You may use frozen fruits in many of the same ways as fresh or canned. Serve them slightly frozen with some ice crystals remaining. Fully thawed fruit will have a softer, mushier texture. To retain the fruit's shape, do not thaw it before cooking.

Cook frozen vegetables from the frozen state using the same methods you use for fresh vegetables. However, use slightly shorter cooking times.

You may serve dried fruits right from the package or use them as is in baked products. To rehydrate dried fruits, soak them in hot water for about an hour and then cook as directed.

Soaking and cooking methods for dried beans and peas were covered in Topic 15-1. Remember, cooking times for dried vegetables are much longer than for fresh or frozen vegetables. Simmer or bake dried vegetables in liquid until they are tender.

Check It Out!

1. What is the value of buying produce that is in season?
2. True or false. Most fruits and vegetables should be washed before storing in the refrigerator.
3. True or false. Most fruits and vegetables should be cooked in a covered pan to reduce cooking time and nutrient loss.

Topic 15-3
Grain Products

Objectives

After studying this topic, you will be able to
▼ list factors to consider when buying grain products.
▼ use proper storage methods for grain products.
▼ describe methods used to prepare grain products.

Topic Terms

cereal
refined
pasta
starch
leavening agent
biscuit method
muffin method

Cereals are starchy grains used as food, including wheat, corn, rice, and oats. These grains can be used in their natural form. They can also be used to make products such as flour, pasta, breakfast cereals, and breads, 15-18.

Buying Grain Products

Grain products are plentiful sources of food energy. In addition, they are economical, easy to store, and easy to prepare. Knowing what is available will help you choose the products that meet your needs and food budget.

15-18
These nutritious foods are all made from grains.

Flour

Flour is made by grinding grains into powder. **Refined** flour has had parts of the grain kernel removed during the milling process. Removing parts of the kernel also removes nutrients contained in those parts. Refined flour can be *enriched* to add back B vitamins and iron lost during milling.

In the United States, wheat flour is the most common type. However, flour can be made from any grain. At the supermarket, you can choose among several types of flour. These include all-purpose flour, self-rising flour, cake flour, and whole wheat flour.

All-purpose flour is used for general cooking and baking purposes. When a recipe merely calls for flour, all-purpose flour is usually intended.

Self-rising flour has a leavening agent (a substance that makes baked goods rise) and salt added. This flour is often used to make quick breads.

Cake flour is made of softer wheat and may be milled more finely than the other flours. This flour is used for delicately textured cakes and other baked products.

Whole wheat flour has a coarser texture than other flours. It is made from the entire grain kernel. Whole wheat flour is often used in breads. It gives them a coarser texture and nuttier flavor. For best results, use this flour in recipes calling for whole wheat flour.

Pasta

Pasta is the family name for a group of products that includes spaghetti, macaroni, and noodles. These products add interest to meals because they offer such a wide variety of shapes, 15-19. Whatever the shape, however, all pastas are made of the same ingredients: flour and water. Noodle products also contain eggs. Most pastas are enriched by the addition of thiamin, niacin, riboflavin, folic acid, and iron.

Pasta products are made from *semolina*, which is made from durum wheat. Durum wheat is specially grown for use in pasta products. This hard wheat yields pasta that will cook to a firm yet tender texture.

15-19
These are only a few of the shapes available when selecting pasta.

Rice

The two major types of rice are white rice and brown rice. In the United States, people tend to consume more white rice. *White rice* is produced when the bran layer of the rice kernel is removed. When shopping for white rice, look for the word *enriched. Brown rice* is whole grain rice. Because the whole grain is used, brown rice is higher in fiber than white rice.

Precooked or *instant rice* is an expensive form of rice, but it is popular with many people. It is white rice that has been fully cooked and dried. It can be prepared very quickly to restore the moisture.

Rice grains come in various sizes. Short and medium grains tend to cling together when cooked. Long grain rice cooks to a fluffy texture, and the grains are more likely to stay separate. See 15-20.

In spite of its name, *wild rice* is not rice at all. It is the seed of a wild grass that grows in marshes. Wild rice is much more expensive than rice. To lower the cost, wild rice is often mixed with brown rice.

15-20
Properly cooked long grain rice is tender and fluffy.

Breakfast Cereals

Both ready-to-eat and cooked cereals come in a variety of flavors, textures, and forms. Use nutrition labeling to compare different cereals for nutritive value. Many are high in sugar or may contain fat. Some are low in fiber. In general, however, whole grain, enriched, and fortified cereals are nutritious and filling. Served with milk and fruit, cereal can be a nourishing meal.

Some types of cereal are more expensive than others. Ready-to-eat cereal is more expensive than cereals that require cooking. Cereals with dried fruits or nuts added and presweetened cereals are more costly than plain cereals. Although convenient to serve, quick-cooking and instant cereals are also more costly than regular cereal.

When evaluating cereal cost, it is best to compare cost per serving. Cereals differ greatly in weight. Packages of the same size may not contain the same number of servings. Also, compare the size of the serving before you decide which cereal to choose.

Breads

A wide variety of breads are available, 15-21. White, whole wheat, raisin, and rye bread are just a few examples. Rolls, muffins, and bagels are other types of bread products you can find at your local supermarket or bakery. For the best flavor and texture, look for freshness dates stamped on the products.

You can choose from commercially prepared bread products or in-store bakery products. Commercial breads are prepared in large quantities, so they are reasonably priced. They are prepackaged and then sold on grocery store shelves. Grocery store bakeries sell freshly baked bread products

15-21
Breads can come in different shapes, sizes, and flavors.

15-22
Pasta and other grain products should be stored in tightly covered containers to keep out moisture and pests.

directly to you. Although these products are more costly, you may prefer the fresh-baked taste.

Convenience bread products also come in many forms. *Brown-and-serve products* are partially baked; you finish baking them at home. *Refrigerated doughs* need only to be baked at home. *Frozen doughs* must be thawed and then baked.

Storing Grain Products

Grain products, including flour and pasta, should be stored in tightly covered containers in a cool, dry place, 15-22. For short-term storage, store breads, cakes, and cookies in airtight bags, bread boxes, or cake boxes.

Storage times vary depending on the product. Breads stored in a cool, dry place will last about one week. Ready-to-eat cereals keep well for two to three months. Wild rice and brown rice will keep for six months. Refined flour, pasta, and white rice will keep for one year.

Some grain products may require refrigeration. Whole grain products, which contain some fat, stay fresher in the refrigerator. Cakes and cookies with perishable fillings and frostings will need refrigeration. Bread may be stored in the refrigerator to prevent mold growth.

Baked products can be frozen for several months. Wrap tightly to keep out excess moisture. Frozen bread defrosts quickly, so you can use slices as you need them. Stored properly, most baked goods will taste as fresh as when you purchased them.

Preparing Grain Products

The preparation methods used for grain products depend on the product you are preparing. Products prepared from the grains group include sauces, gravies, and puddings thickened with flour or cornstarch. Pasta, rice, cooked cereals, and breads also have special preparation methods.

Cooking with Thickeners

Starch is the complex carbohydrate part of plants. It makes up the major portion of grain products. When starch and water are heated, the starch granules swell. This is because the granules absorb the water, which makes them soft and thick. As a result, grain products increase in volume as they cook.

The key to smooth, lump-free mixtures is proper temperature and gentle stirring. Low heat slows the absorption of water by the starch granules. High heat causes granules to lump together. Gentle stirring prevents lumps; overstirring causes the granules to break down.

Flour, cornstarch, and other starches are grain products often used to thicken sauces, gravies, and puddings. When preparing these foods, lumps may form if starch is added directly to hot liquid. Separating the starch granules before adding them to the hot liquid can prevent this.

You can use three methods to keep starch granules separated. The first is to coat the starch granules with melted fat to make a paste. Then add the liquid slowly, stirring constantly. This method is used for sauces and gravies, 15-23. The second method is to combine the starch with sugar, then stir in the liquid slowly. This method is used when making puddings. Mixing the starch with a cold liquid to form a paste is the third method. The paste is slowly stirred into the hot mixture. Mixtures thickened with flour or cornstarch should be stirred constantly during cooking to achieve a smooth texture.

15-23
To achieve the smooth texture, this gravy was stirred constantly during cooking.

Pasta

"Tender but firm" describes properly prepared pasta. You must cook pasta in a large amount of rapidly boiling water to keep it from becoming sticky. To test for doneness, remove a piece of pasta from the water and bite into it.

Rice

Properly cooked rice is tender and fluffy. Combine the rice with water or other liquid in the proper size pan. Bring it to a boil and then stir. Lower the heat and cover the pan. As the rice cooks, it absorbs the liquid and swells. Rice may also be baked in the oven.

Cooked Cereals

Cooked cereals, such as oatmeal and grits, should be smooth and free of lumps. See 15-24. Like all starch products, when cereals are cooked, they absorb liquid and increase in volume.

There are some general rules to follow when preparing cooked cereals. Add cereal slowly to boiling water, stirring constantly. (This will help prevent lumps.) While the cereal is cooking, keep stirring it constantly. Cook the cereal for as long as directed on the package. Be sure to use the recommended pan or bowl size.

Cereals cooked in a microwave oven can be prepared and served in the same dish. Use a dish large enough to allow for boiling and swelling. Microwave cereals according to package directions, stirring as directed. Let stand a few minutes before serving to complete the cooking process.

Breads

The two main groups of breads are yeast breads and quick breads. Breads need air, steam, and leavening agents to rise. Air is added as ingredients are mixed. Steam is produced when liquid ingredients are heated during baking. **Leavening agents** are ingredients used to produce carbon dioxide. Yeast breads and quick breads are prepared with different leavening agents and mixing methods.

Yeast Breads

Yeast is a tiny plant used as a leavening agent in yeast breads. When mixed with the right ingredients, yeast produces carbon dioxide, which causes the bread to rise. Yeast breads must be mixed, kneaded, and allowed to rise before they are ready for baking. The basic steps in preparing yeast breads are shown in 15-25.

Quick Breads

As their name implies, quick breads are faster to make than yeast breads. You can mix and bake quick breads in a short period.

Quick bread mixtures can be divided into three classes of batters and doughs. *Pour batters* are thin. Typical pour batters are used for pancakes, waffles, tortillas, and some coffee cakes. *Drop batters* are thick. Typical drop batters are used for muffins, drop biscuits, and coffee cakes. *Soft dough* is sticky but can be handled. Soft doughs are used for rolled biscuits, dumplings, and some coffee cakes.

You prepare some quick breads using the biscuit method and others using the muffin method. With the **biscuit method**, you mix the dry ingredients together, and then cut fat into the mixture. Next, you add the liquid ingredients. Then you knead the dough before cutting or shaping it. Biscuits and doughnuts are among the quick breads produced by the biscuit method.

In the **muffin method**, you mix the dry ingredients. Mix the liquid ingredients together in a separate bowl. Make a well in the center of the dry ingredients and then pour in the liquid. Stir the batter until all the dry ingredients are just moistened. Then spoon the batter into a loaf pan or muffin pan and bake it. (Fill muffin cups about two-thirds full with batter.)

15-24

This oatmeal swelled to at least twice its original size by absorbing the water in which it was cooked.

A — Combine ingredients and beat until smooth. Stir in enough additional flour to make a moderately stiff dough.

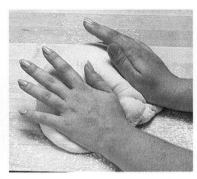

B — On a lightly floured pastry board or cloth, knead dough until smooth and elastic.

C — Place dough in a lightly greased bowl; turn once to grease top.

D — Let dough rise in a warm place until double in bulk. Test dough for lightness with two fingers.

E — When dough is light, punch down.

F — Shape dough into loaves or rolls and bake as directed. Use of these preparation techniques can produce successful yeast breads.

15-25

These are the basic preparation steps you would follow to prepare yeast breads from scratch.

Cakes and Cookies

Cakes and cookies are popular baked products served as desserts. You can prepare all types of cakes from scratch or from convenience cake mixes sold at the grocery store. Homemade cookies are just about everyone's favorite. Many varieties are available at the grocery store, too.

Success in cake and cookie baking depends on a number of factors. You need to measure accurately and use quality ingredients. You must have an understanding of the mixing method and follow the baking directions correctly.

Preparing Cakes

Cakes are divided into two main groups: shortened and unshortened. *Shortened cakes* contain fat, such as butter, margarine, or vegetable shortening. Baking powder or baking soda plus buttermilk are used to make them rise. Layer cakes and pound cakes are shortened cakes, 15-26.

Unshortened cakes contain no fat. Beaten egg whites and steam formed during baking makes them rise. Angel food and sponge cakes are unshortened cakes.

Chiffon cakes are a combination of the two types described above. They contain fat and beaten egg whites to make them rise.

Setting the Scene: How Would You Trim Your Food Budget?

Your family needs to cut the cost of food in your household budget while still preparing healthful and satisfying meals. You analyze your family's typical shopping list. It includes such items as tender cuts of meat, instant rice, three types of ready-to-eat cereal, several boxes of cake mix, and out-of-season fruit.

Analyze It: What do you think is contributing to your family's high food costs? What changes can you make without sacrificing nutrients? What changes can you make without sacrificing convenience?

15-26
This pound cake, garnished with fresh fruit and raspberry sauce, is a classic shortened cake.

Baking Guidelines

Shortened and unshortened cakes have different ingredients and different mixing procedures. The finished products look and taste different. Whichever type you make, follow recipe directions carefully and use the right size pans. The following tips will help you prepare cakes successfully.

▼ Prepare the pans. For shortened cakes, grease cake pans with solid shortening. Then coat the pans lightly with flour to allow the layers to turn out easily. Fill the pans half full with batter. Unshortened cakes are baked in ungreased tube pans. This allows the batter to cling to the sides of the pan. Fill the pan almost full of batter.

▼ Preheat the oven to the correct temperature.

▼ Allow at least one inch between pans and the sides of the oven when baking. This will allow heat to circulate freely.

▼ Check cakes for doneness at the end of the shortest recommended baking time. The cake should slightly pull away from the sides of the pan when done. Check the recipe for the proper doneness test.

▼ Follow the recipe directions for cooling and removing the cake from the baking pan. Some cakes should be removed from the baking pan immediately. Some should be cooled on a rack about ten minutes before removing. Unshortened cake pans are turned upside down over a bottle for cooling.

Preparing Cookies

Many varieties of cookies are easy to make at home. Among them are dropped, refrigerator, bar, rolled, molded, and pressed cookies. These types differ in the ingredients used, the consistency of the dough, and the way the dough is handled.

Dropped cookies are made from soft dough that is pushed from a spoon onto a baking sheet. Space the dough on the baking sheet to allow for spreading while baking. Chocolate chip cookies are one of the most popular dropped cookies. See 15-27.

Refrigerator cookies are made by shaping stiff dough into a long, smooth roll. Wrap the roll in waxed paper or plastic wrap and place in the refrigerator. Chill the dough until it is firm enough to slice easily. Cut the dough with a thin, sharp knife to ensure even slices.

Bar cookies are made from soft dough that is spread in a greased baking pan. The cookies are baked, cooled, and cut into squares. Carefully remove bars from the baking pan with a spatula. Brownies are a favorite bar cookie.

Rolled cookies are made from stiff dough that is chilled, rolled, and cut into desired shapes. Many decorative cookie shapes, such as gingerbread people, can be made using this method. Sugar cookies are another popular type of rolled cookie, 15-28.

Molded cookies are formed from stiff dough that is broken off and shaped by hand. For some types of molded cookies, the dough is shaped into crescents or tied into knot shapes. Some types, such as peanut butter cookies, are flattened before being baked. Others are filled with jelly or candied fruits.

Pressed cookies are made of rich dough. The dough is forced through a cookie press onto an ungreased baking sheet. The cookie dough can be pressed into a variety of shapes by changing the tip on the cookie press. Spritz cookies are one common type of pressed cookie.

Baking Guidelines

As with cakes, the best cookies result from following the recipe directions. Here are some baking tips.

▼ Preheat the oven to the correct temperature.

▼ Use the correct pan size. Heavy aluminum cookie sheets or pans work best for many types of cookies.

▼ Follow specified baking times. For chewy cookies, bake long enough to set the dough (the shortest recommended baking time). For crisp cookies, bake a little longer (the longest recommended baking time).

▼ Follow recipe directions for removing cookies from the cookie sheet. Some cookies must be cooled slightly on the

15-27

For best results, follow the recommended mixing method for dropped cookies.

15-28

Cookies that are cut into shapes with cutters are rolled cookies.

baking sheet before removing them to the cooling rack. Others must be removed immediately.

▼ Store cooled cookies to maintain top quality. Keep crisp, thin cookies in a can or jar with a loose cover. Keep soft cookies in an airtight container. See 15-29.

15-29
Store bar cookies in an airtight container to help them keep their soft textures.

Check It Out!

1. Give five examples of foods made from grains.
2. When a recipe lists flour as an ingredient, what type should you buy?
3. Describe how most grain products should be stored.
4. What is the key to smooth, lump-free sauces, gravies, and puddings?
5. True or false. Quick breads must be mixed, kneaded, and allowed to rise before they are ready for baking.
6. Identify the six types of cookies.

Topic 15-4
Milk and Milk Products

Objectives
After studying this topic, you will be able to
▼ list factors to consider when buying dairy products.
▼ use proper storage methods for dairy products.
▼ describe methods used to prepare milk and cheese.

Topic Terms
pasteurization
homogenized
natural cheese
process cheese

Milk is essential for good health. Besides being a good source of calcium, it supplies high-quality protein. Other dairy products, such as lowfat cheese and yogurt, can provide the same nutrients present in milk. If you do not like to drink milk, you should include other calcium rich milk products in your diet.

Comparing different brands and product sizes will help you get the best buys in dairy products, 15-30. Proper storage will ensure their freshness. Following some basic principles will help you obtain good results when cooking with dairy products.

15-30
Comparison shopping will help you make wise choices when shopping for foods in the milk group.

Buying Dairy Products

Many types of dairy products are available to consumers. Milk, cheese, yogurt, frozen milk products, cream, and butter are included in this group of foods. The two most common dairy products—milk and cheese—are covered in this chapter.

All dairy products shipped across state lines for retail sale in the United States are pasteurized. **Pasteurization** is a heating process that destroys harmful bacteria in dairy products. This process prevents illness and helps milk products stay fresh.

Milk

You can purchase milk in several forms at the grocery store. See 15-31. The form you choose usually depends on the following factors:

▼ whether the milk is intended for drinking or cooking
▼ your budget
▼ your storage facilities

Forms of Milk

Fresh Fluid Milks

- *Whole milk* contains at least 3.25 percent milkfat.
- *Reduced fat milk* contains 2 percent milkfat.
- *Lowfat milk* contains 1 percent milkfat.
- *Fat free milk*, also called *skim milk* or *nonfat milk*, contains less than 0.5 percent milkfat.
- *Chocolate milk* is made by adding chocolate to whole milk.

Canned Milks

- *Evaporated milk* is obtained by removing about 50 percent of the water from whole milk.
- *Evaporated fat free milk* is obtained by removing about 50 percent of the water from fat free milk.
- *Sweetened condensed milk* is made by partially removing water from whole milk and adding sweetener.

Dry Milks

- *Nonfat dry milk* is produced by removing the water and fat from fluid whole milk.
- *Dry whole milk* is made by removing the water from fluid whole milk.

Cultured Milk

- *Buttermilk* is produced by adding special bacterial cultures to fluid milk.

15-31
Milk is available in various forms. Buy the form that best suits your needs.

The price of milk is partly determined by its fat content. The higher the proportion of fat, the more the milk costs. Fluid milk must be refrigerated unless it is aseptically packaged. Dry milk and canned milk can be stored on a shelf before being reconstituted for use.

Besides being pasteurized, most milk and milk products are homogenized, and many are fortified. **Homogenized** refers to a process by which the milkfat is broken into tiny particles. As tiny particles, the fat remains evenly suspended throughout the milk. Without homogenization, the fat (also known as cream) would rise to the top. *Fortified* means nutrients, such as vitamins A and D, have been added to the milk.

Cheese

Most cheese is made from milk. In simple terms, cheese is made by *coagulating* milk, or setting milk into a thickened mass. The *curd* (solid portion of the milk) is separated from the *whey* (liquid portion).

Food values vary in different cheeses. Cheddar cheese, for example, contains milkfat, protein, minerals, and vitamins. Cottage cheese is not as rich in fat, minerals, and vitamins, but it is a good source of protein. Cream cheese has a high fat content, but it is not a good source of protein.

Hundreds of varieties of cheeses are available. They differ in aroma, body, flavor, color, and texture. Cheeses also vary in cost. All cheeses, however, have some common characteristics. They can be divided into two classes: natural and process.

Natural Cheese

Natural cheeses are made from milk, whey, or cream. The type of cheese produced depends on the

▼ source of the milk (cow, sheep, or goat)
▼ seasonings used
▼ method of preparation
▼ ripening or curing process

Unripened cheeses, such as cream cheese and cottage cheese, have soft textures and mild flavors. As soon as the whey is removed from them, they are shipped to the grocery store.

Ripened cheeses are stored for certain lengths of time at specific temperatures to develop their flavors and textures. Cheddar and Swiss are typical examples of ripened cheeses. See 15-32.

Process Cheese

Blending and melting two or more natural cheeses results in **process cheeses**. The natural cheeses are grated and shredded. The cheeses are then combined and heated.

There are two types of process cheese. *Process cheese food* has slightly higher moisture content than natural cheese. However, the fat content for process cheese

15-32
Ripened cheeses have distinctive flavors and textures that are developed through an aging process.

food is lower than natural cheese. *Process cheese spread* has a higher moisture content and lower fat content than process cheese food. Process cheese products may contain meats, fruits, or vegetables. They are sold as slices, in blocks, or in jars.

Consumers often choose process cheeses for their convenience. These mild-flavored cheeses melt easily when heated, making them popular for sauces and casseroles. Spreadable forms are popular for serving on crackers, raw vegetables, and sandwich breads.

Storing Dairy Products

Dairy products are perishable, so you must store them properly to keep them fresh and wholesome. Before you buy, look for the date stamped on the product. Choose the latest date possible. When you get the products home, be sure to store them promptly.

Store milk, yogurt, sour cream, and butter in the coldest part of the refrigerator. Because these foods may absorb off-flavors from other foods, keep them tightly covered.

The dates stamped on milk products are called *pull dates*. A pull date is the last day a product should be sold. Dairy products will remain fresh and wholesome in your refrigerator for a few days after the pull date.

Keep all cheese—whether natural or process—tightly wrapped and refrigerated. After opening, cheese tends to dry out quickly and may pick up strong odors from other foods. Re-cover or tightly wrap any unused portions.

Preparing Dairy Products

Many recipes for puddings, cream soups, casseroles, and sauces call for milk or milk products. As you know, milk products contain protein. This is important to remember because protein foods are sensitive to heat. For best results when cooking with milk products, always use low cooking temperatures, 15-33.

Cooking with Milk

Milk and milk products are often used as ingredients in heated mixtures, such as sauces and puddings. The proteins in milk will *scorch* (burn) if they are cooked over high heat. Scorching causes milk to develop a bitter taste. Cooking milk slowly over low heat will prevent scorching. Using a double boiler when preparing heated mixtures also helps.

15-33
Low cooking temperatures help keep foods prepared with milk, such as this soup, smooth and creamy.

High cooking temperatures can cause milk proteins to *curdle* (form clumps). High acid foods, such as fruits and vegetables; salt cured meats; and certain enzymes can also cause curdling. Using low cooking temperatures and fresh milk prevents curdling.

Sometimes a film will form on the surface of milk as it is being heated. This is called *scum*. Scum can cause the milk to boil over. Beating milk to produce a foam layer on top of the milk will keep scum from forming. Covering the milk during heating will also prevent scum formation. If scum does form, you should remove it because it will cause lumps in the milk or milk mixture.

Cooking with Cheese

Cheese can become tough and rubbery when it is cooked at a high temperature. To prevent overcooking, add cubed or shredded cheese to sauces and casseroles at the end of the cooking time, 15-34. Sprinkle cheese on casseroles after they are baked.

To melt cheese in a microwave oven, use a medium to medium-high power setting. Using high power will cause cheese to become rubbery.

15-34
To keep a cheese sauce for broccoli smooth, add the cheese at the end of the cooking time.

Check It Out!

1. Explain the difference between pasteurized and homogenized milk.
2. A process cheese _____ has more moisture and a lower fat content than a process cheese _____.
3. How should milk, cheese, and butter be stored?
4. True or false. For best results, when cooking with milk and cheese, use high cooking temperatures.

Chapter Review

Summary

Knowing how to buy, store, and prepare foods are basic skills. When buying foods, choose the products that best meet your needs. Learn to select nutritious foods at the lowest possible prices.

Consider factors such as grade, age, quality, appearance, form, and preparation time when making your choices.

Proper storage helps maintain the quality of foods you buy. Follow the recommended guidelines for storing foods on the shelf or in the refrigerator or freezer. For best quality, use the products within the suggested storage times.

Learn to prepare foods successfully by following the recommended preparation techniques. Choose the techniques best suited to the type of food you are preparing. When using a recipe, follow directions and methods carefully for best results.

Think About It!

1. If you were trying to reduce the fat in your diet, which grade of meat would you buy? Explain your answer.
2. Why do you think meat alternates, such as legumes, are becoming more popular as main dish choices?
3. Why is it important to cook fruits and vegetables properly?
4. Evaluate the pros and cons of making your own breads, cakes, or cookies from scratch versus buying them from the store.
5. How would you encourage other teens to use more milk and milk products in their diets?

6. Describe some cultural differences among people that would affect the purchase, storage, and preparation of foods.
7. Compile a list of family and consumer sciences careers that relate to buying, storing, and preparing food.

Try It Out!

1. Perform a market survey comparing the cost of various egg sizes available. Determine the best buy. Report your findings to the class.
2. Create a checklist for evaluating fresh produce.
3. Compare various types of milk, such as whole, lowfat, fat free, nonfat dry (reconstituted), evaporated, and buttermilk. Which would you buy for drinking? Which would you buy for cooking purposes? Compare the cost per serving of these products.
4. Select several foods from each of the food groups. Write the name of each food item on an individual slip of paper. Distribute these to the members of your class. Let each person tell how to properly store the food listed on the slip of paper.
5. Plan with your teacher to prepare and serve foods from each of the food groups discussed in the chapter. Review the preparation principles you must consider when preparing foods from each group.

Chapter 16
Serving Food and Dining Out

Careers

These careers relate to the topics in this chapter:
▼ fast-food restaurant worker
▼ chef trainee
▼ flight kitchen manager
▼ school lunch program director
As you study the chapter, see if you can think of others.

Topics

Topic 16-1
Serving Food

Objectives

After studying this topic, you will be able to
▼ state how family mealtime can affect family relationships.
▼ describe four types of meal service.
▼ identify tableware included in a place setting.
▼ demonstrate how to set a table properly.

Topic Terms

meal service
tableware
place setting
cover

16-1
Taking the time to set an attractive table can set the mood for entertaining guests.

Thought should go into serving foods just as it goes into planning and preparing them. After taking time to prepare delicious meals or refreshments, take care to serve them properly. A casual setting is suitable for an informal meal, but an elegant meal deserves an elegant setting. There are no rigid rules for how you should serve meals or refreshments. However, by following some general guidelines, you can help make your meal a success. Whether you are serving family members, friends, or honored guests, you can make the people who eat with you feel special. See 16-1.

Family Mealtime

Families are busily involved in numerous activities. In many homes, the evening meal is one of the few opportunities family members have to get together during the day. This makes family mealtime more than just a chance to satisfy hunger. It becomes a time of important social interaction. Family members can use this time to discuss what is going on in their lives. Together they can make plans and share hopes for the future. This type of communication helps build family strength and unity. Members learn to develop tolerance and respect for individual differences. See 16-2.

Family mealtime provides a chance for parents to teach children. One area on which parents often focus is table manners. As children practice good manners, parents can provide positive reinforcement. This will help children remember to use these social skills as they grow up and begin interacting with people outside the family.

Many parents use family mealtime to help children develop a healthful appreciation for food. Parents can teach children family customs and food traditions. They can encourage children to try a variety of new tastes. Parents can help children select nutritious diets by offering them choices from each of the groups in MyPyramid. Parents can also teach children to eat slowly and chew food

16-2
Busy families can enjoy interacting with each other during meals.

thoroughly. Learning to approach food this way aids digestion and helps children avoid overeating.

You can play a role in making mealtime a positive experience in your home. You might set the table attractively and put on some soft music. Giving a little extra attention to details will show that you respect and care for family members.

You can also make meals enjoyable by keeping conversation pleasant. Save upsetting issues to discuss at another time. Treat your family members as you would treat your best friends. Show genuine interest as they share stories and ideas.

Types of Meal Service

Meal service is the way a meal is served. There are several types of meal service. The type you use will depend partly on the menu and the number of people you are serving. The formality of the occasion will also affect your choice of meal service.

Family Service

Family service, also known as *American service*, begins with a table that has been set with plates and flatware. The beverage is also on the table. All foods are placed in serving dishes and placed on the table. Family members pass the food from one person to another. Everything should be passed in one direction. People serve themselves as the foods come to them. This style of meal service is popular. However, it is inconvenient when serving dishes are hot or heavy. It may also be difficult if children at the table are too young to handle dishes of food.

Plate Service

Plate service is often used in restaurants. Individual portions are placed on each person's plate in the kitchen. The plates are then brought to the table and placed in front of each diner. Breads and condiments are usually passed at the table where family members may help themselves. This style of service is convenient when there are small children. It is also a good choice when some family members have special diets.

Buffet Service

Buffet service allows both large and small groups to be served with ease. Food is placed in serving dishes on a buffet table, with special care taken to keep everything at the proper temperature. Guests walk around the buffet and help themselves. Serving dishes are refilled as needed.

When serving a buffet, arrange items on the table in the order in which guests will pick them up. Plates are first. Flatware and beverages are often placed last. Gravies and sauces should come after the foods they accompany. Place serving utensils to the right of each dish. Leave space between serving dishes for people to rest their plates while serving themselves. See 16-3.

You may not have enough table space to seat a large group of guests. In this case, you may invite guests to sit in any available space and hold their plates in their laps. However, be sure the menu includes foods that can be cut with a fork or eaten with the fingers.

English Service

Some families use *English* or *head-of-table service* for special occasion meals, such as Thanksgiving dinner. This formal type of service requires the table to be set with flatware in advance. Salads may be set at each person's place. All plates are stacked at the head of the table. The server sits at the head of the table. He or she fills each plate and passes it to a diner seated at the table. Bread and condiments are passed so individuals can serve themselves. Eating begins after everyone has been served.

There are no hard and fast rules for meal service. You can vary and combine different styles of service to meet your needs.

Tableware

Regardless of the type of meal service being used, tableware can enhance the dining atmosphere. **Tableware** refers to dinnerware, flatware, and glassware.

You can buy tableware in sets, as place settings, or as open stock. A set includes

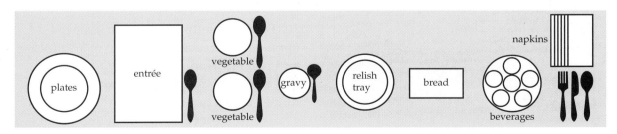

16-3

This diagram of a buffet table shows the arrangement of the items in the order they will be picked up. Guests can take a plate, serve themselves the entree, and then move to the side dishes.

all the tableware needed to serve a group of people. Most sets include four or eight place settings. A **place setting** is the dinnerware or flatware that one person would need. A place setting of dinnerware might include a dinner plate, salad plate, cup, and saucer. A place setting of flatware might include a knife, dinner fork, salad fork, teaspoon, and soup spoon. See 16-4.

When selecting tableware, consider its care requirements. For instance, you might want to be sure your tableware is dishwasher-safe.

Setting the Table

An attractive table setting can enhance any meal. There is no prescribed formula for setting a table. The primary goals in table setting are convenience and comfort. A pretty table helps diners relax and enjoy meals more.

When setting a table, you should place tableware to look similar to the **cover** (individual place setting) shown in 16-5. The dinner plate should mark the center of the space allowed for each person.

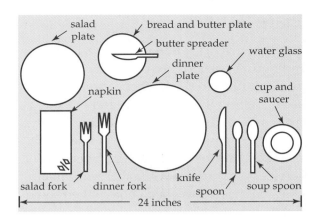

16-5

This diagram of an individual cover shows the proper placement of dinnerware, flatware, and glassware.

Place the salad plate to the upper left of the dinner plate. Place the cup and saucer to the lower right. Position the bread and butter plate above and slightly to the left of the dinner plate.

Flatware should be placed in the order in which it will be used. Place the knife to the right of the plate with the blade toward the plate. Place the spoons to the right of the knife. Lay the butter knife on the bread and butter plate. You will usually place forks to the left of the plate. However, if a fork is the only utensil needed for a meal, you should place it on the right. Place cocktail forks to the right of the spoons.

Set the water glass above the knife. Place other glasses to the right of the water glass.

For most settings, you can simply fold napkins into rectangles. You can also fold and pleat napkins in a variety of ways to add a creative touch. Place napkins on the dinner plates or to the left of the forks.

Try to achieve a balanced, organized look when setting the table. Items need not match, but they should harmonize with one another. What is important is the way the table looks when it is complete, 16-6.

16-4

This dinnerware, flatware, and glassware are used together to create an elegant table setting.

16-6
Items on a properly set table are neatly arranged for the convenience of diners.

Clearing the Table

At the end of a course, you should remove everything that will not be needed for the next course. Remove serving dishes first. Then remove dinnerware, beginning with the guest of honor. Clear each person's cover, moving around the table in sequence. Be careful not to reach in front of another person when clearing the table.

When clearing a cover, remove the dinner plate first. Pick it up with your left hand and transfer it to your right hand. Next, remove the salad plate and place it on top of the dinner plate. Then remove the bread and butter plate and place it on top of the salad plate.

Setting the Scene: Serving as a Volunteer

You are volunteering for a community service project, and you want to learn more about serving food. You know about an opportunity to help at a local food kitchen. You are not yet sure about working there and want to think over this decision.

Analyze It: What can you learn about food service from working in a food kitchen? What might be the advantages and disadvantages? What could you learn about yourself from this exercise?

Check It Out!

1. True or false. Family mealtime provides a chance for parents to teach children table manners.
2. In what type of meal service are serving dishes passed from one person to another, allowing people to serve themselves?
3. True or false. When setting a table, flatware should be placed in the order in which it will be used.

Topic 16-2
Making Dining Enjoyable

Objectives

After studying this topic, you will be able to

▼ list responsibilities of someone hosting a meal.

▼ describe appropriate manners to use when dining.

Topic Term

etiquette

Using a formal style of meal service and setting an attractive table can make any meal a special occasion. However, the easiest way to make dining truly enjoyable is to use proper etiquette. **Etiquette** refers to approved social conduct, or good manners. At the table, using proper etiquette is an essential social skill. See 16-7. Rules of etiquette apply to those who serve meals as well as to those who eat meals.

Hosting a Meal

Offering food to guests is a common gesture of hospitality. When you host a meal, you can make it a pleasant experience for diners by practicing good manners. This includes being willing to accept a guest's offer of assistance.

As host, you should invite guests to the table when a meal is ready to be served. You need to inform guests where they are to sit at the table. After all guests are seated, serving may begin.

You should see that all guests are served before serving yourself. (Family style service can be an exception to this guideline. If someone else begins passing a dish, you may take a serving as the dish comes to you.) Guests generally wait for the host to begin eating. Therefore, if you are busy serving, invite those who have been served to begin eating. This allows guests to enjoy their food while it is still hot. During the meal, you should offer second helpings of food if they are available.

You should be able to enjoy a meal with your guests. Proper planning and preparation will keep you from leaving the table repeatedly to attend to kitchen tasks. As a host, you have a responsibility to guide conversation during the meal. You may suggest topics of interest and encourage all guests to become involved in the conversation. Controversial or unappetizing topics are best saved for another time. Continue eating until all guests have finished. At the end of the meal, you may invite guests to move to another room. You may need to do some after-dinner cleanup. For health and safety, store leftover foods promptly after the meal. You may also want to remove dirty dishes from the view of your guests. However, save detailed cleanup for later so you can return to your guests as quickly as possible.

Manners When Dining

Everyone should assume a role in making dining an enjoyable experience. As a dinner guest, plan to arrive on time. Come to the table in a pleasant frame of mind. Be prepared to help those dining with you to relax and enjoy themselves.

Knowing proper etiquette can enhance your self-esteem. You will feel good about yourself when you know how to behave in social situations. Using appropriate behavior will help you feel comfortable in

Mealtime Manners

- Sit up straight and avoid placing your elbows on the table during a meal.
- At the beginning of a meal, lay your napkin across your lap. A luncheon napkin may be unfolded completely. However, leave a dinner napkin folded in half. Never tuck a napkin in your collar.
- Use the serving utensils offered with each dish of food. Never put a utensil from which you have eaten into a serving dish.
- Try a small portion of all foods that are offered to you. Do not discuss foods that you do not like or those that you are unable to eat for dietary reasons.
- Flatware is usually placed on the table in the order of use. Use the outermost pieces first.
- If you drop your flatware on the floor, leave it there. The host will offer you another piece. Unless the host invites you to begin eating, you should wait for him or her to start the meal. (At very large gatherings, you may begin eating when those seated near you have been served,)
- Never chew with your lips open so others can see the food in your mouth.
- Never talk when your mouth is full.
- Eat and drink quietly. Smacking your lips, slurping, gulping, and making other noises is inappropriate at the table.
- When in doubt about how to eat a food, follow the lead of your host. In a restaurant, you may quietly ask your waiter for advice.
- Never spit food out of your mouth at the table. If it tastes spoiled, quietly leave the table and go to the bathroom. If it is too hot, quickly take a swallow of a cold beverage. (This is the only time it is appropriate to consume a beverage when your mouth has food in it.)
- Inconspicuously remove fish bones or fruit pits from your mouth with your thumb and forefinger.
- Use fingers to eat only those foods that can be eaten without leaving traces of the food on your fingers. For instance, carrot sticks and cookies are finger foods. Barbecued chicken and cakes with sticky frosting are fork foods.
- Cut food one or two bites at a time as you are ready to eat it.
- Do not gesture with flatware in your hand.
- Cut sandwiches in halves or quarters before eating them.
- Break off small pieces of bread rather than biting into a whole slice. Break rolls in the same way. Butter one small portion of bread at a time.
- Place used flatware on the edge of a plate or saucer, not on the table.
- Never use toothpicks or dental floss while at the table.
- If you spill something at the table, be as inconspicuous as possible. If cleanup is necessary, offer to help. Apologize briefly, but do not allow the incident to spoil your meal or that of others.
- When you have finished your meal, lay your knife and fork together across the center of your plate. Before you leave the table, lay your napkin beside your plate.
- After the meal, avoid leaving the table until the host rises. If you must leave, ask the host if you may be excused.

16-7
Following these guidelines will help you appear polite and feel comfortable at any meal.

almost any setting. Using good manners will also help others feel comfortable in your presence. See 16-8.

Many employers consider the ability to use proper etiquette an important employability skill. If you are invited to lunch when you are on a job interview, be sure to use your best table manners. The employer may be evaluating how you will behave when dining with future clients and customers.

You do not need a special occasion to practice good table manners. You should use proper etiquette whenever you eat. Using good manners should become a habit. Table manners are influenced by culture. Rules of table etiquette vary in different countries. However, following some basic guidelines will help you feel comfortable no matter where you are.

16-8
Knowing proper table etiquette helps people feel more at ease in social settings.

Check It Out!

1. Approved social conduct is known as _____.
2. Why might a host invite guests who have already been served to begin eating?
3. True or false. If a guest drops a fork, he or she should pick it up, wipe it off, and quietly continue eating.

Topic 16-3
Dining Out

Objectives

After studying this topic, you will be able to
▼ describe several types of restaurants.
▼ interpret a restaurant menu.
▼ select nutritious foods when eating out.
▼ give etiquette guidelines to follow when dining in a restaurant.
▼ explain the process of paying and tipping in a restaurant.

Topic Terms

table d'hôte
a la carte
gratuity

People used to dine out as a luxury or for special occasions. Today, many people choose to eat out rather than prepare meals at home. Recognizing different types of restaurants and knowing menu terms can help make dining out more enjoyable. Understanding how to make wise food choices can make eating in restaurants more healthful.

Types of Restaurants

When eating away from home, you can choose from several types of restaurants. Sometimes you will choose a restaurant where you can eat quickly because you are hungry. At other times, you will choose a restaurant with fine food and a nice atmosphere because you want to be pampered.

People who do not want to spend much time eating like the quick service fast-food restaurants deliver. For extra fast service, customers often prefer using the drive-up window offered at many fast-food restaurants.

Cafeterias and buffets have a variety of foods placed along a serving line, 16-9. You choose the items you wish to eat. Cafeterias price each food item separately. At the end of the line, you pay for the specific items you chose. You can control the cost of your meal by choosing foods that fit your budget.

Buffets are offered at a fixed price. Most food items are self-serve. Customers can take as much or as little of each food as they like. They may also return to the buffet for additional servings.

The atmosphere is casual in most family restaurants. Menus list a variety of foods that appeal to all age groups. Prices are reasonable to make dining affordable for the entire family.

Formal restaurants offer customers an elegant dining atmosphere. Customers enjoy attractive surroundings, dine on

16-9
Buffet customers walk along a serving line and select the foods they want.

excellent food, and receive superb service. Prices in formal restaurants tend to be high due to these features.

Specialty restaurants serve specific types of food. Pizza parlors, steak and seafood houses, and ethnic restaurants are examples. See 16-10.

Ordering from a Restaurant Menu

Fast-food and some casual restaurants post their menus on the wall. After reading your choices, you place your order at a counter. Most other restaurants provide printed menus listing the foods available. A waiter will come to your table to take your order. He or she may mention other food specials that you can select.

When you are given a menu, you can quickly determine if you will order table d'hôte or a la carte. **Table d'hôte** means the entire meal has one price. Usually the meal will include a salad or soup, a main course, a side dish, and bread. Sometimes table d'hôte meals also include a beverage, appetizer, and dessert. **A la carte** menus feature items that are priced individually. A separate charge will be made for the soup, salad, and main dish.

Some menus use French terms to describe the way food has been prepared. See 16-11. Do not hesitate to ask questions when you do not understand the menu. Your waiter should be happy to assist you. Also, do not be afraid to ask the price of specials described by the waiter. These items may be the most expensive dishes the restaurant serves.

16-10
The décor in this ethnic restaurant enhances the customers' dining experiences.

Menu Terms

a la Kiev. Containing butter, garlic, and chives.

a la king. Served with a white cream sauce that contains mushrooms, green peppers, and pimentos.

a la mode. Served with ice cream.

almondine. Made or garnished with almonds.

au gratin. Served with cheese.

au jus. Served with natural juices.

du jour. Of the day. For instance, *soup du jour* means *soup of the day*.

en brochette. Cooked or served in small pieces on a skewer.

en coquille. Served in a shell.

en croquette. Breaded and deep-fried.

en papillote. Cooked in parchment paper to seal in juices.

Florentine. Prepared with spinach.

julienne. Cut into long, thin slices.

Marengo. Sauteed with mushrooms, tomatoes, and olives.

picata. Prepared with lemon.

Provençale. Prepared with garlic, onion, mushrooms, tomato, herbs, and olive oil.

16-11
Becoming familiar with these terms will help you read restaurant menus.

Making Healthful Food Choices

You need to consider the impact of meals eaten away from home on your overall health. When you select foods from a menu, keep MyPyramid in mind. Consider how your food choices will contribute to your daily needs.

An ideal meal would supply 25 to 30 percent of your calorie needs for the day. It would also provide a perfect balance of needed nutrients. Few meals meet this ideal description. However, you do not have to get a full range of nutrients at each meal. Your goal should be to meet your needs throughout the day. You can balance food choices made at one meal with those made at the next.

A fast-food meal of a hamburger, French fries, and a milk shake is rather high in calories. This meal is also high in fat while being low in vitamins, minerals, and fiber. You can make lowfat choices that are rich in vitamins, minerals, and fiber at other meals. This will help offset your fast-food selections.

If you eat out often, you must learn to choose foods carefully. This may require you to choose restaurants carefully as well. Plan to eat in those restaurants that offer nutritious options.

Restaurant Etiquette

When you are in a restaurant, you should be as polite as if you were a guest in someone's home. The same good table manners you use daily will make you comfortable in any restaurant. You should also keep a few special pointers in mind when in restaurants.

The More You Know: Healthful Eating Away from Home

What can you do to make healthful choices in restaurants? For starters, select broiled, roasted, or grilled foods rather than fried. Opt for a plain baked potato instead of French fries. Choose steamed vegetables rather than buttered or creamed vegetables. Select whole grain breads and rolls, which are higher in fiber than white bread products. Ask to have items such as salad dressings, sour cream, cheese and barbecue sauces, and butter served on the side. Choose water instead of soda to drink.

Before going to a restaurant, call to see if you will need reservations, 16-12. If you make reservations, be sure to arrive on time.

Upon arrival, tell the host the name in which your reservation is made and the number in your party. If you are asked where you would like to sit, respond promptly. When your table is ready, the host will seat you. (In more casual restaurants, a sign may indicate that you should seat yourself.)

If you are unfamiliar with a restaurant, ask to see a copy of the menu before being seated. Evaluating the menu in advance allows you to decide if the foods and prices suit your tastes and budget. Many restaurants post menus outside their doors for this reason.

16-12

Calling for reservations may be necessary for especially popular restaurants.

While in a restaurant, talk in a low but comfortable tone of voice. Others in the restaurant will not want to hear your conversation.

If you get the wrong order, or if your food is not prepared correctly, tell your waiter. He or she should be happy to help correct the error. If you need to talk with your waiter and cannot catch his or her eye, try raising your hand slightly. If this does not get attention, you may quietly call "Waiter" when he or she is near. If this still does not get the attention you need, ask another waiter to send your waiter over. If you have finished your meal and the waiter has not presented your check, you may request it. Simply say "May I please have the check?"

16-13

If you are paying with exact change, you can place your cash securely in the folder.

Paying the Check

At the end of a meal in a restaurant, the waiter will bring your check. The waiter may lay the check on the table. This indicates you should pay the cashier on your way out the door. Sometimes the waiter will place the check in a folder or on a small tray, 16-13. This indicates the waiter will return to take your payment. The waiter will also usually tell you if he or she will return for the payment when you are ready.

You may place cash or a credit card in the folder or on the tray with the check. The waiter will return your change if you pay cash. He or she will return with a receipt for you to sign if you pay with a credit card. Be sure your bill is accurate before you sign the receipt.

Tipping

A **gratuity**, or tip, is a measure of your gratitude for good service. A gratuity usually ranges from 15 to 20 percent. You may want your tip to be toward the higher end of the range if you receive excellent service.

The type of restaurant influences the amount of your tip. Since no meal service is provided, fast-food customers are not expected to leave a tip. Ten percent is an appropriate tip for services offered at cafeterias and buffets. A tip of 15 percent is considered appropriate in family restaurants. When waiters have to clean up after messy children, a larger tip is in order. A tip in a formal restaurant may be as much as 20 percent of the cost of your food. No tip is expected for carryout service. However, customers are expected to tip delivery people.

You may leave your gratuity for the waiter on the tray or in the folder with the check. If you are paying with a credit card, you may add the tip to the receipt before writing the total. If there is no folder or tray provided, you may leave your tip inconspicuously on the table.

Check It Out!

1. Which type of restaurant offers food at a fixed price and allows customers to serve themselves as much as they like?
2. Briefly describe what would be served if a diner ordered roast beef au jus with green beans almondine and julienne potatoes.
3. Give three tips for making healthful food choices in restaurants.
4. How should a restaurant guest get the attention of his or her waiter?
5. What would be an appropriate tip when the check total is $17.96 in a cafeteria? at a family restaurant? in a formal restaurant??

Chapter Review

Summary

After planning and preparing your meals, you will want to serve the food attractively. Such attention to detail can even make family meal time a more pleasant experience. Choose a style of meal service that suits your menu and the people you are serving. Select tableware that harmonizes and complements the dining area. Set the table with both convenience and appearance in mind.

To make dining enjoyable, be considerate of every person at the table, especially guests. Know and practice good table manners so they become second nature to you.

Dining out can be just as enjoyable as eating at home. There are several types of restaurants from which to choose. Becoming familiar with menu terms will help you order your meal. Learning to make wise food choices will allow you to fit restaurant meals into a healthful diet. Being aware of restaurant etiquette will enable you to feel more comfortable when dining out. Knowing about methods of payment and tipping will also help you feel more at ease when eating away from home.

Think About It!

1. Which type of meal service do you think your family would most enjoy? Why?
2. What would you consider to be the three most important table manners?
3. Suppose you are served a lobster tail in a restaurant. You suddenly realize you do not know how to get the meat out of the shell. What will you do?
4. Suppose you were in another country and noticed that your table manners were different from those of your host. What would you do? If you were the host and your international guest used different table manners, what would you do?
5. What is your favorite type of restaurant? Explain your answer.
6. What negative consequences might arise when dining with family members or coworkers if you did not know proper restaurant etiquette?
7. In what careers other than homemaking would the information in this chapter be helpful?

Try It Out!

1. Plan a menu for a buffet. Sketch how you would set the table for the buffet so guests could easily serve themselves.
2. Demonstrate for the class how to properly set the table.
3. Role-play various dining situations showing a lack of table manners. Discuss the situations. Then repeat the role-plays using appropriate manners.
4. Collect menus from several restaurants. Working in small groups, look for terms from Chart 16-11 on the menus.
5. Select two or three healthful meal options from each menu gathered in the previous activity.

Good manners make social gatherings more enjoyable for everyone.

Culinary Arts and Hospitality Careers

Career Ladder for Culinary Arts and Hospitality

▶ **Advanced Degree**

Human resources trainer
Consumer consultant
Market researcher

▶ **Bachelor's Degree**

Marketing specialist
Hotel manager

▶ **Associate's Degree**

Restaurant manager
Airline flight attendant
Cafeteria manager
Chef
Butcher

▶ **High School Diploma**

Waiter/waitress
Housekeeping assistant
Cashier
Chef trainee
Host/hostess
Pantry/stockroom worker

▶ **Pre-High School Diploma**

Service as an intern with
    any of the above
Food checker
Dietary aide
Volunteer in a community
    kitchen, food-distribution
    center, or a meal-delivery
    service for shut-ins

Those employed in the culinary arts prepare and serve food in commercial settings. This field is important to the hospitality industry, which provides places for people to stay when away from home.

Employment Opportunities

People working in the culinary arts include chefs, bakers, short-order cooks, salad makers, catering directors, hosts, and servers. They often work in restaurants, hotels, and businesses that offer food services for employees.

The desk clerks, porters, and cleaning staff in hotels are part of the hospitality industry. Hospitality jobs are also found in motels, spas, inns, camps, resorts, and country clubs.

Entrepreneurial Opportunities

Catering, a cleaning service, and cake decorating are some of the many options for those wishing to be self-employed. Entrepreneurs also run their own restaurants or hotels. For those entrepreneurs willing to share their homes, running a bed and breakfast or a guesthouse is a popular option. Home-based businesses also include teaching private cooking classes or preparing specialty baked goods and pastries for a local business.

Rewards and Demands

A special reward in culinary arts and hospitality is the gratitude of repeat customers. People tend to return for those services they enjoy.

Demands of this field include standing for many hours and dealing with difficult customers. Busy periods such as the dinner hour and check-in time can be very stressful. Workers must meet tight deadlines and are often asked to do extra work.

Preparation Requirements

Job options are greater for those with more education, but many occupations do not require training beyond high school. Much of the training in culinary arts and hospitality occurs on the job. However, job candidates can profit from having prior experience and taking related courses in high school. A foodservice and hospitality course and other family and consumer sciences classes are good choices.

Entry-Level Jobs

A baker, cook, busperson, or waiter is often trained on the job and will find many openings for entry-level work. These jobs require a high school diploma.

Midlevel Jobs

A two-year degree will prepare a worker for midlevel jobs such as foodservice manager, kitchen supervisor, party planner, and food stylist. Specialty schools and community colleges teach many culinary arts and hospitality programs.

Professional-Level Jobs

Jobs at the professional level include chef, school foodservice director, test kitchen manager, and hospitality director. Chefs use their creativity and food knowledge to prepare dishes that appeal to the eye as well as the palate. Their skills can make or break a business. A four-year degree, perhaps in hotel and restaurant management, helps workers move into the top jobs faster.

Personal Qualities Needed for Success

Guests of the hospitality industry expect first-rate service, so workers in this field must pay close attention to detail. They need an interest in people and a desire to serve them. Workers must be focused, poised, eager to accept responsibility, and tactful. Skill in organizing tasks, making decisions, communicating well, and working with business records and machines are important assets. A neat appearance, good health, and sense of humor are also needed.

Future Trends

Culinary arts and hospitality is a fast-growing career area that continues to have many job openings. Workers skilled in culinary arts will be in high demand in restaurants, clubs, and private homes. The hospitality industry keeps growing as more people travel and services such as fitness rooms and continental breakfasts expand. As a rule, entry-level salaries in this field are low, but opportunities are numerous.

Career Interests, Abilities, and You

A key question to ask yourself is whether you enjoy making people—especially strangers—feel comfortable and happy. If so, try a part-time job in a restaurant or work in a summer camp to confirm your interest in culinary arts. Part-time work as a porter, waiter, or desk clerk can help you decide if hospitality suits you.

You can gain experiences in culinary arts by working with a catering service. Festivals that include food vendors are other possibilities for career experience. You could also volunteer in a soup kitchen, where workers welcome an extra pair of hands. Keep in mind that adults are willing to help responsible young people get started on their career path. Do not hesitate to make contacts and ask for chances to gain experience.

Chefs use their creativity and knowledge of food to prepare dishes that appeal to the eye as well as the palate.

Part Five
Managing in Today's World

Chapter 17
Learning to Manage

Careers

These careers relate to the topics in this chapter:
- ▼ comparison shopper
- ▼ bookkeeper
- ▼ financial planner
- ▼ life management specialist

As you study the chapter, see if you can think of others.

Topics

Topic 17-1
Goals and Resources

Objectives

After studying this topic, you will be able to
▼ describe the different types of goals
▼ identify your resources, recognize their limits, and apply techniques to make the most of them.

Topic Terms

management
resources
goals
short-term goals
long-term goals
visionary goals
material resource
human resource
community resource
natural resource

You live in a busy world. You have to keep track of responsibilities, assignments, and deadlines. Keeping all these details straight is not always easy. Learning some management skills can help you maintain control of your life.

Management can be defined as wisely using what you have to achieve goals. The means used are called resources. **Resources** may be time, objects, services, or abilities.

Setting and Prioritizing Goals

Goals are the aims people consciously try to reach. When you reach one of your goals, you attain something you wanted and considered important. Your efforts are regarded with satisfaction.

People set goals that reflect their values. Perhaps one of your values is physical fitness. You might set a goal of jogging one mile each day. Perhaps you value knowledge. You might set a goal of earning a degree.

Your goals help to make you unique. Even when you have the same values as someone else, your goals may differ. Some goals involve only yourself. Some involve your family and friends. Some involve groups, 17-1. Some even involve people and organizations you don't know yet. For instance, you may want to work in the sales department of a large company, but you may not know at which company.

Short-Term and Long-Term Goals

You may have several goals at the same time. Some are **short-term goals**. You can reach these goals in an hour, a day, or even

17-1
Through teamwork, group members can accomplish many goals they might not achieve alone.

a week. Others are **long-term goals**. You may need several months or even several years to reach these goals.

Suppose you want to be the best high jumper in your state. This would be a long-term goal. As a freshman, you could join the track team. During the next four years, you could try to reach many short-term goals. You could work to get in good shape. You could set a goal of jumping a little higher each week. You could try winning the high jump events at track meets. Finally, you might be ready to reach your long-term goal. Perhaps you could win first place in the high jump event at the state track meet.

Visionary Goals

You may have a few goals that you don't really expect to achieve. These can be called **visionary goals**, 17-2. Though you know you probably won't reach these goals, they are worthwhile. They can inspire you to do more than you thought you were capable of doing. They may also add some interesting experiences to your life.

Suppose you had a visionary goal of winning an Olympic gold medal for high jumping. The effort you put into reaching this visionary goal could yield interesting experiences. This mental image could help you win a local meet. You might get the chance to talk to and work out with other prospective members of the Olympic team. You may even have the chance to compete in the Olympic games.

Fixed and Flexible Goals

Some goals are *fixed*. This means they are related to a specific date in time. For example, your term paper is due on a certain date. You must achieve your goal of finishing your paper by this date or receive a failing grade.

17-2
A visionary goal of becoming an astronaut may inspire you to join your high school science club.

Other goals are *flexible*. They can be achieved at any time. For instance, you may be trying to achieve a goal of having $1000 in your savings account. This can be done over a period of time with no particular end date. You can just keep saving until you have achieved your goal.

Steps in Setting and Achieving Goals

Have you thought about your goals? What careers interest you? What do you want from life? Setting goals is an important part of achievement. Goals give you a sense of direction. They add motivation to keep you moving forward.

The first step in setting and achieving goals is to make a list of what you want out of life, 17-3. Be as honest with yourself as possible as you make your list. Be sure to include both short- and long-term goals. You may want to set some visionary goals for yourself, too. Just remember to keep them in their proper perspective. Don't feel disappointed if your visionary goals are never achieved.

The second step is to consider your values. Determine which ideals and objects are the most important. Make a list of them. How will they influence the goals you have listed? You will not want to give up what you consider important to achieve your goals. For instance, suppose owning a car was one of your goals. You could ask your parents to give you the money you need. However, if you value independence and personal achievement, you would find another way to reach your goal.

17-3

Owning a home one day may be one of your life's goals.

The third step is to list ways you could achieve your goals. Give yourself several options. Life continuously changes. You change, and the people around you change. Likewise, the situations and problems you face change. Having a few alternate plans is always a good idea.

Although you need to include options in your list, you should keep the list realistic. You should not count on luck to help you achieve your goals. You might win a huge sweepstakes, but your chances are not very good. You probably will have to find another way to achieve your goals.

The fourth step is to make some definite plans. Goals will not be reached unless specific steps are taken. Try to group some short-term goals with related long-term goals. Perhaps achieving some short-term goals will lead you closer to the achievement of your long-term goals. On the other hand, you may find you have to sacrifice some goals to achieve others. For instance, you may have to give up some free evenings to take courses at a nearby school. You may have to give up a summer vacation to earn money for a new car. You may have to delay marriage until you have become established in a career.

The final step in setting and achieving goals is to establish deadlines and rewards. *Deadlines*, or time goals, help you direct your efforts. They state what needs to be done first, what should be done next, and what can wait. A final deadline or time goal can help you work efficiently to get a job done.

Meeting Your Goals

When you meet a deadline, you deserve a reward. You can challenge yourself more fully when you know your efforts are worthwhile. Unpleasant tasks need special rewards. You can promise yourself a weekend vacation, a free afternoon, or a new shirt. See 17-4. The size of the reward is not as important as feeling good about completing the task and achieving the goal.

The key to success in setting and achieving goals is knowing yourself and what you want to accomplish. Some people do not know what they really want in life. They simply try a variety of activities. By keeping their options open, many find what is right for them. You can save yourself a great deal of time and frustration by trying to know yourself. You can do this by thinking about your values, your goals, and the methods you use to achieve your goals.

Recognizing Your Values and Standards

You tend to take actions that support your values and maintain your standards. Therefore, you need to recognize the values and standards that relate to your problem. They will affect the way you choose to reach your goal. For instance, if you think health and exercise are important, you might consider walking to the game. If you value convenience, you may ask a friend to pick you up. Suppose you have a high standard for promptness. You may not want to ride with a friend who cannot get to the stadium in time for the kickoff.

Determining Your Resources

The types and amounts of resources people have vary. Look at and try to assess your resources. This will help you determine which to use to reach your goal.

Material and Human Resources

Resources can be classified as material or human. See 17-5. **Material resources** are not physically or mentally part of a person. They include time, money, possessions, and community resources.

Human resources come from within people. They include skills, knowledge, talents, energy, and people themselves. Athletic skill is a human resource that helps ballplayers achieve the goal of winning a game. Teachers are human resources that help students reach the goal of getting an education. Energy needed to walk is a human resource you could use to get to the game.

17-4
You may buy a new pair of athletic shoes as a reward for finishing a project.

Resources	
Human	**Material**
abilities	appliances
communication	car
creativity	clothing
dedication	fire and police
enthusiasm	protection
flexibility	food
interests	housing
knowledge	libraries
optimism	money
people	parks
skills	schools
talents	time

17-5
Both human and material resources can be used to meet goals.

People do not always recognize the value of their human resources. These resources can often be used in place of material resources. For instance, sewing skills can be used instead of money to make clothes rather than buy them. Although fabric and sewing items cost money, they cost a lot less than a finished garment. Also, cooking skills can be used to prepare food at home instead of spending considerably more money to eat out.

Many times, human resources need to be used with material resources to reach goals. For instance, skill in operating a computer is a human resource. However, it must be coupled with the material resource of a computer in order to be useful. With this blend of resources, countless goals can be reached. You could write reports and calculate math problems to reach goals at school. You could type letters and send e-mail to reach communication goals. You could access information to achieve research goals.

Time is a special resource. All people have the same amount of time, 24 hours a day, but use it differently. Because the use of time is unique to every person, this resource will be given individual treatment in Topic 17-3.

Community Resources

Community resources are parks, schools, libraries, and other facilities that are shared by many people. Kitchen equipment and food supplies are material resources that could help you reach a goal of satisfying hunger. Public transportation is a material resource that could help you reach your goal of getting to the game.

Natural Resources

Natural resources are taken from the land. Agricultural products, forest products, and fossil fuels are examples.

Resource Limitations

All people have a variety of resources. However, they have limited amounts of each resource. No one has an endless amount of money, time, energy, or any other resource.

The limits on resources will be different at different points in your life. For instance, the longer you work, the greater your income is likely to be. This means you will have more money available when you are older than you do now. On the other hand, as you get older, you are likely to have less energy than you do now.

In addition to being limited, many resources are *expendable*. In other words, they can be used up. For instance, a piece of paper is an expendable resource. It can be used to reach the goal of sending a letter. The piece of paper cannot be used again to reach a future goal of writing a report. See 17-6.

17-6
Food is an expendable resource. It can be used only once to meet the goal of satisfying hunger.

Not all expended resources are gone forever. Some can be renewed. For instance, taking a nap or eating a snack can restore your energy. The piece of used paper can be recycled to make more paper.

Some resources are actually *expandable*. Solving problems, making decisions, and using skills, for example, tend to improve with use. In fact, they may weaken when not used.

Conserving Human and Material Resources

Knowing which resources are limited and which can be renewed or expanded can help you plan. You need to think about how future goals might be affected before deciding to use resources for present goals. You do not want to deplete a resource now if you will need it in the future. In your goal of getting to the game, taking public transportation would require money. Money is an expendable resource. If you have a goal of buying a gift next week, you might not want to use this resource

now. Walking to the game might be a better choice since it requires energy—a renewable resource.

Flexibility of Resources

Resources are flexible. They can be decreased and increased in a number of ways. For instance, breaking your leg would temporarily decrease your athletic skill. Taking a computer class would increase your knowledge and skill with computers. Losing your job would decrease your income. Winning a contest would suddenly increase the amount of money you have available.

You cannot plan to win a contest. However, you can use various techniques to help you make the most of limited resources. These techniques include substituting, combining, and exchanging resources.

Substituting Resources

One resource can often be substituted for another because most goals can be reached in more than one way. People often substitute a plentiful resource for one that is more limited. Friendship, money, and energy are all resources. They could all be used to reach the goal of getting to the game. If you have too little money, you could substitute friendship or energy.

Combining Resources

Most goals are reached through the use of a combination of resources. For instance, walking to the game would require both time and energy. Riding with a friend would require the friend's car as well as the friend.

Family members often combine their resources. Together, a family unit has more resources than any one person in the family. Each family member can contribute human resources. Some members may cook; others may be able to repair appliances. All family members may contribute to cleaning and other home care tasks. Families often have an easier time meeting goals when they work together, 17-7.

Exchanging Resources

Resources must often be exchanged to achieve a goal. Money is probably the resource that is exchanged most frequently. Money can be exchanged for a wide range of goods and services. Food, clothing, furniture, vacations, and the services of doctors, plumbers, and mechanics can all be obtained in exchange for money.

Money is not the only resource that is exchanged. People exchange time, energy, and skills, too. For instance, you might use your math skill to tutor your friend in exchange for a ride to the game. You might use your sewing skills and several hours of time to create clothes too expensive to buy.

Check It Out!

1. Wisely using resources to achieve goals is known as _____.
2. Give an example of a short-term goal, a long-term goal, and a visionary goal.
3. True or false. Possessions are human resources.
4. What are three techniques that can be used to help make the most of limited resources?

17-7
Family members combine resources when they work together to complete a task, such as preparing a meal.

Topic 17-2
Decision Making and the Management Process

Objectives

After studying this topic, you will be able to

▼ explain the importance of management skills.

▼ outline the steps in the decision-making process.

▼ explain the management process.

Topic Terms

decision
emulation
decision-making process
management process
implement

The way you manage your daily life will greatly influence the quality of your life. You are the manager of your life. That means you are responsible for making the choices and decisions that will move you toward your goals. Management skills will help you solve problems and make decisions. By the decisions you make on a daily basis, you move closer to your goals. You move toward something you want to achieve—something that is important to you. If you are a good manager, you will be more likely to achieve the quality of life you desire.

Solving Problems and Making Decisions

A **decision** is a conscious or unconscious response to a problem or an issue. Whenever you make up your mind about what you will do or say, you are making a decision. Some decisions are made without thinking; they just happen. Some decisions are actively made after much thought. Either way, your values, goals, standards, needs, and wants will affect the decisions you make.

Making Routine Decisions

Some decisions seem simple. These *routine decisions* are made often and without much thought. For instance, you need to brush your teeth every morning. You probably do this when you first wake up or after you finish breakfast. You do it without thinking about the pros and cons. Habit causes you to make many daily decisions without even thinking about them. There are other ways to make routine decisions as well.

Impulsive decisions are made on the spot. You see something; you want it; you get it, 17-8. Perhaps you are in the supermarket. A product promoter is serving bite-size portions of a new brand of pizza to shoppers. It looks good, so you pick up a portion and pop it into your mouth. You never asked yourself "should I taste this?" You just tasted it impulsively.

Emulation is a regular source of decisions for teens. **Emulation** means you do what most other people around you are doing. What do you wear to school? Students often dress like other students. If your school has an official uniform, you get up in the morning and put it on. If your school has an "unofficial uniform" such as jeans, sweatshirts, and athletic shoes, you probably emulate that dress code.

17-8
People often buy items they see on an impulse.

Creativity is the motivator for some decisions. You just want to do something different. For instance, when Sara's family decided to spend more time together, she suggested an old-fashioned marsh-mallow roast.

Default is the act of not making a decision. For example, you could not decide whether to go to the movies or go to the dance. You ended up doing neither. You stayed home. By not deciding between the two options you had considered, you ended up making a decision by default.

Steps in Decision Making

Some decisions are more complex. Deciding whether or not to get a part-time job, making a career choice, or buying a car are examples. These will need to be made more carefully as many of these decisions tend to have long-lasting effects.

When you have important decisions to make, the decision-making process can help you make the decisions that are best for you. The **decision-making process** is a set of logical steps to follow when making complex decisions.

1. *Define the problem or the decision to be made.* Be sure that you recognize the real problem and its importance to your life.
2. *Establish your goals.* Review your long-term goals and what you want out of life. Review the short-term goals you have set for yourself, too. Then establish new, additional goals related to the problem.
3. *Prioritize your goals.* List your goals in order of importance, placing the goals you want to accomplish most first on your list. Direct most of your efforts

toward your major goals. Your less important goals can be put on a waiting list.

4. **Look for resources.** Make a list of everything available to you that will help you reach your goals.

5. **Identify alternatives.** Make a list of all the pros and cons of each alternative. Try to keep an open mind as you do this. Avoid letting any personal prejudices become stumbling blocks to progress. A good way to test alternatives is to ask yourself these questions:

   ▼ Would I want to keep this decision a secret from others?

   ▼ Will this decision hurt anyone (including myself) either emotionally or physically?

   ▼ Can this decision have a negative influence on my goals?

Answering *yes* to any of these questions means caution. You may want to reconsider the decision and choose another alternative.

6. **Make a decision.** If you have been guided by your most objective thinking, you will probably be happy with the decision you make. Decision making often involves taking risks. You may make some errors and create some conflicts. However, if you follow these steps, most of your decisions should produce good results.

7. **Carry out the decision.** After thinking through and making your decision, take action to carry it out. This can be a difficult step, but it is important. You must make the effort to follow through.

8. **Evaluate the results of your decision.** Once a decision is made and action is taken, the result cannot be changed. This is part of learning to take responsibility for your decisions by accepting the consequences. You can, however, benefit from past experience by using it to help you make a future decision. To do this, you need to evaluate your decision. That means looking back on your decision and judging its success. Did your decision solve your problem? Did the decision help you reach your desired goal? Are you satisfied with the results? Try to see what did or did not work. In evaluating your decisions, you learn from your mistakes as well as from your successes, 17-9.

As you can see, the decision-making process can be applied to all kinds of decisions and problems. You can use it for important decisions you make every day. The steps can also be applied to more complex decisions such as those involving your education, your career, parenthood, or major purchases. These major decisions can impact your family, friends, society as a whole, and your future.

17-9

This bulletin board reminds students to evaluate results on a daily basis.

The Management Process

Management involves following a series of steps called the **management process**. This process helps you plan how to use resources to achieve goals. In some ways, the management process is similar to the decision-making process. The management process can be used by families and other groups as well as by individuals. It helps all members know what goals have been set and what plans are to be followed. Otherwise, group resources may not be used efficiently and group goals might not be met.

Planning

The first step in the management process is to form a plan. Begin forming your plan by deciding exactly what steps to take to reach your goal. Think about the best order for accomplishing the steps.

When working toward a short-term goal, like your goal to get to the game, this step may be brief. You might plan to check the bus schedule, walk to the bus stop, and get on the bus. Long-term goals, however, will require more in-depth planning.

Organizing

For long-term goals, you should write down the steps of your plan for frequent review. Be sure to list everything you must do. Note people you must see and materials you will need. When you make a thorough plan, you are less likely to forget little details.

Determine standards for each step in your plan. This will help you know when you have accomplished the step to your satisfaction. Set deadlines, too. Deadlines keep you working toward the goal by preventing you from getting sidetracked.

Implementing

To **implement** a plan simply means to carry it out. Putting your plan into action is the next step of the management process. Again, this step may take little effort when working toward short-term goals. It would involve actually checking the schedule, walking to the bus stop, and getting on the bus.

For a long-term goal, you might want to divide large tasks into several smaller tasks that are easier to accomplish. Check off the items listed on your plan as you complete them. Try to honor the deadlines you set for yourself. This will give you a feeling of success.

The More You Know: Managing Cleaning

In some families, members set aside a certain day for cleaning the house. Therefore, members do not plan to meet other goals on this day. Activities such as seeing a movie with friends are out. When cleaning starts, the family members make a plan outlining each person's responsibilities. This prevents such problems as having two people dust the furniture at different times during the day.

Evaluating

You will probably find yourself evaluating each step in your plan as you complete it. You will check to see if you have met your deadlines and maintained the standards you set.

After you have completed all the steps in your plan, you will want to do a final evaluation. See 17-10. You might ask yourself the following questions: Were my goals reasonable? Did I use my resources as I had anticipated? Was I able to follow my plan? How can I improve when I do this again? Your evaluation might tell you that walking to and from the bus stop took more energy than you had planned. You might decide that next time you will do just as well to walk to the game.

Many people like to keep records of their evaluations that can be used for reaching future goals. Such records can make planning easier the next time.

17-10
After achieving a goal, evaluating the results is the final step in the management process.

Check It Out!

1. Explain what it means to be the manager of your life.
2. List the eight steps in the decision-making process.
3. List the steps of the management process.

Topic 17-3

Managing Your Time

Objectives

After studying this topic, you will be able to

▼ explain the importance of time management.

▼ list some ways to help manage time.

Topic Terms

time management
dovetail

Sometimes people remember exactly what they did yesterday or last week. At other times, they cannot recall. Was the time well spent, or was it wasted? Managing time is very important because once this resource is wasted, it is never regained. It is lost forever.

Why Plan Your Time?

Time management is the ability to plan and use time well. It is not a way to change time but to change people. Time management is really about self-management. By managing time, you accomplish more of what you want to do. This is the main reason for time management.

In addition, there are several other benefits of managing time. You meet your deadlines. You are ready to face each day's responsibilities. By managing time, you can put small periods of time to good use so none is wasted. You complete your short-term goals, work toward long-term goals, and even find time for visionary goals.

Short-Term Goals Are Met

Short-term goals are your immediate aims for today and this week. For example, you attend classes, do homework, and meet deadlines for term papers. You also do household tasks and possibly hold a part-time job. Fulfilling all these duties does not happen automatically. It is the result of managing time well, 17-11.

Long-Term Goals Are Met

A long-term goal, such as choosing a career, takes more than a month or even a year to achieve. These goals require considerable thought and preparation. By dividing long-term goals into smaller steps, however, you can work on them gradually. As a result, you will be better prepared to make major life decisions when the time comes.

17-11
People who manage their time well always try to remain aware of what time it is.

Some long-term goals involve perfecting skills and finding helpful resources to make decisions. Related activities include looking ahead to foresee and prevent problems that may stop you from reaching your goals.

Visionary Goals Are Addressed

Managing time allows you to dream, explore, and fit unexpected opportunities into your schedule. Staying ahead of deadlines can help you do this.

Preparing in advance for scheduled events gives you flexibility when unplanned opportunities suddenly arise, 17-12. You can then adjust your schedule to take advantage of them without sacrificing your performance in other areas.

17-12
This student stays up-to-date on her school assignments so she can attend special events that are suddenly announced.

Steps in Time Management

Busy people who handle many tasks well make time management look easy. With practice, it can be. Time is managed in three steps: planning, carrying out the plan, and evaluating the results.

Planning

Before planning actually begins, you need a clear work area. You also need to review your goals and values. Only then can you develop a to-do list and weekly plan.

Organizing

Good planning begins with an organized work area. Not being able to grab a pencil and paper to record your thoughts will slow the planning process. It is important to have a neat workspace with storage for all your tools. Returning tools to their proper places will allow you to find them when needed.

Consider Goals and Values

Before planning starts, think about your goals and values. There are many worthwhile ways to spend time, but some may not benefit or interest you. Consider where you want to direct your life and spend time on related activities. Occasionally you must skip some interesting activities to allow room for those most important to you. See 17-13.

Make To-Do Lists

Activities that are not part of a routine should be added to a to-do list. Some people arrange their lists in priority order. This means they rank the most important activity 1, the next important 2, and so on. This type of system is helpful when activities must be done in a specific order.

17-13
These students prefer to spend their spare time preparing for a science fair.

Map each day on paper so you can see which hours are filled and which are open. Look ahead to assignments due later in the month that should be started this week. Then take one day at a time, determining what to do on each to be prepared for the next. Transfer items from your to-do list to the weekly plan, scheduling them to suit your needs.

If you have to mesh your plan with those of others, coordinate them. See 17-14. Then, write out your plan and put it in view so you can refer to it as needed. At first you may need to glance at it often. Later, referring to it at the end or start of each day may be sufficient. After much planning experience, you may find that each daily to-do list is firmly imprinted on your mind.

Other people with long to-do lists simply use a four-letter rating system. They rank the must-do tasks *A*; the next-do tasks *B*; the should-do tasks *C*; and the can-wait tasks *D*. All A and B tasks are included in the day's plan. C and D tasks are handled as time allows. If not completed that day, C and D tasks eventually become A and B tasks. This system is useful when many tasks must be accomplished by the day's end, but not in a specific order. It allows more flexibility in fitting tasks into individual schedules.

Create a Weekly Plan

Planning is usually done on a weekly basis. Look ahead to next week and note any special assignments due. For example, a student may have a test on Tuesday, an oral report to give on Thursday, and a book report due on Friday. Knowing this, the student can make a schedule that flags these important deadlines. In that way, no important task is left to the last minute.

17-14
When plans involve other people, discuss as many details as possible before beginning, then update others as needed.

Implementing

Now it is time to put your plan into action. Remember your standards of excellence. Think: "Do it well so it reflects the pride I have in myself."

Do not be afraid to think creatively. Find new ways to do old tasks. Creativity can help you implement your management plan and give you a greater sense of accomplishment.

Evaluating

Evaluation may be as simple as noting whether or not the plan worked. If you finish all the tasks scheduled for the day, you can begin working on tomorrow's. That will help you get ahead of your deadlines. If some tasks could not be completed, ask yourself why. Did you misjudge the amount of time needed for each task? This is quite likely to occur with your first few efforts at planning. With practice, you will be able to set more realistic deadlines.

Remember that a time management plan is simply a guide. It is not meant to be a perfect balance between available time and tasks to do. If you scheduled too few tasks one day, use your spare time well. If you fall behind in completing your A list, reschedule whatever you can for later.

Managing Time Wisely

To get started on managing time well, look for some helpers. See what tools are available to help you create your weekly plans. Then keep your plans on track by using strategies that help you use time effectively.

Using Time Management Aids

All you really need to get started is pencil and paper. Also, you will need a calendar to see the "big picture" so you can stay on schedule.

Visit an office supply store and browse the planners, calendars, and schedules. Also check the calendars and task lists that can be created by computer. Handheld electronic organizers are quite useful tools. Also consider the features of your cell phone. Some include a calendar for recording important dates such as due dates for projects and assignments. (Keep in mind your school's rules regarding use of cell phones in class.)

Experiment with several tools to see which work best for you. If you find what you need in one tool, your plans will be easier to manage. Use a tool that shows an entire week in a glance and allows you to easily add new tasks, 17-15. Do not get complex tools that require great effort to operate. This could cost you more time than it saves!

17-15
This planning tool shows the week, month, and year at a glance.

Using Time Management Strategies

Using time well is a skill that requires practice. Here are several strategies to help you reach that goal.

▼ *Steer clear of time wasters.* Do television programs or phone calls from friends sidetrack you from scheduled tasks? Discipline yourself to follow your plan as closely as possible.

▼ *Avoid procrastination.* Do you stare into space, only to realize later that too much time has passed? Make a point of starting each task in a timely manner.

▼ *Combine tasks whenever possible.* For example, combine family time with your fitness schedule by encouraging everyone to walk, bike, or run together. If cleaning up after meals is your assignment, combine it with some form of recreation. You can listen to radio, glance at a favorite television program, or socialize with the family. When you combine or fit tasks together, you **dovetail** them. Many tasks cannot be dovetailed, but look for those that can be.

▼ *Break tasks into smaller steps.* In this way, time-consuming or complex tasks are much easier to do. Also, the satisfaction of crossing the finished steps off your list will motivate you to tackle the remaining steps.

▼ *Compensate for lost time.* Review your priorities, combine tasks when possible, and eliminate unnecessary tasks. This will help to get a schedule back on track.

▼ *Be prepared to use spare time.* Waiting to see a doctor or to take a sibling home from practice often lasts longer than expected. When you find yourself with spare time, be prepared to use it. If you go somewhere, always take a project along, such as a book to read or homework to do. See 17-16.

17-16
These students wisely use the time when they are waiting to be picked up after school to study.

With time management, you are in the driver's seat, determining the direction your life will take.

Energy and Task Management

Time is a limited resource and so is energy. All people have the same amount of time each day, but all people do not have the same amount of energy. A time management plan must take into consideration the energy a person has to give. No amount of goal setting can force you to accomplish more than your body can handle.

Some students finish homework and go to bed at 11 p.m. Others must finish homework by 10 p.m. or they fall asleep. Do the students who go to bed earlier have fewer responsibilities? No. They may have more. How do they accomplish their tasks? They use time management techniques. They schedule their time well and avoid wasting it.

Sometimes you may feel inefficient and unable to do all you should. In these cases, ask yourself, "Am I getting enough sleep? Am I energized when I wake up in the morning?" Enough rest and recreation is needed for physical growth and for motivation to work, 17-17. *All work and no play* is not a formula for healthy living. Rest and recreation should be included in your daily schedule.

Creativity is a helpful resource to use when you feel unable to keep up with your schedule. Look for shortcuts that take less time without cutting quality. Remember, you are in the driver's seat. When beginning a project, ask yourself, "How can I best accomplish this without sacrificing quality?" Consider your energy and ways to manage the tasks efficiently.

17-17
To perform at your peak, always get all the sleep and rest your body needs.

Managing Your Study Time

Study management begins by listening carefully to your teacher during class. Teachers often provide guidance on what portions of your text or assignment are most important. Paying attention in class can allow study time to be used more efficiently later.

Note taking is also an important study skill. Notes taken in class identify and clarify important points. They also remind you of what was emphasized in class. Notes are absolutely essential when information not included in your text is presented in class. Test taking becomes much easier when you have written notes from which to study.

To manage your study time at home, try to determine how you study best. Maybe this is at the dining room table or in your room at your desk. Try to work without the distractions of music or television. Once you have determined your best location for studying, map out time that you will use *only* for studying. Do not let yourself be distracted during this time by phone calls, visitors, or even other chores.

Balancing Personal, Family, Work, and Leisure Time

Balancing your time means making sure that everything you value is included in your schedule. Your obligations at school, home, and work absorb most of your daytime hours. Meeting these obligations also requires spending time with others and learning to communicate and work well with them. In addition, time must be devoted to physical activity, rest, and sleep—all of which your body requires. See 17-18.

Besides these common activities, your values will prompt you to add others to the list. For example, you will want to spend some time helping others in need and beautifying your community. Satisfying your spiritual needs and practicing your religious beliefs is another important way to spend time.

Everyone has only 24 hours each day. To accomplish all the tasks that become a part of a busy schedule means managing yourself first. Then you can use your time to pursue your priorities.

Check It Out!

1. Why plan for the use of time?
2. Which goals are addressed by a time management plan?
3. Name four aids to time management.
4. Name four strategies for time management.

17-18
This family uses leisure time to get physical activity *and* spend time together.

Topic 17-4

Managing Your Money

Objectives

After studying this topic, you will be able to
▼ discuss work compensation.
▼ describe the deductions taken from an employee's paycheck.
▼ distinguish between gross income and net income.
▼ prepare a personal budget.
▼ list ways to reduce flexible expenses.
▼ explain how a computer can be used to help manage money.

Topic Terms

budget
hourly wage
salary
fringe benefits
gross income
net income
fixed expense
flexible expense

Money is an important resource. A **budget** is a plan to help you manage your money wisely. A budget will help you time your purchases so you can reach both short and long-term goals. If you do not have a plan, it is easy to spend money on immediate wants without saving for future goals. The ability to plan purchases and stick with a budget is a mark of maturity.

Earning an Income

Employees who are paid a set amount of money for each hour they work earn an **hourly wage**, 17-19. If they work more than 40 hours per week, they are usually paid overtime. *Overtime* pay is usually one and one-half times the employee's hourly wage. For instance, an employee who earns $6.50 per hour would receive $9.75 per hour of overtime pay.

In certain types of jobs, employees earn a salary. A **salary** is a set amount of money paid for a certain period of time. For instance, teachers sign a contract to do a specific job for a certain salary amount. To fulfill their contract, they spend time in and out of the classroom. Some full-time employees earn an annual salary, with the amount divided into equal payments during the period. If salaried employees in professional positions work more than 40 hours a week, however, they do not receive overtime pay.

17-19
Many teens who work part-time earn an hourly wage.

Many full-time workers receive financial extras called **fringe benefits**. These benefits are provided by the employer in addition to the worker's regular paycheck. What types of fringe benefits can you expect when you work full-time? This depends on the company where you work. However, many companies offer the following benefits: health and life insurance, paid vacation time, paid sick days, savings plans, and retirement plans.

Understanding Your Paycheck

One of the benefits of employment is earning an income. When you receive your first paycheck, you may be surprised. The amount you were promised when you were hired will be different from the amount you receive in your paycheck. Why do you not get to keep all the money you earned? A part of your earnings are deducted from each paycheck by your employer for taxes and other benefits. An important part of understanding your paycheck is knowing what comes out of your paycheck and where it goes.

Paychecks and Paycheck Deductions

The paycheck stub attached to your paycheck provides important information about your earnings and deductions. The total amount of money you earn *before* deductions is your **gross income**. The actual amount of your paycheck *after* deductions is your **net income**, sometimes called your *take-home pay*. Though payroll deductions vary for individuals, about two-thirds of a person's wages remain after deductions are made. The paycheck stub in 17-20 shows an example of earnings and common deductions.

Taxes and Other Deductions

Your paycheck stub lists the various deductions your employer subtracts from your gross pay. The following list includes some of the most common paycheck deductions:

▼ federal and state income taxes
▼ Social Security taxes
▼ health and life insurance
▼ savings and retirement plans
▼ union dues
▼ charitable contributions

Income Taxes

Your employer deducts federal and state income taxes from your paycheck. This tax money is the government's main source of income. The government uses the tax money to provide services, programs, and facilities to all citizens. The amount of tax taken out of your paycheck is based on how much you earn. The more you earn, the higher the rate of taxes you will have to pay.

Social Security Taxes

Another deduction is made for Social Security taxes. This amount may be listed under the letters *FICA* (Federal Insurance Contributions Act) on your paycheck stub. The federal government administers the Social Security program. It provides retirement, disability, and survivor benefits to eligible working citizens. As with federal income tax, your contribution is a percentage of your earnings. Whatever you pay, your employer pays a matching amount for you.

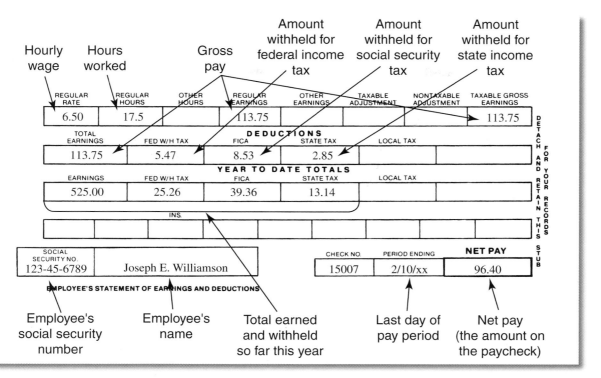

17-20
As this paycheck stub shows, your net pay will be less than your gross pay.

Other Deductions

The taxes already described are mandatory—you must pay them. Other deductions from your paycheck are made with your permission. Health insurance and life insurance may be available to you through your employer. Premiums may be deducted from your paycheck, or your employer may pay the insurance premiums at no cost to you.

Many other possible payroll deductions exist. Deductions may be made for benefits such as a retirement plan or a credit union savings plan. If you join a union, your employer will deduct your union dues. Any contributions you make toward raising funds for a company-endorsed charity may also be deducted by your employer.

The Basics of Budgeting

Budgets are designed to reflect income and expenses for a given period of time. Many families prepare annual budgets. Some people prefer monthly budgets because most of their bills must be paid monthly. If you receive a weekly paycheck or a weekly allowance, you may find a weekly budget helpful.

Setting up a budget involves only a few basic steps. Once you learn these steps, you can develop a budget of your own. A sample weekly budget is shown in 17-21.

Establish Financial Goals

The first step in developing a budget is to set goals for your spending. Your primary goal will be to meet all your

	Weekly Budget	
Income		
Allowance	$20.00	
Babysitting	25.00	
Total Income	45.00	
Expenses		
Fixed Expenses		
Lunch	$7.50	
Scout dues	1.00	
Savings	10.00	
Flexible Expenses		
Entertainment	11.00	
Snacks & eating out	10.00	
Clothes and accessories	5.50	
Total Expenses	$45.00	

17-21
A teen might use a weekly budget to balance income and expenses.

commitments and pay for all of your basic needs. However, you are also likely to have financial goals to purchase certain items. You may have short-term goals for items you would like to buy soon. You may also have long-term goals for items you want to purchase in the future. Long-term goals often center on more costly items. Attaining such goals will require saving money over an extended period.

Once you determine your goals, list them with an estimate of each item's cost. This will help you budget money for basic needs in a way that allows you to save for goals. Keep in mind that your goals may change. Review your goals from time to time so you can make any needed adjustments in your budget.

Determine Sources of Income

The second step in making a budget is to list your sources of income. List the amount of money you receive from each source during the time period of your budget.

Income is all the money you receive. Most income is *earned income*. This is money received for working. It may be in the form of a salary, wages, tips, or commissions. Some income is *unearned income*. This includes interest on bank accounts, dividends on stocks, and money received as prizes or gifts.

When you record income, remember to count only your take-home pay. Any deduction from your paycheck is money already spent. Also, count only income that you are certain to receive. Income that might be available from overtime work or gifts should not be included.

Estimate Expenses

The third step in developing a budget is to estimate your expenses for the time period of your budget. Make a list of items and services you buy and what they cost. See 17-22. This list will reflect your spending patterns. Later, you can review the list to see if you need to change your spending patterns.

Expenses can be divided into two general groups—fixed and flexible expenses. These groups are further divided into various budget categories according to your spending patterns.

Fixed expenses are items that cost set amounts that you are committed to pay. Included in this group are mortgage or rent payments, installment payments, insurance premiums, and pledged charitable contributions. Savings are also considered a fixed expense. If you do not make a commitment to save a certain amount, you might end up not saving anything.

17-22
Preparing a written list will help you estimate your expenses more accurately.

Flexible expenses are costs that occur repeatedly, but which vary in amount from one time to the next. These expenses commonly include food, clothing, transportation, and recreation.

Compare Income and Expenses

The fourth step in developing a budget is to compare your income and expenses. If your income is greater than your expenses, you can put the extra money toward your goals. If your income equals your expenses, you will be able to meet all your commitments. However, you will not be able to work toward your goals. If your income is less than your expenses, you will not have enough money for your commitments.

If you are not able to meet your commitments, you must look again at your income and expenses. You must either increase your income or decrease your expenses. You may wish to take these steps even if your income and expenses are equal. This will allow you to have extra money to put toward your goals.

Write the Budget and Keep Records

Putting your budget in written form is the fifth step in budget planning. Written records will help you keep track of your spending and stay within your budget. When you set up a record-keeping system, keep it simple. The simpler your system is, the more likely you are to use it regularly and accurately.

Your written budget can be prepared in one of several styles. Choose the style that is easiest and most logical to you. You may decide to buy a record book and set up different accounts for budget categories, 17-23. With this method, you allocate a certain amount of money to each category and keep a running balance. You can easily see just how much you can afford to spend. You can also see which expenses, if any, are getting too large.

Some people decide how much money they will need to cover their expenses for a month. They divide this amount by the number of paychecks they will receive during the month. Then they set aside the appropriate amount from each check. They use the balance for goals or spending money. For instance, assume you need $1,000 a month for expenses. Suppose you receive four paychecks a month. Divide $1,000 by 4 to get $250—the amount to set aside from each check. Managing your money in this way takes a certain amount of discipline. You must train yourself not to use money set aside to cover expenses. Big-budget items such as annual insurance premiums require extra planning. Start preparing to pay them several months in

Food Budget for March

Mar.						Balance	
Mar.	1	Budget allocation				200	00
	1	Lunch at the deli	4	75	195	25	
	3	Supermarket	34	20	161	05	

Recreation Budget for March

Mar.	1	Budget allocation			50	00
	5	Movie for two	12	00	38	00

17-23

Listing purchases in a record book can quickly show how much money is left in each budget category.

advance. Set aside a certain amount from each paycheck so you will be ready when the premium is due.

Evaluate the Budget

Like any good planning process, the final step in planning a budget is evaluation. Evaluate your spending every few months to see how well you are following your budget. If you have money left over, be proud of yourself. If you overspent, try to find out why. Perhaps you allowed too little for certain expenses.

You may need to make adjustments in your budget. Perhaps you will want to increase your allotment in one category to more accurately reflect your spending patterns. However, remember that this will require you to reduce your allotment for another category to keep your budget balanced.

A budget is not a rigid schedule that must remain constant. When there is a need to change the budget, do so. Your budget should work for you, not against you.

Reducing Flexible Expenses

If you want to cut down your food spending, look at what you buy and where you buy it.

Food

Fast-foods and restaurant meals tend to be the most costly items. If you eat out often, you can probably save money by cooking at home instead. See 17-24. If you already do a lot of cooking, think about what you buy at the grocery store. If you buy expensive convenience foods, you will find cooking from scratch can save

17-24

Preparing this meal at home would be less costly than purchasing it in a restaurant.

you money. If you are short on time, try preparing dishes on weekends and freezing them for weekday use.

Snack foods purchased on the go can add a lot to the food budget. If you buy a snack every day, add up the cost over a year. You may be surprised when you discover how much you are spending.

Clothing

You can save money by purchasing good-quality clothes. Well-made, durable garments may cost a little more, but they need not be replaced often. Buy clothes made for laundering to avoid dry-cleaning costs. If you know how to sew, you can save money by making your own clothes. You can also do your own repairs and alterations instead of paying someone to do them for you.

Transportation

The transportation category includes the cost of cars and other vehicles used. Gasoline, oil, and upkeep are in this category. Also included are fares for those who travel by bus, train, or plane. Saving money in this category may seem difficult. If you must drive to work, you need a car. However, you may be able to save quite a bit if you can form a car pool with friends. Another option might be to use public transportation instead of driving.

Recreation

Any money spent solely for relaxation and pleasure belongs in this category. The amount of money you spend depends on the types of activities you do. Bowling costs less than skiing. Renting a video is cheaper than buying a theater ticket. Going camping is less costly than taking a cruise, 17-25. Evaluate recreation expenses

17-25
Fishing is an inexpensive recreational activity that adults can share with children.

in relation to other expenses. Then decide how much money you are willing to spend on recreational activities.

Other Expenses

Miscellaneous expenses can make or break your budget. Such expenses might include grooming products and services, school supplies, and gifts. Evaluate how much money you spend on these items. You might decide that you need to have separate budget categories for them.

Future Expenses

Your budget categories are likely to change as you grow older. As you gain independence, you will become responsible for more of your own expenses. Such expenses include utilities, home repairs, furnishings, and health care. Learning to plan your spending now will help you live within a budget in the future.

Unexpected Expenses

Sometimes expenses occur that are not anticipated. Every person needs an emergency fund they can tap to meet unexpected needs. These can include loss of income or health emergencies. Many people build a savings account to meet these needs. You will read more about savings accounts in Chapter 18.

Budgeting with a Computer

A computer with appropriate software can make money management and record keeping easier. A year-end printout can help you quickly complete income tax forms and plan a budget for the next year.

Most bills can be paid online. You can set up billing accounts to electronically deduct the payment amount from your checking or savings account. You can even set the transfer to happen automatically on a certain day each month. If you choose to pay bills online, take steps to protect yourself from identity theft. Make sure Web sites are secure before transmitting any personal or financial information.

A computer is also helpful for keeping track of investments. It can easily calculate figures for dividends, rates of return, capital gains, and depreciations. This saves time and improves accuracy when planning future investments. See 17-26.

17-26
A home computer can make family budgeting, bill paying, and investment analysis easier.

Check It Out!

1. Give three examples of fringe benefits.
2. Explain the difference between gross income and net income.
3. What are the six steps in developing a budget?
4. True or false. Fast-foods and restaurant meals tend to be the most costly items in a food budget.
5. How can a computer be used to help manage money?

Chapter Review

Summary

Learning to manage involves identifying your goals, recognizing your values and standards, and determining your resources. You can learn to use both human and material resources to reach your goals. Then you must form a plan, put it into action, and evaluate the results.

Managing your life also involves learning how to solve problems and make decisions. Some decisions are routine, while others are more complex. Using the decision-making process is a skill you can use to help make the best decisions for you. To be an effective manager, you need to learn to use the management process.

One of the most important material resources to manage is time. By managing it well, you can achieve short- and long-term goals. You can even address your visionary goals.

In return for your hard work on the job, you receive a paycheck. Understanding what comes out of your paycheck is important for budgeting. A budget is a helpful tool for managing money to reach financial goals. To establish a budget, you must determine your sources of income and estimate your fixed and flexible expenses. After evaluation, you may find it necessary to reduce some of your flexible expenses to balance your budget.

Think About It!

1. State a long-term or short-term personal goal that you would like to achieve. What resources do you already have to help you reach that goal? What other resources will you need?
2. Do you have any visionary goals? How does this goal influence the way you approach short-term goals and long-term goals?
3. What community and natural resources do you use most frequently?
4. Discuss the relationship between problem solving and decision making.
5. How do you think the management process would be useful to teens?
6. Which time management strategies would be especially useful for teens to try?
7. List some of your flexible expenses and give suggestions for reducing them.
8. How might the information you learned in this chapter help you in your career?

Try It Out!

1. Write a biographical sketch of an imaginary person. Set a long-term goal for this person. Then set several short-term goals to help the person reach his or her long-term goal. Finally, list the resources the person could use to reach the goals.
2. Choose a real or imaginary problem. Write a paper explaining how you could use the decision-making process to solve the problem.

3. Write a short story about a family who learned to use the management process. Show how it improves their family life.

4. Next month, create to-do lists and weekly plans. Then write a brief report on what you learned about how well you use time.

5. Create a bulletin board showing how paycheck deductions are used to fund government programs and facilities.

6. Prepare a weekly budget for yourself. After following it for two weeks, write an evaluation describing its usefulness. Also note any adjustments you would want to make in the budget.

Chapter 18
Achieving Financial Strength

Careers

These careers relate to the topics in this chapter:
▼ credit counselor
▼ account manager
▼ insurance broker
▼ family economics specialist

As you study the chapter, see if you can think of others.

Topics

Topic 18-1

Using Financial Services

Objectives

After studying this topic, you will be able to
▼ describe various services offered by financial institutions.
▼ write and endorse checks correctly.
▼ balance a checkbook.

Topic Terms

certified check
cashier's check
endorse
account statement
reconciling
overdraft

18-1
Money saved at home will not earn interest or be protected from theft as it would at a financial institution.

As a child, you may have kept pennies in a piggy bank. That method of handling money may have worked well for you then. When you start earning money, however, you should start dealing with financial institutions. Piggy banks lack the safety and earnings potential found at financial institutions. See 18-1.

Financial Services

Commercial banks, mutual savings banks, savings and loan associations, and credit unions are all financial institutions. Though there are differences among them, each offers a range of financial services.

When selecting a financial institution, you will want to consider its services. Saving money, making payments, and obtaining loans are the most common financial services used. These services and

their features differ from one institution to another. You must decide which financial services are important to you. Then you should look for an institution that offers the services that meet your needs.

Savings Accounts

Savings accounts are a key service available through financial institutions. These accounts pay various amounts of interest. Some accounts have restrictions regarding the length of time money must stay on deposit. (Section 18-2, "Saving for the Future," will discuss savings accounts in more detail.)

Checking Accounts

One of the main financial services people want is a checking account. Checking accounts are sometimes called *demand deposits*. That means money in them is available on demand. You can demand a sum of money from a checking account simply by writing a check. Several types of checking accounts are available. Some earn interest; others do not.

Debit Cards

A *debit card* shows that you have an established checking account with the financial institution identified on the card. It looks like a credit card and is swiped through a point-of-sale terminal in much the same way. However, swiping the card immediately transfers payment from your checking account. You may have to key in a security code called a *PIN* (personal identification number.) Using a debit card is a quick, easy method of payment that does not require showing other forms of identification.

You will need to record each transaction immediately in your checkbook, just as you do when writing checks. Debit purchases are itemized on your monthly checking account statement.

Electronic Banking

Electronic banking, or *e-banking*, is banking through your telephone or computer. Through e-banking, you can retrieve information about your accounts, move money between accounts, or make payments. To do this, you will need to set up a phone account through your bank. For Internet banking, your bank's Web site will guide you in setting up usernames and passwords for your account.

One of the greatest advantages of e-banking is that you can do your banking from home at any time of day. You can pay bills without mailing checks and worrying about the time it takes for them to be delivered. E-banking also allows you to more easily manage your accounts. See 18-2.

18-2
Once you have set up your account for Internet banking, you can easily pay bills using your computer.

One disadvantage is that you will not be able to e-bank when your computer or the bank's computer system is down. There are also concerns about the security of e-banking. However, banks are working hard to make the systems secure. You can also take precautions. Always make sure you are at a secure Web site before transmitting any personal or financial information. Never transmit usernames or passwords through e-mail.

Automated Teller Machines (ATMs)

Automated teller machines offer people the flexibility of banking at any time. ATMs are available locally in a variety of convenient locations, including shopping malls and convenience stores. See 18-3. To use an ATM, you need a special banking card with a PIN. The card and PIN number allow a customer to access his or her accounts, withdraw cash, and make deposits.

Some ATM cards can also be used as debit cards. When making a debit purchase

18-3
Automated teller machines provide routine banking services 24 hours a day.

or using the ATM card to withdraw cash, always record the transaction immediately in your checkbook.

Loans

Loans are another service many people seek from financial institutions. People apply for both short- and long-term loans. They may borrow money to pay existing bills or make purchases, such as major appliances, cars, and houses.

Different types of financial institutions make loans for different types of purchases. For instance, some institutions loan money for a home purchase, but not a car purchase. Check to be sure your financial institution makes the type of loan you are seeking.

Certified and Cashier's Checks

Some individuals and businesses will not honor personal checks from people they do not know well. In these cases, a certified check may be a more acceptable form of payment. A **certified check** is simply a personal check for which the financial institution guarantees payment. When the institution certifies your check, the amount of the check is immediately deducted from your account to reserve it for the payee.

If you do not have a checking account, you may have a financial institution issue a **cashier's check**. This is a check drawn on the institution's own funds and signed by an officer of the institution. You present the money to the institution along with the name of the payee. The institution then issues a check made out to that person or business. If you have a savings account in the financial institution, the money can be withdrawn from that account.

Traveler's Checks

Many financial institutions offer traveler's checks. They are a convenient source of money for travelers who do not want to carry large amounts of cash. These checks are accepted around the world. If traveler's checks are lost, they can be quickly replaced by providing the serial numbers of the lost checks.

Safe-Deposit Boxes

Many financial institutions have safe-deposit boxes that can be rented by their customers. These boxes are usually located in a vault for protection from theft and fire. Safe-deposit boxes are used to store valuable items, such as jewelry and coins. They are also used to store important papers, such as a marriage license, deed to property, citizenship papers, or stocks and bonds.

Other Financial Services

Financial institutions may offer a number of other services for customer convenience. These include credit cards, drive-up windows, estate management, brokerage accounts, and financial counseling. Special services like these are worth considering when you select financial institutions.

Types of Institutions

You can choose from among several types of financial institutions to provide the services you desire. When people speak of banks, they usually mean *commercial banks*. See 18-4. They are owned by stockholders and are run for a profit. Commercial banks offer a great variety of services to both businesses and individuals.

All *mutual savings banks* are owned by their depositors rather than by stockholders. The owners/investors decide the interest rates. The interest paid to depositors will depend on profits from the banks' investments. *Savings and loan associations* may be operated either like commercial banks or like mutual savings banks.

Credit unions are nonprofit financial institutions owned and operated by members. A credit union is usually sponsored by a company or professional association. Membership is open only to people associated with the sponsoring organization. At credit unions, the rate of interest is usually high for deposits and low for loans.

Before choosing a financial institution, do some comparison shopping. Interest rates vary among different institutions. This applies to interest earned on savings accounts as well as interest charged on loans. When saving or borrowing money, compare the rates of all institutions available to you. Find the one that best suits you.

18-4
Commercial banks are the most common type of financial institution.

Using a Checking Account

A checking account is convenient for making purchases and paying bills. Money needed for these expenses can be held in a checking account. Anytime payment needs to be made, you can simply use a debit card or write a check, 18-5. When a check is cashed, the amount of the check is withdrawn from your account. Use of a debit card, on the other hand, withdraws money immediately.

Types of Accounts

Different types of checking accounts are available. With some checking accounts, you need a minimum amount to open the account. Interest earned by the bank on this balance pays for the costs of handling the account. You usually do not pay service

18-5
A customer can write a check for a purchase rather than paying cash.

charges, except for purchasing personal checks. If the account balance falls below the minimum required, however, you must pay a service charge.

Some checking accounts do not require a minimum balance. For such an account, you usually pay a service charge. This covers the financial institution's cost of handling the account. This charge may be a monthly fee, a set fee for each check written, or both.

Some checking accounts pay interest if you maintain a balance over a certain amount. This is an advantage for people who keep a large amount of money in their checking accounts. They will not lose the interest they would otherwise be earning in a savings account.

When deciding which type of account to open, determine how much money you can afford to keep in the account. Think about how much you are willing to pay for service fees. Consider how important it is for you to earn interest. Then choose the type of account that best meets your needs.

Opening an Account and Making a Deposit

When you open a checking account, you will be asked to sign a *signature card*. The financial institution keeps this card on file to compare with signatures made during transactions. This helps to eliminate forgeries. When opening a checking account, you will need to specify the type of account you want. If you are the only person who will write checks on the account, you will open an individual account. If someone else, such as a spouse, will also use the account, you will open a joint account.

To add money to your checking account, you simply fill out a deposit slip. Write the date on the appropriate line. Sign the slip if you want to receive cash from the deposit. List specifically what is being deposited—currency, coins, or checks—and the exact amount of each. Total the amount of the deposit. Subtract the amount you want to receive, if any. Then figure the net deposit. See 18-6.

Writing a Check

A check instructs your financial institution to pay a certain sum of money to a person or company. Checks should be clearly written in ink. Be sure to fill in all the following information in the appropriate spaces, as shown in 18-7:

▼ *date*
▼ *name of the individual or group to whom you are paying the money*—Be sure the name is spelled correctly.
▼ *amount of payment in numerals*—Write close to the dollar sign to prevent anyone from inserting a number to change the amount.
▼ *amount of payment in words*—Begin writing as far to the left as possible.

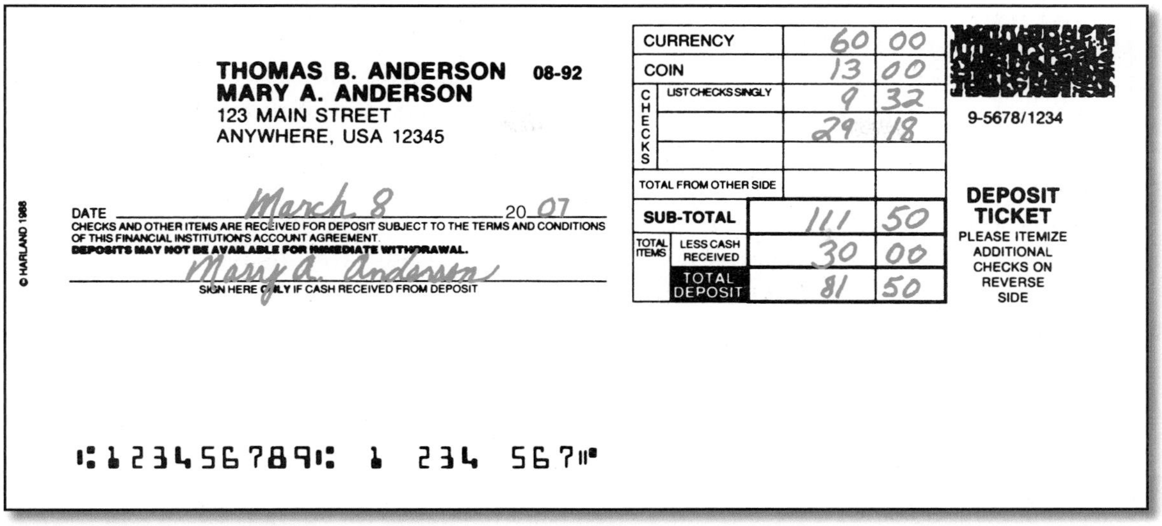

18-6

A deposit slip must accompany cash or checks being deposited in a checking account.

After writing the dollar amount, write the word *and*. Then write the amount of cents as a fraction of 100. For instance, 37 cents is written as 37/100. When writing a check for an even dollar amount, write *00/100* or *no/100*. Draw a line through the remaining space.

▼ *purpose of the check*—This brief note serves as a quick reference when you balance your checkbook.

▼ *your signature*—Sign the check exactly as you signed the signature card when you opened the account.

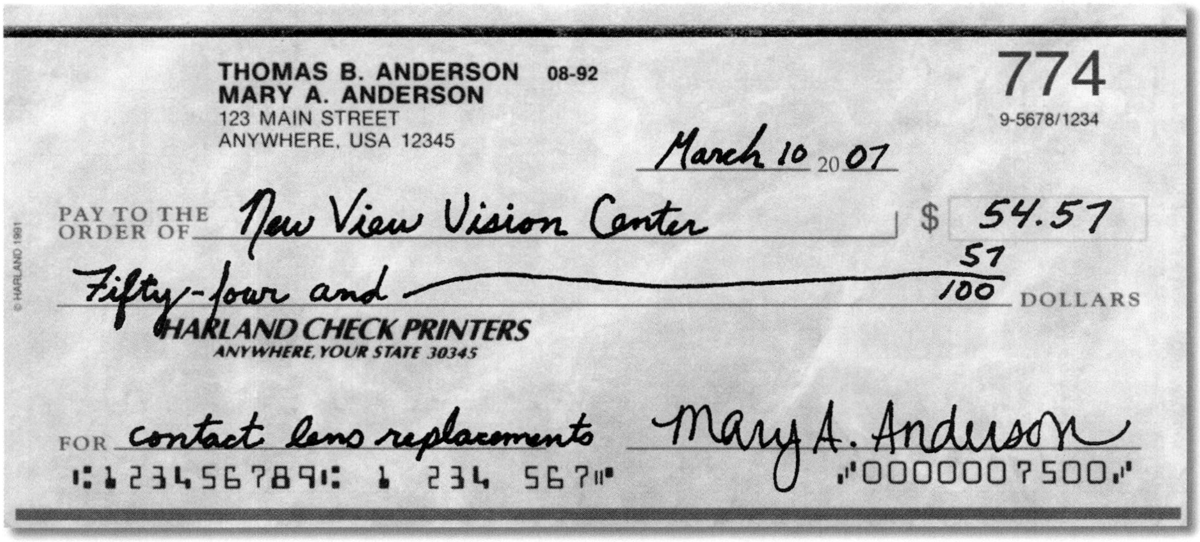

18-7

This check is correctly written.

Keep an accurate record of all checks written. A check stub or register is provided for record keeping. Complete the check stub or fill in the register at the time that you use your debit card or write a check. Record the number of the check, date, payee, and amount. Subtract the amount from your balance so you always know how much money is in your account. This will keep you from writing checks when you do not have sufficient funds. See 18-8.

Endorsing a Check

Before you can cash or deposit a check that has been written to you, you must **endorse** it. This means you must sign your name on the back, at the left end of the check. The signature on the back must match the name on the face of the check.

There are two kinds of endorsements. The first type of endorsement, a *blank endorsement*, is the payee's signature only.

If a check bearing a blank endorsement is lost, it can be cashed by anyone. The

RECORD ALL CHARGES OR CREDITS THAT AFFECT YOUR ACCOUNT							
NUMBER	DATE	DESCRIPTION OF TRANSACTION	PAYMENT/DEBIT (-)	√ T	FEE (IF ANY) (-)	DEPOSIT/CREDIT (+)	BALANCE $ 143 | 38
	3-8	Deposit	$		$	$ 81 | 50	81 | 50
							224 | 88
774	3-10	New View Vision Center contact lens replacements	54 | 57				54 | 57
							170 | 31
775	3-13	Edison Electric electric bill	44 | 40				44 | 40
							125 | 91
776	3-18	Image Salon haircut	24 | 00				24 | 00
							101 | 91
	3-22	Deposit				467 | 20	467 | 20
							569 | 11
777	3-28	Sloan Realty rent	395 | 00				395 | 00
							174 | 11
778	3-2	Alum Creek United Church offering	30 | 00				30 | 00
							144 | 11
779	3-3	Brownie's Market groceries	27 | 63				27 | 63
							116 | 48
780	4-4	Lakeshore Home Economics April meeting	20 | 00				20 | 00
							96 | 48
	4-5	Deposit				420 | 48	420 | 48
							516 | 96

18-8

A check register keeps track of how much money is in a checking account.

finder needs only to sign the check below the first signature. For this reason, always wait until you are ready to cash or deposit the check before using a blank endorsement.

The second type of endorsement is a *restrictive endorsement*. It states specifically what is to be done with the check. *For deposit only* is a common restrictive endorsement. When used, it means the check cannot be exchanged for cash. The amount of the check must be deposited in the account of the person named in the endorsement.

Pay to the order of is another common restrictive endorsement. This type of endorsement names the person who will endorse the check. No one but the person named in the endorsement can cash the check. See 18-9.

Balancing Your Checkbook

Your financial institution will send you a monthly, bimonthly, or quarterly summary of your checking account. This summary is called an **account statement**. This statement lists checks, deposits, withdrawals, charges, and interest earnings on the account.

When you receive an account statement, you will begin a process called **reconciling**. You will compare the account statement to your check stubs or register. The institution's record should match yours. This is known as balancing your checkbook.

In most cases, the financial institution will enclose *canceled checks* with the account statement. The checks you wrote that are not returned with the statement are called *outstanding checks*. These checks were not yet cashed when the statement was made.

Some financial institutions do not return canceled checks. However, the statements they issue will list each check by amount and check number. In this way, you will be able to tell which checks were cashed.

Compare the canceled checks with those listed on the statement. Then compare them with your record of checks written. In your check register or on the

18-9

A check must be endorsed with a blank or restrictive endorsement before it can be cashed or deposited.

check stubs, mark off the checks that have been returned to you. Also mark off any deposits and other withdrawals shown on the statement. If the financial institution has made any service charges, subtract them from the balance in your checkbook. Likewise, if you have earned interest on your account, add that amount to your checkbook balance.

At this point, a little math will help you see if your checkbook has balanced. Most account statements have a worksheet printed on the back to help you with the math. See 18-10. Complete the following steps in the spaces provided on the worksheet:

1. Write the closing balance shown on the bank statement.
2. List the deposits you have made that are not shown on the statement.
3. Add the amounts from steps 1 and 2 and record the total.
4. List by number and amount all outstanding checks and withdrawals. Find the total and record it.
5. Subtract the total in step 4 from that in step 3. The difference should match the balance shown in your checkbook. What should you do if the balance on the statement does not match yours? Begin by double-checking your math. Be sure you have made no errors before you question the financial institution about its statement.

Balancing your checkbook promptly is always wise. Financial institutions can make errors. You should not depend completely on them to keep your account in order. The sooner you notice an error, the sooner it can be corrected.

There is another good reason for balancing your checkbook promptly. People who neglect this task are more likely to write **overdrafts**. These are checks written when there is not enough money in the account to cover them. They are also known as checks that bounce.

Most financial institutions fine account holders for writing overdrafts. Many businesses also fine customers who write overdrafts in payment for goods or services. The total fines for an overdraft can easily exceed $40. Thus, writing an overdraft can be costly as well as embarrassing. See 18-11.

BALANCING WORKSHEET

CHECKS OUTSTANDING
(Written but not shown on statement because not yet received by Bank.)

MONTH _March 1-31_, 20 _07_

BANK BALANCE shown on this statement $ _174.11_

ADD + $ _420.48_

DEPOSITS made but not shown on statement because made or received after date of this statement.

TOTAL $ _594.59_

SUBTRACT –

CHECKS OUTSTANDING ..... $ _77.63_

BALANCE .... $ _516.96_

The above balance should be the same as the up-to-date balance in your checkbook.

NO.	$	
778	30	00
779	27	63
780	20	00
TOTAL	77	63

18-10

A form such as this is often printed on the back of a bank account statement to help customers balance their checkbooks.

18-11
Retail businesses often post signs warning customers of a fee charged on returned checks.

Check It Out!

1. List six financial services offered by financial institutions.
2. How does a debit card differ from a credit card?
3. What are the two types of check endorsements?
4. Give two reasons for balancing a checkbook promptly.

Topic 18-2
Saving for the Future

Objectives

After studying this topic, you will be able to
▼ explain why it is important to save money.
▼ list five factors to consider when deciding how to save.
▼ describe various types of savings accounts.
▼ determine why people need to plan their estates.

Topic Terms

liquidity
certificate of deposit
securities
stock
dividend
bond
mutual fund
portfolio
diversified
estate
will

Putting some money in savings before making other purchases is a wise decision. Later, if you need money, it will be available. You also earn additional money on savings in the form of interest.

Why Save?

Why should I save? When should I use the money in my savings? The answers to these two common questions vary for different people. A few facts about savings might help reveal the right answers for you.

▼ Money in a savings account will be available to spend for future wants and needs.

▼ Savings can be the most direct path to your long-term goals. By saving, you can make purchases that would otherwise be beyond your reach.

▼ Money in a savings account can be considered an emergency fund. As a rule, a person should have at least three-months' income saved to cover any emergencies that might arise.

▼ Savings can ensure that retirement will not put a strain on your standard of living. The sooner you begin to plan and save for retirement, the more money you will have when you retire. See 18-12.

Factors in Deciding How to Save

You should consider five factors in deciding how to save. These factors are safety, returns, liquidity, purchasing power, and convenience.

18-12
People can enjoy financial freedom during their retirement if they budget well and save money while employed.

Safety is the most important factor regarding savings. Savings should be protected against loss, theft, fire, and other risks. Financial institutions offer built-in safety through guards and vaults. However, most of them also insure savings accounts up to $100,000.

Another consideration is the *rate of return* you will earn on your savings. Savings institutions offer different interest rates on accounts. They also calculate interest in a variety of ways. You should investigate each savings option to find the highest rate of return available to you.

When deciding how to save you will need to evaluate the **liquidity** of your funds. This is the degree to which you will be able to get cash quickly. A high degree of liquidity is important for savings that must quickly be used for emergencies. Some savings accounts pay very high interest, but withdrawal of funds is restricted. Planning your savings so that some cash will be immediately available without loss of interest is always wise.

Purchasing power is a fourth factor in deciding how to save. Your savings should be protected against inflation. Savings in stocks, bonds, and real estate are usually considered better protection against inflation than savings accounts. These investments usually increase in value in step with inflation. They do not offer liquidity, however. Once money is invested in them, you may not be able to get it back for several years.

Convenience is also a factor you will want to keep in mind when deciding how to save. A financial institution near your home or along your route to work is very convenient for routine services, 18-13.

18-13

A drive-up feature at a local financial institution makes it convenient for saving money.

Savings Accounts

Savings institutions offer several types of savings accounts. Be sure you understand the terms of the account you select.

Regular Savings Accounts

Regular savings accounts allow deposits and withdrawals to be made in any amount at any time. This savings account pays the lowest interest rates, but provides the greatest liquidity.

Certificates of Deposit

Another type of savings account is a **certificate of deposit (CD)**. CDs pay a set rate of interest on money that is deposited for a set period of time. A higher interest rate is paid on CDs than on regular savings accounts. Interest rates on such accounts vary according to the length of time the money must be left on deposit.

Setting the Scene: Pay Yourself First

Tameka has taken her first job and is excited about her forthcoming paycheck. Her grandfather says, "You have a lifetime of earning power ahead of you. Pay yourself first. Start with an amount you know you can afford and increase the amount periodically. You will have it when you need it most."

Analyze It: What does Tameka's grandfather mean by "pay yourself first"? Assuming she is earning minimum wage, what percentage of Tameka's income would you suggest she save? If she pays herself first, how can she manage to pay her other bills? How can she ensure the greatest financial gain on her savings?

A minimum deposit is required for most CDs. All CDs can be cashed before maturity. However, doing this will result in a loss of interest income and a penalty fee.

Decisions About Securities

Most people invest money in one way or another to provide for their future needs. When people talk about investments, they often are referring to securities. **Securities** are proof of debt or ownership of a company or government. This proof is often in the form of stocks and bonds.

Why Invest in Securities?

Investments put your money to work for you. Securities have a few advantages over savings accounts.

▼ Long-term prices of securities have increased almost steadily. This has made their average annual increase in value greater than interest rates on savings accounts.

▼ Inflation is an economic factor commonly at work in the economy. It causes money to decrease in value. Due to the higher long-term returns on securities, however, they offset the effects of inflation better than savings accounts do.

▼ The long-term trend of the U.S. economy has been upward for many years. Purchasing securities provides a way to participate in this economic growth, which is not offered by savings accounts.

Stocks

Stocks are certificates that represent ownership of a small portion of a company. When people buy shares of stock in a company, they are actually buying part of that company. By selling stock, the company makes money to conduct its business. Stockholders take part in the business by electing the board of directors. The directors run the company for the benefit of all the owners.

A stockholder shares in the profits and losses of the company. Some of the company's profits are distributed to stockholders as **dividends**. Some of the profits are reinvested in the company to help it grow. If the company makes no profit, the value of its stock usually goes down. If the company fails, the investment will be completely lost. See 18-14.

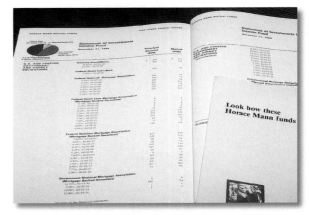

18-14
A stockbroker can provide information on the stock of individual companies as well as on funds that combine stock from several companies.

Bonds

Bonds are certificates that represent a promise by a company or government to repay a loan on a given date. Companies sell corporate bonds. In effect, the companies are borrowing money from the people who buy the bonds. Companies promise to pay a certain amount of interest on these loans. The loans are repaid in full when the bonds reach maturity.

Governments also sell bonds. The federal government issues Series EE savings bonds that can be bought for half their face value. For instance, a $50 bond can be bought for $25. If the bond is held until its maturity date, it can be cashed for $50. Bonds can be cashed before maturity at a reduced interest rate. These savings bonds can be bought at most savings institutions. They are a safe investment. See 18-15.

Local governments sell bonds, too. These are called *municipal bonds*. Voters are often asked to approve bond sales in local elections. Funds from municipal bonds may be used for such projects as building schools or improving streets.

18-15
U.S. savings bonds are a good investment, especially if held until the maturity date.

Mutual Funds

A **mutual fund** is a group of many investments purchased by a company representing many investors. These funds are classified according to the types of investments purchased and called a **portfolio**. When you buy a share of a mutual fund, you become part owner of everything in that portfolio. There are stock funds, bond funds, and balanced funds that include stocks and bonds.

Many people prefer to invest in mutual funds rather than directly in stocks or bonds. The investment is basically the same, but there is less risk. A mutual fund offers three advantages to the casual investor.

▼ A professional fund manager does the buying and selling. Individual investors rely on that person's expertise to manage the fund.

▼ The investment is **diversified**. This means money is invested in many different stocks and bonds, so decreases in some are offset by increase in others. Overall, the investor is likely to make good returns on the total investment.

▼ Mutual funds have good liquidity. They are much easier and quicker to buy and sell than individual stocks and bonds.

401k Retirement Plans

A *401k retirement plan* is offered by some employers. The employer sets up a *trust*, a legal entity that holds assets benefiting more than one person. Full-time employees are allowed to contribute money from their paychecks before it is taxed. This savings builds retirement funds. It also delays and perhaps reduces taxes. You will pay taxes when you withdraw the funds. If you wait to withdraw the funds until after you have retired, you may be in a lower tax bracket.

Individual Retirement Accounts (IRA)

An *individual retirement account (IRA)* is another investing tool. You invest money into the account, and the interest compounds over time. Taxes are usually deferred until retirement. Rules establish the amount that can be invested. You save in the long term by paying taxes on your savings at a lower rate when you retire.

Planning an Estate

An **estate** is what a person leaves behind when he or she dies. People who have saved and invested throughout their lives generally have plans for their estates. They want their property to be distributed in a certain way. Perhaps they want to be sure to provide support for their survivors. Maybe they want to donate funds to a favorite charity. In order for their wishes to be fulfilled, they must take appropriate legal steps. Otherwise, their estates will be distributed according to state laws.

A **will** is a legal document describing how a person wants his or her property to be distributed after death. It specifies who will be in charge of carrying out the deceased person's wishes. See 18-16.

18-16
A lawyer can help a person make a will that directs how his or her estate will be handled.

One main reason parents need to prepare wills is to name legal guardians for their children. If they do not do this, the court will become responsible for the children. The court can then name any legal guardian. This guardian may or may not be the person whom the parents would have chosen.

Wills may be written or oral. However, a written will prepared by an attorney is the most legally binding. This type of will provides the greatest protection against disputes by unhappy heirs.

People have many options as they plan their estates. The size of the estate and the goals of the individual affect those options. Lawyers, bankers, investment counselors, insurance agents, and accountants can assist with estate planning.

Check It Out!

1. Give two reasons for saving money.
2. What are the five factors that should be considered when deciding how to save?
3. Which type of savings account allows deposits and withdrawals to be made at any time?
4. A portfolio of diversified investments purchased by a company representing many investors is called a _____ _____.
5. List four professionals who can assist people with estate planning.

Topic 18-3

Meeting Insurance Needs

Objectives

After studying this topic, you will be able to
▼ describe different kinds of insurance protection.
▼ evaluate the types of insurance that you will need.

Topic Terms

policy
policyholder
premium
beneficiary
cash value
loan value
deductible
co-insurance
copayment
health maintenance organization (HMO)
preferred provider organization (PPO)

Nobody likes to think about getting sick, injured, or killed. However, these events are realities of life. Preparing for them can make them less devastating. One way to prepare is to purchase insurance. Insurance can protect your investments, provide for your loved ones, and cover costs of damage repairs and medical treatments. See 18-17.

Insurance Basics

Insurance is a risk-sharing plan. Insurance companies offer a way in which many people can unite to protect each other from income losses. These losses may be

18-17
Homeowner's insurance will cover the cost of replacing a home destroyed by a fire.

due to death, disability, natural disasters, thefts, accidents, or other misfortunes.

Insurance contracts are called **policies**. A person who has a policy is called a **policyholder**. A policyholder agrees to regularly pay a certain amount of money, called a **premium**, to the insurance company. In return, the insurance company provides financial protection for the policyholder in the event of a misfortune covered in the policy.

When an insurance company collects premiums from policyholders, the money is promptly invested. In this way, the premiums earn money for the insurance company. The insurance company uses part of the earnings to pay the claims made by policyholders. Some earnings are also used to cover the company's operating expenses.

A good insurance agent will help you determine the types of insurance you need. The agent will also help you find a plan you can afford to provide the amount of coverage you need.

The information that follows describes several types of insurance that you are likely to buy.

Life Insurance

Life insurance is protection against financial loss due to death. This type of protection is especially important for people who have dependents. A *dependent* is someone, such as a spouse, child, or elderly parent, who relies on another person for financial support. See 18-18. Life insurance should be bought when a person begins to have financial responsibility.

Most families carry life insurance on the parent who is the chief wage earner. However, some insurance should be carried on both parents. Should either parent die, survivors need protection against the loss of that parent's income and services.

When a life insurance policyholder dies, the insurance company pays the *death benefit* of the policy, called *face value*. The person who receives the death benefit is called the **beneficiary**.

Two basic types of life insurance are available—term and whole life. Many variations of each type are available. You should know the difference between the basic types, then obtain the advice of a reliable agent to help determine your needs.

Term Insurance

Term insurance covers the owner of a policy for a specific number of years. The most common term policies available are annually renewable, 5-year renewable, 10-year renewable, 20-year renewable,

18-18
Life insurance protects dependents from a loss of income due to a wage earner's death.

The More You Know: Tips for Financial Well-Being

You will need to plan for your financial well-being just as you plan other aspects of your life. Some key tips can help you do this.

First, know the difference between needs and wants and focus on your needs. Try to pay as you go instead of using credit. If you do use credit, know the amount of interest you are paying. Keep accurate records so you can take advantage of tax deductions. Prepare for possible devastating losses by maintaining a regular savings plan and buying insurance coverage.

and term to age 65. At the end of the term, coverage stops. Benefits are payable only if the policyholder dies within the term.

If you buy term insurance, look for a policy with a *renewal privilege*. This allows the policyholder to renew the policy without having a physical examination. Without a renewal privilege, you might not be able to obtain more insurance when the term expires. A term policy may also carry a *convertible clause*. Under this clause, the owner may later exchange the term policy for a whole life policy without a physical examination.

Whole Life Insurance

Whole life insurance covers the policyholder for a lifetime rather than for a specific number of years. Whole life policies acquire cash value and loan value after premiums have been paid for at least two years. **Cash value** is the amount the policyholder can collect if he or she decides to give up the policy. **Loan value** is the amount the policyholder can borrow from the insurance company using the cash value as collateral. The cash value and the loan value are usually equal.

When choosing whole life policies, you have two basic options. One option is called a *straight life policy*. Fixed premiums based on your age at the time you buy the policy are paid throughout your lifetime. The second option is a policy that can be purchased outright over a shorter period of time. These policies are called *limited payment life policies*.

Universal Life Insurance

A relatively new form of life insurance is universal life insurance. It combines term insurance with an investment feature. The cash value accumulated on the policy is invested to earn interest. The return will vary from year to year as a result of the insurer's investment success.

Health Insurance

Health care is expensive. The costs of medical checkups, medicine, and hospital care can add up quickly. Health insurance helps cover these costs.

Many people are able to get health insurance coverage through a group plan. Companies, unions, and professional organizations often offer group plans. With these plans, all members of the group can buy the insurance at reduced rates. Employers may pay all or part of the cost of premiums as an employee benefit.

People who do not have group plans available to them may purchase health insurance individually. However, the premiums are generally higher. See 18-19.

18-19
For many people, a key factor in selecting health insurance is being able to see the doctor of their choice.

Health insurance policies differ in terms of what they cover. Evaluate a policy carefully before making a purchasing decision. Find out whether certain illnesses are excluded from coverage. See if there are any limits on the amount of costs that will be covered.

Most insurance policies do not pay 100 percent of a policyholder's medical expenses, even for items that are covered. Some policies have provisions for deductibles, co-insurance, and copayments. A **deductible** is an amount that a policyholder must pay before the insurance company will pay anything. If you have a $250 deductible, you would pay the first $250 of medical expenses covered by the insurance. The insurance company would pay the remaining expenses covered. **Co-insurance** requires the policyholder to pay a certain percentage of medical costs. Many co-insurance policies cover 80 percent, requiring policyholders to pay the remaining 20 percent. **Copayments** are small, fixed fees for certain items or services. For instance, you may have a $20 copayment for each doctor visit. These provisions help defray the costs of settling insurance claims and therefore reduce premiums.

Types of Health Coverage

Like health care, health insurance is expensive. The cost of insurance premiums may seem high. However, medical expenses can lead to financial ruin if you do not have insurance. Think about whether you could afford to pay medical bills without insurance coverage. If so, you might decide not to purchase a certain type of coverage.

Three main types of health insurance coverage are available. These are basic medical coverage, major medical coverage, and disability insurance.

Basic medical coverage pays standard hospital costs. These costs include room, meals, nursing care, drugs, X rays, and laboratory tests. Some policies also pay for doctor visits and simple medical procedures.

Major medical coverage pays the bulk of expenses resulting from major illness or serious injury. It covers surgery and other expenses not covered by a basic medical policy. See 18-20.

Disability insurance provides payments for people who are unable to work because of illness or injury. It generally pays two thirds of a person's gross salary.

Workers' Compensation

Workers' compensation is a type of health insurance required by state law. It is carried by employers to provide benefits for employees who suffer illness or injuries due to their work environment. Private insurance companies handle the policies. Medical expenses, hospitalization, lost wages, and a disability pension are included in the coverage.

Health Maintenance Organizations

A **health maintenance organization (HMO)** is a group of medical professionals and facilities that provides health care services to members. HMO members pay a flat fee regularly. When medical service is needed, members go to a doctor associated with their HMO. They receive care at little or no added cost.

It is less costly to prevent an illness than to cure one. Therefore, HMOs focus on preventative health care. Because the charge, if any, for office visits is minimal, members are encouraged to get regular checkups. This eliminates the need for more costly health procedures that result from a lack of routine care.

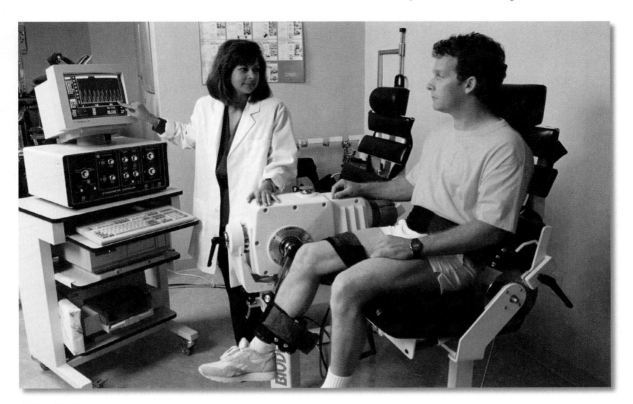

18-20
Major medical coverage often includes the cost of rehabilitation after surgery.

Preferred Provider Organizations

A **preferred provider organization (PPO)** is a group of doctors and medical facilities that contract to provide services at reduced rates. PPOs make agreements with employers or insurance companies. They designate fixed fees and terms for the health care services to be provided.

PPOs benefit all involved. The employer or insurance company can better control medical care costs. The doctors and hospitals have more clients. Patients pay less for health care when they use the preferred provider.

Before you choose a PPO, know who the preferred providers are. Find out what services are provided. Be aware of the costs. All doctors do not participate in PPOs; neither do all hospitals. You may see a doctor who is not a member of the PPO, but it will cost you more. Be sure you have access to the health services you will need before you join.

Automobile Insurance

Because automobile insurance premiums are high, many people are tempted to drive without insurance. This is not a wise decision. The losses from a single accident could destroy a family's financial security. In addition, states require drivers to be responsible for accidents in which they are at fault. Having insurance is one way to prove responsibility. See 18-21.

18-21
Everyone who drives a car should be protected by automobile insurance.

Types of Auto Coverage

An automobile insurance policy usually includes several kinds of coverage. The six basic types of coverage are: bodily injury liability, property damage liability, medical payments, uninsured motorists, comprehensive physical damage, and collision.

Bodily injury liability covers you if you are legally liable for the death or injury of others. Bodily injury pays for any loss of earning ability as well as medical expenses of the injured. It pays the legal fees and the damages assessed against you, up to the limits of the policy. Liability insurance covers the car's owner. It may also cover anyone else who drives the car with the owner's permission. The amount of coverage is usually stated in two amounts.

For instance, $100,000-$300,000 coverage means the insurance company will pay up to $100,000 for any single injury and up to $300,000 for any single accident.

Property damage liability pays for damages that your car causes to the property of others. Like bodily injury liability, it will also pay legal fees. It does not pay for damages to your property—your car.

Medical payments coverage pays medical costs resulting from an accident regardless of who was at fault. It covers anyone in your car if your car is involved in an accident. It also covers you and your family if you are injured while riding in another car or while walking.

Uninsured motorist coverage pays for bodily injuries for which an uninsured motorist or hit-and-run driver is responsible. You and your family are covered as drivers, passengers, and pedestrians. Guests in your car are also covered.

Comprehensive physical damage coverage protects your car from damage by something other than another vehicle. Such damage may be caused by fire, theft, water, hail, and vandalism.

Collision insurance pays for damages to your car caused by collision with a vehicle or other object. Damages are paid regardless of who was at fault. Collision coverage usually has a deductible option. With a $100 deductible option, if damages to your car amount to $250, you will pay the first $100. The insurance company will pay the $150 balance. You can get coverage with different deductible options.

Automobile Insurance Premiums

Premiums for auto insurance vary greatly and depend on a number of factors. Your age, your driving record, and the year and model of your car affect your insurance premium. Where you live and the distance you drive in a year are factors as well.

Some companies offer discounts on premium costs. Have you completed a driver education course? Are you a good student? Does your family own more than one car? If you can answer yes to any of these questions, you may be eligible for a discount. See 18-22.

When buying auto insurance, shop carefully. Check several companies to get the best price for the coverage you need. Research the company's long-term ratings before you make a final decision.

Housing-Related Insurance

If you own or rent your home, insurance can provide financial protection in the event of loss or damage. The cost of this insurance will depend on the type and amount of coverage and the insurance rates in your area.

Homeowner's insurance provides two basic types of coverage: property protection and liability protection. Property coverage insures you against such dangers as fire, lightning, vandalism, burglary, theft, and explosions. It covers the damage or loss of the dwelling and your personal possessions, such as clothes and furnishings. It also pays for your living expenses if you must move out of your home because of damages to the property.

Liability coverage protects you against financial loss if others are injured on or by your property. It also offers protection if you or your property accidentally damages the property of others. It pays for legal costs if you are sued because of injuries to others or damages to their property. It pays for damages assessed against you if you are held legally liable for injuries or property damage.

18-22
Many insurance companies offer a multiple-car discount for families who insure more than one vehicle.

Renter's insurance is similar to home owner's insurance. It covers a renter's personal possessions and liability.

Insurance coverage should be kept in line with the value of your home and belongings. Make an inventory of your possessions and estimate their values. This will help you decide how much coverage you need. Periodically update your coverage as you make major purchases. See 18-23.

Some policies pay *actual cash value*, which equals today's costs less depreciation for the use of the item. Thus, an old item may have depreciated to the point where it is no longer considered to have value. Such an item may not be covered in the case of loss. Other policies pay *replacement costs*, which equal today's costs without considering any depreciation. Replacement cost protection generally is somewhat more expensive. However, the expense may be worthwhile in the event of a major loss.

18-23
A videotape of valuable possessions serves as an accurate inventory for purchasing homeowner's insurance and making future claims.

Check It Out!

1. Regular payments made by a policyholder to an insurance company are called ———.
2. What is the difference between term and whole life insurance policies?
3. True or false. Co-insurance is an amount of money that a policyholder must pay before the insurance company will pay.
4. What kind of automobile insurance coverage pays for damages that your car causes to the property of others?
5. What factors affect the cost of homeowner's and renter's insurance?

Chapter Review

Summary

Several types of financial institutions can help you manage your money. Your choice of institutions will be based partly on the services you need. One of these services is sure to be a checking account. Learning how to correctly write and endorse checks and balance your checkbook will give you convenience and flexibility in managing your money.

The unexpected can happen to even the best of money managers. Having some money in savings can help you prepare for the unexpected. Your savings options range from regular savings accounts and CDs to stocks, bonds, and mutual funds. When deciding how to save, you will want to consider safety, rate of return, liquidity, purchasing power, and convenience. Your savings will become part of your estate when you die. Preparing a will enables your wishes to be observed regarding the distribution of your estate.

Insurance can protect you against huge losses. You may need life insurance to provide for dependents in the event of your death. You are likely to want health insurance to help cover the high costs of medical treatments, drugs, and hospitalization. If you drive a car, you need to be protected by automobile insurance. If you own or rent a home, insurance will cover your property and protect you against liability.

Think About It

1. Which of the different financial services do you see yourself using in the next five years? Which type of financial institution do you think would be best able to provide you with the services you will need?
2. If you had a checking account, explain why you would or would not make a habit of balancing your checkbook each month.
3. Determine a rank order of the five factors that will influence how you save your money. Rank from 1 to 5, with 1 being most important.
4. In which type of security would you most prefer to invest? Explain your answer.
5. At what age do you think you should open an IRA account? Why do you think this is an appropriate age to begin saving for retirement?
6. Imagine you are 25 years old. You are married, and both you and your spouse work. You do not have any children. What specific types of insurance would you choose to purchase? Explain your choices.
7. How might the information you learned in this chapter help you in your career?

Try It Out

1. Working with three or four classmates, investigate the services offered by one financial institution in your area. After an oral report from each group presenting facts about all area institutions, compare them.

2. Use sample checks to practice writing and endorsing checks properly.

3. Invite an investment counselor to speak to your class about the advantages and disadvantages of various savings options. Ask the speaker to also discuss the importance of planning an estate.

4. Do independent research on one type of insurance and explain how it helps provide security for individuals and families.

Chapter 19
Consumer Decisions

Careers
These careers relate to the topics in this chapter:
▼ personal shopper
▼ customer service representative
▼ family financial counselor
▼ consumer information specialist
As you study the chapter, see if you can think of others.

Topics

Topic 19-1
Making Shopping Decisions

Objectives

After studying this topic, you will be able to
▼ evaluate options available when deciding where to shop.
▼ analyze the factors affecting consumer buying decisions.
▼ relate comparison shopping guidelines to your shopping decisions.

Topic Terms

impulse buying
sale
comparison shopping
warranty

Informed consumers are smart shoppers. They use the decision-making process in many ways as they make choices in the marketplace. They learn as much as they can about goods and services before making buying decisions. They plan their shopping in advance by deciding where to shop and when to buy. In deciding what to buy, they consider factors such as price, quality, suitability, and use and care. They know how to compare goods and services, and what to look for in warranties.

Being an informed consumer can help you get the most for your money. With practice, you can learn to recognize the best buys among your choices and to shop wisely. Improving your buying habits will also help you become a better consumer.

Deciding Where to Shop

As a consumer, you will have many choices to make when you shop. One of your first choices will be to decide where to shop for the items you want. Retail stores, catalogs, and electronic shopping are some of the more popular choices you may consider.

Retail Shopping

In deciding where to shop, you consider many factors. Which types of stores carry the item you want to buy? Store location, product price and quality, and product selection will also influence where you choose to shop.

Department stores are large retail firms that offer a wide variety of consumer goods and services, all under one roof. Departments within the stores offer many lines of merchandise including clothing, cosmetics, jewelry, household goods, and home furnishings. See 19-1. Department stores also offer customers extra services such as personal shopping, gift registries, gift wrapping, delivery, and charge accounts. Because of higher operating costs to provide these services, department store prices are often higher.

Discount stores sell a wide assortment of goods at lower prices. Unlike department stores, services such as delivery and consumer credit are usually not available. Discount stores save money by offering fewer customer services and having smaller sales staffs. They pass their cost savings on to consumers.

Specialty stores specialize in selling one line of goods such as shoes, videos, or books. These stores are often found in shopping centers or malls. Since they carry one type of product, their salespeople

19-1
Most department stores sell apparel and accessories on the street-level floor and nonapparel items on a separate level.

know the merchandise well. For consumers who want to select from one complete product line, these stores often carry a wider selection. The prices in these stores vary depending on how unique their products are and how high their sales volume is. See 19-2.

Off-price retail stores buy designer label products or brand name products at low prices from manufacturers. Then they pass the cost savings on to consumers. However, because they often purchase excess merchandise from manufacturers, the types of products they offer frequently change. Prices are lower than retail department stores and fewer customer services are offered.

Factory outlet stores are one type of off-price retail store. These stores, owned by the manufacturer, sell directly to the

19-2
This specialty store offers a wide selection of baked goods and beverages.

consumer. Sometimes the goods are irregulars or closeouts on discontinued lines. Merchandise that is not bought by retailers is sold to consumers as *overruns*. Because the manufacturer sells directly to the consumer, the merchandise is sold for less. Many of these stores are located in outlet malls, which are shopping centers consisting of off-price retail stores.

In-Home Electronic Shopping

Two types of in-home electronic shopping methods exist: television and Internet retailing. Instead of fighting crowded stores and heavy traffic, shoppers can order merchandise from their homes at any hour. Then orders are delivered to the shipping address of their choice.

Television retailing involves showing merchandise on certain television channels. TV channels devoted to 24-hour home shopping focus on clothing, accessories, and beauty care products. Viewers order by phone and pay by credit card. See 19-3.

Internet shopping is an option that continues to grow rapidly. Most retailers now have Web sites, and many of these show merchandise for sale online as well as store information. The items are shown in sharp detail and include extensive product information. The ability to locate difficult-to-find items is a key reason for shopping online. Some sites have a search agent that tracks down rare items or items that meet certain criteria. Many sites offer free standard shipping or upgrades to express shipping.

Popular online purchases include books, compact discs, computer software, travel services, and furniture. Before giving credit card information online, always make sure you are at a secured site. A special icon, such as a padlock, is an indication sign that a retailer's Web site is secure.

19-3
Many people buy clothing via TV home shopping channels because viewers can see how the clothing appears on others.

The biggest drawback to electronic shopping is not being able to inspect items before purchase. This is especially important in the case of clothing. Consequently, garments with "roomy fit" tend to be the leading sellers among clothing items. Some of the advantages of in-home shopping are as follows:

▼ It saves time. You can quickly visit hundreds of merchants offering almost limitless choice.
▼ Prices are comparable to or slightly lower than in-store prices. The lower operating costs of electronic retailers make this possible.
▼ You can choose to have an item shipped more quickly if you need it.
▼ Ordered items are delivered to the address of your choice.
▼ Policies on returning merchandise are usually generous.

There are also drawbacks to at-home electronic shopping. These include the following:

▼ You do not have the personal assistance of a salesperson.

▼ Some manufacturers will not allow their products to be sold through electronic channels, thus eliminating those options.

▼ You cannot check or test a product before purchasing it. However, you can return or exchange it later.

▼ You will have to wait at least a day for an item to be shipped.

▼ Shipping costs usually add to the cost of the purchase.

▼ You are not contributing to your local economy. When you shop locally, your purchases help to keep area stores in business. That, in turn, provides jobs for people in the community. With their salaries, they buy local products and services. This cycle contributes to making your town a better place to live.

▼ You need to be sure the vendor from whom you are buying is legitimate and not someone who will cheat you.

Catalog Shopping

Almost any product imaginable is available through a catalog. This type of shopping offers many advantages. However, catalog shopping has some drawbacks, too. Convenience and time-savings are the main advantages of catalog shopping, 19-4. Busy people can shop at home from a catalog, and then order items online or by phone or mail. Although consumers pay charges for shipping and handling, they save time, energy, and driving expenses by shopping at home.

Selection and price savings are other advantages. Some catalogs offer a wide variety of goods. Others specialize in one

19-4
Catalog shoppers save time and money by shopping at home.

type of item, such as shoes or clothing. Prices are often lower than in department stores.

Catalog shopping has some disadvantages, too. You cannot see the item before you buy it. The color, size, or material may not be exactly as it appears in the catalog. You may have to wait for the item to be shipped. If you are not satisfied with the item after you receive it, you are responsible for returning it and paying for the shipping.

Shopping Guidelines

Buy wisely when shopping by catalog by following these guidelines:

▼ Read the catalog before you place an order. Find out the company's policy for returning items in case you are not satisfied.

▼ Fill out the order form accurately and completely before sending in your order.

▼ Avoid sending cash through the mail to pay for your order. Pay by check, money order, or credit card.

▼ Keep a record of your order until you receive the goods. Keep a copy of the company's name, address, and telephone number in case you need to contact the company.

▼ When the order arrives, check it over carefully. If something is wrong or not completely satisfactory, return the item to the company.

Other Shopping Options

Thrift stores, consignment shops, garage or yard sales, and *flea markets* are other popular shopping options. These businesses sell new and used merchandise at greatly reduced prices. Shoppers with limited budgets who know quality may find true bargains. Impulse shoppers may be enchanted by amazingly low prices and buy items they really do not need. **Impulse buying** is making an unplanned or quick purchase without giving it much thought. To buy wisely, consumers must analyze their shopping goals and buy only what they need. Also, they must realize that purchases are usually final. These vendors rarely accept returns.

The More You Know: Consignment Shops

Consignment shops are gaining popularity as a shopping option. The owner of the shop accepts merchandise that is resalable from people like you. For example, maybe you have outgrown some clothes that you have not worn or that are still in good condition. The shop will accept them for a designated period of time and try to sell them. You agree on a price that is fair to yourself, the shop owner, and the prospective buyer. You also agree to give the shop owner a percentage of the sale price for the services provided. If the item sells, there is an income from the sale for both you and the shop owner.

Deciding When to Buy

Knowing when to buy is as important as knowing where to shop. Smart shoppers plan their purchases ahead of time and watch for sales. Those who can anticipate their needs save money by shopping at sales. They are also aware of factors that can affect their shopping decisions.

Shopping at Sales

Wise shoppers try to get the most value for their shopping dollars. Shopping at store sales is one way they can save money. A **sale** is a special selling of goods at reduced prices. Smart shoppers buy items because they need them, not because the sale price is low. Shoppers carefully plan their purchases to match the timing of sales. See 19-5.

Many stores offer *preseason sales* when new merchandise arrives. For example, winter coats may be on sale in August to encourage people to shop early. For consumers who need new coats and want the best selections, preseason sales usually offer good savings.

End-of-season sales, or *clearance sales*, take place when retailers are making room for new merchandise for the next season. For instance, snow blowers may be on sale in March so retailers can make room for lawn

19-5

Do you need the item? Is the sale price really lower than the regular price? Is the item in good condition and unflawed? Can you return it if necessary, or is it a final sale?

19-6

Clipping coupons for items you use regularly can help you save money.

furniture. Consumers who are able to wait until the end of the season often receive large discounts on merchandise. However, disadvantages of an end-of-season sale are that selection may be limited and return policies may be strict.

Seasonal sales take place throughout the year. This type of sale often offers consumers the best sale price. Knowing when to expect these sales helps consumers plan their purchases. Winter clothing, for example, is usually on sale in January. Sports equipment is a good buy in August. Holiday sales take place throughout the year. These are good times to buy needed items at reduced prices.

Coupons and Rebates

Coupons are small discounts on products offered by a store or manufacturer, 19-6. They are often found in newspaper advertisements and direct mailings. Coupons usually offer a direct reduction in price when the proper coupon is presented at the time of a purchase.

Rebates are sometimes instant reductions in price offered at the time of purchase. However, they more commonly require initial payment of full price. Then, after submission of proof of purchase, a rebate check is mailed to the purchaser. It may take several weeks for the rebate check to arrive.

Other Factors Affecting Buying Decisions

Certain factors can affect consumer-buying decisions. Being alert to these factors can help consumers decide when to buy. Two major factors are the shopper's mood and the time available for shopping. How people feel when they shop affects their buying decisions. People who feel down when they shop tend to buy items they do not need to make themselves feel better. People who are hungry, tired, or rushed tend to buy impulsively. If they shop when they are tired or not feeling well, they will not be as alert to details. They may make hurried decisions because they are too tired to evaluate the merchandise properly.

Time is another factor that affects consumer-buying decisions. It is a resource that should be used wisely. Not allowing enough time to shop, shopping when the store is crowded, or shopping late in the day encourages impulsive shopping. Smart shoppers plan their shopping to allow plenty of time for making buying decisions.

Deciding What to Buy

When you decide to make a purchase, do you buy the first item you see? Probably not. Most likely you shop around to find the right product at the right price. There are other factors to consider in your buying decisions. The ability to judge quality, suitability, use and care, and product warranties is also an important part of your decision.

Comparison Shopping

Comparison shopping means comparing products and prices in different stores before buying. Comparison shopping helps you get the best value for your money. Look at features, price, quality, use and care, and other characteristics that are important to you. It takes time to make such comparisons. However, you will get better quality and find the product that best suits your needs for the money you invest. See 19-7. Comparison shopping helps you avoid impulse buying. Impulse buying may seem like fun at the time of the purchase. Later, though, you may regret spending money for the item. You may pay too much for an item or buy something you really do not need. A sale item may be hard to resist, but it is no bargain if you do not use it.

You save time, energy, and money by comparison shopping. This is because you plan your shopping in advance. You first

19-7
Some consumers prefer a local shopping mall for convenient one-stop comparison shopping.

consider what features are important to you. Then make a list of the features you want and the price you want to pay. At this point, you are ready to shop for what you need.

Judging Quality

Price is not always the most important factor to consider in your buying decision. Shopping for value also means judging the quality of a product.

Product price is not always a guide to a product's quality. Although better-quality products usually cost more, a lower-cost product sometimes offers the same quality. When you shop, compare nationally advertised name brands with lesser-known brands. If the lesser-known brand is the same quality as the more expensive brand and costs less, it is a better buy. As a smart shopper, you will learn that a store's own brand is often worth considering.

Learn to inspect products as you shop so you can recognize different quality levels, 19-8. Checking the quality is

19-8
When you comparison shop, compare the price, quality, and features of similar items. This will help you get the best value for the money you have to spend.

important if you plan to use the product often or for a long time. Higher-quality products are made to higher standards, so they usually last longer. This makes them a better value, too. For example, leather shoes may be more costly than vinyl shoes, but will be a better value in the long run. Since leather is a more durable material that will wear longer, the shoes should last for several seasons. You will not need to replace them as often as vinyl shoes, which saves money in the long term. Consumer research publications also offer helpful information to help you judge quality.

Sometimes a lower-priced, good-quality item may best meet your needs. For instance, if you are learning to play tennis, a less expensive racket may suit your needs until you improve your skills.

Suitability

Before you go shopping, find out as much as you can about a product. When you are ready to shop, you will be prepared to make a wise selection from all the choices. You will be able to find the most suitable product to meet your needs.

Use and Care

Read labels and care instructions on the product to be sure it is what you want. Suppose you are shopping for a casual shirt that you plan to wear often. You find one you like that must be dry-cleaned. You must then decide if you want the added expense of dry cleaning, or if you want to look for a machine washable shirt instead. Your shopping decision will be affected by the use and care information.

Warranties

Studying the warranty or guarantee on a product is also an important part of comparison shopping. A **warranty** is a written promise that a product will meet specified standards of performance. It is a form of consumer protection. See 19-9. A warranty states the procedures the manufacturer or vendor will follow if the product fails to perform as stated. It covers the product for a stated period of time, such as 90 days or 5 years. If the product fails because of customer abuse, the warranty does not apply.

Two basic types of warranties may be found on products. The first type is a full warranty. A *full warranty* is required by law to provide broad coverage on a product. It includes the following:

▼ free repair or replacement of defective parts or products

▼ repair or replacement within a reasonable time frame

▼ replacement if attempts to repair the product are unsuccessful

▼ no unreasonable demands on the consumer as a condition for receiving repair or replacement service

▼ transfer of warranted coverage to a new owner if the product changes ownership during the warranted period

The second type of warranty is a *limited warranty*, which provides less coverage. It always specifies the degree to which it is limited. For example, a limited warranty may cover repairs, but not replacement. It may also require the product be returned to the manufacturer for servicing. A product may carry a full warranty on service and a limited warranty on parts. You must read the warranty carefully to know the exact coverage offered.

When you comparison shop, carefully read product warranties. Determine what

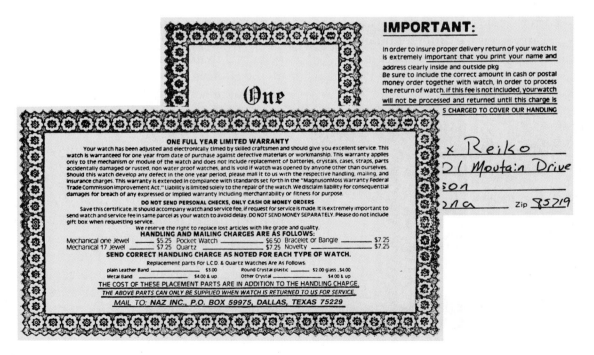

19-9

This limited warranty clearly states what is and what is not covered by the manufacturer.

protection they guarantee. Are they full or
limited warranties? Know what you must
do if the product does not comply with its
warranty. If you have a problem with the
product, who is responsible for carrying
out the warranty? Warranty information
can help you make a more informed choice.

Check It Out!

1. A _____ store sells a certain type of
   product such as athletic shoes, toys,
   or jewelry.
2. List four advantages and four
   disadvantages of catalog shopping.
3. Explain the difference between a
   seasonal sale and an end-of-season sale.
4. What is the purpose of comparison
   shopping?
5. Name the two types of warranties
   found on consumer products.

Topic 19-2
The Impact of Technology on Consumers

Objectives

After studying this topic, you will be able to
▼ list information technology available to
   consumers.
▼ analyze the impact of information
   technology on the lives of consumers.
▼ summarize ways to manage
   technology.

Topic Terms

computer
handheld organizer
computer-aided design (CAD)
real-time
simulation software
obsolescence

Technology provides ways to perform
complicated tasks more quickly and easily.
What is learned with each new technology
translates into applications in other areas.
Technological advances can help people
manage resources, solve problems, and
achieve goals.

Technology Options Available

Some definitions of technology are
complex. Very simply, technology is
the practical application of knowledge.
Reviewing everything that technology has
achieved would be a huge task. The task

would be never-ending because as each second passes, more new processes and inventions are created.

Of the many inventions created by applying scientific principles, the computer is perhaps the most influential. It is responsible for the current era known as the *Information Age*. At home, computers help control the car, heating and cooling equipment, and home appliances. Computers also control the television and practically all other types of electronic equipment. Instead of focusing on these inventions, however, this text will discuss the information technology important now and into the future.

High-Tech Products and Services

The array of information products and services is increasing each year. Of those used most often, several stand out as particularly important in their impact on consumers. These items include computers, the Internet, and handheld organizers.

Computers

Computers are found in schools, homes, and the workplace. A **computer** is an electronic device that processes information according to instructions. Computers are available in desktop and laptop models, 19-10. Data is either stored in the computer's memory or sent to an output device.

Computers are generally becoming less expensive. Prices begin around $200 but can be much more expensive depending on the type chosen and accessories purchased. Consumers often buy additional software and accessories after purchasing a computer to make it perform more functions.

19-10
Laptop computers provide all the computing power of desktop models plus the convenience of portability.

Internet Access

Many computer owners are Internet users. By linking to the Internet, consumers can send and receive e-mail. They can explore various Web sites for information and entertainment. They can also download software programs and join special interest message boards and chat groups.

Handheld Organizers

A pocket-size computer that serves as a personal planner is a **handheld organizer**. These tools display schedules and deadlines, recall dates and phone numbers, and figure budgets. They also permit you to input information as needed. Most handheld organizers can be connected to a home or office computer to interchange information. Some models also let you link to the Internet. See 19-11.

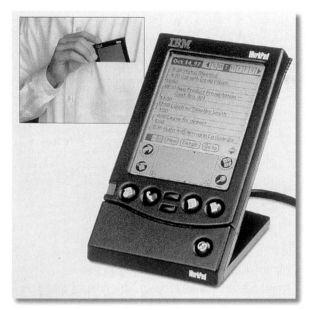

19-11

Handheld organizers with Internet connections allow owners to receive information from their favorite Web sites and databases.

The Functions of High-Tech Equipment

Computers and computer-related equipment help to perform many everyday functions faster. Shopping is one function that was discussed in Topic 19-1. In addition, people can process information, manage money, and keep records better by using the equipment. Also, high-tech equipment can help people gather information, learn, enjoy entertainment, and communicate.

Information Processing

Computers can process many kinds of information—words, numbers, images, and sound. The word processing feature is the main reason computers became popular. Computers are helpful for doing reports, writing letters, and creating charts and graphs.

Landscapes or interiors for homes can be created with the use of special design software. This is called **computer-aided design (CAD)**, which is graphics software that assists in creating a design. CAD software lets you electronically change the color, size, shape, and arrangement of various elements. This prevents costly mistakes and allows last-minute changes to occur on screen or paper before implementing the final design.

Money Management

Creating budgets is easy with the computer's rapid ability to process numbers, 19-12. Software and Web sites devoted to money management help you prepare worksheets of various savings and spending plans. You can also write checks and balance a checkbook with special software. With an Internet link to your bank, you can bank from home.

19-12

A tiny computer chip has enormous computing power.

Information Gathering and Learning

Perhaps the greatest value of the computer today is accessing the wealth of information available on the Internet. Any given subject can be explored on numerous Web sites. You can search online libraries of major universities and government agencies. Encyclopedias, databases, magazines, and newspapers are also available. In addition, major television news organizations provide **real-time** information. This refers to an event happening now.

Besides finding factual information, discussion groups on the Internet provide opinions about various products, services, and issues. You can read their comments and join the discussion by posting a message. At least one special-interest group exists on practically every subject imaginable. By joining a special-interest group, you learn about the latest facts and events scheduled for the featured topic.

Entertainment

Sometimes software programs and Web sites present information in such an entertaining way that the line between information and entertainment is blurred. Some products, however, are designed specifically to entertain, such as computer games, 19-13. Also, **simulation software** imitates an actual experience. For example, you can sense some of the fun of piloting a hot-air balloon, surfing the Pacific, and investigating other adventures while sitting at your computer. You can also observe real-time entertainment events broadcast on the Internet, such as concerts in other countries.

Communication

As families and friends are separated by distance, the desire to stay in touch is strong. This is the main reason for the

19-13
Colorful graphics and a speedy response to commands are the key reasons for the popularity of computer games.

popularity of e-mail among consumers. E-mail transmits written and visual messages. These messages can include documents, photos, charts, sounds, and graphs. E-mail permits the exchange of messages without the cost of postage or telephone calls. It is a particularly convenient way for people living in different countries to communicate. Also, it can get someone's prompt attention anywhere in the world. See 19-14.

Managing Technology

Just as pencil and paper are neither good nor bad, the same is true for technology. How high-tech devices are used is what really matters. To get full value from information technology, you must make good buying decisions and use the items to enhance your life. You should also be aware of some cautions in the use of technology.

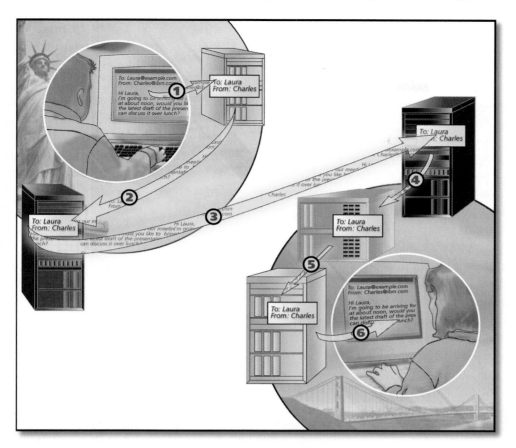

19-14
This illustration shows how e-mail travels between computers linked together electronically.

Making Buying Decisions

Acquaint yourself with the high-tech market and the basic types of items available before buying anything. This market is so vast that you will quickly become overwhelmed if you try to shop before becoming informed. Talk with friends about the products and services they recommend. Also talk with knowledgeable people who can offer good advice. These are some of the questions to answer before buying high-tech equipment.

▼ *What equipment features do you need?* It is best to buy equipment that satisfies your current and short-term needs. Do you simply want to send and receive e-mail, or do you also need to create professional-looking reports and records? Determining what features to shop for will help you determine what you need.

▼ *What new products will be introduced soon?* Every 12 to 18 months, technological advances create new products with more speed, convenience, and feature options. Learn what will be available in the next few months. Check what new products are being planned for Christmas or back-to-school sales. Read magazines from the computer and Internet industries to see what new features to expect in the coming months.

▼ *What nonproduct factors should you consider before buying?* Besides examining equipment features, you will want to consider other important questions. For example, is the dealer reputable and established in the community? What is the provision of the warranty? What must you do to get service? How available and reliable is the service? Is a training program offered? See 19-15. Does your equipment come with a trade-in option so you can upgrade to a more powerful computer later if you want?

▼ *What is the total cost?* Sometimes a great deal includes signing up for a multiyear service contract or buying other extras. Computers are often advertised in conjunction with one- to three-year contracts for Internet service. If costs for competing services should drop in the future, you could be stuck with an expensive obligation to pay off. To make a wise decision, research the average costs and fees involved in getting everything you will need to use your equipment. Then you can judge whether the item purchased with the advertised extras represents a good buy for you.

Drawbacks to Using High-Tech Equipment

Technologies can impact lives in a negative way as well as a positive one. Sometimes having information equipment available leads to undesirable or harmful

19-15
A free or low-cost training program provided with a new computer is a very valuable benefit.

effects. You will want to recognize that these possibilities exist so you can avoid them in your life. These are some of the possible drawbacks of using high-tech equipment.

▼ *Personal privacy may be threatened.* Many fear the invasion of their privacy as a result of data collecting through computers. Because computers can compile and access data quickly, it is possible to combine all the existing information on each person. Purchases made with a credit card, data provided in a loan application, facts in your medical records—all can be combined to develop a profile of you.

Some people worry that a personal profile created by computer can include wrong information that is never corrected. They also worry that a computerized personal profile would give marketers and others special insight. It could reveal who you are, how you think, and what you are likely to do. Consequently, many experts recommend giving only as much information as needed. For example, when filling out a product warranty form, it is not necessary to answer the unrelated questions about educational status and annual income. Also, it is appropriate to ask data collectors to explain all the uses of any personal information you may provide.

▼ *Health and development can be adversely affected.* Too much time spent alone with the computer can lead to loneliness and isolation. By interacting with people, you develop social skills that cannot be gained by simply exchanging e-mail. Physical inactivity is another factor associated with frequent computer use. While sitting for hours at the computer can promote intellectual growth, it does not help—and can actually harm—your physical, emotional, and social growth. See 19-16.

▼ *The natural environment could be endangered.* The pace of high-tech advances is fast, resulting in rapid **obsolescence**. This is the state of uselessness. When items that were high-tech just a few years ago are not powerful enough for today's uses, they are quickly discarded. Often they end up in landfills, which are fast filling up. Citizens concerned about the environment should find ways to recycle their equipment or discard it in a responsible way. Contacting the local waste collection authority and the product manufacturer should provide alternatives.

19-16

Fascination with a computer can lead some to spend too much time with it while sacrificing important social and physical events.

▼ *Spending can occur too easily.* With instant access to cash and credit, online purchases can be made in seconds. When purchases are not planned or budgeted, people can quickly find themselves in a serious financial crisis.

▼ *Too much pressure can be exerted on other family resources.* Money and time are the resources most often affected. A student's desire to keep up with peers and have the very latest equipment can test the family budget. The burden is even greater when a family has several children, all wanting their own equipment. If items must be shared, prepare a schedule showing who gets them and when.

▼ *Family life may be threatened.* High-tech equipment does not encourage family interaction. Constant competition for the family computer can leave no time available for all family members to get together. Relationships are threatened if members skip family activities for solitary entertainment with their computers.

Check It Out!

1. Name three examples of information technology.
2. List five functions in which information technology can assist.
3. What four questions should be asked before buying high-tech equipment?
4. List five ways in which technology can negatively impact your life.

Topic 19-3
The Role of Advertising

Objectives
After studying this topic, you will be able to
▼ explain the role of advertising in promoting goods and services.
▼ identify how advertising influences consumer spending.
▼ evaluate various types of advertising.

Topic Terms
advertisement
bait and switch

As a consumer, are you aware of the methods businesses use to promote their goods and services? Through advertising, businesses inform you about their goods and services. They use various media such as radio, television, magazines, direct mail, the Internet, and billboards to convey their messages. Businesses are interested in increasing sales and profits. Their ads are designed to attract your attention and get you to buy.

Before you buy any goods or services, you need to understand the role of advertising. If you understand that the main purpose of advertising is to sell, you can make advertising work for you. You can use the information to buy what you need.

Advertising plays an important role in the economy. It benefits both consumers and businesses. Through ads, consumers are informed about the many goods and services available to them. Businesses are able to market their goods and services more efficiently. Advertising helps businesses introduce new or improved products to the marketplace. As a result, the economy grows as consumers make more purchases.

How Advertising Affects Consumer Spending

An **advertisement** is a paid public message communicated through various media that promotes the sale of goods and services. You see and hear many different types of advertisements every day. However, you may not be aware of the effects these ads have on your buying behavior. See 19-17.

Do you look for a certain brand of shoes or jeans when you shop? When you go out to eat, do you meet your friends at a certain restaurant? Do you watch the latest movies when they arrive at your local theater? In some way, advertising likely influenced your decisions about all these issues.

19-17
Even if you had not planned to shop at this store, the ad in the window might prompt you to come in.

As a wise consumer, keep in mind that the main goal of all ads is to convince you to buy something. Ads are designed to show products in the best possible ways, so only persuasive information appears. If you realize this, you can benefit from it. Carefully evaluate the information presented in ads. Look for factual information, such as features and price, to help you make buying decisions. Do not be sold on a product just because of the ad. Beware of ads that try to persuade you to buy unneeded, unwanted, or unaffordable items. This cautious approach can help you improve your buying decisions.

Types of Advertising

Advertisers use certain types of ads to influence consumer choices. Effective ads gain your attention and hold your interest. Six of the most common types of ads are described here. As you read about these ads, think how each type may influence your buying decisions.

Factual ads provide useful consumer information. They describe a product's features, benefits, and cost, and tell where the product is sold. Some factual ads are used to introduce a new product to the market so consumers become aware of it. See 19-18.

Comparison ads make comparisons with competing products. They stress the advertised product's beneficial features over the other choices. Some may also spotlight new or improved product features.

Testimonial ads use celebrities, sports professionals, or experts to endorse products. This makes the products' claims seem more believable. Some consumers may be persuaded to buy a product if they think a well-known person likes it. However, keep in mind that these people

19-18

This factual ad provides important information on a community recycling program. Do you think this form of advertising will influence consumers?

are usually paid to endorse the products. In some of these ads, average people who use the product tell how they like using it.

Attention-getter ads are designed to be entertaining. These ads use creative techniques, such as humor or visual images, to gain and hold consumers' attention.

Bandwagon ads try to be persuasive. These ads imply that many people use and enjoy the product and you should, too.

You are encouraged to become part of the crowd by using the product.

Sex-appeal ads have strong emotional appeal. These ads make consumers feel they will be more attractive and popular if they use the product.

In addition to these six types, *infomercials* are 30-minute blends of information and commercials on one product. Most are shown at off-hours. An infomercial may appear to be a talk show or news program with product demonstrations. Household, cooking, and fitness products are often sold via infomercials.

Direct mail is the process of mass mailings. A variety of information is sent to people selected as the most likely to respond positively. Direct mailings are often used by charities and political organizations as well as companies selling products to consumers. See 19-19.

Advertising on the Internet

A great deal of advertising takes place on the Internet. Most Web sites include advertisement banners or pop-up

19-19

This type of direct mail is usually an incentive for you to buy additional products.

ads. If the pages of a Web site try to persuade you to make a purchase, they are advertisements.

Before accepting any advice from an Internet site at face value, determine who sponsors the Web site. If the sponsor is a manufacturer or retailer, recognize the information provided by the site reflects just one viewpoint. If the sponsor of the site cannot be determined, it is best to remain skeptical of any information provided.

Evaluating Advertisements

Remember, no matter what method advertisers use, their final purpose is to get you to buy. As a consumer, you have the responsibility of evaluating advertisements. By using helpful information and ignoring the rest, you will improve your buying decisions. Use these evaluation questions to help you sort through the information presented in ads.

▼ Can you determine the purpose of the ad?
▼ Is it designed to inform you or persuade you to buy a product or service?
▼ Is the information in the ad useful to you?
▼ Is it factual and easy to understand?
▼ Does it tell what you want to know about the features, quality, and price?

As part of your evaluation, you also need to determine whether the ad is using a persuasive or deceptive advertising method.

Persuasive Advertising

Remember, persuasive advertising offers little or no useful information about a product or service. Be aware of this type of advertising so you can avoid being

influenced by it. When you are gathering information about products or services, focus on the facts conveyed by advertising. Then you can make choices based on the quality of the product or service.

Deceptive Advertising

Some types of advertising are misleading. Although the illegal methods used in the past have been stopped, some deceptive advertising still occurs.

Bait and switch is one deceptive advertising method used to lure shoppers who are looking for bargains. The advertiser offers a low-priced item as bait to get shoppers in the store. Once shoppers are there, the advertiser tries to switch them to a more expensive item. They may do this by telling shoppers the advertised item is sold out. See 19-20. Another approach advertisers use is convincing shoppers the advertised item is poor quality and will not meet their needs.

In another type of deceptive advertising, consumers are informed by mail or by phone that they have won a free gift. They may be required to come to a store to receive the gift. Once there, they may have to answer questions, listen to a sales presentation, or fill out a coupon to earn their gift. The advertiser may give the consumers a catalog of merchandise as well. More gifts are offered to the consumers for ordering additional merchandise from the store's catalog. The "free" gift may turn into an expensive purchase.

Offering free items or services to consumers who buy their product is another common sales strategy for some advertisers. For instance, a book club may offer free books if you agree to buy a certain number of monthly selections. However, the cost of the free books is actually figured into the cost of the books

19-20
Nonfood stores are required to have a minimum supply of advertised items on hand to meet reasonable demand, unless "limited supply" is clearly stated in the ad.

you buy. This practice is legal because all terms are advertised. Taking the time to figure the costs involved may help you understand that the books are not really free.

Consumer Protection Against Deceptive Advertising

To help protect consumers, advertising is regulated by federal government agencies. The *Federal Trade Commission (FTC)* is responsible for preventing false advertising and deceptive advertising practices. The *Federal Communications Commission (FCC)* regulates ads aired on television or radio. These agencies can impose steep fines on advertisers who violate advertising laws. They can also challenge advertisers to prove claims made in ads.

If you observe false or deceptive advertising practices, what can you do? It is your responsibility to bring them to the attention of the advertiser immediately. If they are not corrected, report them to a consumer protection agency promptly. More information about these agencies and their responsibilities will be covered in Topic 19-5.

Check It Out!

1. Explain how advertising can affect consumer spending.
2. Name six types of advertisements.
3. True or false. Being aware of deceptive or persuasive advertising helps consumers make wiser buying decisions.

Topic 19-4

Using Consumer Credit

Objectives

After studying this topic, you will be able to
▼ identify different types of credit.
▼ analyze the pros and cons of using credit.
▼ describe how to establish a credit rating.

Topic Terms

credit
creditors
collateral
credit rating
finance charges
interest
annual percentage rate (APR)
credit contract

Consumer credit is widely used in the United States. **Credit** is an arrangement that allows consumers to buy goods or services now and pay for them later. Credit has been called savings in reverse because it involves the present use of future income.

Credit can be a successful buying tool, but if misused, it can cause many problems. As a consumer, you have choices to make in determining whether or not to use credit. Use it wisely and it may help you enjoy a more comfortable lifestyle. Take it for granted and it can lead to serious financial difficulties.

Types of Credit

Consumer credit can be classified as either sales credit or cash credit. Those who have goods or services to sell offer sales credit. Department stores, car dealers, repair services, and professional services offer sales credit. Those who have money to loan offer *cash credit*. Lending and financial institutions offer cash credit.

Sales and cash credit can then be divided into one of two categories based on how they are repaid. Credit to be repaid in full at the end of the month is called *noninstallment credit*. Dentist bills, utility bills, and repair bills are examples of noninstallment credit.

Installment credit is repaid in a series of regular, equal payments. Such payments may be made at regular intervals over several weeks, months, or years. The period of time depends on the contract between you and the creditor. Installment credit is used primarily for major purchases—homes, cars, household furnishings, and large cash loans. See 19-21.

Sales Credit

Sales credit is widely used because it is convenient. The cost of using sales credit varies. Three types of sales credit are commonly used.

Regular charge accounts are forms of noninstallment credit. They are used as a shopping convenience and as a way for customers to avoid carrying large amounts of cash. The customer can charge as much as is needed as long as the account is paid in full at the end of the billing period. These accounts are a form of open-end credit. This means that any number of items can be charged. Finance charges are not usually added to regular charge accounts if bills are paid promptly.

19-21

An expensive item such as this car might be bought using installment credit.

Installment charge accounts are forms of installment credit, as the name suggests. The buyer signs a contract and agrees to make a fixed number of payments at certain intervals over a set period of time. This contract is known as a *closed-end credit contract*. This means that no further items may be purchased on the contract. If other purchases are made, other contracts must be signed. This type of credit is usually used for major purchases, such as furniture.

Revolving charge accounts combine the features of noninstallment and installment credit plans. They are a form of open-end credit. Consumers are allowed to make purchases up to a credit limit established in the credit contract. Consumers may pay their bills in full each month. When

this is done, no finance charge is applied to the account. Consumers also can pay in installments over a longer period. Then a finance charge is applied to the unpaid balance. Department stores often offer this type of account.

Credit Cards

A credit card shows that the company or bank that issued the card honors your credit. See 19-22. Most credit cards are revolving charge accounts. You are billed at the end of each billing period. There is no charge for use of credit if the bill is paid in full each month. If payment is spread over a period of several months, a finance charge is made on the unpaid balance.

19-22

The credit card itself will show such information as the user's name, account number, validity dates, and issuing bank.

What happens if you lose a credit card? Under the law, you are responsible for no more than $50 worth of charges made by someone else on each lost or stolen card. You are still responsible for the charges you have made. Most credit card issuers furnish you with a form to use in reporting the loss or theft of a card. They also furnish a phone number to call to report the loss. It is important to report the loss immediately.

Loans

A loan is a financial transaction in which the lender agrees to give the borrower a certain amount of money. Total repayment is expected by a specified time. Sometimes payment is due in a lump sum on a certain date. More commonly, regular payments are spread over a period of time agreed to by lender and borrower. Usually interest is paid in addition to the principal.

A promissory note or contract spells out the details of the transaction. Financial penalties are often incurred for missed or late payments. Loans are often used in the purchase of major items such as a new car or house.

19-23
Credit can be a useful buying tool only if it is used sensibly and carefully.

The Pros and Cons of Using Credit

The use of credit has advantages, but it has several dangers, too. The main advantage of credit is convenience. You do not need to carry large amounts of cash when shopping or vacationing. In an emergency, credit can provide temporary help for an unexpected expense. Credit allows you to use expensive goods and services, such as a car or a home, as you pay for them. See 19-23.

One great danger of credit is that it makes spending too easy. It can encourage impulse spending. Also, merchandise bought on credit does not really belong to you until the debt has been paid.

If payments are not made on schedule, you may lose the merchandise. Some **creditors** (people who give credit and to whom debts are owed) ask for collateral. **Collateral** is something of value that you own and that you pledge to a creditor as security for a loan. If you fail to make credit payments, you may lose more than the money you have already paid and the merchandise. You may also lose the items that were pledged as collateral.

Using credit is expensive. The more you use and the longer you take to repay, the higher the cost. By using credit now, you are reducing future income. That means you will have less money to spend in the future. Misusing credit can have serious long-term effects. It can lead to a bad credit rating, repossession of goods, or bankruptcy.

Applying for Credit

How do creditors determine if you are a good credit risk? When you apply for credit, prospective creditors will evaluate you. The creditors will determine if they think you can handle credit.

Establishing a Credit Rating

Your credit rating is the most important factor affecting your ability to get credit. A **credit rating** is the creditor's evaluation of your ability to repay debts. Your credit rating is determined by a variety of personal attributes that relate to your repayment ability. In most cases, you must be at least 18 years old to get credit.

You may be thinking, "How am I going to get credit if I need a credit rating to do so? How can I have a credit rating if I never bought anything on credit?" Young people are at a disadvantage when they first apply for credit. Proving their abilities to handle credit is not easy. Here are some tips that you might use to establish a credit rating.

▼ Open a checking account and a savings account. A good banking record can serve as a reference if your accounts have been handled responsibly, 19-24.

▼ Buy something on a layaway plan. Some stores will give charge accounts to customers who have successfully handled layaway purchases.

▼ Be prepared to make a big down payment in your first attempt to get credit. Most creditors are more willing to extend credit if you are able to make a sizable investment in the purchase.

19-24
A good banking record may help you obtain credit.

▼ Apply to a local department store for a charge account. If you are offered even a small amount of credit, accept it. Buy small items and make payments promptly. Stores that cater to young people are also likely to help you establish credit.

▼ Ask a relative to *cosign* (guarantee repayment of) a loan for you. This method gives you credit on your cosigner's record. When the debt is paid, you will have established your own credit record.

Keeping a Good Credit Rating

Credit is a privilege that should not be taken lightly. Once you build a good credit rating, you need to protect it. Be truthful whenever you apply for credit. Use credit only in amounts you can afford to repay. If you meet all the terms of your credit agreement and pay on time, you will have a good credit rating. Late payments or failure to pay will lead to a poor credit rating. A poor credit rating will make it difficult for you to get credit in the future.

Checking Your Credit Rating

Consumer reporting agencies gather information about your credit activities. The agencies then charge a fee for providing the information to lenders. You may obtain a free credit report once each year. You can do this by visiting www.anualcreditreport.com, which was created by the three consumer reporting agencies. You can also fill out and mail an Annual Credit Report Request form. These can be downloaded from www.ftc.gov/credit.

Check your credit rating prior to applying for a major loan to make sure there are no errors in your report. If you find errors, contact the consumer credit reporting agency immediately and request that they be corrected.

The Three Cs of Credit

The three Cs of credit will be used to evaluate you. They are *character*, *capital*, and *capacity*. See 19-25.

Character is an important consideration to creditors. Personal attributes, such as your honesty and reliability, will be studied. Creditors will also review your established record of financial responsibility. For instance, they will see if you consistently paid your bills on time.

Your *capital* is important. This refers to your income. Your occupation and years you have held your job will be considered. The length of time you expect to remain at your job will also be considered. In addition, your other financial resources will be examined. Do you have savings or insurance? Do you own an automobile or a home?

Your *capacity* to repay will also be examined. Other debts that you have and your general living expenses will be reviewed. Creditors must know that you have the capacity to repay before they can extend credit to you.

The first time you use credit, you establish a record at your local credit reporting agency. Your file will grow as you use credit throughout your life. Maintaining a good credit record is important. Then you can prove your character, capital, and capacity when you need to use credit.

Why Credit Costs

Providing credit for consumers is costly for businesses. Businesses often have to borrow money to cover operating costs until debtors begin to pay. These businesses have to pay interest on the money they borrow. In addition, they have to pay the costs involved in running a credit department. Employees must be hired to interview credit applicants and to check over the information on completed credit applications. Bookkeepers are needed to keep credit accounts up-to-date. Bills must be sent and payments accepted and recorded. Because all people do not pay on schedule, businesses have to pay for additional help to collect bad debts. They must compensate for losses on unpaid bills.

How can businesses afford to extend credit? They make up part of their expenses by slightly raising the prices of their goods and services. They collect a credit charge from their credit customers. The credit charge is related to the cost of providing credit. The more money a business spends to provide credit, the more it must charge its credit customers.

Shopping for Credit

Wise consumers shop for credit as they shop for other goods and services. As with any form of purchase, they shop for the best value. They compare the total

BELK CREDIT APPLICATION

EMPLOYEE NO.	DATE

I WANT	☐ REVOLVING	☐ 30-60-90	☐ BOTH	Type of Account Requested: ☐ INDIVIDUAL ☐ JOINT

PLEASE TELL US ABOUT YOURSELF

FIRST NAME (TITLES OPTIONAL)	MIDDLE INITIAL	LAST NAME	AGE

STREET ADDRESS (IF P.O. BOX — PLEASE GIVE STREET ADDRESS)	CITY	STATE	ZIP

☐ OWN ☐ LIVE WITH RELATIVE ☐ RENT ☐ OTHER	MONTHLY PAYMENT $	YEARS AT PRESENT ADDRESS	HOME PHONE NO. ( )	NO. OF DEPENDENTS

PREVIOUS ADDRESS	CITY	STATE	ZIP	HOW LONG

NAME OF NEAREST RELATIVE NOT LIVING WITH YOU	RELATIONSHIP	PHONE NO. ( )

ADDRESS	CITY	STATE

NOW TELL US ABOUT YOUR JOB

EMPLOYER OR INCOME SOURCE	POSITION/TITLE	HOW LONG EMPLOYED YRS. MOS.	MONTHLY INCOME $

EMPLOYER'S ADDRESS	CITY	STATE	TYPE OF BUSINESS	BUSINESS PHONE ( )

MILITARY RANK (IF NOW IN SERVICE)	SEPARATION DATE	UNIT AND DUTY STATION	SOCIAL SECURITY NO.

SOURCE OF OTHER INCOME (Alimony, child support, or separate maintenance need not be revealed if you do not wish to have it considered as a basis for repaying this obligation)	SOURCE	INCOME $	☐ MONTHLY ☐ ANNUALLY

AND YOUR CREDIT REFERENCES ARE

NAME AND ADDRESS OF BANK/SAVINGS AND LOAN	☐ CHECKING ☐ SAVINGS ☐ LOAN	PREVIOUS BELK OR LEGGETT ACCOUNT? ACCOUNT NO. HOW IS ACCOUNT LISTED?	☐ YES ☐ NO

List Bank cards, Dept. Stores, Finance Co.'s, and other accounts:	NAME	ACCOUNT NO.	BALANCE	PAYMENT
			$	$
			$	$
			$	$
			$	$

INFORMATION REGARDING JOINT APPLICANT

COMPLETE THIS AREA IF   ☐ JOINT ACCOUNT IS REQUESTED   ☐ YOU ARE RELYING ON SPOUSE'S INCOME OR CREDIT HISTORY TO OBTAIN CREDIT

FIRST NAME	MIDDLE INITIAL	LAST NAME	AGE	RELATIONSHIP	SOCIAL SECURITY NO.

JOINT APPLICANT'S ADDRESS IF DIFFERENT FROM APPLICANT ADDRESS	CITY	STATE	ZIP

JOINT APPLICANT'S PRESENT EMPLOYER	ADDRESS	HOW LONG EMPLOYED YRS. MOS.

BUSINESS PHONE ( )	POSITION/TITLE	MONTHLY INCOME $

YOUR SIGNATURE PLEASE

Store Stamp Below

I have read and agree to the Terms and Conditions of the Belk Retail Charge Agreement as set forth on attached. Belk is authorized to investigate my credit record and exchange credit experience with other creditors and Credit Reporting Agencies. This information is given to obtain credit, and is true and complete.

FOR OFFICE USE ONLY
Letter _____
CB. RPT. _____
EMP. VER _____

Applicant's Signature _____   Date

DATE	EMP.	#CARDS	T/C	CR/LN.	APPROVED
☐	☐	☐	☐	☐	☐

Joint Applicant's signature
(required if joint applicant section completed) _____   Date

19-25

When applying for credit, you will fill out an application such as this one. The information you provide helps creditors determine if you are a good credit risk.

costs of using credit at several different places. They also compare terms of credit agreements. Since credit charges vary from source to source, comparison shopping is smart.

When shopping for credit, compare sources. A car dealer may offer credit for the purchase of a car or truck. A store may offer credit for major purchases. Credit unions, savings and loan associations, and banks are other sources. Finance companies specialize in offering credit, but their interest rates are usually high.

Find out the exact cost of using credit. This helps you compare finance charges and determine how much credit you can afford. **Finance charges** are the total amounts a borrower must pay the creditor for the use of credit. These charges include interest, service charges, and any other fees. Creditors are bound by law to tell borrowers the dollar amount of all finance charges.

The Cost of Credit

Three factors determine the total cost of using credit. These factors are the size of the loan or amount of credit used, the annual percentage rate, and the repayment time. By comparing these factors, you can shop for the best deal.

The Amount of Credit Used

As you borrow or charge greater amounts, you will pay more in interest. **Interest** is the price you pay the creditor for the use of money over a period of time. Interest is a rate, expressed as a percentage. For example, the interest rate paid on a credit card account may be 1.5 percent a month.

The Annual Percentage Rate

To compare credit costs fairly, be sure to consider the **annual percentage rate (APR)**. This is the actual percentage rate of interest paid per year. A monthly 1.5-percent rate equals an APR of 18 percent.

Comparing APRs from different sources is an easy way to choose the lowest interest rate. The higher the APR is, the more you will pay in interest. For instance, an 18-percent APR would mean higher interest payments than a 15.5-percent APR.

The Repayment Time

The longer you take to repay your credit debt, the larger the amount you will pay in interest. For instance, the interest on a $100 loan at 18-percent APR repaid in two years would cost $36. If the same loan is repaid in one year, the interest would be $18.

Credit Contracts

A **credit contract** is a legally binding agreement between creditor and borrower. It details the terms of repayment. A contract provides protection for both creditor and borrower, 19-26. It tells what is expected of each party. If either party fails to carry out the terms of the contract, the other may take legal steps to enforce the terms.

Read all contracts carefully before signing. Make sure you understand every term and the meaning of each statement. Question any point that you do not understand. Be sure that all blank spaces on the contract have been filled. Look for dates, total finance charges, and the annual percentage rate. This information is required on the contract by law.

A credit contract is a serious commitment. Before you sign, ask the creditor these important questions:

KEEP THIS NOTICE FOR FUTURE USE
BELK RETAIL CHARGE AGREEMENT

1. Each time I receive the monthly statement (at about the same time each month) I will decide whether to pay the New Balance of the account in full or in part. If full payment of the New Balance shown on the statement is received, by BELK, by the Payment Due Date, No FINANCE CHARGE will be added to the account. Any month I choose not to pay the New Balance in full, I will make at least the minimum partial payment listed on the statement as Minimum Payment Now Due. Each month the Minimum Payment Due will be calculated according to the following schedule:

If New Balance Is	Less Than $10	$10-100	$101-150	$151-200	$201-250	$251-300	Over $300
Minimum Monthly Payment Is	Balance	$10	$15	$20	$25	$30	1/10 of account balance rounded to next highest $5 increment

2. If payment in full is not received by the Payment Due Date, I agree to pay a FINANCE CHARGE at the rate described below for my State of residence.

Annual Percentage Rate for Purchases	10% to 21% (see table below)		
State of Residence	Periodic Rate	Annual Percentage Rate	Portion of Average Daily Balance To Which Applied
DE., KY., VA., MS., GA., OK., MD.	1.75%	21%	ENTIRE
NC., PA., TN., FL., TX and all other states	1.50%	18%	ENTIRE
AL.	1.75%	21%	$750 or less
	1.5%	18%	over $750
WV.	1.5%	18%	$750 or less
	1.0%	12%	over $750
SC.	1.75%	21%	$650 or less
	1.5%	18%	over $650
MO.	1.5%	18%	$1,000 or less
	1.0%	12%	over $1,000
AR.	.083%	10%	ENTIRE
Grace Period:	You have until the next billing date which on average is 23 days if the balance is paid in full, before a finance charge will be imposed.		
Method of Computing the Average Daily Balance.	Average Daily Balance Method: We figure a portion of the finance charge on your account by applying the periodic rate to the "average daily balance" of your account (including current transactions). To get the "average daily balance", we take the beginning balance of your account each day, add any new purchases and subtract any payments or credits, and unpaid finance charges. This gives us the daily balance. Then, we add up all the daily balances for the billing cycle and divide the total by the number of days in the billing cycle. This gives us the "average daily balance".		

3. Credit for returned merchandise will not substitute for a payment.

4. BELK has the right to amend the terms and conditions of this agreement by advising me of its intentions to do so in a manner and to the extent required by law.

5. If any payment is not received by BELK by the Payment Due Date, the full unpaid balance of the account may, at the option of Belk, become due and payable. If the account is referred for collection by Belk to any outside agency and/or attorney, who is not a salaried employee of BELK, I will, to the extent permitted by law, pay all costs including attorney fees.

6. BELK reserves the right to charge a handling fee, not to exceed the amount permitted by law, on any check used for payment on the account that is returned by the bank for insufficient funds or otherwise unpaid.

7. If this is a joint account, both of us agree to be bound by the terms of this agreement and each of us agrees to be jointly and severally liable for payment of all purchases made under this agreement.

8. The credit card issued to me in connection with this account remains the property of BELK and I will surrender it upon request. I understand that BELK is not obligated to extend to me any credit and, without prior notice, may refuse to allow me to make any purchase or incur any other charge on my account. Such refusal will not affect my obligation to pay the balance existing on my account at the time.

9. If any provision of this agreement is found to be invalid or unenforceable, the remainder of this agreement shall not be affected thereby, and the rest of this agreement shall be valid and enforced to the fullest extent permitted by law. No delay, omission, or waiver in the enforcement of any provision of this agreement by BELK will be deemed to be a waiver of any subsequent breach of such provision or of any other provision of this agreement.

10. I hereby authorize BELK, or any credit bureau employed by BELK, to investigate references, statements, and other data contained on my application or obtained from me or any other source pertaining to my credit worthiness. I will furnish further information if requested. I authorize BELK to furnish information concerning its credit experience with me to credit reporting agencies and others who may lawfully receive such information.

11. Except as provided in paragraph 2 above, this agreement will be governed by the laws of the State of North Carolina.

19-26

This is an example of a typical credit contract. When you are issued a credit card, you agree to abide by rules such as these.

1. What action can be taken if I skip a payment or make it late?
2. Can I repay the debt in advance? For example, if the contract states I have a total of 24 monthly payments, can I repay in 12 months instead?
3. If I pay in advance, will part of the finance charges be refunded to me?

When a contract that involves a large sum of money is being considered, you may need legal advice. Do not hesitate to hire a lawyer. The fee you pay an attorney may save you a lot of money later. People who have either a weak credit rating or no credit rating may need a cosigner or *guarantor* on a contract. The cosigner may be a parent, older sibling, or family friend. Anyone who cosigns a contract agrees to pay the debt if the debtor fails to pay.

Using Credit Wisely

Managing credit wisely is an important consumer skill. When used carefully and sensibly, you get more of what you need, when you need it. You can learn to manage your credit wisely by following the guidelines in 19-27.

Using Credit Wisely

- Stay within your credit limits. Use credit sparingly and only after much thought.
- Shop around for the best credit terms before you borrow or charge.
- Deal only with reputable creditors.
- Read credit agreements before signing. Make sure you understand all the credit terms and can fulfill your obligation.
- Keep records of all credit transactions. Include receipts, payments, contracts, and correspondence. Keep records neatly organized in a file.
- Pay off balances on revolving charge accounts each month to avoid finance charges.
- Keep a good credit rating by paying promptly.
- Correct billing errors immediately.
- Notify creditors promptly if your credit card is lost or stolen.
- If you have trouble making credit payments, contact your creditors right away.

19-27

Following these guidelines can help consumers use credit wisely.

Here are some other helpful ways to manage your credit wisely:

▼ Before using credit, determine how much credit you can afford. Analyze your budget to see the expenses you must meet. Limit your use of credit to an amount you can safely pay each month.

▼ Evaluate whether or not to use credit. Compare credit terms to paying cash, using savings, or waiting.

▼ If you decide to use credit, shop for the best terms to meet your needs.

Handling Credit Problems

Credit problems can result when difficult situations arise. Sometimes an unexpected illness, job loss, or accident can lead to financial problems. If this happens, do not ignore your credit bills. Notify your creditor promptly and be honest about your situation. Most creditors will let you delay or decrease your monthly payments until your situation improves.

Credit problems can also result from misusing credit. Some people spend more than they can afford. Financial problems also may result from poor management, lack of management skills, loss of income, illness, or an emergency. Learning to use credit wisely can help people avoid some of these problems.

Once a problem becomes serious, notify your creditors promptly. If they are aware of the facts and your sincere intention to repay, they may defer payments for a while. They may allow you to return merchandise for credit. They may offer to extend the payment period, thus decreasing the size of your monthly payments.

Setting the Scene: Credit Trouble

Pat always used credit cards for routine purchases. She tried to pay most bills off at the end of the month, but she wasn't always able to. Her major debt was a car loan. Then Pat bought a new town house and found a roommate to share expenses. She wanted nice furniture and made purchases at several different stores. Each store allowed her at least one year to start making payments.

A few months later, Pat's roommate lost her job and could no longer pay rent. Pat could not make her house payment. Also, it was almost time to start making payments on the furniture. Pat was on the brink of bankruptcy and didn't know what to do. She knew that bankruptcy would destroy her credit rating for ten years. She felt guilty, embarrassed, and afraid.

Analyze It: What danger signals did you see for Pat before she bought the town house? How can Pat reduce her financial commitments? What can she do to increase her income? How could this situation have been avoided?

When creditors will not offer a more lenient plan for paying, you may need to *consolidate* your debts. To do this, you must find a financial institution that will loan you enough money to pay all other debts. This institution will then arrange a monthly payment plan that you can afford. Monthly payments may be smaller, but the repayment schedule may be longer.

Credit Counseling

When credit problems get out of control, people can seek help from nonprofit credit counseling services, 19-28. Credit counseling services can help debtors in two ways. First, an effort is made to work out a reasonable budget based on available income. This budget must allow a certain amount of income to be applied to paying debts. Sometimes the difference between income and living expenses is not enough to pay debts. Then the credit counselors will try to help the debtor to arrange new payment schedules.

The second kind of help is training in money management. Counselors teach people management skills so future problems can be avoided.

Court Protection

People who cannot resolve serious long-term credit problems on their own may seek legal protection through the court system. Two choices are available: a Wage Earner Plan or bankruptcy.

The *Wage Earner Plan* is a legal arrangement by the courts that schedules debt repayment. With this plan, the debtor's income, property, and other assets are protected while the debtor repays all debts. This plan may be very costly, but the debtor does not have to file bankruptcy.

When a person files *bankruptcy*, the court declares that the person is unable to pay debts. The debtor's possessions are sold. The cash from the sales, with the exception of a small amount, is distributed to creditors. Filing bankruptcy will probably prevent you from obtaining credit for at least 10 years.

19-28
Credit counselors can help debtors manage their payments.

Check It Out!

1. List three advantages and three disadvantages of using credit.
2. Explain the difference between sales credit and cash credit.
3. List five ways to establish a credit rating.
4. What three factors do creditors use to evaluate people who are applying for credit?
5. True or false. The three factors affecting the cost of credit are capital, annual percentage rate, and the repayment schedule.
6. A _____ is a legally binding agreement between the creditor and borrower that details the terms of repayment.
7. List two ways in which credit counseling services help debtors handle credit problems.

Topic 19-5

Consumers and the Law

Objectives

After studying this topic, you will be able to

▼ identify consumer protection laws.

▼ practice techniques for protecting your privacy.

▼ describe your consumer rights and responsibilities.

Topic Terms

Food and Drug Administration (FDA)
Consumer Product Safety Commission (CPSC)
recourse

Businesses and consumers are active participants in the United States economy. In the free enterprise system, businesses produce goods and services. Consumers then buy and use these goods and services. This puts money back into businesses so they can continue producing. Keeping this economic cycle strong depends on businesses and consumers treating each other fairly. Laws that prohibit unfair business practices protect consumers' rights. To protect these rights, consumers must act responsibly.

Understanding your consumer rights and responsibilities can help you become a better consumer. As you use your rights and take on your responsibilities, you help keep the economy strong. See 19-29.

Consumer Protection Laws

In recent years, much attention has been focused on protecting consumers against unfair business practices. As a result, the federal government passed several laws aimed at protecting consumers' rights. How do these laws aid consumers? They help consumers understand and compare credit costs. The laws provide guidelines for consumers if they are denied credit, find a billing error, or receive an inaccurate credit rating. These four laws are summarized as follows.

The *Truth in Lending Law* requires creditors to provide a complete account of credit costs and terms. Ask for this information before you sign any credit contracts. This law also requires creditors to send debtors regular statements. These statements must show the unpaid balances of the accounts and any finance charges that have been made.

The *Equal Credit Opportunity Act* protects people from discrimination because of sex, marital status, race, religion, or age. In other words, credit can be denied only for financial reasons. People who have been denied credit can demand to receive written explanations of why credit was denied.

The *Fair Credit Billing Act* states the rules by which consumers and creditors must settle disputes about billing. If a debtor thinks there is a mistake in a bill, the creditor is required by law to pay attention to the complaint. If an error is found, it must be corrected without charge to the debtor.

Consumers who wish to complain must follow certain rules. They must send the complaint *in writing* to the creditor within 60 days after the bill was mailed. The consumer's name and account number plus the amount and description of the error must be clearly stated.

19-29
The economy is stimulated by consumers making purchases.

The *Fair Credit Reporting Act* protects you against an inaccurate credit record. Your credit rating is based on information in your credit file. Under this act, you have a right to see the contents of your file. In addition, you can file a letter to explain any information in the file that you feel is not correct.

Protecting Your Privacy

You have the right to decide who has access to your personal information. This includes such information as your social security number, credit card numbers, and e-mail address.

How do you make sure your personal information is kept private? There are several steps you can take to protect yourself. First, do not share personal information with others who do not have the right to know. Be wary about sharing your social security number or credit card numbers. Only do so if you are confident about the reliability of the person or company with whom you are dealing. Ask your bank to notify you in writing when someone wants to check your records. Check your bank records carefully to make sure that no one is tapping into your account electronically.

Be cautious when giving information over the phone or Internet, 19-30. Online privacy is especially difficult. Take care when providing information to Web sites you browse. If you are placing an order online, make sure you are at a secure Web site.

19-30

Protect your private information from other Internet users—be sure a company is legitimate and reliable before making an online purchase.

Identity Theft

One of the dangers of not controlling your personal information is identity theft. *Identity theft* occurs when someone wrongfully obtains and uses another's personal information in a way that involves fraud.

Some scam artists send bogus e-mails that appear to come from a legitimate source. The e-mails may request credit card or other personal information. If you receive a request for personal information or passwords, make sure the e-mail is genuine before complying. Most Internet providers, online stores, and banks will *not* request such information, especially in an e-mail. Such a request could be an attempt to steal your identity.

If someone uses your personal information to pretend they are you, they can make purchases that will be charged to you. In some cases, unauthorized people take funds from their victims' bank accounts and run up huge credit debts. Some even commit crimes while using the names and private information of others.

While laws project you from such losses, it is still a long, difficult task to clear up the confusion. You may lose some money. If your credit rating is damaged, you will have to reestablish it and your reputation. The thief may use your insurance or set up new credit accounts in your name. If this happens, working through the red tape to set things right can take years.

To prevent identity theft, memorize your social security number and keep your card in a safe place—not in your wallet. Carry only those credit cards you use regularly. Cut up old cards before you throw them away, 19-31. Make sure the number and your signature are unreadable.

When choosing PIN numbers, do not use obvious numbers such as those from your address, phone number, or birthday. Memorize your PIN. Do not write it down on your card. Be constantly aware of the need to protect your personal information.

19-31

Expired credit cards should be cut before they are thrown out so all personal information is destroyed.

Fraud

Fraud is a deliberate misrepresentation that causes another person to suffer damages, usually the loss of money. Fraud can take many forms.

Telemarketing schemes involve using the phone to take money from victims. Telemarketers will call victims and promise goods or services for a fee. Some may offer prizes in exchange for personal information. Then the promised goods, services, or prizes are never provided.

Pyramid schemes and *chain letters* depend on a continuing supply of people investing in the system. They depend on people recruiting more and more people to join in the scheme. The problem is that eventually, they always wind down. The people who come in late lose their money. To protect yourself from these schemes, always be wary of the following:

▼ an investment that promises quick profit with no risk

▼ an investment that does not indicate how and where your money will be invested

▼ an offer to sell an item at much less than the known value

Internet fraud may involve the same kinds of schemes already discussed. One reason Internet fraud is easy is because the thief has the ability to carry it out quickly. In addition, many potential victims can be reached anywhere in the world.

Consumer Rights and Responsibilities

Fairness to both buyer and seller is the basis of the free enterprise system. Unfair business practices hurt both consumers and producers. For this reason, monopolies, price fixing, and deceptive business practices are illegal. When consumer rights are protected, the whole economic system benefits. In accepting these rights, consumers must meet certain responsibilities as well. These rights and responsibilities are outlined in 19-32.

The Right to Be Informed

As a consumer, you have a right to accurate information about products and services. Such information can help you make good buying decisions and use products wisely after purchase.

You have the right to be informed through reliable sources. Information should be available on product cost, features, benefits, and uses. An honest, knowledgeable salesperson can answer questions about product quality and performance. See 19-33. Consumer publications provide comparison shopping

---

Your Consumer Rights and Responsibilities

You have the right to

- information
- selection
- performance
- safety
- recourse

You have the responsibility to

- seek and use information when making consumer decisions
- select wisely
- follow instructions
- guard against carelessness
- let dissatisfactions be known

19-32

When you accept your consumer rights, you must meet certain responsibilities as well.

19-33
When you order merchandise from a catalog, the salesperson should be able to answer any questions you have.

advice and product test results. They also inform consumers on many other related issues. *Consumer Reports* is one such publication. Product labels include information about use and care, features, and warranties.

The Responsibility to Seek and Use Information

You have a responsibility to seek and use reliable information about products and services. Advertising simply informs; it is not intended to provide all the information you need to make good buying decisions. Read consumer articles in reputable newspapers and magazines. Read product labels and service agreements. Ask reliable, experienced sources to share their opinions. Carefully compare competing products and services before you buy.

The Right to Selection

Consumers have a right to choose the products they want. However, this presupposes that a variety is available.

Suppose that only the Make-Believe Company supplies a certain product. Also, suppose this company has used unfair business practices to drive competing products out of the market. Then the Make-Believe Company would have a *monopoly* on the product since it would be offered nowhere else. Without competing products, you would have to buy from the Make-Believe Company at whatever price it charged.

Laws prohibit monopolies to ensure that competing products and services remain available to consumers. Sellers then compete for consumers' money with products of different price and quality levels. The result of competition is the creation of more selection at better prices.

The Responsibility to Select Wisely

When variety is available, you are responsible for wise choices. Select the product or service that best meets your needs. Shop carefully for the right quality. This does not mean that you should always look for the very best quality or lowest prices. Make a wise selection by purchasing the best quality to meet your needs at a price you can afford.

The Right to Performance

As a consumer, you have the right to expect that the product you buy will perform as it should. Suppose an ad claims that a certain cleaning fluid will not injure the finish of your furniture. Then you have the right to expect that it will not remove varnish from your dining room table. What if you buy a laundry detergent that claims it is safe to use with all fabrics? Then your best shirt should not fall apart after being washed with it.

The Responsibility to Read and Follow Instructions

To get good performance from a product, you must use it as it is meant to be used, 19-34. Suppose the label on a bottle of cleaning fluid reads *Use on tile only; may be harmful to wood finishes.* If you used it on your dining room table and ruined the finish, you would have only yourself to blame.

Clothing manufacturers are required to put care labels on the garments they make. Read and follow the manufacturer's directions carefully. What if the label on your new sweater reads *dry clean only* and you wash it? Then you cannot complain if it shrinks.

Most manufacturers provide use and care booklets with the products they sell. These booklets give detailed instructions for using and maintaining products. You are responsible for reading and following these instructions. If you do not operate products properly, you could damage them or cause an injury. The products you buy will give you the performance you expect only if you do your part.

The Right to Safety

Consumers have a right to protection against harmful products. They have the right to know the products and services they buy will be safe if used properly. Several government agencies were developed to protect this right. These agencies provide consumer protection by screening products for safety and taking steps to prevent unsafe products in the market.

The **Food and Drug Administration (FDA)** watches over sales of food, drugs, and cosmetics. The FDA may prohibit the sale of or require safety warnings on products that may harm people.

The **Consumer Product Safety Commission (CPSC)** handles complaints about unsafe products such as household appliances, toys, and tools. It protects consumers from unsafe products and encourages safe product use at all times. This agency investigates reports of dangerous products and bans hazardous products.

Each year the CPSC receives thousands of complaints from unhappy consumers. When a pattern becomes evident, the agency studies the product and reviews news reports about it. If a product is considered hazardous, the CPSC takes steps to ban it. For example, one study resulted in the recall of several million coffeemakers. Defective wiring made the coffeemakers a fire hazard.

The Responsibility to Use Products Safely

As a consumer, you have a responsibility to use products safely. Read product labels to find out if products may

19-34
You can expect good performance from products only if you read and follow product instructions.

be dangerous if used in a certain way. Some products that are perfectly safe when new may become unsafe after lengthy storage. Ingredients may deteriorate or become unstable.

Always review guidelines, operating instructions, and other product materials provided by the manufacturer. One of the greatest mistakes is dismissing instructions for products that you do not regard as potentially dangerous. Always follow all guidelines. Use products for the purposes for which they were designed.

One of the greatest consumer responsibilities in the area of safety is that of making hazards known. Return a dangerous product to the store where you bought it. Notify its manufacturer of your action. You can also report hazards to appropriate government agencies.

The Right to Recourse

If you buy a product and it does not perform as expected, you have the right to recourse. **Recourse** is asking for help. In other words, you have the right to express your dissatisfaction. You also have the right to have your complaint heard and to have action taken on it. You have the right to complain if

▼ a product you bought is defective
▼ services or product repairs are not satisfactory
▼ merchandise you ordered was not received
▼ a warranty or guarantee is not honored
▼ a refundable deposit is not refunded

Some consumer problems are difficult so consumer agencies may help resolve some of them. When problems are beyond the help of consumer agencies, legislation may be needed. State legislators can be contacted for problems confined to one state. Federal legislators can be contacted for nationwide problems. If enough people appeal to their state or federal government representatives, legislation may be considered to handle the problem. See 19-35.

A sampling of private and government agencies to contact for help with consumer problems are described here.

Letters to Legislators

- Be clear! State the issue and how you want your legislator to handle it in the first few sentences.
- If you are writing about a specific bill that has already been introduced, identify the bill by name and number. (If you do not know the name and number, give some description of its contents.)
- Write about only one issue in each letter.
- Be persuasive. Tell why you feel the way you do.
- Be brief. Write legibly or type. Legislators do not have time to read long, scribbled letters.
- Be courteous. Anger and threats may work against you.
- Do not pretend to have vast influence.
- Be constructive. Do not just say what is wrong. Go further and say what is right.
- Write only to legislators who represent you.
- Send notes of appreciation when your legislators do something you like.

19-35
Legislation may be needed to solve some consumer problems.

Chambers of commerce usually have divisions that accept and act on consumer complaints. Your chamber of commerce may keep a file on local businesses, including complaints that consumers have filed against them. If you need information about a local business, you can call your local chamber of commerce for a reference.

Better Business Bureaus (BBB) perform services similar to those of a chamber of commerce. Their information usually covers more than just local businesses. The BBBs are nonprofit organizations sponsored by private businesses. They try to settle complaints against local businesses.

Media complaint desks of newspapers, radio stations, and television stations provide outlets for consumer complaints. Complaints reported by the media reach the greatest number of people in the quickest possible way.

Licensing boards have been set up by state governments to issue licenses to persons who are qualified to perform certain services. These boards set standards that must be met before a license to perform a service is granted. Boards may also cancel a license. For example, suppose someone who is licensed to perform a service has acted unethically. The board may suspend or cancel the person's license to practice in that state. Licensing boards cover many areas of service. If you have a complaint, report it to the appropriate board in your state.

State government consumer protection divisions are under the direction of the state's attorney general. These agencies aim to protect consumers from unfair and deceptive business practices.

Small claims courts handle claims that involve relatively small amounts of money. Consumers represent themselves instead of hiring attorneys. Booklets that describe such courts can be obtained from your local

government, from consumer agencies, or from your state's attorney general.

Private or public legal services may be needed to settle larger claims. Persons who can afford legal services must pay for them. Persons who cannot afford private legal aid may ask for public legal aid.

The Responsibility to Let Dissatisfactions Be Known

When you pay for a product or service and are dissatisfied, you have a responsibility to voice your dissatisfaction. By complaining, you bring problems to the only people who can do something about correcting them—the providers of goods and services.

When you complain to a company, do so in an organized way. Whether you call or make a personal visit, state your name, address, and account number. Describe the nature of your complaint (for example, poor service or faulty merchandise). Tell when and where the incident happened. Tell what goods or services you purchased and how much you paid. Briefly explain what happened. Finally, tell what action you want the company to take.

For a more serious problem, you may decide to write a complaint letter to the manufacturer. Address your letter to the consumer affairs department of the company. If you feel top management should know about the problem, write to the president of the company. In either case, include a clear, concise explanation of the problem. Give the date and place of purchase, model number, and purchase price. Enclose a photocopy of the receipt or bill in question. At the close of the letter, suggest the action you want taken, such as a refund or replacement. A sample complaint letter appears in 19-36.

Do not let your temper interfere with your complaint. If you are angry, cool off before you call or write. This will make

Complaint Letter

2201 Mountain Drive
Tucson, Arizona 85719
March 21, 2007

Hillary Willis
Consumer Relations Manager
Great Time Watch Company
12 North Hunter Trail
Carol Stream, IL 60188

Dear Ms. Willis:

I purchased a Great Time watch for $25.99 on March 10, 2007, from the Discount Center in Tucson. The model number is 923. A photocopy of my receipt and the warranty is enclosed.

After one week of use, the watch stopped working. I changed the battery, but it still doesn't work. I carefully followed your directions for use, so I think the watch was defective. I am concerned that other consumers who buy this watch may have the same problem.

The warranty states that I should receive a replacement if the product is defective. Even after explaining my problem to the manager at the Discount Center, he said he could not help me. Since I am not satisfied with this product, I would like my watch replaced within the next month.

If you need more information about this problem, please call me at (602) 555-1700. I appreciate your help and look forward to receiving a replacement watch.

Sincerely,

Alex Reiko

Alex Reiko
Enclosures

19-36
When writing a complaint letter, clearly explain the problem and suggest a solution.

your complaint easier to understand. Remember that the person who reads your letter or answers your call is not personally responsible for your problem. He or she is just trying to help settle it.

Resolving Consumer Problems

Knowing and practicing both your consumer rights and responsibilities is the key to resolving consumer problems. There are consumer laws that protect you, but you certainly will not want to go to court to resolve every problem.

Sometimes people are responsible for creating their own consumer problems. This happens when they ignore their consumer responsibilities. Not using information available, buying unwisely, ignoring instructions provided, and ignoring safety precautions means they lose their right to complain.

How to Resolve a Consumer Problem

When you have a legitimate complaint, follow a step-by-step procedure to resolve it. Begin by contacting the place where you bought the product or service. If that fails, write a letter to the manufacturer. As a final step, contact a consumer protection agency, such as the BBB. Government agencies at the local, state, and federal levels can also assist you with your complaint.

Here is an example of how to resolve a product complaint. Suppose you bought athletic shoes that came apart after you wore them for one week. First, ask yourself if the shoes were truly defective or if your dog chewed a hole in them before they started to rip. If the dog chewed a hole due to your carelessness, you have no right to complain.

If you have shoes that are truly defective, what should you do? Go back to the store where you bought the shoes. Show them to the manager of the shoe department and explain your problem. If the department manager does not resolve your problem, talk to the store manager. If the problem remains unresolved, contact the manufacturer of the product. If the problem still remains, contact the appropriate private or government agency. As a last resort, contact your legislator. The legislature may need to amend an old law or write a new law to cover some consumer problems.

Check It Out!

1. Name the consumer protection law that requires creditors to provide a complete account of credit costs and terms.
2. List the five basic consumer rights and their corresponding responsibilities.
3. Outline the step-by-step procedure for resolving a consumer complaint.

Chapter Review

Summary

Consumers must choose from a variety of goods and services in the marketplace every day. It pays to be an informed consumer and shop wisely to get more value for the money. Knowing where to shop, when to buy, what to buy, and how to use the decision-making process keeps smart shoppers on target.

The computer and other types of high-tech equipment are common purchases in today's Information Age. When used well, they provide many useful functions including information processing, money management, information gathering, and communicating. When not managed well, high-tech equipment does not improve the quality of life and even creates drawbacks.

One of the strongest influences on consumer spending is advertising. Advertising affects consumer attitudes, tastes, and preferences. It can be informative as well as persuasive. Understanding the types of advertising and how to evaluate them can help consumers make informed choices.

Deciding whether or not to use credit is an important consumer decision. It involves knowing how each type of credit works and the pros and cons of credit use. Shopping for the best credit terms helps consumers compare finance charges and get the best deal. Misusing credit can lead to serious financial problems. Those consumers who cannot handle serious credit problems should seek help from credit counseling services or through legal protection.

To help keep the economy strong and productive, consumers must understand their rights and be prepared to exercise them. Consumers have the right to information, selection, performance, safety, and recourse. In turn, consumers must recognize that every right carries a basic responsibility that must also be followed.

Think About It!

1. What factors do you consider in deciding to shop at each of the following: specialty store, department store, factory outlet, and flea market?
2. Why do you think it is important to read and understand the terms specified in a warranty?
3. Explain why comparison shopping is a useful consumer skill to develop.
4. What are some everyday activities that are made easier by computers?
5. What are some possible drawbacks associated with using high-tech equipment?
6. Who benefits when a consumer like yourself complains about fraudulent and deceptive advertising?
7. Give three examples of how you have been influenced by advertising to buy goods and services. For each example, describe the type of advertising used. How did each ad make you feel about buying the product?
8. Explain how the following factors influence your consumer decisions:
   A. culture
   B. economics
   C. society
   D. environment

9. Topic 19-4 suggested several ways people can establish a credit rating. State the three tips you would most likely use when you attempt to establish a credit rating.

10. Since buying with credit usually costs more than buying with cash, when is it financially feasible to use credit? Why should you find out the cost of credit before using it?

11. What information should you seek before signing a credit contract?

12. Suppose you lost your job and had no means of paying your creditor. How do you think you would handle your problem?

13. Choose to agree or disagree with one of the following statements. Explain your response.
    A. Consumer rights are more important than consumer responsibilities because…
    B. Consumer responsibilities are more important than consumer rights because…
    C. Consumer rights and responsibilities are equally important because…

14. Share an experience you had with an unsatisfactory product or service. What steps did you take to solve the problem?

15. Review this chapter and suggest five related careers that would interest you.

Try It Out!

1. Brainstorm as a class to name the different shopping alternatives available in your area.

2. Determine an item that would be of interest to members of your class. Go through the process of comparison shopping. Consider quality, suitability, use and care, warranty, and cost. Choose the best buy.

3. As a class, evaluate examples of printed advertisements for high-tech equipment. Evaluate each ad to determine whether it is informative or persuasive and what type of advertising is used. Based on your evaluation, which type seems to be most commonly used?

4. Have a class discussion about the wise and unwise use of consumer credit. Design a bulletin board to illustrate the conclusions made during the discussion.

5. Collect credit contracts from three local stores where teens shop. Read and discuss the contracts in class. Make sure you understand the terms for each one. Determine how much interest you would have to pay for $100 worth of credit used over a three-month period.

6. Divide the class into groups. Each group should select and interpret one of the consumer rights and its corresponding responsibility. The groups may use any method—skits, bulletin board displays, posters, or videotapes—to convey their messages to the class.

career.guide

Consumer Services Careers

Career Ladder for Consumer Services

▶ **Advanced Degree**

Consumer affairs director
Consumer attorney
Certified financial planner

▶ **Bachelor's Degree**

Consumer affairs journalist
Customer service
   representative
Product tester
Consumer correspondent
Credit manager

▶ **Associate's Degree**

Consumer safety officer
Insurance agent

▶ **High School Diploma**

Bank teller
Telephone operator
Personal shopper
Product demonstrator

▶ **Pre-High School Diploma**

Club treasurer
School newspaper reporter
   on teen consumer issues

People in this field discuss, demonstrate, and ensure the quality and proper use of the goods and services they sell to customers. These professionals also help consumers use their resources well.

Employment Opportunities

Manufacturers of food, clothing, cars, and other products have departments devoted to handling consumer questions and complaints. Workers for cable, phone, and utility companies help customers identify service plans that are right for them. Financial advisers help clients develop financial goals and make plans to reach them. Credit counselors work with people who have credit problems to help solve them. Many businesses and government agencies employ workers to help callers with their questions.

Entrepreneurial Opportunities

Many money managers and financial advisers begin their careers working for someone else. After gaining experience, they open their own offices. Insurance agents often follow a similar career path. Someone with consumer services experience in several industries may write a book or newspaper column or offer tips through a radio show. A person who has an eye for value may start a business as a personal shopper.

Rewards and Demands

People in consumer services say their chief reward is the feelings of fulfillment from helping others. The demands of this field, on the other hand, are often the hurdles to providing help. Some people resent advice about their financial affairs and resist assistance. Sometimes the work can be emotionally draining. Consumer services workers must be cheerful, understanding, and open to the needs of their clients. They must stay focused on their roles as representatives of their company.

Preparation Requirements

Consumer services jobs are available for people with all levels of training. The type of consumer service a worker wishes to provide shapes the kind of preparation needed.

Entry-Level Jobs

Aids to consumer affairs specialists and product testers have entry-level jobs. These workers do a limited number of tasks. Someone at a higher level oversees the work of entry-level employees. People who do entry-level work may need only a high school diploma.

Midlevel Jobs

Research clerks in credit bureaus have mid-level consumer services jobs. Assistant loan officers, insurance agents, and collection agents also work at this level. These workers usually need two-year degrees from a business college.

Professional-Level Jobs

Skilled workers in this field include credit managers, survey specialists, loan officers, mediators, consultants, and consumer representatives. These professionals must understand consumer issues, consumer law, and their companies' policies. As a rule, skilled workers need at least a four-year degree. Some employers also want employees to have prior experience and demonstrate an ability to communicate well under stress.

Personal Qualities Needed for Success

An interest in consumer affairs and a commitment to helping people are needed for success in this field. Workers must know the laws protecting consumers and keep their information confidential. Successful workers have good problem-solving ability, excellent communication skills, and a winning strategy for counseling customers.

Future Trends

The future is likely to bring more job openings for people skilled in helping others manage their lives. A growing number of people will need help to meet financial goals. As businesses offer more online shopping, they need enough staff to handle customer questions and concerns. Companies will also need consumer service workers to maintain good customer relations. All these opportunities should provide more job options.

Career Interests, Abilities, and You

How would your interests, skills, and abilities stack up to the demands of a consumer services career? Taking a consumer skills or consumer issues class in high school could help you answer this question. Another way to see if you should plan a career in consumer services is to talk with someone who works in the field. Working with an aid organization that helps people resolve problems can give you insight into consumer services work.

You can practice using your consumer skills by setting up a budget for your money. Joining a junior investment club may be helpful if you have an income that you can invest. You might serve as treasurer of a school club to practice keeping financial records. Consider talking with peers about their problems in the marketplace as inspiration for writing a "consumer advice" column for the student newspaper.

Financial advisors assist clients with decisions about savings and investments.

Part Six
Meeting Your Clothing Needs

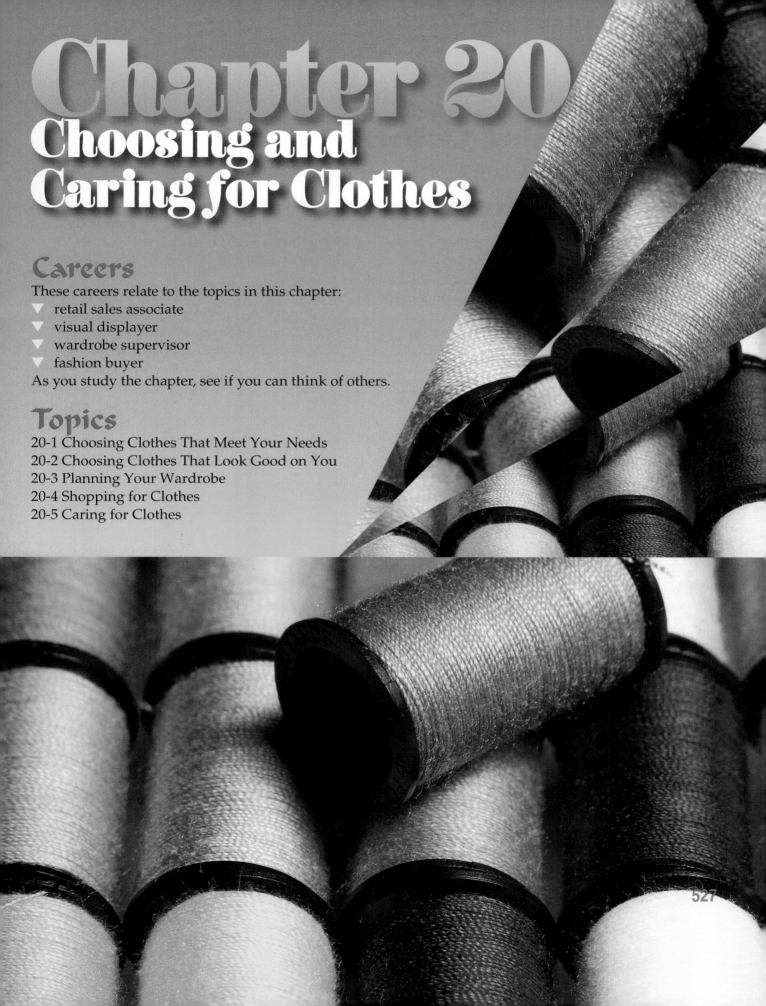

Chapter 20
Choosing and
Caring for Clothes

Careers

These careers relate to the topics in this chapter:
- ▼ retail sales associate
- ▼ visual displayer
- ▼ wardrobe supervisor
- ▼ fashion buyer

As you study the chapter, see if you can think of others.

Topics

Topic 20-1

Choosing Clothes That Meet Your Needs

Objectives

After studying this topic, you will be able to
▼ list ways in which clothing meets physical needs.
▼ explain how clothing satisfies psychological and social needs.
▼ choose clothing that would be appropriate for specific occasions.

Topic Terms

lifestyle
uniform
dress code
modesty
status
conformity
individuality

Buying clothes can take a big bite out of your budget. Deciding what to wear can take time out of your day. These statements indicate that clothing choices are important decisions. Thinking about your choices helps you choose clothes that will meet your needs.

Factors That Influence Clothing Decisions

A number of factors influence your clothing decisions. Besides your basic needs, you are likely to consider your peers' opinions when you are choosing clothes. You may think about what your clothes say about you. You will undoubtedly think about what activities you will be doing when you wear the clothes.

Physical Needs

Clothes help meet your basic *physical needs* to protect your body. Your body requires protection from the weather, environmental dangers, and occupational hazards.

Weather can be a threat to the body. People need to be protected from cold and heat and such elements as sun, rain, and snow. Jackets, gloves, scarves, hats, heavy socks, and boots keep people warm and dry on cold days. In warm weather, lightweight clothes in light colors help keep people cool. Garments that repel water provide protection from rain.

The environment poses certain physical dangers that can be moderated through clothing. Life jackets provide safety for those who work and play near water. In areas where insects are bothersome, some people wear special jackets and hoods to protect their skin from bites. Hiking boots help prevent skids and falls and protect feet from the impact of harsh, rocky terrains.

Clothes protect many people from hazards in their workplaces. Road workers wear brightly colored, reflective clothing so they will be visible to drivers. Firefighters wear heat- and fire-resistant garments. See 20-1. Health care workers often wear masks and gloves when working with patients. These items protect patients as well as workers from the possible transfer of germs.

Lifestyle

Many of your physical needs for clothing are determined by your **lifestyle**. This is your way of life or your style of living. You may own a few garments

20-1
Special clothing protects firefighters from flames, water, and fire-extinguisher chemicals. Gloves and boots also repel these elements and provide slip-resistance.

to wear for special occasions such as weddings. However, you probably do not wear these clothes often. Most of your clothing choices are dictated by your daily activities. If you enjoy playing sports, you probably own several pieces of activewear. If you spend much time outside, you are likely to own more outerwear than someone who prefers being indoors.

Psychological Needs

Any garment might meet a physical need. However, clothes must have certain characteristics to meet psychological needs. Certain colors, fabrics, and styles of clothing can affect how you feel. For

instance, bright colors might make you feel happy, 20-2. Perhaps you feel relaxed in soft fabrics and confident in formal styles.

Choosing clothes you find appealing gives you a sense of well-being by helping to meet your psychological need for attractiveness. Wearing clothes that enhance your appearance can boost your self-esteem.

Social Needs

The social need for acceptance plays a big role in the clothing choices most people make. This is especially true during the school years when children and teens are seeking the approval of their peers. Teens often wear clothes that identify them with a specific group. They may use clothing to exhibit a desired level of status. Teens also tend to choose clothing that conforms to styles worn by their friends.

Group Identification

People who identify with a group often use clothing as a sign of belonging. Members of certain groups wear uniforms as marks of identification. Other groups choose less rigid attire.

20-2
Feeling good about the clothes you wear is an important psychological need.

Uniforms are distinctive outfits that identify those who wear them with a specific group. See 20-3. You can look at athletes in their uniforms and immediately identify their sports and their teams. Military personnel on duty always wear uniforms. During war or peace, you can identify a person in military service by the uniform he or she wears.

Many schools, especially private schools, require students to wear uniforms. The uniforms of exclusive schools often serve as symbols of prestige. Some public school systems require students to wear uniforms as an antiviolence measure. Wearing uniforms sends a message that all students belong to the same "team." This results in less competition and more cooperation among "team members." Uniforms keep fashion from being an issue so students can focus more on learning.

Some groups do not have specific uniforms. However, they use certain colors or symbols to identify their members. For instance, members of sororities and fraternities often own garments with Greek letters representing the names of their organizations.

Many people show group identity simply by yielding to the influence of their peers. Your peers form an informal group. By wearing the kinds of clothes your friends wear, you are showing you are a member of that group. Jeans and T-shirts are typical attire of many teen peer groups.

20-3
These uniforms are worn by guards assigned to England's Buckingham Palace.

Dress Codes

Dress codes are standards of dress that are enforced in a social setting. Formal dress codes are based on the belief that how people dress tends to affect their behavior. For instance, many businesses have formal dress codes for their employees. Employers believe requiring employees to wear professional clothing encourages them to act professionally. See 20-4. Likewise, most school systems have written dress codes. These policies are designed to keep both teachers and students from wearing clothes that detract from teaching and learning.

Informal dress codes exist in society. People within a culture commonly accept these unwritten standards of dress. Societal dress codes reflect popular beliefs about **modesty**, or the proper way to cover the body in various settings. For instance, the social dress code in the United States considers swimsuits suitable for wearing at a beach, but not the office. There, swimsuits are viewed as immodest attire because they do not cover enough of the body.

Some religious and ethnic groups have informal dress codes that are stricter than the society in which they live. These stricter codes are based on standards of modesty that are more conservative.

Status

Status is a person's rank within a group. People often use clothing as signs of their status. Certain garments, styles, and brands carry a higher status than others. For instance, a Gucci purse and a Hermes scarf have a prestigious status because they are expensive. Such accessories suggest the wearers are wealthy. In many high schools, varsity jackets are signs of status. They indicate the wearers rank high among their classmates in athletic or academic skill.

People who want a certain status often desire clothes that reflect that status. In some teen groups, this means clothes that display names and logos of specific brands. Wearing these clothes can cause some teens to feel they have a higher status just because they are fashion conscious.

Conformity Versus Individuality

What other people wear greatly influences clothing choices. For most people, clothing selection is a balance between conformity and individuality. **Conformity** in dress means wearing garments similar to those worn by others. Early in life, children begin expressing a desire to wear the same kinds of clothes they see other people wearing. This kind of conformity gives children a feeling of belonging.

20-4

People who work in fashion or design careers, such as this apparel buyer, must meet a dress code requiring a stylish appearance.

In contrast, **individuality** in dress means choosing clothes that set you apart from others. See 20-5. You express your unique personality when you wear what you like without being swayed by what others wear. Wearing pants with a tailored shirt when others are wearing jeans and T-shirts is an example of expressing individuality.

People who conform too much give up their individuality. This occurs when someone wears only what is worn by peers. Most people, however, also select garments that are unique. This allows people to dress to suit their moods and create different impressions with their clothing.

Special Needs

Some people, such as older adults or people with disabilities, have special clothing needs. Older people may choose more casual, comfortable clothes for their daily activities. Easy care is another important factor. People with disabilities may want clothes that are stylish, yet easy to get on and off. Elastic waists and knit fabrics allow both comfort and ease of movement. People with physical limitations or low vision also need simple fasteners and larger openings.

Choosing Clothes for Specific Occasions

You need different types of clothes for different occasions. For instance, you would probably wear formal attire to a wedding or prom. You will need clothing that reflects your career choice when you go to a job interview. You will want your clothes looking their best when you go on a date, 20-6.

20-5
As teens mature, they tend to choose clothing styles that reflect their self-concept rather than prevailing trends.

Choosing the right clothes for the occasion can greatly influence your personal effectiveness. For instance, at a job interview, you need to emphasize your qualifications. You will be able to do this more easily if your clothing is not distracting to your potential employer.

If you are uncertain about what to wear for an occasion such as a party, check with your host. You could also ask others planning to attend the event. For an occasion such as a job interview, you could call the place of business. Someone there will be able to tell you what type of attire is appropriate.

Check It Out!

1. What are three factors from which clothing provides physical protection?
2. A distinctive outfit that identifies someone who wears it with a specific group is a _____.
3. How does conformity differ from individuality?
4. True or false. Choosing the right clothes for a specific occasion can greatly influence a person's effectiveness.

20-6

Choosing a simple, attractive outfit is the best way to make a good "first impression" on your date's parents.

When choosing clothes for specific occasions, you will not want to emphasize your individuality. Conformity is a safer policy in these situations. If an occasion is formal, choose formal clothing. If an event is in a business setting, look prepared for business.

Topic 20-2

Choosing Clothes That Look Good on You

Objectives

After studying this topic, you will be able to
▼ identify the colors that look best on you.
▼ explain how line, texture, and form can affect the way clothes look on you.
▼ apply the elements and principles of design to clothing selection.

Topic Terms

elements of design
hue
value
intensity
color wheel
primary colors
secondary colors
intermediate colors
neutrals
line
texture
form
principles of design
balance
proportion
rhythm
emphasis

Earlier you learned that good grooming and health habits can improve your appearance. Now you will see how the clothes you choose can enhance your appearance, too. Clothes can highlight your best features. At the same time, they can draw attention away from problem areas.

Which of your clothes are most flattering to you? Do those clothes have anything in common? Are most of them the same color? Do they have distinct lines? Are the textures mostly rough or mostly smooth? Do the forms of the garments enhance your body shape?

Color, line, texture, and form are the **elements of design**. These are factors that affect the appearance of a garment. Each element influences the way you look in your clothes. Whether you buy or make garments, you can consider these elements. Using the elements effectively can help you dress to look your best.

Color

Of all the design elements, color is the most exciting in clothing selection. Color is an expression of you. It reveals something about your looks, feelings, and moods. Knowing how to use color will help you achieve a pleasing appearance by enhancing your best features.

Color Characteristics

The color used in clothing is *pigment*, which is a substance that gives color to other materials. Color has three distinct characteristics. First, color can be defined in terms of hue. **Hue** is the name given to a color. Red, blue, violet, and orange are hues. Hue is what distinguishes one color from another. It makes red different from green or blue. If you make red lighter or darker, you will not change the hue—the changed color is still red.

A second characteristic of color is value. **Value** refers to the lightness or darkness of a color, such as light green and dark green. The value of a color changes when either black or white is added to it. Adding black to a color creates a *shade*. For instance, burgundy is a shade of red. A *tint* results when white is added to a color. Pink is a tint of red.

Intensity is the third characteristic of color. **Intensity** is the brightness or dullness of a color. Bright colors such as red or yellow have a high intensity. See 20-7. Pale colors such as pink or violet have a softer, less intense appearance.

The Color Wheel

How do colors relate to one another? The **color wheel** is a tool that shows this relationship, 20-8. The color wheel is very helpful for choosing and studying color in design. It shows the primary, secondary, and intermediate colors.

Yellow, blue, and red are known as **primary colors** because they cannot be created from other colors. The primary

colors are equally spaced from one another on the color wheel. By mixing, darkening, or lightening the primary colors, you can fill in the rest of the color wheel.

Mixing equal amounts of two primary colors produces a **secondary color**. Green, violet, and orange are the three secondary colors. You get green by mixing yellow and blue. Mixing blue and red produces violet. Mixing red and yellow results in orange. On the color wheel, each secondary color lies halfway between the two primary colors used to make it.

Intermediate colors are produced from equal amounts of one primary color and one secondary color. These colors lie between the colors used to make them. Intermediate colors take their names from the colors that produce them. The primary color is always listed first. Yellow-green, blue-green, blue-violet, red-violet,

20-7
Apparel made for bad weather often has bright colors for motorists to clearly see.

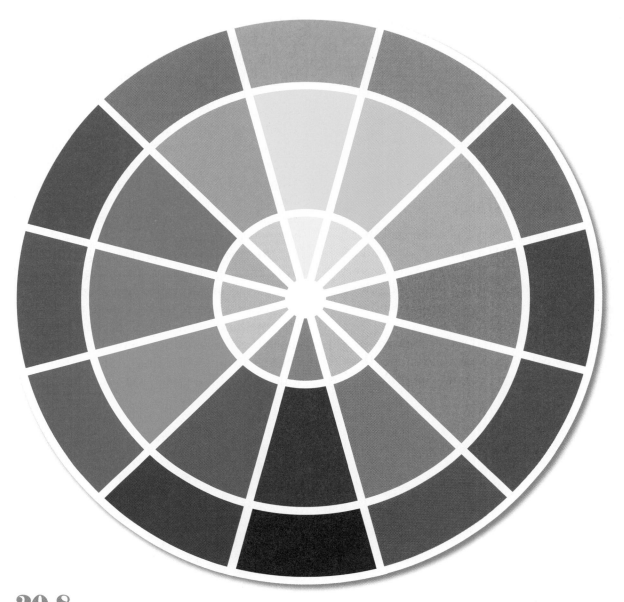

20-8
Study the color wheel to understand color relationships.

red-orange, and yellow-orange are the names of the intermediate colors.

Color Schemes

When you select clothing, you can use the color wheel to create a color scheme. Three common color schemes are monochromatic, analogous, and complementary. See 20-9.

Using different values of the same hue creates a *monochromatic color scheme*. A maroon skirt and a pink blouse or brown pants and a beige shirt are examples of this color scheme.

Combining adjacent colors on the color wheel creates an *analogous color scheme*. Wearing an outfit with blue and green, or orange and yellow, are examples of this color scheme.

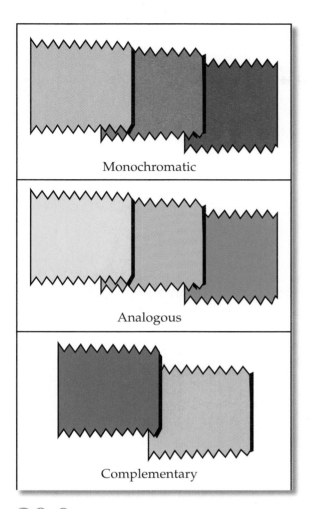

20-9

As you select clothes for an outfit, try these common color schemes.

Combining two colors that are directly across from each other on the color wheel creates a *complementary color scheme*. Because these colors are contrasting, they make each other look intense. Wearing an orange T-shirt with blue jeans is an example of this color scheme.

Warm and Cool Colors

Colors on the color wheel are considered either warm or cool. *Warm colors* are related to red, orange, and yellow. They are also described as *advancing colors*.

This means the colors visually stand out. Clothes in warm, advancing colors seem to make the body appear larger.

Cool colors are related to blue, green, and violet. These colors seem to move away, so they are called *receding colors*. Receding colors make the body appear smaller.

White and black are considered **neutrals**. Neutrals are not true colors. White is the absence of color; it reflects all light. Black absorbs all color and light. Combining varying amounts of white and black creates another range of neutrals, the grays. Neutrals can be used alone or in combination with colors. See 20-10.

20-10

When combined with neutrals, colors tend to stand out.

Choosing Your Best Colors

When choosing colors for clothes, keep your skin tone, hair and eye color, and body shape in mind. All these factors help you determine which colors to wear or avoid.

Personal Coloring

Skin tone, and hair and eye color are factors that determine your personal coloring. Which colors look best with your skin tone? Which colors complement your hair and eye color? There is an easy way to determine this. Sit in front of a mirror and drape fabrics of different colors near your face. Keep in mind that different tints and shades of colors can have different effects.

Study the effects of each color on your skin tone and hair color to find those most flattering. Good color choices will brighten and complement your face. Avoid colors that appear to drain color from your face. Once you find a few basic colors that work well for you, try to build your wardrobe around them, 20-11.

Body Shape

Another factor to consider when choosing colors for clothes is your body shape. Take an honest look at yourself in the mirror. Are you happy with your basic body shape? Would you like to look thinner or heavier? Would you like to look taller or shorter? Color can help you make the most of your appearance.

White, bright, and light colors tend to make the body look larger. Use these colors for areas you want to emphasize. Black, dark, and dull colors tend to make the body appear smaller. Use these colors for areas you want to play down or hide. Dressing in one color will make you appear taller. Outfits that create strong color contrasts between your upper body and your lower body make you appear shorter. This is because the eye stops at the line of contrast.

20-11
Bright colors are flattering to darker skin tones.

The Other Design Elements

Color may seem like the most interesting element of design. However, it is not the only one. Line, texture, and form also affect how your clothes will look on you.

Line

Line is the design element that gives direction to a design. Vertical, horizontal, curved, and diagonal lines are the most common types of lines used in clothing design. Vertical lines move the eye up and down. Horizontal lines carry the eye from side to side. Gently curved lines add softness to clothing designs. Diagonal lines, which slant or slope, give a feeling of motion.

Clothing has both structural and decorative lines. *Structural lines* are seams. They are created as the various pieces of the garment are sewn together. An example is a rounded collar versus a pointed one. *Decorative lines* are those added to the fabric or garment to make it visually appealing. Striped fabric, for example, has decorative lines. Braids, buttons, and other trims are sometimes used to add decorative lines to garments.

Structural and decorative lines can be used to create optical illusions. Vertical lines in clothes tend to make the body look taller and thinner, 20-12. Horizontal lines have the opposite effect; they tend to make the body look shorter and wider. Diagonal lines add a feeling of movement to any design. They may add visual height or width to the body, depending on their angle.

Texture

The **texture** of fabric refers to the way the fabric looks and feels. Fabric textures can be rough or smooth, shiny or dull, crisp or soft, bulky or silky. Each texture gives garments a different overall appearance.

Garments made from soft and silky fabrics slenderize a figure, but they also reveal the silhouette. Such garments are most flattering on those who have few flaws in their body shapes.

Some fabrics are crisp and stiff. They are great for either making a body appear larger or hiding flaws in a body shape. Rough and bulky textures also make a body look larger.

Fabrics with dull textures absorb light. They have a slenderizing effect. Shiny textures reflect light and increase the apparent size of the body.

Stripes, checks, plaids, geometric shapes, flowers, and other patterns add *visual texture* to fabrics. Bold color, large plaids, and wide stripes will make a person look shorter and wider. Small patterns with little contrasting color tend to make the body look smaller. See 20-13. The most suitable patterns are those that harmonize with a person's body size. Very large patterns overpower a small body frame, while a tiny pattern seems lost on a large frame.

Form

The shape of a three-dimensional object is its **form**. Your body outline and the clothes you wear create your form. Clothes that produce a *full form*, such as a full skirt

20-12
Vertical lines can be dramatic as well as slenderizing.

20-13
The colored shapes add visual texture to this bulky sweater.

or wide-legged pants, may make you appear larger and heavier. A *tubular form*, such as a one-color suit or straight-legged pants, may make you appear taller. The *bell-shaped form*, which flatters most people, is created by flared designs.

Consider the Principles of Design

The **principles of design** are the guides for combining the elements of design. The four principles of design are balance, proportion, rhythm, and emphasis. Using each principle correctly creates a feeling of *harmony* in the design. That is, all parts of the design appear to belong together.

Balance

A garment with equal visual weight on both sides of a central point has **balance**. This means the garment is equally interesting when examined from side to side, or above and below the waist. No one part of the design overpowers the other.

Balance can be formal or informal. *Formal balance* creates a centered balance, meaning both sides are the same. A solid-colored shirt is a garment with formal balance. This is the most common type of balance. *Informal balance* means the two sides are different, but have the same visual impact. A child's blue shirt with one red sleeve and one yellow sleeve has informal balance. This type of balance is more visually appealing than formal balance.

Proportion

Proportion is the spatial relationship of the parts of a design to each other and to the whole design. In other words, the size of one part should balance the size of another part. Picture a man's suit with a knee-length jacket. The jacket would not be proportional to the pants. In a well-proportioned outfit, all parts are in scale with one another. See 20-14.

Rhythm

Rhythm creates a feeling of movement. Your eye moves from one part of the design to another. All parts of the design seem related. Rhythm is achieved through repetition, gradation, and radiation of colors, lines, shapes, or textures. Imagine a white knit shirt with a navy collar worn with navy shorts and sport socks with navy stripes. The repeated use of navy in this outfit gives it rhythm. An outfit of dark green pants, a light green shirt, and a medium green vest would have rhythm through gradation of color.

Topic 20-3

Planning Your Wardrobe

Objectives

After studying this topic, you will be able to
▼ build a wardrobe that will be appropriate for various activities.
▼ develop a wardrobe inventory.
▼ describe techniques for extending your wardrobe.

Topic Terms

wardrobe
accessory

20-14

Both the vest and jacket show pleasing proportions through the use of contrasting colors.

Emphasis

What do you first see when you look at an outfit? You see the center of interest in the design, which is called **emphasis**. You can use emphasis to draw attention to or away from an area. For instance, a colorful belt draws attention to the waist. A bright tie draws the eye upward, away from the waistline.

Check It Out!

1. What are the four elements of design?
2. Identify the three characteristics of color.
3. What factors should you consider in choosing your best color?
4. Name the four principles of design.

Your **wardrobe** is all the clothes and accessories you have to wear. **Accessories** are items that accent your clothes, such as shoes, hats, belts, jewelry, neckties, and scarves. A well-planned wardrobe will include appropriate clothing and accessories for all your activities.

Building a well-planned wardrobe takes time. It is like putting a puzzle together. Your goal will be to make all the pieces fit.

Factors to Consider in Wardrobe Planning

As you plan your wardrobe, you should consider four factors. These factors address needs versus wants, lifestyle, climate, and approvals. First, you need to separate your needs from your wants. Recall that *needs* relate to items required for survival, but *wants* simply reflect desires. Wants can persuade you to fill a closet with garments you seldom wear. Buying clothes you really need that fit your lifestyle will help you look well dressed on every occasion.

Second, you need to select clothes that are appropriate for your lifestyle. See 20-15. Casual clothes worn for relaxation are different from dressy clothes worn for special occasions. Informal clothes you wear to school are different from formal styles you might wear to a prom.

A third factor in determining your clothing needs is climate. Do you live in a warm or cold climate? Select clothes that will suit both your activities and the climate in which you live.

The fourth factor is approval. You know what kinds of clothes make you feel best. You know what your personal tastes

are. You also know what your friends and employers consider acceptable. Research shows that wearing appropriate clothing influences social as well as business success. It is up to you to determine what kinds of clothes meet your approval and the approval of others.

Taking an Inventory

Wardrobe planning begins by taking an inventory of what you already have. This will help you decide what garments you need to add.

Begin your inventory by making a detailed list of every wearable garment you own. Do not forget accessories—they are part of your wardrobe, too. Use the wardrobe inventory in 20-16 as a guide for developing and completing your own inventory.

Once you know what you have, you can set specific goals. Make a list of new clothes you need to buy to replace any basic items that have worn out. Also consider what garments or accessories would help update your existing wardrobe.

Extending Your Wardrobe

After completing your wardrobe inventory, you may decide to extend your wardrobe. You can do this by choosing multipurpose clothing and mixing and matching garments. You can also use accessories to extend your wardrobe.

Choosing Multipurpose Clothing

As the name implies, *multipurpose clothing* can be worn several ways to satisfy different needs. These clothes can make

20-15
Clothing should match a person's lifestyle, such as the casual dress preferred by these students for most school activities.

Wardrobe Inventory				
Clothes/Accessories	Description (Colors)	Keep	Repair	Need to Add
Jeans	2-blue cotton	✓		
Slacks	1-tan, dressy	✓		
Shirts/Blouses	1-tan/blue plaid 1-white			need new dress blouse
Sweaters	1-tan cardigan 1-lt. blue turtleneck	✓		
Suits				
Sport coats (men's)				
Dresses (women's)	1-navy			
Skirts (women's)	1-jean skirt 1-tan/blue flowered	✓	fix hem	
Jackets	1-jean jacket 1-navy blazer	✓	missing button	
Coats	1-all-weather coat	✓		
Belts	1-navy blue			
Shoes/Boots	1-pair for school 1-navy dress shoes	✓		need new pair
Socks				
Underwear				
Jewelry				
Headwear				
Other				

20-16

A form like this can help you complete your own wardrobe inventory.

your wardrobe much more versatile and practical. For example, a long-sleeved shirt might be worn

▼ with an open neck for a casual look
▼ with the collar buttoned and a tie or scarf added for a formal look
▼ over a knit shirt for a jacketed effect
▼ over a bathing suit as a cover-up

Mixing and Matching Garments

Mixing and matching is an easy way to stretch your wardrobe and make many outfits from a few clothing items. First, look at the clothes you have. If you notice one color repeated in several items, consider using that as a base color.

Suppose navy blue is your base color. If you have a navy and white striped shirt, you can wear it with navy pants, jeans, or white shorts. By mixing and matching, you create three outfits. If you have a navy sweater that flatters all three outfits, you then create six outfits.

As you can see, adding just one new piece of clothing can extend your existing wardrobe. Keep this in mind when shopping for wardrobe additions. A few well-chosen items can create several new outfits.

Using Accessories

Accessories can give a finished look to your outfits and let you express your personality. Well-chosen accessories are great wardrobe extenders, too. They add variety to the clothes you wear.

Accessories can change the appearance of a basic outfit. They can make the same outfit appear either dressy or casual. Accessories also blend separates together to give a unified look to an outfit. For example, you could accessorize a navy blazer and tan pants with a tan and navy print scarf or tie. See 20-17.

You can wear basic accessories with many different garments. For instance, gold or silver jewelry goes well with any color. Some accessories, such as a green belt or an orange tie, may be color keyed to wear with a few garments. Choosing accessories wisely can help you create a variety of looks.

20-17
Well-chosen accessories help to express your personality and add diversity to your wardrobe.

Check It Out!

1. What factors should you consider in wardrobe planning?
2. What is the purpose of a wardrobe inventory?
3. State three ways to extend your wardrobe.

Topic 20-4
Shopping for Clothes

Objectives

After studying this topic, you will be able to
▼ give guidelines to follow when shopping for clothes.
▼ recognize common fashion terms.
▼ evaluate the quality of garments by considering their durability and fit.
▼ use the information on labels and hangtags to make wiser clothing selections.
▼ analyze factors that affect a garment's cost.

Topic Terms

fashion
style
classic
fad
label
hangtag

By shopping wisely, you will find the right clothes to complete your wardrobe at the right price. First, you must decide where to shop. Learning to judge quality and read labels are very important factors to consider when shopping for clothes.

Shopping Guidelines

Before you decide where to shop, you need to plan what to buy. Based on your wardrobe inventory, make a list of the clothes and accessories you need. Then decide how much money you have to spend. Next, prioritize your list so you know which wardrobe additions to buy first. You may want to give the highest priority to items you will wear most often, such as a coat or shoes.

As you read in Chapter 19, you can shop in many different types of stores. You can also shop at home electronically. In deciding where to shop, consider the pros and cons of each retail site. To be a wise shopper, try to get the best quality at a price you can afford.

Get the most for your money by following these shopping tips:

▼ Refer to the shopping list you made when completing your wardrobe inventory. This will show you exactly what you need to buy.
▼ Comparison shop at several different retail sites before making a buying decision. Check for sales or end-of-season clearances.
▼ Buy only what you really need, 20-18. Avoid impulse buying and expensive trendy styles.

20-18

If you shop with friends, beware of advice that steers you away from your shopping list.

Technology Brings New Ways to Shop

When you cannot make purchases locally, online retail sites are another option. Although the sensory experience of seeing and feeling merchandise is missing, Internet shopping offers many advantages over in-store shopping. For example, comparison shopping is much easier. You can compare products and prices from the convenience of your own home at any hour. Items are displayed in sharp detail with extensive product information. Customer service is generally very reliable. Delivery of items to your home is quick, and you can easily return them if dissatisfied.

Web sites offer much more opportunity for tailoring your wardrobe around your personal tastes. This is possible because of the vast assortment of products available. Stores cannot always carry a wide assortment because their limited space must be devoted to merchandise that appeals to everyone. Online retailers are not bound by this restriction. They offer a wider array of items that appeal to smaller segments of consumers, 20-19.

The ability to locate difficult-to-find items is a key reason for shopping online. Some shopping sites have a search agent that tracks down specific colors, sizes, or prices. In some cases, you can create your own electronic catalog of favorite selections. You can even view merchandise next to items resembling what you already own. This feature allows you to judge how well the garment works with your existing wardrobe.

The main drawback to Internet shopping is not being able to try on garments before ordering. However, this is being addressed in several ways. Some Web sites display garments on various

20-19
Internet shoppers can usually find more in-stock clothing styles, colors, and sizes than are available in stores.

body frames so you can judge how it might look on you. You can also view garments on mannequins from various angles. Eventually, you will be able to view a garment just as it would appear in a mirror. This requires *body scanning*, a technology that electronically measures your size and determines your body shape. By sending scanned data to an online site, the garment for sale can be adjusted to your body proportions. Body scanning will ultimately let consumers redesign garments to order the specific length, color, and fabric desired.

To be a wise online shopper, always follow the shopping guidelines. These apply equally to in-store and online purchasing.

Understanding Fashion Terms

Do you have an awareness of what it takes to achieve a well-dressed look? This is called *fashion sense*. Learning about fashion terms will help you build your wardrobe-planning fashion sense. Fashion terms include *fashion*, *style*, *classic*, and *fad*.

Fashion

In wardrobe planning, the term **fashion** refers to the current mode of dress. This is the manner of dress being worn by the majority of people at a given time. Some typical fashion looks are narrow-leg pants, fitted waistlines, ankle-length hemlines, and double-breasted jackets. Fashion looks can change from year to year, and even from season to season. For example, pants with wide legs may be in fashion one year and out of fashion the next.

Style

The term **style** refers to specific construction details that make one garment differ from another garment of the same type. For instance, gathered skirts and pleated skirts are just two of the many skirt styles. Straight legs, flared bottoms, and cropped length are examples of pant styles.

Classic and Fad Styles

A **classic** style is one that is in fashion year after year. A classic never changes drastically. Business suits, shirtwaist dresses, men's dress shirts, crew-neck sweaters, and wrap coats are examples of classic styles. Investing in durable, classic clothing will enable a person to feel well dressed and fashionable for many years. See 20-20.

20-20
Well-fitting clothing in classic styles will be fashionable for many years.

A **fad** is a style that is popular for a short time and then disappears. In other words, consumers heartily accept the style for a time and then reject it. People who invest in fad items often discard them as soon as they go out of fashion.

Some designs are destined to become classics while others will become fads. Blue jeans, T-shirts, and athletic shoes were initially thought to be fad items. Because of their long-lasting popularity, however, they are now considered casual classics.

Fashion Cycles

To keep people buying new clothes, the fashion industry must constantly produce new designs. After a new clothing style is introduced, it goes through a period when it gains popularity. Then the style reaches its height of acceptance before consumers begin to tire of it. The time from the introduction of a new fashion idea to its eventual decline in popularity is called a *fashion cycle*.

Look in magazines and store ads to spot current fashions. Think about how long these fashions have been popular.

This will help you determine where current styles are in their fashion cycles.

As you assemble your wardrobe, you will want to make all the pieces fit. Identify garments in your wardrobe that are classic styles and garments that are fads. Note items that are in line with current fashions and recognize those that seem out-of-date. This analysis will help you make decisions as you shop.

As a general rule, you will get the most wear from classic garments that last for many seasons. For variety, add a few inexpensive fad items you will be able to reuse in a different way when fashions change.

Judging Quality

When you consider buying a garment, inspect it for quality. Quality is an important factor in clothing. It affects a garment's look, durability, and fit.

Durability

Durability refers to how a garment will hold up under use. A garment's construction and the fabric from which it is made affect durability.

Before buying, examine a garment carefully. Signs of poor construction are most noticeable inside the garment, but also show on the outside. Check for quality construction features, such as secure buttons, neatly stitched buttonholes, smooth seams, and matched patterns. A well-constructed garment will provide many seasons of use. A poorly constructed garment will show wear and tear after using and cleaning it a few times.

Evaluate the type of fabric used for the garment. Some fabrics wear better than others. Fabrics that snag and bag easily will not wear as well as sturdier fabrics that will hold their shape.

Crushing a corner of the garment tightly between two fingers will show you how easily the fabric wrinkles. If creases or wrinkles remain, the garment will crease or wrinkle when you wear it. Chart 20-21 describes features you would find in quality-made clothing.

Fit

An important point to consider when buying clothes is fit. The *fit* of a garment refers to how it conforms to the size and shape of the body of the wearer. The three categories of a garment's fit are fitted, semifitted, and loose. A fitted garment is shaped to conform closely to the lines of your body. If a fitted garment does not fit properly, it will not lie smoothly. Semifitted and loose garments do not conform to the body as closely as fitted garments. However, they must still fit properly to look neat and move freely as you move.

You must try on a garment to determine whether it fits. The best time to do this is before you buy the garment. Doing this will prevent the needless step of returning items that fit poorly. If possible, try the garment on with the accessories you plan to wear with it. That way, you can see if the new garment matches the accessories you already have.

When you try on a garment, you should move normally. Try sitting, bending, and raising and crossing your arms and legs. Note how comfortable the garment feels with each movement. Also notice how the garment looks. Does it pull or wrinkle anywhere? If the garment feels or looks too tight or too loose in a given body posture, it does not fit right.

Look for Quality Clothing

- **Garment construction**—Are plaids, stripes, and large designs matched at the seams? Are shoulder pads or other supports giving proper shape to the garment? Do linings lie flat? Are they secured at the seams so they will not show when the garment is worn?
- **Fabric**—Is it easy to clean and maintain? Is it loosely or tightly constructed? The tighter the construction, the better the fabric will hold its shape.
- **Trim**—Do decorative features appear as durable as the rest of the garment? Are they securely attached?
- **Fasteners**—Do buttonholes appear sturdy and free from raveling? Are the buttons appropriate for the garment? Are extra buttons included for replacements? Are buttons, snaps, hook, and eyes firmly attached? Are zippers inserted neatly and working smoothly?
- **Hem**—Are the stitches invisible on the outside of the garment? Is the hem wide enough for future adjustments? Is the edge finished to prevent raveling?
- **Seams**—Are all stitches straight, even, and free of puckers? Are they secured so they will not pull apart? Are edges finished to prevent raveling? Is there enough fabric at the seams to widen for future adjustments?
- **Reinforcements**—Are points of strain, such as armholes and crotches, reinforced with extra stitching? Wherever fasteners and pockets are sewn to a single thickness of fabric, are they reinforced?

20-21

Check for quality before you buy. As you examine garments, keep these questions in mind.

Reading Labels and Hangtags

Is this garment the right size? What kind of fabric is it? Can it be machine-washed? Does it need ironing? If you have questions about a garment, carefully read the label and hangtags attached to it. Labels and hangtags on clothing provide useful information for the shopper. See 20-22.

Labels are informative cloth tags permanently attached to garments. They provide important facts to the consumer, many of which are established by laws. These include the following:

▼ *The Textile Fiber Products Identification Act* requires all products to identify fiber content, the name of the manufacturer, and country of origin.

▼ *The Care Labeling Rule* mandates the listing of specific instructions for a garment's care. (More details of this law will be discussed in Topic 20-5.) Look for whether the garment needs machine washing or dry cleaning. Dry cleaning can significantly add to the upkeep cost of a garment over time.

▼ The *Wool Products Labeling Act* calls for the type of wool, the percentage of wool, and its country of origin to be listed.

▼ The *Fur Products Labeling Act* requires the identification of a fur's animal source and its country of origin.

▼ The *Flammable Fabrics Act* prohibits the sale of very hazardous materials for use in clothing. It also requires fabrics used in children's sleepwear to stop a flame.

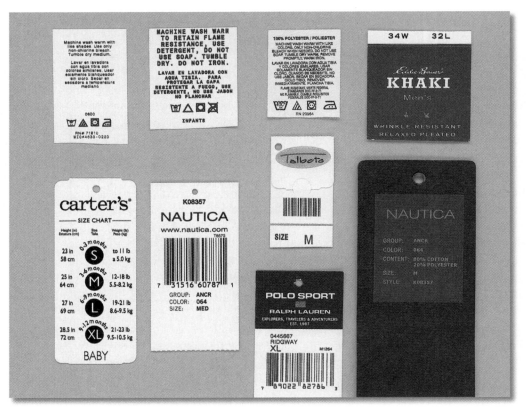

20-22
Careful shoppers read labels and hangtags so they can make informed choices.

In addition to the required information, labels may also list the brand name, size, special finishes, and construction features.

Hangtags are larger tags attached to new garments. Before wearing a garment, you would remove these tags. Unlike labels, hangtags are not required by law. They include useful information, such as trademarks, guarantees, style numbers, sizes, and prices. See 20-23.

Consider the Cost

Cost is a key factor affecting clothing purchases. When shopping for clothes, you must decide whether you can afford a garment. You must also assess whether an item fits into your price range. For instance, if you have $50 in your wallet, you can afford a $45 shirt. However, $45 may be more than you are willing to spend for a shirt.

You might want to evaluate how much psychological benefit you will get from a garment. This can help you set your price range. You may be willing to spend more for a garment that really makes you look and feel your best. Your evaluation can also help you decide whether you should wait for an item to go on sale. When you do not feel strongly about an item, you may be more willing to wait for a sale price. However, this might mean losing the garment to another buyer while you wait.

Think about how many times you will wear a garment. That will determine the cost per wear. For example, a prom dress

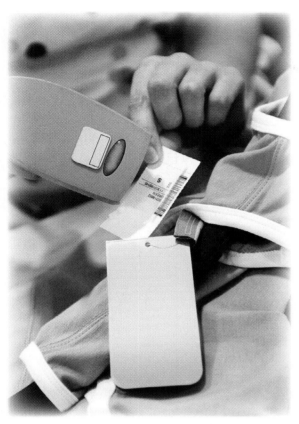

20-23
A hangtag like this one is scanned to record your purchase.

20-24
An example of a wise purchase is the easy-care casual top this teen found on sale in her favorite color.

that sells for $180 may be worn only once. Thus, the prom dress will cost $180 per wear. A jacket costing $180 may be worn every day for several years. Therefore, the jacket costs only pennies per wear. You may be able to save money by borrowing or renting garments that you intend to wear only once.

You should also evaluate how long you will be able to wear a garment. If you are still growing, the garment may not fit you very long. If the item is not well made, it may wear out quickly. If it is a fad style, it may go out of fashion before long.

Another factor you need to consider when evaluating the cost of a garment is how much it will cost to maintain, 20-24.

For instance, a silk shirt may seem like a bargain at $15. However, spending $5 each time it is dry-cleaned will soon exceed the cost of the shirt. Carefully considering upkeep costs will help you determine if a garment purchase is right for your budget.

Economizing with Vintage Values

Another way to hold down clothing costs is to buy vintage clothing. *Vintage* literally means something that is aged. In clothing terms, it means garments that are used, but still classic. Think of the time you received a great hand-me-down that a family member or friend outgrew. By shopping carefully, you can find attractive, used garments as good as new, but at a fraction of their normal costs.

Good clothing "finds" show up in thrift stores, garage sales, and resale clothing shops. Used garments are put on sale when people outgrow them or clean their closets before moving or adding new purchases. The shopping guidelines to follow for buying used clothes are the same as those for new items. Purchases of used clothing should always be cleaned before storing and wearing.

Check It Out!

1. Give three guidelines to follow when shopping for clothes.
2. Explain the difference between fashion and style.
3. How is clothing quality judged?
4. List the information found on a label versus a hangtag.
5. True or false. A garment's care requirements can exceed the garment's cost.

Topic 20-5
Caring for Clothes

Objectives
After studying this topic, you will be able to
▼ explain daily clothing care.
▼ care for your clothes by using proper laundering, drying, ironing, and storing techniques.

Topic Terms
ironing
pressing
dry cleaning

After spending your time and money to get the right clothes, you will want to take good care of them. Proper care of clothes helps to ensure a neat personal appearance. Your clothes will look better and last longer if you care for them properly.

Daily Clothing Care

Setting a daily routine will help you keep your clothes in good condition. You will always have clean clothes ready to wear. See 20-25.

When you dress and undress, try not to damage or soil your clothes. Open fasteners so garments will slip easily over your head, arms, and hips. Avoid placing undue strain on any part of the garment. Strain can result in rips, broken zippers, and missing buttons. Taking the extra seconds to open fasteners can save hours in repairing damages.

As you pull garments over your head, try to protect the clothing. Avoid letting the garment touch your head or face to prevent stains from hair products, makeup, skin

20-25
Proper care of your clothes will help you look your best.

lotions, or sunscreens. It is better to apply these products after you are dressed.

Allow an extra minute or two to care for your clothes when you undress. Inspect garments closely for stains, rips, hanging threads, and missing buttons. Put clothes with any of these problems in a special place. This will remind you to take care of the problems before wearing or cleaning the garments. Items that need dry cleaning should be set aside and taken to the dry cleaner promptly.

Laundering Steps

Washable garments will look their best and last longer when you launder them properly. Laundering not only cleans

garments, but also removes wrinkles and perspiration odors. To care for clothes properly, you need to know some basic laundry principles.

Read Care Labels

The Care Labeling Rule, issued by the Federal Trade Commission, requires care labels to clearly identify the correct procedures for each garment's upkeep. The label must also warn against care procedures that are likely to damage the item. The label must remain readable for the life of the garment.

Symbols, as shown in Chart 20-26, indicate the various care methods used. If the clothing is to be washed, the following information must be included on the label:

▼ washing method
▼ water temperature
▼ drying method
▼ drying temperature
▼ type of bleach that can be used safely
▼ use of iron
▼ ironing temperatures

Always follow care labels to keep clothes looking neat and colors staying bright.

Sort Clothes Properly

The purpose of sorting is to separate items that could cause damage to others. One key way to sort clothes is by color. Separate whites from colors, and light colors from bright or dark colors. Different wash water temperatures are needed to keep some colors from either fading or bleeding onto other garments. When fabrics *bleed*, they emit color to adjacent clothing. *Colorfast* means the color will withstand washing, dry cleaning, perspiration, sunlight, and rubbing.

Sorting clothes by fabric will help you determine what wash cycle to use. White cottons and linens require hot water and a

20-26

This chart explains the clothing-care symbols and instructions printed on garment labels.

regular wash cycle for cleaning. Permanent press fabrics require warm wash water and a cold rinse. Other fabrics require cold water and a short, gentle wash cycle to prevent fading and shrinking.

Sort clothes by their surface texture to separate lint-catchers from lint-producers. Corduroy, velveteen, and fabrics of

manufactured fibers catch lint. On the other hand, chenille and terry cloth produce lint.

Another factor you should consider when sorting clothes is the degree of soil. Heavily soiled clothes require different laundry procedures than lightly soiled items.

Prepare Clothes for Laundering

Visually inspect your clothes before laundering. Remove surface soil by shaking or brushing it away. Be sure all zippers and hooks are closed. They may get damaged or may cause damage to other items when left open. Repair snags and mend rips and tears to prevent greater damage from occurring during washing or drying.

Check pockets carefully before putting garments in the washing machine. A pen, tissue, or other object left in a pocket can produce stains or lint. This could damage every item in a wash load.

Pretreat Stains and Heavy Soil

Treat and wash stains promptly, when they are easiest to remove. Follow the directions of a stain-removal guide, such as Chart 20-27. Heavily soiled items should be pretreated by soaking, or by applying a liquid detergent or a prewash product.

Read the package labels on all soil and stain removers before using them. Always test the product first to see if it discolors the fabric. Use an unseen part of the garment, such as the back of a hem. Test the product by waiting 5-10 minutes after applying it and rinsing the area thoroughly.

Understand Laundry Products

Many types of laundry products are available. For best laundry results, you need to use the right types of products and follow package directions carefully.

Soaps and Detergents

Soaps and detergents are designed to remove soil from fabrics. The main difference is the way they work in hard water.

Soap reacts with the minerals in hard water to form white cloudy curds that cling to fabrics. These curds make whites look dingy and colors look dull. Because of this drawback, soaps work best in soft or softened water.

Detergents work well in hard or soft water and give a whiter, brighter wash in hard water. Detergents are either high-sudsing or low-sudsing. Both types are usable in top-loading washers, but the low-sudsing type is best for front-loaders.

Detergents come in both liquid and powder forms. In cold water, powdered detergents may dissolve slowly, so liquid detergents are recommended. Detergent should always be mixed into wash water before clothes are added to allow it to dilute or dissolve completely.

Because detergents differ in concentration, following package directions is important. Always use the recommended amount of detergent. Using too little or too much detergent is one of the most common laundry errors.

Bleach

Bleach helps remove stains and whitens, disinfects, and deodorizes clothes. The two types of bleach are chlorine and oxygen.

Chlorine bleach is a strong chemical mixture. It can weaken fabric fibers if it is used too often or too concentrated. It should not be used on wool, silk, spandex, noncolorfast fabrics, or on some fabric finishes. Refer to the care labels in garments for cleaning instructions.

Carefully follow the directions on the bleach container for best results. If your washer has a built-in bleach dispenser, read the use and care instructions for exact directions. If your washer does not have a bleach dispenser, the bleach must be diluted and added after agitation begins.

Oxygen bleach helps remove stains and whiten clothes. It is milder than chlorine bleach and safe for all washable fibers. For best results, oxygen bleach should be used regularly to keep clothes white and bright.

Stain	Procedure for Bleachable Fabrics (white and colorfast cotton, linen, polyester, acrylic, triacetate, nylon, rayon, permanent press)	Procedure for Nonbleachable Fabrics (wool, silk, spandex, noncolorfast items, some flame-retardant finishes)
Blood	Soak in cold water 30 minutes or longer. Rub detergent into any remaining stain. Rinse. If stain persists, put a few drops of ammonia on the stain and repeat detergent treatment. Rinse. If stain persists, launder in hot water using chlorine bleach.	Same method, but if colorfastness is questionable, use hydrogen peroxide instead of ammonia. Launder in warm water. Omit chlorine bleach.
Chewing gum, adhesive tape	Rub stained area with ice. Remove excess gummy matter carefully with a dull knife. Sponge with a safe cleaning fluid. Rinse and launder.	Same method.
Chocolate, cocoa	Soak in cold water. Rub detergent into stain while still wet, then rinse thoroughly. Dry. If a greasy stain remains, sponge with a safe cleaning fluid. Rinse. Launder in hot water using chlorine bleach. If stain remains, repeat treatment with cleaning fluid.	Same method. Launder in warm water. Omit chlorine bleach.
Coffee, tea	Soak in cold water. Rub detergent into stain while still wet. Rinse and dry. If grease stain remains from cream, sponge with safe cleaning fluid. Launder in hot water using chlorine bleach.	Same method. Launder in warm water. Omit chlorine bleach.
Cosmetics	Rub detergent into dampened stain until outline of stain is gone, then rinse well. Launder in hot water using chlorine bleach.	Same method. Launder in warm water. Omit chlorine bleach.
Egg, meat juice, gravy	If dried, scrape off as much as possible with a dull knife. Soak in cold water. Rub detergent into stain while still wet. Launder in hot water using chlorine bleach.	Same method. Launder in warm water. Omit chlorine bleach.
Fingernail polish	Sponge white cotton fabric with nail polish remover. Use amyl acetate (banana oil) on other fabrics. Launder. Repeat if necessary.	Same method.
Fruit juices	Soak in cold water. Launder in hot water using chlorine bleach.	Soak in cold water. If stain remains, rub detergent into stain while still wet. Launder in warm water.
Grass	Rub detergent into dampened stain. Launder in hot water using chlorine bleach. If stain remains, sponge with alcohol. Rinse thoroughly.	Same method. Launder in warm water. Omit chlorine bleach. If colorfastness is questionable or fabric is acetate, dilute alcohol with two parts water.

20-27

This chart applies only to prewash stain removers for washable items. It does not apply to in-wash stain removers or garments that must be dry-cleaned.

Stain	Procedure for Bleachable Fabrics (white and colorfast cotton, linen, polyester, acrylic, triacetate, nylon, rayon, permanent press)	Procedure for Nonbleachable Fabrics (wool, silk, spandex, noncolorfast items, some flame-retardant finishes)
Grease, oil (car grease, butter, shortening, vitamin oils)	Rub detergent into dampened stain. Launder in hot water using chlorine bleach and plenty of detergent. If stain persists, sponge thoroughly with safe cleaning fluid. Rinse.	Rub detergent into dampened stain. Launder in warm water using plenty of detergent. If stain persists, sponge thoroughly with safe cleaning fluid. Rinse.
Ink (ballpoint)	Sponge stain with rubbing alcohol, or spray with hair spray until wet looking. Rub detergent into stained area. Launder. Repeat if necessary.	Same method.
Ink (felt tip)	Some may be impossible to remove. Rub household cleaner into stain. Rinse. Repeat as many times as necessary to remove stain. Launder.	Same method.
Mayonnaise, salad dressing	Rub detergent into dampened stain. Rinse and let dry. If greasy stain remains, sponge with safe cleaning fluid. Rinse. Launder in hot water with chlorine bleach.	Same method. Launder in warm water. Omit chlorine bleach.
Mildew	Rub detergent into dampened stain. Launder in hot water using chlorine bleach. If stain remains, sponge with hydrogen peroxide. Rinse and launder.	Same method. Launder in warm water. Omit chlorine bleach.
Milk, cream, ice cream	Soak in cold water. Launder in hot water using chlorine bleach. If grease stain remains, sponge with safe cleaning fluid. Rinse.	Soak in cold water. Rub detergent into stain. Launder. If grease stain remains, sponge with safe cleaning fluid. Rinse.
Mustard	Rub detergent into dampened stain. Rinse. Soak in hot detergent water for several hours. If stain remains, launder in hot water using chlorine bleach.	Same method. Launder in warm water. Omit chlorine bleach.
Perspiration	Rub detergent into dampened stain. Launder in hot water using chlorine bleach. If fabric has discolored, try to restore it by treating fresh stains with ammonia or old stains with vinegar. Rinse. Launder.	Same method. Launder in warm water. Omit chlorine bleach.
Soft drinks	Sponge stain immediately with cold water. Launder in hot water with chlorine bleach. Some drink stains are invisible after they dry, but turn yellow with aging or heating. This yellow stain may be impossible to remove.	Same method. Launder in warm water. Omit chlorine bleach.

20-27
(Continued)

Water Softeners

A sign that your home has hard water is a ring appearing around your sink or bathtub after the water drains. Clothes washed in hard water may look gray or dull. To keep clothes looking bright, you can add a water softener to laundry water before adding the soap or detergent. Water softeners neutralize the calcium and magnesium ions of hard water. This keeps dulling residue from settling on your clothes.

Fabric Softeners

Fabric softeners make fabrics soft and fluffy. They help reduce wrinkling and control static electricity. Different liquid softeners are designed for adding to wash or rinse cycles. Fabric softener sheets are used in the dryer.

Using the Washing Machine

For good cleaning action, distribute items evenly in the washer. This balances the wash load. Do not overload the washer. Too many garments in the wash prevent good circulation of water and cleaning agents. See 20-28.

Select a wash cycle suitable for the wash load. Delicate items need a *gentle* or *delicate cycle* with warm or cold water. Permanent press garments will need a *permanent press cycle* with a cold-water rinse if they are to remain free of wrinkles. The *regular cycle* handles all other laundry items. Select wash temperature according to fiber content and care labels. A cold-water rinse is suitable for all fabrics and saves energy, too.

Drying Clothes

Clothes can be dried in an automatic dryer, on a clothesline, or on a flat surface. Check garment care labels for drying directions.

20-28
Cleaning aides should be blended into the water before adding clothes.

Tumble-drying clothes in an automatic dryer is convenient, especially for large loads. Most clothes are softer and more comfortable when tumble-dried.

Never overload the dryer. If clothes are too crowded to tumble freely, they will probably wrinkle. Larger loads take longer to dry. You should remove clothes as soon as the tumbling stops to prevent wrinkles. Remember to clean the lint filter after each use.

Different brands and models of dryers have different cycles, but three are common. The *regular cycle* is used for items that are not heat sensitive. The *permanent press cycle* provides moderate heat at the start and no heat for the last 10 minutes. The *air-dry cycle* provides unheated air to freshen or fluff items. Follow the use and care instructions that come with the dryer for best results.

Line drying is recommended for some fabrics and is often done indoors. Garments are hung above a bathtub or in a shower stall to drip-dry. In areas not affected by smog or high humidity, line drying can be done outdoors. Line drying gives clothes a fresh smell, while saving the cost of using an electric or gas dryer.

The flat-drying method is used for garments such as sweaters to avoid shrinking or stretching them out of shape. Remove excess moisture first by rolling the garment in a towel. Then unroll and shape the garment by hand on a clean, absorbent surface, such as a towel. Keep the garment away from direct heat.

Ironing and Pressing

The terms ironing and pressing are often used interchangeably, but they have slightly different meanings. **Ironing** is a process of moving an iron across fabric to smooth wrinkles, usually after laundering.

Pressing is a process of lifting the iron up and down to apply pressure in one area at a time. Pressing is done on seams and curves as garments are sewn or to touch up wrinkles after laundering.

Always use a heat setting that is safe for the fabric and any attached trim, 20-29. A too-hot iron will scorch some fabrics, melt others, or create permanent wrinkles.

Dry Cleaning

Some care labels indicate that garments require dry cleaning instead of laundering. **Dry cleaning** is a process that cleans clothes using organic chemical solvents. Water is not used in this process. Because dry cleaning is a delicate cleaning process, clothes should be cleaned before they become heavily soiled.

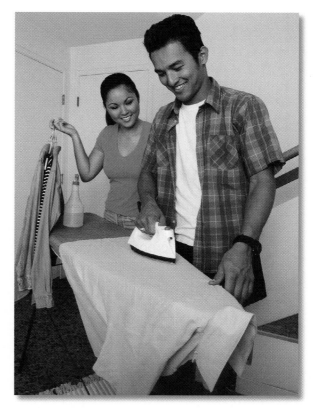

20-29

When setting the iron, use a safe temperature for the fabric and increase heat gradually if necessary.

Professional dry cleaners know how to treat various fabrics and most spots and stains. You can assist them, however, by pointing out stains when you take garments to be cleaned. Explain the cause of the stain and how old it is. You may also want to request the addition of sizing to make a limp garment look fresh again. Likewise, you can have a water-repellent finish restored to a garment after cleaning. See 20-30. To air out any cleaning fumes, gang dry-cleaned garments in an open area awhile before storing.

Another choice for garments marked "dry-clean only" is a home in-dryer kit. Home dry-cleaning kits can remove odors, wrinkles, and light stains in most linen, silk, wool, and rayon clothing. The

20-30
Professional dry cleaning can often make difficult-to-clean garments look new.

The More You Know: Ironing Tips

Ironing may look easy, but careless ironing can ruin a garment. The following tips can help you iron your clothes properly.

Always read the care label first and turn the iron to the proper setting for the fabric. Press an inside area—such as the hem—to test the effects of the temperature on the fabric. Do this before touching the garment in a visible spot to prevent scorching. Iron or press along the lengthwise grain of the fabric to keep it from stretching out of shape.

Some fabrics develop a shine when heat is applied directly to them. Place a pressing cloth over such fabrics. When in doubt, use a pressing cloth just to be safe. For a smoother finish, press the underside of areas such as collars, cuffs, and pockets first.

convenient process takes about half an hour in the dryer. The kit also works well on garments with beads, sequins, and other trims. Currently three companies market the easy-to-use kit. It is an economical way to freshen a special-care garment when you cannot get to a dry cleaner. However, the kit may not remove all stains and will not give the "pressed" look of a professional dry cleaner.

Cleaning your clothes properly will help them look their best. Your clothes, in turn, will help you look your best.

Environmental Awareness in Clothing Care

Modern technology has developed laundry appliances that use energy and water very efficiently. Laundry products are continually improved, too, with formulas and packaging that are environmentally sound. As a consumer, you can also play a part in protecting the environment by following the recommendations in Chart 20-31.

The Environmental Laundry List

General

- Do laundry at times other than peak energy-use hours.
- Buy laundry products in concentrated form and recycle containers.
- Use and dispose of each product in the manner directed on its label.

Washing

- Pretreat heavily soiled spots and stubborn stains to avoid the need for additional washings.
- Sort and wash full loads of compatible garments.
- Adjust the water level to the size of the load.
- Select a wash cycle that matches the degree of soil.
- Use cooler wash water whenever possible. Hot water may be needed for heavily soiled clothes, but warm water handles light soil, and cold water is fine for very light soil.
- Use cold-water rinses since warm water is never a necessity for this task.

Drying

- Save energy by line-drying whenever possible.
- Clean the lint filter before each load.
- Check the vent system regularly to avoid obstructions that will slow the airflow in a dryer.
- Avoid overloading the dryer.
- Remove clothes from the dryer promptly to prevent wrinkling and unnecessary ironing.
- Dry consecutive loads of wash to use residual heat left from the preceding load.

Ironing

- Iron as many items as possible at one time to prevent the repeated heating of the iron for individual uses.
- Sort garments according to the ironing temperature needed to avoid heating and cooling the iron between uses.

20-31

These simple steps show how to handle laundry tasks and express concern for the environment at the same time.

Storing Clothes

If your clothes are clean and in good condition, store them properly. Drawer space is often more plentiful than closet space. Therefore, it is a good idea to store as many garments in drawers as possible. Always store knit garments in drawers to prevent the stretching and sagging that occurs when they are hung.

Store similar garments together. For instance, put all your T-shirts in the same drawer and hang all pants together in the same corner of the closet. When you need the items later, you will do less searching to find them. Mixing and matching garments to create outfits will be easier, too.

Clothes stored in the closet should be neatly hung on hangers. Close top buttons, zippers, and other fasteners so clothes will

Setting the Scene: Dressing to Impress?

You are almost late for a special date. Your grab your favorite black T-shirt from the closet. There is a grease stain on the front and imprints made by the hanger on both shoulders. Lint is scattered all over it. About four inches of the hem is ripped and hanging down. There is a fold across the front where the shirt was wedged too tightly between other garments.

Analyze It: Would you really wear this shirt on a date? Could you do anything quickly to make the shirt wearable? What steps might have prevented this situation? What storage advice would you be likely to follow in the future?

the best shape. Hangers covered with a thin layer of foam keep garments made from slippery fabrics from falling. Hangers with clips conveniently hang skirts and pants from the waistline.

Many accessories are available to increase the clothing storage space in your home. With some ingenuity, you can create other storage containers. Large boxes that slide under beds are one storage option that works well for clothes. This frees up closet and drawer space for the garments you use most often.

When storing out-of-season clothes, be sure to consider the possibility of insect damage. Moths and crickets can eat holes in your clothes, especially woolens. To protect wool garments, store them in cedar-lined closets or chests. If these are not available, place mothballs or crystals into their drawers or containers.

retain their shape and not slip off hangers. Have a clothes brush handy to remove any lint or dust. Allow enough space in the closet for clothes to hang loosely without becoming wrinkled.

Specialty hangers can help you store certain garments more easily. Hangers designed for blazers, jackets, and coats are curved to simulate the curve of the shoulders. This helps the garments retain

Check It Out!

1. List five steps to take daily to keep your clothes in great shape.
2. List four factors to consider when sorting clothes for laundering.
3. Which drying method is preferred for garments that might stretch or shrink?
4. Moving an iron across fabric to smooth wrinkles is called _____.
5. What are five steps you can take to conserve energy as you care for your clothes?

Chapter Review

Summary

A number of factors affect your clothing decisions. Clothes meet a basic physical need by protecting your body from weather and various safety hazards. How a garment makes you feel is a result of clothing's effect on your psychological needs. Clothes also meet some of your social needs by helping you identify with groups and serving as status symbols. The occasion for which you will wear clothes is another factor that sways your clothing decisions.

Use the elements and principles of design in choosing clothes that reflect your personal tastes and style. Choose colors that flatter your skin tone and hair and eye color. Use line, texture, and form in clothing design to complement your body shape. Apply the principles of design to create well-coordinated outfits that enhance your appearance.

Planning your wardrobe takes skill. A wardrobe inventory helps you identify what clothing you own and what you need to add. Wearing multipurpose clothing, as well as mixing and matching garments, extends your wardrobe options. Accessories can give your outfits a finished look. You can also use them to make a statement about your individuality.

Understanding fashion terms can help you shop for a basic wardrobe to suit your activities and lifestyle. Try to get the best quality you can afford. As you shop, watch for sales. Use the information on labels and hangtags to make informed decisions. Also, consider the cost of garments and their care as you shop for clothes to fit your budget.

Proper care of clothing always means longer wear. Establish a daily routine for clothing care. Read clothing labels for care instructions. Follow proper steps for laundering, drying, ironing, or dry cleaning clothes. Take steps to care for the environment as you care for your clothes, too. When storing clothes, handle them properly so they will look their best on you.

Think About It!

1. Describe clothing that is appropriate for four of your most frequent activities.
2. Analyze your skin color and body shape. Which colors, lines, and textures do you think will make you look your best?
3. Evaluate the garments you already have. What garments and accessories do you need to add to your wardrobe in the future?
4. Assess your clothing-selection habits. What changes would you make to improve your shopping skills?
5. Why is it important to establish a daily clothing care routine?
6. Name five job opportunities in your area that relate to the topics in this chapter.

Try It Out!

1. Illustrate what clothes you would choose to wear to a prom. Also illustrate what you would wear to a job interview as a salesperson in an apparel department. You may draw sketches or clip pictures from catalogs or magazines.

2. Design a bulletin board to illustrate how the elements and principles of design affect personal appearance.

3. Invite a fashion coordinator from your favorite clothing store to discuss and demonstrate wardrobe extenders.

4. Use Chart 20-21 to evaluate the quality of several pieces of clothing.

5. Assemble a wide variety of fabric swatches. Then review the procedures given in the chapter for properly sorting clothes. Sort the fabric swatches into suitable laundry loads.

6. Research the cost of dry cleaning an all-weather coat in your area. Assume you will be wearing the coat for three years. Determine how much you would need to spend to keep it clean.

Chapter 21
Fabrics, Patterns, and Sewing Equipment

Careers

These careers relate to the topics in this chapter:
- ▼ fabric salesperson
- ▼ sewing demonstrator
- ▼ textile lab technician
- ▼ pattern designer

As you study the chapter, see if you can think of others.

Topics

21-1 Understanding Fabrics
21-2 Selecting Patterns, Fabrics, and Notions
21-3 Sewing Equipment

Topic 21-1

Understanding Fabrics

Objectives

After studying this topic, you will be able to
▼ explain how fibers, yarns, and fabrics are produced and manufactured.
▼ distinguish various fabric finishes.

Topic Terms

fiber
yarn
fabric
natural fibers
manufactured fibers
microfibers
spun yarns
filament yarns
weaving
knitting
nonwoven fabrics

The freedom to choose design, color, and fabric is yours when you learn how to sew. By using your imagination, you can create original garments that reflect your fashion taste and style.

Today's clothes are made from a variety of fabrics. The textile industry continues to introduce new fibers, yarns, blends, and finishes for fabrics. All these choices make shopping for fabric fun, but rather confusing. You can make wise fabric selections if you know the facts about how fabrics are made.

Fibers

The **fiber** is the basic unit of all fabrics. Fibers are combined to form a continuous strand called a **yarn**. The weaving and knitting of yarns make **fabrics**.

Fibers have certain characteristics that determine the texture, strength, warmth, absorbency, and durability of fabrics. The characteristics of a fiber depend on its source. Fibers are obtained from either natural or chemical sources. Thus, the two major groups of fibers are natural fibers and manufactured fibers.

Natural Fibers

Natural fibers are those that exist in nature. Their composition does not change during processing. Plants such as cotton and flax are sources of natural fibers. The wool of sheep, specialty hair fibers such as mohair and cashmere, and silk are also natural fibers. See 21-1.

Cotton

Cotton fibers come from the seedpod of the cotton plant. Different varieties of cotton plants produce fibers of different lengths. Long fibers make fine, smooth, lustrous fabrics. Shorter fibers go into coarser fabrics such as the cotton denim used to make blue jeans.

Cotton is a versatile, absorbent, and durable fiber. These qualities make cotton the most widely used natural fiber, 21-2. Although cotton wrinkles and shrinks easily, finishes can be applied to fabrics to prevent these undesirable qualities.

Linen

Flax is obtained from the woody stalk of the flax plant. Flax is the fiber used to make linen. Flax is the oldest known fiber used for fabrics. Remnants of linen have

The Natural Fibers

Cotton

Advantages

Absorbent; soaks up water easily

Comfortable and cool to wear in warm weather

Dyes and prints well

Does not build up static electricity

Withstands high temperature; can be boiled to sterilize

Combines with other fibers easily

Wide variety of uses

Disadvantages

Wrinkles easily unless treated with special finish

Shrinks in hot water if not treated

Mildews if left damp or stored in damp area

Weakened by wrinkle-resistant finishes and by prolonged exposure to sunlight

Highly flammable unless treated with flame-retardant finish

Linen (Flax)

Advantages

Strongest of natural fibers

Cool to wear; absorbs moisture from skin and dries quickly

Looks smooth and lustrous

Withstands high temperatures; will not scorch easily when ironed

Durable; withstands frequent laundering

Lint-free; used for dish towels and for cloths in medical profession

Disadvantages

Wrinkles and creases easily unless treated

Shines if ironed

Expensive if of good quality

Poor resistance to mildew and perspiration

Wool

Advantages

Warmest of natural fibers

Highly absorbent; absorbs moisture without feeling wet

Resists wrinkles

Holds and regains shape

Creases well

Durable

Combines well with other fibers

Disadvantages

Expensive

Will shrink and mat when moisture and heat are applied

Usually requires dry cleaning

Burns easily

Attracts moths and carpet beetles

Silk

Advantages

Looks and feels smooth and luxurious

Very absorbent

Strong but lightweight

Resists wrinkling

Resists soil

Combines well with other fibers

Disadvantages

Usually requires dry cleaning

Yellows with age

Weakened by detergents, perspiration, and long exposure to sunlight

Attacked by insects such as silverfish

Spotted by water unless specially treated

Expensive

21-1

The natural fibers have advantages and disadvantages.

21-2
Cotton is often used for baby clothes because of its softness and absorbency.

21-3
After wool is sheared from sheep, it goes through several processes before becoming cloth.

been found in Egyptian tombs as old as 5000 B.C. Linen was the fabric used to wrap bodies for burial.

Linen is best known for its strength, durability, absorbency, and luster. Flax makes linen the coolest fabric you can wear. The flax fibers absorb perspiration quickly and carry it away from the body. Like cotton fabric, linen wrinkles and creases easily unless treated with a special finish. Ironing makes the fiber shiny.

Wool

Wool, a protein fiber, comes from the fleece of sheep, 21-3. Wool is an absorbent, resilient, and elastic fiber and the warmest of all fibers. Even though wool fabric is warm, it can also feel cool in lightweight fabrics. Wool fibers allow the fabric to breathe. This lets heat out and air in to keep the body dry and cool. These and other qualities make wool a very comfortable and durable fabric.

Consumers cannot know the type and quality of wool simply by looking at wool fabric. To inform and protect consumers, Congress passed the Wool Products Labeling Act in 1939. This legislation requires that wool in any garment or fabric must be labeled as new or recycled. Wool, as defined by the act, means fibers from the coat of a living animal that are being used for the first time. This wool is often called *virgin wool*.

Recycled wool refers to fibers from previously made wool fabrics that were never used. This wool often comes from cutting scraps, mill ends, or garments. These fabrics are converted back into fibers and then used to make new yarns and fabrics. Fabrics made from recycled wool are not as resilient (springy) as fabrics made from virgin wool. They are often used as interlinings in heavy coats.

Silk

Silk was first produced in China where the process of *sericulture* (silkworm cultivation) was kept a secret for more than 2,000 years. Gradually, the silk industry spread westward, but silk production is still confined mainly to China, Japan, and other Asian countries. Silk, characterized by long, lustrous filaments, is often called the luxury fiber. See 21-4.

Silk is a fiber excreted from the silkworm when it builds its cocoon. The cocoons are then soaked in warm water and unwound (either by hand or machine) as one continuous filament about 1,000 feet long. These long filaments are twisted to form yarns for the manufacture of silk fabrics.

Silk is strong, lustrous, elastic, and absorbent. Most silk garments should be dry-cleaned, but washable silk fabrics are now more common.

Ramie

Ramie fibers are obtained from the stalks of China grass, which is grown in Southeast Asia. Ramie is a linenlike fiber that is strong, durable, washable, and lustrous. Ramie absorbs body moisture, dries quickly, and absorbs dyes readily. It is often blended with other fibers in making fabrics.

21-4
Silk is often used to make fine scarves.

Manufactured Fibers

Manufactured fibers are produced through chemical and technical means from natural cellulose or crude oil products. For centuries, clothing consisted of animal pelts and fabric made from natural fibers. In 1924, the first manufactured fiber, *rayon*, was produced. *Acetate* was developed a few years later, and more manufactured fibers followed.

Today, the Federal Trade Commission recognizes 26 generic names of manufactured fibers. Within each group, the fibers share a similar chemical composition. Some categories are not made in this country, and several are only used in specialized industrial uses. See 21-5 for manufactured fibers that are commonly used in fabrics and apparel.

Rayon, acetate, triacetate, and lyocell are made from *cellulose*, the fibrous substance from plants. Wood pulp is used most often. The other manufactured fibers are called *noncellulosic fibers* because they are completely chemical based. Both cellulosic and noncellulosic fibers require the same basic production steps.

1. Solid materials are changed to a liquid form.
2. The liquid is extruded or forced through a *spinneret*, a small nozzle with many holes.
3. The liquid hardens into continuous strands of fibers.

As with all fibers, manufactured fibers have both advantages and disadvantages. Noncellulosic fibers are generally *thermoplastic*, which means they soften at high temperatures. Fabrics made of these fibers can be heat-treated to form pleats, shape fabrics, or emboss fabric designs.

Rayon and lyocell are somewhat absorbent, while acrylic moves moisture away from the skin. Other manufactured fibers are less comfortable to wear in hot,

The Manufactured Fibers

	Acetate	Acrylic	Aramid	Lyocell	Metallic	Modacrylic	Nylon	Olefin	Polyester	Rayon	Saran	Spandex
Absorbent				●						●		
Colorfast		●			●		●	●	●	●	●	
Easy to dye	●		●	●		●			●			
Easy to launder		●	●	●	●	●	●	●	●			●
Easy to iron			●			●		●	●			
Elastic						●						●
Exceptional durability			●	●	●	●	●	●		●		
Flame resistant			●			●					●	
Good drapability	●		●	●		●			●			
Good shape retention		●				●	●		●			●
Quick drying		●				●	●	●	●			●
Resilient		●	●	●		●			●			
Resistant to: ■ abrasion		●				●	●	●	●			
■ chemicals		●	●			●	●	●	●		●	
■ moths	●	●	●		●	●	●	●	●	●	●	●
■ mildew	●	●	●		●	●	●	●	●		●	●
■ oil/grease		●	●			●						●
■ pilling	●								●			
■ stretching		●							●			
■ soil		●						●				
■ shrinking		●	●	●	●		●		●		●	
■ weather		●			●	●		●	●	●	●	
Soft	●	●		●	●		●			●		
Strong			●	●			●	●	●		●	
Warm		●				●	●		●			
Wide color range	●	●		●		●	●		●	●		
Wrinkle resistant		●							●			●

21-5
This chart lists the most important properties of common manufactured fibers.

humid weather. Because they don't absorb or move moisture, they can generate static electricity. Fiber blends and special finishes can overcome some of these limitations.

Microfibers

A relatively recent development in textile technology is the creation of microfibers. A **microfiber** is an extremely thin filament of a manufactured fiber. The thinness of a microfiber is determined in step 2 of the manufacturing process, described earlier. The result is a fabric having all the qualities that are characteristic of the fiber plus a luxurious look and feel.

Polyester microfiber, for example, often looks like fine silk. Yet it has the strength, durability, and easy-care qualities associated with polyester. In addition, the fabric has a natural resistance to water since the thin fibers pack together so closely that a water molecule cannot penetrate. However, body heat can escape so the wearer remains comfortable. Acrylic, rayon, nylon, and polyester are available as microfibers.

Yarns

A yarn is a continuous strand made by combining staple fibers or filaments. *Staple fibers* are short fibers. All natural fibers except silk are staple fibers. *Filaments* are continuous strands of fibers. Manufactured fibers are made in filament form, but can be cut to form staple fibers.

Spinning staple fibers together produces **spun yarns**. These yarns have a fuzzy appearance. Rubbing and wearing may cause the tiny fiber ends of spun yarns to *pill*, or form little balls. You may have noticed pilling on sweaters and other clothes.

Filament yarns are made from filaments. One or more types of filament fibers may be combined to form a filament yarn. See 21-6.

Many yarns on today's market are either blends or combinations. Spinning different staple fibers together makes a *blended yarn*. Twisting two different yarns together forms a *combination yarn*.

Blends and combinations are often used to make fabrics with better performance. In the case of a polyester/cotton shirt,

21-6
An ordinary spool of all-purpose thread usually has continuous filament yarns made of polyester.

the two fibers blended together give very good performance. Polyester is wrinkle-resistant, but it absorbs very little moisture. Cotton is absorbent, but it wrinkles easily. By blending the fibers, the shirt can have the best characteristics of both fibers. Sometimes blends and combinations are used to make less-expensive fabrics.

Fabric Construction

Two common methods of fabric construction are weaving and knitting. Other methods are felting, fusing, braiding, knotting, and quilting.

Weaving

A woven fabric is composed of two sets of yarns crossing at right angles. The process of interlacing these two sets of yarns to produce a fabric is known as **weaving**. Weaving is done on machines called *looms*.

Passing crosswise yarns over and under different numbers of lengthwise yarns creates different weaving effects. The plain, twill, and satin weaves are the three basic weaves.

Plain Weave

The plain weave is the simplest form of weaving. It is made by passing a crosswise yarn alternately over and under the lengthwise yarns. See 21-7. The plain weave produces a fabric that is strong, reversible, and durable. Examples of the plain weave include muslin, percale, dress linen, gingham, and broadcloth.

Twill Weave

The twill weave is formed when a crosswise yarn passes, or *floats*, over two or three lengthwise yarns. See 21-8. Each float begins at least one yarn over from the last one. The twill weave is characterized by a diagonal line or *wale*. The angle of a wale may vary from a low slope to a very steep one.

Twill weaves are often used to produce strong, durable fabrics such as denim and gabardine. Twill-weave fabrics resist wrinkles and hide soil.

Satin Weave

A satin weave is made when a crosswise yarn floats over four or more yarns and under one. See 21-9. Satin-weave fabrics are characterized by their lustrous shine. This shine is a result of long floats on the surface of the fabric reflecting light.

21-8
In this twill weave, crosswise yarns pass two lengthwise yarns in a continuous over-and-under pattern.

Since the floats tend to snag easily, the satin weave does not produce durable fabrics. Durability increases if the yarns are woven closely together. Satin weave fabrics are often used as lining fabrics because they are smooth and slippery.

Knitting

The process of looping yarns together to form a fabric is called **knitting**. The loops are varied to create numerous patterns and textures. One yarn can form the entire fabric.

Knit fabrics are best known for their stretch, which allows the fabric to move with, and fit, the body. See 21-10. They

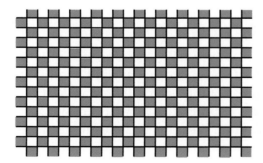

21-7
A plain weave is created by passing single crosswise yarns continuously over and under single lengthwise yarns.

21-9
In this satin weave, each crosswise yarn passes under one lengthwise yarn and over four to create long floats.

21-10

Knits are popular because they are very comfortable, especially during vigorous activity.

also resist wrinkles well. When threads are broken, however, a *run* can form, as in nylon stockings. Knits also can snag or ravel if a yarn is pulled.

Other Fabric Constructions

Not all fabrics are knitted or woven. Some are made by locking fibers together or by braiding, knotting, or quilting yarns.

Nonwoven fabrics are made by pressing, bonding, or interlocking fibers together directly without using yarns. This can be done with mechanical action, chemicals, and/or heat. Nonwoven fabrics have many industrial and medical uses. They are also used as interfacings in garments. *Interfacings* give support to collars, waistbands, and cuffs. Batting, a lightweight layer of insulation used inside quilts, is also a nonwoven fabric.

Applying heat, moisture, agitation, and pressure to wool fibers results in *felt*. Due to the nature of wool fibers, the *felting* process causes fibers to permanently interlock. Felt is easy to mold and is often used to make hats and craft items. It has many industrial uses, too.

Braiding is the process of interlacing three or more yarns lengthwise and diagonally to make fabrics. Braided fabrics are usually narrow. They are used for decorative trims and shoelaces. Braids are often joined together to make rugs.

Knotting or twisting yarns produces *laces* and *nets*. These fabrics can be constructed by hand or machine. Lace and net fabrics can be fine and sheer, or coarse and open.

Quilting is the process of stitching a layer of insulating material between two layers of fabric. Often the stitching is regular and consistent to produce an all-over pattern. Sometimes decorative stitching is used, especially to emphasize a unique design. Quilting is used to make warm articles such as jackets, coats, and bed coverings. When quilting for crafts and home-decorating items, hot glue is sometimes used to seal the fabric layers.

Fabric Finishes

All fabrics go through some type of finishing process before they are ready for use. Most finishes add certain characteristics to the fabrics. Common fabric finishes are listed in 21-11. They improve the appearance, feel, or performance of fabrics.

Check It Out!

1. Name the five most commonly used natural fibers and list two characteristics of each.
2. What substances are used in making manufactured fibers?
3. Name five common manufactured fibers and list two characteristics of each.
4. Explain the basic difference between weaving and knitting.
5. Why are finishes applied to fabrics?

Common Fabric Finishes

Type of Finish	Description
Antistatic	Prevents garments from clinging to the body.
Bleaching	Whitens fabrics and removes impurities. Is usually used on cotton and linen fabrics.
Brushing	Uses circular brushes to remove short, loose fibers from the surface and produce an even, soft pile.
Calendering	Is the process of pressing fabric between heated rollers to make it smooth and glossy.
Dyeing	Adds color to fabric. *Colorfast* means the color will withstand washing, dry cleaning, perspiration, sunlight, and rubbing.
Flame Retardant	Prevents the fabric from supporting a flame by cutting off the oxygen supply. Is used on children's sleepwear, general wearing apparel, carpets, rugs, and mattresses according to flammability standards set by the Flammable Fabrics Act.
Mercerization	Is most often used on cotton, linen, and rayon fabrics to increase luster, strength, and affinity (attraction) for dyes.
Permanent Press	Helps fabric retain its original shape and resist wrinkling after washing and drying. Is also called *durable press*.
Preshrinking	Shrinks fabrics in a heat-and-moisture process. Garments labeled *preshrunk* will not shrink more than three percent. *Sanforized*™ is a trademark name, guaranteeing less than one percent shrinkage in length or width.
Sizing	Is a solution of starch, glue, or resin applied to fabric to increase weight, body, and luster. May be temporary or durable.
Soil Release	Helps water-resistant fibers become more absorbent so detergents can release soil. Makes possible the removal of oily stains from durable-press fabrics.
Stain Resistance	Makes fabrics less absorbent to resist water and oil stains so spills can be lifted or sponged off easily. *Scotchguard*™ is a trademark for a stain-resistant fabric.
Water Repellence	Makes a fabric resistant to wetting, but must be renewed after several launderings. Does not waterproof the fabric against heavy rain.

21-11

Fabric finishes are applications and processes that affect how a cloth looks, feels, and functions.

Topic 21-2

Selecting Patterns, Fabrics, and Notions

Objectives

After studying this topic, you will be able to
▼ determine your figure type and pattern size.
▼ identify a suitable pattern and interpret the information on its envelope.
▼ select appropriate fabric for your garment.
▼ purchase the correct amount of fabric.
▼ identify the necessary sewing notions.

Topic Terms

figure type
pattern view
notions

Successful sewing begins with choosing the right pattern. Pattern catalogs will show you many style choices.

In order to buy a pattern, you will need to know what size to request. Since pattern sizes vary slightly from ready-to-wear sizes, you will need to first take your measurements. These measurements will help you identify your figure type and size. After selecting a pattern, you will follow the information on the back of the envelope.

Determine Your Figure Type and Size

Pattern companies have standard pattern sizes for various figure types. **Figure types** are based on height and general body proportions. Six basic figure types apply to most teens and adults, 21-12. Body-measurement charts for all body types appear in pattern catalogs at fabric stores. The charts usually appear near the last page. Choosing a pattern of the correct figure type will result in a garment that fits well.

If you are a female, two measurements are used to determine your figure type—your height and back waist length. The *back waist length* is the distance from the most prominent bone at the center back of the neck to the waistline. Females must also analyze body proportions and shape to determine figure type. If uncertain about which figure type to use, it is best to choose the one with the closest back waist length. For males, choosing the right pattern size is simpler.

Select your pattern size by comparing your measurements to those for your figure type. If your measurements fall between two sizes, select the smaller size if you want a garment with a closer fit.

Basic Figure Types for Teens and Adults

Females
- Junior
- Junior Plus
- Misses'/Miss Petite
- Women's/Women's Petite

Males
- Boys' and Teen Boys'
- Men's

21-12
Most young men and women fit into one of these figure types.

The More You Know: What Measurements Should You Take?

Learning to take your measurements accurately will help you choose the best pattern sizes. To measure the *head* for a hat or cap, bring the tape measure around the head at the fullest part of the forehead. *Hips* should be measured around the fullest part of the hip section. This is about seven or eight inches below the waistline. The *waist* should be measured at the smallest part of the midsection on females. For males, it may be where the waistband of pants usually falls. The *bust* or *chest* is measured with the tape straight across the back and around the fullest part of the bust or chest while holding your arms at your sides.

Taking Your Measurements

To ensure accuracy, ask someone to help you take your measurements. Measure over the undergarments you normally wear. Do not try to take measurements over bulky clothing. When taking measurements, put the tape measure snugly around the body, but not too tight. Be sure the tape measure is always parallel to the floor.

Deciding on a Pattern

After determining your figure type, you can turn to the sections of the pattern book that feature your figure type. In making your decision, you will want to consider your sewing skill. You will probably be wise to limit yourself to one new learning experience each time you choose a pattern.

Beginning with a simple garment will assure your success. A clue to a pattern's sewing ease is its number of pieces. Fewer pattern pieces usually mean the pattern will be easier to sew, 21-13.

You will also want to select a style that suits you. Try to visualize how the finished garment will look on you. Apply what you have learned about design lines that flatter your figure. Study the drawings in the pattern book. Look for the design details that you prefer.

The Pattern Envelope

After selecting the pattern, read the information on the front and the back of the pattern envelope. The front of the

21-13
Patterns that have only a few pattern pieces are easiest to sew.

envelope usually has drawings or photos of more than one image, or pattern view. Each **pattern view** shows a variation of the basic pattern. For instance, a pattern may show a shirt with long sleeves next to one with short sleeves. Skirts may be shown in different lengths. In addition, the front of the pattern envelope usually shows the pattern number, company name, figure type, and size. See 21-14.

The back of the pattern envelope includes the following information:

▼ price of the pattern (usually on back flap)
▼ the number of pattern pieces included
▼ a written description of the garment
▼ fabric recommendations
▼ supplies needed to complete the garment

▼ a drawing of the back of each garment view
▼ a measurement chart
▼ directions for how much fabric to buy
▼ any interfacing or lining fabrics needed

Choosing a Fabric

On the back of the pattern envelope, you will find a section that identifies fabrics appropriate for the pattern, 21-15. Beginning sewers will want to follow these recommendations closely. This section also alerts you to fabrics that should not be used, such as pile fabrics or diagonal patterns.

Also consider your sewing skills when choosing fabric. A medium-weight fabric is easiest to sew. Very heavy or light fabrics are more challenging. The same is true for fabrics that ravel easily, are slippery, or

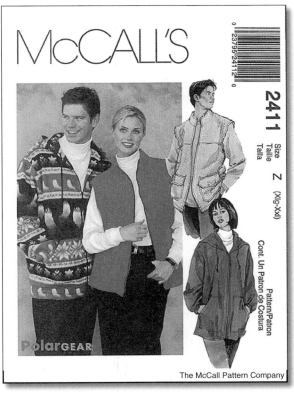

21-14
The front of a pattern envelope usually shows the different ways that a pattern can be varied.

Setting the Scene: Fabric Care

You have realized that the type of care some fabrics require can be costly. You cannot afford to add the cost of dry cleaning to the price of a garment. You also have little time for washing clothes. While choosing a fabric, you read its care requirements. You will need to wash the garment separately in cold water, avoid chlorine bleach, let it drip dry, and press with a cool iron.

Analyze It: Would you consider this fabric a good buy? What other factors might prompt you to buy the fabric anyway?

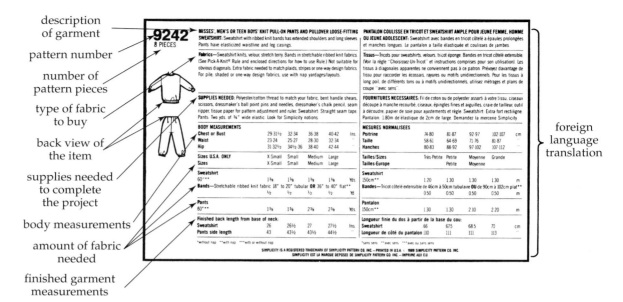

description of garment

pattern number

number of pattern pieces

type of fabric to buy

back view of the item

supplies needed to complete the project

body measurements

amount of fabric needed

finished garment measurements

foreign language translation

21-15

The back of the pattern envelope includes information you will need when purchasing your supplies.

have a design that must be matched at the seams. You should also consider the care requirements of a fabric before making a purchase.

How Much Fabric Is Needed?

To determine how much fabric to buy, again refer to the back of the pattern envelope. A chart shows the amount of fabric to buy based on fabric width and pattern size. Fabric widths vary, so you will need to know the width of your fabric.

To use the chart, first locate the section for the pattern view you will make. Then find the column for the size of your pattern. Go down the column until you come to the width of the fabric you have chosen. Circle this figure. This is the number of yards of fabric you should buy. It will also tell you how much interfacing is needed.

Choosing Notions

To complete your garment, you must have notions. **Notions** are small items needed to construct a garment. They include thread, buttons, trims, fasteners, seam binding, and bias tape. The notions needed to complete the garment are listed on the back of the pattern envelope. Purchase these items when you buy your fabric. Then you can make sure your thread, buttons, and other notions match your fabric.

If you cannot match the exact color, choose a slightly darker color. Thread will appear lighter when sewn. See 21-16. Polyester or cotton-covered polyester thread is good for working with most fabrics on a standard sewing machine.

21-16

Sometimes a contrasting color of thread is chosen to create interest and add design.

Check It Out!

1. What should you look for when choosing a pattern that will be easy to sew?
2. What are pattern views?
3. List three factors to consider before choosing a fabric.
4. What three factors will help you locate the number of yards of fabric to buy on a yardage chart?
5. What should you do when you cannot find thread that is an exact match for your fabric?

Topic 21-3
Sewing Equipment

Objectives

After studying this topic, you will be able to
- determine the basic sewing supplies.
- describe how to operate and care for a sewing machine.
- list the uses of a serger.

Topic Terms

lockstitch
bobbin
presser foot
feed dogs
thread-tension regulator
serger
looper

Having the proper equipment and knowing how to use it will help you become a successful sewer. There are certain supplies every sewer needs. Begin by purchasing the basics, 21-17. As you progress, you may want to add equipment that will simplify construction and reduce sewing time.

Small Equipment

One of the first things you will need is a sewing box. It can be any kind of container or box that will help you keep your small equipment organized. Use dividers or small containers to hold pins, needles, a tape measure, and other small items.

You will need several types of small sewing equipment. These include measuring tools, cutting tools, marking

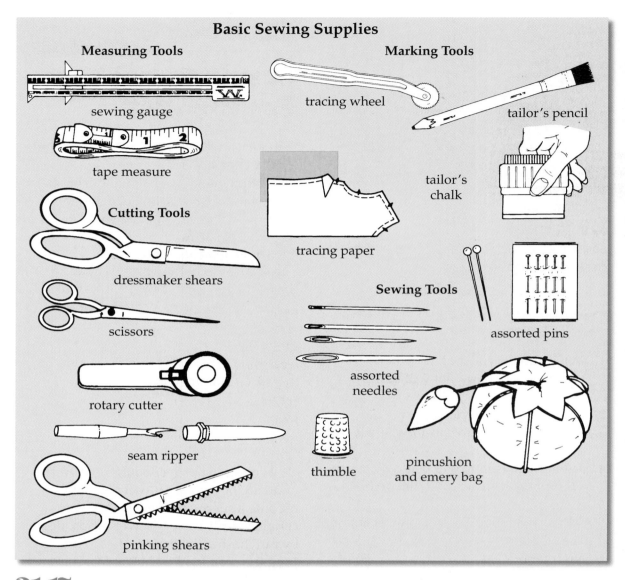

21-17
These are the basic sewing supplies you will need.

tools, pins and needles, and pressing equipment. Most of these items can be bought in department or fabric stores.

Measuring Tools

A *tape measure* is essential for taking body measurements. Most tape measures are 60-inches long. Make sure the tape is made from a material that will not stretch. Choose one that has protectors on the ends to give the tape durability. Also check to be sure the numbers are clearly visible and printed on both sides of the tape.

A *sewing gauge* is a 6-inch metal or plastic ruler with a sliding marker. It is used to measure small areas, such as hems, cuffs, and the space between buttons.

Cutting Tools

Having sharp, quality shears and scissors is very important in sewing. Before buying cutting tools, always test them to be sure they cut cleanly. Shears and scissors come in various sizes and have many different uses. Make your selections based on what you will be cutting.

Dressmaker shears are used to cut pattern pieces from the fabric. A bent handle (rather than a straight handle) allows the fabric to lie flat on the worktable while cutting. This makes it easier to cut smooth, accurate edges. Shears are available in right- and left-handed versions.

Scissors are smaller and shorter than shears and have round handles. They are used for trimming, grading, and clipping seams and snipping threads.

A *rotary cutter* also cuts pattern pieces from the fabric. It cuts with a round blade as the tool is pushed along the pattern cutting lines. The tool must be used with a mat specially designed for rotary cutting on a table surface.

A *seam ripper* is used to neatly open unwanted seams.

Another cutting tool you may want to buy later is *pinking shears*. These shears are used to finish the cut edge of seams so they will not ravel. Pinking shears cut a zigzag edge.

Marking Tools

Tracing wheels, tracing paper, tailor's chalk and *tailor's pencil* are types of marking tools. They are used to transfer pattern markings from a pattern piece to the fabric. These markings help you put pattern pieces together for sewing.

Always test your marking tool on a scrap of the actual fabric. If the mark comes off easily without marring the fabric, it is okay to use. If the fabric is marred or the mark is difficult to remove, try a different marking tool.

Pins and Needles

Dressmaker pins are used to hold garment pieces in place until stitched together permanently. These pins have sharp points, 21-18. *Ballpoint pins* are best for pinning knit fabrics since their rounded points slide between the yarns of the fabric. (Pins with sharp points could cut the yarns and cause snags.)

Needles are used to bring thread through the fabric. They have a small hole, called the *eye,* which holds the thread. Needles range in size from 1 to 12. Smaller numbers indicate larger needles. Needles called *sharps,* in size 7 or 8, are most often used for hand sewing.

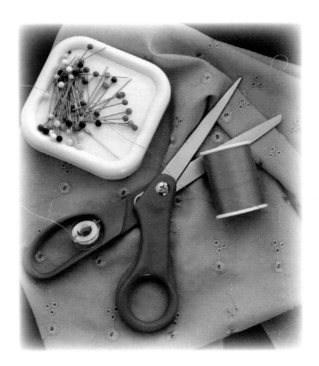

21-18

After seams are sewn, dressmaker pins are then used for adjusting fit and holding hemlines.

A *pincushion* holds pins and needles when not in use. Pincushions come in many sizes and shapes. Some sewers find a wrist pincushion very convenient to wear while fitting and sewing. Some pincushions have an *emery bag* attached for sharpening pins and needles.

When sewing by hand, you may want to use a *thimble* to prevent the needle from pricking your finger. It should fit snugly on your middle finger. If you are a beginning sewer, a thimble may feel awkward at first. With a little practice, you will see how useful it can be.

Pressing Equipment

When sewing a garment, pressing is as important as stitching. Careful construction alone will not result in a well-made garment. "Press as you sew" is a good rule to follow. Each construction line you sew should be pressed before another seam is stitched across it.

Several pieces of pressing equipment are recommended, but an *iron* is the most important. Most irons have a temperature guide that gives the proper heat setting for various types of fabric. A steam iron is more convenient to use for pressing, but a dry iron can also be used.

A *pressing cloth* is used to protect the fabric from overheating and shining when an iron is used. These cloths are made of cheesecloth, organdy, or muslin.

The *ironing board* needs to be sturdy, level, and tapered to a narrow width at one end. The ironing board should be covered with a pad and cover. A silicone treated cover will prevent scorching and sticking. Keep the cover clean and smooth since a wrinkled cover can cause wrinkles in a garment.

A *tailor's ham* is a firmly stuffed, oval cushion used to shape curved areas while pressing. It is used for pressing a rounded shape into darts, sleeve caps, and curved seams.

The Sewing Machine

The sewing machine is a complex piece of equipment requiring a skilled operator. Learning how to operate a sewing machine is easier when you have a basic understanding of how it works. Then knowing how to care for the sewing machine will assure its smooth and continued operation.

How a Sewing Machine Works

There are many different brands and models of sewing machines, but all operate essentially the same way. The basic parts of a sewing machine are shown in 21-19. The job of the sewing machine is to secure pieces of fabric together with a **lockstitch**. This stitch uses thread from both the upper and lower parts of the machine. Thread from the upper part of the machine is carried by way of the needle down through the fabric to pick up the lower thread. The lower thread comes from the **bobbin**. The two threads lock in the middle of the fabric layers to make a secure stitch.

A knee or foot control sends power to the machine when pressure is applied. The **presser foot** holds the fabric in place as the machine stitches. The **feed dogs** are two small rows of teeth that move the fabric forward under the presser foot. Stitches are made when power is applied. The needle should always be in the highest position before sewing begins.

Two **thread-tension regulators** are found on the sewing machine. The tension, or pull between the upper and lower threads, must be balanced for a proper stitch to form. A perfectly balanced stitch looks identical on the top and bottom of the fabric. Generally, any adjustment can be made with the upper-tension regulator that applies tension to the upper thread. The instruction manual with your machine will show you how to adjust the tension.

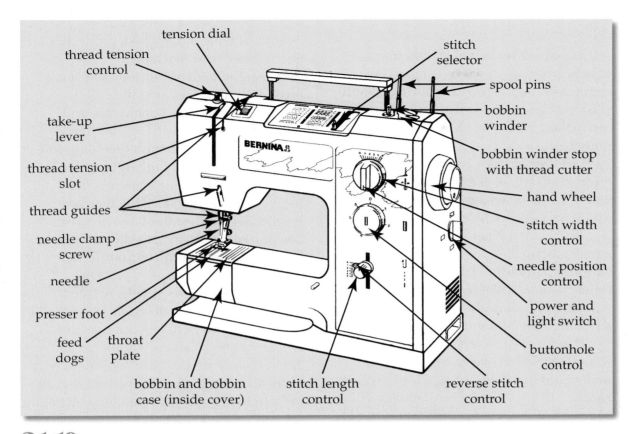

21-19
Knowing the names of the parts of the sewing machine is a first step in learning how to operate it.

Two basic types of sewing machines are in use today—mechanical and computerized machines. With mechanical machines, you dial the stitch you want and adjust the length, width, and tension. With computerized machines, the preferred length, width, and tension are preprogrammed for you. However, you can change the settings and override the computer. Some computerized machines have hundreds of decorative and special stitches programmed into them. Most feature simple, one-step buttonhole operations.

Threading the Machine

Different sewing machines thread differently. A diagram in your instruction manual will show how to thread your machine.

From one machine to another, the basic steps are the same. At the upper part, the thread is guided from the spool pin through the upper tension control. From there the thread goes to a take-up lever and down to the needle. Several thread guides keep the thread from tangling while directing it. The thread guide nearest the needle is always placed on the side from which the needle is threaded.

Threading the lower part of the machine begins with threading the bobbin. Your instruction manual will tell you how to do this. The bobbin is then placed in the bobbin case. The bobbin thread must always be brought up through the needle hole before beginning to sew. If the thread is not pulled up, a knot will form as the first stitch is attempted.

Types of Stitches

Almost all sewing machines make at least two basic types of stitches—the common straight stitch and the frequently used zigzag stitch. Most sewing machines can make a variety of stitches in addition to these two.

The *straight stitch* is a lockstitch used for holding layers of fabric together. Its length can be adjusted to correspond with different purposes. A typical stitch length is 10 to 15 stitches per inch. A long stitch length, six stitches per inch, can be used for temporarily holding fabric pieces in place, called *machine basting*. A length of 18 to 21 stitches per inch is often used to reinforce stress areas in garments.

The *zigzag stitch* is a sideways stitch. It is often used to overcast seam edges that would otherwise ravel, 21-20. A short zigzag stitch is used for buttonholes. A variation of the zigzag stitch is also used to sew stretch-knit fabrics. This allows seams to give slightly with the fabric. The zigzag stitch can be adjusted by using the stitch length and stitch-width regulators.

Caring for the Machine

A sewing machine is an expensive piece of sewing equipment that requires special care. Regular cleaning will result in

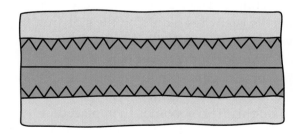

21-20
When sewing a zigzag seam finish, the needle will move on and off the fabric edge.

fewer machine problems. Your instruction manual will have step-by-step directions for cleaning your machine.

Cleaning with a soft cloth and small brush is a must. Use a small brush to remove lint from the bobbin case and under the feed dogs.

Always use the correct type of needle for your machine and the right size for your fabric. Your instruction manual will have guidelines for selecting the correct needle. Replace needles if they become bent, nicked, or rusty. Needles dull easily and can damage both your fabric and your machine.

Sewing machines should be oiled periodically. Your instruction manual will tell you how often to oil your machine. It will also show where oil should be applied. After oiling your machine, be sure to wipe away any excess oil. Then sew on a scrap of cloth to remove any remaining oil before sewing your good fabric.

The Serger

Sergers are high-speed sewing machines that can stitch, trim, and finish seams in one simple step, 21-21. They were originally designed for the ready-to-wear industry. Now they are available for home use.

The home sewer can obtain professional results by using a serger. The outer edges of garments can be finished without the need for facings, ribbings, or bands. Narrow or rolled hems can be made, such as those found on scarves or tablecloths. Sergers can also produce a blind hemming stitch. Stretch fabrics are easily sewn with a serger. Decorative stitching is popular for embellishing T-shirts, sweatshirts, and similar garments.

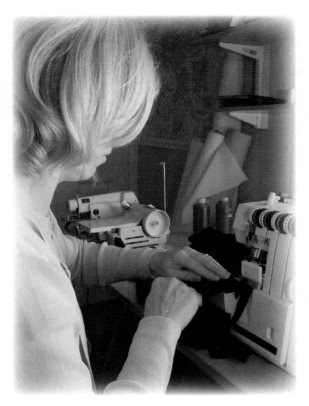

21-21
Learning to use the serger can save you time as you create your own unique fashions.

Sergers use two, three, four, or five threads and one or two needles. Sergers do not have bobbins. Instead they have one to three **loopers**, both upper and lower. The needle threads intertwine with the looper threads to form stitches. Sergers also have upper and lower knives that trim the seam allowance before the seam is finished.

Though sergers are fast and perform many functions, they cannot replace a conventional sewing machine. A conventional sewing machine is needed for topstitching and buttonholes. Some people also prefer to insert zippers with a conventional machine.

Safety with Sewing Tools

Safety is an important consideration in everything you do. Sewing and pressing are no exceptions. Following basic safety precautions is important for keeping the sewing area safe for you and others:

▼ Read all instructions before using any tool.
▼ Use each tool only for its intended purpose.
▼ Never leave tools unattended when others are around. Put tools away when not being use.
▼ Closely supervise any children or pets in the area. Tools should not be used as toys.

Besides these basic steps, follow the safety recommendations pertaining to the tools used in the sewing area, 21-22. Irons can cause fires and burns. Scissors, pins, and other common tools can cause cuts and wounds. When using electricity, electric shock is always a possibility. In addition, appliance cords can cause people to trip and fall.

Check It Out!

1. Explain how the use of dressmaker shears differs from the use of scissors.
2. True or false. A size 5 needle will be larger than a size 10 needle.
3. What is the "press as you sew" rule?
4. If a machine stitch does not look the same on both the top and bottom of the fabric, what needs to be adjusted?
5. Give two uses for the zigzag stitch.
6. What three functions can sergers perform in one fast operation?
7. State four safety hazards that can take place in a sewing area.

Preventing Sewing-Area Hazards	
Fires and Burns	• Fill a steam iron with water while unplugged. Let a hot iron cool before emptying it. • Keep your hands and face, especially your eyes, away from steam and heated water. • Rest a hot iron on its heel between uses, and turn it off during periods of nonuse. • Do not allow the electrical cord or any other item to rest against the iron's hot surface. • Let the iron cool before returning it to storage.
Cuts and Wounds	• Keep the blades of scissors and shears closed when not in use. Keep fingers away from moving needles and the serger's cutting blades while sewing. • Use rotary cutters on an appropriate cutting mat, always cutting away from the body. • Avoid placing pins and other tools in your mouth. • Immediately pick up pins and tools that fall to the floor. • Put tools away that are not being used. • Do not point sharp tools at others. When passing a sharp tool to another person, carefully grasp the dangerous end of the tool so the other person can grasp the handle or blunt end.
Electric Shock	• Make sure the switch of an electrical appliance is in the *off* position before connecting it to, or disconnecting it from, the outlet. • Do not operate an appliance with a damaged electrical cord. • Do not handle electrical appliances with hands that are wet or immersed in any solution. • Unplug an appliance by grasping the plug, not yanking the cord.
Trips and Falls	• Keep paths free of electrical cords. • Unplug and roll up the cord of any appliance not in use.

21-22
Keep your sewing area safe by removing potential hazards.

Chapter Review

Summary

Knowledge of fabrics—their fiber content, construction, and finishes—will help you select the right fabric for your project. This knowledge will also help you when purchasing ready-to-wear garments and other fabrics for your home.

Before you can select a pattern, you must determine your figure type and size. Taking accurate body measurements is the first step. Your height and body proportions determine your figure type. Match your measurements to those listed for your figure type. Then select a pattern appropriate for your skill level. You will also want to consider your wardrobe needs and your activities when choosing a pattern.

The pattern envelope will list recommended fabrics as well as the notions needed to complete the project. Some fabrics are more difficult to sew than others. Some fabrics can be laundered and others must be dry-cleaned. These are some of the factors that need to be considered when selecting a fabric.

Some basic pieces of equipment are needed for sewing. Measuring, cutting, and marking tools are needed, as well as pins, needles, and pressing equipment. The sewing machine is the most important piece of equipment and the most expensive. Learn how the sewing machine operates and give it proper care to keep it running smoothly. As you gain sewing experience, you may decide a serger would be useful. No matter what sewing tools you use, always use them safely.

Think About It!

1. How can knowledge about fibers and fabrics help the person who sews? How can the same knowledge help someone who does not sew?
2. Which fabric finishes would you like applied to the garments you wear? Which finishes would you like applied to the fabrics you use in your home? Explain your answers.
3. What criteria would you consider when selecting a pattern for yourself? Since trade-offs sometimes need to be made, list your criteria in order of priority.
4. Why is it best not to select your pattern size solely by the size of your ready-to-wear clothes?
5. Why is the pattern envelope an important resource for the person who sews?
6. In what careers would sewing skills be particularly helpful? somewhat helpful?
7. List some of the advantages of sewing your own clothes. Name some disadvantages.
8. What do you see as the future for home sewing? How have changes in society impacted the home sewing industry?
9. What can you do to keep your sewing area safer?

Try It Out!

1. Collect samples of many fabrics. Identify and label how each fabric was constructed.

2. From your collection of fabrics, unravel some of the samples. Identify the types of yarns used.

3. Cut out eight advertisements of textile products from newspapers, magazines, or catalogs. Circle the fiber content in each ad. List two reasons you think a particular fiber or fiber blend was used for each product. Discuss your advertisements with the class.

4. At fabric shops, look through different brands of pattern catalogs. Become familiar with the pattern sections and the information given in the catalogs. Find one pattern that would be a good sewing project for you. Look at the fabrics recommended for the pattern and read the fabric care labels.

5. Look through magazines or department store catalogs. Find five examples of clothing or home furnishings that have been treated with a special finish.

6. Practice your measuring skills with two classmates. Each person is to be measured by the other two people in the group. If the two measurements differ, determine why and measure again. Record each person's measurements on a chart.

7. At a fabric shop, identify several kinds of sewing equipment. In class, explain or demonstrate how each piece of equipment (if available) is used in sewing.

8. Invite a sewing machine salesperson to bring a portable model of the latest sewing machine to class and demonstrate its features.

9. Sew a practice seam using a serger. If possible, construct a simple garment using a serger.

Chapter 22
Sewing Techniques

Careers

These careers relate to the topics in this chapter:

▼ tailor
▼ pattern maker or grader
▼ sewing instructor
▼ clothing specialist

As you study the chapter, see if you can think of others.

Topics

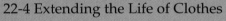

589

Topic 22-1

Begin with the Pattern

Objectives

After studying this topic, you will be able to
▼ explain the meaning of pattern symbols.
▼ adjust pattern length and width.

Topic Terms

pattern guide sheet
cutting line
notch
dot
multisize pattern
stitching line
seam allowance
grain
grainline arrow
adjustment lines
alteration

Like other projects that you complete yourself, sewing projects require instructions. That is why you need a pattern. Sewing patterns include not only the pattern pieces, but also a detailed set of instructions. Most of the instructions are found on the pattern guide sheet.

The Pattern Guide Sheet

Every pattern has a set of instructions called the **pattern guide sheet**. See 22-1. The guide sheet has step-by-step directions that will lead you through each phase of your sewing project. Read and study the guide sheet before beginning your project.

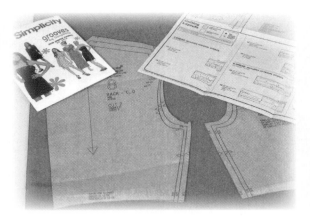

22-1
The pattern guide sheet is somewhat like a road map. By following it, you can reach your destination.

Most pattern guide sheets also contain other types of information you will find helpful:
▼ front and back views of each garment
▼ line drawings of the pattern pieces
▼ explanations of marking symbols found on pattern pieces
▼ explanations of terms used in the sewing directions
▼ suggested ways to transfer pattern markings to fabric
▼ ways to adjust the pattern for fit
▼ sewing directions
▼ layout directions for each garment and view

Understanding Pattern Symbols

Each pattern piece contains a pattern number, size, view number, piece name, and identification letter. The pattern guide sheet tells you which pattern pieces are needed for each view you make. From the pattern envelope, remove the pattern pieces you need. If the pieces are wrinkled, press them with a warm, dry iron.

The pattern pieces contain many lines, terms, and symbols. It is important to know what these mean. Many of the symbols are used when you lay the pattern pieces on the fabric. Others are used when you sew the pieces together. A pattern with the most common pattern symbols is shown in 22-2.

Cutting Lines

The **cutting line** is indicated with a bold line. On this line you will see several diamond-shaped symbols. These are called **notches**. There may be single notches, double notches, and even triple notches. Cut precisely around them. You will match these notches when you sew the pieces together. **Dots** are also used for matching seams and other construction details.

Practically all patterns available today are multisize. **Multisize patterns** contain three or more sizes on one tissue pattern. You simply cut along the appropriate line for your figure size.

Making adjustments in multisize patterns is easy. Wherever an adjustment is needed, simply cut on the cutting lines for one of the other sizes. For instance, if you need to increase the waistline, gradually angle as you cut to the line for the next larger size.

When making separates, there is another advantage in using multisize patterns. If a person is a different size above the waist than below, there is no need to buy two patterns.

Stitching Lines

The **stitching line** is the seamline, which is ⅝-inch inside the cutting line. On single-size patterns, it appears as a broken line. On multisize patterns, however, the stitching line is not marked. The space between the cutting line and the stitching line is the **seam allowance**. It generally is ⅝-inch wide. Sometimes the pattern guide sheet uses small arrows to indicate the best direction for stitching.

A ⅝-inch gauge is a standard feature at the throat plate of sewing machines. It alerts sewers where to align the edge of the fabric while sewing. When the fabric touches the ⅝-inch mark, the sewing needle is positioned directly over the stitching line.

Grainline Arrows

The two basic directions that yarns run in a woven fabric is called the **grain**. Fabrics have a lengthwise and a crosswise grain. A **grainline arrow** indicates the direction a pattern piece should be placed on the fabric. Usually, this arrow should align the lengthwise grain of the fabric.

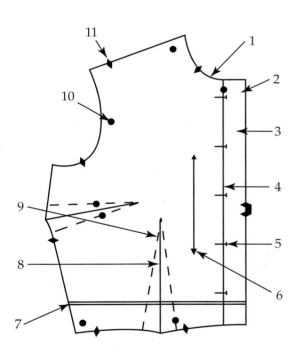

1. cutting line
2. seam allowance
3. stitching line
4. center front
5. buttonhole placement
6. grainline arrow
7. adjustment lines
8. fold line for dart
9. dart stitching line
10. dot
11. notch

22-2

Knowledge of pattern symbols is important to successful sewing.

Sometimes short arrows point to the edge of a pattern piece. This means the piece must be placed on a fold of the fabric. A cutting line is absent at a fold line to signal that fabric should not be cut.

Adjustment Lines

Lines that indicate where to shorten or lengthen a pattern piece are called **adjustment lines**. These two parallel lines usually extend across the pattern piece. Some pattern pieces will tell you to adjust the length at the hemline.

Altering Your Pattern

How should a garment fit? A well-fitted garment is comfortable to wear and well proportioned to your body. The garment is neither too big nor too small. It conforms to body contours without binding, pulling, sagging, or hanging unevenly. Proper fit is one of the keys to successful sewing, 22-3.

Patterns cannot be made to fit every person perfectly. **Alterations** are changes to the size of a pattern or garment. Carefully selecting a pattern according to your body measurements and figure type will reduce the need for alterations.

If you are using a multisize pattern, alterations to the bust, waist, and hip are easily made. At the point where your size changes, simply draw tapering lines to connect one size to the other.

Alterations should be made on pattern pieces before laying them out on the fabric. To see how well your pattern fits you, you can *pin fit* the pattern. To do this, pin the darts closed. Then pin the pattern pieces together at the seamlines and carefully try on the pattern. Pin the center front and back to your clothing. Then check sleeve, skirt, and pant lengths. You can also check the back and front waist lengths. Check the widths of various pattern pieces, too. Note changes that need to be made.

22-3
Spending time and effort on proper fit will result in a well-fitting garment.

Adjusting Pattern Length

Adjusting length is one of the most common and least difficult alterations to make. For example, you may be long waisted or short waisted. You may have short arms or long arms. Sometimes length must be adjusted in more than one area of the pattern. Alterations are made where they will not interfere with the lines of the garment.

To shorten a pattern piece, make a fold in the pattern piece between the adjustment lines. The fold should be half the amount to be shortened. Measure the fold to see that it is even. Then tape it in place.

To lengthen a pattern piece, cut between the adjustment lines. Place a piece of paper under the two pattern pieces. Measure the needed distance between the lines. Tape the pattern to the paper. Measure the distance again to check your accuracy. See 22-4.

Adjusting Pattern Width

Width adjustments may need to be made in the sleeve, waist, hips, or thighs. These adjustments should be made in both front and back pieces. Making adjustments to multisize patterns is easy, as described earlier.

With single-size patterns, however, adjusting the width of pattern pieces is more difficult. Waistline alterations in pants and skirts are made at the side seams. See 22-5. To increase the waistline, tape a

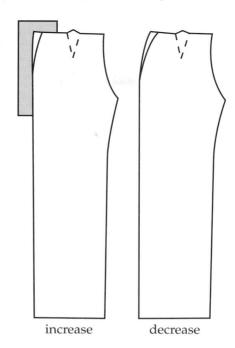

increase   decrease

22-5

To increase or decrease the width of the waist, measure in or out one-fourth of the needed amount at the side waistline edge. Redraw the cutting lines, tapering to the hipline.

strip of paper along the side edges of the front and back pattern pieces. Measure from the side cutting line at the waist edge of the front pattern piece. The width added to this pattern piece should be one-fourth of the total waistline increase. (One-fourth of the increase times four edges—each edge at both side seams—equals the total increase.) Make a dot at the extended point and redraw the cutting line, tapering to the hipline. Do the same with the back pattern piece.

To decrease the waistline, measure in from the cutting line one-fourth of the total amount to be removed. Redraw the cutting line, tapering to the hipline. If there is a waistband, lengthen or shorten it the same amount as the total waist adjustment.

If a garment is too small for the hips, wrinkling and pulling will occur around

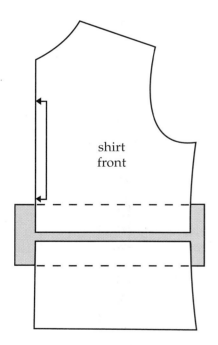

shirt front

22-4

To lengthen a pattern piece, cut between the adjustment lines. Allow room between the pattern pieces for the amount of fabric to be added.

the hipline. If a pants or skirt pattern is too large, there will be extra fullness. Hipline width is altered the same as waistline width. One-fourth the needed fullness is added or removed along the length of the side seams. Taking bigger or smaller darts is another way to adjust waistline width.

Check It Out!

1. True or false. The pattern guide sheet includes directions for taking your measurements.
2. What pattern symbols are used to match garment pieces when sewing?
3. True or false. To shorten a pattern, make a fold that is half the total amount to be shortened.
4. True or false. To widen a pattern piece, add half of the total alteration needed to the front side seam.

Topic 22-2
Pattern Layout, Cutting, and Marking

Objectives

After studying this topic, you will be able to
▼ choose the appropriate cutting layout.
▼ pin the pattern pieces to the fabric correctly.
▼ cut the fabric and transfer pattern markings.

Topic Terms

cutting layout
selvage

After your pattern and fabric are prepared, you are ready to lay out your pattern. For this step, you will again need to refer to your pattern guide sheet.

The Pattern Layout

The pattern guide sheet shows many cutting layouts, 22-6. A **cutting layout** is a drawing that shows how to fold fabric and place pattern pieces for cutting. Layouts are shown for different garments, views, sizes, and fabric widths. You will need to find the layout for the pattern version you make. Then look for your size and your fabric width. Circle the layout you will use. This will help you find your layout quickly each time you need to refer to it.

Different layouts are also shown for fabrics with surface texture such as velvet, suede, flannel, velour, and corduroy. When these fabrics are viewed in one direction,

JACKET
use pieces 1 thru 8

58" 60" (150cm)
fabric
with nap
size extra-small

sizes small, medium

sizes large, extra-large

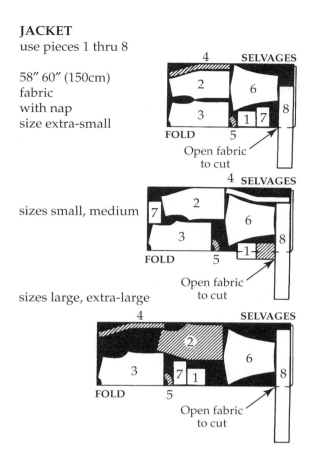

22-6
Several cutting layouts will be shown on the pattern guide sheet.

they appear light and shiny. When viewed in the opposite direction, they appear darker. To prevent a garment from having a two-tone look, pattern pieces must all be cut in the same direction. The layout for fabrics *with nap* is your guide to placing pattern pieces on these fabrics.

Folding the Fabric

Fold your fabric according to the instructions given for your layout. Fabric is usually folded with the right sides together. The guide sheet may tell you to use a lengthwise fold or a crosswise fold. A *lengthwise fold* brings the two selvages

together. A **selvage** is one of two finished lengthwise edges on a piece of fabric. These edges are stronger than the rest of the fabric and will not ravel.

A *crosswise fold* brings the two cut edges together. Sometimes a *doublefold* is used, which brings each selvage edge toward the center. Measure to be sure you fold the fabric the same amount for the entire length of the fabric. Watch for layout notes, such as the words *selvage*, *single thickness*, and *double thickness*.

Placing Pattern Pieces

Place pattern pieces on the fabric as pictured in the pattern layout. Most pattern pieces are placed on the fabric with the printed side up. Pattern pieces to be placed with the printed side down will appear shaded on the guide sheet.

Lay all pattern pieces on the fabric before pinning any in place. See 22-7. This allows you to make sure they all fit on the

22-7
Place all the needed pattern pieces on the fabric before you begin pinning.

fabric. Plaids, stripes, and checks need special attention during layout so designs will match at seamlines and front openings.

Pinning

Before pinning the pattern pieces to the fabric, they must be placed on the fabric grain. To do this, pin one end of the grainline arrow to the fabric to hold it in place. Measure from the pinned end of the arrow to the fabric selvage. Then measure from the other end of the grainline arrow to the selvage. See 22-8. If measurements differ, adjust them so the grainline arrow is a uniform distance from the selvage edge. Then pin the pattern piece in place.

Gently smooth the pattern from the grainline. Finish pinning by placing pins every 6 inches inside the cutting lines. Place pins at right angles, perpendicular to the pattern edges. Pin diagonally in corners.

Watch for pattern pieces that must be placed on the fold of the fabric. Pin the fold edge of the pattern piece along the fold

22-8
Each end of the grainline arrow should measure the same distance to the selvage.

first. You will never cut the edge of a fold. Then smooth out the pattern and pin the remaining edges to the fabric.

After pinning each pattern piece, compare your work with the layout guide. Your pattern layout should be accurate before you start to cut.

Cutting the Fabric

Dressmaker shears are best for cutting out pattern pieces. Because the handle is bent, the blades glide along the tabletop. This allows the fabric to lie flat so cutting lines are obvious.

Find the cutting line on the pattern piece for your size. This is especially important when using multisize patterns since the cutting lines lie close together and occasionally cross one another. The patterns usually have three sets of cutting lines, but sometimes there are as many as six. Pay attention to any size adjustments you have made to the pattern.

Marking the Fabric

Markings on the pattern guide you in putting the garment together. Markings for center front, center back, darts, buttons, buttonholes, dots, and pockets all need to be transferred to the fabric. Seamlines do not need to be marked since a ⅝-inch seam is presumed.

When marking, remove only the pins that are in the way. Leave enough pins to hold the pattern and fabric in place.

Using Tracing Paper

Several methods can be used to transfer pattern markings. Tracing paper and a tracing wheel are often used to mark firmly woven and knitted fabrics. Tracing quickly and accurately transfers the marks.

Test the tracing paper on a scrap of your fabric first since it may mark some fabrics permanently. Make sure its marking is visible on the wrong side of the fabric. Also, check to be sure it does not show on the right side. Before marking, place a magazine or piece of cardboard under the fabric. This will protect the table from the sharp teeth of the tracing wheel.

Two pieces of tracing paper are needed to mark both fabric layers. Place one piece of paper right side up, under the bottom layer of fabric. Slip the other piece right side down, between the pattern and the top layer of fabric. Make sure both sheets of tracing paper face the wrong sides of the fabric.

Carefully roll the wheel along the markings. To ensure accuracy, use a ruler to help trace straight lines, 22-9. Use only

enough pressure to make the markings visible on the wrong side of the fabric. Too much pressure may mar the fabric with holes or transfer color to the right side of the fabric.

Check It Out!

1. Name five factors that determine which cutting layout you will use.
2. What are you to do with the grainline arrow on a pattern piece?
3. True or false. Notches should be cut inward.
4. Explain the use of a tracing wheel to transfer pattern markings to fabrics.

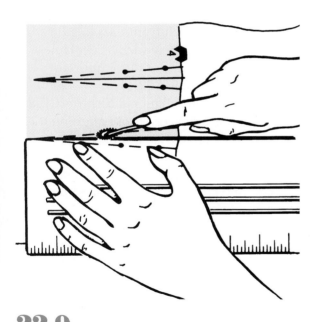

22-9
A ruler will help you trace straight lines when marking with a tracking wheel and tracing paper.

Topic 22-3

Basic Sewing Techniques

Objectives

After studying this topic, you will be able to
▼ perform directional stitching and staystitching.
▼ construct darts and gathers.
▼ sew seams.
▼ complete the construction of sewing projects that include fasteners and hems.

Topic Terms

directional stitching
staystitching
dart
easing
gathering
seam
backstitching
trimming
grading
clipping
notching
thread shank

Sewing can be both fun and productive. If you follow good sewing techniques, you can make clothes that you will be proud to wear. They will look as good as, or even better than, clothes purchased from stores. Custom-made clothes will probably fit you better, too. To make a good-looking garment, you must follow good sewing techniques from beginning to end.

Stitching Techniques

Before you begin constructing your project, you need to be familiar with basic stitching techniques. These are directional stitching and staystitching.

Directional Stitching

Stitching in the direction of the grain is called **directional stitching**. It makes the yarns lie flat and feel smooth, 22-10. Directional stitching prevents garments from puckering or stretching along seamlines. It should be used whenever a seam is sewn.

Staystitching

Staystitching is a line of machine stitching that keeps the edges of garment pieces from stretching out of shape as you sew. Staystitching is done through a single layer of fabric ½-inch from the cut edges. Bias and curved edges, such as necklines and armholes, are especially important areas to staystitch. See 22-11.

Bias means any diagonal direction. Bias edges include all except those aligning the lengthwise or crosswise grain.

Staystitching is needed to stabilize knits, other stretchy fabrics, and loose weaves. Staystitching is not needed on

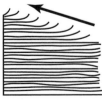

against the grain   with the grain

22-10

For directional stitching, you sew in the direction of the grain so seams lie flat for a smooth appearance.

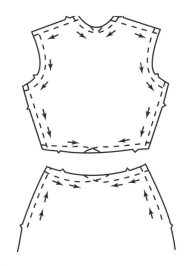

22-11
Staystitch bias and curved edges of garment pieces to prevent them from stretching out of shape as you sew.

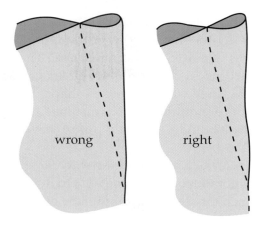

wrong   right

22-12
The last three stitches of a dart should be made on the fold to prevent puckering at the point of the dart.

fabrics that do not stretch. Some fabric finishes permanently set yarns in place, preventing the fabric from stretching.

Darts and Gathers

After your garment is staystitched, the guide sheet usually instructs you to make any darts or gathers. These begin to give shape to your garment. Since darts and gathers cross seamlines, they are made before seams are sewn.

Darts

A **dart** is a construction element used to give shape and fullness to a garment. A dart helps fit a flat piece of fabric to the curves of the body. It is made by stitching to a point through a fold in the fabric, 22-12. The last three stitches should be made in the fold to prevent the point of the dart from puckering. The larger the body curves, the larger the darts need to be.

All darts point to the fullest part of body curves. On skirts and slacks, darts begin at the waistline and taper to the hipline, allowing fullness around the hips. In jackets, shirts, and blouses, darts taper to the fullest part of the chest.

Gathering and Easing

Gathering and easing are techniques used when two seamlines of unequal length are sewn together. **Easing** involves making a piece of fabric fit a slightly smaller piece of fabric as a flat, curved seam is sewn. Easing provides needed fabric fullness at certain points on the body, usually where sleeves meet front and back sections.

To ease a longer piece of fabric into a shorter one, pin the two ends first. Then distribute the rest of the fullness evenly between these two pins, being sure to match notches, dots, and other markings. Insert additional pins at right angles to the seamline. Stitch the seam with the longer piece on top. Remove the pins only as you come to them. Try to avoid stitching any ripples or puckers into the seam.

When ripples and soft folds are desired at a seamline that joins two different lengths of fabric, **gathering** is used. The ripples and soft folds that result are called *gathers*. They yield a rounded shape. Gathers are often used at waistlines, cuffs, and the shoulder seams of puffy sleeves. See 22-13.

To make gathers, set the stitch length regulator on your machine for 6 to 8 stitches per inch for medium-weight fabrics. Two rows of long stitches are needed to make smooth, even gathers. Place the first row of stitches near the ⅛-inch seamline. Place the second row of stitches ¼-inch from the first row, inside the seam allowance. Do not backstitch. Leave at least three inches of thread at the ends of the stitching lines.

Pin the right sides of the two fabric pieces together, matching notches and other markings. Gently pull both bobbin threads at one end, working toward the center of the edge being gathered. (You will gather one side before the other.) Gather half of the longer fabric piece until it lies flat against half of the shorter one. Fasten the bobbin threads by wrapping them in a figure eight around the pin located where you began gathering. See 22-14.

Repeat the gathering process at the other end. Distribute the gathers evenly and insert pins across the gathering stitches. Set your machine to a regular stitch length of about 12 stitches per inch. Stitch the two fabric pieces together with the gathered side up. Hold the fabric to prevent any folds from forming in the seam.

Seams

A **seam** is a row of stitching that joins garment pieces together. There are many types of seams used in sewing. The choice of a seam depends on the type and weight of the fabric and the durability desired. Fashion trends in structural and decorative lines may dictate seam choice.

The *plain seam* is the most common seam. A plain seam is made by placing right sides of the fabric together. Sew along

22-13
A shiny fabric highlights gathers in a garment.

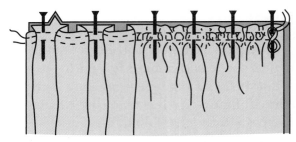

22-14
Secure threads by wrapping them around a pin. Then pull the opposite ends to form gathers.

the seamline with a ⅝-inch seam allowance, backstitching at both ends. **Backstitching** means to sew backward and forward in the same place for a few stitches to secure the thread ends. Press the seam to one side. Then press the seam open.

Trimming, Grading, Clipping, and Notching

When a curved seam is stitched, such as an armhole or neckline, it will need one of the following treatments to look neat and smooth. Always make sure not to cut the stitching.

Trimming means cutting away part of a seam allowance to reduce bulk in lightweight and medium-weight fabrics. Trimming removes a ⅜-inch strip of fabric along the length of the seam. Trimming is also used to remove bulk from corners and points. See 22-15.

Grading means trimming each layer of the seam allowance to a different width. This is the best way to treat seams on heavier fabrics or seams with three or more fabric layers. Trim each layer

⅛-inch narrower than the next, keeping the smallest layer at least ¼-inch thick, 22-16. When all the seams of a heavy fabric are cut alike, they form a noticeable ridge along seam lines.

Clipping is making straight cuts toward the stitching line, usually at ½-inch intervals. Clipping is used on seams that have an inward curve so the seam will not pucker when turned. **Notching** means cutting small wedges from the seam allowance. This removes excess fabric that would create noticeable bulk in seams with an outward curve. Clipping and notching are shown in 22-17.

Seam Finishes

Seam finishes are treatments done after seams are sewn to prevent the raw edges of the seam allowances from raveling. They also improve the appearance of the inside of the garment. The choice of a seam finish depends on the weight of the fabric and the degree to which it ravels. Some fabrics ravel very little and, therefore, need no further work on the raw edges. Others are loosely woven and require a seam finish.

A *pinked finish* is the easiest finish to do. Simply use pinking shears and cut close to the edge of the seam allowance through

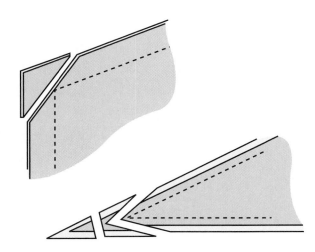

22-15
Trim corners and points as shown to reduce bulk when seams are turned to the inside of the garment.

22-16
Grading a seam means trimming each seam allowance to a different width.

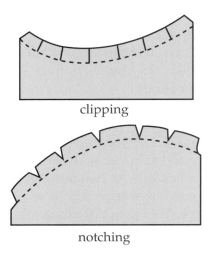

clipping

notching

22-17

Clipping is used on inward curves. Notching is used on outward curves.

both fabric layers. Then press the seam open. Use a pinked finish only on fabrics that ravel slightly. To make a sturdier finish, you can also stitch close to the pinked edge of each seam allowance.

A *zigzag finish* is a quick and easy seam finish used on fabrics that ravel easily. To make a zigzag finish on a seam, press it open before stitching. Stitch through one seam allowance at a time.

Fasteners

Snaps, hooks and eyes, buttons, and hook-and-loop tape are types of fasteners used to close garments. When sewing on fasteners, make sure they are placed correctly. Garment edges should meet evenly and lie smoothly when fasteners are closed. Buttons are the most common fasteners.

Buttons

The key to sewing on buttons correctly is to allow space for a thread shank. The **thread shank** provides room for the button to lie over the buttonhole fabric. It uses two strands of thread. The length of the shank depends on the thickness of the garment. To make a thread shank, place a toothpick over the button while sewing. Then remove the toothpick and pull the button up. Bring the threaded needle between the button and garment. Wind thread around the stitches several times. Then bring the thread to the wrong side of the garment and fasten with several stitches. See 22-18. Some buttons have shanks already attached. Simply sew these buttons securely in place.

Transfer buttonhole markings from the pattern. Follow the directions for making a buttonhole that came with your sewing machine.

Hems

Hemming is the final step in garment construction. A hem should be flat and unnoticeable on the outside of the garment. Having a neat, level hem is important to the overall appearance of the garment.

22-18

Make a thread shank as you sew on a button.

Marking the Hem

To mark the hem, have someone pin the hem as you stand straight and still. Use a yardstick or hem marker to measure from the floor to the length you like. Mark the hemline with pins, placing them parallel to the floor about 3 inches apart. Now turn up the hem and pin it to the inside of the garment. Match hem and garment seamlines. Press a light crease at the hem edge. Using a ruler, mark the width of the hem with pins or tailor's chalk. Trim along this line, cutting an even hem width.

Finishing the Hem Edge

The hem edge needs to be finished before it is stitched to the garment. Hem finishes are similar to seam finishes. The choice of a finish depends on the fabric and style of the garment. The four methods of finishing hem edges described below are shown in 22-19.

▼ The *turned and stitched finish* is used for medium-weight and lightweight fabrics that ravel. Turn the cut hem edge under ¼-inch and stitch close to the fold.

▼ The *stitched and pinked finish* is used for fabrics that do not ravel, such as knits. Machine stitch ¼-inch from the cut edge. Pink the edge with pinking shears. Be careful not to cut through stitching.

▼ The *zigzag finish* is used most often for knits where stretch and flexibility are needed. It is also used on bulky fabrics that ravel. To finish, zigzag ¼-inch from the cut edge of the hem.

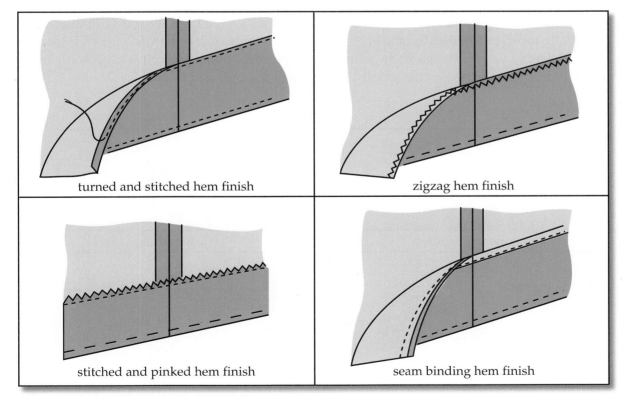

turned and stitched hem finish

zigzag hem finish

stitched and pinked hem finish

seam binding hem finish

22-19
Use one of these hem finishes along the raw edge of your garment.

▼ *Seam binding tape* is used as a hem finish for medium-weight and heavyweight fabrics that ravel. On the right side of the fabric, lap the tape over the cut edge. Stitch the tape ¼-inch from the cut edge of the hem.

Stretch-lace binding tape is used to finish curved hems and hems of fabrics that stretch. It is applied like seam binding tape.

Stitching the Hem

Most hems are stitched by hand using a single thread. Make stitches somewhat loose to avoid puckers and to allow ease in the hemline. Space stitches evenly and sew neatly. Always begin hemming at a seam and secure the thread knot in the seam allowance. Refer to the diagrams in 22-20 as you read the following descriptions.

Hemming Stitch

This stitch is used for all types of hems, especially those finished with binding tape. Pick up a yarn of the garment with the needle, bring the needle diagonally through the edge of the hem, and pull the thread through. Continue stitching around the hem at ¼-inch intervals, spacing stitches evenly.

Slip Stitch

This nearly invisible stitch is hidden in a fold along the hem edge. A hem with a turned and stitched finish creates the fold. Pick up a yarn of the garment close to the hem, slide the needle into the fold about ¼-inch, and bring the needle out, picking up another garment yarn. Continue around the hem.

Blind Stitch

This stitch is often used for hems on coats and suits. The stitch is hidden from view between a finished hem and the garment. The line of machine stitching in the hem's finish serves as a guide for making blind stitches. You will need to hold the hem edge back while hemming. Pick up a yarn from the garment followed by a yarn from the hem in ¼-inch intervals. Continue, making stitches loose so the hem will not pull and pucker.

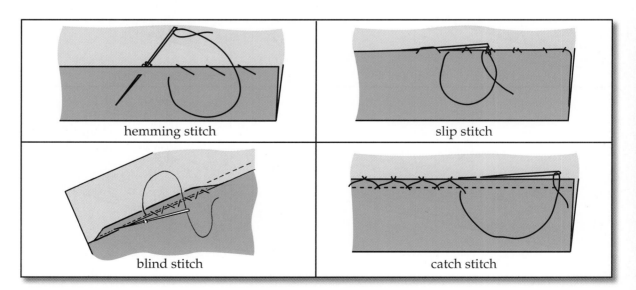

hemming stitch

slip stitch

blind stitch

catch stitch

22-20

The stitch you use to hem your garment will depend on its hem finish and type of fabric.

Catch Stitch

This flexible stitch is good for hemming knit fabrics. You will work from left to right with the needle pointing left. In ¼-inch intervals, pick up a yarn below the hem edge followed by a yarn in the garment diagonally above the edge. Keep the thread loose so the zigzag pattern of stitches will allow some stretch.

Other Hemming Methods

Machine stitching can be used to secure hems. Some machines have a special hemming stitch. Hems can also be topstitched or zigzagged to add a decorative finish. Sergers are particularly good at making hems. Check your sewing machine manual and follow its directions.

Fusible material can also be used to secure hems. The steam heat of an iron causes it to fuse the hem and the garment together. Follow the manufacturer's directions for fusing. The fusible material should be suitable for the garment fabric. Test the material between fabric scraps. Fusing should not change the color or texture of the fabric.

Check It Out!

1. What two stitching techniques are used to prevent stretching of the edges of the seamlines?
2. Explain how to stitch a dart.
3. How does trimming differ from grading?
4. What is the purpose of making a thread shank when sewing on a button?
5. Which hemming stitch is best for knit fabrics?

Topic 22-4
Extending the Life of Clothes

Objectives

After studying this topic, you will be able to
▼ describe common repairs clothes may need.
▼ alter the seams and hems of clothes.
▼ suggest ways to restyle clothes.
▼ identify ways to recycle clothes you can no longer wear.

Topic Term

restyle

Do you have any clothes that you no longer wear? Most people do. Ask yourself why they are not worn. Are you tired of them? Are some clothes too short or too long? Do some have stains that you cannot remove? Do rips and tears need repairing? Are buttons or other fasteners loose or missing? Maybe some clothes seem too plain or too fancy. Others may no longer fit you because your weight or height has changed.

You can probably extend the life of most of these clothes by repairing, altering, or restyling them. If they no longer fit, there are ways to recycle clothes so other people can use them.

Repairing Clothes

Often garments that are not worn just need simple repairs. That is why basic sewing skills are helpful. Even if you never want to sew your own clothes, you can still make repairs for yourself and your family, 22-21.

22-21
Simple repair skills can extend the life of a garment.

To repair a split seam, turn the garment inside out. Pin the seam together and sew on the seamline. If the seam is one that receives a lot of stress, stitch the seam twice, using small stitches.

Buttons and other fasteners often loosen with normal wear. When they become loose, secure them immediately. A lost button cannot always be replaced with an identical one. One lost button may force you to replace them all, which can cost considerable time and money.

Zippers sometimes break with normal wear. They may also be damaged during laundering or dry cleaning. Though you may be able to repair them, some will need to be replaced. Purchase a zipper of the same style and color as the previous one. Replace the zipper using the same application method as the garment originally used.

Hems often come loose in garments. If you need to repair a hem, use one of the hemming stitches described earlier.

Snags detract from the appearance of knitted garments. When left unattended, a small snag can catch and become a large "run." To repair it, slip a needle threader, a needle with a large eye, or a small crochet

The More You Know: Zipper Applications

The four most common zipper applications are centered, lapped, invisible, and fly front. The location of the zipper and the look you desire will determine which method to use.

When zippers are intended for center front or center back seams, a *centered zipper application* is often used. The zipper coils are centered in the seamline. A row of stitches appears on both sides of the seamline. A *lapped zipper application* has only one row of stitching showing on the outside of the garment. It can be used at front, back, or side openings. An *invisible zipper* looks like a regular seam because no stitches show on the outside of the garment. *Fly front zipper applications* are used on front openings of jeans and slacks.

hook through from the back of the fabric next to the snag. Grasp the snag and pull it to the backside of the garment. Carefully stretch the fabric to smooth the snagged area.

Holes can be patched in several ways. Iron-on patches are easy to use and appropriate for casual garments. Select a patch that matches the color of the garment. Follow the package directions for ironing the patch onto the garment. If a piece of the garment fabric is available, it can be placed behind the hole. Turn under the torn edges of the garment and secure with small, neat hand stitches.

Altering Clothes

Altering differs from repairing. To repair is to restore something to its original condition. To alter is to change the size. If a garment is too large or small, you may be able to make it fit by altering the seams. If the garment is a little too long or short, you may be able to alter the hem.

Altering Seams

Making the garment smaller is fairly simple. Begin by putting the garment on inside out. Ask someone to pin new seams so the garment will have the snugness you want. Be sure the garment still hangs properly after it is pinned. Take the garment off and baste along the pinned lines, removing pins as you stitch. Try the garment on again to check the fit. Make adjustments as needed. Stitch the new seam with a regular machine stitch. Remove the old stitches. Trim the seam allowance to ⅝-inch and press the new seam open.

Letting out a seam to enlarge a garment is more difficult. First, determine how much wider the garment should be. Then measure the seam allowance to see how much room can be added by letting out one or more seams. (The minimum seam allowance is ¼-inch.) If letting out seams will provide the needed space, you can begin.

Altering Hems

Changing a hemline can make a garment fit better or appear more fashionable. Hems can be adjusted on pants, skirts, dresses, sleeves, and jackets.

To shorten a garment, first remove the old hemming stitches. Steam press the crease until it disappears, 22-22. Put the garment on and have someone mark the desired length. Turn the hem to the inside and pin it in place. Lightly press the hem

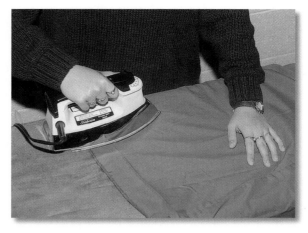

22-22
Thoroughly press the old hem flat before marking a new hem.

near the folded edge. Try the garment on again to be sure the length is satisfactory. Then complete the hem as explained earlier. Trim away any excess hem width.

If you want to lengthen a garment, check to see if the existing hem is deep enough to add the desired amount. If so, remove the existing hem and press out the crease. Have someone mark the new hem and complete the hemming of the garment.

Restyling Clothes

You can extend the life of clothes by restyling them. When you **restyle** a garment, you change it to create a different look. Ask yourself why you are not wearing a certain garment. Maybe by restyling you can give it a new look or function. You might try some of the following ideas:

▼ If a collar is worn and frayed, remove it. You can wear a garment collarless, or you might add a contrasting collar.

▼ Cover holes or permanent stains with an applique or a fancy patch.

▼ If pants are too short, cut them off. They can be worn as shorts. Sweatshirts can be cut off and made into crop tops.

▼ If the shape of pant legs is out of fashion, restyle the legs by altering the seams.

▼ If cuffed pants are out of fashion, shorten the pants to eliminate the cuffs. If the elbows of sweaters or jackets are wearing thin, cover them with elbow patches.

▼ Give a garment a new look by changing the buttons or adding snap-on button covers. Trims can also be added.

▼ Try giving an old garment new dazzle with decorative trims or creative additions. See 22-23.

▼ Some dresses can be shortened to make tunic tops.

▼ If a garment is a light color, you may want to dye it or tie-dye it. Review the literature that comes with the dye so you know what colors to expect. For example, yellow fabric that is dyed blue will result in a green color. Orange fabric that is dyed blue will result in a brown tone.

Recycling Clothes

When you have exhausted the usefulness of a garment, it is time to recycle it. When you recycle a garment, you reuse it in a different way. This may mean passing clothes along to others who can wear them. Have you thought of doing any of the following?

▼ *Give wearable clothes to someone else.* A family member or a friend may be happy to receive your hand-me-downs.

▼ *Have a garage sale.* Then use the money you make to buy new clothes.

▼ *Take garments in good condition to a consignment shop.* They will try to sell the garments for you and give you a portion of the income.

22-23
Decorative trims can give a garment a whole new look.

▼ *Donate unwanted garments to a charitable organization.* Contact such groups as the Red Cross, Salvation Army, or Goodwill Industries. The garments are repaired and given to people in need. Also consider donating old garments to the craft department of a senior center. They will find many uses for the fabric and trims.

Setting the Scene: Sewing for Profit

You have an idea to use your sewing skills to start a small business. You want to reuse portions of old clothing creatively to produce unique items to sell. You will be able to get plenty of recyclable old clothes, including the trims and buttons, by shopping yard sales. Expenses for the business will be minimal. Your imagination and available sewing time are your limits.

Analyze It: What sewing skills will you find most useful? What useful items can you create to sell?

22-24
Use fabric from clothes you no longer wear to make quilts or stuff toys.

▼ *Reuse portions of old clothes to create new items.* Use the fabric in old garments to make crafts, room decorations, or children's toys, such as doll clothes or stuffed animals. See 22-24. Make clothes for children, or let them use old garments to play "dress-up." Remove and save trims, buttons, zippers, and fasteners for future use. Convert soft cotton garments into cleaning and polishing cloths. Cut soft fabrics and nylon hose into small pieces and use as stuffing material in craft projects.

As a last resort, check if your community recycles cloth. In some places, you can drop cloth off at a recycling center along with your paper, glass, and cans.

Check It Out!

1. How might time and money be saved by renewing loose buttons immediately?
2. How does altering clothes differ from restyling clothes?
3. Name two ways to recycle clothes.
4. How can a consignment shop help you recycle clothes?

Chapter Review

Summary

Studying the pattern guide sheet and knowing the symbols and terms on pattern pieces are important to successful sewing. You can pin fit your pattern to check for any needed alterations. Making alterations prior to cutting is easier than making them after construction.

Follow the appropriate cutting layout. Lay out the fabric and place pattern pieces as shown. Pin all pattern pieces securely to avoid slipping. Leave the fabric flat on the table as you take long cutting strokes with your shears. After you transfer the pattern markings to the fabric, you can begin sewing.

Sewing involves many different techniques. As you learn and practice them, your skills will develop and you can expand your wardrobe. You can also save money and express your creativity by using sewing skills to extend the life of clothes.

You can save a lot of money by repairing, altering, or restyling clothes. If you can no longer wear a garment, it can be recycled or given to others to wear. Portions of garments can also be reused in other ways. Therefore, consider all your options before throwing old clothes away.

Think About It!

1. Why is it important to understand the information on the pattern guide sheet and pattern pieces before you begin sewing?
2. What is the point of pin fitting a pattern and altering the pattern pieces before cutting the fabric?
3. What kind of pattern do you think would be best for sewing plaids and stripes?
4. What types of garments do you own that have darts or gathers?
5. When might you skip the step of finishing seams when constructing a garment?
6. Suggest several reasons why people might want to extend the life of their clothes.
7. What charitable groups collect used clothing in your community? Have you donated clothing to any of these groups?
8. Which of the sewing techniques described in this chapter do you think you will use most frequently? Why?
9. List careers including entrepreneurial opportunities that might utilize sewing skills.

Try It Out!

1. Demonstrate to the class how to pin fit a pattern to determine if any alterations are needed.
2. Demonstrate to the class how to make one of the alterations discussed in this chapter.
3. Patterns can be altered in many ways in addition to those shown in this chapter. Many people have figure variations that require very specific pattern alterations. Choose a pattern alteration not discussed in this chapter to demonstrate to the class.
4. Make samples of darts. Demonstrate to the class the correct way to press them.
5. Make a bulletin board display showing sample darts and gathers.

6. On several fabric samples, practice gathering fabric. Vary the stitch length and the sewing matching tension with each sample to see how these affect gathering ease.

7. Practice sewing seams. Make a sample of a plain seam.

8. Cut two 12-inch circles of scrap fabric. Stitch the circles together with a ⅝-inch seam around the edge. Divide the circle into four sections. Show trimming on one quarter of the circle, grading on another quarter, clipping on another, and notching on the last section. Label each section.

9. Try different seam finishes on different fabrics. Which finish works best on light, medium, and heavy fabrics?

10. Practice sewing on buttons, incorporating a thread shank.

11. Practice making hemming stitches on fabric samples. Use a 12-inch square of fabric for each sample. Press a mock hem in place and use a different hemming stitch on each sample.

12. Bring an item of clothing to class that can be repaired, altered, or restyled. Explain to the class what you intend to do to make the garment wearable again.

career.guide

Textiles and Apparel Design Careers

Career Ladder for Textiles and Apparel Design

▶ **Advanced Degree**

Market researcher
Fiber analyst
Quality control engineer
Fashion historian

▶ **Bachelor's Degree**

Buyer
Fabric tester
Merchandise manager
Fashion editor
Textile lab technician

▶ **Associate's Degree**

Fashion illustrator
Fabric dyer
Sewing center director
Personal color analyst
Buyer's assistant

▶ **High School Diploma**

Fabric finisher
Dry cleaner
Pattern cutter

▶ **Pre-High School Diploma**

Intern with a professional
    dressmaker
Stock clerk
Fabric store salesclerk
Volunteer in a community
    clothing center

Careers in textiles and apparel design range from making fibers to selling garments and other textile products. This career area has positions for people with high school diplomas as well as those with advanced degrees.

Employment Opportunities

Professionals who work in the textile industry develop fibers and finishes or design fabrics. Workers in apparel design and production turn fabrics into fashions for each new season. Designers sketch designs, make samples, and draft patterns. Production workers cut fabric, run sewing machines, and press garments. Managers help plan and supervise each stage of the production process. Costing engineers figure the cost of producing each item. Quality control engineers check to be sure finished apparel is well made.

The fashion merchandising industry promotes new products through creative displays. Buyers predict the types and numbers of items customers will buy for the season. Fashion illustrators, models, photographers, and writers create ads that entice shoppers into stores. Salespeople help customers find the items they want.

Jobs in textiles and apparel design are clustered in Los Angeles and New York City, but sales jobs exist in all parts of the country. The same is true for laundry and dry-cleaning work. Dry cleaners hire people to clean clothing and wait on customers. Dry cleaners also hire pressers and specialists in garment alterations.

Entrepreneurial Opportunities

Many jobs in textiles and apparel design are well suited for people who would like to be entrepreneurs. Someone with skill and drive might start a business in fashion design, photography, or tailoring. Those wishing to be entrepreneurs need good business management skills.

Rewards and Demands

Many textile and apparel careers call for creativity. People who work in this field often view using their creative skills as one of the rewards of their careers. Many workers also feel satisfaction in producing products that meet a basic human need.

Demands of textile and apparel careers may include long hours. Some employees perform repetitive tasks and are pushed to meet production quotas. People working in production and sales jobs are often under pressure to meet deadlines.

Preparation Requirements

Careers in textiles and apparel design do not all carry the same responsibilities. So, they require different levels of education and training.

Entry-Level Jobs

Entry-level jobs require little training or prior work experience. Training is often provided on the job. Entry-level jobs are usually helper positions that involve repeating simple tasks. Stock clerks, tailor's aides, and production workers are all considered entry-level workers.

Midlevel Jobs

Textile and apparel workers in mid-level jobs need specific skills. These workers usually have a two-year degree or specialized training. Textile technicians, weaving instructors, dressmakers, and tailors all have jobs at this level.

Professional-Level Jobs

Textile and apparel workers who design, manage, or do research are at the professional level. Most people who work at this level need at least a four-year degree. Key specialty areas include fashion design, merchandising, and textile science. All levels of textile and apparel workers must keep up with new technology.

Fabric store managers must have knowledge of textiles and garment construction to help customers make wise choices.

Personal Qualities Needed for Success

Many positions in the textile and apparel field require creative flair and an ability to foresee fashion trends. Skills in solving problems and working under pressure are important, too, since good timing is all-important in the fashion world. Having the right fashions available at the right time is the key to success.

Future Trends

Fashion trends and technological advances will continue to shape future textiles and apparel. Designing stylish fabrics and fashions and the equipment needed to make them will generate jobs for U.S. workers. The same holds true for merchandising and selling the apparel. Most textile and apparel production, however, will continue to be handled by workers in other countries. As a result, the number of entry-level U.S. jobs in this field will continue decreasing.

Career Interests, Abilities, and You

Assess your skills, interests, and abilities for this field by enrolling in a clothing design course in high school. Consider taking part in a job shadowing experience at a department store. Hold a part-time job as a retail salesperson volunteer to help make costumes for local school productions.

Part Seven
Meeting Your Housing Needs

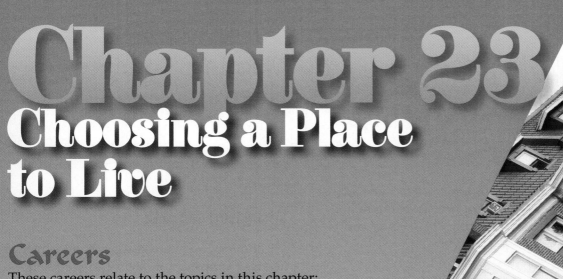

Chapter 23
Choosing a Place to Live

Careers

These careers relate to the topics in this chapter:

▼ real estate assistant
▼ apartment building manager
▼ drafter
▼ architect

As you study the chapter, see if you can think of others.

Topics

Topic 23-1

Housing Options

Objectives

After studying this topic, you will be able to
▼ give examples of how housing helps you meet your physical, social, and psychological needs.
▼ list different types of housing.
▼ explain the difference between single-family houses and multifamily dwellings.
▼ describe how cooperatives and condominiums differ.

Topic Terms

housing
single-family house
attached house
freestanding house
custom house
tract house
manufactured house
multifamily dwelling
cooperative
condominium

People have many choices to make when choosing a place to live. That is because housing is more than walls and a roof. Housing can affect the way people feel and behave. The housing you choose will reflect your lifestyle and who you are. You may be surprised at the many types of housing available.

Meeting Housing Needs

Housing is any dwelling that provides shelter. Housing should satisfy the needs—physical, social, and psychological—of all residents of the dwelling.

Physical Needs

Shelter, food, and rest are basic physical needs. For protection from bad weather, people turn to housing. The dwelling should also have room for preparing and eating food. It should provide adequate, comfortable space for sleeping and space for personal belongings. When one or more friends or family members share housing, it should meet everyone's physical needs. Individual needs usually change over time.

Social Needs

The need to interact with other people is a basic social need. Before you choose a place to live, you should decide which social needs you want to meet. Will you want the space to enjoy friends and family? Do you need indoor or outdoor space for recreation? Do you want to live close to many people or do you prefer a quieter setting? People express their social needs differently, 23-1.

Psychological Needs

Although psychological needs cannot be measured as accurately as physical and social needs, they have a very strong influence on how you feel about your living space. Sometimes people base their housing choices on their psychological needs before their physical needs. In most cases, however, the following psychological needs will not be more important than physical needs.

23-1
Your housing should provide enough space for fun activities with friends.

▼ *Security.* Housing should provide safety from physical harm. Injury and suffering can result from exposure to the dangers of the outside world and destructive forces of nature.

▼ *Familiarity.* An unfamiliar place makes people feel uneasy. Housing in a familiar place makes people feel comfortable and secure.

▼ *Beauty.* Almost everyone wants beautiful surroundings, but there are many different standards of beauty.

▼ *Privacy.* Most people need to be away from others occasionally. A bedroom or other empty room often fills this need. Sometimes people need an outdoor setting that provides privacy, 23-2.

▼ *Self-expression.* People express themselves through the design and location of their homes. A bustling city street, a flower-filled yard, and a river's edge all say something about home owners in these different locations.

23-2
A quiet outdoor sitting area may satisfy a person's need for privacy.

Types of Housing

After determining your housing needs, you can start deciding which type of housing will best meet those needs. A wide variety of housing is available. All housing can be classified as either single-family housing or multifamily housing.

Single-Family Houses

A **single-family house** is designed to shelter one family. The house can be attached to others or a freestanding house.

Attached Houses

Some single-family houses share a common wall with houses on one or more sides. These dwellings are called

attached houses. *Town houses* and *row houses* are common names for attached houses. The owners possess the dwelling, the land under it, and a small yard. They often pay a monthly fee for maintaining the common grounds.

Freestanding Houses

A **freestanding house** is a house that stands alone. The basic types of freestanding houses include custom, tract, and manufactured houses.

Custom houses are specifically designed and built for the new owner. They tend to be very distinctive. The need for an architect and a building contractor also causes them to cost more than other houses in both time and money. See 23-3.

Tract houses, also called *developer-built houses*, are part of an entire neighborhood built at once. To save money, the houses are generally limited to a few basic designs. The houses are not as distinctive, but are less expensive than custom houses. Landscaping, painting, and additions can give the houses individuality.

Manufactured houses are made in a factory and moved to a site. There are many different kinds, sizes, and prices of factory-built houses. Practically all require assembly at the final site. The use of mass-produced parts saves labor costs. A manufactured house can be less expensive than a same-size custom house or developer-built house.

The smallest manufactured houses, called *mobile homes*, are completely assembled at a factory. They usually come equipped with plumbing, heating, electrical wiring, lights, and furnishings. When wheels are attached, mobile homes can be moved to another location. Be aware

23-3
A custom house can reflect an owner's particular tastes, but is usually more costly than other types of housing.

that many laws impact how manufactured houses are transported to and secured at a site's foundation.

Multifamily Dwellings

Multifamily dwellings are buildings designed to house more than one family. Apartments, cooperative units, and condominiums are common types of multifamily housing. You cannot tell by looking at these buildings which type of housing they provide. See 23-4.

Apartments

Apartments range from small, low-cost units to plush units in expensive high rises. Some apartment buildings also include laundry rooms, recreational facilities, stores, or parking spaces on lower floors. Residents pay a monthly fee.

23-4
These town houses could be apartments, cooperatives, or condominiums.

Cooperative Units

A **cooperative** is a multiunit building owned by and operated for the benefit of the residents. A person buys stock in the corporation owning the property and receives a housing unit in return. The stockholders decide as a group how the cooperative, or *co-op*, is run and who can live there. Stockholders pay a monthly fee for upkeep and repairs.

Condominium Units

A **condominium** is an individually-owned housing unit in a multiunit structure. Condominium, or *condo*, owners can sell their units without the approval of other owners. Common areas such as hallways, swimming pools, and parking lots are shared. Each owner has a vote in concerns relating to them and pays a monthly fee for their upkeep.

Check It Out!

1. Give examples of how housing helps people meet the physical needs of shelter, food, and rest.
2. List three psychological needs that can be met through housing.
3. List five housing alternatives available for families.
4. Describe the difference between single-family houses and multifamily dwellings.
5. How do cooperatives and condominiums differ?

Topic 23-2
Renting or Buying Housing

Objectives

After studying this topic, you will be able to
▼ discuss the factors to consider when choosing housing.
▼ identify advantages and disadvantages of renting or buying housing.
▼ give examples of what you need to know before you rent or buy housing.

Topic Terms

rent
lease
sublease
security deposit
eviction
mortgage

After considering all basic housing options, you will need to decide how to acquire the housing of your choice. You can rent or buy almost all types of housing.

Choosing Housing

There are many factors you need to consider as you choose a type of housing. The two main factors are your income and the location of the housing.

Income

Housing prices keep going up, and most people cannot afford to live in their dream home. However, they can decide which housing aspect is most important to them and budget their income to achieve it.

The More You Know: The Ancestry of Modern Housing

Do you ever wonder why there are so many different housing styles? The main reason is the cultural factors linked to the many different groups that settled in this country. Native Americans lived in dwellings such as hogans and teepees. Early European settlers copied the architecture of their homelands, bringing English, Dutch, Italian, Spanish, and French housing styles. For instance, the style of houses in the Southwest shows the influence of Spanish missions. New England housing reflects the cottage styles of the English Pilgrims. When people from different cultures began to move to other areas of the country, they brought their housing preferences with them. Today, as the ethnic diversity among Americans continues to increase, many people still choose housing based on the cultural traditions of their ancestors.

Suppose you dream of living in a large high-rise with a view. You quickly learn that people on your budget cannot afford it. You may then decide that space is more important than a view. However, a roomy high-rise is still out of your price range. You realize that living in a high-rise is not worthwhile without the view. At this point, it is clear that space is the most important aspect of your housing dream. You look for a spacious town home that you can afford.

The housing you can afford depends on your income. One of the following guidelines can help you determine the amount of your income you can spend on housing:

1. Allow no more than two and one-half times your gross annual income for the purchase price of a house.
2. Budget one-third of your net monthly income for housing costs.
3. Divide your gross annual income by 60 and limit monthly housing costs to this amount.

The first guideline refers only to the purchase price of a house. The second and third guidelines can be applied to both renting and buying housing. For these two guidelines, you should consider other housing expenses as well. These include utility bills, property insurance, taxes, maintenance, and city services.

Location

Where your housing is located has a great impact on the lives of you and your family members. It can affect both the job you have and your family's lifestyle.

Job

Some people choose housing that is close to their jobs or transportation that will take them to their jobs. For instance, doctors need to live close to their offices so they can quickly treat patients in emergencies.

People also choose to live in areas that have jobs available in their fields. For instance, a marine biologist would have more job opportunities living near an ocean than in the desert.

Lifestyle

The number and ages of family members should be taken into consideration when choosing housing.

You should make sure the house is accessible to community facilities your lifestyle demands. Such facilities may include shopping centers, entertainment, athletic and cultural attractions, public transportation, and recreational areas, 23-5.

You should also make sure the house meets the needs of the family. Families with children may want a bigger house with more space. They will need schools and playgrounds, too. Single people and childless couples may want smaller houses that are easy to maintain and are in quiet neighborhoods.

Renting Housing

Rental housing is popular with single people, young married couples, older people, and families with low incomes. Many people think of apartment buildings when they consider rental housing. However, some single-family houses can be rented, too.

23-5
Some choose housing near parks so they can spend time outdoors.

Rent is a fee paid to the owner each month. This fee may or may not include utilities, such as heat, water, gas, and electricity.

Advantages and Disadvantages of Renting

Many people rent housing because it is convenient. See 23-6. It lets them get acquainted with a new community before they make a long-term housing commitment. They can move when their leases expire and not worry about selling the property. They also do not have to worry about whether the value of the property is increasing or decreasing.

Renting is economical, too. Renters know how much their housing is going to cost them, and they can budget for it. There also won't be any surprise expenses, such as the cost of a new water heater. The owner of the property is responsible for the maintenance and repair of the building.

Before you rent housing, you need to know what your rights and responsibilities are as a tenant. A *tenant* is the temporary occupant of a rented housing unit. You also need to understand the rights and responsibilities of the owner.

23-6
People rent apartments for many reasons including convenience, flexibility, and location.

Responsibilities

A lease is written by the property owner to protect the property. A **lease** is a contract between a tenant and a property owner. It lists the rights and responsibilities of both parties. A lease covers a specified rental period, which is often one year.

Leases identify the amount of rent to be paid each month. In addition, they list what tenants must do and must not do. See 23-7. You must understand everything stated in the lease before you sign it. Once your signature is on the lease, you are responsible for fulfilling all the terms. When you sign a lease, you are saying you will pay your rent promptly. You are agreeing to keep the property clean and free from damage. In turn, the owner agrees to keep the building and grounds in good condition. He or she also promises to obey health and safety laws.

A lease protects you from a rent increase after you move into rental housing. The lease also protects the owner if you want to move out after a short time. If you move, you are still responsible for paying the rent until the lease expires.

Many owners let tenants sublease rental property to someone else. To **sublease**, or sublet, means you have the right to pass the lease over to a second tenant. This person pays rent directly to the owner. If he or she fails to pay, you are still responsible for the rent being paid on time. The owner usually has to approve the new tenant.

A security deposit is commonly required in a lease. A **security deposit** is a sum of money, usually one month's rent, paid by the tenant before moving into the property. It is used to cover possible damages to the property. When the tenant moves out, the owner refunds the security deposit if the terms of the lease have been met. The owner can keep all or part of the deposit if the tenant damages the property.

ENGLISH MANOR APARTMENTS
I N C O R P O R A T E D
203 WINDSOR ROAD   •   LAKE SHORE, N.C. 28001

THIS AGREEMENT OF LEASE, MADE THIS _1st_ DAY OF _March_ 20_08_ BETWEEN ENGLISH MANOR APARTMENTS, INC., HEREINAFTER CALLED LESSOR: AND _____ _____ HEREINAFTER CALLED TENANT, WHETHER ONE OR MORE.

WITNESSETH, That the Lessor leases and lets unto the Tenant, premises known as _____ Lake Shore, N.C. 28401, for a term of not less than thirty (30) days from this date at the rental of $___600⁰⁰___ per month, to be paid in advance at the office of English Manor Apartments on the first day of each month without formal demand. This lease shall be renewed automatically for successive terms of one month each so long as the terms hereof are complied with at the same rental as hereinabove set forth payable in advance on the first day of each said renewed term, which renewed term shall expire of its own limitation at midnight on the last day of said term.

This will acknowledge the receipt of $___700⁰⁰___ as a deposit to cover any indebtedness to the Lessor for charges made for breakage or damage to the property. Any or all of deposit to be returned to the Tenant upon proper termination of the lease providing (1) THE TENANT HAS REMAINED IN POSSESSION AND PAID RENT ON ABOVE PROPERTY FOR AT LEAST SIX (6) MONTHS: (2) KEYS TO THE ABOVE PROPERTY HAVE BEEN RETURNED (3) THE PREMISES ARE LEFT IN A CLEAN CONDITION, AND ALL OTHER CONDITIONS OF THIS AGREEMENT HAVE BEEN MET TO THE SATISFACTION OF THE LESSOR. IT IS FURTHER UNDERSTOOD AND AGREED THAT THE TENANT SHALL GIVE A FIFTEEN (15) DAYS WRITTEN NOTICE BEFORE VACATING PREMISES. IF SAID NOTICE IS NOT GIVEN, TENANT WILL BE CHARGED FOR SAME.

TENANT will pay for any damage other than normal deterioration, wear and tear to the premises of Lessors property and will be responsible for the stoppage of sewer and drainage facilities chargeable to his use of the premises. Tenant will pay all utility bills as they come due. TENANT AGREES TO PAY A $50.00 GAS SERVICE CHARGE UPON VACATING.

LESSOR and its agents reserve the right to cancel this lease for any reason at any time by mailing a written notice to Tenant specifying a day of termination of the lease, which date shall be seven (7) days from the date of mailing the notice of cancellation. The mailing of such written notice by first class mail will constitute the giving of this notice. Any unearned portion of the rent will be refunded to the Tenant.

Should Tenant fail to make payment of the rental herein specified in advance by the first day of the month, this lease shall terminate at midnight of the last day of the preceding month without the necessity of any written notice; and Tenant agrees upon such termination to immediately vacate the premises. Should Tenant fail to vacate the premises, Lessor shall have the absolute right to lock the premises and forbid the use thereof by the Tenant.

The Lessor and its agents shall have the right to enter upon the premises at any reasonable time to assure that this agreement is being complied with and not being violated.

Time shall be of the essence of this agreement. It is agreed that no failure of the Lessor to insist on the strict terms hereof shall constitute a waiver of its rights to insist on such terms on any later occasion. Tenant will comply with the general rules and regulations promulgated by the Lessor for the operation of the apartment of which the subject premises are a part.

I/We accept the foregoing conditions.   ENGLISH MANOR APTS.

_____   _____
Tenant   Agent

_____
Tenant

23-7
Always read a lease carefully before you sign it.

The owner also keeps the deposit if the tenant moves without giving the owner proper notice.

If you are renting property and fail to live up to the terms of the lease, you can be evicted. **Eviction** is a legal procedure that forces a tenant to leave the property before the rental agreement expires. An owner has the right to evict tenants if they fail to uphold the terms of the lease. Failing to pay rent or keeping pets when they are prohibited are grounds for eviction.

Rights

As a tenant, you also have rights. You have the right to housing that is safe and secure. Suppose the owner does not take proper care of the property or follow health and safety laws. You can turn to your local government for help. For instance, if there are fire hazards in the building, you can call the fire department. Your city hall can help you locate the right agency to solve the problem. If your problem cannot be solved through these channels, you can seek legal advice.

Buying Housing

Many people choose to own their own houses instead of renting. They can buy either single-family houses or units in multifamily housing.

Advantages and Disadvantages of Buying

People buy houses for many different reasons. They may prefer the emotional security of buying a home to the convenience of renting. They may decide to stay in one location for a number of years. Some need the space a single-family house offers.

Setting the Scene: Can They Afford It?

Tasha and Bill have been living in an apartment. All utilities were included in the monthly payments. They now want to buy a house and have found one they like. The monthly payments will take approximately 33% of their combined incomes. They have no experience in judging the cost of utilities.

Analyze It: Is the cost of the house in keeping with their income? What financial programs help people like Tasha and Bill buy housing? Are they overlooking other important expenses? What might happen if either of them lost their job or developed health problems? What advice would you give them?

People may choose to buy houses for financial reasons. Houses usually increase in value faster than the rate of inflation. Therefore, many homeowners regard their house payments as a type of savings plan. Home ownership improves credit ratings. Money paid for real estate taxes and interest on a home mortgage can be deducted from income taxes.

To buy a house, you will pay a down payment and get a loan to pay the rest. This type of loan is called a **mortgage**. It is usually paid monthly over 15 to 30 years, depending on the terms.

In addition to the down payment and monthly payments, there are other mortgage expenses. These include closing costs, homeowner's insurance, taxes, and other costs. See 23-8. Purchasing a home

Expenses Included in Closing Costs

- Appraisal
- Property survey
- Deed
- Title search
- Title insurance
- Tax stamp
- Recording fees
- Notary fee
- Credit report
- Escrow fees

23-8

Home buyers need to remember that closing costs must be added to the purchase price of a home.

and shopping for the best mortgage may become very involved. Be sure to seek the advice of professionals when you are ready to buy. You should get estimates of the costs and be sure to have enough money available to pay for them.

New houses usually need some decorating, furniture, and landscaping. Previously owned houses may need improvements such as painting, new plumbing, or even rewiring. Buying a house usually involves moving expenses, too. Besides the mortgage, all these costs need to be considered when budgeting for a house.

Check It Out!

1. Why do you need to consider location when choosing housing?
2. List three advantages of renting housing and two advantages of buying it.
3. What are a tenant's responsibilities after signing a lease?
4. In addition to the down payment and the mortgage, what are three other expenses a home buyer will pay?

Chapter Review

Summary

When choosing a place to live, you start by considering your physical, social, and psychological needs. Your physical needs include shelter, food, and rest. Your social needs may require some space for enjoying family, friends, and individual needs like recreation. Your psychological needs are for security, familiarity, beauty, privacy, and self-expression.

Once you identify your needs, you can evaluate how well different types of housing meet these needs. You will choose between a single-family house or a unit in a multifamily dwelling. Single-family houses are either attached or freestanding. Multifamily dwellings include apartments, cooperative units, and condominium units.

After deciding what type of housing will meet your needs, you will decide whether to rent or buy. Both your income and the location of the housing will impact your decision. There are advantages and disadvantages to both options. You need to choose what works best for you.

Think About It!

1. How would you feel if your housing did not meet your physical needs for food and rest?
2. How does your housing help you meet your social needs?
3. Which of the five psychological needs discussed in this chapter is most important to you? Why?
4. Would you rather live in a multifamily dwelling or a freestanding house? Why?
5. What would you do if you owned a co-op and you disagreed with a decision made by the other stockholders in the corporation?
6. How does cultural diversity influence your choice of where you would like to live?
7. Under what circumstances would it be best for you to rent housing?
8. How would you plan to meet the financial responsibilities of home ownership?

Try It Out!

1. Locate a recent news story about a problem occurring because physical housing needs were not met. Write a paragraph explaining how this could be prevented.
2. Think about how your housing needs will change in the next 5 years and in the next 15 years. Discuss your thoughts in a small group setting.
3. Look through the classified section of your local newspaper. Make a list of single-family housing available in your area. Then make a list of multifamily housing available. Compare the two lists to see which type of housing is the most plentiful in your area.
4. Prepare a brochure that highlights your community. Be sure to give examples of the benefits of living in the area.
5. Obtain a copy of a lease. Examine it to see how the tenant's and owner's rights and responsibilities are defined.
6. Interview a person who recently bought housing. Write a report on the steps taken before actually buying the house. Then discuss what the owner sees as advantages and disadvantages of owning a house.

colors that satisfy everyone. In private areas, such as a bedroom, colors that appeal to individual family members can be used.

▼ Choose a dominant color when decorating. Smaller amounts of other colors can be used to accent it and add interest and variety.

▼ A sharp contrast can emphasize an object. For instance, a dark sofa will stand out against a light background. The same sofa will blend in with a room decorated in similar dark colors.

▼ Light colors make items and rooms look larger. Dark colors make items and rooms look smaller. For instance, long, narrow rooms can look shorter if a dark color is used on the end walls.

▼ Using a variety of color values, especially in unequal amounts, can make a room more interesting. For example, large areas of light values can be set off by small areas of dark values.

▼ Make greater use of low-intensity colors, especially as backgrounds and in large areas. High-intensity colors are better suited for small areas and as accents. Color intensity is more effective when used with variety.

▼ Using warm colors, shades, and high intensity colors will make a room appear smaller.

▼ Using cool colors, tints, and low intensity colors will make a room appear larger.

▼ Warm colors suggest informality, while cool colors suggest formality.

Line

Vertical, horizontal, diagonal, and curved lines are all used in house design. See 24-2. *Vertical* lines suggest height, confidence, and dignity. They are visible in tall furniture, such as secretaries and armoires; long, narrow draperies; striped

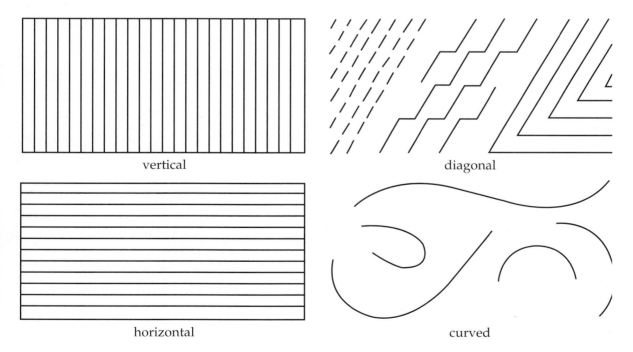

vertical

horizontal

diagonal

curved

24-2
Different types of lines are used to create various visual effects in design.

wallpaper; and pillars or columns. They can make ceilings seem higher and rooms more spacious.

Horizontal lines suggest relaxation and informality. They are seen in long, low furniture, such as sofas and chests. They can make ceilings seem lower and rooms seem wider.

Diagonal lines suggest activity and movement. They are found in slanted ceilings, staircases, and fabric designs. They provide variety in design, but can be overpowering and tiring unless used in small amounts.

Curved lines can suggest either activity or relaxation, depending on the degree of the curve. Soft curves appear restful and graceful. Upward curves give an impression of rising. Small curves look playful. Tight curves look busy and action packed. Curves can be seen in arches, tabletops, ruffled curtains, and rounded furniture.

Using a variety of lines can create interest, but it can also cause confusion. Therefore, when designing a home, one type of line should dominate. For example, vertical lines may dominate a room. Small amounts of curved or diagonal lines can be used in accessories to create interest.

Texture

Texture provides much of a home's character because it strongly stimulates the imagination and affects the senses of touch and sight. Rough textures and bold patterns tend to make a room appear smaller. Uneven surfaces cast small shadows and absorb light. This makes the actual color seem deeper, the room darker, and the objects larger and heavier. On the other hand, shiny, smooth textures reflect light and make a room appear brighter and lighter.

The room shown in 24-3 has a variety of textures. Rough textures are in the bed covering and pillows. The smooth textures of the polished wood, glass tabletop, sleek lamp base, and metal handles provide good contrast. A variety of textures gives the room an inviting, pleasant look.

Form

Form is three-dimensional. It has length, width, and depth. In housing, it is found in architecture, furniture, equipment, and accessories. Forms should not be chosen only for how they look. They should also be chosen for their **function**, or how they will be used. For example, a lounge chair is designed to let a person stretch out and relax. A dining

24-3
The various textures used in this room give it character.

room chair is designed for eating at a table in an upright position. You could not comfortably stretch out on a dining room chair. Room design works best when the forms are functional and relate to one another while also providing variety.

The Principles of Design

The principles of design are guidelines for working with the elements of design. The principles of design are proportion, rhythm, balance, and emphasis.

The More You Know: The Goals of Design

Keep the goals of design in mind as you use the elements and principles of design. The goals are beauty, appropriateness, and unity with variation.

Beauty is a quality that gives pleasure to the senses. However, what one person finds beautiful may not be beautiful to another. *Appropriateness*, or suitability, means a design is right for its purpose. To make your design appropriate for all members of the family, take their personalities, needs, wants, and lifestyles into consideration. To create *unity with variation*, choose an element of design to serve as a dominant theme in each room. Then add variety using small, contrasting amounts of the same element.

Proportion

Proportion is the ratio of one part to another part and to the whole. Unequal proportions, such as 2:3, 3:5, and 5:8, are pleasing to the eye. They are more interesting than equal proportions, such as 2:2 or 2:4. For example, a rectangle is more pleasing in a design than a square. See 24-4 to see how proportion affects furniture and accessories.

Think about proportion when choosing furniture and accessories. If they are too large in proportion to a small room, they will make the room seem crowded. The room will seem too small, and the furniture will look too large.

Rhythm

Rhythm leads the eyes smoothly from one feature to another in a design. The five types of rhythm are repetition, opposition, gradation, radiation, and transition. All five types can be seen in 24-5, which shows good use of rhythm.

By repeating color, line, form, or texture in a design, you can achieve rhythm by *repetition*. The use of the same wood in the furniture pieces creates repetition.

Opposition is rhythm formed by lines meeting at right angles. You can see opposition in the corners of the windows, picture frames, and cabinet doors.

Gradation is rhythm created by a gradual change. The room setting shows gradation in color value from light to dark in the color of the carpeting, furniture, wooden floor, and wallpaper.

In rhythm by *radiation*, lines extend outward from a central point. This is evident in the ornate light fixture.

Transition is rhythm created by curved lines. Transition carries the eyes easily over an architectural feature or piece of furniture. In this case, the rounded backs of the chairs create rhythm.

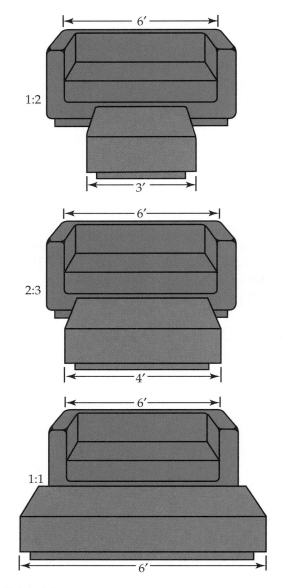

24-4

The table in the middle is in a 2:3 ratio with the sofa. This unequal proportion is considered more pleasing than the 1:2 and 1:1 ratios seen above and below.

Balance

Balance gives design a sense of *equilibrium*, or a sense of weight on both sides. Balance can be formal or informal.

Formal balance is the arrangement of identical objects on opposite sides of a central point. Formal balance gives a

24-5

A good sense of rhythm creates a comfortable, relaxing room.

restful, orderly, sophisticated look to a room. However, too much use of formal balance can become dull. With *informal balance*, the two sides are different, but have the same visual impact. Various forms, sizes, and colors can be used together to achieve informal balance.

For instance, the hutch in 24-6 is an example of formal balance when it is empty. One side is a mirror image of the other. However, when dinnerware and accessories are added, the hutch appears balanced because of the informal arrangement of items within and above. The various colors and sizes of dinnerware plus interesting accessories make the difference. Although the items vary from side to side, they appear to have equal visual weight.

24-6
Notice how all the items are arranged informally to create a sense of equal visual weight.

24-7
Among the many attractive features in this bathroom, the curved lines of the window stand out.

Combining formal and informal balance in a room creates variety. However, as with other elements and principles of design, balance works best when either formal or informal balance dominates.

Emphasis

Emphasis refers to the center of interest, or focal point, in a design. A sense of unity and order in room design is achieved when your eyes are repeatedly drawn to one feature. A fireplace, window, or special piece of artwork or furniture can be a point of emphasis. See 24-7. The special item should blend with other objects in the room.

When using emphasis in design, two guidelines need to be followed. First, the point of emphasis should dominate. No other features should compete with it. Second, the focal point should not overpower the room.

Check It Out!

1. How do warm colors affect the appearance of a room's size?
2. What are the five types of rhythm?
3. What two rules should be followed when using emphasis in design?

Topic 24-2

Furnishing Your Home

Objectives

After studying this topic, you will be able to
▼ explain how to choose good furniture.
▼ demonstrate ways to organize living space.
▼ give examples of ways to use accessories.

Topic Terms

veneer
finish
activity center
scale floor plan
traffic pattern

Furnishing your home involves choosing good-quality furniture that meets your needs. It also involves organizing living space and using accessories to tie the room's design together.

Choosing Furniture

Your basic furnishings should be comfortable, tasteful, and suitable to your lifestyle. Furniture should also be durable enough to last for several years. The furniture you choose will depend on your preferences for certain materials, styles, and finishes. Your decisions should complement your lifestyle and personal taste.

Factors to Consider

As you select furniture, choose furniture that is functional. Look for pieces that can have multiple uses. For example, a bedroom dresser might be used as a buffet in a dining room. Flexibility of furniture pieces provides more options if you want, or need, to change room arrangements. See 24-8.

Consider proportion, too. All furniture should be in proportion to the size of the room as well as other furnishings. For instance, select armchairs appropriate for the room. Then choose end tables that are about the height of the chairs. Finally, choose table lamps that are in proportion to the tables.

You also need to think about who will be using the furniture. Furniture used by children should be sturdy. Its fabrics should be durable and not show dirt easily. Choose lighter colors and decorative fabrics for furniture used infrequently.

Furniture Styles

Common furniture styles include traditional, modern, and contemporary. Furnishings in a traditional design are based on popular styles of the past. An

24-8

These chairs are lightweight and attractive enough to move to the living room when more seating is needed.

example is Early American furniture, which originated in the colonial period. The result was rustic, sturdy furniture often made of pine, birch, or maple.

Modern furniture has simple lines. It reflects the theme of "form follows function." For instance, the basic purpose of a chair is to provide a comfortable place to sit. Unnecessary frills are omitted in the design of modern furniture.

Contemporary furnishings are based on the latest designs and materials. The pieces usually have plain lines and geometric shapes. Contemporary furnishings often use metal, plastics, and glass with or without wood. Textures are emphasized more than decoration.

Judging Quality in Furniture

The type of materials used is one factor to consider when judging furniture quality. The second factor is how well the furniture is made.

Wood Furniture

Wood furniture is beautiful and practical, but very expensive when made of solid wood. For that reason, most furniture is made of veneered wood. A **veneer** is a thin slice of fine-quality wood. It is bonded to inexpensive wood, which provides the structure and support. The result is affordable furniture with surfaces having the look of fine wood. Good veneered furniture is strong, durable, and more resistant to breaking and warping than solid wood.

Another aspect of wood furniture that influences cost is the joints. You should not spare expense in this area. Look for sturdy joints when deciding between pieces of wood furniture. Quality joints are pricey and usually hidden from view, 24-9. By comparison, joints held together by glue, screws, or nails are weaker.

24-9
These high-quality chairs are constructed with sturdy joints.

Most wood has one or more finishes. A **finish** is a treatment to wood to improve its surface. Some finishes are decorative, affecting the wood's color, grain pattern, and sheen. Other finishes are protective. They help the surface resist moisture and scratches.

Upholstered Furniture

Upholstered furniture, such as chairs and sofas, has padding and a fabric covering. The frame for an upholstered piece should feel sturdy. It should be reinforced with corner blocks or steel plates. The joints should be secure. Since many of the important details are completely hidden, you should read all labels carefully.

The best way to judge the quality and performance of springs and cushions is to sit on the piece of furniture. Be sure to check the comfort of the seat, back, and arms.

The upholstery fabric affects the quality and durability of the piece. Fine fabrics such as silk or loosely woven fabrics are not durable. Soil-repellent and fire-resistant finishes may be used to improve safety and durability. Seams and stitches should be neat and straight. Upholstered furniture with plaids, stripes, or large patterns that match at the seams is one sign of good-quality, 24-10.

24-10
The striped pattern in this chair is perfectly matched at all seams.

Organizing Living Space

The appearance, convenience, and comfort of a room depend partly on how the living space is organized. How the furniture is arranged should reflect how the room is used. Before arranging furniture, review the space available as well as the activities planned for it. Activities that occur in shared family space will differ from those that take place in personal space.

Shared Space

Most homes have areas where members can gather and spend time with one another. Kitchens, dining areas, and family rooms are examples of indoor family space. Porches, patios, and yards are examples of outdoor family space.

Family space is shared space. Areas where family members can communicate and enjoy the company of one another are important in fostering family unity. Sharing family space also helps build relationships outside the family. You are more prepared for sharing space with others, such as a roommate or spouse.

Shared space should reflect the needs and tastes of all family members. Everyone in the house should feel comfortable in family areas. There should be enough furniture to accommodate all family members as well as guests. Also, the furniture in these areas should be arranged to make communication easier.

Many families maximize their living space by using it in multiple ways. Examples are a hide-a-bed sofa that converts to sleeping space for an overnight guest and a kitchen table used for homework. See 24-11.

Shared spaces often contain one or more **activity centers**. This is a grouping of

24-11
When shopping for a kitchen table, many families look for a smooth, durable top so children can use it to do homework.

all the furnishings needed for a particular activity. For instance, you might plan an activity center for using the computer. It would include a desk or similar surface, chair, lamp, and anything else needed by those who share the computer.

Personal Space

All people need some personal space where they can be alone and store their belongings. Many teens prefer private bedrooms, but they are not always possible. When siblings share a room, they often arrange furniture to achieve greater privacy. They may use bookcases as visual barriers. They may choose bunk beds to separate their sleeping areas. Some siblings

arrange their beds with headboards back-to-back so they face away from each other.

Some shared spaces are designed to include quiet sitting or reading areas used as personal spaces. Family members can use these to seek privacy if desired. People may also find private space outdoors.

Making a Scale Floor Plan

As you plan furniture arrangements for your home, you need to consider the space available. A very useful tool for doing this is a scale floor plan. A **scale floor plan** is a drawing that shows the size and shape of a room. A certain fraction of an inch on the scale floor plan is equal to a certain number of feet in the room.

To make a scale floor plan for a room, begin by measuring the floor. Draw a scale floor plan on graph paper. Then measure the width and depth of each piece of furniture in the room. Draw the pieces of furniture on graph paper using the same scale as the floor plan. Color the pieces of furniture the color you want the furniture to be. This will help give you a good idea of the color balance in the room. Cut out the furniture pieces. Arrange them on the scale floor plan until you find the best arrangement for your room.

As you arrange furniture pieces on your floor plan, you need to keep traffic patterns in mind. **Traffic patterns** are the paths people follow as they move within and between rooms. These patterns should allow people to walk through a room freely. They should avoid cutting through a conversation area or in front of someone's view. See 24-12.

After deciding how to arrange furniture on your scale floor plan, you can begin placing furniture in your room. There are several guidelines you should follow.

▼ Avoid too much furniture in a room.
▼ Place large pieces first.
▼ Place large pieces parallel to the walls.
▼ Allow enough space to use the furniture. For example, you need space in front of a dresser to open drawers.
▼ Arrange upholstered furniture among pieces of wood furniture.

Computer Programs

Some computer programs, such as computer-aided drafting and design (CADD), can help you create floor plans and design interiors. You must input the dimensions of the room and the location of doors, windows, electrical outlets, and other important features. The program will then draw the room to the scale you designate.

Most programs also have a wide variety of symbols shaped like furniture and appliances. You select the furnishings desired and arrange them. The computer program makes it easy to arrange the symbols and replace those that prove unsuitable. You can keep making changes until you design the scale plan that fits your needs.

By making a floor plan before attempting to arrange furniture, you save a great deal of time and physical effort. You can also avoid mistaken purchases and store returns.

Using Accessories

Accessories can transform an ordinary room into a unique living space. Many accessories, such as pictures, flowers, and statues, are purely decorative. They simply add beauty and pleasure. Other accessories are functional, too. They accent the decor while serving a purpose. For example, clocks display the time and lamps provide lighting.

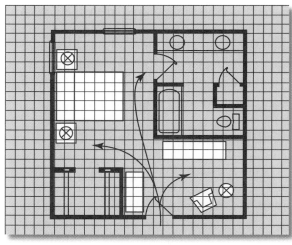

24-12
Using a scale floor plan can save you time when arranging furniture and planning traffic patterns.

Setting the Scene: Dual-Purpose Accessories

You live in a small apartment with little storage space. Every accessory needs to be functional as well as attractive. Available items include cosmetic items, books, baskets, fresh fruit to be eaten within a few days, seasonings and spices, bath towels, saucepan lids, and decorative serving trays.

Analyze It: In what rooms might you use these items as accessories? In what different ways could you use them? What are some other necessities that can also be used as accessories?

24-13
The use of plants and accessories give this room a cozy, informal look.

The accessories you choose should harmonize with the other details of the room. See 24-13. As you choose accessories, try different ideas. Be creative and try making accessories from items you use. Hang cooking utensils in the kitchen instead of storing them in a drawer. Display serving bowls on shelves and mantels. Use kitchen bowls as fruit bowls in other rooms. Well-arranged flowers, plants, twigs, and leaves add variety and interest to a room.

Gift shops, garage sales, and fund-raisers are good sources of unique accessories. Small neighborhood stores may offer special local art. Arts-and-crafts festivals are also good places to look.

As you work with accessories, keep these additional hints in mind:

▼ Select accessories with textures and colors that go well with the rest of the room.
▼ Keep proportion in mind. You may choose a tiny vase with one flower for a small shelf, but a large table needs something bigger.
▼ Consider the design element of line. Some spaces need vertical lines, while others would benefit from horizontal, diagonal, or curved lines.

Check It Out!

1. List two criteria for choosing upholstery fabric when shopping for upholstered furniture.
2. Paths people follow as they move within a room are called _____ _____.
3. What is the difference between functional and decorative accessories? Give two examples of each type.

Chapter Review

Summary

The elements of design—color, line, texture, and form—are the building blocks of design. The principles of design—proportion, balance, rhythm, and emphasis—are the guidelines for using the elements of design.

Furnishing your home is an important step and should be considered carefully. You will need to determine which areas are shared space or personal space. After choosing furniture from the many styles available, you need to think about how to arrange it. This can be done by using a scale floor plan and furniture cutouts or a computer program. Accessories can be added as the final touch. Accessories should coordinate with other furnishings.

Think About It!

1. Think about the colors used in your bedroom. How do these colors reflect your personality?
2. If you were decorating a small room, how would you decorate the walls to make the room look larger?
3. How would you feel if the furniture in your house was too large in proportion to the rest of the house?
4. Why do you feel it is important to check the quality of furniture before you purchase it?
5. Do you feel using a scale floor plan would help you arrange furniture in your bedroom?
6. Although accessories are not necessary, why do you think people use them in their homes?

Try It Out!

1. Find magazine pictures or photographs that illustrate each color scheme, element of design, or principle of design. Make a bulletin board display for your class. For each picture, write a caption explaining what point is being illustrated.
2. Using colored pencils, design and sketch a small room that appears more spacious than it really is.
3. Find examples of vertical, horizontal, diagonal, and curved lines in your classroom. Imagine you are given the job of redesigning the room. List ways you would create greater interest through the use of line.
4. Visit a furniture showroom. Have a salesperson explain the signs of quality construction. Study the labels and keep a list of the information they contain.
5. Draw a scale floor plan of a room in your house. Make cutouts of the furniture in the room. Rearrange the furniture, keeping activity centers and traffic patterns in mind. Determine the best possible arrangement for the room.
6. Working in small groups, arrange pictures of accessories to create formal balance and informal balance.

Chapter 25
A Safe and Healthful Environment

Careers

These careers relate to the topics in this chapter:
- ▼ safety instructor aide
- ▼ housekeeping assistant
- ▼ environmental specialist
- ▼ home energy consultant

As you study the chapter, see if you can think of others.

Topics

Topic 25-1

Home Safety and Security

Objectives

After studying this topic, you will be able to
▼ explain how to prevent accidents in the home.
▼ identify ways to provide for personal security.
▼ describe basic emergency procedures.

Topic Term

accident

Most people think of their homes and surrounding environments as safe, secure places. However, safety and security cannot be taken for granted, even in familiar settings. You can prevent accidents and protect yourself by following safety precautions and preparing for the unexpected.

Preventing Accidents in the Home

Accidents are unexpected events that cause losses, injuries, and sometimes death. They are the leading cause of death for teenagers. Accidents kill or injure thousands of people in homes annually. Most can be prevented.

What causes accidents? Human error is a major factor. People who are ill, tired, in a hurry, or under stress get careless. They are less observant and tend to use poor judgment. The most common types of household accidents are falls, fires, poisonings, and electric shock.

Falls

Falling from high places, tripping, or slipping on a wet surface are common accidents in and around the home. Of these, falls are the most common. Older adults and young children are the most frequent victims. Prevent falls and help make your home safer by doing the following:

▼ Never stand on chairs, tables, or counters instead of a ladder.
▼ Use steady ladders or step stools and stay off the top step.
▼ Do not exceed the weight limit of the ladder. If no label is present, assume the limit is 200 pounds for the person plus any carried items. See 25-1.

25-1
The label on the side of this ladder specifies a weight limit.

- ▼ Look for and put away items on the floor, such as toys, shoes, or boxes that may cause someone to trip.
- ▼ Wipe up spills on counters and floors immediately.
- ▼ Use sturdy, nonskid rugs on wood or tile floors.
- ▼ Use nonskid strips in bathtubs and on shower floors.
- ▼ Avoid walking on wet floors indoors and slippery surfaces outdoors.
- ▼ Place a night-light in hallways and bathrooms to help see at night.
- ▼ Keep outdoor walkways clear of ice, snow, and objects.

Fires

Fires are the second leading cause of deaths at home. Careless smoking, kitchen fires, electrical shorts, and mishandled chemicals are common fire hazards.

Kitchen Safety

The kitchen can be a very dangerous place. Safely store matches beyond the reach of children. Keep hot appliances away from materials that can catch fire. Also keep paper towels, potholders, and kitchen towels away from hot cooking surfaces.

Kitchen fires start suddenly, often without warning. When food is cooking, never leave it unattended. Grease can ignite if it gets too hot. Keep kitchens clean since grease buildup is highly flammable. Pay special attention to the range hood and areas near the range. Always keep a fire extinguisher in the kitchen area and know how to use it.

Another part of kitchen safety is preventing burns. Turn pot handles away from the front of the range when you are cooking. Do not reach over lighted burners. Use dry, heat-resistant oven mitts to remove hot pans from the oven. Lift lids and covers away from your face to prevent steam burns. Turn off appliances and range controls when you finish cooking.

Electrical Hazards

Electrical shorts caused by frayed cords, faulty wiring, or misused appliances start many fires. If electrical cords are frayed or cracked, replace them. Do not run cords or wires under carpets or rugs. Avoid overloading electrical outlets with too many plugs. Use appliances and cords that meet current safety standards. To make sure they do, look for a safety seal such as the Underwriters Laboratories (UL) seal. Use appliances properly, and when finished, unplug them and put them away.

Flammable Chemicals and Heating Equipment

It is important to store flammable chemicals, such as cleaning fluids and aerosol sprays, in safety containers. Always read the label to find out if a product is flammable. Some chemicals, such as glues and nail polish remover, produce flammable vapors that could ignite. Never store or use flammable chemicals near a heat source.

Always follow the instructions for proper use and care of fireplaces, wood-burning stoves, and space heaters. Use a fire screen or glass doors on a fireplace and have the chimney cleaned regularly. Make sure wood-burning stoves are properly installed and maintained. Keep space heaters in top-notch condition and use them away from water and flammable materials.

Fire Safety Precautions

Most deaths and injuries from home fires are caused by smoke inhalation. Deadly smoke and gases may be produced before flames appear. More importantly, most fires start at night when people are asleep. This is why having efficient smoke detectors and an escape plan is so important, 25-2.

Battery-operated smoke detectors are very affordable. Smoke detectors should be on every level of the home. Hallways, bedrooms, and attics are the best sites. Attach the detector on or near the ceiling according to the manufacturer's instructions. Check each detector once a month to make sure it works properly. Replace dead batteries immediately.

An emergency escape plan can be a lifesaver if a fire strikes. To get prepared, draw a floor plan of your home and map two escape routes. Then conduct a fire drill that involves all family members. Be sure everyone knows the plan perfectly as well as where to meet outdoors.

If a fire occurs, gather everyone and move quickly through the nearest reachable escape route. If the room is filled with smoke, stay close to the floor as you exit. Feel each door before opening it. If a door is hot, take another route. Close all doors behind you when leaving and do not re-enter the home for any reason. If clothing catches on fire, the person should drop to the ground and roll over to smother the flames. When everyone is safely out, call the fire department.

Poisoning

Another leading cause of death at home is poisoning. Children are especially in danger because they are curious and tend to put things into their mouths, 25-3. Store

25-2
Smoke detectors usually alert residents to a fire in enough time for a safe escape.

25-3
Children are especially attracted to the different colors of pills and tablets.

all poisonous chemicals out of children's reach, preferably in locked cabinets. This includes cosmetics, cleaning products, pesticides, fertilizers, and medications. All can be hazardous when improperly used. Securely replace child-resistant caps on products after every use.

Common causes of poisonings among adults include consuming toxic substances from mislabeled containers and overdosing on medications. Store chemicals in their original, properly labeled containers. Chemicals that could be mistaken for food products or seasonings should never be stored in the kitchen. Before taking any medications, labels should be carefully checked for the correct dosage.

Electric Shock

Electricity always presents the potential for hazards. It can spark fires as well as cause electric shock. The shock can range from minor to life threatening. Low-voltage electric current can cause burns by passing through the body, while high-voltage current halts breathing and heart activity. It may even cause death.

Household wiring, electrical outlets, power tools, and appliances should always be used with safety in mind.

▼ Cover unused outlets with safety covers when children are around. This prevents them from sticking fingers or objects into outlets.

▼ Keep electrical appliances and cords in good repair. Never use appliances that don't work properly, especially those with damaged cords. Do not use electrical cords with broken plugs or exposed wires.

▼ Never use electrical appliances near water.

Water and electricity is a deadly combination because water conducts electricity. Sinks, bathtubs, and showers are obvious areas for electrical hazards, but stay alert to unexpected places. For example, do not stand on a damp or wet floor when using an electrical appliance. Do not use power tools on an aluminum ladder near water. In the kitchen, wipe up spills immediately and keep damp cloths away. Always dry your hands before turning power switches on and off or when using electrical appliances or tools. Electrical appliances such as hair dryers, shavers, and radios should not be used around water.

Providing for Security

No home or neighborhood is completely safe from break-ins and attacks. However, certain measures can help make these places safer. You can help prevent break-ins by making it more difficult for intruders. Your best defense against an attack is to be alert and avoid unsafe situations.

In Your Home

Taking extra precautions will help you feel secure when you are home alone. The first step is to identify security hazards that might make your home an easy target. Taking action to reduce or eliminate these hazards is the next step.

Conduct a Home Security Inspection

The main purpose of a security inspection is to identify security hazards in your home. This inspection should include a check of your home's doors, windows, lights, locks, and landscaping. For a complete checklist of items to inspect, contact your local police. Some departments have officers assigned to conduct the inspections. An example of a home security checklist is shown in 25-4.

Make the Home Secure

Would-be intruders are more likely to strike a home that looks vacant or easy to enter. Increase your home's security by following these tips.

▼ Create the appearance of activity in your home, even when you are not there.

▼ Vary your daily routines slightly so you are not leaving and arriving daily at the same times.

▼ Keep doors and windows locked at all times—even when at home. Heavy solid wood or metal doors with secure locks offer the best protection against break-ins. Keyed locks on windows provide extra security.

▼ Leave exterior lights on at night since lighting is the greatest deterrent to intruders. All entrance doors, parking areas, and courtyards should be well lighted.

▼ Consider installing an alarm system for added security, no matter when the home is occupied or empty. A sensory

Home Security Inspection Checklist

Front, Side, Rear, and Basement Entrances

- Are the doors of solid wood construction or metal with secure locks?
- Are the door frames strong enough to prevent forced entry?
- Does each entrance have a screen or storm door with a secure lock?
- Are all entrances well lighted?
- Can the entrances be observed from the street?
- Are all entrances clear of landscaping (trees, shrubs, bushes) that could conceal an intruder?

Ground Floor and Upper Floor Windows

- Do all windows have secure locks in working condition?
- Do windows have screens or storm windows that lock from the inside?
- Are window areas well lighted and clear of overgrown landscaping that could conceal an intruder?

Garage Doors and Windows

- Is the overhead door equipped with a secure lock?
- Is the entry door kept closed and locked at all times?
- Are tools and ladders stored in the garage?
- Are all doors well lighted on the outside?

25-4

Law enforcement agencies use this type of checklist to perform home security inspections for residents.

device that sounds an alarm in case of burglary is one type. Prices vary based on the complexity of the system. See 25-5.

25-5
Affordable alarm systems can give you peace of mind in addition to detecting intruders.

Protect Yourself When Home Alone

You need to protect yourself from dangerous situations when you are home alone. You also need to know how to get help in an emergency.

▼ Leave a spare house key with a trusted neighbor. Never hide extra keys outside. If you come home and find a door unlocked or open, do not go inside. Go to a neighbor's home or a public phone and call the police. Have them check the house first in case an intruder is inside.

▼ If someone calls or comes to the door, do not tell the person you are alone.

▼ When the doorbell rings, look through a nearby window or a door peephole to see who is there. Ask the person for identification before you open the door.

▼ If you must go out for a short time, lock all doors.

▼ Use nightlights in several rooms. Keep outside areas, especially door entrances, well lit. If you must go out at night, make sure lights are left on inside and outside for your return.

▼ If you are returning home at night, ask a friend to accompany you and wait until you are safely indoors. If you must return home alone, have your key ready and get inside quickly.

▼ Keep a list of emergency telephone numbers posted near the phone. These numbers should include your parents' workplace, a neighbor or nearby relative, and police and fire departments.

In Your Neighborhood

You can help make your neighborhood safer and more secure by joining a group of neighbors who work together to reduce crime. They look out for each other's homes to discourage break-ins, too.

As part of a watch group, you learn to look for suspicious people, vehicles, or activities. Watch for anything that appears strange and note descriptions of the people and their vehicles. Also, record their license numbers. If they behave suspiciously, immediately call police. Your actions may protect a neighbor and prevent a crime.

Away from Home

If you feel a place or a situation is dangerous, avoid it. If you find yourself in a situation that makes you feel uncomfortable, leave as quickly as possible. Whether you are walking or driving, a commonsense approach can help you avoid danger.

As You Walk

Avoid walking alone, especially at night. A lone person is an easier target for attack. See 25-6. If you must walk alone, stay alert to your surroundings and watch for suspicious people. Choose well-lighted, busy streets, not dark paths, vacant lots, alleys, parks, and shortcuts across parking lots.

Walk at a steady pace, appearing calm and confident. The more vulnerable you appear, the more susceptible you are to

The More You Know: Walking Safely

Walking may be a means of transportation or a form of exercise. Whatever your reason for walking, you need to walk safely to protect yourself from hazards. Walk in safe places and scan the traffic around you. Face the oncoming traffic and always use existing sidewalks. Cross streets at marked crossings. Watch for cars backing out of parking spaces. Pedestrians have the right of way but may need to yield to aggressive drivers.

Wear light-colored clothes to reflect light; it will be easier for others to see you. Walk during daylight hours when possible. When walking at night, wear reflective accessories such as shoes or armbands to be more visible. Use a flashlight to scan ahead. This will help you avoid obstacles while making you more visible.

25-6
Walking with a friend or in a group is the safest way to reach your destination.

as you could get hurt. It is better to give up the item than to risk your life. Notice the attacker's face and clothing so you can describe the person to police.

In Your Car

Have your keys ready so you enter the car quickly. Before opening the door, check front and back seats to make sure no one is hiding. Once inside, immediately lock the car. When driving, avoid empty streets and unsafe areas.

If you think a vehicle is following you, drive to a well-lighted public area or the nearest police station. If immediate help is not available, honk the horn nonstop and turn on the emergency signals. Do not drive home, as the other car may follow. Never stop for the other car.

attack. If you think you are being followed, head for a well-lighted public area. A store or restaurant is a good choice. Get to a phone in a safe area and call police.

Avoid wearing jewelry or clothing that looks expensive and draws attention. Keep your valuables in your front pockets. If you carry a purse, keep it tightly tucked under your arm or out of sight. Keep extra money safely hidden (not in your wallet) for an emergency phone call, bus fare, or cab fare.

If an attacker wants your money or jewelry, let him or her have it. Do not resist,

Keep your car in good running condition with a full tank of gas to lessen the chance of stopping for car problems. If you must stop, raise the car hood and turn on the emergency signals. If you have a cellular phone, call for help. If someone stops, do not roll down your window, open the door, or leave the car. Ask the person to call for help, but stay inside your car with the doors locked until help arrives.

It is important to always park your car in well-lighted areas. If you cannot start your car in a parking lot, call home or the nearest service station for help. Do not accept help from strangers or get into a stranger's car.

Emergency Procedures

An *emergency* is an unexpected event that requires immediate action. Emergencies frequently result from accidents, but are also caused by bad weather and many other factors. In an emergency, you need to remain as calm as possible so you can think clearly. You do not want to upset a scared or injured person.

A well-stocked first aid kit contains basic supplies to care for someone sick or mildly injured. Keep first aid kits at home, in your car, and with camping and hiking gear.

If someone appears seriously injured, call 911 or your local emergency number right away. Immediate treatment is the best chance of lessening any damage from injuries. Give the location of the accident. Tell what happened, what seems to be wrong, and what first aid is being given. Be sure to stay on the line long enough to answer all the dispatcher's questions. Let the dispatcher be the first to hang up the telephone. See 25-7.

Some emergency victims require specialized procedures such as rescue breathing. The American Red Cross regularly offers such courses. Learning first aid skills may help you save someone's life. However, you should never perform a medical procedure if unsure how to do it.

In a weather emergency, stay tuned to a local news station on a portable radio. You will hear weather updates and important safety instructions. In case you need them, keep a three-day supply of food, water, and other necessities on hand for each family member and pet.

Check It Out!

1. True or false. One cause of accidents is a person's emotional state.
2. Name the four most common types of household accidents.
3. If you are home alone, what safety precautions should you follow?
4. True or false. When away from home, the best way for people to prevent being attacked is to avoid dangerous situations.
5. What information should you give when calling for help in an emergency?

1

In an emergency, while one person gives care, another can call for help.

2

Dial 911 or the local emergency number. Tell the dispatcher... (see steps 3, 4 and 5)

3

Location of the emergency. Include cross streets, room number, and telephone number you are calling from.

4

What happened. For example, motor vehicle crash, sudden illness

What seem to be wrong. For example, victim is bleeding, unconscious

5

What first aid is being given. For example, rescue breathing, control of bleeding.

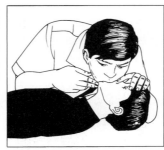

6

Don't hang up until the dispatcher hangs up The dispatcher may tell you how to take care for the victim

Return to the scene. Help to care for the victim until help arrives.

25-7

Knowing how to respond and give first aid in an emergency may help you save someone's life.

Topic 25-2
Keep It Clean!

Objectives

After studying this topic, you will be able to

▼ explain reasons for keeping the home clean.

▼ select the right cleaning products and equipment for different household cleaning tasks.

▼ plan a cleaning schedule that involves everyone in your home.

▼ list measures you can take to help make household cleaning easier.

Topic Terms

pesticides
cleaning agents
cleaning schedule

Cleaning tasks can seem overwhelming and dreary at times, but certain steps can make them less tiresome. Household cleaning becomes easier if you know what products and tools to use. Tasks are more likely to get done on time if the family follows a cleaning schedule that uses the help of all family members.

Why Clean?

There are many reasons for keeping a home neat and clean. A well-kept house provides more than just an attractive appearance. Besides a pleasant living environment, cleaning provides these additional benefits:

▼ *Health*. Cleanliness reduces harmful bacteria. This helps prevent foodborne illnesses and other disease-causing organisms.

▼ *Safety*. Residents of a clean, organized home are less prone to the hazards of clutter, such as accidents and injuries.

▼ *Organization*. Tools and materials are stored in their proper places, so you know where to find them. Work and play areas are free of clutter and ready for use.

▼ *Efficiency*. Tools and power equipment that are clean and well maintained work more reliably. They have a longer service life, too.

▼ *Pest control*. Good housekeeping habits help prevent rodents, insects, and other pests, 25-8. When using **pesticides,** the strong chemicals designed for pest control, carefully follow label directions. Persistent problems may need a professional exterminator.

Routine cleanup keeps household tasks manageable and relatively brief. Putting off small tasks for too long only compounds the workload. It can also jeopardize the family's safety.

25-8
Cereal and grain products should be tightly covered to keep out insects.

Cleaning Products and Equipment

Having the right cleaning supplies on hand makes cleaning faster and easier. Understanding the uses of household cleaners, waxes, polishes, and cleaning tools and appliances will help you get started.

Household Cleaners

Household cleaners are available as liquids, gels, powders, solids, sheets, and pads. They are used on painted, plastic, metal, porcelain, and other surfaces. Some leave a shiny finish for a polished look. While all-purpose cleaners are designed for general use, many work best on specialized jobs. Rug shampoos, glass cleaners, and oven cleaners are some examples.

Water dissolves many kinds of dirt and flushes it away. Water is safe for cleaning most surfaces and fabrics, 25-9. However, water that is too hot or remains in contact with surfaces for too long can cause damage.

Many **cleaning agents**, the materials used to remove soil, are added to water. They are used as *wetting agents* to improve the cleaning ability of water. Cleaning agents reduce water's *surface tension*. This force causes water molecules to cling together and form beads. Surface tension keeps water from penetrating soil. Some cleaning agents are not mixed with water, such as those in spray containers.

Soaps and detergents are well-known cleaners. *Soaps* are based on cleaning agents found in a natural state. Since they are less effective than detergents, pure soap is rarely used today.

The term *detergent* refers to nonsoap products that are put together chemically from various raw materials. The materials include petroleum and the fats and oils

25-9

Always read labels to see which cleaning products are designed to be mixed with water.

of plants and animals. Detergents are specially designed for dishwashing and other cleaning tasks. They do not react with minerals in hard water to create curds. Alone or combined with soap, detergents also make up the bars, gels, and liquids used for personal cleansing.

Various household cleaners work well for certain cleaning tasks.

▼ *Alkalies* allow water to penetrate and pick up dirt more readily. Examples are soaps, washing sodas, lye, water softeners, and some all-purpose cleaners.

▼ *Acid cleaners* cut grease and also act as a mild bleach. Examples are ammonia, vinegar, and lemon juice.

▼ *Fat solvents* are compounds used to dissolve greasy or oily soil.

▼ *Fat absorbents* are dry materials that are sprinkled over greasy soil. They absorb the oils that are then brushed away.

▼ *Abrasives* rub dirt away with a scraping or polishing action. Their texture can be fine like silver polish or scouring powder, or harsh like steel wool and soap pads.

Household cleaners must be selected and used with care. Always read labels to choose the right product for the job. Follow instructions carefully to avoid fire and health hazards.

Waxes and Polishes

Wax products protect surfaces from soil and abrasions. Most waxes are a combination of materials that will clean, polish, and protect in one application, 25-10. Most waxes come from plants, insects, or petroleum.

Floor Polishes

Easy-care floor polishes have either a solvent base or water base. Choose the polish recommended for the type of floor material being cleaned.

Solvent-based cleaning waxes are a blend of natural waxes mixed with a solvent. They are available as either a paste or liquid. Solvent-based cleaning waxes loosen soil, remove old layers of polish, and form a new protective wax coating.

Solvent-based cleaning waxes are safe to use on most wood, cork, and resilient types of flooring. They should not be used on asphalt and rubber tile.

Water-based cleaning waxes use water as a carrier for wax. Water-based products lift soil out and form a new coat of protective wax. They do not remove old wax coatings and should be stripped off periodically.

25-10
The cleaning agents for woodlike surfaces leaves a polished finish.

Water-based polishes should never be applied to wood or cork because water deteriorates them. These polishes are generally used on resilient vinyl floor coverings. They also can be used on slate, marble, other types of stone, and concrete floors.

Furniture Polishes

Wood furniture and paneling with sealed wood surfaces can be cleaned and protected with polishes. Spray polishes are good cleaners and time-savers. Creamy liquid polishes are more time-consuming. They require two cloths: one for application and one for polishing. Paste wax is used where a more-durable protective coating is desired.

Multipurpose Cleaner Waxes

For plastic furniture, a creamy liquid or multipurpose cleaner wax may be used. Products in this group provide cleaning and wax protection. Most can be used on countertops, tile, appliances, wallboard, and wood-like surfaces.

Cleaning Tools

After choosing your cleaning products, you will need appropriate tools. They are necessary for removing the two types of household dirt—loose dirt and adhesive dirt, which sticks to a surface. Most cleaning tools are inexpensive and can be used for different jobs. See 25-11.

Vacuum Cleaners

The cleaning appliance that removes loose dirt and dust is the vacuum cleaner. You will need one to care for floors, woodwork, furniture, upholstery, and draperies. Vacuum cleaners come in upright or canister (tank) models.

Some vacuum cleaners beat stiff brushes into the carpet as well as supply vacuum action. The attachments clean surfaces other than carpeting. An upholstery brush is useful for cleaning furniture and draperies. A crevice tool is helpful for getting into small areas. Choose a model with attachments to meet your cleaning needs.

Vacuum cleaners are more costly than other cleaning equipment. Consider cost and efficiency in your buying decision. Reports from consumer testing agencies can help you decide which unit is best for you.

Some homes have a built-in vacuum system concealed in their walls. The vacuum hose and attachments can be plugged into special outlets in each room. For lighter-duty floor cleaning, an electric broom is a less-expensive alternative.

Cleaning Tools

Cleaning Loose Dirt

- Broom—for sweeping floors, porches, and sidewalks
- Cloths—for dusting and polishing
- Dust mop—for picking up dust on hard flooring
- Dustpan—for collecting small piles of debris
- Soft-bristled brushes—for cleaning upholstery and fabrics

Cleaning Adhesive Dirt

- Lint-free cloths or paper toweling—for cleaning windows and mirrors
- Long-handled brush—for cleaning toilet bowls
- Pail or bucket—for holding water and cleaning solutions
- Scrub brush—for tasks requiring abrasive cleaning action
- Soft cloths—for polishing brass and chrome fixtures
- Sponges—for washing walls, woodwork, and appliances
- Stepladder or stool—for reaching high places
- Wet mop—for cleaning floors

25-11
A few basic, inexpensive cleaning tools will take care of most household cleaning tasks.

Making a Cleaning Schedule

If all family members understand and agree on cleaning goals, organizing cleaning tasks is much easier. A cleaning schedule helps the family achieve its cleaning goals. A **cleaning schedule** is a written plan identifying what tasks must be done, by whom, and how often. See 25-12. The schedule reminds everyone what to do and when.

A Cleaning Plan

Cleaning Tasks	Frequency				Person In Charge
	Daily	Weekly	Monthly	Seasonally	
Bathroom:					
Replace and launder soiled washcloths and towels.					
Empty wastebasket.					
Wash sink, bathtub, shower, and toilet exterior with hot, sudsy water.					
Damp-mop floor.					
Use toilet bowl cleaner.					
Scrub bowl with brush.					
Clean mirror.					
Launder towels, bath mat, and rug.					
Organize medicine cabinet.					
Bedrooms:					
Make beds.					
Hang up clothes, or fold and put them in drawers.					
Dust furniture and woodwork (such as windowsills).					
Vacuum or sweep floor.					
Put fresh linens on bed.					
Dust light fixtures and accessories.					
Turn and vacuum mattress.					
Clean closet and store seasonal clothes.					
Clean curtains, other window coverings, and bedspreads.					
Kitchen:					
Wash dishes.					
Wipe off tables, counters, and appliances.					
Clean oven and broiler to remove spilled or spattered food.					
Empty garbage container and install fresh liner.					
Scrub kitchen sink.					
Sweep or dry-mop floor.					
Scrub floor. Wax as needed.					
All Areas (could be separated by room):					
Wash windows and clean woodwork.					
Dust walls and ceilings.					
Clean window coverings.					
Shampoo rugs and carpets.					
Living and Dining Area:					
Dust and polish furniture and woodwork.					
Dust upholstery with vacuum, tool, or brush.					
Dust light fixtures, bulbs, and lamp shades. Wash as needed.					
Wash or dry-clean curtains, other window coverings, and slipcovers.					
Wash or polish china, glass, silver, brass, copper, or pewter accessories.					

25-12

A cleaning plan tailored to fit your living space helps keep you on target.

A cleaning schedule is not meant to run your life. If it does, the schedule is too rigid. A healthy amount of flexibility should be allowed in the schedule to fit your lifestyle.

How Clean Is Clean?

The people who share a home should decide how it should be kept. There must be agreement on what is important. Do housekeeping tasks and cleanliness standards conflict with other interests and values? Do people sharing the home agree on the importance of the home's appearance?

Before you can make a cleaning schedule, you need to establish standards for cleaning. All family members should be involved in setting the standards. It is hard for one person to set standards acceptable to all. What is clean to one person may fail to meet another's standards. Likewise, what might suggest clutter to one person might be a peaceful, lived-in atmosphere to another. Family members should seek a balance between demanding a spotless home and lowering their standards.

Writing the Schedule

Develop a schedule by writing down all cleaning tasks that come to mind. Then separate the tasks by room. Try to determine how long each task should take and how often it needs to be done. Finally, decide who will be responsible for each job.

Unless you live alone, divide the workload among all capable family members. Even small children can handle simple chores. Occasionally rotating tasks can promote understanding and cooperation.

When assigning housekeeping tasks, keep the personalities and lifestyles of family members in mind. If one person enjoys cleaning floors, give the task to that person. If one family member has a busy schedule, he or she might be given less time-consuming tasks. This arrangement makes it much easier for everyone to contribute, 25-13. Everyone pitches in to make the home a more pleasant place to live.

Planning for Easy Cleaning

To prevent big messes and cleanup headaches, you can stop dirt before it enters your home. You can also make cleanup easier by providing storage space for items that cause clutter. With good planning, you can even reduce the size and frequency of certain cleaning tasks.

25-13
Accepting and maintaining standards of cleanliness is easier when you help define them.

Use Preventive Measures

Try to prevent dust and dirt from entering the home by focusing on the source. Keep outside walks, steps, and porches swept to reduce the amount of dirt brought indoors. Use doormats and foot scrapers outside each entrance and a small rug just inside. Have boot storage near entrances to prevent the tracking of soil through the home.

Try to keep windows closed on windy days to prevent dust from blowing in. Change furnace filters often to avoid circulating dust indoors during heating and cooling seasons. A furnace humidifier helps keep dust down as it conditions dry air.

Lay out old newspapers before starting projects that create dirt or litter. Debris can be wrapped up in the paper and thrown away when the project is finished. No additional cleanup may be necessary.

You can avoid a lot of future cleaning jobs by choosing easy-care fabrics and durable finishes on your furnishings. For example, a family room with light-colored carpeting and upholstery is sure to need constant care and cleaning.

Provide Adequate Storage

Finding a place for everything is not always possible, but clutter can be stopped if most items are organized. Try to store items where they are used. For instance, hanging up coats is easy when a coat closet or coatrack is next to the door, 25-14.

Each room should have some type of storage space, ideally a closet or built-in area. If not available, furnishings and accessories can be adapted for storage.

25-14
Some type of storage near entrances encourages neatness in the home.

Organize Cleaning Tasks

The key to organizing cleaning tasks involves your answers to three questions:

▼ *What is the best time to do them?* This answer depends on the schedule of the person responsible for handling the cleaning task.

▼ *What is the best cleaning method to use?* This is often outlined in use-and-care instructions, on labels, and or in related booklets or brochures.

▼ *What is the best order for doing the tasks?* If not immediately apparent, follow this general rule for cleaning a room: Clean from top to bottom, and from outside edges to the center.

You will develop methods of your own for making housekeeping easier and faster. Much can be learned from the experience of others. See 25-15 for suggestions.

Scheduling General Maintenance

Routine maintenance is an important part of caring for your home. Sometimes a drain gets clogged, a faucet leaks, or a fuse blows. These routine problems are usually minor and easy to fix. Occasionally, a more-serious problem occurs. It may involve the building's structure or the plumbing, heating, or electrical systems. Watching for problems and keeping everything in good working condition will make your home safer and more secure.

A plan for regular inspections and maintenance will keep you ahead of costly major repairs. Conduct inspections weekly, monthly, and seasonally.

▼ *Weekly maintenance* helps you notice minor problems as soon as they occur. Checking for leaky faucets is an example.

Housekeeping Tips

- Try not to let household tasks accumulate.
- Carry a container for small items that are out of place. Pick up paper clips, pencils, pens, and magazines as you clean. Then go from room to room, dropping off items where they belong.
- Carry a small trash bag for collecting bits of trash as you straighten up a room.
- Consider using a portable cleaning caddy to hold supplies as you clean. Stock it with items you need for dusting, cleaning glass surfaces, and polishing furniture and metals.
- Try to work with both hands. You can dust and polish furniture and appliances in much less time.
- Talk to others and share ideas. Ask parents or relatives how they perform certain cleaning tasks.
- Look for cleaning tips in magazines and newspapers.

25-15

Following a few simple tips can help make cleaning tasks easier.

▼ *Monthly maintenance* allows you to take care of necessary tasks before major problems develop. Changing the filters on heating and cooling equipment is an example.

▼ *Seasonal maintenance* is linked to the onset of hot or cold weather. Actual tasks depend on the climate in which you live. For example, fall maintenance on a home in Florida will differ from that on a home in Minnesota, 25-16.

You will probably think of other maintenance chores your family performs to keep your home in good repair. Make these chores a part of your cleaning schedule. Repairs made by family members

25-16
An important seasonal task in many areas is the removal of fallen leaves from gutters.

cost less than hiring a professional. Also, most maintenance tasks can be done at the family's convenience.

Check It Out!

1. True or false. A home should meet certain cleaning standards for sanitation and safety reasons.
2. Give three examples of cleaning tools for each of the two types of household dirt.
3. A _____ _____ is a written plan identifying what tasks must be done, by whom, and how often.
4. List three preventive measures that will keep soil from entering the home.

Topic 25-3

A Sound Environment

Objectives
After studying this topic, you will be able to
▼ explain the importance of a healthful environment.
▼ identify the causes of different types of pollution.
▼ relate how pollution affects people's health.
▼ discuss ways people can protect and build a healthful environment.

Topic Terms
fossil fuels
pollution
hazardous waste
toxic waste
radon
recycle

Some of the most serious world problems threaten the environment. Limited natural resources, rapid population growth, and pollution are a few of these. People must think about how they use the environment. They must be willing to examine how they affect it. They should learn what they can do to protect and preserve it.

A Healthful Environment

A *healthful environment* promotes good physical and mental health and enables people to reach their goals. It has clean air, unpolluted water, rich soil, a continuing supply of natural resources, and pleasant surroundings, 25-17. The surroundings are spacious enough to allow individuals some privacy and room for recreation. A healthful environment also supports diverse plant and animal life.

Does such an environment exist only in secluded or primitive areas? Can it co-exist with an advanced standard of living? Many people believe that, with care and effort, everyone can enjoy a healthful environment.

Factors Affecting the Environment

Two factors play major roles in the increase of environmental problems—rapid population growth and shrinking natural resources.

25-17
The natural beauty of the environment can be preserved for future generations through the wise use of resources today.

Rapid Population Growth

The human population is increasing at a rapid rate and living longer. This affects the environment. As the population increases, the available living space for each person decreases. Existing resources must be divided among more and more people. Food, one of these resources, is sometimes not available to some people.

A growing population needs more goods and services, and industry uses more energy to provide them. As more goods are produced and used, solid waste is created. Ever-growing amounts of waste can mix with the air, water, and soil. Without controls, the end result is a polluted environment.

Shrinking Natural Resources

The earth has two categories of resources—renewable and nonrenewable. Understanding the difference is important. Plants and animals are *renewable resources*. These resources are replaced rapidly enough to provide people with a continuing supply.

If land continues to be fertile, plant resources can be renewed and even increased as people grow new crops each year. Healthy animals can also grow and reproduce. Some energy resources, such as the sun and wind, are also renewable. They will probably play a much greater role in supplying the energy needs of the future. Water is a renewable resource, too. Maintaining it in an unpolluted state, however, is difficult and costly. See 25-18.

Oil, coal, and natural gas are called **fossil fuels**. Their energy is derived from the partly decayed plants and animals that lived long ago. The earth's supply of fossil fuels is limited and replaced very slowly. Fossil fuels are therefore called *nonrenewable resources*. Minerals

25-18
Water is considered unpolluted if it is safe to use for swimming and fishing.

such as copper and gold belong in this category, too. When present supplies of these resources are depleted, no more will be available. The cost and availability of fuel supplies has been a source of tension among world powers.

Pollution

The environment greatly affects people's health. One unhealthful side effect of society is pollution. **Pollution** is all the harmful changes in the environment caused by human activities. It occurs when people mismanage the air, water, or land. Substances that actually cause pollution are called *pollutants*.

Air Pollution

People must have clean air to breathe and remain healthy. Air pollution is linked to respiratory ailments, such as bronchitis, asthma, lung cancer, and other lung diseases. Pollutants are dangerous because they build up over time and may stay in the air. Long-term exposure to air pollution is especially harmful to young children, older adults, and people who are ill. Limiting the volume of pollutants that become airborne is the focus of many nations.

Smoking cigarettes and using pesticides also cause airborne pollutants, but the burning of fossil fuels causes the biggest problem. Industries and consumers use fossil fuels to run cars, produce heat and light, and power tools and equipment. See 25-19. Burning these fuels creates airborne pollutants, particularly carbon dioxide and carbon monoxide.

25-19
Exhaust from automobiles is a major source of air pollution.

Scientists believe air pollution has other harmful effects on the environment. These include the greenhouse effect, the diminishing ozone layer, and acid rain.

The Greenhouse Effect

Scientists think putting more carbon dioxide into the atmosphere may have a dramatic *greenhouse effect* on future weather patterns. They believe carbon dioxide acts like a blanket to prevent the earth's warmth from escaping. This would raise average temperatures and produce major changes in regional climates.

The Thinning Ozone Layer

Closely related to the greenhouse effect is the apparent weakening of the natural ozone layer in the stratosphere. The ozone layer filters ultraviolet radiation so less reaches the earth. Scientists think the layer is thinning, thus allowing more solar radiation to penetrate. Increased solar radiation would likely increase skin-cancer rates and the greenhouse effect. Scientists believe certain gases combining with oxygen cause the thinning. The new gases add to the greenhouse effect. Ozone-depleting chemicals are now banned in many countries.

Acid Rain

Acid rain is a term used to describe acids that fall from the atmosphere in either a wet or dry form. The acids are created from the emissions of electric power plants and motor vehicles, 25-20. The chief cause is sulfur dioxide. Acid rain can pollute rivers, damage the surface of cars and buildings, and harm or kill plant and aquatic life. Efforts are underway to limit the use of the chemicals causing acid rain.

The U.S. Government, especially the *Environmental Protection Agency (EPA)*, is very involved in all air pollution matters. It sets standards for air and water quality

25-20
The generation of electricity is a major cause of acid rain.

and regulates the disposal of wastes. State and local governments also have laws to reduce pollution.

Water Pollution

Water pollution is the accidental or careless addition of waste materials to rivers, lakes, oceans, and underground water supplies. Industrial wastes, sewage, and agricultural chemicals are the main causes. In recent years, oil tankers have spilled their loads into ocean waters. Some industrial plants have discharged lead, mercury, and other toxic waste. Untreated sewage causes problem in areas with inadequate sanitation systems. Rains wash agricultural chemicals, especially fertilizers and pesticides, into nearby streams. Animal wastes from feedlots have seeped through soil, contaminating some water supplies.

Water is a vital resource in sustaining all forms of life. Pollution slows or halts the natural purification process of streams and rivers. It reduces the supply of fresh water and can cause disease. Pollution can kill plant and animal life, thus affecting the balance of nature. Some pollutants accumulate in the tissues of fish and seafood. This affects the food supply, possibly causing illness.

Noise Pollution

Noise pollution is the excessively high sound level to which people are subjected in their everyday lives. Modern machines, such as jet planes and jackhammers, introduce dangerously loud noises to the environment. Amplified sounds from concerts and CD players add to the problem.

One of the major dangers of noise pollution is loss of hearing since constant exposure can damage it. Another danger of high noise levels is increased stress. People are more likely to become short-tempered

and irritable. Long-term noise may promote the development of stress-related ailments, such as stomach ulcers, heart disease, and high blood pressure.

EPA standards limit the noise level of newly built vehicles and equipment. Many communities enforce local rules to reduce loud, irritating noises in residential neighborhoods.

Hazardous Waste

Hazardous waste is a by-product of society that poses a danger to human health or the environment when not properly managed. Hazardous waste has at least one of four characteristics. It may ignite, corrode, chemically react with another material, or be toxic. **Toxic waste** can cause injury if inhaled, swallowed, or absorbed through the skin.

Industry, government, and consumers all create hazardous waste, but proper disposal eliminates the danger. It is the careless and illegal dumping of this waste that contaminates land, water, and air. Laws and regulations identify proper disposal methods for all hazardous materials, and some are quite costly. Industrial polluters who try to escape the high cost of proper disposal are brought to trial. When found guilty, they usually must pay all cleanup costs plus a high penalty for ignoring their legal responsibilities.

Smaller contaminated sites, however, are caused by the careless acts of individuals who may never be identified. Cleanup operations can take many years and vast amounts of money. Sometimes communities hold fund-raisers to pay for the cleanup since government funds for this purpose are limited. See 25-21.

What can be done to reduce hazardous waste in the environment? Become an advocate of continued EPA monitoring of illegal dumping. Support community

25-21
People need to responsibly dispose of every piece of waste they handle.

programs that inform the public about hazardous waste and provide collection sites for their proper disposal.

At home, make sure items requiring special disposal are handled appropriately. For instance, used motor oil, antifreeze, certain batteries, and empty pesticide containers should be taken to special collection sites. The products should not be placed with other household trash. Look for labels on paints, pesticides, solvents, and other consumer products that contain special disposal alerts.

Radiation

People are exposed to low levels of radiation from natural sources every day. The sources include the sun and radioactive gases from rocks and soil.

In small, infrequent doses, the exposure usually causes no health problems. Prolonged exposure can cause serious health problems, such as skin cancer from too much sunlight.

More powerful doses of radiation, such as an X-ray, can cause greater damage if taken frequently. X-rays are necessary for medical diagnosis, but dosage and timing are strictly monitored. Large doses of radiation can damage reproductive cells and disturb normal cell activity. They can even cause death. Nuclear explosions cause high doses of radiation.

Radon in the Home

In recent years, radon in the home has become another environmental health concern. **Radon** is a colorless, odorless, radioactive gas produced by the breakdown of radium. It is released gradually into the atmosphere from soil, rocks, and well water. Outdoors, the air dilutes radon. Indoors, it becomes an environmental problem if levels reach high concentrations.

Radon finds its way into houses through cracks in foundations, floors, and walls. Radon may also enter through plumbing systems that use well water. High concentrations of radon can cause lung cancer. Tightly sealed, energy-efficient buildings increase the problem by trapping radon inside. Ventilation that brings outside air into the home is important. A well-ventilated home is the best insurance against a radon buildup.

Radon is present everywhere in the United States, but only a small percent of homes have unhealthy levels. You can learn whether your home has a radon problem by using an inexpensive test kit from a home improvement center. You can also have a radon-reduction contractor perform the test for you. If radon levels are high, you will need the services of a qualified contractor to remedy the problem. Your state's environmental department can help find a registered contractor in your area.

Some states and municipalities require radon testing before a house can be sold. Some banks and loan companies require radon testing before granting a home mortgage. Because radon causes about 10 percent of lung cancer cases, the EPA named January "Radon Awareness Month."

How You Can Help

Individuals can play an important role in preserving and protecting the environment. They can learn how to use natural resources to achieve a better standard of living. They can recognize that misused resources lead to pollution and other negative consequences. Finally, they can make a strong commitment to maintaining the health of the environment.

Conserve Resources

One way you can help conserve natural resources is by recycling. To **recycle** means reprocessing resources to use them again. See 25-22. Some recyclable items are aluminum cans, glass and plastic bottles, and paper. Old furniture and appliances can also be recycled.

Take recyclable trash to recycling centers instead of throwing it away. Ask your friends to pitch in and do their part, too. Some companies will pay you for recyclable items, so you can earn money as you lessen pollution.

Old clothing is another recyclable resource. Give outgrown clothes to someone who can wear them or consider restyling them for yourself. In many instances, you can make new garments from old ones. Often there is enough fabric

25-22

Collecting materials for recycling instead of throwing them away helps conserve limited natural resources.

in adult garments to make clothing for children. Donate clothing you cannot use to charitable organizations that collect it.

Reduce Pollution

To reduce air pollution in your area, try walking, riding a bicycle, or taking public transportation. If you must drive, use the car efficiently by carpooling or combining several errands in one trip.

To reduce water pollution, avoid dumping waste on the ground or into bodies of water.

Do your part to reduce noise levels and help insulate your home from noise pollution. Carpeting, draperies, and acoustical tile deaden outdoor noise. If you are exposed to high noise levels on your job, protect your hearing by wearing ear protectors.

Carelessly tossed gum wrappers and soda cans may not seem like pollution. However, they create litter, which is a sign of mismanaging the land. Always keep the environment clean and dispose of your waste properly. Think of ways to make others want to stop littering and do their part, too.

Learn how your community handles waste. Enlist the support of your parents and other adults to insist that local leaders use safe practices at all times. Join community groups that address environmental issues or help clean up problems, 25-23. Write your legislators to express your views on pending environmental legislation. Much can be done to control pollution if each person makes an effort.

25-23
Cleaning up littered landscapes is an effective way for individuals to get involved in the fight against environmental pollution.

Make Responsible Decisions

Making responsible decisions regarding the environment can be challenging. For instance, one source says using plastic bags will save the trees used to make paper bags. Another source says paper bags will save the fossil fuels used to make plastic bags. Reusing your own cloth bags is the best choice here.

Many consumers end up making environmental tradeoffs. In other words, they exchange one resource to save another resource. As a citizen, you have a duty to carefully evaluate your choices to the best of your ability.

Seek out environmental information from reputable sources. Begin with information from the EPA and the sources linked to its Web site. The Agency's information is thoughtfully composed and reviewed by many experts. When some disagree with its opinion, consider whether they have something to gain personally by holding other views.

Check It Out!

1. List five requirements for a healthful environment.
2. Name the two primary factors responsible for the increase of environmental problems.
3. Explain the difference between a renewable and nonrenewable resource.
4. Name five types of pollution.
5. List five ways for people to promote the health of the environment.

Topic 25-4
Conserving Energy in the Home

Objectives

After studying this topic, you will be able to
▼ identify renewable and nonrenewable energy sources.
▼ discuss ways you can help conserve energy at home.

Topic Terms

solar energy
biomass
wattage
lumens

Another important part of caring for your home involves using energy wisely. Electrical power and gas energy are the main energy sources used in homes. You use electrical power for appliances, such as stereos, washers, ranges, refrigerators, and hair dryers. Gas is used as a heat source in furnaces, clothes dryers, water heaters, and ranges. Conserving these natural resources means using as little energy as possible to get household jobs done. Conserving energy can also lower your utility bills.

Energy Sources

Energy could be defined as something that gives a machine the power to perform an action. There are many different kinds of energy: light energy, heat energy, and electrical energy. Energy can be stored. The energy stored in gasoline is harnessed when an engine burns it. Energy stored in batteries can power tools and appliances.

People have many ways to supplement their own physical energy with energy from other sources. For example, they burn gasoline to run their cars, thereby saving the energy of walking or pedaling a bicycle. They use electricity to run a clothes washer, thereby saving the labor of washing clothes by hand. People also use energy to heat and light their homes and run household equipment. See 25-24. There are two major sources of energy—nonrenewable and renewable.

Nonrenewable Energy Sources

You learned earlier in this chapter that once current supplies of nonrenewable energy are used, no further supplies would be available. This is why fossil fuels are classified as *nonrenewable resources*. Because they have been so affordable for so long, much of the world operates on fossil fuels.

These fuels are available in the liquid, gaseous, and solid states. Crude oil, often just called oil, is unrefined petroleum. It is a dark, thick liquid. Natural gas is a mixture of gases beneath the earth's surface, usually in petroleum deposits. Coal is the only solid fossil fuel.

Uranium ore is another nonrenewable energy source. It is used to provide nuclear power that is converted into electricity. Supplies of this energy source are limited and there are problems related to safety.

Renewable Energy Sources

Sources of energy that can be replaced are called *renewable energy sources*. These sources can produce additional supplies of energy in a relatively short period. However, producing a large supply of energy from these sources at an affordable

25-24
Dams generate a large share of the country's electricity.

cost may require more research and investment. Energy can be produced from five renewable sources—water, wind, solar, biomass, and geothermal.

Water

The energy of falling water can be converted into electrical energy called *hydroelectric* energy. The amount of power generated at a given plant is limited, but another plant built downstream can generate more power from the same water. As water evaporates and falls again as rain, water supplies are replaced. More flowing water allows the plant to generate more electrical power. This cycle is a renewable source of energy.

Building more hydroelectric plants is not likely. Most of the practical power-generating sites in the United States have already been developed. Building other sites could damage the environment.

Wind Energy

An average wind speed of about 14 miles per hour is needed to economically convert wind to electricity. Wind turbines can convert the energy of the wind into electrical energy, which can be stored in batteries and used as needed. See 25-25. Good wind sites are often located far from where most energy is needed. Wind energy is the fastest growing energy technology in the world. Good sites are abundant and the technology produces no pollution.

Solar Energy

The greatest renewable source of energy is the sun. Energy from this source is called **solar energy**. The sun's energy can be captured and used in several ways. Solar collectors absorb it to provide hot water for household use or for space heating. See 25-26. Photovoltaic systems convert sunlight to electricity that may be used directly or stored in batteries for

25-26
A solar heat collector traps the heat of the sun to heat water and living spaces.

25-25
Giant wind-powered electric generators can convert wind energy to electrical energy.

future use. Special reflectors focus sunlight into a fiber optic system to light the interior of buildings. Solar energy has two advantages: the supply is almost limitless, and it does not have harmful effects on the environment. However, the technology is still relatively expensive.

Biomass

Energy is stored in dry, decayed plant and animal matter called **biomass**. When burned, biomass produces heat and steam, both of which can be converted to electricity. Many types of biomass exist, but the three main types burned to create energy are wood, crops, and solid waste.

▼ *Wood* once provided all the energy needed for heating homes and cooking. Today it is used in fireplaces, but this is a minor use. Burning wood is restricted in many areas because the smoke contains pollutants. Industries that convert wood to paper, chemicals, and building products use wood waste to produce their own steam and electricity.

▼ *Crops* like corn and sugar are fermented to produce the transportation fuel called *ethanol*. Another such fuel, *biodiesel*, is made from oil extracted from soybeans. Although in limited supply, these new types of fuel will become more available in the future.

▼ *Solid waste* is considered biomass if it is the type that rots, such as food scraps and lawn clippings. (Trash also contains glass, metals, and plastics, which are not biomass.) Americans create an average of 4.4 pounds of trash daily, of which over a pound is biomass. Burning this waste generates steam and an ash by-product, often used for roads. When the waste is placed in a landfill, it releases a gas that can be converted to a fuel source.

Geothermal Energy

Geothermal energy is derived from heat produced within the earth. This source of energy is only possible in unique, geographic locations, where it is collected as steam to generate electricity. Only 43 U.S. generating plants use geothermal energy. Since nature dictates how many plants can be built, this source is not likely to contribute greater U.S. energy supplies.

Outlook for the Future

The energy picture for the future is clouded. Oil and natural gas supplies are heavily used and being depleted. Coal is one fossil fuel that is still abundant, but it presents some concerns. Unless properly controlled, the by-products of burning coal can add to air pollution.

Renewable sources currently account for only 6 percent of U.S. energy supplies. Renewable sources offer promise, but there are many challenges. Switching U.S. consumption away from fossil fuels requires public support as well as new processes and facilities. Greater investment in research and development is needed to make newer energy forms more available and affordable. Historically low fossil-fuel costs have discouraged those investments. Record-high prices for fossil fuels increase interest in the renewable fuels.

You Can Help Conserve Energy

An important goal for everyone is to reduce the use of fossil fuels. This goal is partly met by newer, energy-efficient appliances, which are designed to run on less energy. Another factor that affects energy use is how people live with and use their appliances. The checklist shown in 25-27 will help you discover ways to conserve energy in your own home. Using less energy can also lower utility bills.

Heating and Cooling a Home

About 56 percent of the energy used by a household is for heating and cooling. A whole-house approach is the only way to lower the amount of energy used by the furnace and air conditioner. Controlling indoor temperature, sealing air leaks, and using appropriate window coverings are simple steps. Other steps include increasing the home's insulation, installing energy-efficient windows, and landscaping wisely.

Use a programmable thermostat to regulate temperatures that make sense for your family. Take into account the periods when less heated (or cooled) air is needed, as when everyone is away or asleep. Set your thermostat as low in winter and as high in summer as is comfortable. Consider 65°F in winter and 78°F in summer. Wear layered garments so clothing can be removed or added as needed.

If indoor air is leaking outdoors, sealing these areas can save 10 percent or more of your energy bill. Begin by sealing and weather-stripping all cracks and openings around doors and windows. Indoors, look for possible paths to the outdoors that streams of air may take and seal them. Examples include fireplace chimneys, electrical outlets, ceiling fixtures, and entrances to the attic. Also seal ducts that leak heated air into crawl spaces and other unheated areas.

Make sure all windows have draperies, window shades, blinds, or other window coverings that can be opened and closed. Let the sunlight in to warm a room, but block it for cooling. To let in the most sunlight, keep windows on south and west sides clean.

Residential Energy Checklist

The Home's Shell
- Are plants properly located around the house to provide a break against wind and unwanted sun?
- Are drapes and furniture located so they do not obstruct heating, air conditioning, or ventilation?
- Are exterior house doors closed quickly after use?
- Do you have double-pane windows or storm windows and doors?
- Are all doors and windows properly caulked and weather-stripped?
- Are draperies and shades closed at night, on cloudy days during the heating season, and on sunny days during the cooling season?
- Are draperies opened to admit sunlight on sunny days in the heating season?
- Is the attic well ventilated and insulated?
- Are the walls well insulated?
- Is the house shaded from the western sun?
- Is your home sealed from drafts? Is it free from cracks and holes?

Environmental Control
- Does your home have as much fluorescent lighting as possible?
- Is the fireplace damper closed when not in use?
- Are lights and appliances turned off after use?
- Are ducts, radiators, or air conditioners closed off in unused areas?
- Are air ducts and hot-water pipes insulated in spaces that lack heating and cooling?
- Is the thermostat set at 65°F or lower during the heating season and at 78°F or higher during the cooling season?
- Is the thermostat turned back at night and when the house is empty?
- Are furnace and air conditioner filters kept clean?
- Is the air conditioning unit properly sized for your needs?

- Are windows and doors tightly closed while heating or cooling the home?
- Is an attic fan used in the summer?
- Is the water heater insulated or located in a heated space?
- Do you use natural ventilation as much as possible?
- Are radiators and other heating or cooling equipment clean and dust free?

Housing Selection
- If you live in an apartment, is it an "inside" apartment?
- If you live in a mobile home, does it have a "skirt"?
- If you live in an older home, has the plumbing, wiring, insulation, and chimneys been checked by experts?
- Is the den, game room, or family room oriented to the south?

Appliance Use
- Are the refrigerator and freezer kept free of frost buildup?
- Is the refrigerator set at 40°F?
- Is the freezer set at 0°F?
- Is the cooking range turned off immediately after use or a short time beforehand?
- Are appliances clean and dust free (particularly cooling coils)?
- Is a timer used to avoid overcooking?
- Is the dishwasher's air-dry cycle used?
- Are dishes washed only when there are full loads?
- When washing clothes, is cold or warm water used in place of hot water as often as possible?
- Are clothes always rinsed with cold water?
- Is the lint screen cleaned after each dryer load?
- Do the members of your family limit water use when showering or bathing?
- Is an outside air conditioning unit located on the shady (north) side of the house?

25-27

Can you answer yes to these questions? If so, you are doing your part in helping to conserve energy.

Adding insulation to a home built before 1980, if not done already, is probably a good long-term investment. Good insulation controls the movement of air and moisture into and out of the home. Some insulation additions are easy to make, while others may need an insulation expert. That person can measure how well your home's insulation compares to the recommendations for your region.

Single-pane windows, which are on nearly half of all U.S. homes, are big energy wasters. They should be covered with storm windows or replaced with double-pane windows of high-performance glass. In cold climates, gas-filled panes with "low-e" coatings reduce heat loss. In warm climates, windows should have one or more coatings that block the sun's rays.

Another way to better insulate a dwelling is through landscaping. Use trees, shrubs, and vines to help shield a home from sun, wind, and noise, 25-28.

Water Heating

After the climate-control appliances, the single biggest energy user in the home is the water heater. It averages about

25-28
Trees and foundation plantings help insulate a home against heat, cold, and wind.

16 percent of the home's energy budget. Water-heating bills can be cut by using more energy-efficient appliances and less hot water.

There are several easy ways to cut back on hot water. Taking quick showers instead of baths and using aerating showerheads are two ways. Running the dishwasher and clothes washer only when loads are full is another. Insulating the hot water storage tank and first six feet of pipes saves energy, too. You can also lower the temperature setting of your water heater so less energy is needed to heat the water. Lowering it to 120°F should provide enough hot water for most families.

Using cooler water whenever possible spares the water heater from heating more water. For example, hot water is a must for washing dishes, but not for cleaning most loads of laundry. Cold and warm water are often effective for most clothes washer cycles. Cold water is appropriate for rinsing all types of laundry. Heavily soiled laundry, however, needs hot-water washes to get clean.

Homes with heated pools use considerable energy, perhaps doubling their water-heating bill. Because few households own pool heaters and pumps, they are not figured into the national averages.

Lighting and Appliances

After considering furnaces, air conditioners, and water heaters, all other energy users average about 28 percent of the home's energy budget. This group includes lighting, appliances, and power-using equipment such as TVs and office machines.

Lighting

The average home uses 5 to 10 percent of its total energy budget on lighting. Advances in lights and lighting controls can cut that energy use by half or more. See 25-29. Tube-fluorescent and compact-fluorescent bulbs are examples of new lighting choices. They give off the brightness and color of traditional lightbulbs, but last 4 to 10 times longer.

To reduce the energy used for lighting, focus light where it is needed rather than brightly lighting an entire room. Turn lights off in any room not being used. For outdoor lights, choose bulbs with a photocell, motion sensor, or both so they operate only when needed.

Always use the lowest wattage lightbulb that gives adequate light for the specific need. **Wattage** indicates the amount of energy required to operate the bulb. The amount of light produced is stated in **lumens**. Both figures are usually labeled on packages.

Refrigerated Food Storage

Refrigerators and refrigerator/freezers use about 5 percent of the home's energy budget, much less than in earlier decades. Most refrigerator/freezers sold today are frost free, but those that are defrosted manually are available, too. These require

25-29
A good way to hold back lighting costs is to allow as much sunlight into the home as possible.

periodic defrosting to keep the buildup less than ¼-inch thick. A frost-free feature uses extra energy. Water or water/ice dispensers in the door further increase energy use.

Family members should think before opening refrigerator or freezer doors. Getting food quickly helps prevent the escape of cold air. Make sure to cover all food containers before storing them to prevent the release of moisture. Added moisture makes the refrigerator work harder. Keep refrigerator temperatures between 37°F and 40°F, but a separate freezer section should be kept at 0°F.

Other Kitchen and Laundry Appliances

Avoid prewashing dishes before loading the dishwasher. Scrape off food scraps without rinsing to keep water use to a minimum. Don't run the rinse-and-hold feature for just a few soiled dishes since it uses 3 to 7 gallons of water. Use the air-drying feature when quick drying is not essential.

Among cooking appliances, one type uses about as much energy as any other similar model. For ovens and ranges, the main difference in the energy used in different homes is the cooking habits of the owner. There are many ways to save energy when cooking. For example, match the size of a pan to the heating element. Always use covers to hold heat in, especially when boiling water. If the flame on a gas appliance looks yellow instead of blue, gas is burning inefficiently. This is a sign to call for service.

When using the oven, cook several dishes at the same time. Turn the oven off a few minutes early so the existing heat finishes the cooking. This principle also applies to cooking on top of an electric range. To reduce cooking time, use microwave ovens and pressure cookers when convenient.

When washing clothes, be sure to adjust the water level to the size of the load. To run the clothes dryer efficiently, clean the lint filter after every load. Dry heavier items such as towels separately from lighter items. Avoid overdrying the laundry load.

Home Electronics and Office Equipment

Home electronics refers to televisions, audio systems, video recorders, and all the equipment that links to them. Home office equipment includes computers, copiers, fax machines, monitors, printers, and scanners. Many U.S. homes contain several of these items, but because they are used for short periods, their total energy use is small. For example, an average television equals the energy use of a microwave oven. When in constant use, these appliances may add significantly to the utility bill if they are not energy-efficient models.

Few people know that items plugged into electricity continue to draw a small amount of power when turned off. For home electronics and office equipment, 75 percent of the energy they use occurs while turned off. Unplugging the items or plugging them into a power strip that is switched off stops this wasteful "leakage."

Shopping for Energy Efficiency

When shopping for appliances, electronics, and powered equipment, there are two prices to consider. The first is the purchase price, which is clearly labeled. The second is the operating cost. Operating cost is a very important consideration, especially if you plan to use the item for many years.

Bright yellow *EnergyGuide labels* help you compare the operating costs of major appliances. These labels, developed by the U.S. Department of Energy, appear on gas and electric appliances. They display each model's yearly energy use on a scale showing comparisons to the least-efficient and most-efficient models. Labels for refrigerators, refrigerator-freezers, freezers, dishwashers, water heaters, and clothes washers also show the average yearly bill for running the appliance. See 25-30.

Another label to look for is the *Energy Star label*, developed by the EPA. See 25-31. This label appears in 40 product categories on only the most energy-efficient models. Besides appliances, the label appears on home electronics, office equipment, fluorescent lighting, windows, and even new homes. When products save energy, they deliver environmental benefits as well.

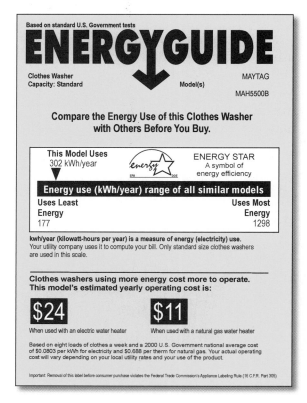

25-30

EnergyGuide labels help you compare the operating costs and energy use of appliances.

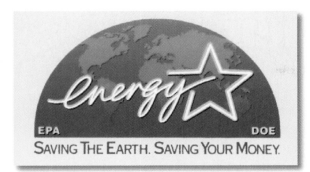

25-31
Energy Star labels identify the appliances and other consumer products that use the least energy.

Check It Out!

1. List four renewable energy sources.
2. What is preventing some renewable energy sources from being used more widely as fossil fuel replacements?
3. Name five ways you can help conserve energy in your home.

Chapter Review

Summary

The quality of life depends on important factors such as safety, security, and a healthful environment. Accidents and attackers can threaten your safety and security. To keep them from harming you at home or away from home, you need to identify and eliminate hazards.

Cleaning is an important part of caring for a home. While people have different cleaning standards, regular care is needed for safety and comfort. Preventive maintenance, easy-care decor, adequate storage space, and the right cleaning supplies make cleaning tasks easier.

A healthful environment is one that promotes good physical and mental health and allows people to reach their goals. Pollution and other environmental problems are concerns that directly affect everyone's health. Each person must assume a responsibility for protecting the environment that supports all living things.

Conserving energy is an aspect of home care that has environmental implications. By using less energy, the fossil fuels are spared. Every person must be willing to do his or her part. Knowing conservation issues helps people make energy-saving practices a habit.

Think About It!

1. What steps can you take to prevent accidents at home? How can you get family members involved in making your home safer?
2. Suggest three of the most effective ways to provide for your security at home and away from home.
3. Suppose, while walking through your neighborhood one summer evening, you see someone following. What action would you take to avoid an attack?
4. Why do you think it is important to define household cleaning standards?
5. If you were planning a weekly home maintenance schedule, what tasks would you include on it?
6. Imagine you are adapting this chapter to be studied by teens in another part of the world. What other topics would you want to add? What topics could you delete because they would not be applicable?
7. In what ways does the content of this chapter relate to the family? In what ways does it relate to work outside the home?
8. Which of the nonrenewable energy resources do you think the global community should try hardest to conserve? Which of the renewable energy resources do you think is most reliable?
9. Suppose you are planning to build a house and cannot use fossil fuels. Which of the renewable energy sources would you choose to supply power to your home?
10. Outline seven steps you can take to conserve energy in your home.

Try It Out!

1. Develop a safety checklist for each room in your home and use it to conduct a safety inspection. Identify potential hazards and determine how they should be corrected.
2. Invite a safety specialist from the police department to discuss personal safety and security issues in your community.
3. Collect magazine pictures of rooms that are easy, moderately easy, and difficult to clean. Label each picture and use them to design a bulletin board showing the positive and negative features of cleaning each room.
4. Invite a technology teacher to speak to your class about factors to consider when selecting tools.
5. Plan and organize a class recycling project to benefit your community. Sponsor a drive to collect paper, bottles, aluminum, clothing, or other recyclable materials.
6. Research ways your community and state are working to stop pollution. Report your findings to the class.
7. Invite a speaker from the health department to discuss the presence of radon in your area.
8. Research and report to the class the various ways that energy is produced for your community.
9. Develop a brochure of tips teens could follow to conserve energy at home, at school, and on the job.
10. Write an article for the school newspaper detailing how teens in your community can get involved in conserving natural resources.

Housing, Interiors, and Furnishings Careers

Career Ladder for Housing, Interiors, and Furnishings

▶ **Advanced Degree**

Architect

Furniture and equipment specialist

Housing educator

Historic preservationist

▶ **Bachelor's Degree**

Kitchen designer

Building materials engineer

Textile chemist

Furniture designer

▶ **Associate's Degree**

Design technologist

Home furnishings lab technician

Lighting specialist

Model maker

▶ **High School Diploma**

Cleaning service contractor

Decorator's assistant

Drapery maker

Furniture-making apprentice

Upholsterer

▶ **Pre-High School Diploma**

Intern in a housing-related business

Volunteer builder for an organization that houses people in need or as a decorator for a women's shelter

Careers in this field involve all types of buildings. The exteriors and interiors of structures in which people live, work, and play are all affected by workers in this field.

Employment Opportunities

Of the many career options available in this field, some focus on planning and constructing housing. These jobs involve architects, building contractors, and trades workers such as carpenters, masons, and plumbers. Interior designers plan the inside environments, making homes useful as well as attractive. Interior decorators sometimes carry out the work of interior designers by doing the actual painting, reupholstering, and arranging of furniture. Other professionals design and make the fabrics and fibers that become carpeting, upholstery, curtains, linens, and other household textiles. Equipment designers and testers make sure appliances work reliably.

Entrepreneurial Opportunities

This field presents numerous opportunities for self-employment. Architects, interior designers, and decorators often have their own firms. Before these professionals can enjoy career success, they must be able to refer potential clients to satisfied customers.

Many building contractors own their own construction businesses and hire workers in various trades on a project basis. Most carpenters, plumbers, roofers, drywallers, electricians, and other tradespeople work as self-employed subcontractors for their entire careers.

Rewards and Demands

Those who choose housing careers find it rewarding to help people. The environments these workers create improve the efficiency and add to the quality of their clients' lives.

Demands of this field often involve working with difficult clients. Clients may reject designs or change their minds several times. They are not always happy with the products and services they receive or their bills. Workers may wish they could use their creativity more freely. Workers may also have to put in long, irregular hours to meet deadlines.

Preparation Requirements

The training needed for a career in this field depends on the specific job. Some firms hire people with vocational training. Others accept workers with associate's degrees. However, a four-year degree is needed for many design positions or highly technical jobs.

Entry-Level Jobs

Most of the work available to people with only a high school education are low-skill jobs that involve assisting carpenters, painters, and other tradespeople. The situation is similar for interior decorators. With supervision and hands-on experience, however, these opportunities help workers build the skills needed to develop a craft and get better jobs.

Midlevel Jobs

Some workers at this level receive their training as apprentices, perhaps in one or more years of a work-study program. They work under highly skilled employees who excel at their trades. In design firms, model makers construct three-dimensional miniatures of complex buildings and interiors. These help clients and building contractors envision the final results.

Professional-Level Jobs

Architects, building engineers, and interior designers require a four-year degree and credentials from a respected organization. For example, having *ASID* after a person's name means the American Society of Interior Design includes the person as a member. To be eligible, a person must successfully complete an internship plus written and practical exams.

Many products and services are needed to build, decorate, and furnish a home.

Personal Qualities Needed for Success

People who work in housing, interiors, and furnishings must be creative, persistent, and detail-oriented. They also need to stay alert to cutting-edge trends and relate well to clients, suppliers, and coworkers. Designers also need good visual communication skills to accurate depict their ideas. Successful people in this field work independently and manage time and money well.

Future Trends

Jobs in this field are strongly affected by the economy. In times of prosperity or low mortgage rates, there is high demand for housing and the necessary workers. Professionals who are talented, creative, and competitive will likely find success.

Career Interests, Abilities, and You

Skills needed in the field of housing, interiors, and furnishings vary widely from one career to another. Classes in housing and interior design can teach you the basics of creating a living environment. Consider learning a housing craft, such as furniture refinishing or upholstering, or a building trade.

A part-time job as a helper to someone working in the field can give you hands-on experience. You might volunteer with an organization such as Habitat for Humanity that provides housing for people in need. This could give you a chance to work more closely with carpenters, electricians, plumbers, and painters.

Appendix

Developmental Charts

The following charts list a number of skills and characteristics typical of children at various ages. Also listed are activities that caregivers can do with children to help them develop these skills and characteristics. When reviewing these charts, you must remember that each child develops at his or her own rate. Some children will acquire certain skills and characteristics earlier or later than indicated in the charts.

The Infant

(Three to Twelve Months)

Skills and Characteristics	Activities
Begins to focus eyes.	Hang a colorful mobile on the crib and place colorful pictures in the room.
	Move a rattle or toy slowly in front of the baby's face so the eyes will follow the toy.
Develops eye-hand coordination.	Hold an object such as a rattle or a stuffed animal in front of the baby. Let the baby grasp it, bang it, and shake it.
	Have different-shaped objects such as blocks and containers for the baby to pick up and hold. The baby will probably put the objects in his or her mouth, so be sure they are clean and too large to swallow.
	Provide objects the baby can place into a larger container.
Develops eye-hand-hearing coordination.	Shake a rattle behind the baby's head. Let the baby turn and grab the rattle.
Becomes aware of different textures.	Offer the baby toys with a variety of textures such as fuzzy, hard, and soft. Talk to the baby about how the toys feel.
Becomes aware of self.	Allow the baby to look at himself or herself in a safe mirror.
Grabs and pulls.	Attach a toy to a string so the baby can pull it across the floor, table, or bed.
Develops reasoning skills.	Play hide-and-seek by covering the baby's face with your hands.
	Partially hide a toy under a blanket and let the baby recover it.
	Hide a toy completely with a blanket. Let the baby find it. In this way, the baby learns that out-of-sight objects still exist.
	Put a toy in a container with a top and let the baby find it.

(Continued)

The Infant (Continued)

(Three to Twelve Months)

Skills and Characteristics	Activities
Develops muscle coordination.	Allow the baby to play on the floor. Encourage the baby to stretch, turn over, creep, crawl, and pull up.
	Roll a ball and let the baby crawl to it.
Becomes interested in sounds and words.	Talk to the baby. Point out parts of his or her body such as toes, nose, eyes, ears, and arms. Identify dolls, balls, and other toys with which the child plays. Talk about pictures that are in the baby's books.

The One-Year-Old

Skills and Characteristics	Activities
Shows curiosity about self.	Encourage free play with safe mirrors.
	Stand or sit with the child before a mirror. Talk to the child about his or her reflection. Encourage the child to make movements before the mirror.
Can recognize objects, animals, and people from pictures or toy reproductions.	Provide a set of plastic farm animals for free play. Talk to the child about each animal's name, the sound it makes, its color, and other characteristics.
	Look at simple picture books. Let the child point to objects, animals, and community helpers as you name them. Talk about the pictures.
Is very active; enjoys running, climbing, and throwing.	Provide many opportunities for active free play both indoors and outdoors.
	Encourage climbing on small, safe climbing equipment, such as a wooden rocking boat that can be overturned to make steps.
	Encourage play with small balls and beanbags. The child can throw the ball to an adult or at an object.
Can manipulate objects with hands and fingers.	Encourage play with blocks, containers, and other stackable toys.
	Encourage play with large plastic nuts and bolts that can be easily manipulated.
	Encourage the child to place small objects into a container.
	Encourage the child to open and close containers with loose-fitting lids.
Understands some basic concepts such as *cause and effect*, *texture*, and *size*.	Talk about cause and effect relationships. For instance, you might say "If you turn over the cup, the juice will spill" or "If you stand in the rain, you will get wet."
	Talk about textures of objects the child feels. Say "The rock is hard" or "The blanket is soft."
	Talk about the size of objects. Say "This is a big ball" or "This block is smaller than that block."

The Two-Year-Old

Skills and Characteristics	Activities
Is very active; has a short attention span.	Provide pushing and pulling toys.
	Encourage play with toys such as pounding benches or punching bags that allow the child to release energy.
	Provide opportunities both indoors and outdoors for active free play that involves climbing, running, sliding, and tumbling.
Shows interest in manipulation. Can stack several items, pull objects apart, and fill and empty containers.	Provide stacking cups or blocks for stacking and unstacking.
	Provide pop-apart toys such as pop beads for taking apart.
	Provide large beads for stringing.
	Provide opportunities for filling and emptying containers with materials such as sand, water, rice, and beans.
Shows increased development in language skills.	Encourage the child to talk with you.
	Use pronouns such as *I, me, you, they,* and *we.* Encourage the child to use these words.
	Talk with the child about pictures. Ask the child to point to objects you name. Ask the child to name objects to which you point. Always correct the child if he or she does not identify an object accurately.
	Give directions for the child to follow, such as "Close the door" or "Pick up the doll." Be sure to make this a fun game.
	Teach the child the names of unusual objects such as fire extinguishers, thermometers, or screwdrivers.
Likes to imitate.	Encourage finger play.
	Recite nursery rhymes. Encourage the child to repeat them.
	Play "I am a mirror." Stand or sit facing the child and have him or her copy everything you do.
Shows interest in dramatic play.	Provide items such as dolls, dress-up clothes, carriages, doll beds, and telephones for the child to use in role-playing.
Shows increased development of fine motor skills.	Provide crayons, chalk, paint, and paper for scribbling and painting. Allow the child to "paint" the sidewalk, building, and play equipment with clear water and a brush.

The Three-Year-Old

Skills and Characteristics	Activities
Shows increased development of large motor skills.	Provide opportunities for vigorous free play both indoors and outdoors. Provide opportunities for climbing, jumping, and riding wheel toys. Play "Follow-the-Leader" using vigorous body movements.
Has greater control over small muscles.	Provide opportunities for free play with blocks of various sizes and shapes. Provide a variety of manipulative toys and activities such as pegboard and peg sets, building blocks, and puzzles. Encourage the child to dress and undress himself or herself. Also encourage the child to do other manipulative tasks such as serving food, setting the table, and watering plants.
Shows increased development of language skills and vocabulary.	Read to the child each day. Encourage the child to tell stories. Encourage the child to talk about anything of interest.
Begins to understand number concepts. Can usually grasp the concept of *1, 2, 3*. Can count several numbers in a series, but may leave some out.	Count objects of interest such as cookies, cups, napkins, or dolls. When possible, move the objects as you count. Also allow the child to count the objects. Display numbers in the child's room. Use calendars, charts, rulers, and scales.
Enjoys music and is beginning to be able to carry a tune and express rhythm.	Provide music activities. Sing songs and create rhythms. Encourage the child to move his or her body to music. Encourage the child to make up songs.
Shows curiosity about why and how things happen.	Provide new experiences that arouse questions. Answer the questions simply and honestly. Use reference books with the child to find answers. Conduct simple science activities such as picking up items with a magnet, freezing water, planting seeds, making a terrarium, and flying kites on a windy day.
Enjoys art activities.	Encourage free expression with paint, crayons, chalk, colored pens, collage materials, clay, and play dough.

The Four-Year-Old

Skills and Characteristics	Activities
Uses good balance and body coordination. Shows increased development of small and large motor skills.	Provide opportunities for vigorous free play. Provide opportunities for the child to walk on a curved line, straight line, and low balance beam. Encourage the child to walk with a beanbag on his or her head. Devise games that encourage the child to test the speed, height, and distance of his or her hopping and jumping skills. Provide opportunities for throwing items such as balls and beanbags.
Can group items according to similar characteristics.	Play lotto games. Group buttons by color or size. Provide a mixture of seeds to sort by variety. At clean-up time, sort blocks according to shape. Play rhyming word games.
Has increased understanding of concepts related to numbers, size and weight, colors, textures, time and distance, and position.	In conversation, use words related to these concepts. Play games such as "Simon Says" that require the child to follow directions. Provide swatches of fabric and other materials that vary in texture. Talk to the child about the different textures. Blindfold the child and ask him or her to match duplicate textures.
Uses symbols in drawings and art.	Provide opportunities for the child to do a variety of art projects. Encourage the child to tell a story or talk about his or her finished project. Encourage the child to mix primary colors to produce secondary colors. Name the colors with the child.
Becomes more aware of nature.	Build a simple bird feeder and provide birdseed. Identify for the child the kinds of birds observed. Take the child to a park, zoo, or farm. Help the child plant a small flower or vegetable garden.
Has a vivid imagination; enjoys dramatic play.	Provide a variety of dress-up clothes. Encourage dramatic play through props such as a cash register, empty food containers, a tea set, and child-size furniture.

The Five-Year-Old

Skills and Characteristics	Activities
Has a good sense of balance and body coordination.	Encourage body movement with records, stories, and rhythms. Encourage the child to skip to music or rhymes. Teach the child simple folk dances.
Has a tremendous drive for physical activity.	Provide free play that encourages running, jumping, balancing, and climbing. Play "Tug-of-War" games. Allow the child to tumble on a mat.
Can distinguish right from left.	Play games that emphasize right and left. These games might require the child to respond to directions. You might say "Put your right hand on your nose" or "Put your left foot on the green circle."
Can evaluate different weights, colors, sizes, textures, and shapes.	Play sorting games. Ask the child to sort rocks by weight; marbles or seeds by color; and blocks by size or shape. Ask the child to match fabric swatches by texture.
Develops greater coordination of small muscles in hands and fingers.	Encourage the child to paint, draw, cut, paste, and mold clay or playdough. Provide small peg games and other manipulative toys. Help the child sew with a large needle and thread. Provide carpentry experiences.
Shows increased understanding of number concepts.	Count anything of interest such as cookies, cups, leaves, acorns, trees, children, teachers, chairs, tables, books, cymbals, drums, and bells. Identify numbers the child sees on calendars, clocks, measuring containers, and other devices.
Enjoys jokes, nonsense rhymes, and riddles.	Read humorous stories, nonsense rhymes, and riddles.
Enjoys creative dramatic activities.	Encourage the child to use body movements to dramatize movements seen in nature. These might include a flower opening; snow, leaves, or rain falling; worms and snakes wiggling; and wind blowing. Have the child dramatize stories as they are read. Good stories to use include *Caps for Sale, Three Billy Goats Gruff,* and *Goldilocks and the Three Bears*.

Adapted From *Children*, North Carolina Office of Day Care Licensing, North Carolina Office for Children.

Acknowledgments

Preparation of a manuscript is never completed without assistance. Appreciation is due to many people who helped make this venture possible. It is impossible to name all those to whom I am indebted, but the following provided special assistance.

My chief indebtedness is to my husband, Dr. James F. Parnell, for his encouragement, advice, and moral and professional support as well as his willingness to help me with the numerous skills needed in the preparation of a manuscript.

Appreciation is due to my parents, Mr. and Mrs. W.O. Baynor and Mr. and Mrs. C.K. Parnell (all deceased, but whose influence lingers on), as well as my sisters and brothers for the "in-service" training they have given me in the art and science of work and family skills.

Mrs. Jan Reid, SAGA yearbook adviser; the SAGA photographers; and Mrs. Arleta Oldfield assisted with photographs in classrooms and on school campuses.

Elizabeth A. Bordeaux, retired Director of Exceptional Children, Wayne County Schools, Goldsboro, NC, provided valuable assistance by reviewing the book.

Finally, much credit goes to my own teachers and those many students who, over the years, have been sources of inspiration and motivation as I have continued to grow as a professional.

Frances Baynor Parnell

Photo Credits

Agricultural Research Service, USDA, 12-7, 13-3, 15-7, 15-18

American Fiber Manufacturers Association, 21-5

American Red Cross, 25-7

Apple Computer, 4-12, 5-12, 8-5, 8-17, 9-23

Bernina® of America, 21-19

Cabela's, 7-11

Cape Fear Community College, 4-16, 8-8, 11-10

Cerebral Palsy Center of Wilmington, 10-11, 10-12, 10-18, 10-27

Constructive Playthings, 10-5, 10-24, 10-32, 10-33, 11-3

FCCLA, 8-6

Fleischmann's Yeast, Inc., 15-25

GE Appliances, 4-17, 12-10, 14-2, 14-3, 14-5

Hamilton Beach/Proctor-Silex, Inc., 14-6A

Photo Courtesy of IGA, INC., 15-30

Courtesy of International Business Machines Corporation. (Unauthorized use not permitted.) 19-10, 19-11, 19-12, 19-14, 19-15

Holbrook Early Learning Years Catalog, 10-23, 10-30, 10-34

©Imaginations Advertising, Wilmington, NC, 19-18

Johnson and Wales, Part 4 career spread

Keep America Beautiful, 25-23

Mabry, Marty, 4-13, 17-25

Maready, Millie, 7-10

The McCall Pattern Company, 21-13, 21-14, 21-15, 22-3, 22-6, 22-23, 22-24

Men's Fashion Association, 20-13

Mirro, 14-10

National Chicken Council, 15-4

National Pork Board, 12-3, 15-33

Originally published in *Lowe's Creative Ideas* magazine. Copyright 2006 SPC Custom Publishing, 5-7, 14-22

Parnell, James F., 2-18, 4-7, 8-11, 13-1, 14-15, 17-15, 18-14, 19-2

Rubbermaid, 14-14, 15-16, 25-8

SAGA, 2-12, 3-2, 3-17, 4-11, 5-16, 6-1, 6-7, 6-10, 6-17, 9-3, 12-19, 12-24, 17-13, 19-7

Simplicity Pattern Company, 20-10, 20-11, 20-12, 20-14, 21-13, 21-15, 22-13

Spiegel, 16-1

Sunbeam/Thalia, 14-25

Tupperware™ Home Parties, 13-19

University of North Carolina at Wilmington, 25-6

Geri Vital, photographer, 1-2, 6-11, 8-1, 8-16

Michael Wolt, photographer, 2-10

U.S. Department of Energy, 25-30

U.S. Department of Labor, Secretary's Commission on Achieving Necessary Skills, 9-26

Glossary

A

ability. Skill in doing tasks developed through training and practice. (9-1)

abstinence. A choice to refrain from sexual intercourse until marriage. (6-2)

accessory. An item that accents clothing and gives an outfit a finished look. (20-3)

accident. An unexpected event that causes loss, injury, or sometimes death. (25-1)

account statement. A monthly, bimonthly, or quarterly summary of a checking account. (18-1)

acquaintance rape. Rape that occurs between people who know each other. This may be a friend, someone at school, a coworker, or someone the victim just met. (6-3)

acquired immune deficiency syndrome (AIDS). A deadly sexually transmitted disease caused by the human immunodeficiency virus, which breaks down the immune system, leaving the body vulnerable to disease. (2-3)

active listener. A listener who gives the speaker some form of feedback. (3-1).

active-physical play. Play that helps children develop their large-muscle skills. They use their large muscles for movements like walking, running, hopping, jumping, and skipping. (10-3)

activity center. A grouping in a room of all the furnishings needed for a particular activity. (24-2)

addiction. A dependence of the body on a continuing supply of a substance, such as a drug. (5-3)

adjustment lines. Two parallel lines that extend across a pattern piece, indicating where to shorten or lengthen the pattern piece. (22-1)

adolescence. The period of life from when puberty begins until growth ceases and adulthood is reached. (1-2)

advertisement. A paid public message about goods and services for sale, which is communicated through various media. (19-3)

aerobic capacity. A measure of endurance and the condition of the heart and lungs. (2-1)

a la carte. Items on a restaurant menu that are priced individually. (16-3)

alcoholic. A person who suffers from the disease of alcoholism. (5-3)

alcoholism. A disease in which a person develops a physical and psychological addiction to alcohol. (5-3)

alteration. A change made to the size of a pattern or garment to make the garment fit the wearer perfectly. (22-1)

amino acid. A component of proteins. (12-1)

analogous color scheme. A color scheme that combines three to five hues found next to each other on the color wheel. (20-2)

annual percentage rate (APR). The actual percentage rate of interest paid for an entire year. (19-4)

anorexia nervosa. A complex eating disorder in which the victim avoids eating, sometimes to the point of starvation. (12-4)

apprenticeship. A work-based learning program that provides training for a skilled trade. (9-1)

aptitude. A person's natural talent and his or her potential for learning. (9-1)

aseptic packaging. A packaging technique in which foods and containers are sterilized separately before food is packed in the container in a sterilized chamber. (13-4)

attached house. A single-family house that shares a common wall with houses on one or more side; also called a townhouse or rowhouse. (23-1)

autocratic leadership. A style of leadership in which the leader has full control of the group and makes all the decisions for the group. (8-1)

B

backstitching. Sewing backward and forward in the same place for a few stitches to secure thread ends. (22-3)

bait and switch. A deceptive advertising method in which the advertiser offers a low-priced item as bait to get shoppers in the store. Once shoppers are in the store, the advertiser tries to switch them to a more expensive item. (19-3)

bakeware. Utensils used for baking foods in an oven. (14-1)

balance. Equal visual weight on both sides of a central point. (20-2)

basal metabolism. Life-sustaining activities that account for energy expended when the body is at physical, emotional, and digestive rest. (12-4)

beneficiary. A person who receives the death benefit of a life insurance policy. (18-3)

biomass. Plant and animal matter that provides energy when burned. (25-4)

biscuit method. A mixing technique used in food preparation in which dry ingredients are mixed together, and then fat is cut into the mixture before liquid ingredients are added. (15-3)

bobbin. A small metal or plastic spool that feeds the lower thread on a sewing machine, which is needed in making a lockstitch. (21-3)

body language. Body movements, such as facial expressions, gestures, and posture, used to send messages to others. (3-1)

body mass index (BMI). A calculation used by health professionals to assess an adult's weight in terms of his or her height. (12-4)

bond. A certificate that represents a promise by a company or government to repay a loan on a given date. (18-2)

brainstorming. A group method of solving problems in which members offer any and all ideas. (8-1)

budget. A plan to help manage money wisely. (17-4)

bulimia nervosa. An eating disorder, also known as the binge-purge syndrome, in which the victim consumes large amounts of food and then vomits or takes laxatives or diuretics to avoid weight gain. (12-4)

bylaws. A set of specific rules that expand upon an organization's constitution by giving more information. (8-2)

C

calorie. The unit of measurement of food energy. (12-4)

carbohydrate. A nutrient that serves as the major source of energy in the diet. (12-1)

career. A series of jobs, often in the same field, a person has over a period of years. (9-1)

career plan. A list of steps to achieve a career goal. (9-1)

caregiver. A person who provides care for someone else. (11-1)

cashier's check. A check drawn on a financial institution's own funds and signed by an officer of the institution. (18-1)

cash value. The amount a policyholder can collect if he or she decides to give up a whole life insurance policy. (18-3)

cereal. A starchy grain used as food, such as wheat, corn, rice, and oats. (15-3)

certificate of deposit (CD). A type of savings account that pays a set rate of interest on money that is deposited for a set period of time. (18-2)

certified check. A personal check for which a financial institution guarantees payment. (18-1)

character. Inner traits, such as conscience, moral strength, and social attitudes, that guide a person's conduct and behavior into acceptable standards of right and wrong. (1-1)

child care cooperative. A child care program formed by groups of parents who share in the care of their children, allowing parents more control over the program. (11-2)

childless family. A couple without children. (4-2)

children with special needs. Children with disabilities and gifted and talented children. (10-2)

cholesterol. A fatty substance found in every body cell. (12-1)

chronological growth. Increase in age, which takes place at the same rate for all people. (1-2)

civil law. A type of law that deals with disputes between private citizens. (8-3)

classic. A fashion that never changes drastically and is therefore worn year after year. (20-4)

cleaning agents. Materials used to remove soil; often added to water. (25-2)

cleaning schedule. A written plan identifying what household cleaning tasks need to be done, who is responsible for which tasks, and how often the tasks are to be completed. (25-2)

clipping. Making straight cuts in a seam allowance toward the stitching line, usually at ½-inch intervals, to prevent puckering. (22-3)

coded message. A means of communication in which people fail to say what they really mean. (3-2)

codependency. A pattern of unhealthy behaviors that is used by family members to cover up a problem. (5-1)

co-insurance. An insurance policy provision that requires the policyholder to pay a certain percentage of medical costs. (18-3)

collateral. Something of value a person owns that he or she pledges to a creditor as security for a loan. (19-4)

color wheel. A tool that shows how colors relate to one another. (20-2)

communicable diseases. Illnesses that can be passed on to other people. (10-3)

communication. The process of conveying information so messages are received and understood. (3-1)

community resources. Facilities that are shared by many people, such as parks, schools, and libraries. (17-1)

comparison shopping. Comparing products and prices in different stores before making a purchase. (19-1)

complementary color scheme. A color scheme using colors opposite each other on the color wheel for a strong contrast. (20-2)

compromise. A technique used in negotiating conflicts in which all parties agree to give up something of importance to reach a mutual agreement. (3-3)

computer. An electronic device that processes information according to instructions. (19-2)

computer-aided design (CAD). Graphics software that assists in creating a design. (19-2)

condominium. An individually owned housing unit in a multiunit structure. (23-1)

conflict. A struggle between two people or groups who have opposing views. (3-3)

conflict resolution process. A step-by-step form of communication that allows conflicts to be resolved in a positive manner. (3-3)

conformity. Wearing garments similar to those worn by others. (20-1)

consequences. Results that follow an action or behavior. (10-4)

consistency. Enforcing rules the same way each time. (10-4)

constitution. A set of major laws used to govern an organization. (8-2)

Consumer Product Safety Commission (CPSC). A government agency that sets and enforces safety standards for consumer products and handles consumer complaints. (19-5)

convection cooking. A method of cooking that involves circulating hot air over all food surfaces, allowing food to cook quickly and evenly. (14-1)

convenience food. A food product that requires minimal preparation. (13-1)

cookware. Utensils, including saucepans and skillets, used for cooking on top of a range. (14-1)

cooperative. An multiunit building owned and operated for the benefit of the residents; also called co-op. (23-1)

cooperative education. A work-based learning program that prepares students for an occupation immediately after high school through a paid job experience. (9-1)

cooperative play. A stage of play when two or more children play complementary roles and share play activities. (10-2)

copayment. A small, fixed fee paid by a policyholder for certain insured items or services. (18-3)

cover. The individual place setting and allotted space needed by each person at a table. (16-1)

credit. An arrangement that allows consumers to buy goods or services now and pay for them later. (19-4)

credit contract. A legally binding agreement between creditor and borrower that details the terms of repayment. (19-4)

creditor. A person who gives credit to consumers and to whom debts are owed. (19-4)

credit rating. A creditor's evaluation of a person's ability to repay debts. (19-4)

crisis. An event that greatly influences people's lives and causes them to make difficult changes in their lifestyles. (5-3)

cross-contamination. The spread of bacteria from a contaminated food to other food, equipment, or surfaces. (14-2)

cultural heritage. Learned behaviors, beliefs, and languages that are passed from generation to generation. (1-1)

custom house. A house specifically designed and built for the new owner. (23-1)

cutting layout. A drawing showing how to fold fabric and place pattern pieces for cutting. (22-2)

cutting line. A bold line on pattern pieces used as a guide for cutting fabric. (22-1)

D

dart. A construction element used to give shape and fullness to a garment made by stitching to a point through a fold in the fabric. (22-3)

date rape. The rape of a dating partner. (6-3)

decision. A conscious or unconscious response to a problem or issue. (17-2)

decision-making process. A logical, step-by-step method people can use to make the decisions that are best for them. (17-2)

deductible. An amount that a policyholder must pay before his or her insurance company will pay on a claim. (18-3)

defense mechanism. A behavior pattern used to protect a person's self-esteem. (2-2)

dehydration. The depletion of body fluids during periods of activity. (12-3)

democratic leadership. A style of leadership that stresses the needs and wishes of individuals and in which members are encouraged to participate in decision making by voting. (8-1)

demographics. Statistical qualities of the human population. (4-2)

depression. An emotional state that ranges from mild, short-lived feelings of sadness to a deep, despairing sense of dejection. (2-2)

developmentally appropriate practices. Techniques suited to the developmental characteristics and needs of the individual child. (10-4)

Dietary Guidelines for Americans. Suggestions made by the U.S. Departments of Agriculture and Health and Human Services to help people choose healthful diets. (12-2)

Dietary Reference Intakes (DRIs). Four types of reference values that outline nutrient requirements for each sex and for several age groups, including needs for energy, protein, and many vitamins and minerals. (12-1)

direct tax. A type of tax that is charged directly to the taxpayer. (8-3)

directional fabric. A fabric with nap, pile, texture, a border print, or one-way design. (21-3)

directional stitching. Stitching in the direction of the grain. (22-3)

diverse. Differing from one another. (3-2)

diversified. Money is invested in many different stocks and bonds, so decreases in some are offset by increases in others. (18-2)

diversity. Condition of a group whose members represent many different cultures. (8-1)

dividend. A distribution of a company's profits to a stockholder. (18-2)

dot. A pattern symbol used to match seams and other construction details. (22-1)

dovetail. To combine or fit tasks together. (17-3)

dramatic play. A form of play involving role-playing. A child imitates another person or acts out a situation, but does so alone. (10-5)

dress code. A standard of dress that is enforced in a social setting. (20-1)

dry cleaning. The process of cleaning clothes using an organic chemical solvent instead of water. (20-5)

drug abuse. The use of a drug for a purpose other than it was intended. (5-3)

dual-career family. A family in which both spouses are employed. (5-2)

dysfunctional family. A family that provides a negative environment that discourages the growth and development of family members. (5-1)

E

easing. Making a piece of fabric fit a slightly smaller piece of fabric as a flat, curved seam is sewn to provide fabric fullness at certain points on the body. (22-3)

elements of design. Color, line, texture, and form as used in artistic design. (20-2)

emotional abuse. A form of abuse that happens when one person purposely hurts another's self-concept through constant yelling, teasing, or insulting. (5-3)

emotional disorder. A disorder that limits the way a person functions emotionally and socially; sometimes marked by extremes of behavior. (10-2)

emotional growth. Development of the ability to express feelings. (1-2)

emotional neglect. The failure to provide loving care and attention to family members. (5-3)

empathy. The quality of understanding how others feel even when personal feelings may differ. (1-1)

emphasis. The center of interest in a design. (20-2)

emulation. The act of imitating the behavior of other people around you. (17-2)

enabler. Someone who unknowingly acts in ways that contribute to an alcoholic's or addict's drug use. (5-3)

endorse. Signing the back, left end of a check before cashing or depositing it. (18-1)

enriched. A term used to describe a food product that has nutrients added back to it that were lost during processing. (12-1)

entrepreneur. A person who starts and manages his or her own business. (9-2)

environment. Everything that surrounds a person. (1-1)

estate. What a person leaves behind when he or she dies. (18-2)

ethnic group. A group of people who share common racial and/or cultural characteristics, such as national origin, language, religion, and traditions. (1-1)

etiquette. Approved social conduct, or good manners. (16-2)

eviction. A legal procedure that forces a tenant to leave a property before the rental agreement expires if he or she fails to uphold the terms of the lease. (23-2)

expiration date. A date stamped on food products such as yeast and baby formula indicating the last day the product should be used or eaten. (13-3)

extended family. A family structure that includes other relatives, such as grandparents, aunts, uncles, and/or cousins, living with parents and their children. (4-2)

F

fabric. A textile product usually made by weaving or knitting yarns together. (21-1)

fad. A style that is popular for a short time and then disappears. (20-4)

family. Two or more people related by blood, marriage, or adoption; two or more persons who share resources, responsibility for decisions, personal priorities, and goals and who have commitment to one another over time. (4-1)

family life cycle. Basic stages of growth and development experienced by families. (4-3)

family structure. The makeup of a family group based on the relationships of the members in the family. (4-2)

fashion. The manner of dress being worn by the majority of people at a given time. (20-4)

fat. A nutrient that provides a concentrated source of food energy. (12-1)

feedback. A clue that lets the speaker know the message is getting through to the listener and how it is being received. The feedback can be a nod, a smile, or even a comment. (3-1)

feed dogs. Two small rows of teeth that move the fabric forward under the presser foot. (21-3).

felony. A serious criminal offense. (8-3)

fiber. The basic unit of all fabrics. (21-1)

figure type. A category developed by pattern companies to standardize pattern sizes based on height and general body proportions. (21-2)

filament yarns. One or several continuous strands of fibers. (21-1)

finance charges. The total amount a borrower must pay a creditor for the use of credit. These charges include interest, service charges, and any other fees. (19-4)

finfish. Fish that have fins and backbones. (15-1)

finish. A treatment to improve the surface of wood. (24-2)

first aid. Emergency care or treatment given to people right after an accident, which relieves pain and prevents further injury. (10-3).

fixed expense. A set amount of money that a person is committed to pay, such as a monthly car payment. (17-4)

flexible expense. A cost that occurs repeatedly, but which varies in amount from one time to the next. (17-4)

flexible workweeks. Employees may work four-day, 40-hour workweeks with 10-hour workdays. (5-2)

flextime. Employees set their own work schedules within certain company terms. (5-2)

follower. A person who supports a group by helping put goals into action. (8-1)

food additive. A substance added to a food for a specific purpose. (13-3)

food allergy. An abnormal reaction of the body's immune system to a particular food. (12-3)

Food and Drug Administration (FDA). A government agency that helps protect consumer safety by regulating the production, packaging, and labeling of foods, drugs, and cosmetics. (19-5)

foodborne illness. A sickness caused by eating contaminated food. (14-2)

food intolerance. An adverse reaction to the consumption of certain foods. (12-3)

food rotation. Storing the freshest food at the back of the shelf in order that the oldest foods, stored at the front of the shelf, will be used first. (13-4)

form. A design element that defines the shape of an object. (20-2)

fortified. A term used to describe a food product that has had nutrients added to improve its nutritional value. (12-1)

fossil fuels. Energy sources, such as oil, coal, and natural gas, derived from the partly decayed plants and animals that lived long ago. (25-3)

foster care. Care provided for a child who needs a home temporarily. (11-1)

freestanding house. A single-family house that stands alone. (23-1)

freshness date. A date stamped on food products such as baked goods that indicates the end of a product's quality peak. (13-3)

fringe benefits. Employee benefits provided by an employer such as insurance, profit-sharing plans, and paid vacations. (17-4)

function. The way in which architecture, furniture, equipment, and accessories will be used. (24-1)

functional family. A family that provides a positive environment that encourages each family member to grow and develop to his or her fullest potential. (5-1)

G

gathering. Creating ripples and soft folds in a fabric that is attached to a shorter length of fabric. (22-3)

generic product. A product that has a plain label containing only required information. (13-2)

gifted or talented. A person who shows outstanding ability in either a general sense or in a specific ability. (10-2)

goal. An aim a person is consciously trying to reach. (17-1)

grading. Trimming each layer of a seam allowance to a different width. (22-3)

grain. The two basic directions that yarns run in a woven fabric. (22-1)

grainline arrow. A pattern symbol indicating that a pattern piece is to be placed on fabric parallel to its lengthwise edge. (22-1)

gratuity. A sum of money left for a waiter in a restaurant as a measure of gratitude for service received, usually fifteen to twenty percent of the total bill; also called a tip. (16-3)

grooming. Cleaning and caring for the body. (2-1)

gross income. The total amount of money an employee earns before deductions. (17-4)

group dating. A type of dating in which a number of people of both sexes go out together. (6-2)

guidance. Everything caregivers do and say to promote socially acceptable behavior in children. (10-4)

H

handheld organizer. A pocket-size machine that serves as a personal planner. (19-2)

hangtag. A tag attached to a garment to provide information, such as trademarks, guarantees, style number, size, and price. (20-4)

hazardous waste. A by-product of society that poses a danger to human health or the environment when not properly managed. (25-3)

health maintenance organization (HMO). A group of medical professionals and facilities that provides health care services to members. (18-3)

heredity. The sum of all traits passed on through genes from parents to children. (1-1)

homogenized. Refers to a process by which milkfat is broken up into tiny particles that remain suspended throughout milk. (15-4)

hormone. A substance in the body that triggers cellular activity, such as growth and the development of adult characteristics. (1-2)

hot line. A telephone number people can call for information or other assistance with a specific problem. (11-1)

hourly wage. A set amount of money paid to an employee for each hour of work. (17-4)

house brand. A brand that is sold by a store or chain of stores. (13-2)

housing. Any dwelling that provides shelter. (23-1)

hue. The name given to a color. (20-2)

human immunodeficiency virus (HIV). The virus that breaks down the immune system, leaving the body vulnerable to disease, and causes AIDS. (2-3)

human resource. A resource, such as knowledge, energy, a skill, or a talent, that comes from within a person. (17-1)

I

imitative-imaginative play. Form of play in which children use their imaginations as they pretend to be other people or objects; begins at about two years of age. (10-5)

immunizations. Injections or drops given to a person to provide immunity from a certain disease. (10-3)

implement. To carry out. (17-2)

impulse buying. Making an unplanned or quick purchase without giving it much thought. (19-1)

inclusion. The placing of students of varying abilities in the same class. (10-2)

indirect tax. A type of tax that is included in the price of taxed items. (8-3)

individuality. Choosing clothes that set a person apart from others. (20-1)

individual rates of growth. Children grow and develop at different rates based on heredity, environment, and motivation. (10-2)

infant. A baby up to 12 months old. (10-1)

infatuation. An intense feeling of admiration. (6-2)

insomnia. The inability to get the amount of sleep needed when it is needed. (2-1)

intellectual growth. A developing ability to reason and form complex thought patterns. (1-2)

intensity. The brightness or dullness of a color. (20-2)

interest. The price a borrower pays a creditor for the use of money over a period of time. (19-4)

interests. All the activities a person likes to do. (9-1)

intermediate color. A color produced from equal amounts of one primary color and one secondary color. (20-2)

intermittency of love. When love seems to fade and then reappear. (7-1)

Internet. An international network of computers that are joined together. It is available to anyone who has a computer, an Internet service provider, and a means of connection. (3-1)

internship. A work-based learning program that offers paid or unpaid work experience to learn about a job or industry. (9-1)

interrelated development rates. Interactions between physical, emotional, social, and intellectual aspects of growth. (10-2)

ironing. A process of moving an iron across fabric to smooth wrinkles. (20-5)

J

job. The work a person does to earn a living. (9-1)

job shadowing. A program to explore career options through a student's one-day visit with an experienced person to his or her job. (9-1)

job sharing. Two people divide the work responsibilities of one job, each working on a part-time basis. (5-2)

K

kitchen utensil. A hand-held kitchen tool used for measuring, cutting, mixing, cooking, or baking tasks. (14-1)

knitting. A process of looping yarns together to form a fabric. (21-1)

L

label. A cloth tag permanently attached to a garment to provide important information usually required by law, such as fiber content, manufacturer, country of origin, and care instructions. (20-4)

lactose intolerance. A form of food intolerance in which the body is unable to digest dairy products that contain lactose. (12-3)

laissez-faire. A style of leadership in which members may do whatever they want to do and leaders are on hand only to serve as resources. (8-1)

leader. A person who has the power to influence the behavior of others. (8-1)

learning disability. A limitation in the way a person's brain sorts and uses certain types of information. (10-2)

lease. A contract between a tenant and a property owner, listing the rights and responsibilities of both parties. (23-2)

leavening agent. An ingredient used to produce carbon dioxide in baked goods. (15-3)

legumes. Seeds that grow in the pods of some vegetable plants. (12-1)

lifestyle. A person's way of life or style of living. (20-1)

line. A design element that gives direction to a design. (20-2)

liquidity. The degree to which a person will be able to get cash quickly from a savings account or financial investment. (18-2)

loan value. The amount a policyholder can borrow from an insurance company using the cash value of a whole life insurance policy as collateral. (18-3)

lockstitch. A stitch made by a sewing machine with thread coming from both the upper and lower parts of the machine and locking securely in the middle of the fabric layers being sewn. (21-3)

long-term goal. A goal that takes several months or years to achieve. (17-1)

loopers. Serger sewing machine parts that form upper and lower stitches. (21-3)

lumens. A measurement of the amount of light produced by a given source. (25-4)

M

management. Wisely using means to achieve goals. (17-1)

management process. A series of steps that helps people plan how to best use resources to achieve goals. (17-2)

manipulative-constructive play. Play that helps children develop small-muscle skills. The small muscles are those that control the wrists, hands, ankles, fingers, and thumbs. (10-3)

manners. Rules to follow for proper social conduct. (3-1)

manufactured fibers. Fibers that are produced artificially from substances such as cellulose, oil products, and chemicals. (21-1)

manufactured house. A house made in a factory, moved to a site, and assembled if not already self-contained. (23-1)

material resource. Resources that are not physically or mentally part of a person, including time, money, possessions, and community resources. (17-1)

maturity. The change that occurs between childhood and adulthood, during which physical, personal, and behavioral characteristics become more adult. (1-2)

meal management. Using resources of skills, money, and time to put together nutritious meals. (13-1)

meal service. The way a meal is served. (16-1)

measurement equivalent. An amount that is equal to another amount, such as one-fourth cup equaling four tablespoons. (14-3)

meat. The edible portion of animals, including muscles and organs. (15-1)

meat analog. A plant-based protein product made to resemble various kinds of meat. (15-1)

media. Channels of mass communication, such as magazines, television, radio, and the Internet. (4-2)

mediation. Technique in which a third person is called upon to help reconcile differences between conflicting parties. (3-3)

mental disability. A disability that limits the way a person's brain functions, causing a limited learning capacity. (10-2)

mentor. A person at a job site who knows how to do a job and teaches a student to do it well. (9-1)

microfiber. An extremely thin filament of a manufactured fiber. (21-1)

mineral. An inorganic substance needed for building tissues and regulating body functions. (12-1)

misdemeanor. A minor criminal offense. (8-3)

modeling. The act of adults exhibiting behaviors in front of children, which the children then copy. (10-4)

modesty. A standard held by a cultural group about the proper way to cover the body in various settings. (20-1)

monochromatic color scheme. A color scheme based on only one hue, which may be used in various values and intensities for variety. (20-2)

mortgage. A loan used to pay for a home. (23-2)

motivation. A force that gives people a reason to take action. (8-1)

muffin method. A mixing technique used in food preparation in which dry ingredients and liquid ingredients are mixed together in separate bowls, and then the liquid ingredients are poured into a well made in the center of the dry ingredients. (15-3)

multicultural book. A book that involves characters from a variety of racial and ethnic groups. (10-5)

multicultural society. People from many different cultures living in the same communities. (6-2)

multifamily dwelling. A building designed to house more than one family. (23-1)

multiple roles. Two or more roles, such as work and family roles, being filled by one person. (5-2)

multisize pattern. A garment pattern designed with two or more sizes on one pattern tissue. (22-1)

mutual fund. A group of many investments purchased by a company representing many investors. (18-2)

mutual respect. Regard held by two people who each view the other with honor and esteem. (6-1)

MyPyramid. Symbol representing the USDA's food guidance system, which features a personalized approach to healthy eating and physical activity. (12-2)

N

nanny. A trained individual who provides quality child care in a parent's home. (11-2)

national brand. A product that is advertised nationwide. (13-2)

natural cheese. Cheese made from milk, whey, or cream. (15-4)

natural fibers. Fibers that exist in nature. (21-1)

natural resources. Resources taken from the land, such as agricultural products, forest products, and fossil fuels. (17-1)

need. A basic item, such as food, clothing, or shelter, that all people require for living. (1-2)

negotiation. Communicating with others in order to reach a mutually satisfying agreement, usually through compromise. (3-3)

net income. The amount of money left after all deductions have been taken from an employee's gross pay. (17-4)

networking. Forming an interconnected group whose members work together to help one another. (6-1)

neutrals. Black, white, and gray, which are not true colors but are used as colors in design. (20-2)

newborn. A baby in the first month of life. (10-1)

nonverbal communication. A process of communication that involves sending messages without words. (3-1)

nonwoven fabrics. Fabrics made by bonding or interlocking fibers together directly without using yarns. (21-1)

notch. A diamond-shaped pattern symbol located on the cutting line and used to match garment pieces before sewing them together. (22-1)

notching. Cutting small wedges out of the seam allowance to remove excess fabric. (22-3)

notions. Small items needed to construct a garment, including thread, buttons, trims, fasteners, seam binding, and bias tape. (21-2)

nuclear family. A family group that consists of a man, woman, and their children. (4-2)

nutrient. A chemical substance provided by food and used by the body to function properly. (12-1)

nutrition. The science of how nutrients support the body. (12-1)

O

obese. A term used to describe an adult who has a body mass index over 30. (12-4)

object permanence. The concept that objects and people exist even when they cannot be seen. (10-2)

obsolescence. The state of uselessness. (19-2)

online. Having access to the Internet. (3-1)

open communication. A free flow of ideas, opinions, and facts among the people communicating. (3-2)

open dating. A dating process that gives information about the freshness of foods. (13-3)

overdraft. A check written when there is not enough money in a checking account to cover it. (18-1)

overweight. A term used to describe an adult who has a body mass index of 25 up to 30. (12-4)

P

pack date. A date stamped on food products such as canned goods that tells when the food was processed. (13-3)

parallel play. A stage of play in which a child will play beside other children rather than with them. (10-2)

parenting. The name given to the process of raising a child. (7-2)

parliamentary procedure. Guidelines followed by many organizations to help them conduct meetings in an orderly fashion. (8-2)

passive listener. A listener who does not respond to the speaker in any way. The speaker does not know if the message is being received or not. (3-1)

passive smoking. Inhaling smoke in a smoke-filled environment. (2-3)

pasta. Grain products such as spaghetti, macaroni, and noodles. (15-3)

pasteurization. A heating process that destroys harmful bacteria in dairy products. (15-4)

pattern guide sheet. A set of instructions included with every pattern that has step-by-step directions for the sewing project. (22-1)

pattern view. A drawing on the front of a pattern envelope showing a garment design that can be made from the pattern included in the envelope. (21-2)

pediatrician. A doctor who specializes in the care and development of children. (10-1)

peer mediators. Students who are trained in the conflict resolution process and are called upon to act as mediators when conflicts arise among their peers. (3-3)

peer pressure. The influence a person's peers have on him or her. (6-3)

peers. Other people in a person's age group. (1-2)

personal fact sheet. An organized list of information, such as education, work experiences, skills, honors and activities, hobbies, interests, and references, used to fill out job applications. (9-2)

personality. The total behavioral qualities and traits that make up an individual. (1-1)

personal space. The area surrounding an individual. (3-1)

pesticide. A strong chemical used for pest control. (25-2)

physical abuse. The physical injury of one person by another through such behaviors as hitting, kicking, biting, or throwing objects. (5-3)

physical disability. A disability that limits a person's body or its functions. (10-2)

physical fitness. The condition of the body. (2-1)

physical growth. Changes in body stature influenced by heredity and health habits. (1-2)

physical neglect. Failure to provide proper food, clothing, shelter, medical care, and parental supervision to meet family needs. (5-3)

physical wellness. A state of health in which the body is able to fight illness and infection and repair damage. (2-1)

place setting. The tableware that one person would need, such as a dinner plate, salad plate, cup, and saucer. (16-1)

policy. An insurance contract. (18-3)

policyholder. A person who has an insurance policy. (18-3)

pollution. All the harmful changes in the environment caused by human activities. (25-3)

portable appliance. A cooking aid that can be easily moved from one place to another. (14-1)

portfolio. A group of securities purchased by a mutual fund for an investor. (18-2)

positive reinforcement. Rewarding positive behavior as a way to encourage children to repeat the behavior. (10-4)

poultry. Any domesticated bird used for meat and/or eggs. (15-1)

preferred provider organization (PPO). A group of doctors and medical facilities that contract to provide services at reduced rates. (18-3)

prejudices. Preconceived ideas or judgments of people or objects that are based on a lack of understanding. (3-2)

premium. A regular payment made for an insurance policy. (18-3)

preschooler. A child who is between the ages of three and five years old. (10-2)

preshrinking. Allowing fabric to shrink before cutting out garment pieces. (21-2)

presser foot. A sewing machine part that holds fabric in place as the machine stitches. (21-3)

pressing. The process of lifting an iron up and down to apply pressure in one area of a garment at a time. (20-5)

primary colors. Colors that cannot be created from other colors, such as yellow, blue, and red. (20-2)

principles of design. Balance, proportion, rhythm, and emphasis used as guides for combining the elements of design. (20-2)

priorities. A list of items or tasks that have been ranked in order of importance. (5-2)

process cheese. Cheese made by blending and melting two or more natural cheeses. (15-4)

procreation. The bearing of children. (4-1)

produce. Fresh fruits and vegetables. (15-2)

progressive tax. A type of tax that increases in rate as the price of the item being taxed increases. (8-3)

prompting. Asking questions to prompt children to exhibit desired behavior. (10-4)

proportion. The spatial relationship of the parts of a design to each other and to the whole design. (20-2)

protein. A nutrient that is found in every cell of the body and is needed for growth, maintenance, and repair of body tissues. (12-1)

puberty. A stage of physical growth in which an individual becomes capable of sexual reproduction. (1-2)

public law. A type of law that governs the relationship between people and the government. (8-3)

pull date. A date stamped on food products such as dairy products and cold cuts that shows the last day a store should sell the product. (13-3)

R

radon. A colorless, odorless gas that is produced by the radioactive breakdown of radium. (25-3)

random dating. A type of dating, also called casual dating, that allows people to date more than one person at a time. (6-2)

rape. The crime of forcing another person to submit to sexual relations. (6-3)

real-time. Refers to an event happening now. (19-2)

recipe. A list of ingredients with a complete set of instructions for preparing a food product. (14-3)

reconciling. The process of comparing the account statement to your check stubs or register to make sure they match. (18-1)

recourse. A consumer's right to express dissatisfaction about a product or service. (19-5)

recycle. To reprocess resources so they can be used again. (25-3)

redirection. Focusing the child's attention on something else by providing an appealing substitute. (10-4)

references. People a person knows who can vouch for his or her good work. (9-2)

refined. A term used to describe flour that has had parts of the grain kernel removed during the milling process. (15-3)

reflection. The listener repeats in his or her own words what he or she thinks the speaker said. (3-1)

rent. A monthly fee paid to the owner of a property in return for living accommodations. (23-2)

resource. Time, object, service, or ability used to achieve goals. (17-1)

restyle. To change a garment to give it a different look. (22-4)

resume. A brief account of your education, work experience, and other qualifications for employment. (9-2)

retort packaging. A shelf-stable food packaging method in which foods are sealed in a foil pouch and then sterilized. (13-4)

rhythm. A principle of design that creates a feeling of movement in a design. (20-2)

role expectation. A pattern of socially expected behavior in which people learn to behave the way they think society expects them to behave. (3-2)

S

salary. A set amount of money paid to an employee for a certain period of time. (17-4)

sale. A special selling of goods or services at a reduced price. (19-1)

sanitation. The process of maintaining a clean and healthy environment. (14-2)

saturated fat. A fat that is generally solid at room temperature. (12-1)

scale floor plan. A drawing that shows the size and shape of a room, with a fraction of an inch equaling a certain number of feet in the room. (24-2)

scapegoating. An attempt to resolve conflicts by blaming others. The person blamed for the problem is the scapegoat. (3-3)

seam. A row of stitching that joins garment pieces together. (22-3)

seam allowance. The space between the cutting line on a pattern and the stitching line, usually $\frac{5}{8}$-inch wide. (22-1)

secondary colors. Colors created by mixing equal amounts of two primary colors. (20-2)

securities. Proof of debt or ownership of a company or government, often in the form of stocks or bonds. (18-2)

security deposit. A sum of money, usually one month's rent, paid by a tenant before moving into a property to cover possible damages. (23-2)

self-concept. A person's view of himself or herself. (1-1)

self-esteem. The sense of worth a person attaches to himself or herself. (1-1)

self-help feature. A clothing design detail that makes clothes easier for children to put on and take off. (10-3)

self-image. The way a person sees himself or herself. (10-4)

selvage. One of two finished lengthwise edges on a piece of fabric. (22-2)

serger. A high-speed sewing machine that can stitch, trim, and finish seams in one simple step. (21-3)

sequential steps. A series of patterns during which children grow and develop. (10-2)

setting limits. Giving children guidelines, or rules, of what they may and may not do. (10-4)

sexual abuse. A form of abuse in which one person forces another to engage in sexual activities. (5-3)

sexual harassment. Unwanted or unwelcome sexual advances, requests for sexual favors, or other verbal or physical sexual conduct. (6-3)

sexually transmitted disease (STD). A disease spread mainly through sexual contact with symptoms and side effects ranging from an outbreak of blisters to blindness to death. (2-3)

shellfish. Fish that have shells instead of backbones. (15-1)

short-term goal. A goal that takes a short time to reach, such as an hour, a day, or a week. (17-1)

sibling. A brother or sister. (6-1)

simulation software. Computer software that imitates an actual experience. (19-2)

single-family house. A house designed to shelter one family. (23-1)

single-parent family. One adult living with one or more children. (4-2)

smokeless tobacco. A product, such as chewing tobacco or snuff, that is placed in the mouth for chewing or dipping. (2-3)

social growth. A developing ability to get along with other people. (1-2)

socialization. The teaching process used to help children learn to conform to social standards. (4-1)

socio-dramatic play. A stage of play where several children imitate others and act out situations together. (10-5)

solar energy. Energy produced from the sun. (25-4)

solitary play. A stage of play in which a child will play by himself or herself. (10-2)

spun yarns. Yarns made by spinning staple fibers together. (21-1)

standard. An accepted level of achievement. (1-2)

starch. The complex carbohydrate part of plants. (15-3)

status. A person's rank within a group. (20-1)

staystitching. A line of machine stitching that keeps the edges of garment pieces from stretching out of shape while being sewn. (22-3)

steady dating. A type of dating in which two people agree to date only each other. (6-2)

stepfamily. A family structure formed when a single parent marries. (4-2)

stereotype. A set belief that all members of a group are the same. (3-2)

stitching line. The seamline, which is ⅝-inch inside a pattern's cutting line; is unmarked in multisize patterns, but marked as a broken line in single-size patterns. (22-1)

stock. A certificate that represents ownership of a small portion of a company. (18-2)

stress. The body's reaction to the events in a person's life. (2-2)

style. Specific construction details that make one garment differ from another garment of the same type. (20-4)

sublease. Passing a lease over from a renter to a second tenant who pays rent directly to the owner. (23-2)

substance abuse. The use of illegal drugs or the misuse of legal drugs such as alcohol. (5-3)

sudden infant death syndrome (SIDS). The sudden death of an apparently healthy baby during sleep. (10-1)

support group. A group of people who share a similar problem or concern. (5-3)

support system. A network of people and organizations family members can turn to during a crisis. (5-3)

T

table d'hôte. A type of menu in which one price is charged for an entire meal. (16-3)

tableware. Dinnerware, flatware, and glassware. (16-1)

tact. Knowledge of what to do or say to avoid offending others. (8-1)

tailored paycheck. A program that allows employees to choose benefits that best meet their own wants and needs. (5-2)

team. A group of people organized around a common goal. (8-1)

technology. The use of scientific knowledge for practical purposes. (3-1)

tech prep. A work-based learning program that often combines two years of high school courses with two years of postsecondary education. (9-1)

telecommuting. An arrangement where an employee works from an office set up at home. The employee is connected to the office by electronic technology—e-mail, facsimile (FAX) machines, wireless phones, GPS (global positioning systems), and video conferencing. (9-3)

texture. A design element that affects the way a design looks and feels. (20-2)

thread shank. A short stem of thread that provides room for a button to lie over the buttonhole fabric. (22-3)

thread-tension regulator. Two separate controls found on a sewing machine that balance tension or pull between the upper and lower threads to form the proper stitch. (21-3)

time management. The ability to plan and use time well. (17-3)

time out. Moving a child away from others for a short period of time when a child's disruptive behavior cannot be ignored. The child calms down and gains self-control. (10-4)

toddler. A child who is one or two years old. (10-2)

toxic waste. Waste that can cause injury if inhaled, swallowed, or absorbed through the skin. (25-3)

tract house. A house built by a developer who builds an entire neighborhood at once. (23-1)

traffic pattern. The path people follow as they move within and between rooms. (24-2)

trimming. Cutting away part of a seam allowance to reduce bulk. (22-3)

U

underweight. A term used to describe an adult who has a body mass index below 18.5. (12-4)

uniform. A distinctive outfit that identifies a person who wears it with a specific group. (20-1)

unit pricing. A consumer aid that shows the cost per standard unit of weight or measure for a product. (13-3)

universal product code (UPC). A group of bars and numbers appearing on a product that contains price and product information. (13-3)

unsaturated fat. A fat that is most often liquid at room temperature. (12-1)

V

value. The lightness or darkness of a color. (20-2)

values. The beliefs, feelings, and experiences a person considers to be important and desirable. (1-2)

vegetarian diet. A pattern of eating that is made up largely or entirely of foods from plant sources. (12-3)

veneer. Thin slice of fine-quality wood. (24-2)

verbal communication. A form of communication that involves the use of words. (3-1)

visionary goal. A goal that inspires people to do more than they thought they were capable of achieving. (17-1)

vitamins. Organic substances needed in small amounts for normal growth and the maintenance of good health. (12-1)

volunteers. People who provide valuable services by offering their time, talents, and energy free of charge. (8-3)

W

wants. Items people desire, but don't need to survive. (1-2)

wardrobe. All the clothes and accessories a person has to wear. (20-3)

warranty. A written promise by a manufacturer that a product will meet specified standards of performance. (19-1)

wattage. A measurement of the amount of energy required to operate an electrical device. (25-4)

weaving. The process of interlacing two sets of yarns to produce a fabric. (21-1)

will. A legal document describing how a person intends for property to be distributed after his or her death. (18-2)

work ethic. A standard of conduct for successful job performance. (9-3)

work plan. A detailed list of all the duties that must be completed during a lab experience. (14-4)

Y

yarn. A continuous strand formed from combined fibers. (21-1)

Index